P9-EDT-781

## DATE DUE

| | | | |
|---|---|---|---|
| | | | |
| | | | |
| | | | |
| | | | |
| | | | |
| | | | |
| | | | |
| | | | |
| | | | |
| | | | |
| | | | |
| | | | |
| | | | |
| | | | |
| | | | |
| | | | |
| | | | |

DEMCO 38-296

# Connecting Cultures

# CONNECTING CULTURES™

A Guide
to Multicultural Literature
for Children

——➤•◄——

*Rebecca L. Thomas*

R. R. Bowker®
A Reed Reference Publishing Company
New Providence, New Jersey

Published by R. R. Bowker, a Reed Reference Publishing Company
Copyright © 1996 by Reed Elsevier Inc.
Printed and bound in the United States of America

**Library of Congress Cataloging-in-Publication Data**

Thomas, Rebecca L.
    Connecting cultures : a guide to multicultural literature for
children / Rebecca L. Thomas.
        p.        cm.
    ISBN 0-8352-3760-5
    1. Minorities—Juvenile fiction—Bibliography. 2. Minorities—
Juvenile poetry—Bibliography. 3. Children's fiction, English—
Bibliography. 4. Children's poetry, English—Bibliography. 5. Folk
literature—Bibliography. 6. Minorities—Songs and music—
Juvenile—Bibliography. 7. Minorities—United States—Juvenile
fiction—Bibliography. 8. Minorities—United States—Juvenile
poetry—Bibliography. 9. Folk literature, American—Bibliography.
10. Minorities—United States—Songs and music—Juvenile—
Bibliography. I. Title.
Z1037.T465    1996
[PS509.M5]
011.62—dc20                                            96-25944
                                                          CIP

ISBN 0-8352-3760-5

9  780835  237604

# CONTENTS

# FOREWORD

As an Armenian American, my cultural heritage has been central to my personal and professional experiences. My father immigrated to America from Karput, Turkey, in 1915; my mother in 1922. I grew up in a home that included regular family gatherings to celebrate with stories, songs, and food. In my home, there was an emphasis on our heritage, a need to remember traditions and values. One of my favorite memories of childhood is hearing my parents tell Hodja stories, traditional stories of the Armenian culture. I still look for Armenian recipes in international cookbooks, often judging the quality of these books by the number and variety of recipes from my heritage.

As an adult, I read *The Road from Home: The Story of an Armenian Girl* by David Kherdian (Greenwillow, 1979). In Kherdian's reminiscence about his mother's life, I recognized a connection to my own family and childhood. It was as though I was reading my mother's story. Reading this personal reflection reinforced my knowledge of the importance of having your own stories and of making connections with other people.

In my capacity as director of library media for the Shaker Heights City Schools for over 25 years, I have encouraged the use of multicultural literature with our children during the librarians' monthly review meetings, with teachers on curriculum committees, and by bringing authors and illustrators from many cultures to our district to talk about their life and work. I have a commitment to introducing young people to the many opportunities that are available to them through literature and reading. As president of the Association for Library Service to Children, I worked on the planning for the ALSC/REFORMA Book Award, a new award planned for Latino literature. This award is being developed to recognize outstanding works written or illustrated by a Latino author or illustrator that affirm Chicano/Latino/Hispanic ethnicity, heritage, and experiences in the United States. Encouraging publishers, librarians, teachers, and others who work with young people to present diverse experiences through quality literature has been central to my advocacy role.

I have also been involved in a project undertaken by Ann Cameron and her husband, Bill Cherry, in Panajachel, Guatemala. They have worked to restore the public library there, focusing particularly on the children and their needs. Many colleagues and I have supported this project by donating books in Spanish as well as money, some of which was earned through special student projects. Visiting this library in the summer of 1994, I saw for myself the joy of children poring over beautiful new books, there because they wanted to be, not because they had to.

Educators so often become accustomed to using books they know and miss opportunities to bring new and varied materials into their classrooms and libraries. *Connecting Cultures* will serve as a resource to expand the awareness of available multicultural books. Its Subject Access will help teachers and librarians add books that feature diverse experiences into programs and units that are already established. *Connecting Cultures* will enable educators to make connections between literature and the heritage of the children in their classrooms.

In 1966, Charlemae Rollins spoke to my graduate children's literature class at the School of Library Science, Rosary College. She emphasized the importance of being sensitive to the portrayal of African Americans in literature and to be alert to images that promoted stereotypes. She reinforced the fact that knowledge about others is one step toward understanding, tolerance, and acceptance. Her words have shaped my professional life, spurring me to encourage all those who work with young people to share literature that promotes cultural diversity and to let children see and find themselves in quality children's books.

ELLEN M. STEPANIAN

Director of Library Media
Shaker Heights (Ohio) City Schools

# PREFACE

In recent years, literature featuring the experiences of people from many cultures has become increasingly available. As a member of the 1994 Caldecott Committee, I was amazed to see the number of multicultural books that were published during the previous year. Our committee's choice, *Grandfather's Journey* by Allen Say (Houghton, 1993), captured the emotions of one man who knew life in two diverse communities. Several of the Honor Books we selected also incorporated diversity into themes, such as *Raven: A Trickster Tale from the Pacific Northwest*, retold and illustrated by Gerald McDermott (Harcourt, 1993), which is a folktale from the native peoples of the Northwest Coast, and *Yo! Yes?* by Chris Raschka (Orchard, 1993), in which two boys from different cultures establish a friendship.

Reading many books about diverse experiences and seeing different peoples presented in the illustrations provides children with opportunities to learn about the similarities and differences among peoples. They learn about customs and habits, families and friends, schools and homes. They learn about the world around them and they learn about themselves. Children develop an appreciation for the needs of other people and begin to understand these needs. There are many different interpretations of what constitutes multicultural literature. For *Connecting Cultures*, two definitions were considered: "books by and about people of color" (Ginny Moore Kruse, "No Single Season: Multicultural Literature for All Children," *Wilson Library Bulletin*, February 1992, p. 30) and literature that "emphasizes respect for the different historical perspectives and cultures in human society" (quote from Elizabeth Martinez, in "The Politics of Multicultural Literature for Children and Adolescents: Combining Perspectives and Conversations," by Dan Madigan, *Language Arts*, March 1993, p. 169).

As an elementary school librarian in the Shaker Heights (Ohio) City Schools since 1976, I have been involved in developing curriculum to meet the needs of children from diverse backgrounds and with a variety of interests and abilities. It has often been frustrating to find that many children's books are not given culturally specific subject headings, particularly those books where the illustrations feature diversity but the text is more general. The use of literature and the incorporation of a whole language philosophy in classrooms and libraries has encouraged teachers and librarians to become more knowledgeable about books. In many elementary schools, children's literature is the focus of reading and language arts activities. Teachers and librarians have become more involved in using quality children's literature in their classrooms and libraries.

Many educators are choosing specific books to use with their students and devising units around themes and topics. It is essential to have resources that connect general subject areas to books that feature a wide variety of experiences. Children need to see themselves in books to become involved in their reading and research. *Connecting Cultures* evolved from a need to include more multicultural literature in the established units and curricula in libraries and classrooms. It has been developed as a resource to link children with literature that presents diverse experiences, celebrates common bonds, and introduces the wonderful variety of our world.

Finding and selecting the books for *Connecting Cultures* was a challenge with consideration given to several issues. One important issue was choosing books of quality that would be generally available in school and public libraries. Standard selection sources were consulted first, including *Children's Catalog*, 16th edition and supplements (Wilson, 1991–1994); *Elementary School Library Collection*, 18th edition (Brodart, 1992); *A to Zoo*, 4th edition (Bowker, 1993); *Beyond Picture Books*, 2nd edition (Bowker, 1995), and other similar titles. Specialized reference books were also examined, for example, *Our Family, Our Friends, Our World* (Bowker, 1992); *Multicultural Literature for Children and Young Adults*, 3rd edition (Cooperative Children's Book Center, 1993); *Black Authors and Illustrators of Children's Books* (Garland, 1992); *Through Indian Eyes* (New Society Press, 1992); *American Indian Resource Manual* (Wisconsin Dept. of Public Instruction, 1992); *The Multicolored Mirror* (Highsmith, 1991); and *The Black Experience in Children's Literature* (New York Public Library, 1989). Major children's literature textbooks were consulted, including *Children's Literature in the Elementary School*, 5th edition (Harcourt, 1993) and *Literature and the Child*, 3rd edition (Harcourt, 1993). Some general reviewing journals were also examined, particularly *Horn Book Guide*, which features recommended titles, and *Booklinks*, which organizes titles around themes. From these and other related resources, a database was prepared. Every title was personally examined and annotated and subject headings were assigned.

Another selection issue that was considered was the currency of the titles. In *Connecting Cultures*, the focus is on relatively recent titles that are still available in school and public libraries. Selections have been included from the 1970s, 1980s, and 1990s, with some earlier titles being considered; however, an attempt has been made to exclude titles that were dated in their presentation of the issues of cultural relationships and civil rights (unless those issues were presented in the context of historical fiction). Some out-of-print books have been included, especially if they were still generally available in libraries. To keep the emphasis on more current books that reflect the needs and interests of contemporary children, the Annotated Bibliography includes books that were published through spring 1995. *Books in Print Plus* was consulted to provide information about the availability of the included books. The currency of the information was validated through July 1995.

*Connecting Cultures* includes 1,637 fiction, folktale, poetry, and song books suitable for use with preschoolers through children in sixth grade. Books for a middle school or junior high audience were not included except when they continued a series. *Connecting Cultures* is not meant to be a comprehensive list; it is meant to be a starting point to generally available titles. This edition is just a beginning—the database continues to grow even as this book has been readied for publication. Suggestions for future editions from librarians, teachers, publishers, and others who use this resource would be greatly appreciated. A focus for future editions would be to include more resources from less well-known publishers so that there is more access to materials featuring diverse experiences.

*Connecting Cultures* is organized into six sections:

1. Annotated Bibliography
2. Subject Access
3. Title Index
4. Illustrator Index
5. Culture Index
6. Use Level Index

The Annotated Bibliography is arranged alphabetically by author surname (except for a few main entries arranged by title). Each entry has been assigned an entry number which is referenced in the various indexes. Each title in the Annotated Bibliography includes:

1. Bibliographic Information: Author, Title, Publisher (hardback and paperback, as available), date of publication, and International Standard Book Number (ISBN) or o.p. (out-of-print) information.

2. Use Level: PS = Preschool
   P = Primary Grades
   M = Middle Grades
   U = Upper Grades

   Of course, depending on the needs and interests of specific children, there could be some overlap.

3. Cultural/Regional Designation: This features the specific culture or region of the book, for example, African, African American, Asian, Asian American, Native American, Hispanic, Hispanic American, and so on. When possible, a more specific culture or region is appended, for example, Central American—Costa Rica or African—Akan. This allows the user to be aware of the heritage featured in the book and to select a variety of materials.

4. Summary: Each book has a brief summary to assist in the selection and use by teachers and librarians.

5. Subjects: The subject headings used for *Connecting Cultures* are based on the subjects in another Bowker guide, *A to Zoo*. Some subjects have been added or revised to meet the specific needs of this project.

The Subject Access is a guide to the 1,637 numbered titles in the Annotated Bibliography that have been catalogued under more than 730 alphabetically arranged subject headings. Each annotated title has been assigned up to six subject headings. The author, title, entry number, use level, and culture are listed for each entry. The Subject Access has been designed to present books in theme or topic groupings that would be appropriate to the needs in schools and public libraries. In addition, books in a series are listed by their series title under the heading "Series." Teachers and librarians will find this a quick reference to titles that feature diversity and that would fit into their already established programs and units. The Title Index, Illustrator Index, Culture Index, and Use Level Index provide additional access points for selecting books about diverse peoples and experiences.

Preparing *Connecting Cultures* was an opportunity for me to create a resource based on my own experiences with children and children's literature. It allowed me to become more knowledgeable about many new books that are available and rediscover older books that present diverse images and experiences. It let me build on the doctoral work that I had done with Charlotte S. Huck at the Ohio State University. I received a great deal of support and encouragement in this process.

Throughout my affiliation with Bowker, which included the compilation of picture book bibliographies *Primaryplots* (1989) and *Primaryplots2* (1993), I have been fortunate to work with outstanding professionals: Catherine Barr, formerly Editorial Director, Professional and Reference Books, supervised the preparation of the manuscript and organized the arrangement for *Connecting Cultures*; and Nancy Bucenec, Managing Production Editor, assisted in all stages of the book. Their contributions to this book were especially important and much appreciated.

Several libraries served as the resource for books, including the Shaker Heights (Ohio) City Schools, the Cleveland Public Library system, the Shaker Heights Public Library, the Cleveland Heights-University Heights Public Library, and other member libraries of the CLEVNET system. Many hours were spent browsing through these collections, especially seeking books that presented diversity through visual representations. These libraries all have policies that are user friendly, which made preparation of this book possible

During the work on this book I received the support of many of my friends. Mary Underwood listened to most of my struggles; Hylah Schwartz looked at different phases of the manuscript; Bill Scherer and Gary Raymont provided much encouragement, as did my library colleagues, Pat Baird, Madeleine Obrock, and Ruth Robbins. Brenda Spivey and her daughter, Alex, shared insights into their cultural heritage. Dr. Rosemary Weltman, principal of Onaway Elementary, was very understanding about the writing process and has been an advocate for providing more multicultural resources in our schools. Ellen Stepanian, Director of Library Media for the Shaker Heights City Schools, first connected me with Bowker. Through her mentoring and friendship, I have had many opportunities. It is a pleasure to work for such a committed professional and such a caring person. My family has always encouraged me to take risks, and their support for this project was essential to its completion. I would like to dedicate this book to the memory of my parents, who taught me the importance of being proud of your heritage.

# ANNOTATED
# BIBLIOGRAPHY

AARDEMA, VERNA, RETELLER

1
*Anansi Finds a Fool: An Ashanti Tale.* Ill. by Bryna Waldman.
Dial, 1992 (0-8037-1164-6); LB (0-8037-1165-4). USE LEVEL:
M
*African—Ashanti*
Anansi thinks he can find someone to catch fish for him but
Bonsu tricks Anansi into doing all the work.
BEHAVIOR—TRICKERY; CHARACTER TRAITS—FOOLISHNESS; FOLKTALES—
AFRICA—ASHANTI; SPORTS—FISHING.

2
*Bimwili & the Zimwi: A Tale from Zanzibar.* Ill. by Susan
Meddaugh. Dial, 1985 (0-8037-0212-4); LB (0-8037-0213-2);
pap. (0-8037-0553-0). USE LEVEL: M
*African—Zanzibar*
A little girl is abducted by an ogre, Zimwi, and must find a way
to escape.
BEHAVIOR—TRICKERY; FOLKTALES—AFRICA—ZANZIBAR; MONSTERS.

3
*Borreguita and the Coyote: A Tale from Ayutla, Mexico.* Ill. by
Petra Mathers. Knopf, 1991 (0-679-80921-X); LB (0-679-
90921-4). USE LEVEL: M
*Mexican*
Borreguita, a lamb, must outwit the coyote that wants to eat
her.
ANIMALS—COYOTES; ANIMALS—SHEEP; BEHAVIOR—TRICKERY;
FOLKTALES—MEXICO.

4　*Bringing the Rain to Kapiti Plain: A Nandi Tale*. Ill. by Beatriz Vidal. Dial, 1981 (0-8037-0809-2); LB (0-8037-0807-6); pap. (0-8037-0904-8). USE LEVEL: P/M
*African—Nandi*
In this cumulative rhyme, Ki-pat sees the drought around him. Using an eagle's feather for an arrow, he aims at the cloudy sky, piercing the cloud and causing the rain to fall.
CUMULATIVE TALES; FOLKTALES—AFRICA—NANDI; POETRY, RHYME; WEATHER—DROUGHTS; WEATHER—RAIN.

5　*Jackal's Flying Lesson: A Khoikhoi Tale*. Ill. by Dale Gottlieb. Knopf, 1995 (0-679-85813-X); LB (0-679-95813-4). USE LEVEL: M
*African—Khoikhoi*
The jackal tricks the dove into giving him her two babies, and he swallows them. Then the crane tricks the jackal into thinking he can fly. When the jackal falls, the two baby doves come out of him and are returned to their mother.
ANIMALS—JACKALS; BEHAVIOR—TRICKERY; BIRDS; FOLKTALES—AFRICA—KHOIKHOI.

6　*Ji-Nongo-Nongo Means Riddles*. Ill. by Jerry Pinkney. Four Winds, 1978, o.p. USE LEVEL: P/M
*African*
Riddles from a variety of African peoples are presented in this collection.
FOREIGN LANDS—AFRICA; RIDDLES.

7　*Oh, Kojo! How Could You! An Ashanti Tale*. Ill. by Marc Brown. Dial, 1984 (0-8037-0006-7); LB (0-8037-0007-5); pap. (0-8037-0449-6). USE LEVEL: M
*African—Ashanti*
Kojo causes problems for his mother, Tutuola. He spends her money and does not work. He does not listen to her warnings and is tricked by Anansi. A cat and a dog try to help Kojo.
ANIMALS—CATS; ANIMALS—DOGS; BEHAVIOR—TRICKERY; CHARACTER TRAITS—LAZINESS; FOLKTALES—AFRICA—ASHANTI; POURQUOI TALES.

8　*Pedro and the Padre: A Tale from Jalisco, Mexico*. Ill. by Friso Henstra. Dial, 1991 (0-8037-0522-0); LB (0-8037-0523-9). USE LEVEL: M
*Mexican*
Pedro's father is vexed with his laziness and sends him off to find work. The padre gives Pedro work, but Pedro lies to the padre. Pedro's lies get him into trouble and he learns the importance of telling the truth.

CHARACTER TRAITS—HONESTY; CHARACTER TRAITS—LAZINESS; FOLKTALES—MEXICO.

9    *Princess Gorilla and a New Kind of Water: A Mpongwe Tale.* Ill. by Victoria Chess. Dial, 1988 (0-8037-0412-7); LB (0-8037-0413-5); pap. (0-8037-0914-5). USE LEVEL: M
*African—Mpongwe*
King Gorilla devises a test for those who would marry his daughter. They must drink a barrel of vinegar.
ANIMALS—GORILLAS; CHARACTER TRAITS—CLEVERNESS; CONTESTS; FOLKTALES—AFRICA—MPONGWE; HUMOR.

10   *Rabbit Makes a Monkey of Lion: A Swahili Tale.* Ill. by Jerry Pinkney. Dial, 1989 (0-8037-0297-3); LB (0-8037-0298-1). USE LEVEL: M
*African—Swahili*
Two times, Rabbit eats Lion's honey and is not punished. Even Rabbit will not try to trick Lion a third time.
ANIMALS; ANIMALS—RABBITS; BEHAVIOR—TRICKERY; FOLKTALES—AFRICA—SWAHILI; JUNGLES.

11   *Sebgugugu the Glutton: A Bantu Tale from Rwanda.* Ill. by Nancy L. Clouse. Africa World, 1993 (0-86543-377-1). USE LEVEL: M
*African—Bantu*
Sebgugugu does not listen to his wife, or to Imana, the Lord of Rwanda. Each time that Sebgugugu's needs are being met, his greediness makes him spoil his good fortune and he loses everything.
BEHAVIOR—GREED; CHARACTER TRAITS—QUESTIONING; FOLKTALES—AFRICA—BANTU.

12   *Traveling to Tondo: A Tale of the Nkundo of Zaire.* Ill. by Will Hillenbrand. Knopf, 1991, LB (0-679-90081-0); pap. (0-679-85309-X). USE LEVEL: M
*African—Zaire*
Bowane, a civet cat, has chosen his bride. She lives in Tondo, a nearby village. However, it takes Bowane and his friends so long to reach Tondo that his bride-to-be has married another.
ACTIVITIES—TRAVELING; ANIMALS; CUMULATIVE TALES; FOLKTALES—AFRICA—ZAIRE.

13   *The Vingananee and the Tree Toad: A Liberian Tale.* Ill. by Ellen Weiss. Puffin, 1988, pap. (0-14-050890-2). USE LEVEL: M
*African—Liberia*

Spider has a large farm and has hired animals to work for him. When the huge Vingananee tries to take their food, Tree Toad is able to overcome him.
ANIMALS; FOLKTALES—AFRICA—LIBERIA; FROGS AND TOADS; MONSTERS; SPIDERS.

14 *What's So Funny, Ketu? A Nuer Tale.* Ill. by Marc Brown. Dial, 1982 (0-8037-9364-2); LB (0-8037-9370-7); pap. (0-8037-0646-4). USE LEVEL: M
*African—Nuer*
Ketu rescues a snake and is given the gift of being able to hear what animals think. What he hears makes him laugh.
ANIMALS; BEHAVIOR—SECRETS; FOLKTALES—AFRICA—NUER.

15 *Who's in Rabbit's House? A Masai Tale.* Ill. by Leo Dillon and Diane Dillon. Dial, 1977 (0-8037-9550-5); LB (0-8037-9551-3); pap. (0-8037-9549-1). USE LEVEL: M
*African—Masai*
Someone is in Rabbit's house and she must find a way to get her house back.
ANIMALS; ANIMALS—RABBITS; BEHAVIOR—TRICKERY; CUMULATIVE TALES; FOLKTALES—AFRICA—MASAI; INSECTS—BUTTERFLIES, CATERPILLARS.

16 *Why Mosquitoes Buzz in People's Ears: A West African Tale.* Ill. by Leo Dillon and Diane Dillon. Dial, 1975 (0-8037-6089-2); LB (0-8037-6087-6); pap. (0-8037-6088-4). USE LEVEL: M
*African—West Africa*
In this sequential story, a mosquito's silly behavior creates fear in the jungle. Now we know why mosquitoes are such annoying pests.
CALDECOTT AWARD; CUMULATIVE TALES; FOLKTALES—AFRICA—WEST AFRICA; INSECTS—MOSQUITOES; POURQUOI TALES.

## ACKERMAN, KAREN
17 *By the Dawn's Early Light.* Ill. by Catherine Stock. Macmillan, 1994 (0-689-31788-3); LB (0-689-31917-7). USE LEVEL: P
*African American*
Mom works nights in a factory, so Rachel and Josh stay with their grandmother. Sometimes, the children wake up just as Mom gets home and they share some quiet time together.
CAREERS—FACTORY WORK; FAMILY LIFE—GRANDMOTHERS; FAMILY LIFE—MOTHERS; NIGHT.

**ADA, ALMA FLOR**

18    *The Gold Coin.* Translated from the Spanish by Bernice Randall.
Ill. by Neil Waldman. Macmillan, 1991 (0-689-31633-X); pap.
(0-689-71793-8). USE LEVEL: M
*Central American*
Juan wants to steal an old woman's gold coin. He follows her
and learns that she helps everyone. He is touched by her gen-
erosity and when he finally meets her, he offers to help her.
BEHAVIOR—STEALING; CHARACTER TRAITS—GENEROSITY; CRIME;
FOREIGN LANDS—CENTRAL AMERICA.

19    *My Name Is María Isabel.* Ill. by K. Dyble Thompson.
Macmillan, 1993 (0-689-31517-1). USE LEVEL: M
*Hispanic American—Puerto Rico*
After her teacher decides to call her Mary, María Isabel finds it
difficult to concentrate at school. In an essay, she tells her
teacher the important family heritage associated with her name.
CHARACTER TRAITS—PRIDE; NAMES; SCHOOL; SELF-CONCEPT.

20    *The Rooster Who Went to His Uncle's Wedding: A Latin
American Folktale.* Ill. by Kathleen Kuchera. Putnam, 1993 (0-
399-22412-2). USE LEVEL: M
*Latin American*
On his way to his uncle's wedding, rooster stops to eat a kernel
of corn and he dirties his beak. Each character he asks to help
clean his beak refuses. Finally the sun helps him, setting off a
chain of events.
BIRDS—ROOSTERS; CUMULATIVE TALES; FOLKTALES—LATIN AMERICA.

21    *Where the Flame Trees Bloom.* Ill. by Antonio Martorell.
Macmillan, 1994 (0-689-31900-2). USE LEVEL: M
*Caribbean—Cuba*
These 11 stories all relate to the author's memories of growing
up in Cuba. Many feature family members, like her grandfather
Modesto, who lost his fortune but stayed with his dying wife,
and her grandmother Lola, who was a gifted teacher.
ACTIVITIES—REMINISCING; FAMILY LIFE; FOREIGN LANDS—CARIBBEAN
ISLANDS—CUBA; SHORT STORIES.

**ADAMS, JEANIE**

22    *Going for Oysters.* Ill. by the author. Whitman, 1994 (0-8075-
2978-8). USE LEVEL: P
*Australian—Aborigine*

A girl describes a family weekend at the seashore—fishing, boating, and eating oysters.

FAMILY LIFE; FOREIGN LANDS—AUSTRALIA—ABORIGINE; SEA AND SEASHORE; SPORTS—FISHING.

**ADOFF, ARNOLD**

23　*All the Colors of the Race: Poems.* Ill. by John Steptoe. Lothrop, 1982 (0-688-00879-8); LB (0-688-00880-1). USE LEVEL: U
*Multicultural*
The poems in this collection describe the activities in a family where the father is white and the mother is black. Written from the point of view of a child, the poems celebrate the diversity and capture feelings.

CORETTA SCOTT KING AWARD; EMOTIONS; FAMILY LIFE; RACE RELATIONS.

24　*Black Is Brown Is Tan.* Ill. by Emily Arnold McCully. HarperCollins, 1973 (0-06-020083-9); LB (0-06-020084-7); pap. (0-06-443269-6). USE LEVEL: P
*Multicultural*
In free verse, this book focuses on the daily life and experiences of a racially mixed family.

FAMILY LIFE; POETRY, RHYME; RACE RELATIONS.

25　*Flamboyán.* Ill. by Karen Barbour. Harcourt, 1988 (0-15-228404-4). USE LEVEL: P
*Caribbean—Puerto Rico*
Flamboyán enjoys her life in Puerto Rico, playing among the beautiful flowers. She dreams that she can fly like the many island birds.

ACTIVITIES—FLYING; DREAMS; FOREIGN LANDS—CARIBBEAN ISLANDS—PUERTO RICO; TREES.

26　*Hard to Be Six.* Ill. by Cheryl Hanna. Lothrop, 1991 (0-688-09013-3); LB (0-688-09579-8). USE LEVEL: P
*Multicultural*
A little boy is frustrated that he cannot do everything his older sister can do. This multiracial family enjoys many activities together.

FAMILY LIFE—SIBLINGS; POETRY, RHYME; SELF-CONCEPT; SIBLING RIVALRY.

27　*I Am the Darker Brother: An Anthology of Modern Poems by Negro Americans.* Foreword by Charlemae Rollins. Ill. by

Benny Andrews. Macmillan, 1968, pap. (0-02-041120-0). USE
LEVEL: M/U
*African American*
Included in this collection are poems by Gwendolyn Brooks,
Langston Hughes, Paul Lawrence Dunbar, and other poets.
EMOTIONS; POETRY, RHYME.

28   *In for Winter, Out for Spring.* Ill. by Jerry Pinkney. Harcourt,
1991 (0-15-238637-8). USE LEVEL: P/M
*African American*
Playing in the snow, finding the first flower, going barefoot, and
collecting walnuts are some of the seasonal activities featured in
these poems.
FAMILY LIFE; POETRY, RHYME; SEASONS.

29   *Ma nDa La.* Ill. by Emily Arnold McCully. HarperCollins,
1971, o.p. USE LEVEL: P
*African*
The poetic text celebrates the joy and togetherness of this family
in Africa.
FAMILY LIFE; FOREIGN LANDS—AFRICA.

30   *My Black Me: A Beginning Book of Black Poetry.* Dutton, 1974
(0-525-35460-3). USE LEVEL: M/U
*African American*
These poems explore several themes including prejudice, urban
life, and heroes.
EMOTIONS; POETRY, RHYME; PREJUDICE; URBAN LIFE.

31   *My Black Me: A Beginning Book of Black Poetry.* rev. ed. Dutton,
1994 (0-525-45216-8); LB (0-525-35460-3). USE LEVEL: M/U
*African American*
This book contains the same poems as the 1974 edition but has
a revised introduction. Some of the poets included are Langston
Hughes, Sam Cornish, Nikki Giovanni, and Ray Patterson.
EMOTIONS; POETRY, RHYME; PREJUDICE; URBAN LIFE.

32   *OUTside INside Poems.* Ill. by John Steptoe. Lothrop, 1981 (0-
15-200224-3). USE LEVEL: M
*African American*
In free verse, a boy reflects on familiar images inside and outside. Playing baseball and worrying about doing well are some
of his concerns.
EMOTIONS; POETRY, RHYME; SPORTS—BASEBALL.

33　　*Where Wild Willie?* Ill. by Emily Arnold McCully. HarperCollins, 1978, o.p. USE LEVEL: P
*African American*
Willie enjoys many activities in her urban neighborhood. As her family looks for her, she pretends to be hiding and running away, but she comes home at the end of the day.
BEHAVIOR—RUNNING AWAY; POETRY, RHYME; URBAN LIFE.

## AGARD, JOHN
34　　*The Calypso Alphabet.* Ill. by Jennifer Bent. Henry Holt, 1989 (0-8050-1177-3). USE LEVEL: P
*Caribbean*
Letters of the alphabet feature the life and language of the Caribbean, including "O for Okra" and "S for Sugarcane."
ABC BOOKS; FOREIGN LANDS—CARIBBEAN ISLANDS.

## AGARD, JOHN, AND GRACE NICHOLS, EDS.
35　　*A Caribbean Dozen: Poems from Caribbean Poets.* Ill. by Cathie Felstead. Candlewick, 1994 (1-56402-339-7). USE LEVEL: M/U
*Caribbean*
Thirteen poets from the Caribbean Islands describe their experiences in this region. Among those included are James Berry, Valerie Bloom, and Pamela Mordecai.
FOREIGN LANDS—CARIBBEAN ISLANDS; POETRY, RHYME.

## AGELL, CHARLOTTE
36　　*Dancing Feet.* Ill. by the author. Harcourt, 1994 (0-15-200444-0). USE LEVEL: PS/P
*Multicultural*
Children from diverse backgrounds are depicted enjoying their feet, hands, hair, arms, legs, eyes, and mouths.
ACTIVITIES; ANATOMY; POETRY, RHYME.

## ALBERT, BURTON
37　　*Where Does the Trail Lead?* Ill. by Brian Pinkney. Simon & Schuster, 1991 (0-671-73409-1); pap. (0-671-79617-8). USE LEVEL: PS/P
*African American*
After enjoying a day on the beach, a young boy returns to his family and a campfire where dinner is cooking.
ACTIVITIES—EXPLORING; ACTIVITIES—WALKING; ISLANDS; SEA AND SEASHORE.

**ALEXANDER, ELLEN**

38 *Chaska and the Golden Doll.* Ill. by the author. Arcade, 1994 (1-55870-241-9). USE LEVEL: M
*South American*
Chaska wants to go to school but the school in her little village is too small for all the children to be able to attend. When Chaska finds an Inca doll, she sells it to fund a school.
CHARACTER TRAITS—GENEROSITY; FOREIGN LANDS—SOUTH AMERICA; SCHOOL.

39 *Llama and the Great Flood: A Folktale from Peru.* Ill. by the author. HarperCollins, 1989 (0-690-04727-4); LB (0-690-04729-0). USE LEVEL: M
*South American—Peru*
A llama warns his master of the coming of a flood and they seek refuge on a mountain peak in the Andes.
ANIMALS—LLAMAS; FOLKTALES—SOUTH AMERICA—PERU; WEATHER—FLOODS.

**ALEXANDER, LLOYD**

40 *The Fortune-Tellers.* Ill. by Trina Schart Hyman. Dutton, 1992 (0-525-44849-7). USE LEVEL: P/M
*African—Cameroon*
A young man visits a fortune-teller to learn about his future. The fortune-teller's predictions allow for many options, and they do come true.
BEHAVIOR—TRICKERY; CAREERS—FORTUNE TELLERS; FOREIGN LANDS—AFRICA—CAMEROON; HUMOR.

**ALEXANDER, MARTHA**

41 *Bobo's Dream.* Ill. by the author. Dial, 1970, o.p. USE LEVEL: PS/P
*African American*
In this wordless story, a dachshund dreams of rescuing his young owner from a gang of older boys.
ANIMALS—DOGS; DREAMS; IMAGINATION; WORDLESS BOOKS.

**ALEXANDER, SUE**

42 *Nadia the Willful.* Ill. by Lloyd Bloom. Pantheon, 1983, o.p. USE LEVEL: P
*Middle Eastern—Arabia*
After her brother dies, Nadia's father forbids the family to talk about him, but Nadia finds that sharing her grief helps her family, including her father.

CHARACTER TRAITS—WILLFULLNESS; DEATH; EMOTIONS—LOVE;
EMOTIONS—SADNESS; FAMILY LIFE; FOREIGN LANDS—MIDDLE EAST—
ARABIA.

**ALLEN, JUDY**

43  *Eagle.* Ill. by Tudor Humphries. Candlewick, 1994 (1-56402-143-2). USE LEVEL: P
*Philippine*
On a trip into the jungle, Miguel is afraid of an eagle, but his fear is released when the eagle catches a cobra that was near Miguel.
BIRDS—EAGLES; FOREIGN LANDS—PHILIPPINES; JUNGLES.

44  *Elephant.* Ill. by Tudor Humphries. Candlewick, 1993 (1-56402-069-X). USE LEVEL: P
*African*
Hannah finds an ivory necklace that had belonged to her great-grandmother. Her dreams are haunted by the elephant whose ivory was used. On a trip to the game reserve, Hannah throws the necklace to the elephants.
ANIMALS—ELEPHANTS; ANIMALS—ENDANGERED ANIMALS; ECOLOGY;
FOREIGN LANDS—AFRICA; NATURE.

45  *Tiger.* Ill. by Tudor Humphries. Candlewick, 1992 (1-56402-083-5). USE LEVEL: P
*Asian—China*
The people of the village are worried that there is a tiger nearby. Lee, a young boy, does not want the tiger killed. When a hunter comes, Lee is worried. But the hunter is really a photographer who takes pictures of the tiger.
ACTIVITIES—PHOTOGRAPHY; ANIMALS—ENDANGERED ANIMALS;
ANIMALS—TIGERS; FOREIGN LANDS—ASIA—CHINA.

**ALTMAN, LINDA JACOBS**

46  *Amelia's Road.* Ill. by Enrique O. Sanchez. Lee & Low, 1993 (1-880000-04-0). USE LEVEL: M
*Hispanic American*
Amelia and her family are migrant workers, and Amelia dreams of having a permanent home. Although that does not happen, Amelia does create a special place to come back to.
BEHAVIOR—SEEKING BETTER THINGS; FAMILY LIFE; MIGRANT WORKERS.

**ALTMAN, SUSAN, AND SUSAN LECHNER**

47  *Followers of the North Star: Rhymes about African American*

*Heroes, Heroines, and Historical Times.* Ill. by Byron Wooden. Childrens Pr., 1993, LB (0-516-05151-2); pap. (0-516-45151-0). USE LEVEL: M/U
*African American*
These poems celebrate the accomplishments of prominent African Americans. Among those included are Rosa Parks, Jackie Robinson, Matthew Henson, Malcolm X, and Leontyne Price. Sit-ins, escaped slaves, and integration efforts are also featured.
BIOGRAPHY; CIVIL RIGHTS; POETRY, RHYME; SELF-CONCEPT; U.S. HISTORY.

### ANCONA, GEORGE
48 *The Piñata Maker/El Piñatero.* Photos by the author. Harcourt, 1994 (0-15-261875-9); pap. (0-15-200060-7). USE LEVEL: M
*Mexican*
Don Ricardo makes piñatas in a small village in Mexico. He also makes masks, puppets, and other figures. This book describes the process that is used to make a piñata and shows a birthday celebration where children break one open.
ACTIVITIES—MAKING THINGS; ART; BIRTHDAYS; FOREIGN LANDS—MEXICO; FOREIGN LANGUAGES.

49 *Powwow.* Photos by the author. Harcourt, 1993 (0-15-263268-9); pap. (0-15-263269-7). USE LEVEL: M
*Native American*
Color photos and correlating text describe the events of the Crow Fair in Montana, which celebrates the heritage of several native peoples.
ACTIVITIES—DANCING; CELEBRATIONS.

### ANDERSEN, HANS CHRISTIAN
50 *The Nightingale.* Translated by Eva Le Gallienne. Ill. by Nancy Ekholm Burkert. HarperCollins, 1965 (0-06-023780-5); LB (0-06-023781-3). USE LEVEL: M
*Asian—China*
The nightingale enchants the emperor with her singing. When an artificial nightingale is given to the emperor, the real nightingale is banished. She returns to sing for the emperor when he is ill.
BIRDS—NIGHTINGALES; CALDECOTT AWARD; FOREIGN LANDS—ASIA—CHINA; GIFTS.

### ANDERSON, BERNICE G., COLLECTOR
51 *Trickster Tales from Prairie Lodgefires.* Ill. by Frank Gee. Abingdon, 1979, o.p. USE LEVEL: M
*Native American*

Stories from Blackfoot, Kiowa, Crow, Ponca, Dakota, and Cheyenne peoples are included in this collection.

BEHAVIOR—TRICKERY; FOLKTALES—NATIVE AMERICAN; SHORT STORIES.

## ANDERSON, JANET S.

52    *The Key into Winter.* Ill. by David Soman. Whitman, 1994 (0-8075-4170-2). USE LEVEL: M

*African American*

Clara's mother, Mattie, tells the story of four treasured family keys—keys that cause the seasons to change. As a child, Mattie took the key for winter, hoping that if the season did not change, her grandmother would not die.

DEATH; FAMILY LIFE—GRANDMOTHERS; FANTASY; SEASONS.

## ANDERSON, JOY

53    *Juma and the Magic Jinn.* Ill. by Charles Mikolaycak. Lothrop, 1986 (0-688-05443-9); LB (0-688-05444-7). USE LEVEL: M

*African*

Juma often dreams instead of paying attention in school. When he disobeys his mother and opens the jinn jar, he releases the magic jinn, who grants him three wishes.

BEHAVIOR—WISHING; FOREIGN LANDS—AFRICA; MAGIC.

## ANDERSON/SANKOFA, DAVID A., RETELLER

54    *The Origin of Life on Earth: An African Creation Myth.* Ill. by Kathleen Atkins Wilson. Sights Productions, 1991 (0-96299/8-5-4). USE LEVEL: M

*African—Yoruba*

In this story from the Yoruba, Obatala leaves the sky and creates the earth and all the people.

CORETTA SCOTT KING AWARD; CREATION; FOLKTALES—AFRICA—YORUBA; RELIGION.

55    *The Rebellion of Humans: An African Spiritual Journey.* Ill. by Claude Joachim. Sights Productions, 1994 (0-9629978-6-2). USE LEVEL: M

*African*

After being created by Obatala, the people and their descendants lose contact with their heritage. After many years, one family taught their son, Sankofa, to respect the earth.

FOREIGN LANDS—AFRICA; NATURE; TREES.

## ANDREWS, JAN

56    *Very Last First Time.* Ill. by Ian Wallace. Macmillan, 1985 (0-689-50388-1). USE LEVEL: P/M

*Native American—Inuit*

Eva Padlyat is an Inuit girl living in northern Canada. When the tide is out, she will gather mussels from under the ice. This is the first time she will be alone.

ARCTIC LANDS; CHARACTER TRAITS—BRAVERY; FOOD; FOREIGN LANDS—CANADA; SEA AND SEASHORE.

### ANGELOU, MAYA
57    *My Painted House, My Friendly Chicken, and Me.* Photos by Margaret Courtney-Clarke. Crown, 1994 (0-517-59667-9). USE LEVEL: M
*African—South Africa*
Thandi is a Ndebele girl in South Africa. She describes her family and their activities, including painting their houses, making beaded clothing, going to the city, and keeping a pet chicken.

BIRDS—CHICKENS; COMMUNITIES, NEIGHBORHOODS; FAMILY LIFE; FOREIGN LANDS—AFRICA—SOUTH AFRICA.

### ANNO, MITSUMASA, AND RAYMOND BRIGGS
58    *All in a Day.* Illustrated by ten artists. Putnam, 1986 (0-399-61292-0). USE LEVEL: M
*Multicultural*
Ten artists depict the daily life of children around the world, showing the variety of experiences and the similarities. Featured areas include Brazil, Japan, Kenya, and China. Artists include the authors and Eric Carle, Akiko Hayahi, and others.

FAMILY LIFE; FOREIGN LANDS; WORLD.

### ANZALDÚA, GLORIA
59    *Friends from the Other Side/Amigos del Otro Lado.* Ill. by Consuelo Méndez. Children's Book Pr., 1993, LB (0-89239-113-8). USE LEVEL: M
*Mexican American*
Prietita tries to help Joaquín and his mother, who are illegal immigrants from Mexico. When the Border Patrol comes, she finds them a place to hide.

FOREIGN LANGUAGES; FRIENDSHIP; IMMIGRATION; POVERTY.

### APPIAH, PEGGY
60    *Ananse the Spider: Tales from an Ashanti Village.* Ill. by Peggy Wilson. Pantheon, 1966, o.p. USE LEVEL: M
*African—Ashanti*
A collection of 13 stories about Ananse the spider, including "Why Kwaku Ananse Stays on the Ceiling."

BEHAVIOR—TRICKERY; FOLKTALES—AFRICA—ASHANTI; POURQUOI TALES; SHORT STORIES; SPIDERS.

**APPIAH, SONIA**

61  *Amoko and Efua Bear.* Ill. by Carol Easmon. Macmillan, 1988 (0-02-705591-4). USE LEVEL: P
*African—Ghana*
Amoko loves her toy bear, but when Auntie Dinah brings her a drum, Amoko leaves Efua outside all night. Her father finds Efua, her mother repairs him, and Amoko is happy.
BEHAVIOR—LOSING THINGS; FOREIGN LANDS—AFRICA—GHANA; TOYS—TEDDY BEARS.

**ARKHURST, JOYCE COOPER, RETELLER**

62  *The Adventures of Spider: West African Folk Tales.* Ill. by Jerry Pinkney. Scholastic, 1964; Little, Brown, pap. (0-316-05107-1). USE LEVEL: M
*African—West Africa*
Six stories about Spider include "Why Spiders Live in Dark Corners."
FOLKTALES—AFRICA—WEST AFRICA; POURQUOI TALES; SHORT STORIES; SPIDERS.

63  *More Adventures of Spider: West African Folk Tales.* Ill. by Jerry Pinkney. Scholastic, 1972, o.p. USE LEVEL: M
*African—West Africa*
These six stories about Spider include "Why Spiders Live on the Ceiling."
FOLKTALES—AFRICA—WEST AFRICA; POURQUOI TALES; SHORT STORIES; SPIDERS.

**ARMSTRONG, JENNIFER**

64  *Chin Yu Min and the Ginger Cat.* Ill. by Mary Grandpré. Crown, 1993 (0-517-58656-8); LB (0-517-58657-6). USE LEVEL: P
*Asian—China*
A proud Chinese widow learns humility with the help of a ginger cat. She also learns the importance of friendship.
ANIMALS—CATS; CHARACTER TRAITS—PRIDE; FOREIGN LANDS—ASIA—CHINA; FRIENDSHIP.

65  *Steal Away.* Orchard, 1992 (0-531-05983-9); LB (0-531-08583-X); Scholastic, pap. (0-590-46921-5). USE LEVEL: U
*African American*
In 1855, Susannah, who is white, and Bethlehem, who is black, escape from a southern farm to freedom in the north. Years later, they tell their story to two young girls.

CHARACTER TRAITS—BRAVERY; SLAVERY; U.S. HISTORY; UNDERGROUND RAILROAD.

66  *Wan Hu Is in the Stars.* Ill. by Barry Root. Morrow, 1995 (0-688-12457-7); LB (0-688-12458-5). USE LEVEL: M
*Asian—China*
Wan Hu is absent-minded about everyday concerns. His interest is in the stars. He tries several plans to reach the stars. When he rides off on rockets, he never returns, but a constellation shaped like a lotus appears in the sky.
FOREIGN LANDS—ASIA—CHINA; STARS.

**ARMSTRONG, WILLIAM H.**
67  *Sounder.* Ill. by James Barkley. HarperCollins, 1969 (0-06-020143-6); LB (0-06-020144-4); pap. (0-06-440020-4). USE LEVEL: U
*African American*
When his father takes a ham for his hungry family and is taken to work on the chain gang, the boy works to help his family and learns the importance of education.
ANIMALS—DOGS; FAMILY LIFE; NEWBERY AWARD; PREJUDICE; RACE RELATIONS.

**ARNEACH, LLOYD, RETELLER**
68  *The Animals' Ballgame: A Cherokee Story from the Eastern Band.* Ill. by Lydia G. Halverson. Childrens Pr., 1992, LB (0-516-05139-3); pap. (0-516-45139-1). USE LEVEL: M
*Native American—Cherokee*
To encourage storytelling, the illustrations are presented without words and the text appears on two pages at the end of the book. To settle an argument, the animals and birds have a contest. The bat helps the birds and is given the gift of flight.
ANIMALS; BIRDS; CONTESTS; FOLKTALES—NATIVE AMERICAN—CHEROKEE; POURQUOI TALES; STORYTELLING.

**ASHLEY, BERNARD**
69  *Cleversticks.* Ill. by Derek Brazell. Crown, 1991 (0-517-58878-1); LB (0-517-58879-X). USE LEVEL: PS/P
*Asian American*
Ling Sung feels that other children at his school can do more than he can—like tie their shoes and write their names. When he uses paint brushes like chopsticks, he feels good knowing that he can do something, too.
SCHOOL; SELF-CONCEPT.

ATA, TE, RETELLER

70 *Baby Rattlesnake*. Adapted by Lynn Moroney. Ill. by Veg Reisberg. Children's Book Pr., 1989 (0-89239-049-2); pap. (0-89239-111-1). USE LEVEL: M
*Native American*
Baby Rattlesnake insists on having a full-size rattle, only to cause trouble with it.
FOLKTALES—NATIVE AMERICAN; REPTILES—SNAKES.

THE BABOON'S UMBRELLA

71 *The Baboon's Umbrella: An African Folktale*. Ill. by Ching. Childrens Pr., 1991, LB (0-516-05131-8); pap. (0-516-45131-6). USE LEVEL: M
*African*
The illustrations are presented without words and the text follows to encourage children to retell the story. Because his umbrella will not close, baboon cuts holes in it. Of course, when it rains he gets wet.
ANIMALS—BABOONS; CHARACTER TRAITS—FOOLISHNESS; FOLKTALES—AFRICA; STORYTELLING; UMBRELLAS.

BAER, EDITH

72 *This Is the Way We Eat Our Lunch: A Book about Children Around the World*. Ill. by Steven Björkman. Scholastic, 1995 (0-590-046887-1). USE LEVEL: P
*Multicultural*
This description of the way children around the world eat includes information about the locations.
ETIQUETTE; FOOD; FOREIGN LANDS; POETRY, RHYME.

73 *This Is the Way We Go to School: A Book about Children Around the World*. Ill. by Steven Björkman. Scholastic, 1990, pap. (0-590-49443-0). USE LEVEL: P
*Multicultural*
A rhyming text describes the ways many children go to school. After the story there is a list of where each child lives and a map of the locations.
FOREIGN LANDS; POETRY, RHYME; SCHOOL; TRANSPORTATION.

BAHOUS, SALLY

74 *Sitti and the Cats: A Tale of Friendship*. Ill. by Nancy Malick. Roberts Rinehart, 1993 (1-879373-61-0). USE LEVEL: M
*Middle Eastern—Palestine*
On old woman, whom everyone calls Sitti, lives a simple life. When she helps a cat in a tree, Sitti is rewarded with coins for

her kindness. Another villager, Im Yusuf, is greedy, so when she meets the cats, she is given bees and wasps.

ANIMALS—CATS; BEHAVIOR—GREED; CHARACTER TRAITS—KINDNESS; FOLKTALES—MIDDLE EAST—PALESTINE.

**BAILLIE, ALLAN**

75  *Rebel.* Ill. by Di Wu. Houghton, 1994 (0-395-69250-4). USE LEVEL: P

*Asian—Burma*

When a general arrives with guns and tanks to take over this village in Burma, one child throws a thong (shoe) at him, and all the villagers stand together to protect the young rebel. This is based on an incident that occurred in Rangoon.

BEHAVIOR—BULLYING; BEHAVIOR—FIGHTING, ARGUING; CHARACTER TRAITS—COURAGE; FOREIGN LANDS—ASIA—BURMA.

**BAKER, KEITH**

76  *The Magic Fan.* Ill. by the author. Harcourt, 1989 (0-15-250750-7). USE LEVEL: M

*Asian—Japan*

Yoshi's skill as a builder allows him to accomplish things that surprise the people in his village.

CAREERS—CARPENTERS; FOREIGN LANDS—ASIA—JAPAN; IMAGINATION.

**BAKER, OLAF**

77  *Where the Buffaloes Begin.* Ill. by Stephen Gammell. Viking, 1981 (0-670-82760-6); Puffin, pap. (0-14-050560-1). USE LEVEL: M

*Native American—Plains Indians*

Little Wolf wonders about the legend of his people telling of the sacred land where the buffaloes began.

ANIMALS—BUFFALOES; CALDECOTT AWARD; FOLKTALES—NATIVE AMERICAN—PLAINS INDIANS.

**BANDES, HANNA**

78  *Sleepy River.* Ill. by Jeanette Winter. Putnam, 1993 (0-399-22349-5). USE LEVEL: M

*Native American*

A mother and her son go out in their canoe to watch the world as night falls.

ANIMALS; BEDTIME; NATURE; NIGHT.

**BANG, BETSY, ADAPTER**

79  *Cucumber Stem: From a Bengali Folktale.* Ill. by Tony Chen. Greenwillow, 1980, o.p. USE LEVEL: P

*Asian—India*

A woodcutter and his wife have a son as small as a cucumber. Little Finger's bravery and kindness are rewarded and he grows to full height.
CHARACTER TRAITS—BRAVERY; CHARACTER TRAITS—SMALLNESS; ELVES AND LITTLE PEOPLE; FOLKTALES—ASIA—INDIA.

80    *The Old Woman and the Red Pumpkin: A Bengali Folk Tale.* Ill. by Molly Garrett Bang. Macmillan, 1975, o.p. USE LEVEL: M
*Asian—India*
A bear, a tiger, and a jackal want to eat the old woman, but she tricks them by hiding in a pumpkin.
ANIMALS; BEHAVIOR—TRICKERY; CHARACTER TRAITS—CLEVERNESS; FOLKTALES—ASIA—INDIA.

81    *Tuntuni the Tailor Bird: From a Bengali Folktale.* Ill. by Molly Garrett Bang. Greenwillow, 1978, o.p. USE LEVEL: P
*Asian—India*
In the first of two stories, when Tuntuni the bird has a thorn in her foot, she needs the help of many animals to get it out. In the second story, she shows she is more clever than the raja.
BIRDS; CHARACTER TRAITS—CLEVERNESS; FOLKTALES—ASIA—INDIA; ROYALTY.

**BANG, MOLLY**
82    *The Grey Lady and the Strawberry Snatcher.* Ill. by the author. Macmillan, 1980 (0-02-708140-0). USE LEVEL: P
*African American*
In this wordless book, the strawberry snatcher chases the grey lady, trying to take her strawberries.
CALDECOTT AWARD; FOOD; IMAGINATION; WORDLESS BOOKS.

83    *One Fall Day.* Ill. by the author. Greenwillow, 1994 (0-688-07015-9); LB (0-688-07016-7). USE LEVEL: P
*African American*
Collages of toys, cut paper, fabrics, and objects from nature illustrate the activities of a child on a fall day. Included are playing outside, enjoying a rain storm, and painting a picture.
ACTIVITIES—PLAYING; BEDTIME; SEASONS—FALL; TOYS.

84    *The Paper Crane.* Ill. by the author. Greenwillow, 1985 (0-688-04108-6); LB (0-688-04109-4); pap. (0-688-07333-6). USE LEVEL: P
*Asian*
In this blend of fantasy and reality, the kindness of a restaurant owner is magically rewarded by a stranger.

BEHAVIOR—FACING CHALLENGES; BIRDS—CRANES; CHARACTER TRAITS – KINDNESS; FOREIGN LANDS—ASIA; MAGIC.

85    *Ten, Nine, Eight.* Ill. by the author. Greenwillow, 1983 (0-688-00906-9); LB (0-688-00907-7); pap. (0-688-10480-0). USE LEVEL: PS/P
*African American*
As a little girl prepares for bed, she and her father count backward from ten and describe some of the things in her room.
BEDTIME; CALDECOTT AWARD; COUNTING, NUMBERS; FAMILY LIFE—FATHERS; POETRY, RHYME.

86    *Tye May and the Magic Brush.* Ill. by the author. Greenwillow, 1981 pap. (0-688-11504-7). USE LEVEL: M
*Asian—China*
Tye May is a poor beggar girl. She is given a magic brush and the things she paints become real. The greedy emperor tries to make her paint for him.
ACTIVITIES—PAINTING; ART; BEHAVIOR—GREED; FOREIGN LANDS—ASIA – CHINA; MAGIC.

87    *Wiley and the Hairy Man: Adapted from an American Folktale.* Ill. by the adapter. Macmillan, 1976 (0-02-708370-5); pap. (0-689-71162-X). USE LEVEL: P
*African American*
The Hairy Man wants Wiley. Three times he tries to get Wiley, and three times he fails. Now he cannot harm Wiley again.
BEHAVIOR—TRICKERY; CHARACTER TRAITS—CLEVERNESS; FOLKTALES—UNITED STATES; MONSTERS.

88    *Yellow Ball.* Ill. by the author. Greenwillow, 1991 (0-688-06314-4). USE LEVEL: PS/P
*African American*
Three children build a sand castle on the beach and their yellow ball floats away, into the hands of another child.
ACTIVITIES—PLAYING; SEA AND SEASHORE; TOYS—BALLS.

**BANIM, LISA**
89    *American Dreams.* Silver Moon Press, 1993, pap. (1-881889-68-8). USE LEVEL: M
*Asian American—Japan*
Amy Mochida and her family live in California. After the bombing of Pearl Harbor, the Mochidas are sent to an internment camp and Amy must say good-bye to her best friend, Jeannie.

FAMILY LIFE; FRIENDSHIP; PREJUDICE; RACE RELATIONS; RELOCATION; U.S. HISTORY—WORLD WAR II.

**BANKS, JACQUELINE TURNER**

90    *Egg-Drop Blues.* Houghton, 1995 (0-395-70931-8). USE LEVEL: U
*African American*
Judge and Jury Jenkins and their friends at Plank Elementary School return in this novel. Judge needs Jury's help to improve his science grade in the egg-drop contest. Judge's dyslexia makes school difficult for him.
FAMILY LIFE—SIBLINGS; HANDICAPS; SCHOOL; SELF-CONCEPT; TWINS.

91    *The New One.* Houghton, 1994 (0-395-66610-4). USE LEVEL: U
*African American*
Twin brothers Judge and Jury are in the sixth grade. When a new girl comes into their class, Jury is distracted. He is also bothered by his mother and her new boyfriend. He and his friends are surprised by the prejudicial behavior of another friend.
FAMILY LIFE; FRIENDSHIP; PREJUDICE; SCHOOL; TWINS.

92    *Project Wheels.* Houghton, 1993 (0-395-64378-3). USE LEVEL: U
*African American*
Judge and Jury Jenkins and their friends are in the sixth grade. For their class Christmas party, they decide to earn money to buy a motorized wheelchair for Wayne DeVoe.
CHARACTER TRAITS—HELPFULNESS; FRIENDSHIP; GIFTS; HANDICAPS—PHYSICAL; SCHOOL; TWINS.

**BANKS, SARA H.**

93    *Remember My Name.* Ill. by Birgitta Saflund. Roberts Rinehart, 1993, pap. (1-879373-38-6). USE LEVEL: U
*Native American—Cherokee*
Annie Rising Fawn, 11, leaves her home to live with her uncle William Blackfeather. On his farm in Georgia, Annie befriends one of his slaves, Righteous, and the two stay together even when Annie and the other Cherokees are relocated to Oklahoma.
RACE RELATIONS; RELOCATION; SLAVERY; U.S. HISTORY.

**BARBER, BARBARA E.**

94    *Saturday at The New You.* Ill. by Anna Rich. Lee & Low, 1994 (1-880000-06-7). USE LEVEL: P
*African American*

On Saturdays, Shauna helps her mother at her beauty parlor, The New You. On this Saturday, Shauna helps find a way to satisfy a difficult customer—Little Tiffany Peters, who is five.

CAREERS; CHARACTER TRAITS—HELPFULNESS; FAMILY LIFE—MOTHERS.

**BARNES, JOYCE ANNETTE**
95 *The Baby Grand, the Moon in July, & Me.* Dial, 1994 (0-8037-1586-2); LB (0-8037-1600-1). USE LEVEL: U
*African American*
Annie Armstrong, ten, worries about the divisiveness in her family. Her parents worry about money and about her brother, Matty, who wants to be a musician. Annie watches the 1969 moon launch and dreams of being an astronaut.

BEHAVIOR—FIGHTING, ARGUING; CAREERS—ASTRONAUTS; FAMILY LIFE; MUSIC; SELF-CONCEPT.

**BARRETT, JOYCE DURHAM**
96 *Willie's Not the Hugging Kind.* Ill. by Pat Cummings. HarperCollins, 1989 (0-06-020416-8); LB (0-06-020417-6); pap. (0-06-443264-5). USE LEVEL: P
*African American*
Willie's friend, Jo-Jo, tells Willie that hugging is silly, but Willie decides that hugging is right for him.

CHARACTER TRAITS—CONFIDENCE; EMOTIONS—LOVE; FAMILY LIFE; FRIENDSHIP.

**BARRETT, MARY BRIGID**
97 *Sing to the Stars.* Ill. by Sandra Speidel. Little, Brown, 1994 (0-316-08224-4). USE LEVEL: P
*African American*
Ephram enjoys playing his violin and talking to Mr. Washington, who is blind and who used to play the piano professionally. When there is a benefit concert, Ephram and Mr. Washington make music together.

FRIENDSHIP; HANDICAPS—BLINDNESS; MUSIC; URBAN LIFE.

**BATTLE-LAVERT, GWENDOLYN**
98 *The Barber's Cutting Edge.* Ill. by Raymond Holbert. Children's Book Pr., 1994 (0-89239-127-8). USE LEVEL: P
*African American*
While he cuts Rashaad's hair, the barber, Mr. Bigalow, discusses vocabulary words. When he does not know a word, Mr. Bigalow pretends he needs something from the back room. He is checking the dictionary.

CAREERS—BARBERS; CHARACTER TRAITS—PRIDE; LANGUAGE.

**BAUMGARTNER, BARBARA**

99 *Crocodile! Crocodile! Stories Told Around the World.* Ill. by Judy Moffatt. Dorling Kindersley, 1994 (1-56458-463-1). USE LEVEL: M

*Multicultural*

Six folktales—two from India, and one each from China, Puerto Rico, the Appalachian area, and Native Americans—are presented along with instructions for making simple stick puppets for putting on a show.

FOLKTALES; PUPPETS; SHORT STORIES.

**BAYLOR, BYRD**

100 *Before You Came This Way.* Ill. by Tom Bahti. Dutton, 1969, o.p. USE LEVEL: P/M

*Native American*

Baylor writes about the ancient drawings that can still be seen on canyon walls. These are messages from the past, telling of another time and another people. The illustrations evoke images of prehistoric cave paintings.

ART; U.S. HISTORY.

101 *The Desert Is Theirs.* Ill. by Peter Parnall. Macmillan, 1975 (0-684-14266-X); pap. (0-689-71105-X). USE LEVEL: M

*Native American—Papago*

People and animals of the desert canyon are described in this poetic text.

CALDECOTT AWARD; DESERT; ECOLOGY; NATURE; POETRY, RHYME.

102 *Hawk, I Am Your Brother.* Ill. by Peter Parnall. Macmillan, 1976 (0-684-14571-5); pap. (0-689-71102-6). USE LEVEL: P/M

*Native American*

Rudy Soto dreams of flying. By helping an injured hawk and then setting it free, Rudy is able to feel the joy of flight as the hawk soars through the sky.

ACTIVITIES—FLYING; BIRDS—HAWKS; CALDECOTT AWARD; CHARACTER TRAITS—FREEDOM.

103 *Moon Song.* Ill. by Ronald Himler. Macmillan, 1982 (0-684-17463-4). USE LEVEL: M

*Native American*

Coyote sees the moon and cries out for his mother. This story explains why coyotes howl at the moon.

ANIMALS—COYOTES; FOLKTALES—NATIVE AMERICAN; MOON; POURQUOI TALES.

104 *The Way to Start a Day.* Ill. by Peter Parnall. Macmillan, 1978 (0-684-15651-2). USE LEVEL: M
*Multicultural*
The importance of the sun to different peoples and cultures is poetically described in this book.
POETRY, RHYME; SUN.

105 *When Clay Sings.* Ill. by Tom Bahti. Macmillan, 1972 (0-684-18829-5); pap. (0-689-71106-9). USE LEVEL: P/M
*Native American*
The images that remain on fragments of clay pots used by the desert people of long ago provide information about their lives.
ART; CALDECOTT AWARD; DESERT; HISTORY.

**BEAKE, LESLEY**
106 *Song of Be.* Henry Holt, 1993 (0-8050-2905-2); Puffin, pap. (0-14-037498-1). USE LEVEL: U
*African—Namibia*
Be lives in the Bushmanland area of Namibia and works as a servant for Mr. and Mrs. Coetzee. As the political situation in her country changes, Be becomes more aware of the uncertainty of her future and of her growing attraction to Khu.
FOREIGN LANDS—AFRICA—NAMIBIA; RACE RELATIONS.

**BEDARD, MICHAEL, RETELLER**
107 *The Nightingale.* Ill. by Regolo Ricci. Houghton, 1991 (0-395-60735-3). USE LEVEL: M
*Asian—China*
This retelling of Andersen's literary tale includes details that reflect the Chinese setting. For example, red is the color of joy, and it is used throughout this book, and yellow is a sacred color and the emperor is shown in yellow.
BIRDS—NIGHTINGALES; FOREIGN LANDS—ASIA—CHINA; GIFTS.

**BEGAY, SHONTO**
108 *Ma'ii and Cousin Horned Toad: A Traditional Navajo Story.* Ill. by the author. Scholastic, 1992 (0-590-45391 2). USE LEVEL: M
*Native American—Navajo*
Ma'ii, the coyote, tricks Horned Toad into giving him food. After Ma'ii swallows Horned Toad, he learns a lesson about causing mischief.
ANIMALS—COYOTES; BEHAVIOR—TRICKERY; FOLKTALES—NATIVE AMERICAN—NAVAJO; FROGS AND TOADS.

109    *Navajo: Visions and Voices Across the Mesa.* Ill. by the author. Scholastic, 1995 (0-590-46153-2). USE LEVEL: U
*Native American—Navajo*
Shonto Begay's paintings are accompanied by poems, chants, and stories that provide insight into contemporary Navajo life and that link them with the heritage of this culture. Respect for the natural world is a theme in several of these writings.
NATURE; POETRY, RHYME.

**BEGAYE, LISA SHOOK**
110    *Building a Bridge.* Ill. by Libba Tracy. Northland, 1993 (0-87358-557-7). USE LEVEL: P
*Native American—Navajo*
Anna is apprehensive about her first day of kindergarten on the Navajo Reservation. At school, Juanita works with Anna as they share blocks and build a bridge.
ACTIVITIES—PLAYING; BEHAVIOR—GETTING ALONG WITH OTHERS; COMMUNITIES, NEIGHBORHOODS; FRIENDSHIP; SCHOOL.

**BELTING, NATALIA**
111    *Moon Was Tired of Walking on Air.* Ill. by Will Hillenbrand. Houghton, 1992 (0-395-53806-8). USE LEVEL: U
*South American*
This collection of stories features native peoples of South America. Included are several pourquoi tales, like "How the Birds Got New Beaks and Men Got Teeth."
ANIMALS; FOLKTALES—SOUTH AMERICA; NATURE; POURQUOI TALES; SHORT STORIES.

112    *Our Fathers Had Powerful Songs.* Ill. by Laszlo Kubinyi. Dutton, 1974, o.p. USE LEVEL: M
*Native American*
These lyrical verses are based on the legends and writings of different Native American peoples. They celebrate nature and the cycle of life.
NATURE; POETRY, RHYME.

113    *The Sun Is a Golden Earring.* Ill. by Bernarda Bryson. Holt, 1962, o.p. USE LEVEL: M
*Multicultural*
This collection of sayings and thoughts about the sun, moon, and sky is from a variety of peoples and places including the Solomon Islands, India, Malaya, and the Ute Indians.
CALDECOTT AWARD; FOLKTALES; MOON; POETRY, RHYME; SKY; SUN.

114     *Whirlwind Is a Ghost Dancing*. Ill. by Leo Dillon and Diane
        Dillon. Dutton, 1974, o.p. USE LEVEL: M
        *Native American*
        Poetic images from diverse native peoples are presented. Images
        of the natural world are featured, including the seasons, stars,
        and wind.
        NATURE; POETRY, RHYME.

BELTON, SANDRA
115     *From Miss Ida's Porch*. Ill. by Floyd Cooper. Macmillan, 1993
        (0-02-708915-0). USE LEVEL: M
        *African American*
        The children in this neighborhood often end up on Miss Ida's
        porch, listening to the stories of their neighbors, which often
        include their memories of important moments in their lives.
        ACTIVITIES—REMINISCING; FRIENDSHIP; OLDER ADULTS; STORYTELLING.

116     *May'naise Sandwiches and Sunshine Tea*. Ill. by Gail Gordon
        Carter. Macmillan, 1994 (0-02-709035-3). USE LEVEL: M
        *African American*
        Big Mama has a scrapbook and she loves to share memories
        with her granddaughter. Big Mama tells a story about her child-
        hood when she was worried that a friend would not be comfort-
        able in her less affluent home.
        ACTIVITIES—REMINISCING; BEHAVIOR—WORRYING; FAMILY LIFE—
        GRANDMOTHERS; SELF-CONCEPT.

BENCHLEY, NATHANIEL
117     *Small Wolf*. Ill. by Joan Sandin. HarperCollins, 1972 (0-06-
        020491-5); LB (0-06-020492-3); pap. (0-06-444180-6). USE
        LEVEL: P
        *Native American*
        Small Wolf wishes to hunt deer and bears, thinking he will then
        be a man. When he does go hunting, Small Wolf encounters
        white settlers, who threaten him and his people, forcing them to
        move to new lands.
        SPORTS—HUNTING; U.S. HISTORY—COLONIAL TIMES.

BERENDS, POLLY BERRIEN
118     *The Case of the Elevator Duck*. Ill. by Diane Allison. Random,
        1989, LB (0-394-92646-3); pap. (0-394-82646-9). USE LEVEL:
        M
        *African American*
        Gilbert finds a duck on the elevator in his apartment building

To his mother's chagrin, Gilbert brings the duck home. Of course, he must try to find its owner.

BIRDS—DUCKS; MYSTERY AND DETECTIVE STORIES; URBAN LIFE.

**BERGER, TERRY**
119    *Black Fairy Tales.* Ill. by David Omar White. Macmillan, 1969, pap., o.p. USE LEVEL: M
*African*
Tales from the Swazi, Shangani, and 'Msuto peoples are included in this collection. Many of the stories feature kings and queens, princes and princesses.

FOLKTALES—AFRICA; ROYALTY; SHORT STORIES.

**BERNHARD, EMERY, RETELLER**
120    *The Girl Who Wanted to Hunt: A Siberian Tale.* Ill. by Durga Bernhard. Holiday, 1994 (0-8234-1125-7). USE LEVEL: M
*Asian—Siberia*
Little Anga lives on the taiga in Siberia. Anga's stepmother, Unin, makes her do all the work, and it is worse after her father dies. Anga must be brave to face the cruelty of her stepmother.

CHARACTER TRAITS—BRAVERY; FOLKTALES—ASIA—SIBERIA; MAGIC;
SPORTS—HUNTING.

121    *How Snowshoe Hare Rescued the Sun: A Tale from the Arctic.* Ill. by Durga Bernhard. Holiday, 1993 (0-8234-1043-9). USE LEVEL: M
*Native American—Yuit Eskimo*
The demons steal the sun and take it to their home under the earth. The animals of the tundra try to rescue the sun, but Snowshoe Hare is the one who succeeds.

ANIMALS; ANIMALS—RABBITS; ARCTIC LANDS; FOLKTALES—NATIVE
AMERICAN—YUIT ESKIMO; MONSTERS.

122    *Spotted Eagle & Black Crow: A Lakota Legend.* Ill. by Durga Bernhard. Holiday, 1993 (0-8234-1007-2). USE LEVEL: M
*Native American—Lakota*
Black Crow tricks his brother, Spotted Eagle, and leaves him on a cliff with the eagles. The eagles help him survive and escape from the cliff. He returns to lead his people into battle.

BEHAVIOR—TRICKERY; BIRDS—EAGLES; CHARACTER TRAITS—BRAVERY;
EMOTIONS—ENVY, JEALOUSY; FOLKTALES—NATIVE AMERICAN—LAKOTA.

123    *The Tree That Rains: The Flood Myth of the Huichol Indians of Mexico.* Ill. by Durga Bernhard. Holiday, 1994 (0-8234-1108-7). USE LEVEL: M
*Native American—Huichol*

Watakame loves to work. One day, he chops down some trees and they grow back. Watakame learns that a flood is coming and he survives to thank Great-Grandmother Earth for her gifts.

FOLKTALES—NATIVE AMERICAN—HUICHOL; WEATHER—FLOODS.

**BERRY, JAMES**

124 *Ajeemah and His Son.* HarperCollins, 1992 (0-06-021043-5); LB (0-06-021044-3); pap. (0-06-440523-0). USE LEVEL: U

*African*

A father and son are taken from Ghana to Jamaica, where they are separated and sold into slavery. Ajeemah, the father, has the maturity and strength to survive the experience. His son, Atu, does not.

CRUELTY; DEATH; FOREIGN LANDS—AFRICA; FOREIGN LANDS—CARIBBEAN ISLANDS; HISTORY; SLAVERY.

125 *Spiderman Anancy.* Ill. by Joseph Olubo. Henry Holt, 1988 (0-8050-1207-9). USE LEVEL: M

*Caribbean*

There are 20 stories about Anancy, the trickster. Included are stories in which Anancy meets other colorful characters like Bro Tiger and Bro Monkey.

ANIMALS; BEHAVIOR—TRICKERY; CHARACTER TRAITS—CLEVERNESS; FOLKTALES—CARIBBEAN ISLANDS; SHORT STORIES; SPIDERS.

**BESS, CLAYTON**

126 *Story for a Black Night.* Houghton, 1982 (0-395-31857-2). USE LEVEL: U

*African*

During a storm when the electricity is off, Momo tells a tragic story from his childhood. Strangers came to his home in rural Africa, leaving a baby infected with smallpox. His sister died from the disease and his mother was disfigured.

DEATH; FOREIGN LANDS—AFRICA; ILLNESS.

127 *The Truth about the Moon.* Ill. by Rosekrans Hoffman. Houghton, 1983 (0-395-34551-0); pap. (0-395-64371-6). USE LEVEL: M

*African*

Sumu wants to understand the moon. His family cannot answer all his questions so he asks the chief. The chief tells Sumu a folktale about the sun and the moon.

CHARACTER TRAITS—QUESTIONING; FOREIGN LANDS—AFRICA; MOON; POURQUOI TALES.

**BEST, CARI**

128　*Taxi! Taxi!* Ill. by Dale Gottlieb. Little, Brown, 1994 (0-316-09259-2). USE LEVEL: P

*Hispanic American*

Tina's father, her "Papi," drives a taxi. He does not live with Tina and her mother, so Tina looks forward to seeing him on most Sundays.

DIVORCE, SEPARATION; FAMILY LIFE—FATHERS; TAXIS; URBAN LIFE.

**BIBLE, CHARLES, ADAPTER**

129　*Hamdaani: A Traditional Tale from Zanzibar.* Ill. by the adapter. Holt, 1977, o.p. USE LEVEL: M

*African—Zanzibar*

Hamdaani is a beggar. He finds some money and buys a gazelle, who helps him marry the sultan's daughter. But Hamdaani is ungrateful and he loses his wife and his wealth.

ANIMALS—GAZELLES; CHARACTER TRAITS—CONCEIT; FOLKTALES—AFRICA—ZANZIBAR.

**BIERHORST, JOHN, RETELLER**

130　*Doctor Coyote: A Native American Aesop's Fables.* Ill. by Wendy Watson. Macmillan, 1987 (0-02-709780-3). USE LEVEL: M

*Mexican—Aztec*

These Aztec stories focus on Coyote, who is a tricky character in the stories of many Native American people. Like other fables, these stories are short, and the moral lesson is stated at the end.

ANIMALS; ANIMALS—COYOTES; BEHAVIOR—TRICKERY; FABLES; FOLKTALES—MEXICO—AZTEC; SHORT STORIES.

131　*The Fire Plume: Legends of the American Indians.* Ill. by Alan E. Cober. Dial, 1969, o.p. USE LEVEL: M

*Native American*

Eight stories from native peoples of the northeastern United States and Canada are presented, including a story of six falcons who help each other survive the winter.

CHARACTER TRAITS—BRAVERY; FOLKTALES—NATIVE AMERICAN; SHORT STORIES.

132　*Lightning Inside You: And Other Native American Riddles.* Ill. by Louise Brierley. Morrow, 1992 (0-688-09582-8). USE LEVEL: M

*Native American*

"A hand over the world. Darkness." "What is there inside you like lightning? Meanness." This collection of riddles includes those of many native peoples in the Americas, including Aztec, Arapaho, Inuit, and Guarani. Many feature the natural world.

HUMOR; NATURE; RIDDLES.

133 *The Monkey's Haircut: And Other Stories Told by the Maya*. Ill. by Robert Andrew Parker. Morrow, 1986 (0-688-04269-4). USE LEVEL: M/U
**Central American—Mayan**
The 22 stories in this collection depict many of the traditions of the Mayan people of Mexico. An introduction provides background information on these people.
FOLKTALES—CENTRAL AMERICA—MAYAN; SHORT STORIES.

134 *The Naked Bear: Folktales of the Iroquois*. Ill. by Dirk Zimmer. Morrow, 1987 (0-688-06422-1). USE LEVEL: M/U
**Native American—Iroquois**
The 16 stories in this collection reflect the beliefs of the peoples of the Six Nations of the Iroquois. Turtle, a trickster, is included in several stories.
BEHAVIOR—TRICKERY; FOLKTALES—NATIVE AMERICAN—IROQUOIS; MAGIC; SHORT STORIES.

135 *On the Road of Stars: Native American Night Poems and Sleep Charms*. Ill. by Judy Pederson. Macmillan, 1994 (0-02-709735-8). USE LEVEL: M
**Native American**
Charms, poems, and chants from many native peoples feature night and sleep. Included are songs for comfort, dreaming, and animals. Peoples represented include Yoqui, Crow, Inuit, Pima, and Papago.
MAGIC; NIGHT; POETRY, RHYME; SLEEP.

136 *The Whistling Skeleton: American Indian Tales of the Supernatural*. Collected by George Bird Grinnell. Ill. by Robert Andrew Parker. Macmillan, 1982, o.p. USE LEVEL: M/U
**Native American**
The nine legends in this collection are from the Pawnee, the Blackfeet, and the Cheyenne peoples. They are filled with elements of the supernatural, including magic, ghosts, and transformations.
FOLKTALES—NATIVE AMERICAN; MAGIC; SCARY STORIES; SHORT STORIES; SUPERNATURAL.

137 *The Woman Who Fell from the Sky: The Iroquois Story of Creation*. Ill. by Robert Andrew Parker. Morrow, 1993 (0-688-10680-3); LB (0-688-10681-1). USE LEVEL: M
**Native American—Iroquois**
When the sky woman falls to earth, she lands on the turtle's back. She creates the stars and the sun and she brings living creatures to the earth.
CREATION; FOLKTALES—NATIVE AMERICAN—IROQUOIS; POURQUOI TALES.

**BINCH, CAROLINE**

138   *Gregory Cool.* Ill. by the author. Dial, 1994 (0-8037-1577-3).
USE LEVEL: M
*Caribbean*
On a visit to Tobago, Gregory misses his home and familiar routines. Granny and Granpa introduce him to his cousin, Lennox, who becomes his friend.
FOREIGN LANDS—CARIBBEAN ISLANDS; FRIENDSHIP; ISLANDS; POVERTY.

**BIRD, E. J.**

139   *The Rainmakers.* Carolrhoda, 1993 (0-87614-748-1). USE
LEVEL: U
*Native American—Anasazi*
Cricket is a young Anasazi boy living with his family in the American Southwest. With his grandfather, his friend Sheep, and his dancing bear, Cricket travels through the region looking for the kidnappers of Cricket's sister and hunting bison.
ANIMALS—BEARS; DESERT; FAMILY LIFE; FRIENDSHIP; U.S. HISTORY.

**BIRDSEYE, TOM, ADAPTER**

140   *A Song of Stars: An Asian Legend.* Ill. by Ju-hong Chen.
Holiday, 1990 (0-8234-0790-X). USE LEVEL: M
*Asian—China*
As a punishment for neglecting their duties, the Emperor of the Heavens sends the princess and the herdsman to separate parts of the sky.
EMOTIONS—LOVE; FOLKTALES—ASIA—CHINA; SKY; STARS.

**BISHOP, CLAIRE HUCHET**

141   *The Five Chinese Brothers.* Ill. by Kurt Wiese. Putnam, 1938 (0-698-20044-6); pap. (0-698-20642-8). USE LEVEL: M
*Asian—China*
Each of these five brothers can do something special, which helps them save the first brother from being put to death.
CHARACTER TRAITS—CLEVERNESS; FAMILY LIFE—SIBLINGS; FOLKTALES—ASIA—CHINA.

**BLACKMAN, MALORIE**

142   *Girl Wonder and the Terrific Twins.* Ill. by Lis Toft. Dutton, 1991 (0-525-45065-3). USE LEVEL: M
*African American*
Maxine is the girl wonder and her younger brothers, Anthony and Edward, are the terrific twins. They get into scrapes with the neighbor's flowers, a pet cat, and saving energy. Throughout, they support each other and have fun.
FAMILY LIFE—SIBLINGS; TWINS.

**BLOOD, CHARLES L., AND MARTIN A. LINK**

143  *A Goat in the Rug.* Ill. by Nancy Winslow Parker. Macmillan, 1980 (0-02-710920-8); pap. (0-689-71418-1). USE LEVEL: P
*Native American—Navajo*
A goat named Geraldine describes the process of weaving a Navaho rug.
ACTIVITIES—WEAVING; ANIMALS—GOATS; RUGS.

**BLUE, ROSE**

144  *A Quiet Place.* Ill. by Tom Feelings. Watts, 1969, o.p. USE LEVEL: M
*African American*
Matthew loves the library, which is his quiet place. He remembers the different foster homes he has been in and how happy he is now with the Walters family. When his library is closed, Matthew looks for a new quiet place in which to read.
BEHAVIOR—SOLITUDE; FAMILY LIFE—FOSTER FAMILY; LIBRARIES; URBAN LIFE.

**BOGART, JO ELLEN**

145  *Daniel's Dog.* Ill. by Janet Wilson. Scholastic, 1990, pap. (0-590-43401-2). USE LEVEL: P
*African American*
Daniel has an imaginary dog named Lucy. Even when his mother is busy with the new baby, Lucy has time for Daniel.
ANIMALS—DOGS; BABIES, TODDLERS; FAMILY LIFE; IMAGINATION—IMAGINARY FRIENDS.

**BOIVIN, KELLY**

146  *Where Is Mittens?* Ill. by Clovis Martin. Childrens Pr., 1990, LB (0-516-02060-9); pap. (0-516-42060-7). USE LEVEL: PS/P
*African American*
A little girl looks for her cat. She finds her and four new kittens. The simple rhyming text makes this a predictable reader.
ANIMALS—CATS; POETRY, RHYME; PREDICTABLE TEXT.

**BOLOGNESE, DON**

147  *Little Hawk's New Name.* Ill. by the author. Scholastic, 1995, pap. (0-590-48292-0). USE LEVEL: P
*Native American*
Little Hawk picks a horse for himself, goes on a hunt, and rescues his grandfather while he earns his new name, "He-Who-Jumps-Over-Everyone."
BEHAVIOR—GROWING UP; NAMES.

**BONNICI, PETER**

148 *The Festival.* Ill. by Lisa Kopper. Carolrhoda, 1984, LB (0-87614-229-3). USE LEVEL: P
*Asian—India*
In India, Arjuna and his family prepare for the village festival. They discuss many cultural traditions and celebrations.
CELEBRATIONS; FAMILY LIFE; FOREIGN LANDS—ASIA—INDIA.

149 *The First Rains.* Ill. by Lisa Kopper. Carolrhoda, 1985, LB (0-87614-228-5). USE LEVEL: P
*Asian—India*
Arjuna finds the heat oppressive as he waits for the monsoons and the rains they will bring.
FOREIGN LANDS—ASIA—INDIA; WEATHER—RAIN.

**BOSSE, MALCOLM**

150 *Deep Dream of the Rain Forest.* Farrar, 1993 (0-374-31757-1); pap. (0-374-41702-4). USE LEVEL: U
*African—Iban*
In the 1920s, Bayang is an Iban warrior in Borneo. Like his people, Bayang believes in dreams, and he has one about Big Fish. With Tambong, a disabled girl, he goes into the rain forest, seeking the meaning of his dream.
BEHAVIOR—GROWING UP; DREAMS; FOREIGN LANDS—AFRICA; FRIENDSHIP.

**BOWDEN, JOAN CHASE**

151 *Why the Tides Ebb and Flow.* Ill. by Marc Brown. Houghton, 1979 (0-395-29378-7); pap. (0-395-54952-3). USE LEVEL: M
*African*
The Sky Spirit tells the old woman that she may have a rock and the woman chooses the rock that keeps the sea from flowing down the bottomless pit. The Sky Spirit allows the woman to take the rock twice each day, causing the tides.
FOLKTALES—AFRICA; POURQUOI TALES; SEA AND SEASHORE; TIDES.

**BOYD, CANDY DAWSON**

152 *Breadsticks and Blessing Places* (paperback title: *Forever Friends*). Macmillan, 1985 (0-02-709290-9); Puffin pap. (0-14-032077-6). USE LEVEL: U
*African American*
Toni Douglas, 12, wants to enter King Academy, but her schoolwork is not quite good enough. As she struggles to improve, she also struggles to understand her family and to accept the death of one of her friends.
BEHAVIOR—FACING CHALLENGES; DEATH; FRIENDSHIP; SCHOOL.

153     *Charlie Pippin*. Macmillan, 1987 (0-02-726350-9); Puffin,
        1988, pap. (0-14-032587-5). USE LEVEL: U
        *African American*
        Charlie, a sixth grader, is confused by her father's anger. She
        decides to learn more about the Vietnam War, so that she can
        understand her father's past experiences.
        BEHAVIOR—GROWING UP; FAMILY LIFE; U.S. HISTORY—VIETNAM WAR.

154     *Circle of Gold*. Scholastic, 1984 (0-590-49426-0); pap. (0-590-
        43266-4). USE LEVEL: U
        *African American*
        Since her father's death, Mattie Benson finds it difficult to deal
        with her mother's grief. Mattie decides to buy her mother a spe-
        cial present.
        CORETTA SCOTT KING AWARD; FAMILY LIFE; GIFTS; HOLIDAYS—MOTHER'S
        DAY; MONEY.

155     *Fall Secrets*. Puffin, 1994, pap. (0-14-036583-4). USE LEVEL: U
        *African American*
        Jessie wants to be an actress so she auditions and is accepted at
        the Oakland Performing Arts Middle School. At home, Jessie
        has the support of her family but she sometimes resents her
        beautiful older sister, Cass.
        ACTIVITIES—ACTING; BEHAVIOR—GROWING UP; FAMILY LIFE; SCHOOL;
        SELF-CONCEPT.

        **BOZYLINSKY, HANNAH HERITAGE**
156     *Lala Salama: An African Lullaby in Swahili and English*. Ill. by
        the author. Putnam, 1993 (0-399-22022-4). USE LEVEL: P
        *African*
        A little boy says good night to the animals and, finally, to his
        mother. The lullaby appears in both Swahili and English.
        BEDTIME; FOREIGN LANDS—AFRICA; FOREIGN LANGUAGES; LULLABIES;
        POETRY, RHYME.

        **BRENNER, ANITA**
157     *The Boy Who Could Do Anything: And Other Mexican Folk Tales*.
        Ill. by Jean Charlot. Shoe String, 1992 (0-208-02353-4). USE
        LEVEL: M/U
        *Mexican*
        Several of these stories feature Tepozton, who is known as "The
        Boy Who Could Do Anything." Tepozton's father is a god and
        Tepozton has magic powers that help his people
        FOLKTALES—MEXICO; MAGIC; SHORT STORIES.

**BRENNER, BARBARA**

158    *Little One Inch.* Ill. by Fred Brenner. Putnam, 1977, o.p. USE
LEVEL: M
*Asian—Japan*
A couple's wish for a child is granted, but their child is very tiny.
He is clever and brave and he outwits three monsters and mar-
ries his beloved.
BEHAVIOR—TRICKERY; CHARACTER TRAITS—BRAVERY; CHARACTER
TRAITS—SMALLNESS; ELVES AND LITTLE PEOPLE; FOLKTALES—ASIA—
JAPAN.

159    *Rosa and Marco and the Three Wishes.* Ill. by Megan Halsey.
Macmillan, 1992 (0-02-712315-4). USE LEVEL: P
*Hispanic*
Rosa and Marco catch a magic fish who gives them three wish-
es, which they end up wasting.
BEHAVIOR—WISHING; CHARACTER TRAITS—FOOLISHNESS; FAMILY LIFE—
SIBLINGS; MAGIC.

160    *Wagon Wheels.* Ill. by Don Bolognese. HarperCollins, 1978 (0-
06-020668-3); LB (0-06-020669-1); pap. (0-06-444052-4).
USE LEVEL: P
*African American*
This book tells of a black family's westward journey from
Kentucky to Kansas in the 1870s.
ACTIVITIES—TRAVELING; FAMILY LIFE; FRONTIER AND PIONEER LIFE; U.S.
HISTORY.

**BRILL, MARLENE TARG**

161    *Allen Jay and the Underground Railroad.* Ill. by Janice Lee
Porter. Carolrhoda, 1993 (0-87614-776-7); LB (0-87614-605-
1). USE LEVEL: M
*African American*
It is 1842, and Allen Jay and his family are Quakers who hide
escaping slaves on their farm in Ohio.
CHARACTER TRAITS—BRAVERY; EMOTIONS—FEAR; SLAVERY; U.S.
HISTORY; UNDERGROUND RAILROAD.

**BROOKS, BRUCE**

162    *Everywhere.* HarperCollins, 1990 (0-06-020728-0); LB (0-06-
020729-9); pap. (0-06-440433-1). USE LEVEL: M/U
*African American*
A ten-year-old boy is worried that his grandfather is dying.
Dooley, 11, comes up with a plan to arrange a "soul switch"
between the grandfather and a turtle. Reluctantly, the boy
agrees, and they embark on a series of mishaps.

BEHAVIOR—WORRYING; DEATH; EMOTIONS—LOVE; FAMILY LIFE—
GRANDFATHERS; FRIENDSHIP.

163    *The Moves Make the Man.* HarperCollins, 1984 (0-06-020679-
9); LB (0-06-020698-7); pap. (0-06-447022-9). USE LEVEL: U
*African American*
Jerome, 13, loves to play basketball. When he enters an all-
white school, his life is changed. His mother is injured and his
new coach will not let him on the team. Jerome develops a
friendship with a troubled classmate, Bix.
FRIENDSHIP; NEWBERY AWARD; PREJUDICE; RACE RELATIONS; SCHOOL;
SPORTS—BASKETBALL.

**BROOKS, GWENDOLYN**
164    *Bronzeville Boys and Girls.* Ill. by Ronni Solbert. HarperCollins,
1956 (0-06-020651-9). USE LEVEL: P/M
*African American*
Brooks's poems deal with the individual experiences of children.
BEHAVIOR—GROWING UP; POETRY, RHYME; URBAN LIFE.

**BROWN, MARCIA**
165    *The Blue Jackal.* Ill. by the author. Macmillan, 1977, o.p. USE
LEVEL: M
*Asian—India*
By accident, a jackal, called Fierce-Howl, is dyed blue. When he
returns to the forest, the other animals treat him as their king
until they realize that he is still just a jackal.
ANIMALS—JACKALS; BEHAVIOR—TRICKERY; CHARACTER TRAITS—APPEAR-
ANCE; FOLKTALES—ASIA—INDIA.

166    *Once a Mouse: A Fable Cut in Wood.* Ill. by the reteller.
Macmillan, 1961, LB (0-684-12662-1); pap. (0-689-71343-6).
USE LEVEL: P/M
*Asian—India*
A hermit transforms a mouse into progressively larger animals
until the mouse, overcome with his own pride, thinks about
destroying the hermit.
ANIMALS; CALDECOTT AWARD; CHARACTER TRAITS—PRIDE; FABLES;
CONCEPTS—SIZE; FOLKTALES—ASIA—INDIA.

**BROWNE, VEE, RETELLER**
167    *Monster Birds: A Navajo Folktale.* Ill. by Baje Whitethorne.
Northland, 1993 (0-87358-558-5). USE LEVEL: M
*Native American—Navajo*
Monster Slayer and Child Born of Water are twins. They are
taken by Monster Bird to her nest. Monster Slayer kills her and

her mate with his lightning arrows. The twins give their magic feathers to the fledglings and are helped home by Spiderwoman.

BIRDS; FOLKTALES—NATIVE AMERICAN—NAVAJO; MAGIC; WEATHER—RAIN.

### BRUCHAC, JOSEPH, RETELLER

168    *A Boy Called Slow: The True Story of Sitting Bull.* Ill. by Rocco Baviera. Putnam, 1994 (0-399-22692-3). USE LEVEL: M

*Native American—Lakota Sioux*

The son of Returns Again is given a childhood name to reflect his actions. His name is Slow. Slow is eager to earn a new name. After he leads a group against the Crow warriors, his name is changed to Sitting Bull.

CHARACTER TRAITS—BRAVERY; NAMES; SITTING BULL.

169    *The First Strawberries: A Cherokee Story.* Ill. by Anna Vojtech. Dial, 1993 (0-8037-1331-2); LB (0-8037-1332-0). USE LEVEL: M

*Native American—Cherokee*

When man and woman argue, she leaves. With the help of the Sun, who creates strawberries, they reconcile.

BEHAVIOR—FIGHTING, ARGUING; FOLKTALES—NATIVE AMERICAN—CHEROKEE; FOOD; POURQUOI TALES.

170    *Flying with the Eagle, Racing the Great Bear: Stories from Native North America.* BridgeWater, 1993, LB (0-8167-3026-1); pap. (0-8167-3027-X). USE LEVEL: U

*Native American*

Divided into four regions, there are 16 stories from native peoples including the Cherokee, Apache, and Cheyenne.

FOLKTALES—NATIVE AMERICAN; SHORT STORIES.

171    *Fox Song.* Ill. by Paul Morin. Putnam, 1993 (0-399-22346-0). USE LEVEL: P

*Native American*

After her great-grandmother's death, Jamie thinks about all that Grama Bowman had taught her about appreciating nature and her Abenaki heritage.

DEATH; FAMILY LIFE—GRANDMOTHERS; NATURE.

172    *Gluskabe and the Four Wishes.* Ill. by Christine Nyburg Shrader. Dutton, 1995 (0-525-65164-0). USE LEVEL: M

*Native American—Abenaki*

Four Abenaki men travel to Gluskabe, each hoping to be granted a wish. Three men disobey Gluskabe's instructions and, although their wishes are granted, the results are not what they expected. The fourth man does receive his wish to feed his people.

BEHAVIOR—WISHING; FOLKTALES—NATIVE AMERICAN—ABENAKI.

173 *The Great Ball Game: A Muskogee Story.* Ill. by Susan L. Roth. Dial, 1994 (0-8037-1539-0); LB (0-8037-1540-4). USE LEVEL: M

*Native American—Muskogee*

When the Birds and the Animals have a ball game to prove who is better, Bat has trouble choosing sides. The Animals let him be with them and he helps them win.

ANIMALS; BIRDS; CONTESTS; FOLKTALES—NATIVE AMERICAN— MUSKOGEE; POURQUOI TALES.

**BRUCHAC, JOSEPH, AND MICHAEL J. CADUTO, RETELLERS**

174 *Native American Stories.* Ill. by John Kahionhes Fadden. Fulcrum, 1991, pap. (1-55591-094-7). USE LEVEL: M/U

*Native American*

These stories are from many North American native peoples and emphasize creation, the earth, seasons, and other aspects of the natural world.

CREATION; FOLKTALES—NATIVE AMERICAN; NATURE; SHORT STORIES.

**BRUCHAC, JOSEPH, AND JONATHAN LONDON**

175 *Thirteen Moons on Turtle's Back: A Native American Year of Moons.* Ill. by Thomas Locker. Putnam, 1992 (0-399-22141-7). USE LEVEL: M

*Native American*

Legends from many peoples, including the Huron, the Cherokee, and the Lakota Sioux, describe the seasons.

DAYS OF THE WEEK, MONTHS OF THE YEAR; FOLKTALES—NATIVE AMERICAN; SEASONS.

**BRUCHAC, JOSEPH, AND GAYLE ROSS, RETELLERS**

176 *The Girl Who Married the Moon: Tales from Native North America.* BridgeWater, 1994, LB (0-8167-3480-1). USE LEVEL: U

*Native American*

Sixteen stories grouped by regions (Northeast, Southeast, Southwest, and Northwest) present strong images of females in North American societies. Included are stories from the Seneca, Muskogee (Creek), and Dine (Navajo).

FOLKTALES—NATIVE AMERICAN; SHORT STORIES.

BRUSCA, MARÍA CRISTINA

177　*On the Pampas.* Ill. by the author. Henry Holt, 1991 (0-8050-1548-5); pap. (0-8050-2919-2). USE LEVEL: P
*South American—Argentina*
A little girl visits her grandparents in Argentina and learns about the pampas. The endpapers describe items common to life on the pampas.
FAMILY LIFE—GRANDPARENTS; FOREIGN LANDS—SOUTH AMERICA—ARGENTINA; GAUCHOS; RANCH LIFE.

178　*When Jaguars Ate the Moon: And Other Stories about Animals and Plants of the Americas.* Ill. by the author. Henry Holt, 1995 (0-8050-2797-1). USE LEVEL: M
*Multicultural*
Focusing on nature, this book presents information in alphabetical order. Folktales from many cultures are included like the Aymara (Bolivia) story "The Lost Llama" and the Kogi (Colombia) story "The First Tobacco."
ABC BOOKS; ANIMALS; FOLKTALES; NATURE; PLANTS.

BRYAN, ASHLEY

179　*The Adventures of Aku: Or How It Came About That We Shall Always See Okra the Cat Lying on a Velvet Cushion, While Okraman the Dog Sleeps Among the Ashes.* Ill. by the author. Macmillan, 1976, o.p. USE LEVEL: M
*African*
At one time, Cat and Dog were equals. When Aku travels to get items for his mother, he is tricked into taking Okra, the cat, and Okraman, the dog. Spider Ananse tries to take Aku's ring and Okra helps recover it.
ANIMALS—CATS; ANIMALS—DOGS; BEHAVIOR—TRICKERY; FOLKTALES—AFRICA; POURQUOI TALES.

180　*All Night, All Day: A Child's First Book of African-American Spirituals.* Musical arrangements by David Manning Thomas. Ill. by the author. Macmillan, 1991 (0-689-31662-3). USE LEVEL: P/M
*African American*
Twenty spirituals are presented, including "Peter, Go Ring the Bells" and the title song.
CORETTA SCOTT KING AWARD; MUSIC; RELIGION; SONGS.

181　*Beat the Story-Drum, Pum-Pum.* Ill. by the author. Macmillan, 1980 (0-689-31356-X); pap. (0-689-71107-7). USE LEVEL: M
*African*

These five folktales are filled with sounds and rhythms that extend the connection to the traditions of Africa. Included are several pourquoi tales and tales featuring animals.

ANIMALS; CORETTA SCOTT KING AWARD; FOLKTALES—AFRICA; POURQUOI TALES; SHORT STORIES.

182    *The Cat's Purr.* Ill. by the author. Macmillan, 1985 (0-689-31086-2). USE LEVEL: P
*Caribbean—West Indies*
Cat and Rat live happily as friends and neighbors. After the friends fight over Cat's drum, Cat chases Rat, who pushes the drum into Cat's mouth. The drum becomes the cat's purr.

ANIMALS—CATS; ANIMALS—RATS; FOLKTALES—CARIBBEAN ISLANDS; FOLKTALES—CARIBBEAN ISLANDS—WEST INDIES; POURQUOI TALES.

183    *The Dancing Granny.* Ill. by the author. Macmillan, 1977, pap. (0-689-71149-2). USE LEVEL: M
*Caribbean—West Indies*
Granny Anika is a happy woman who loves to dance. Spider Ananse tricks her into dancing while he steals her food.

ACTIVITIES—DANCING; BEHAVIOR—TRICKERY; FOLKTALES—CARIBBEAN ISLANDS—WEST INDIES.

184    *I'm Going to Sing: Black American Spirituals, Vol. 2.* Ill. by the author. Macmillan, 1982, o.p. USE LEVEL: M
*African American*
There are 25 more spirituals in this collection, including "When the Saints," "Joshua Fit the Battle," and "Do Lord Remember Me." Some, like "Steal Away," are associated with both biblical themes and slavery. This is a companion to the author's *Walk Together Children* (see main entry).

CORETTA SCOTT KING AWARD; MUSIC; RELIGION; SONGS.

185    *Lion and the Ostrich Chicks: And Other African Folk Tales.* Ill. by the author. Macmillan, 1986 (0-689-31311-X). USE LEVEL: M
*African*
These four stories are from different areas of Africa. One features Ananse and two feature animals.

ANIMALS; BEHAVIOR—TRICKERY; CORETTA SCOTT KING AWARD; FOLKTALES—AFRICA; SHORT STORIES.

186    *The Ox of the Wonderful Horns and Other African Folktales.* Ill. by the author. Macmillan, 1971 (0-689-31799-9). USE LEVEL: M
*African*

In this collection, there are five stories featuring animals, including "Ananse the Spider in Search of a Fool" and a story with Rabbit as a trickster.

ANIMALS; BEHAVIOR—TRICKERY; FOLKTALES—AFRICA; SHORT STORIES; SPIDERS.

187    *Sh-ko and His Eight Wicked Brothers.* Ill. by Fumio Yoshimura. Macmillan, 1988 (0-689-31446-9). USE LEVEL: M
*Asian—Japan*
Although his eight wicked brothers call Sh-ko ugly, his kindness wins him the favor of Princess Yakami.

ANIMALS—RABBITS; CHARACTER TRAITS—KINDNESS; FOLKTALES—ASIA— JAPAN.

188    *Sing to the Sun.* Ill. by the author. HarperCollins, 1992 (0-06-020829-5); LB (0-06-020833-3). USE LEVEL: M
*African American*
Poems celebrate everyday experiences like enjoying the rain or a flower. Some poems focus on family—"My Dad," "Granny," and "Mama's Bouquets."

FAMILY LIFE; POETRY, RHYME.

189    *The Story of Lightning & Thunder.* Ill. by the author. Macmillan, 1993 (0-689-31836-7). USE LEVEL: M
*African*
Thunder, a sheep, and Lightning, a ram, work together to call the rain, bringing a wonderful harvest. Lightning's impetuous behavior forces them to leave Earth and live in the sky.

ANIMALS—RAMS; ANIMALS—SHEEP; FOLKTALES—AFRICA; POURQUOI TALES; WEATHER—THUNDER.

190    *Turtle Knows Your Name.* Ill. by the author. Macmillan, 1989 (0-689-31578-3). USE LEVEL: M
*Caribbean—West Indies*
A young boy must learn his long name and his grandmother tries to help him.

FAMILY LIFE—GRANDMOTHERS; FOLKTALES—CARIBBEAN ISLANDS—WEST INDIES; NAMES; REPTILES—TURTLES, TORTOISES.

191    *Walk Together Children: Black American Spirituals.* Ill. by the author. Macmillan, 1974, o.p. USE LEVEL: M
*African American*
Many of the 24 spirituals in this collection are familiar, like "Jacob's Ladder," "Go Down Moses," and "Swing Low Sweet Chariot." Many of them have strong rhythmic patterns, captur-

ing the beat of the drum, which was forbidden to many slaves. This is a companion to the author's *I'm Going to Sing* (see main entry).

MUSIC; RELIGION; SONGS.

**BUCKLEY, HELEN E.**

192 *Grandfather and I*. Ill. by Jan Ormerod. Lothrop, 1994 (0-688-12533-6); LB (0-688-12534-4). USE LEVEL: PS/P
*African American*
This little boy loves spending time with his grandfather, who never makes him hurry. This is a newly illustrated version of this title.

ACTIVITIES—WALKING; FAMILY LIFE—GRANDFATHERS.

193 *Grandmother and I*. Ill. by Jan Ormerod. Lothrop, 1994 (0-688-12531-X); LB (0-688-12532-8). USE LEVEL: PS/P
*African American*
This little girl finds sitting in her grandmother's lap is especially comforting. This is a newly illustrated version of this title.

EMOTIONS—LOVE; FAMILY LIFE—GRANDMOTHERS.

**BUFFETT, JIMMY, AND SAVANNAH JANE BUFFETT**

194 *The Jolly Mon*. Ill. by Lambert David. Harcourt, 1988 (0-15-240530-5). USE LEVEL: P
*Caribbean*
Jolly Mon travels among the islands in the Caribbean until he returns to Bananaland to be the king.

ACTIVITIES—TRAVELING; FOREIGN LANDS—CARIBBEAN ISLANDS; MUSIC; ROYALTY—KINGS; SEA AND SEASHORE; SONGS.

**BULLA, CLYDE ROBERT, AND MICHAEL SYSON**

195 *Conquista!* Ill. by Ronald Himler. HarperCollins, 1978, LB (0-690-03871-2). USE LEVEL: M
*Native American*
Little Wolf seeks to learn about himself and his destiny. When he finds a horse that has become separated from Coronado and his men, he must overcome his fear and ride the horse.

ANIMALS—HORSES; EMOTIONS—FEAR; HISTORY.

**BUNTING, EVE**

196 *A Day's Work*. Ill. by Ronald Himler. Houghton, 1994 (0-395-67321-6). USE LEVEL: P
*Mexican American*
Francisco waits with his grandfather, hoping to find work. When they are hired to do gardening, Francisco says they both know

what to do. His lie causes a problem and his abuelo teaches him a lesson about being truthful.

BEHAVIOR—LYING; CHARACTER TRAITS—HONESTY; FAMILY LIFE—GRAND-FATHERS; GARDENS, GARDENING.

197    *Flower Garden.* Ill. by Kathryn Hewett. Harcourt, 1994 (0-15-228776-0). USE LEVEL: PS/P
*African American*
A girl and her father prepare a window box of flowers as a birthday surprise for mother.

BIRTHDAYS; FAMILY LIFE; FLOWERS; GARDENS, GARDENING; POETRY, RHYME.

198    *The Happy Funeral.* Ill. by Vo-Dinh Mai. HarperCollins, 1982 (0-06-020893-7); LB (0-06-020894-5). USE LEVEL: P
*Asian American—China*
When Laura's grandfather dies, she and her family follow the traditions and customs of their Chinese heritage.

CUSTOMS; DEATH; FAMILY LIFE.

199    *How Many Days to America? A Thanksgiving Story.* Ill. by Beth Peck. Houghton, 1988 (0-89919-521-0); pap. (0-395-54777-6). USE LEVEL: M
*Caribbean*
A family leaves their home on a Caribbean island to escape hardship and threats from the military. They are seeking freedom and a better life in America.

CHARACTER TRAITS—FREEDOM; FOREIGN LANDS—CARIBBEAN ISLANDS; HOLIDAYS—THANKSGIVING; REFUGEES.

200    *Smoky Night.* Ill. by David Diaz. Harcourt, 1994 (0-15-269954-6). USE LEVEL: P/M
*African American*
During riots, a young boy, Daniel, and his mother must leave their burning building. At the shelter, they meet some people from their neighborhood, including Mrs. Kim, and they learn about getting along.

ANIMALS—CATS; BEHAVIOR—GETTING ALONG WITH OTHERS; CALDECOTT AWARD; PREJUDICE; COMMUNITIES, NEIGHBORHOODS; RIOTS.

201    *Summer Wheels.* Ill. by Thomas B. Allen. Harcourt, 1992 (0-15-207000-1). USE LEVEL: M
*African American*

The Bicycle Man fixes up old bicycles and then loans them to children in the neighborhood, including Brady and Lawrence. When one angry boy, Leon, purposely wrecks one of the bikes, the Bicycle Man is understanding.

EMOTIONS—ANGER; FRIENDSHIP; OLDER ADULTS; SPORTS—BICYCLING.

**BURCHARD, PETER**

202    *Bimby.* Ill. by the author. Putnam, 1968, o.p. USE LEVEL: M/U
*African American*
As a slave in Georgia before the Civil War, Bimby encounters kindness and cruelty. He becomes more aware of the injustice of slavery and eventually chooses to run away.

CHARACTER TRAITS—BRAVERY; SLAVERY; U.S. HISTORY.

203    *Chinwe.* Ill. by the author. Putnam, 1979, o.p. USE LEVEL: M/U
*African American*
Chinwe is captured from her village in Africa and is taken on a slave ship to America. As a slave, she dreams of freedom.

CHARACTER TRAITS—BRAVERY; SLAVERY; U.S. HISTORY.

**BURCHARDT, NELLIE**

204    *Project Cat.* Ill. by Fermin Rocker. Watts, 1966, o.p. USE LEVEL:
M
*African American*
When Betsy finds a cat, she decides to care for it, even though she knows that pets are not allowed at this city housing project.

ANIMALS—CATS; PETS; URBAN LIFE.

**BURDEN-PATMON, DENISE**

205    *Imani's Gift at Kwanzaa.* Ill. by Floyd Cooper. Simon & Schuster, 1992, pap. (0-671-79841-3). USE LEVEL: P
*African American*
Imani and her family and friends celebrate Kwanzaa together. This is the first time one girl, Enna, has celebrated this holiday and Imani helps Enna understand some of the principles.

CELEBRATIONS; FAMILY LIFE; FRIENDSHIP; HOLIDAYS—KWANZAA.

**BURGIE, IRVING**

206    *Caribbean Carnival: Songs of the West Indies.* Ill. by Frané Lessac. Morrow, 1992 (0-688-10779-6); LB (0-688-11780-X).
USE LEVEL: M
*Caribbean*
Popular songs of this region, including "Jamaica Farewell" and "Day-O," provide images of everyday experiences on these

islands. There are notes about the songs that describe their roots and focus on calypso.

CLOTHING—CARIBBEAN ISLANDS; ISLANDS; MUSIC; SONGS.

### BURTON, MARILEE ROBIN
207 *My Best Shoes.* Ill. by James Ransome. Morrow, 1994 (0-688-11756-2); LB (0-688-11757-0). USE LEVEL: PS/P
*Multicultural*
This rhyming text is accompanied by illustrations of children from diverse backgrounds enjoying different kinds of shoes.

CLOTHING—SHOES; POETRY, RHYME.

### BUSH, TIMOTHY
208 *Three at Sea.* Ill. by the author. Crown, 1994 (0-517-59299-1). USE LEVEL: P
*Multicultural*
Zachariah Jr. and his friends float out to sea and encounter endangered animals who are too concerned about their own safety to help them.

ANIMALS; ANIMALS—ENDANGERED ANIMALS; ENVIRONMENT; SEA AND SEASHORE.

### BUSHEY, JEANNE
209 *A Sled Dog for Moshi.* Ill. by Germaine Arnaktauyok. Hyperion, 1994 (1-56282-631-X); LB (1-56282-632-8). USE LEVEL: P
*Native American—Inuit*
Moshi, an Inuit girl, loves Jessica's pet dog, Tippy. Jessica and her family have moved from New York City to this small Arctic village. Moshi wishes she could have a dog for a pet, but when a sled dog helps rescue the girls, Moshi changes her mind.

ANIMALS—DOGS; ARCTIC LANDS; FRIENDSHIP; PETS; WEATHER—SNOW.

### CAINES, JEANNETTE
210 *Abby.* Ill. by Steven Kellogg. HarperCollins, 1973, LB (0-06-020922-4); pap. (0-06-443049-9). USE LEVEL: PS
*African American*
Abby, who is adopted, is loved by her family, but, as in any family, there can be a problem with an older brother.

ADOPTION; EMOTIONS—LOVE; FAMILY LIFE—SIBLINGS; SIBLING RIVALRY.

211 *Daddy.* Ill. by Ronald Himler. HarperCollins, 1977 (0-06-020924-0). USE LEVEL: P
*African American*

Windy's parents are divorced, but she still shares special times with her father.
DIVORCE, SEPARATION; EMOTIONS—LOVE; FAMILY LIFE—FATHERS.

212 *I Need a Lunch Box.* Ill. by Pat Cummings. HarperCollins, 1988 (0-06 020984-4); LB (0-06-020985-2); pap. (0-06-443341-2). USE LEVEL: PS/P
*African American*
When his older sister gets a new lunch box, a young boy dreams of a different, colorful lunch box for each day of the week.
CONCEPTS—COLOR; DAYS OF THE WEEK, MONTHS OF THE YEAR; EMOTIONS—ENVY, JEALOUSY; FAMILY LIFE.

213 *Just Us Women.* Ill. by Pat Cummings. HarperCollins, 1982 (0-06-020941-0); LB (0-06-020942-9); pap. (0-06-443056-1). USE LEVEL: P
*African American*
A girl and her aunt plan a trip together. The girl describes their preparations and some of the things they hope to do.
ACTIVITIES—TRAVELING; ACTIVITIES—VACATIONING; AUTOMOBILES; CORETTA SCOTT KING AWARD; FAMILY LIFE—AUNTS, UNCLES.

214 *Window Wishing.* Ill. by Kevin Brooks. HarperCollins, 1980, LB (0-06-020934-8). USE LEVEL: P
*African American*
A girl describes the fun she and her brother have when visiting their grandmother. One favorite activity is riding bikes downtown and looking in the store windows and wishing for things.
BEHAVIOR—WISHING; FAMILY LIFE—GRANDMOTHERS.

**CAMERON, ANN**
215 *Julian, Dream Doctor.* Ill. by Ann Strugnell. Random, 1990, LB (0-679-90524-3); pap. (0-679-80524-9). USE LEVEL: M
*African American*
Julian wants to get just the right present for his father's birthday, so he tries to find out what his father is dreaming about by asking him questions while he sleeps.
BIRTHDAYS; DREAMS; FAMILY LIFE—FATHERS; FRIENDSHIP; HUMOR.

216 *Julian, Secret Agent.* Ill. by Diane Allison. Random, 1988, LB (0-394-91949-1); pap. (0-394-81949-7). USE LEVEL: M
*African American*
Julian, Huey, and Gloria decide to be the Crimebusters. They

get a dog out of a hot car and help a toddler out of the fountain, but they would really like to capture the bank robber and collect the $25,000 reward.

FRIENDSHIP; HUMOR; MYSTERY AND DETECTIVE STORIES.

217 *Julian's Glorious Summer.* Ill. by Dora Leder. Random, 1987, LB (0-394-99117-6); pap. (0-394-89117-1). USE LEVEL: M
*African American*
When Gloria gets a new bike, Julian is happy for her. He does not want to tell her that he is afraid to ride a bike.

BEHAVIOR—LYING; EMOTIONS—FEAR; FRIENDSHIP; HUMOR; SPORTS—
BICYCLING.

218 *More Stories Julian Tells.* Ill. by Ann Strugnell. Knopf, 1986, LB (0-394-96969-3); pap. (0-394-82454-7). USE LEVEL: M
*African American*
There are five stories in this book, including one in which Julian, Huey, and Gloria find frogs in their shoes.

FAMILY LIFE; FRIENDSHIP; HUMOR; SHORT STORIES.

219 *The Most Beautiful Place in the World.* Ill. by Thomas B. Allen. Knopf, 1988 (0-394-89463-4); LB (0-394-99463-9); pap. (0-394-80424-2). USE LEVEL: M
*Central American—Guatemala*
In Guatemala, Juan endures many hardships, yet he loves his home.

CHARACTER TRAITS—PRIDE; FAMILY LIFE—GRANDMOTHERS; FOREIGN
LANDS—CENTRAL AMERICA—GUATEMALA.

220 *The Stories Julian Tells.* Ill. by Ann Strugnell. Pantheon, 1981 (0-394-84301-0); LB (0-394-94301-5); pap. (0-394-82892-5). USE LEVEL: M
*African American*
There are six stories about Julian and his family, including one in which Julian tells his brother, Huey, that cats come from catalogues and one where Julian makes a new friend.

FAMILY LIFE; FRIENDSHIP; HUMOR; SHORT STORIES.

**CAREY, VALERIE SCHO, ADAPTER**
221 *Quail Song: A Pueblo Indian Tale.* Ill. by Ivan Barnett. Putnam, 1990 (0-399-21936-6). USE LEVEL: P
*Native American—Pueblo*
Quail must use her wits to trick Coyote.

ANIMALS—COYOTES; ANIMALS—QUAILS; BEHAVIOR—TRICKERY;
FOLKTALES—NATIVE AMERICAN—PUEBLO.

**CARLSON, LORI M., AND CYNTHIA L. VENTURA, EDITORS**

222  *Where Angels Glide at Dawn: New Stories from Latin America.*
Introduction by Isabel Allende. Ill. by José Ortega.
HarperCollins, 1990 (0-397-32424-3); LB (0-397-32425-1);
Trophy, pap. (0-06-440464-1). USE LEVEL: U
*Latin American*
Writers from Chile, Panama, Puerto Rico, and Peru are among
the contributors to this collection of stories. The stories reflect
the current political climate of this region as well as its cultural
traditions.
FOREIGN LANDS—LATIN AMERICA; SHORT STORIES.

**CARLSTROM, NANCY WHITE**

223  *Baby-O.* Ill. by Suçie Stevenson. Little, Brown, 1992 (0-316-
12851-1); pap. (0-316-12840-6). USE LEVEL: P
*Caribbean*
The lively rhythm and repeated words tell about a baby, brother, sister, mama, papa, grandfather, and grandmother who ride
the jitney bus to the market.
FAMILY LIFE; FOREIGN LANDS—CARIBBEAN ISLANDS; ISLANDS; STORES.

224  *Barney Is Best.* Ill. by James Graham Hale. HarperCollins, 1994
(0-06-022875-X); LB (0-06-022876-8). USE LEVEL: PS/P
*Hispanic American*
As he gets ready to go to the hospital to have his tonsils
removed, a young boy has to pick just the right friend to take
along to comfort him—his stuffed elephant, Barney.
BEHAVIOR—WORRYING; EMOTIONS—APPREHENSION; HOSPITALS; TOYS.

225  *Northern Lullaby.* Ill. by Leo Dillon and Diane Dillon. Putnam,
1992 (0-399-21806-8). USE LEVEL: P
*Native American—Eskimo*
A young child says good night to items in the world, including
Grandpa Mountain, Grandma River, and Brother Bear.
BEDTIME; LULLABIES; NATURE; POETRY, RHYME.

226  *Wild Wild Sunflower Child Anna.* Ill. by Jerry Pinkney.
Macmillan, 1987 (0-02-717360-7); pap. (0-689-71445-9). USE
LEVEL: PS/P
*African American*
Anna enjoys being outdoors on a sunny day. She sees flowers,
berries, frogs, and insects as she romps through the fields.
ACTIVITIES—PLAYING; FIELDS, MEADOWS; POETRY, RHYME.

**CARRICK, CAROL**

227　*Aladdin and the Wonderful Lamp.* Ill. by Donald Carrick. Scholastic, 1989, pap. (0-590-41680-4). USE LEVEL: M

*Middle Eastern—Arabia*

An old magician tricks Aladdin into entering the hidden cave and finding the magic lamp. When Aladdin falls in love with the princess, he uses the lamp to try to win her.

FOLKTALES—MIDDLE EAST—ARABIA; MAGIC.

**CASE, DIANNE**

228　*92 Queens Road.* Farrar, 1994 (0-374-35518-5). USE LEVEL: U

*African—South Africa*

In Cape Town, South Africa, in the 1960s, Kathy and her "coloured" family endure the hardships of apartheid, including watching homes destroyed when the government forces families to relocate. Kathy also copes with her own family's problems.

FAMILY LIFE; FOREIGN LANDS—AFRICA—SOUTH AFRICA; PREJUDICE; RACE RELATIONS; RELOCATION.

**CASLER, LEIGH**

229　*The Boy Who Dreamed of an Acorn.* Ill. by Shonto Begay. Putnam, 1994 (0-399-22547-1). USE LEVEL: M

*Native American*

In this original story, three boys go up the mountain to dream their destiny. One dreams of the bear, one of the eagle, and the third of an acorn. The third boy is disappointed with his dream, but he comes to be gentle, kind, and sharing.

DREAMS; SELF-CONCEPT; TREES.

**CASSEDY, SYLVIA, AND KUNIHIRO SUETAKE, TRANSLATORS**

230　*Red Dragonfly on My Shoulder: Haiku.* Ill. by Molly Bang. HarperCollins, 1992 (0-06-022624-2); LB (0-06-022625-0). USE LEVEL: M

*Asian—Japan*

The 13 haiku poems in this book follow the traditional pattern for haiku and are illustrated with collages. Fish, crows, cats, and other creatures are the subjects of these poems.

ANIMALS; FOREIGN LANDS—ASIA—JAPAN; HAIKU; NATURE; POETRY, RHYME.

**CASTAÑEDA, OMAR S.**

231　*Abuela's Weave.* Ill. by Enrique O. Sanchez. Lee & Low, 1993 (1-880000-00-8). USE LEVEL: M

*Central American—Guatemala*

Esperanza's grandmother shows her how to weave tapestries to sell in the market.

ACTIVITIES—WEAVING; FAMILY LIFE—GRANDMOTHERS; FOREIGN
LANDS—CENTRAL AMERICA—GUATEMALA.

232    *Among the Volcanoes.* Dutton, 1991 (0-525-67332-6); Dell,
pap. (0-440-40746-X). USE LEVEL: U
*Central American—Guatemala*
Isabel, a Mayan, lives with her family in Guatemala. She dreams
of being a teacher. When her mother becomes ill, Isabel must
make choices: between modern medicine and native traditions;
between her hopes and the demands of her family.
BEHAVIOR—GROWING UP; BEHAVIOR—SEEKING BETTER THINGS;
FOREIGN LANDS—CENTRAL AMERICA—GUATEMALA.

CAZET, DENYS
233    *Born in the Gravy.* Ill. by the author. Orchard, 1993 (0-531-
05488-8); LB (0-531-08638-0). USE LEVEL: P
*Mexican American*
After her first day of kindergarten, Margarita and her father go
for some ice cream and she tells him about her day. Spanish
phrases are included in their conversation about cubbies, red
week, and story time.
FAMILY LIFE—FATHERS; FOREIGN LANGUAGES; SCHOOL.

CEBULASH, MEL
234    *Willie's Wonderful Pet.* Ill. by George Ford. Scholastic, 1993,
pap. (0-590-45787-X). USE LEVEL: P
*African American*
Willie brings a worm for Pet Day. His classmates say that the
worm cannot do anything, but when the worm crawls on the
floor, it causes a commotion among the other pets.
PETS; SCHOOL.

CENDRARS, BLAISE, AND MARCIA BROWN, TRANSLATOR
235    *Shadow.* Ill. by the translator. Macmillan, 1982 (0-684-17226-
7); pap. (0-689-71875-6). USE LEVEL: P
*African*
This free-verse poem describes images of shadows and their
importance to African peoples.
CALDECOTT AWARD; FOREIGN LANDS—AFRICA; POETRY, RHYME;
SHADOWS.

CHAN, JENNIFER L.
236    *One Small Girl.* Ill. by Wendy K. Lee. Polychrome, 1993 (1-
879965-05-4). USE LEVEL: P
*Asian American—China*
Jennifer Lee is not allowed to touch anything in her grand-

mother's store, so she goes next door to her uncle's store. She is not allowed to touch things there, either. She watches a customer do what she is not allowed to do.

ACTIVITIES—PLAYING; STORES.

### CHANG, CINDY, RETELLER

237  *The Seventh Sister: A Chinese Legend.* Ill. by Charles Reasoner. Troll, 1994, LB (0-8167-3411-9); pap. (0-8167-3412-7). USE LEVEL: M

*Asian—China*

Seven maidens weave the tapestry of the sky. One day, Mei, the youngest, stays with Chang, a farmer. When she returns to her work, her tears become the stars. Chang joins her in the sky, but they are separated by the Milky Way.

FOLKTALES—ASIA—CHINA; SKY; STARS.

### CHANG, HEIDI

238  *Elaine and the Flying Frog* (former title: *Elaine, Mary Lewis, and the Frogs*). Ill. by the author. Random, 1988, LB (0-679-90870-6); pap. (0-679-80870-1). USE LEVEL: M

*Asian American—China*

When Elaine and her family move to Iowa, Elaine finds it hard to make new friends. While working on a class project, Elaine makes friends with Mary Lewis and the girls find a way to make a flying frog—they make a frog kite.

FRIENDSHIP; KITES; MOVING; SCHOOL.

### CHANG, MARGARET, AND RAYMOND CHANG, RETELLERS

239  *The Cricket Warrior: A Chinese Tale.* Ill. by Warwick Hutton. Macmillan, 1994 (0-689-50605-8). USE LEVEL: M

*Asian—China*

When he accidentally releases his family's fighting cricket, a young boy, Wei nian, agrees to be transformed into a cricket and take the cricket's place. After bringing glory to his village, Wei nian is finally returned to his human form.

FOLKTALES—ASIA—CHINA; INSECTS—CRICKETS.

240  *In the Eye of War.* Macmillan, 1990 (0-689-50503-5). USE LEVEL: U

*Asian—China*

During World War II, Shao-Shao, who is ten, is a Chinese boy living in Shanghai, which is occupied by the Japanese. He does not understand his father, who is connected with the resistance, nor does he understand those who support the Japanese.

FAMILY LIFE—FATHERS; FOREIGN LANDS—ASIA—CHINA; WORLD WAR II.

### CHANIN, MICHAEL

241   *Grandfather Four Winds and the Rising Moon.* Ill. by Sally J. Smith. H. J. Kramer, 1994 (0-915811-47-2). USE LEVEL: M
*Native American*
Grandfather Four Winds, who is blind, tells his grandson, Rising Moon, about the special importance of an apple tree—and of all nature—to their people.

HANDICAPS—BLINDNESS; NATURE; TREES.

### CHAPMAN, CHRISTINA

242   *Treasure in the Attic.* Ill. by Pat Hoggan. Raintree, 1993, LB (0-8114-3582-2). USE LEVEL: P
*African American*
Sarah finds a basket in the attic. Her mother and grandmother had made the basket to celebrate their African heritage. Sarah and her mother make a basket and it wins an art contest. This book was written by a sixth grader for a Publish-a-Book Contest.

ACTIVITIES; ART; FAMILY LIFE—MOTHERS.

### CHERRY, LYNNE

243   *The Great Kapok Tree: A Tale of the Amazon Rain Forest.* Ill. by the author. Harcourt, 1990 (0-15-200520-X). USE LEVEL: M
*South American*
While chopping down a kapok tree in the rain forest, a man stops to rest. In his dream, animals and a young child describe the impact of his destruction of this tree.

ECOLOGY; ENVIRONMENT; FOREIGN LANDS—SOUTH AMERICA; NATURE; RAIN FOREST; TREES.

### CHEW, RUTH

244   *Royal Magic.* Scholastic, 1991, pap. (0-590-44742-4). USE LEVEL: M
*African American*
On a visit to the Museum of Natural History, Jack and Cindy are magically transported into the jungle. There they become involved in a mystery involving His Majesty, the Oba of Edo.

FANTASY; MAGIC; MYSTERY AND DETECTIVE STORIES; ROYALTY.

### CHIN, CHARLIE, RETELLER

245    *China's Bravest Girl: The Legend of Hua Mu Lan.* Ill. by Tomie Arai. Children's Book Pr., 1993 (0-89239-120-0). USE LEVEL: M

*Asian—China*

Told in rhyme, this is the story of Hua Mu Lan, a girl who disguised herself as a boy and became a warrior so her elderly father would not have to fight. The text is written in English and Chinese.

CHARACTER TRAITS—BRAVERY; FOLKTALES—ASIA—CHINA; FOREIGN LANGUAGES; POETRY, RHYME.

### CHIN, STEVEN A.

246    *Dragon Parade: A Chinese New Year Story.* Ill. by Mou-Sien Tseng. Raintree, 1993, LB (0-8114-7215-9). USE LEVEL: M

*Asian American—China*

Norman Ah Sing settled in San Francisco's Chinatown. In 1851, he organized a celebration for Chinese New Year, including a dragon parade.

HOLIDAYS—CHINESE NEW YEAR; U.S. HISTORY.

### CHIN-LEE, CYNTHIA

247    *Almond Cookies and Dragon Well Tea.* Ill. by You Shan Tang. Polychrome, 1993 (1-879965-03-8). USE LEVEL: P

*Asian American—China*

Nancy Hong invites her friend Erica to visit her home, where they share cookies and Chinese tea. Erica notices many things that are the same in this Chinese American home, and a few that are different.

BEHAVIOR—ACCEPTING DIFFERENCES; FRIENDSHIP.

### CHOCOLATE, DEBORAH M. NEWTON

248    *Imani in the Belly.* Ill. by Alex Boies. BridgeWater, 1994, LB (0-8167-3466-6). USE LEVEL: M

*African*

Imani lives in Africa with her three children. When she goes to the market, her children disobey her and go out. They are swallowed by Simba. Imani tricks Simba into swallowing her and she rescues her children.

ANIMALS; BEHAVIOR—TRICKERY; CHARACTER TRAITS—BRAVERY; FOLKTALES—AFRICA.

249    *Kwanzaa.* Ill. by Melodye Rosales. Childrens Pr., 1990, LB (0-516-03991-1); pap. (0-516-43991-X). USE LEVEL: P/M

*African American*

Two brothers and their parents celebrate Kwanzaa. When other family members and friends come to visit, they are given special greetings and share food, music, and celebrations.
FAMILY LIFE; FOREIGN LANGUAGES; HOLIDAYS—KWANZAA.

250 *My First Kwanzaa Book.* Ill. by Cal Massey. Scholastic, 1992 (0-590-457262-4). USE LEVEL: PS/P
*African American*
A family describes how they celebrate Kwanzaa. Guests visit, a special flag is flown, greetings are given, and candles are lit.
FAMILY LIFE; FOREIGN LANGUAGES; HOLIDAYS—KWANZAA.

251 *Spider and the Sky God: An Akan Legend.* Ill. by Dave Albers. Troll, 1993, LB (0-8167-2811-9); pap. (0-8167-2812-7). USE LEVEL: M
*African—Akan*
In this story, Ananse needs to bring four things—Python, Hornets, Leopards, and Fairy—to buy the Sky God's stories. He succeeds in tricking each character and he brings the stories to Earth.
BEHAVIOR—TRICKERY; FOLKTALES—AFRICA—AKAN; POURQUOI TALES; SPIDERS; STORYTELLING.

252 *Talk, Talk: An Ashanti Legend.* Ill. by Dave Albers. Troll, 1993, LB (0-8167-2817-8); pap. (0-8167-2818-6). USE LEVEL: M
*African*
Jumaani is a farmer and nothing special ever happens to him, until his yams talk to him, then his dog, then a branch, and then a stone. When he tells others about this talking, they dismiss it, until objects talk to them.
CUMULATIVE TALES; FOLKTALES—AFRICA; MAGIC.

**CHOI, SOOK NYUL**
253 *Echoes of the White Giraffe.* Houghton, 1993 (0-395-64721-5); Dell, pap. (0-440-40770-5). USE LEVEL: U
*Asian—Korea*
In this sequel to *Year of Impossible Goodbyes*, Sookan, 15, is now a refugee in Pusan, hoping to be reunited with her family. She is also developing a forbidden friendship with Junho, a boy she knows from the church choir.
CHARACTER TRAITS—BRAVERY; FOREIGN LANDS—ASIA—KOREA; FRIENDSHIP; WAR.

254 *Gathering of Pearls.* Houghton, 1994 (0-395-67437-9). USE LEVEL: U
*Asian—Korea*

Sookan Bak is now in college in America. She is challenged by her courses and by the different culture and language. She misses her family and feels selfish about her choice. When she learns that her mother has died, Sookan must adjust to the loss.

BEHAVIOR—GROWING UP; DEATH; FAMILY LIFE; FOREIGN LANDS—ASIA—KOREA; SCHOOL.

255 *Halmoni and the Picnic.* Ill. by Karen M. Dugan. Houghton, 1993 (0-395-61626-3). USE LEVEL: P
*Asian American—Korea*
Yunmi loves her grandmother, Halmoni, and she wishes that she could find a way to help her feel more comfortable about being in America.

ACTIVITIES—PICNICKING; FAMILY LIFE—GRANDMOTHERS; SCHOOL.

256 *Year of Impossible Goodbyes.* Houghton, 1991 (0-395-57419-6); Dell, pap. (0-440-40759-1). USE LEVEL: U
*Asian—Korea*
During the 1940s, a Korean girl, Sookan, ten, endures the occupation of northern Korea. As the war ends, Korea is divided and Sookan's family hopes to leave the north for a better life in the south.

CHARACTER TRAITS—BRAVERY; FOREIGN LANDS—ASIA—KOREA; HISTORY; WAR; WORLD WAR II.

**CHRISTOPHER, MATT**
257 *Shortstop from Tokyo.* Ill. by Harvey Kidder. Little, Brown, 1970, pap. (0-316-13992-0). USE LEVEL: M
*Asian American—Japan*
When Sam Suzuki joins the Mohawk baseball team, there is some resentment, especially when Sam replaces Stogie Crane at shortstop.

FRIENDSHIP; SPORTS—BASEBALL.

**CISNEROS, SANDRA**
258 *Hairs/Pelitos.* Ill. by Terry Ybáñez. Knopf, 1994 (0-670-86171-8); LB (0-679-96171-2). USE LEVEL: P
*Hispanic American*
A young girl describes the different kinds of hair of the members of her family.

CHARACTER TRAITS—APPEARANCE; FOREIGN LANGUAGES; HAIR.

**CLARK, ANN NOLAN**
259 *In My Mother's House.* Ill. by Velino Herrara. Viking, 1941 (0-670-83917-5); Puffin, pap. (0-14-054496-8). USE LEVEL: P
*Native American*

Details about growing up in a pueblo are lovingly recounted.
CALDECOTT AWARD; EMOTIONS—LOVE; FAMILY LIFE—MOTHERS;
HOUSES.

260 *In the Land of Small Dragon*. As told by Dan Manh Kha. Ill. by
Tony Chen. Viking, 1979, o.p. USE LEVEL: M
*Asian—Vietnam*
Cám, the younger daughter, is jealous of her beautiful older
stepsister, Tâm, who is her father's Number One Daughter.
Tâm's kindness wins her the heart of the prince.
CHARACTER TRAITS—KINDNESS; EMOTIONS—ENVY, JEALOUSY;
FOLKTALES—ASIA—VIETNAM.

261 *Secret of the Andes*. Ill. by Jean Charlot. Viking, 1952 (0-670-
62975-8); Puffin, pap. (0-14-030926-8). USE LEVEL: U
*South American—Peru*
Cusi lives in the Hidden Valley with Chuto, the Old One, who
treats him like a son. Together, they journey out of the valley
and Cusi learns what is beyond the mountains.
BEHAVIOR—GROWING UP; CHARACTER TRAITS—AMBITION; FOREIGN
LANDS—SOUTH AMERICA—PERU; NEWBERY AWARD.

CLEAVER, ELIZABETH
262 *The Enchanted Caribou*. Ill. by the author. Macmillan, 1985,
o.p. USE LEVEL: M
*Native American—Inuit*
A young woman, Tyya, becomes lost and is helped by three
brothers. A shaman transforms her into a white caribou. One of
the brothers, Etosack, finds Tyya, who returns to her human
form, and they marry. The illustrations are photos of shadow
puppets.
ANIMALS—REINDEER; FOLKTALES—NATIVE AMERICAN—INUIT; MAGIC;
PUPPETS.

CLÉMENT, CLAUDE
263 *The Painter and the Wild Swans*. Ill. by Frédéric Clément. Dial,
1986, pap. (0-8037-084-0-8). USE LEVEL: M
*Asian—Japan*
Teiji's talent as a painter is greatly admired. In his village in
Japan, he is honored and respected. After some swans fly over
him, he begins to search for them. His search takes him to a
frozen island where he is transformed into a swan.
ACTIVITIES—PAINTING; BIRDS—SWANS; FOLKTALES—ASIA—JAPAN; MAGIC.

**CLIFTON, LUCILLE**

264　*All Us Come Cross the Water.* Ill. by John Steptoe. Holt, 1973, o.p. USE LEVEL: P
*African American*
Ujamaa tries to learn about his African heritage. An older man, Tweezer, helps Ujamaa understand his past and that of his people.
CHARACTER TRAITS—PRIDE; SCHOOL; SELF-CONCEPT; SLAVERY.

265　*Amifika.* Ill. by Thomas DiGrazia. Dutton, 1977, o.p. USE LEVEL: P
*African American*
Amifika's father has been away, and now he is coming home. Amifika is not sure his father will remember him.
BEHAVIOR—WORRYING; EMOTIONS—APPREHENSION; FAMILY LIFE—FATHERS.

266　*The Boy Who Didn't Believe in Spring.* Ill. by Brinton Turkle. Dutton, 1973 (0-525-27145-7); pap. (0-525-44365-7). USE LEVEL: P
*African American*
In his urban neighborhood, King Shabazz does not see the signs of spring that others talk about, until he and his friend, Tony, go looking for spring.
COMMUNITIES, NEIGHBORHOODS; SEASONS—SPRING; URBAN LIFE.

267　*Don't You Remember?* Ill. by Evaline Ness. Dutton, 1973 (0-525-28840-6). USE LEVEL: P
*African American*
Tate, a five-year-old girl, thinks she remembers everything, but her family does not seem to remember what she thinks is important. Tate decides they will not remember her birthday, either.
BIRTHDAYS; CORETTA SCOTT KING AWARD; FAMILY LIFE.

268　*Everett Anderson's Christmas Coming.* Ill. by Jan Spivey Gilcrist. Henry Holt, 1991 (0-8050-1549-3); pap. (0-8050-2949-4). USE LEVEL: P
*African American*
The rhyming text describes Everett Anderson's anticipation of Christmas in this newly illustrated version.
HOLIDAYS—CHRISTMAS; POETRY, RHYME; URBAN LIFE.

269　*Everett Anderson's Friend.* Ill. by Ann Grifalconi. Henry Holt, 1976 (0-8050-2246-5). USE LEVEL: P
*African American*
At first, Everett Anderson is disappointed when his new neighbor is a girl, but he and Maria become friends.

CORETTA SCOTT KING AWARD; FRIENDSHIP; POETRY, RHYME; URBAN LIFE.

270    *Everett Anderson's Goodbye.* Ill. by Ann Grifalconi. Henry Holt, 1983 (0-8050-0235-9); pap. (0-8050-0800-4). USE LEVEL: M/U

*African American*

After his father's death, Everett Anderson goes through the stages of grief. These poems capture his emotions, ending with acceptance.

CORETTA SCOTT KING AWARD; DEATH; EMOTIONS—LOVE; EMOTIONS—SADNESS; FAMILY LIFE; POETRY, RHYME.

271    *Everett Anderson's Nine Month Long.* Ill. by Ann Grifalconi. Henry Holt, 1978 (0-8050-0287-1); pap. (0-8050-0295-2). USE LEVEL: P

*African American*

After his mother remarries, Everett Anderson and his parents wait for the birth of a baby.

BABIES, TODDLERS; FAMILY LIFE; POETRY, RHYME; URBAN LIFE.

272    *Everett Anderson's 1 2 3.* Ill. by Ann Grifalconi. Henry Holt, 1977 (0-8050-2310-0). USE LEVEL: P

*African American*

Sometimes, Everett Anderson likes being alone, and he likes being with Mama. He is not sure how he feels about a third person, Mr. Perry, coming over so often.

FAMILY LIFE; POETRY, RHYME.

273    *Everett Anderson's Year.* Ill. by Ann Grifalconi. Henry Holt, 1974 (0-8050-2247-3). USE LEVEL: P

*African American*

There is a verse for each month of the year, chronicling the activities in Everett Anderson's life.

DAYS OF THE WEEK, MONTHS OF THE YEAR; POETRY, RHYME; SEASONS; URBAN LIFE.

274    *The Lucky Stone.* Ill. by Dale Payson. Delacorte, 1979 (0-8446-6592-4); Dell, pap. (0-440-45110-8). USE LEVEL: M

*African American*

Tee loves to sit with her great-grandmother and listen to her stories. Each story tells how a stone was lucky to different generations in the family.

CHARACTER TRAITS—LUCK; CHARMS; FAMILY LIFE—GREAT-GRANDPARENTS; STORYTELLING.

275 *My Brother Fine with Me.* Ill. by Moneta Barnett. Holt, 1975, o.p. USE LEVEL: P
*African American*
Johnetta, eight, who is called Johnny, is glad when her five-year-old brother plans to run away. When she thinks about how much they do together, she is glad that he changes his mind.
ACTIVITIES—BABY-SITTING; BEHAVIOR—RUNNING AWAY; EMOTIONS—LOVE; FAMILY LIFE—SIBLINGS.

276 *My Friend Jacob.* Ill. by Thomas DiGrazia. Dutton, 1980, o.p. USE LEVEL: P
*African American*
Sam's best friend is Jacob, an older boy who is mentally handicapped. Sam understands Jacob's limitations as well as his potential.
CHARACTER TRAITS—HELPFULNESS; FRIENDSHIP; HANDICAPS.

277 *Some of the Days of Everett Anderson.* Ill. by Evaline Ness. Henry Holt, 1970 (0-8050-0290-1); pap. (0-8050-0289-8). USE LEVEL: P
*African American*
Poems follow Everett Anderson through a very busy week of walking in the rain, visiting the candy shop, talking with his mother, missing his father, and watching the stars.
DAYS OF THE WEEK, MONTHS OF THE YEAR; FAMILY LIFE; POETRY, RHYME.

**CLIMO, SHIRLEY**
278 *The Egyptian Cinderella.* Ill. by Ruth Heller. HarperCollins, 1989 (0-690-04822-X); LB (0-690-04824-6); pap. (0-06-443279-3). USE LEVEL: M
*African—Egypt*
In this Cinderella variant, a slave girl, Rhodopes, becomes the pharaoh's queen.
BEHAVIOR—KINDNESS; EMOTIONS—ENVY, JEALOUSY; FOLKTALES—AFRICA—EGYPT; MAGIC; ROYALTY; SIBLING RIVALRY.

279 *The Korean Cinderella.* Ill. by Ruth Heller. HarperCollins, 1993 (0-06-020432-X); LB (0-06-020433-8). USE LEVEL: M
*Asian—Korea*
Pear Blossom is treated cruelly by her stepmother and stepsister. She wears rags and does all the work. At the festival, Pear Blossom loses her shoe. It is found by the magistrate, who looks for Pear Blossom, finds her, and marries her.

CHARACTER TRAITS—KINDNESS; EMOTIONS—ENVY, JEALOUSY; FOLKTALES—ASIA—KOREA; MAGIC.

280    *Someone Saw a Spider: Spider Facts and Folktales.* Ill. by Dirk Zimmer. HarperCollins, 1985 (0-690-04435-6); LB (0-690-04436-4). USE LEVEL: M
*Multicultural*
Spider appears in the folklore of many cultures, including African, Japanese, and American. Information about spiders is featured here, too.
FOLKTALES; SHORT STORIES; SPIDERS.

**CLYMER, ELEANOR**
281    *Luke Was There.* Ill. by Diane deGroat. Holt, 1973, LB (0-03-011161-7). USE LEVEL: M
*African American*
When their mother is ill, Julius and Danny are sent to the Children's House. Julius distrusts adults, who have not given him a secure, stable home. He is wary of Luke, a counselor who befriends him.
EMOTIONS—ANGER; EMOTIONS—FEAR; FRIENDSHIP; URBAN LIFE.

**COERR, ELEANOR**
282    *Chang's Paper Pony.* Ill. by Deborah Kogan Ray. HarperCollins, 1988 (0-06-021328-0); LB (0-06-021329-9); pap. (0-06-444163-6). USE LEVEL: P
*Asian American—China*
Chang and his grandfather work in a mining camp. Although there are hardships, there are also moments of kindness.
ANIMALS—HORSES; FAMILY LIFE—GRANDFATHERS; MINING; U.S. HISTORY.

283    *Mieko and the Fifth Treasure.* Ill. by Cecil H. Uyehara. Putnam, 1993 (0-399-22434-3); Dell, pap. (0-440-40947-0). USE LEVEL: M
*Asian—Japan*
Following the bombing of Nagasaki, Mieko, ten, finds that she cannot find beauty in the world.
ART; FOREIGN LANDS—ASIA—JAPAN; WORLD WAR II.

284    *Sadako.* Ill. by Ed Young. Putnam, 1993 (0-399-21771-1). USE LEVEL: M/U
*Asian—Japan*
Although Sadako Sasaki survived the bombing of Hiroshima, she is later stricken with leukemia. A legend says that folding one thousand paper cranes will bring health to a sick person.

Sadako does die from leukemia, but her spirit is remembered.
CHARACTER TRAITS—BRAVERY; DEATH; EMOTIONS—SADNESS; FOREIGN LANDS—ASIA—JAPAN; HOPE.

285    *Sadako and the Thousand Paper Cranes.* Ill. by Ronald Himler. Putnam, 1977 (0-399-20520-9); Dell, pap. (0-440-47465-5). USE LEVEL: M/U
*Asian—Japan*
The illustrated book *Sadako* is drawn from this longer narrative describing the courage of Sadako Sasaki.
CHARACTER TRAITS—BRAVERY; DEATH; EMOTIONS—SADNESS; FOREIGN LANDS—ASIA—JAPAN; HOPE.

**COFER, JUDITH ORTIZ**

286    *An Island Like You: Stories of the Barrio.* Orchard, 1995 (0-531-06897-8); LB (0-531-08747-6). USE LEVEL: U
*Hispanic American—Puerto Rico*
There are 12 stories about life in the Puerto Rican American community in New Jersey. Some focus on family, friends, and the concerns of teenagers as they face a future that is both bleak and hopeful. Others emphasize the Latino culture.
FAMILY LIFE; SELF-CONCEPT; SHORT STORIES; URBAN LIFE.

**COHEN, BARBARA**

287    *Thank You, Jackie Robinson.* Ill. by Richard Cuffari. Lothrop, 1974, LB (0-688-07909-1); Scholastic, pap. (0-590-42378-9). USE LEVEL: M
*African American*
Sam Green loves baseball, especially the Brooklyn Dodgers and Jackie Robinson. So does his mother's cook, Davy, who becomes Sam's friend. When Davy becomes ill, Sam brings him an autographed baseball, hoping it will help him recover.
DEATH; FRIENDSHIP; SPORTS—BASEBALL.

288    *213 Valentines.* Ill. by Wil Clay. Henry Holt, 1991 (0-8050-1536-1); pap. (0-8050-2627-4). USE LEVEL: M
*African American*
Wade finds it difficult being one of the few black kids in the Gifted and Talented class. He misses his friends at his old school, but he finds a way to make some new friends, including deciding to be a friend to a girl from his old school.
BEHAVIOR—SECRETS; CHARACTER TRAITS—GENEROSITY; FRIENDSHIP; HOLIDAYS—VALENTINE'S DAY; SCHOOL.

COHEN, BARBARA, AND BAHIJA LOVEJOY
289 *Seven Daughters and Seven Sons*. Morrow, 1994, ©1982 (0-688-13563-3). USE LEVEL: U
*Middle Eastern—Arabia*
Buran has six sisters and no brothers to make the family fortune. Her father allows her to be disguised as a boy. In a distant city, she makes a fortune and falls in love. This is a reissue of a book from 1982 and is based on a folktale from Iraq.
ADVENTURE; CHARACTER TRAITS—PERSEVERANCE; EMOTIONS—LOVE; FOREIGN LANDS—MIDDLE EAST—ARABIA.

COHEN, CARON LEE, ADAPTER
290 *The Mud Pony: A Traditional Skidi Pawnee Tale*. Ill. by Shonto Begay. Scholastic, 1988 (0-590-41525-5). USE LEVEL: M
*Native American—Pawnee*
A boy who has no pony shapes one out of mud. When he is separated from his people, Mother Earth gives him a pony. The boy finds his people and becomes a powerful leader.
ANIMALS—HORSES; FOLKTALES—NATIVE AMERICAN—PAWNEE.

COHEN, MIRIAM
291 *Born to Dance Samba*. Ill. by Gioia Fiammenghi. HarperCollins, 1984, LB (0-06-021359-0). USE LEVEL: M
*South American—Brazil*
Maria Antonia has dreamed of being chosen Queen of the Samba at Carnival. When a new girl comes to town, Maria Antonia worries that she will not be chosen.
ACTIVITIES—DANCING; EMOTIONS—ENVY, JEALOUSY; FESTIVALS; FOREIGN LANDS—SOUTH AMERICA—BRAZIL.

COHLENE, TERRI, ADAPTER
292 *Clamshell Boy: A Makah Legend*. Ill. by Charles Reasoner. Rourke, 1990, LB (0-86593-001-5); Troll, pap. (0-8167-2361-3). USE LEVEL: M
*Native American—Makah*
The children do not listen to their parents and are captured by the giant creature, Basket Woman. Clamshell Boy tricks Basket Woman and rescues the children. Information about the Makah follows the story.
BEHAVIOR—MISBEHAVIOR; CHARACTER TRAITS—BRAVERY; FOLKTALES—NATIVE AMERICAN—MAKAH; GIANTS.

293 *Dancing Drum: A Cherokee Legend.* Ill. by Charles Reasoner. Rourke, 1990, LB (0-86593-007-4); Troll, pap. (0-8167-2362-1). USE LEVEL: M
*Native American—Cherokee*
Grandmother Sun becomes angry and burns the land. Dancing Drum tries to stop the drought, but when the Daughter of the Sun is killed, the drought becomes darkness and rain. Information about the Cherokee follows the story.
FOLKTALES—NATIVE AMERICAN—CHEROKEE; SUN; WEATHER— DROUGHT.

294 *Ka-ha-si and the Loon: An Eskimo Legend.* Ill. by Charles Reasoner. Rourke, 1990, LB (0-86593-002-3); Troll, pap. (0-8167-2359-1). USE LEVEL: M
*Native American—Eskimo*
Ka-ha-si sleeps all the time and the villagers mock him, calling him Lazy One. Three times, Ka-ha-si saves his people and now they sing of his deeds. Information about the Eskimo follows the story.
ARCTIC LANDS; CHARACTER TRAITS—BRAVERY; FOLKTALES—NATIVE AMERICAN—ESKIMO.

295 *Little Firefly: An Algonquian Legend.* Ill. by Charles Reasoner. Rourke, 1990, LB (0-86593 005 8); Troll, pap. (0-8167-2363-X). USE LEVEL: M
*Native American—Algonquian*
In this Cinderella variant, Little Firefly is mistreated by her two older sisters. She does all the work and her face has been damaged by fire. She can see The Invisible One and she becomes his bride. Details about the Algonquian follow the story.
CHARACTER TRAITS—APPEARANCE; CHARACTER TRAITS—KINDNESS; FAMILY LIFE—SIBLINGS; FOLKTALES—NATIVE AMERICAN—ALGONQUIAN.

296 *Quillworker: A Cheyenne Legend.* Ill. by Charles Reasoner. Rourke, 1990, LB (0-86593-004-X); Troll, pap. (0-8167-2358-3). USE LEVEL: M
*Native American—Cheyenne*
In her dreams, Quillworker is told to sew seven special garments, which she takes to seven brothers. When the buffalo come for Quillworker, she and the brothers become stars, forming the Big Dipper. Details about the Cheyenne follow the story.
FOLKTALES—NATIVE AMERICAN—CHEYENNE; POURQUOI TALES; STARS.

297 *Turquoise Boy: A Navajo Legend.* Ill. by Charles Reasoner. Rourke, 1990, LB (0-86593-003-1); Troll, pap. (0-8167-2360-5). USE LEVEL: M
*Native American—Navajo*
Turquoise Boy wants to help the people in their struggle to survive. He visits the Talking Gods and then travels to Sun Bearer and he receives horses for the people. Information about the Navajo follows the story.
ANIMALS—HORSES; DESERT; FOLKTALES—NATIVE AMERICAN—NAVAJO.

**COLEMAN, EVELYN**
298 *The Foot Warmer and the Crow.* Ill. by Daniel Minter. Macmillan, 1994 (0-02-722816-9). USE LEVEL: M
*African American*
Hezekiah is a slave who dreams of freedom. Being small in size, he is mocked by his master. Hezekiah's ability to communicate with birds helps him gain his freedom.
BIRDS—CROWS; CHARACTER TRAITS –FREEDOM; EMOTIONS—FEAR; SLAVERY.

**COLES, ROBERT**
299 *The Story of Ruby Bridges.* Ill. by George Ford. Scholastic, 1995 (0-590-43967-7). USE LEVEL: M
*African American*
In 1960, Ruby Coles was six and she was ordered by a judge to go to William Frantz Elementary School. She was the first African American in that school. Although a mob tried to block her attendance, she persevered.
BRIDGES, RUBY; CHARACTER TRAITS—PERSEVERANCE; CIVIL RIGHTS; PREJUDICE; RACE RELATIONS; SCHOOL.

**COLLIER, JAMES LINCOLN, AND CHRISTOPHER COLLIER**
300 *Jump Ship to Freedom.* Delacorte, 1981 (0-385-28484-5); Dell, pap. (0-440-44323-7). USE LEVEL: U
*African American*
Daniel Arabus, 14, is an escaped slave who becomes involved in events surrounding the American Revolution and the Constitutional Convention.
CHARACTER TRAITS—BRAVERY; CHARACTER TRAITS—FREEDOM; SLAVERY; U.S. HISTORY—REVOLUTION.

301 *War Comes to Willy Freeman.* Delacorte, 1983 (0-395-29235-X); Dell, pap. (0-440-49504-0). USE LEVEL: U
*African American*

After her father's death and the imprisonment of her mother, Willy Freeman, 13, disguises herself as a boy and tries to find her mother. As a free black, Willy risks being sent into slavery. The setting is Connecticut during the American Revolution.
CHARACTER TRAITS—BRAVERY; CHARACTER TRAITS—FREEDOM; SLAVERY; U.S. HISTORY—REVOLUTION.

302    *Who Is Carrie?* Delacorte, 1984 (0-385-29295-3); Dell, pap. (0-440-49536-9). USE LEVEL: U
*African American*
After the Revolutionary War, Carrie, a slave, is taken to serve in George Washington's home. While helping her friend, Dan Arabus, find out about the value of his Continental monetary notes, Carrie learns some information about herself.
CHARACTER TRAITS—FREEDOM; FRIENDSHIP; SLAVERY; U.S. HISTORY—REVOLUTION.

COLMAN, WARREN
303    *Double Dutch and the Voodoo Shoes: A Modern African-American Urban Tale.* Ill. by Melodye Rosales. Childrens Pr., 1991, LB (0-516-05133-4); pap. (0-516-45133-2). USE LEVEL: M
*African American*
To encourage children to learn and retell this story, the illustrations appear without words and a brief text follows. Shalesea is challenged to a double dutch jumping contest by a new girl, Mayvelline. Shalesea's shoes seem magical.
ACTIVITIES—JUMPING ROPE; CLOTHING—SHOES; FRIENDSHIP; STORYTELLING.

COMPTON, PATRICIA A., RETELLER
304    *The Terrible EEK: A Japanese Tale.* Ill. by Sheila Hamanaka. Simon & Schuster, 1991 (0-671-73737-6); pap. (0-671-87169-2). USE LEVEL: M
*Asian—Japan*
After overhearing a father tell his son that he is worried about the roof having "a terrible leak," the thief and the animals express their fear of this unknown "EEK" creature.
BEHAVIOR—GOSSIP; CHARACTER TRAITS—FOOLISHNESS; EMOTIONS—FEAR; FOLKTALES—ASIA—JAPAN.

CONWAY, DIANA COHEN
305    *Northern Lights: A Hanukkah Story.* Ill. by Shelly O. Haas. Kar-Ben, 1994 (0-929371-79-8); pap. (0-929371-80-1). USE LEVEL: P
*Multicultural*

In Alaska, Dr. Israel and his daughter Sara spend the first night of Hanukkah stranded by the snow. During their visit with a Yupik Eskimo family, they share information about their culture and traditions.
FRIENDSHIP; HOLIDAYS—HANUKKAH; WEATHER—SNOW.

**COOKE, TRISH**

306 *Mr. Pam Pam and the Hullabazoo.* Ill. by Patrice Aggs. Candlewick, 1994 (1-56402-411-3). USE LEVEL: P
*African American*
When he comes to visit, Mr. Pam Pam brings his baby and describes his encounter with a Hullabazoo. The little boy and his mother are skeptical until, one day, a Hullabazoo does appear.
FRIENDSHIP; HUMOR; IMAGINATION.

307 *So Much.* Ill. by Helen Oxenbury. Candlewick, 1994 (1-56402-344-3). USE LEVEL: P
*African American*
As the family gathers for Daddy's surprise birthday party, everyone wants to play with the baby.
BABIES, TODDLERS; BIRTHDAYS; FAMILY LIFE.

308 *When I Grow Bigger.* Ill. by John Bendall-Brunello. Candlewick, 1994 (1-56402-430-X). USE LEVEL: PS/P
*African American*
Baby Thomas watches as three older children squabble and then he endures as they pull him around.
BABIES, TODDLERS; BEHAVIOR—GROWING UP.

**COOPER, MELROSE**

309 *Life Riddles.* Henry Holt, 1993 (0-8050-2613-4). USE LEVEL: U
*African American*
Janelle, 12, wants to be a writer and she writes about her family. Her father is away looking for work, but when he was home, he and Mama argued a lot. Janelle mu0
st adjust to the changes in her family and in herself.
ACTIVITIES—WRITING; BEHAVIOR—GROWING UP; FAMILY LIFE.

**COOPER, SUSAN**

310 *Jethro and the Jumbie.* Ill. by Ashley Bryan. Macmillan, 1979, o.p. USE LEVEL: M
*Caribbean*
Jethro wants to go fishing with his brother Thomas, but Thomas says he is too small. Jethro walks into the bush down

the jumbie trail and he encounters a jumbie, who helps Jethro get to go fishing.

FAMILY LIFE—SIBLINGS; FOREIGN LANDS—CARIBBEAN ISLANDS; MAGIC; MONSTERS; SPORTS—FISHING.

### COTE, NANCY
311 *Palm Trees.* Ill. by the author. Macmillan, 1993 (0-02-724760-0). USE LEVEL: P
*African American*
When Millie arranges her own hair, her friend, Renee, says something that upsets Millie. Later, Renee arranges her hair to look like Millie's.

CHARACTER TRAITS—APPEARANCE; EMOTIONS—EMBARRASSMENT; FRIENDSHIP; HAIR.

### COURLANDER, HAROLD, COMPILER
312 *The Crest and the Hide: And Other African Stories of Chiefs, Bards, Hunters, Sorcerers, and Common People.* Ill. by Monica Vachula. Putnam, 1982, o.p. USE LEVEL: M/U
*African*
Among the peoples whose stories are presented here are Ashanti, Bemba, Soninke, and Yoruba. There are 20 stories in this collection.

FOLKTALES—AFRICA; SHORT STORIES.

### COURLANDER, HAROLD, AND GEORGE HERZOG
313 *The Cow-Tail Switch: and Other West African Stories.* Ill. by Madye Lee Chastain. Henry Holt, 1947 (0-8050-0288-X); pap. (0-8050-0298-7). USE LEVEL: M/U
*African*
This collection includes 17 stories, many of which feature animals like Guinea Fowl, Rabbit, and Turtle. Others feature Anansi the trickster.

ANIMALS; BEHAVIOR—TRICKERY; FOLKTALES—AFRICA; NEWBERY AWARD; SHORT STORIES.

### COUTANT, HELEN
314 *First Snow.* Ill. by Vo-Dinh Mai. Knopf, 1974 (0-394-82831-3); LB (0-394-92831-8). USE LEVEL: P
*Asian American—Vietnam*
Lien does not understand when she is told that her grandmother is dying. Watching the snow cover the plants helps Lien understand the cycle of life.

DEATH; FAMILY LIFE—GRANDMOTHERS; SEASONS—WINTER.

COWEN-FLETCHER, JANE

315 *It Takes a Village*. Ill. by the author. Scholastic, 1994 (0-590-46573-2). USE LEVEL: P
*African—Benin*
Yemi is supposed to watch her little brother Kokou on market day. When he wanders off, she finds that everyone in her village has been watching Kokou.
ACTIVITIES—BABY-SITTING; BABIES, TODDLERS; COMMUNITIES, NEIGHBORHOODS; FAMILY LIFE—SIBLINGS; FOREIGN LANDS—AFRICA—BENIN.

**THE COYOTE RINGS THE WRONG BELL**

316 *The Coyote Rings the Wrong Bell: A Mexican Folktale*. Ill. by Francisco X. Mora. Childrens Pr., 1991, LB (0-516-05136-9); pap. (0-516-45136-7). USE LEVEL: M
*Mexican*
To encourage retelling, the illustrations appear without the text, which is printed on one page after the pictures. Señor Rabbit tricks Señor Coyote into shaking a tree that is full of hornets.
ANIMALS—COYOTES; ANIMALS—RABBITS; BEHAVIOR—TRICKERY; FOLKTALES—MEXICO.

CRESPO, GEORGE, RETELLER

317 *How Iwariwa the Cayman Learned to Share: A Yanomami Myth*. Ill. by the reteller. Houghton, 1995 (0-395-67162-0). USE LEVEL: M
*South American—Yanomamo Indians*
Iwariwa the Cayman has fire and cooks his food. The other animals eat their food raw. They devise a plan to trick Iwariwa into sharing fire with them.
FIRE; FOLKTALES—SOUTH AMERICA—YANOMAMO; REPTILES—ALLIGATORS, CROCODILES.

318 *How the Sea Began: A Taino Myth*. Ill. by the reteller. Houghton, 1993 (0-395-63033-9). USE LEVEL: M
*Native American—Taino*
Yayael was a great hunter. After he is lost in a storm, his family finds that a gourd holding his bow and arrows continues to provide for the village. When the gourd is broken, the sea is released.
FOLKTALES—NATIVE AMERICAN—TAINO; ISLANDS; POURQUOI TALES; SEA AND SEASHORE.

CREWS, DONALD

319 *Bigmama's*. Ill. by the author. Greenwillow, 1991 (0-688-

09950-5); LB (0-688-09951-3); pap. (0-685-64817-6). USE
LEVEL: P

*African American*

Every summer, Mama and the four children travel to the country to visit Grandmother, who is called Bigmama. They enjoy
the country and the time together. This is based on a reminiscence of the author.

ACTIVITIES—REMINISCING; ACTIVITIES—VACATIONING; FAMILY LIFE;
RURAL LIFE.

320     *Shortcut*. Ill. by the author. Greenwillow, 1992 (0-688-06436-
1); LB (0-688-06437-X). USE LEVEL: P

*African American*

Against the rules, these children take the shortcut home, following the train tracks, and they must jump off the tracks when a
train comes.

ACTIVITIES—WALKING; EMOTIONS—FEAR; RURAL LIFE; TRAINS.

### CREWS, NINA

321     *One Hot Summer Day*. Ill. by the author. Greenwillow, 1995 (0-
688-13393-2); LB (0-688-13394-0). USE LEVEL: PS/P

*African American*

On a hot summer day, a little girl enjoys playing in her neighborhood. When a thunderstorm comes, she dances in the rain.

ACTIVITIES—PLAYING; COMMUNITIES, NEIGHBORHOODS; SEASONS—
SUMMER; WEATHER—RAIN.

### CUMMINGS, PAT

322     *Carousel*. Ill. by the author. Macmillan, 1994 (0-02-725512-3).
USE LEVEL: P

*African American*

Alex's father does not get home from his trip in time for her
birthday party. After she is sent to her room, Alex has a dream
about her new carousel. When she awakens, her father is home.

BIRTHDAYS; DREAMS; FAMILY LIFE; MERRY-GO-ROUNDS.

323     *Clean Your Room, Harvey Moon!* Ill. by the author. Macmillan,
1991 (0-02-725511-5); pap. (0-689-71798-9). USE LEVEL:
PS/P

*African American*

A rhyming text describes Harvey Moon's dismay as his mother
insists he clean his room before watching his favorite Saturday
morning television programs.

ACTIVITIES—CLEANING; BEHAVIOR—MESSY; CHARACTER TRAITS—CLEAN-
LINESS; FAMILY LIFE; POETRY, RHYME.

324     *C.L.O.U.D.S.* Ill. by the author. Lothrop, 1986 (0-688-04682-7); LB (0-688-04683-5). USE LEVEL: P
*African American*
Chuku works in the department of Creative Lights, Opticals, and Unusual Designs in the Sky—C.L.O.U.D.S. His assignment is to design skies for New York City.
CORETTA SCOTT KING AWARD; FANTASY; SKY; WEATHER—CLOUDS.

CUMPIÁN, CARLOS
325     *Latino Rainbow: Poems about Latino Americans.* Ill. by Richard Leonard. Childrens Pr., 1994, LB ( 0-516-05153-9); pap. (0-516-45153-7). USE LEVEL: M/U
*Hispanic American*
The free-verse poems in this collection highlight the achievements of Latinos, including some well-known figures like César Chávez, Roberto Clemente, and Henry Cisneros. A central theme is the pride of accomplishment.
BIOGRAPHY; POETRY; RHYME; SELF-CONCEPT.

CURRY, JANE LOUISE, RETELLER
326     *Back in the Beforetime: Tales of the California Indians.* Ill. by James Watts. Macmillan, 1987 (0-689-50410-1). USE LEVEL: M/U
*Native American*
Creation stories from a variety of native peoples of California are presented in this collection.
CREATION; FOLKTALES—NATIVE AMERICAN; POURQUOI TALES; SHORT STORIES.

CURTIS, EDWARD S., COLLECTOR
327     *The Girl Who Married a Ghost: And Other Tales from "The North American Indian."* Edited by John Bierhorst. With photos from "The North American Indian." Macmillan, 1978, o.p. USE LEVEL: U
*Native American*
These nine stories feature folktales from people of the Northwest Coast, California, the Plains, the North Woods, the Southwest, and Alaska.
FOLKTALES—NATIVE AMERICAN; SHORT STORIES.

CURTIS, GAVIN
328     *Grandma's Baseball.* Ill. by the author. Crown, 1990, o.p. USE LEVEL: P
*African American*

It takes some time for this young boy to get used to having his grandmother come live with his family.
EMOTIONS; FAMILY LIFE—GRANDMOTHERS; SPORTS—BASEBALL.

**CZERNECKI, STEFAN, AND TIMOTHY RHODES**
329 *The Hummingbirds' Gift.* Ill. by Stefan Czernecki. Hyperion, 1994 (1-56282-604-2); LB (1-56282-605-0). USE LEVEL: M
*Mexican*
During a drought, a family helps save the hummingbirds, which then show the family how to weave figures to sell at the festival.
ACTIVITIES—WEAVING; BIRDS—HUMMINGBIRDS; FOREIGN LANDS—MEXICO; WEATHER—DROUGHTS.

330 *The Singing Snake.* Ill. by Stefan Czernecki. Hyperion, 1992 (1-56282-399-X); LB (1-56282-400-7). USE LEVEL: M
*Australian—Aborigine*
There is so much noise on the island that the Old Man decides to have a contest to find the most pleasing voice. Snake catches Lark and wins the contest through trickery, but he is ostracized when the animals realize his deception.
BEHAVIOR—TRICKERY; BIRDS—LARKS; FOLKTALES—AUSTRALIA—ABORIGINE; POURQUOI TALES; REPTILES—SNAKES.

**DALGLIESH, ALICE**
331 *The Courage of Sarah Noble.* Ill. by Leonard Weisgard. Macmillan, 1954 (0-684-18830-9); pap. (0-689-71540-4). USE LEVEL: M
*Native American*
In 1707, when Sarah, eight, and her father go into the Connecticut wilderness to homestead, they encounter Indians who give them help and friendship.
EMOTIONS—FEAR; FRONTIER AND PIONEER LIFE; NEWBERY AWARD; U.S. HISTORY—COLONIAL TIMES.

**DALY, NIKI**
332 *Not So Fast Songololo.* Ill. by the author. Macmillan, 1985 (0-689-50367-9); Puffin, pap. (0-14-050715-9). USE LEVEL: P
*African—South Africa*
Malusi lives with his family near a big city in South Africa. On a trip into the city, Malusi helps his grandmother, and she buys him a new pair of shoes.
CLOTHING—SHOES; FAMILY LIFE—GRANDMOTHERS; FOREIGN LANDS—AFRICA—SOUTH AFRICA; SHOPPING; URBAN LIFE.

333 *Why the Sun and the Moon Live in the Sky.* Ill. by the author.

Lothrop, 1995 (0-688-13331-2); LB (0-688-13332-0). USE LEVEL: M

*African—Nigeria*

Sun and Moon used to live together on the earth. When Sun invites Sea to visit them, she fills their house, forcing Sun and Moon into the sky.

FOLKTALES—AFRICA—NIGERIA; MOON; POURQUOI TALES; SKY; SUN.

**DAVIS, DEBORAH**

334    *The Secret of the Seal.* Ill. by Judy Labrasca. Crown, 1989 (0-517-56725-3); pap. (0-679-86566-7). USE LEVEL: M

*Native American—Inuit*

Kyo wants to hunt seals, but when he encounters a seal, he finds he cannot kill it. He befriends the seal, but, in doing so, he compromises the seal's safety.

ANIMALS—SEALS; ARCTIC LANDS; COMMUNITIES, NEIGHBORHOODS; NATURE; SPORTS—HUNTING.

**DAVIS, OSSIE**

335    *Just Like Martin.* Simon & Schuster, 1992 (0-671-73202-1); Puffin, pap. (0-14-037095-1). USE LEVEL: U

*African American*

It is 1963 and a church has been bombed in Alabama. Stone, 14, plans a children's march to commemorate two of his friends who were killed in the blast.

CIVIL RIGHTS; DEATH; PREJUDICE; VIOLENCE.

**DAVISON, KATHERINE**

336    *Moon Magic: Stories from Asia.* Ill. by Thomas A. Rosborough. Carolrhoda, 1994, LB (0-87614-751-1). USE LEVEL: M

*Asian*

Four stories—from Siberia, Japan, Korea, and Burma—feature explanations about the origin of the moon.

FOLKTALES—ASIA; MOON; POURQUOI TALES; SHORT STORIES.

**DAVOL, MARGUERITE W.**

337    *Black, White, Just Right!* Ill. by Irene Trivas. Whitman, 1993 (0-8075-0785-7). USE LEVEL: PS/P

*Multicultural*

A girl describes her parents. Mama is African American and likes ballet, kittens, and African art. Papa, who is white, likes rap music, Saint Bernards, and modern art. The three of them are a loving family who appreciate their diversity.

FAMILY LIFE; MARRIAGE, INTERRACIAL; SELF-CONCEPT.

**DAY, NANCY RAINES**

338 *The Lion's Whiskers: An Ethiopian Folktale*. Ill. by Ann
Grifalconi. Scholastic, 1995 (0-590-45803-5). USE LEVEL: M
*African—Ethiopia*
Fanaye marries a man, Tesfa, who already has a son, Abebe.
Abebe resents his stepmother. Fanaye travels to the medicine
man, who teaches her that patience will help her win Abebe's
love.
ANIMALS—LIONS; CHARACTER TRAITS—PATIENCE; FAMILY LIFE—STEP
FAMILIES; FOLKTALES—AFRICA—ETHIOPIA.

**DAYRELL, ELPHINSTONE**

339 *Why the Sun and the Moon Live in the Sky: An African Folktale*.
Ill. by Blair Lent. Houghton, 1968, o.p. USE LEVEL: M
*African*
When the Sun and the Moon invite everyone to their home,
they find they must jump into the sky to make room for their
guests.
CALDECOTT AWARD; FOLKTALES—AFRICA; MOON; POURQUOI TALES; SKY;
SUN.

**DeARMOND, DALE, ADAPTER**

340 *The Seal Oil Lamp: Adapted from an Eskimo Folktale*. Ill. by the
adapter. Little, Brown, 1988 (0-316-17786-5). USE LEVEL: M
*Native American—Eskimo*
With the help of the mouse people, a blind boy survives after his
people leave him to die. He grows up to become a famous
hunter and storyteller.
ANIMALS—MICE; ARCTIC LANDS; CHARACTER TRAITS—KINDNESS;
FOLKTALES—NATIVE AMERICAN—ESKIMO; HANDICAPS—BLINDNESS;
SENSES—SEEING.

**DEE, RUBY, RETELLER**

341 *Tower to Heaven*. Ill. by Jennifer Bent. Henry Holt, 1991 (0-
8050-1460-8). USE LEVEL: M
*African*
After the people become too busy to talk to Onyankopon, only
an old woman, Yaa, would speak to him. Onyankopon tires of
her chatter and goes to the sky, but Yaa stands on a tower and
still chatters.
FOLKTALES—AFRICA; SKY.

342 *Two Ways to Count to Ten: A Liberian Folktale*. Ill. by Susan
Meddaugh. Henry Holt, 1988 (0-8050-0407-6); pap. (0-8050-
1314-8). USE LEVEL: M
*African—Liberia*

King Leopard holds a contest to find his successor. The animals compete and the antelope wins.

ANIMALS; CHARACTER TRAITS—CLEVERNESS; CONTESTS; COUNTING, NUMBERS; FOLKTALES—AFRICA—LIBERIA.

**DEETLEFS, RENE, RETELLER**
343 *Tabu and the Dancing Elephants.* Ill. by Lyn Gilbert. Dutton, 1995 (0-525-45226-5). USE LEVEL: P
*African*
Tabu lives in Africa with Temba, his father, and Tandi, his mother. When a mother elephant takes Tabu with her, Mama Tandi must play music for the elephants so they can dance.

ACTIVITIES—DANCING; ANIMALS—ELEPHANTS; FOREIGN LANDS—AFRICA.

**DEGEREZ, TONI, ADAPTER**
344 *My Song Is a Piece of Jade: Songs of Ancient Mexico in English and Spanish.* Ill. by William Stark. Little, Brown, 1984, o.p. USE LEVEL: M
*Mexican*
The poems in this collection celebrate beauty and nature and reflect the beliefs of the Toltecs. They are presented in English and Spanish.

FOREIGN LANDS—MEXICO; FOREIGN LANGUAGES; NATURE; POETRY, RHYME.

**DEGROSS, MONALISA**
345 *Donavan's Word Jar.* Ill. by Cheryl Hanna. HarperCollins, 1994 (0-06-020190-8); LB (0-06-020191-6). USE LEVEL: M
*African American*
Like the other third graders, Donavan Allen likes to collect things. When his collection of words fills his word jar, he shares them with his grandmother and the older adults in her apartment building.

BEHAVIOR—COLLECTING THINGS; BEHAVIOR—SHARING; FAMILY LIFE—GRANDMOTHERS; LANGUAGE; OLDER ADULTS.

**DEJONG, MEINDERT**
346 *The House of Sixty Fathers.* Ill. by Maurice Sendak. HarperCollins, 1956, LB (0-06-021481-3); pap. (0-06-440200-2). USE LEVEL: M
*Asian—China*
During the Japanese occupation of China, Tien Pao is separated from his family and struggles to be reunited with them. With his pig, he travels to his home, helped by 60 American soldiers.

CHARACTER TRAITS—BRAVERY; FOREIGN LANDS—ASIA—CHINA; HISTORY; NEWBERY AWARD; SURVIVAL; WAR.

**DELACRE, LULU, SELECTOR**

347  *Arroz Con Leche: Popular Songs and Rhymes from Latin America*. English lyrics by Elena Paz. Musical arrangements by Ana-Maria Rosado. Ill. by the selector. Scholastic, 1989 (0-590-41887-4). USE LEVEL: P/M
*Latin American*
There are 12 folk songs in this collection, some with fingerplays, some based on popular Latin American games.
FOREIGN LANDS—LATIN AMERICA; FOREIGN LANGUAGES; GAMES; MUSIC; POETRY, RHYME; SONGS.

348  *Las Navidades: Popular Christmas Songs from Latin America*. English lyrics by Elena Paz. Musical arrangements by Ana-Maria Rosado. Ill. by the selector. Scholastic, 1990 (0-590-43548-5); pap. (0-590-43549-3). USE LEVEL: P/M
*Latin American*
This collection introduces children to Christmas songs from Central and South America. Twelve songs are included.
FOREIGN LANGUAGES; HOLIDAYS—CHRISTMAS; MUSIC; POETRY, RHYME; SONGS.

349  *Vejigante Masquerader*. Ill. by the author. Scholastic, 1993 (0-590-45776-4). USE LEVEL: M
*Caribbean—Puerto Rico*
Ramon has made a costume so he can celebrate Carnival as a vejigante. Now all he needs is a mask.
FESTIVALS; FOREIGN LANDS—CARIBBEAN ISLANDS—PUERTO RICO; FOREIGN LANGUAGES; MASKS.

**DEMI**

350  *The Artist and the Architect*. Ill. by the author. Henry Holt, 1991 (0-8050-1580-9). USE LEVEL: M
*Asian—China*
An artist and an architect serve the emperor well. The artist becomes jealous of the architect and plans to destroy him. The architect sees through the plan and uses his wits to survive.
CAREERS—ARTISTS; CHARACTER TRAITS—CLEVERNESS; EMOTIONS—ENVY, JEALOUSY; FOLKTALES—ASIA—CHINA.

351  *A Chinese Zoo: Fables and Proverbs*. Ill. by the author. Harcourt, 1987 (0-15-217510-5). USE LEVEL: M
*Asian—China*
Thirteen fables and proverbs are presented in this collection.
ANIMALS; FABLES; FOLKTALES—ASIA—CHINA; PROVERBS.

352    *Dragon Kites and Dragonflies: A Collection of Chinese Nursery Rhymes*. Ill. by the author. Harcourt, 1986 (0-15-224199-X).
USE LEVEL: P/M
*Asian—China*
There are 22 nursery rhymes in this collection. Many include familiar Chinese images, like New Year's lanterns and silkworms.
FOREIGN LANDS ASIA—CHINA; NURSERY RHYMES; POETRY, RHYME.

353    *The Empty Pot*. Ill. by the author. Henry Holt, 1990 (0-8050-1217-6). USE LEVEL: M
*Asian—China*
To select a successor to rule the kingdom and grow the flowers, the emperor holds a contest. Unbeknown to the children, he gives them seeds that will not grow. Only one child, Ping, does not bring a plant to the emperor, and his honesty is rewarded.
CHARACTER TRAITS—HONESTY; CONTESTS; FOLKTALES—ASIA—CHINA; PLANTS.

354    *In the Eyes of the Cat: Japanese Poetry for All Seasons*. Translated by Tze-si Huang. Ill. by the author. Henry Holt, 1992 (0-8050-1955-2); pap. (0-8050-3383-1). USE LEVEL: M
*Asian—Japan*
These haiku poems feature animals throughout the seasons of the year. Among those included are herons, cats, nightingales, and foxes.
ANIMALS; FOREIGN LANDS—ASIA—JAPAN; HAIKU; POETRY, RHYME; SEASONS.

355    *Liang and the Magic Paintbrush*. Ill. by the author. Henry Holt, 1980 (0-8050-0220-0); pap. (0-8050-0801-2). USE LEVEL: M
*Asian—China*
Liang dreams of painting but cannot afford a brush. An old man on a phoenix gives him a magic paintbrush and whatever he paints becomes real. When the greedy emperor hears of the brush, he takes it, but Liang finds a way to get the brush back.
ACTIVITIES—PAINTING; ART; BEHAVIOR—GREED; FOREIGN LANDS—ASIA—CHINA; MAGIC.

356    *The Magic Boat*. Ill. by the author. Henry Holt, 1990, o.p. USE LEVEL: M
*Asian—China*
Chang rescues a man from drowning and is rewarded. A thief steals his magic boat, but Chang is able to recover it.
BOATS, SHIPS; FOLKTALES—ASIA—CHINA; MAGIC.

357   *The Magic Tapestry: A Chinese Folktale.* Ill. by the author. Henry
      Holt, 1994 (0-8050-2810-2). USE LEVEL: M
      *Asian—China*
      A woman weaves a beautiful tapestry, which blows away. Her
      first two sons search for it but are overcome by greed. Her
      youngest son faces all challenges and returns the tapestry to his
      mother.
      ACTIVITIES—WEAVING; BEHAVIOR—GREED; CHARACTER TRAITS—BRAV-
      ERY; FOLKTALES—ASIA—CHINA.

358   *The Stone Cutter.* Ill. by the author. Crown, 1995 (0-517-
      59864-7); LB (0-517-59865-5). USE LEVEL: M
      *Asian—China*
      A stonecutter is never quite satisfied and keeps wishing for
      more. An angel hears his wishes and changes him into the sun, a
      cloud, the wind, a rock, and finally back to a stonecutter.
      BEHAVIOR—DISSATISFACTION; BEHAVIOR—WISHING; FOLKTALES—ASIA—
      CHINA.

359   *Under the Shade of the Mulberry Tree.* Ill. by the author.
      Prentice, 1979, o.p. USE LEVEL: M
      *Asian—China*
      A rich man lets a poor man buy the shade of his mulberry tree.
      The poor man sits in the shade with his animals, even when the
      shade shifts into the rich man's house.
      BEHAVIOR—GREED; CHARACTER TRAITS—CLEVERNESS; FOLKTALES—
      ASIA—CHINA; TREES.

      **DEPAOLA, TOMIE, RETELLER**
360   *The Legend of the Bluebonnet: An Old Tale of Texas.* Ill. by the
      reteller. Putnam, 1983 (0-399-20937-9). USE LEVEL: M
      *Native American*
      During drought and famine, a young Native American girl sacri-
      fices her most cherished possession to the Great Spirits. Her
      generosity is rewarded as the rain returns and the hills are cov-
      ered with beautiful blue flowers.
      CHARACTER TRAITS—GENEROSITY; FLOWERS; FOLKTALES—NATIVE
      AMERICAN; WEATHER—DROUGHTS.

361   *The Legend of the Indian Paintbrush.* Ill. by the reteller. Putnam,
      1988 (0-399-21534-4); pap. (0-399-21777-0). USE LEVEL: M
      *Native American*
      A Plains Indian boy dreams of bringing the colors of the sunset
      to his land. He finds the colors in the paintbrush flowers.
      ACTIVITIES—PAINTING; FLOWERS; FOLKTALES—NATIVE AMERICAN.

362    *The Legend of the Persian Carpet.* Ill. by Claire Ewart. Putnam, 1993 (0-399-22415-7). USE LEVEL: M
*Middle Eastern—Iran*
King Balash treasures a large diamond that, when the sun shines on it, fills the room with a rainbow of colors. When the diamond is stolen and destroyed, a small boy, Payam, finds a way to bring color to the despondent king by creating a carpet.
FOLKTALES—MIDDLE EAST—IRAN; FURNITURE—CARPETS; PROBLEM SOLVING.

363    *The Legend of the Poinsettia.* Ill. by the reteller. Putnam, 1994, LB (0-399-21692-8). USE LEVEL: M
*Mexican*
When her mother becomes ill and cannot finish the new blanket for the Baby Jesus, Lucinda finds another gift for the Nativity. The green weeds that she brings into the church are transformed into plants with beautiful red flowers.
FLOWERS; FOLKTALES—MEXICO; GIFTS; HOLIDAYS—CHRISTMAS; RELIGION.

**DeSauza, James, reteller, and Harriet Rohmer, adapter**

364    *Brother Anansi and the Cattle Ranch: El Hermano Anansi y el Rancho de Ganado.* Spanish version by Rosalma Zubizarreta. Ill. by Stephen Von Mason. Children's Book Pr., 1989, LB (0-89239-044-1). USE LEVEL: M
*Central American—Nicaragua*
Brother Tiger wins the lottery and Brother Anansi tries to trick him out of his winnings. This story is rooted in African traditions.
ANIMALS; BEHAVIOR—TRICKERY; FOLKTALES—CENTRAL AMERICA—NICARAGUA; FOREIGN LANGUAGES.

**DeSpain, Pleasant**

365    *Thirty-Three Multicultural Tales to Tell.* Ill. by Joe Shlichta. August House, 1993 (0-87483-265-9); pap. (0-87483-266-7). USE LEVEL: U
*Multicultural*
Included among these stories are "The Magic Pot" from China, "The Mirror" from Korea, "The Lion's Whiskers" from Africa, and "Señor Rattlesnake Learns to Fly" from Mexico. The stories are brief and suitable for telling.
FOLKTALES; SHORT STORIES; STORYTELLING.

**DeVeaux, Alexis**

366 *An Enchanted Hair Tale.* Ill. by Cheryl Hanna. HarperCollins, 1987 (0-06-021623-9); LB (0-06-021624-7); pap. (0-06-443271-8). USE LEVEL: M

*African American*

Sudan has wild mysterious hair. Some people tease him about it and he feels sad and mad. Sudan makes some friends who help him feel good about himself.

CHARACTER TRAITS—APPEARANCE; CORETTA SCOTT KING AWARD; HAIR; POETRY, RHYME; SELF-CONCEPT.

**deWit, Dorothy, EDITOR**

367 *The Talking Stone: An Anthology of Native American Tales and Legends.* Ill. by Donald Crews. Greenwillow, 1979, o.p. USE LEVEL: U

*Native American*

Among these 27 stories are familiar characters like Raven, Iktomi, Badger, and Thunderbird. The stories are grouped into nine regions or peoples, like the Iroquois, the Plains, and the Pacific Northwest.

ANIMALS; FOLKTALES—NATIVE AMERICAN; POURQUOI TALES; SHORT STORIES.

**Diller, Harriett**

368 *The Waiting Day.* Ill. by Chi Chung. Simon & Schuster, 1994 (0-671-86579-X). USE LEVEL: M

*Asian—China*

A ferry man sees a beggar and thinks he is waiting for a free ferry ride only to find, after a busy day, that the beggar is watching the sun rise, move through the sky, and set.

BEGGARS; FOREIGN LANDS—ASIA—CHINA; NATURE.

**DiSalvo-Ryan, Dyanne**

369 *City Green.* Ill. by the author. Morrow, 1994 (0-688-12786-X); LB (0-688-12787-8). USE LEVEL: P

*African American*

A group of neighbors work together to turn a vacant city lot into a community garden. One girl, Marcy, tries to involve "Old Man Hammer," who does end up planting sunflowers.

COMMUNITIES, NEIGHBORHOODS; GARDENS, GARDENING; URBAN LIFE.

**Dixon, Ann, RETELLER**

370 *How Raven Brought Light to People.* Ill. by James Watts. Macmillan, 1992 (0-689-50536-1). USE LEVEL: M

*Native American—Tlingit*

In this Tlingit legend, the great chief has three wooden boxes. Raven turns himself into a baby and tricks the great chief out of the sun, the moon, and the stars, but Raven ends up covered with soot.

BEHAVIOR—TRICKERY; BIRDS—RAVENS; FOLKTALES—NATIVE AMERICAN—TLINGIT; POURQUOI TALES.

371    *The Sleeping Lady.* Ill. by Elizabeth Johns. Alaska Northwest, 1994 (0-88240-444-X). USE LEVEL: M
**Native American**
In Alaska, there is a mountain called "The Sleeping Lady." This folktale tells of two lovers, Susitna and Nekatla. When Nekatla is killed in battle, Susitna is asleep. The villagers decide not to tell her the sad news, so she still sleeps.

BEHAVIOR—FIGHTING, ARGUING; FOLKTALES—NATIVE AMERICAN; POURQUOI TALES; WAR.

**DOBKIN, BONNIE**
372    *Collecting.* Ill. by Rick Hackney. Childrens Pr., 1993, LB (0-516-02015-3); pap. (0-51642015-1). USE LEVEL: PS/P
**Asian American**
A young boy talks about all the things he has collected. The rhyming pattern of the text adds to the predictability.

BEHAVIOR—COLLECTING THINGS; PREDICTABLE TEXT.

373    *Everybody Says.* Ill. by Keith Neely. Childrens Pr., 1993, LB (0-516-02019-6); pap. (0-516-42019-4). USE LEVEL: PS/P
**African American**
A young boy celebrates his individuality. He likes to read and draw and to eat raw carrots. This book has a simple, predictable text.

PREDICTABLE TEXT; SELF-CONCEPT.

374    *Just a Little Different.* Ill. by Keith Neely. Childrens Pr., 1994, LB (0-516-02018-8); pap. (0-516-42018-6). USE LEVEL: PS/P
**Multicultural**
An African American girl talks about her friend who is in a wheelchair. The simple text makes this a predictable first reader.

FRIENDSHIP; HANDICAPS—PHYSICAL; PREDICTABLE TEXT.

**DORRIS, MICHAEL**
375    *Guests.* Hyperion, 1994 (0-7868-0047-X); LB (0-7868-2036-5). USE LEVEL: U
**Native American**
Moss is concerned about the strangers who have come to his

village. He runs to the forest and encounters a porcupine and a runaway girl. When he returns to the village, he is more aware of who he is and his place among his people.

BEHAVIOR—GROWING UP; FAMILY LIFE; FRIENDSHIP.

376     *Morning Girl.* Hyperion, 1992 (1-56282-284-5); LB (1-56282-285-3); pap. (1-56282-661-1). USE LEVEL: U
*Native American—Taino*
Morning Girl and her brother, Star Boy, live on an island in the Caribbean in 1492. They describe their activities, ending with the arrival of European explorers.

FAMILY LIFE—SIBLINGS; FOREIGN LANDS—CARIBBEAN ISLANDS; HISTORY—EXPLORERS.

**DORROS, ARTHUR**
377     *Abuela.* Ill. by Elisa Kleven. Dutton, 1991 (0-525-44750-4). USE LEVEL: P/M
*Hispanic American*
Rosalba is riding on the bus with her grandmother. She imagines they can fly and describes their trip. Spanish words are used throughout the story and a glossary is included.

ACTIVITIES—FLYING; FAMILY LIFE—GRANDMOTHERS; FOREIGN LANGUAGES; IMAGINATION; URBAN LIFE.

378     *Radio Man: A Story in English and Spanish/Don Radio: Un Cuento en Inglés y Español.* Translated by Sandra Marulanda Dorros. Ill. by the author. HarperCollins, 1993 (0-06-021547-X); LB (0-06-021548-8). USE LEVEL: P
*Mexican American*
Diego listens to the radio while he travels with his family of migrant workers and while he works in the fields.

FAMILY LIFE; FOREIGN LANGUAGES; MIGRANT WORKERS; RADIOS.

379     *Tonight Is Carnaval.* Illus. Dutton, 1991 (0-525-44641-9); Puffin, pap. (0-14-055467-X). USE LEVEL: P/M
*South American—Peru*
In the Andes Mountains of South America, a family prepares for Carnaval. The illustrations are photographs of fabric wall hangings, "arpilleras." A description of how these were made follows the story, as does a glossary of terms.

CELEBRATIONS; FAMILY LIFE; FESTIVALS; FOREIGN LANDS—SOUTH AMERICA—PERU; FOREIGN LANGUAGES.

**DRAGONWAGON, CRESCENT**
380     *Half a Moon and One Whole Star.* Ill. by Jerry Pinkney.

Macmillan, 1986 (0-02-733120-2); pap. (0-689-71415-7). USE
LEVEL: P
*African American*
The poetic text in this book describes the sounds and activities
that occur as a young girl sleeps.
BEDTIME; CORETTA SCOTT KING AWARD; DREAMS; NIGHT; POETRY,
RHYME.

381 *Home Place.* Ill. by Jerry Pinkney. Macmillan, 1990 (0-02-
733190-3); pap. (0-689-71758-X). USE LEVEL: P
*African American*
When a family finds an old house, they find out about the black
family that lived there.
FAMILY LIFE; HOUSES.

**DUARTE, MARGARIDA ESTRELA BANDEIRA**
382 *The Legend of the Palm Tree.* Ill. by Paulo Werneck. Putnam,
1968, o.p. USE LEVEL: M
*South American—Brazil*
A legend from Brazil tells of a drought that destroyed everyone
in a tribe except a boy and his parents, who travel in search of a
new land. On the trip, a magic palm tree helps them survive.
FOLKTALES—SOUTH AMERICA—BRAZIL; MAGIC; TREES; WEATHER—
DROUGHTS.

**DUBOIS, MURIEL L.**
383 *Abenaki Captive.* Carolrhoda, 1994 (0-87614-753-8); pap. (0-
87614-601-9). USE LEVEL: U
*Native American—Abenaki*
In 1747, Ogistan is 13 when his older brother is killed by the
English. Five years later, John Stark, an English trapper, is captured by the Abenaki. Ogistan treats him with disdain but also
learns about the English and their ways.
ADVENTURE; FOREIGN LANDS—CANADA; HISTORY.

**DUFF, MAGGIE, RETELLER**
384 *Rum Pum Pum: A Folk Tale from India.* Ill. by Jose Aruego and
Ariane Dewey. Macmillan, 1978, o.p. USE LEVEL: M
*Asian—India*
When the king takes Blackbird's wife, Blackbird makes war on
him. On his journey, Blackbird is joined by many animals. When
the king tries to destroy Blackbird, his companions come to his
rescue.
ANIMALS; BIRDS—BLACKBIRDS; CHARACTER TRAITS—BRAVERY;
CUMULATIVE TALES; FOLKTALES—ASIA—INDIA.

**DUNCAN, ALICE FAYE**

385    *Willie Jerome.* Ill. by Tyrone Geter. Macmillan, 1995 (0-02-733208-X). USE LEVEL: P

*African American*

Willie Jerome loves to play jazz music on his trumpet but his family and neighbors don't appreciate him. His sister convinces Mama to sit and listen to him and Mama realizes that he can "play that red hot bebop."

FAMILY LIFE—SIBLINGS; MUSIC; SELF-CONCEPT; URBAN LIFE.

**DUPRÉ, RICK, RETELLER**

386    *Agassu: Legend of the Leopard King.* Ill. by the reteller. Carolrhoda, 1991 (0-87614-764-3). USE LEVEL: M

*African*

Agassu is a slave in Africa and he dreams of freedom. The sea tells Agassu of his fate—to escape from slavery and lead his people.

CHARACTER TRAITS—FREEDOM; FOLKTALES—AFRICA; SLAVERY.

387    *The Wishing Chair.* Ill. by the author. Carolrhoda, 1993 (0-87614-774-0). USE LEVEL: P

*African American*

A young boy likes to visit his grandmother, sit in a special chair, and listen to stories about African American heroes.

FAMILY LIFE—GRANDMOTHERS; STORYTELLING.

**EASMON, CAROL OLU**

388    *Bisi and the Golden Disc.* Ill. by the author. Crocodile Books, 1990 (0-940793-56-3). USE LEVEL: M

*African*

In Africa, Bisi is the daughter of King Olu, who loves her but who is very greedy. When she falls in love with Akin, an evil magician turns him into a snake. Bisi uses a magic disc to destroy the magician.

BEHAVIOR—GREED; FOREIGN LANDS—AFRICA; MAGIC.

**EASTMAN, PATRICIA**

389    *Sometimes Things Change.* Ill. by Seymour Fleishman. Childrens Pr., 1983 (0-516-02044-7); pap. (0-516-42044-5). USE LEVEL: P

*Multicultural*

Children from diverse backgrounds are shown describing changes, many in the natural world, like a butterfly from a caterpillar and a frog from a tadpole. The final group includes "A story was a word." This book has a predictable text.

CONCEPTS; NATURE; PREDICTABLE TEXT.

**ECKEWA, T. OBINKARAM**

390    *The Ancestor Tree*. Ill. by Christy Hale. Dutton, 1994 (0-525-67467-5). USE LEVEL: M

*African*

Nna-nna was the oldest man in the village. He had no living children, but he told stories and cared about all the children. After his death, the children care for him, convincing the adults to plant an ancestor tree for him.

DEATH; FOREIGN LANDS—AFRICA; FRIENDSHIP; TREES.

**EDMISTON, JIM**

391    *Little Eagle Lots of Owls*. Ill. by Jane Ross. Houghton, 1993 (0-395-65564-1). USE LEVEL: M

*Native American*

In this original story, Little Eagle Lots of Owls has a long name, so he is called Little Eagle. His grandfather wants him to know the full meaning of his true name, so he gives him owls as a gift.

BIRDS—OWLS; GIFTS; NAMES; SELF-CONCEPT.

**EDMONDS, I. G.**

392    *Ooka the Wise: Tales of Old Japan*. Ill. by Sanae Yamazaki. Shoe String, 1994 (0-208-02379-8). USE LEVEL: U

*Asian—Japan*

Ooka is a wise judge in the tales of Old Japan. In this collection there are 17 stories of how Ooka searches for justice.

CAREERS—JUDGES; CHARACTER TRAITS—WISDOM; FOLKTALES—ASIA—JAPAN.

**EHLERT, LOIS**

393    *Feathers for Lunch*. Ill. by the author. Harcourt, 1990 (0-15-230550-5). USE LEVEL: PS/P

*African American*

The pet cat would like to eat all the familiar birds in the neighborhood. The illustrations show the hands of a black child reaching to catch the cat.

ANIMALS—CATS; BIRDS; POETRY, RHYME.

394    *Mole's Hill: A Woodland Tale*. Ill. by the author. Harcourt, 1994 (0-15-255116-6). USE LEVEL: M

*Native American—Woodland*

Based on a fragment of a tale from the Woodland Indians, Mole finds a way to keep from having to move her home.

ANIMALS—FOXES; ANIMALS—MOLES; FOLKTALES—NATIVE AMERICAN—WOODLAND.

395    *Moon Rope: A Peruvian Folktale/Un lazo a la luna: Una leyenda peruana.* Ill. by the author. Harcourt, 1992 (0-15-255343-6). USE LEVEL: M

   *South American—Peru*

Mole and Fox are friends. Mole's wants are very simple, but Fox wants to go to the moon.

ANIMALS; FOLKTALES—SOUTH AMERICA—PERU; FOREIGN LANGUAGES; MOON; POURQUOI TALES.

**EISENBERG, PHYLLIS ROSE**

396    *You're My Nikki.* Ill. by Jill Kastner. Dial, 1992 (0-8037-1127-1); LB (0-8037-1129-8); Puffin, pap. (0-14-055463-7). USE LEVEL: P

   *African American*

Nikki is worried that her mother will forget her when she goes to work, so she keeps asking her questions like "What's my favorite color?" and "What do I like to draw the most?"

BEHAVIOR—WORRYING; EMOTIONS—LOVE; FAMILY LIFE—MOTHERS.

**ELLIS, VERONICA FREEMAN**

397    *Land of the Four Winds: Kpa Nieh Kpau.* Ill. by Sylvia Walker. Just Us, 1993 (0-940975-38-6); pap. (0-940975-39-4). USE LEVEL: M

   *African—Liberia*

In the Land of the Four Winds, the world is beautiful and there is plenty for all. Neejee, the evil water spirits, try to take the children. When they fail, they destroy the land, and the winds try to find children who can speak medicine talk.

CONCEPTS—COLOR; FOLKTALES—AFRICA— LIBERIA; MAGIC; WEATHER— WIND.

**ELMORE, PATRICIA**

398    *Susannah and the Blue House Mystery.* Ill. by John Wallner. Dutton, 1980, o.p. USE LEVEL: U

   *African American*

Susannah Higgins has a detective agency with her friend, Lucy. When Mr. Withers dies, the girls and their friends become involved in searching through his collection of antiques.

FRIENDSHIP; MYSTERY AND DETECTIVE STORIES.

399    *Susannah and the Poison Green Halloween.* Ill. by Joel Schick. Dutton, 1982 (0-525-44019-4). USE LEVEL: U

   *African American*

When one of their friends becomes ill from a tampered Halloween treat, Susannah and Lucy investigate. The most likely suspects are at the Eucalyptus Arms Apartments.

FRIENDSHIP; HOLIDAYS—HALLOWEEN; MYSTERY AND DETECTIVE STORIES.

400　*Susannah and the Purple Mongoose Mystery*. Ill. by Bob Marstall. Dutton, 1992 (0-525-44907-8). USE LEVEL: U
*African American*
Susannah and Lucy investigate the mysterious circumstances surrounding two fires in their neighborhood. One clue involves a boy on a purple Mongoose bicycle.
FRIENDSHIP; MYSTERY AND DETECTIVE STORIES.

**ENGEL, DIANA**
401　*Fishing*. Ill. by this author. Macmillan, 1993 (0-02-733463-5). USE LEVEL: P
*African American*
Loretta loves to go fishing with her grandfather. When she and her mother move away, Loretta finds a way to keep fishing.
FAMILY LIFE—GRANDFATHERS; FRIENDSHIP; MOVING; SPORTS—FISHING.

**EQUIANO, OLAUDAH, AND ANN CAMERON, ADAPTER**
402　*The Kidnapped Prince: The Life of Olaudah Equiano*. Knopf, 1995 (0-679-85619-6); pap. (0-679-95619-0). USE LEVEL: U
*African*
This is an adaptation of the memoir of Olaudah Equiano. In 1755 he was captured and taken from his home in Africa. He was a slave in England, the West Indies, and the United States. By learning to read and write, he was able to tell his own story.
EQUIANO, OLAUDAH; FOREIGN LANDS—AFRICA; SLAVERY; U.S. HISTORY.

**ESBENSEN, BARBARA JUSTER, RETELLER**
403　*The Great Buffalo Race: How the Buffalo Got Its Hump/A Seneca Tale*. Ill. by Helen K. Davie. Little, Brown, 1994 (0-316-24982-3). USE LEVEL: M
*Native American—Seneca*
When Young Buffalo ignores the advice of Old Buffalo and angers the Great Spirit Haweniyo, he and all the herd are punished. They are given humps to mark their disobedience and are forced to always look down.
ANIMALS—BUFFALOES; FOLKTALES—NATIVE AMERICAN—SENECA; POURQUOI TALES.

404　*Ladder to the Sky: How the Gift of Healing Came to the Ojibway Nation*. Ill. by Helen K. Davie. Little, Brown, 1989 (0-316-24952-1). USE LEVEL: M
*Native American—Ojibway*
While the people lived in peace, the Great Spirit allowed them

good health. When they became jealous and angry, the Spirit gave them pain, but also the gift of healing.

FOLKTALES—NATIVE AMERICAN—OJIBWAY; ILLNESS; POURQUOI TALES.

405    *The Star Maiden: An Ojibway Tale.* Ill. by Helen K. Davie. Little, Brown, 1988 (0-316-24951-3). USE LEVEL: M
*Native American—Ojibway*
The star maiden wants to come and live on earth. At first she cannot choose how to appear, but she and her star-sisters become water lilies.

FLOWERS; FOLKTALES—NATIVE AMERICAN—OJIBWAY; NATURE; POURQUOI TALES.

### ESKRIDGE, ANN E.

406    *The Sanctuary.* Dutton, 1994 (0-525-65168-3). USE LEVEL: U
*African American*
Little Man, ten, learns that his father was killed trying to help a friend in a fight. In his neighborhood there is an eccentric elderly woman, Lucy Johnson, who has built a shrine, a sanctuary, to others who have died and they add his father to it.

DEATH; EMOTIONS; OLDER ADULTS; URBAN LIFE.

### ETS, MARIE HALL

407    *Gilberto and the Wind.* Ill. by the author. Viking, 1963 (0-670-34025-1); Puffin, pap. (0-14-050276-9). USE LEVEL: P
*Mexican*
A little boy describes all the ways that he interacts with the wind, including watching the laundry flap on the line and flying a kite.

ACTIVITIES—PLAYING; FOREIGN LANDS—MEXICO; IMAGINATION; WEATHER—WIND.

### ETS, MARIE HALL, AND AURORA LABASTIDA

408    *Nine Days to Christmas.* Ill. by Marie Hall Ets. Viking, 1959 (0-670-51350-4); Puffin, pap. (0-14-054442-9). USE LEVEL: P
*Mexican*
Cici is in kindergarten. She is excited about her family's "posada," a special Christmas party, which will be held on the ninth day before Christmas. Cici finds it difficult to wait, but she helps with the preparations, including picking a piñata.

CALDECOTT AWARD; FOREIGN LANDS—MEXICO; HOLIDAYS—CHRISTMAS.

### EVANS, MARI

409    *JD.* Ill. by Jerry Pinkney. Doubleday, 1973, o.p. USE LEVEL: M
*African American*

Four stories about JD, who is growing up in a housing project.
FAMILY LIFE; SCHOOL; URBAN LIFE.

**EVERETT, GWEN**
410    *Li'l Sis and Uncle Willie: A Story Based on the Life and Paintings of William H. Johnson.* Ill. by the author. Rizzoli, 1991 (0-8478-1462-9); Hyperion, pap. (1-56282-593-3). USE LEVEL: M
*African American*
When Uncle Willie comes to visit, he shows his paintings to Li'l Sis and her doll Lillian and he talks about his life.
ART; CAREERS—ARTISTS; FAMILY LIFE—AUNTS, UNCLES; MUSEUMS; U.S. HISTORY.

**FAIRMAN, TONY, RETELLER**
411    *Bury My Bones, But Keep My Words: African Tales for Retelling.* Ill. by Meshack Asare. Henry Holt, 1991 (0-8050-2333-X); Puffin, pap. (0-14-036889-2). USE LEVEL: U
*African*
There are 13 stories in this collection from a variety of African locations, including Kenya, Egypt, Nigeria, and Namibia.
FOLKTALES—AFRICA; SHORT STORIES.

**FALWELL, CATHRYN**
412    *Feast for 10.* Ill. by the author. Houghton, 1993 (0-395-62037-6). USE LEVEL: P
*African American*
As the numbers go from one to ten, the family gathers groceries. Then the numbers go from one to ten again and the family prepares and shares a meal. The text has a simple, rhyming pattern.
COUNTING, NUMBERS; FAMILY LIFE; FOOD; POETRY, RHYME; SHOPPING.

**FEELINGS, MURIEL**
413    *Jambo Means Hello: Swahili Alphabet Book.* Ill. by Tom Feelings. Dial, 1974 (0-8037-4346-7); LB (0-8037-4350-5); pap. (0-8037-4428-5). USE LEVEL: P/M
*African*
This book presents a word for each letter of the Swahili alphabet.
ABC BOOKS; CALDECOTT AWARD; FOREIGN LANDS—AFRICA; FOREIGN LANGUAGES.

414    *Moja Means One: Swahili Counting Book.* Ill. by Tom Feelings. Dial, 1971 (0-8037-5776-X); LB (0-8037-5777-8); pap. (0-8037-5711-5). USE LEVEL: P/M
*African*

The illustrations of the numbers from one to ten include details about life in Africa.

CALDECOTT AWARD; COUNTING, NUMBERS; FOREIGN LANDS—AFRICA; FOREIGN LANGUAGES.

**FEELINGS, TOM,** SELECTOR

415   *Soul Looks Back in Wonder.* Ill. by the selector. Dial, 1993 (0-8037-1001-1). USE LEVEL: M/U
*African American*
Maya Angelou, Langston Hughes, and Mari Evans are among the poets who celebrate the pride of African American life and heritage. Collage illustrations provide layers of images often linking African landscapes with contemporary urban scenes.

CORETTA SCOTT KING AWARD; POETRY, RHYME; SELF-CONCEPT.

416   *Tommy Traveler in the World of Black History.* Ill. by the author. Black Butterfly Children's Books, 1991 (0-86316-202-9); pap. (0-86316-211-8). USE LEVEL: M/U
*African American*
Tommy Traveler reads as much as he can on black history. In his dreams, he finds himself living the history. The comic-book format should attract readers.

IMAGINATION; U.S. HISTORY.

**FENNER, CAROL**

417   *The Skates of Uncle Richard.* Ill. by Ati Forberg. Random, 1978 (0-394-93553-5); pap. (0-679-84923-8). USE LEVEL: M
*African American*
Marsha dreams of being a champion figure skater and she hopes for new skates for Christmas. When she is given her uncle's old hockey skates, she is disappointed.

CORETTA SCOTT KING AWARD; FAMILY LIFE; HOLIDAYS—CHRISTMAS; SEASONS—WINTER; SPORTS—FIGURE SKATING.

418   *Yolanda's Genius.* Simon & Schuster, 1995 (0-689-80001-0). USE LEVEL: U
*African American*
After several events of violence, Yolanda, her mother, and her brother Andrew move to a suburb in Michigan. A fifth grader who is large for her age, Yolanda seems to adjust to the move, but she is concerned as she watches Andrew struggle.

FAMILY LIFE, MOVING; MUSIC; SELF-CONCEPT.

**FICHTER, GEORGE S.**

419   *American Indian Music and Musical Instruments: With Instructions for Making the Instruments.* Drawings and diagrams

by Mari Ostberg and Nils Ostberg. McKay, 1978 (0-679-20443-1). USE LEVEL: M/U
*Native American*
A collection of songs from a variety of peoples, this book also includes instructions for making some of the instruments.
MUSIC; MUSICAL INSTRUMENTS; SONGS.

### FIELDS, JULIA
420    *The Green Lion of Zion Street.* Ill. by Jerry Pinkney. Macmillan, 1988 (0-689-50414-4); pap. (0-689-71693-1). USE LEVEL: M
*African American*
When the bus does not come, a group of children walk to school, past the statue of a lion that seems very real.
ANIMALS—LIONS; IMAGINATION; POETRY, RHYME.

### FINGER, CHARLES J.
421    *Tales from Silver Lands.* Ill. by Paul Honoré. Doubleday, 1924 (0-685-01496-7); Scholastic, pap. (0-590-42447-5). USE LEVEL: U
*South American*
There are 19 stories in this collection from Honduras, Guiana, Brazil, and other areas of South America.
FOLKTALES—SOUTH AMERICA; NEWBERY AWARD; SHORT STORIES.

### FINLEY, MARY PIERCE
422    *Soaring Eagle.* Simon & Schuster, 1993 (0-671-75598-6). USE LEVEL: U
*Multicultural*
In 1845, Julio Montoya's father takes a message from Taos (in Mexico) to Bent's Fort. Julio, 13, goes with him. After his father is killed by Apaches, Julio is aided by the Cheyenne, becoming Soaring Eagle. He cannot forget his Mexican heritage.
DESERT; SELF-CONCEPT; SURVIVAL; U.S. HISTORY.

### FISHER, LEONARD EVERETT
423    *Alphabet Art: Thirteen ABCs from Around the World.* Ill. by the author. Macmillan, 1985 (0-02-735230-7). USE LEVEL: P/M
*Multicultural*
Provides brief facts about 13 alphabets, including Chinese, Greek, Hebrew, and Japanese.
ABC BOOKS; FOREIGN LANDS; HISTORY.

424    *Calendar Art: Thirteen Days, Weeks, Months, and Years from Around the World.* Ill. by the author. Macmillan, 1987 (0-02-735350-8). USE LEVEL: M
*Multicultural*

Aztec, Babylonian, Mayan, and Islamic are among the calendars presented in this book.

CALENDAR; CONCEPTS; DAYS OF THE WEEK, MONTHS OF THE YEAR.

425   *Number Art: Thirteen 1 2 3s from Around the World.* Ill. by the author. Macmillan, 1982 (0-02-735240-4). USE LEVEL: P/M
*Multicultural*
Includes information about 13 numerical systems, including Egyptian, Roman, and Mayan.

COUNTING, NUMBERS; FOREIGN LANDS; HISTORY.

426   *Symbol Art: Thirteen Squares, Circles, and Triangles from Around the World.* Ill. by the author. Macmillan, 1986 (0-02-735270-6). USE LEVEL: M
*Multicultural*
Symbols for many functions, like business, magic, astrology, music, religion, and weather, are presented along with a description of the development of the symbols. The artwork is drawn from many cultures, including Babylonia, Phoenicia, Greece, and Rome.

CONCEPTS; FOREIGN LANDS; HISTORY.

FITZHUGH, LOUISE
427   *Nobody's Family Is Going to Change.* Farrar, 1974, pap. (0-374-45523-6). USE LEVEL: U
*African American*
Emma, 11, is very bright and ambitious. She feels, however, that her parents give more of their attention to her younger brother.

ACTIVITIES—DANCING; FAMILY LIFE; SIBLING RIVALRY.

FLACK, MARJORIE
428   *The Story about Ping.* Ill. by Kurt Wiese. Viking, 1933 (0-670-67223-8); Puffin, pap. (0-14-050241-6). USE LEVEL: P
*Asian—China*
When Ping is separated from his family, he has an unpleasant adventure, but he is willing to receive his punishment in order to get back home.

BEHAVIOR—MISBEHAVIOR; BIRDS—DUCKS; BOATS, SHIPS; FOLKTALES—ASIA—CHINA.

FLEISCHMAN, PAUL
429   *Bull Run.* Woodcuts by David Frampton. HarperCollins, 1993 (0-06-021446-5); LB (0-06-021447-3); pap. (0-06-440588-5). USE LEVEL: U
*Multicultural*

Sixteen characters present their perspectives on the Battle of Bull Run, the first great battle of the Civil War. Included in the accounts are those of a black soldier and a slave woman.
U.S. HISTORY—CIVIL WAR.

**FLEMING, DENISE**

430  *In the Small, Small Pond.* Ill. by the author. Henry Holt, 1993 (0-8050-2264-3). USE LEVEL: PS
*Asian*
An Asian child reaches for a frog that jumps into the pond, encountering many pond animals. The seasons change from spring to winter.
ANIMALS; CALDECOTT AWARD; NATURE; POETRY, RHYME; SEASONS.

431  *In the Tall, Tall Grass.* Ill. by the author. Henry Holt, 1991 (0-8050-1635-X); pap. (0-8050-3941-4). USE LEVEL: PS/P
*Multicultural*
A young child looking into the grass sees many small creatures, including caterpillars, ants, and snakes. Time passes from early morning until night.
ANIMALS; NATURE; POETRY, RHYME.

**FLORA, JAMES**

432  *The Fabulous Firework Family.* Ill. by the author. Macmillan, 1994 (0-689-50596-5). USE LEVEL: M
*Mexican*
Pepito and his family make the finest fireworks in their village in Mexico. They create a wonderful display for the festival but a thief almost spoils the day.
FIREWORKS; FOREIGN LANDS—MEXICO; FOREIGN LANGUAGES.

**FLOURNOY, VALERIE**

433  *The Best Time of Day.* Ill. by George Ford. Random, 1978 (0-394-83799-1). USE LEVEL: PS
*African American*
William enjoys his everyday activities, like eating breakfast, playing at the community center, and going to the supermarket. His favorite time is when Daddy comes home from work.
ACTIVITIES—PLAYING; FAMILY LIFE.

434  *The Patchwork Quilt.* Ill. by Jerry Pinkney. Dial, 1985 (0-8037-0097-0); LB (0-8037-0098-9). USE LEVEL: P/M
*African American*
When Tanya's grandma becomes ill, Tanya decides to work on the quilt her grandmother had begun. When Grandma feels stronger, she returns to work on the quilt, too.

ACTIVITIES—SEWING; CHARACTER TRAITS—HELPFULNESS; CORETTA
SCOTT KING AWARD; FAMILY LIFE—GRANDMOTHERS; ILLNESS; QUILTS.

## FORRESTER, SANDRA

435    *Sound the Jubilee.* Dutton, 1995 (0-525-67468-1). USE LEVEL:
U

*African American*

As a house slave, Maddie dreams of freedom. When the Union
troops capture Roanoke Island in 1862, Maddie and her family
live with a colony of other freed slaves. They still face the hardships of war, including the death of Titus, Maddie's brother.

CHARACTER TRAITS—FREEDOM; SLAVERY; U.S. HISTORY—CIVIL WAR.

## FOURIE, CORLIA

436    *Ganekwane and the Green Dragon: Four Stories from Africa.* Ill.
by Christian Arthur Kingue Epanya. Whitman, 1994, LB (0-
8075-2744-0). USE LEVEL: M

*African*

The four stories in this collection are based on African traditions. One story tells of a monster with a sore tooth; another
tells of a clever chief who wants to find a clever man for his
daughter to marry, but his daughter shows how clever she is.

CHARACTER TRAITS—CLEVERNESS; FOREIGN LANDS—AFRICA; MONSTERS;
SHORT STORIES.

## FOX, MEM

437    *Sophie.* Ill. by Aminah Brenda Lynn Robinson. Harcourt, 1994
(0-15-277160-3). USE LEVEL: P

*African American*

Sophie is welcomed into her loving family. As she grows, her
grandfather ages and becomes weak, finally dying. Sophie and
her family grieve at their loss and then welcome Sophie's child
into the world.

BIRTH; DEATH; FAMILY LIFE.

## FOX, PAULA

438    *How Many Miles to Babylon? A Novel.* Ill. by Paul
Giovanopoulos. Macmillan, 1982 (0-02-735590-X). USE LEVEL:
M

*African American*

James, who is ten, knows his mother is ill, but he imagines she is
in Africa. He decides to leave the people who are caring for him
and go off on his own to find his mother.

BEHAVIOR—RUNNING AWAY; IMAGINATION; URBAN LIFE.

439　*The Slave Dancer: A Novel*. Ill. by Eros Keith. Macmillan, 1973 (0-02-735560-8); Dell, pap. (0-440-40402-9). USE LEVEL: U
*African American*
Jessie, 13, is kidnapped from New Orleans and forced to travel on a slave ship where he must play music for the captured Africans to dance to for exercise.
CHARACTER TRAITS—BRAVERY; CHARACTER TRAITS—FREEDOM; CRUELTY; SEA AND SEASHORE; NEWBERY AWARD; SLAVERY.

**FRANKEL, JULIE E.**
440　*Oh No, Otis*. Ill. by Clovis Martin. Childrens Pr., 1991, LB (0-516-02009-9); pap. (0-516-42009-7). USE LEVEL: PS/P
*African American*
Otis keeps getting into trouble but even when he smears the icing from his birthday cake on himself, his parents still love him. This book has a rhyming, predictable text.
BIRTHDAYS; POETRY, RHYME; PREDICTABLE TEXT.

**FRANKLIN, KRISTINE L.**
441　*The Old, Old Man and the Very Little Boy*. Ill. by Terea D. Shaffer. Macmillan, 1992 (0-689-31735-2). USE LEVEL: P
*African*
In an African village, a little boy enjoys an old man's stories. When the boy is an old man, he remembers this experience and he shares stories with the young boys of the village.
COMMUNITIES, NEIGHBORHOODS; FOREIGN LANDS—AFRICA; OLDER ADULTS; STORYTELLING.

442　*The Shepherd Boy*. Ill. by Jill Kastner. Macmillan, 1994 (0-689-31809-X). USE LEVEL: P
*Native American—Navajo*
A Navajo boy, Ben, watches his father's sheep and, when one ewe's lamb is missing, he searches for her.
ANIMALS—SHEEP; CAREERS—SHEPHERDS; DESERT.

443　*When the Monkeys Came Back*. Ill. by Robert Roth. Macmillan, 1994 (0-689-31807-3). USE LEVEL: P
*Central American—Costa Rica*
As a child, Marta saw monkeys in the trees near her home. Now the trees have been cut down and the monkeys are gone. Marta decides to plant new trees and create a new forest for monkeys. As an old woman, she finally hears the monkeys again.
ANIMALS—MONKEYS; ECOLOGY; FOREIGN LANDS—CENTRAL AMERICA—COSTA RICA; TREES.

FRASER, MARY ANN

444    *Ten Mile Day: And the Building of the Transcontinental Railroad*. Ill. by the author. Henry Holt, 1993 (0-8050-1902-2). USE LEVEL: M
*Asian American—China*
This book describes the building of the transcontinental railroad in the mid-1800s. The work of Chinese immigrants is featured; for example, around 11,000 Chinese worked on this project with almost 2,000 being killed or seriously injured.
TRAINS; U.S. HISTORY.

FREEMAN, DON

445    *Corduroy*. Ill. by the author. Viking, 1968 (0-670-24133-4); Puffin, pap. (0-14-050173-8). USE LEVEL: PS/P
*African American*
During the day, Corduroy, a teddy bear, waits in the department store for someone to buy him. At night, Corduroy leaves the toy department to look for a lost button. Finally, Lisa buys him and gives him a button and a home.
CLOTHING—BUTTONS; EMOTIONS—LOVE; STORES; TOYS—TEDDY BEARS.

446    *A Pocket for Corduroy*. Ill. by the author. Viking, 1978 (0-670-56172-X); Puffin, pap. (0-14-050352-8). USE LEVEL: PS/P
*African American*
When he looks for a pocket, Corduroy is left at the laundry. Lisa comes back to find him, and she sews a pocket on his overalls.
CLOTHING—POCKETS; EMOTIONS—LOVE; LAUNDRY; TOYS—TEDDY BEARS.

FREGOSI, CLAUDIA

447    *The Pumpkin Sparrow: Adapted from a Korean Folktale*. Ill. by the author. Greenwillow, 1977, o.p. USE LEVEL: M
*Asian—Korea*
Wise and his wife, Cheerful, help a wounded sparrow and are rewarded with riches. Fox and his wife, Envy, are greedy and are chased by snakes, toads, and lizards.
BIRDS—SPARROWS; CHARACTER TRAITS—KINDNESS; FOLKTALES—ASIA—KOREA; MAGIC; PLANTS.

FRENCH, FIONA

448    *Anancy and Mr. Dry-Bone*. Ill. by the author. Little, Brown, 1991 (0-316-29298-2). USE LEVEL: M
*African*
In this original story based on African traditions, both Anancy

and Mr. Dry-Bone want to marry Miss Louise. Anancy asks the animals, Tiger, Dog, Alligator, Monkey, and Parrot, to lend him clothes, which he wears to make Miss Louise laugh.
ANIMALS; CLOTHING; CONTESTS; FOLKTALES—AFRICA.

449     *Little Inchkin*. Ill. by the author. Dial, 1994 (0-8037-1478-5).
USE LEVEL: M
*Asian—Japan*
Inchkin is small, no bigger than a thumb, but he is very brave. When he saves the princess from the demons, Lord Buddha rewards him and makes him as tall as other men.
CHARACTER TRAITS—BRAVERY; CHARACTER TRAITS— SMALLNESS; ELVES AND LITTLE PEOPLE; FOLKTALES—ASIA—JAPAN.

**FRIEDMAN, INA R.**
450     *How My Parents Learned to Eat*. Ill. by Allen Say. Houghton, 1984 (0-395-35379 3); pap. (0-395-44235-4). USE LEVEL: P
*Multicultural*
A young girl whose mother is Japanese and whose father is American tells about her family.
BEHAVIOR—ACCEPTING DIFFERENCES; FAMILY LIFE; FOOD; FOREIGN LANDS—ASIA—JAPAN.

**FRITZ, JEAN**
451     *China Homecoming*. Photos by Michael Fritz. Putnam, 1985, (0-399-21182-9). USE LEVEL: U
*Asian—China*
Returning to China as a grown women, the author recounts her experiences, including her visit to her hometown of Wuhan and being declared an honorary citizen. This is a sequel to *Homesick; My Own Story*.
ACTIVITIES—REMINISCING; ACTIVITIES—TRAVELING; FOREIGN LANDS—ASIA—CHINA.

452     *The Good Giants and the Bad Pukwudgies*. Ill. by Tomie dePaola. Putnam, 1982, pap. (0-399-21732-0). USE LEVEL: M
*Native American—Wampanoag*
While the pukwudgies cause mischief, the First People fish, plant corn, and raise their families. Sometimes, the First People need the help of Maushop and the good giants to control the pukwudgies.
FOLKTALES—NATIVE AMERICAN—WAMPANOAG; GIANTS; POURQUOI TALES.

453 *Homesick: My Own Story.* Ill. by Margot Tomes. Putnam, 1982
(0-399-20933-6); Dell, pap. (0-440-43683-4). USE LEVEL: U
*Asian—China*
The author reminisces about her childhood in China. As an
American, she found the British school confusing and she devel-
oped a great appreciation of and respect for the Chinese people
and their customs.
BEHAVIOR—GROWING UP; FOREIGN LANDS—ASIA—CHINA; HISTORY;
NEWBERY AWARD.

GALDONE, PAUL
454 *The Monkey and the Crocodile: A Jataka Tale from India.* Ill. by
the author. Houghton, 1969 (0-395-28806-1); pap. (0-89919-
524-5). USE LEVEL: M
*Asian—India*
A crocodile wishes to catch one of the monkeys that swings in
the mango tree. The crocodile has a plan, but the monkey outwits him.
ANIMALS—MONKEYS; CHARACTER TRAITS—CLEVERNESS; FOLKTALES—
ASIA—INDIA; REPTILES—ALLIGATORS, CROCODILES.

455 *The Turtle and the Monkey: A Philippine Tale.* Ill. by the author.
Houghton, 1983, pap. (0-395-54425-4). USE LEVEL: M
*Philippine*
Turtle and Monkey agree to share the banana tree but Monkey
is greedy and Turtle is clever.
ANIMALS—MONKEYS; BEHAVIOR—GREED; CHARACTER TRAITS—CLEVER
NESS; FOLKTALES—PHILIPPINES; REPTILES—TURTLES, TORTOISES.

GARCIA, ANAMARIE, RETELLER
456 *The Girl from the Sky: An Inca Folktale from South America.* Ill.
by Janice Skivington. Childrens Pr., 1992, LB (0-516-05138-
5); pap. (0-516-45138-3). USE LEVEL: M
*South American—Inca*
To encourage storytelling, wordless pages of illustrations are
presented, followed by one page with the text. A star comes to
the earth as a woman and is kept by a young man. When she
returns to the sky, he tries to join her.
FOLKTALES—SOUTH AMERICA—INCA; SKY; STARS; STORYTELLING.

GARDINER, JOHN REYNOLDS
457 *Stone Fox.* Ill. by Marcia Sewell. HarperCollins, 1980 (0-690-
03983-2); LB (0-690-03984-0); pap. (0-06-440132-4). USE
LEVEL: M
*Native American*

When his grandfather becomes ill, Little Willy tries to run the farm. Little Willy finds that he needs money for taxes, so he enters the dogsled race, competing against Stone Fox.

ANIMALS—DOGS; DEATH; FAMILY LIFE—GRANDFATHERS; SPORTS—SLED RACING.

**GARLAND, SHERRY**

458 *The Lotus Seed*. Ill. by Tatsuro Kiuchi. Harcourt, 1993 (0-15-249465-0). USE LEVEL: P

*Asian American—Vietnam*

A Vietnamese American girl remembers the homeland that her family was forced to leave. Her grandmother had saved a lotus seed from the imperial garden, which has been a treasured possession.

FAMILY LIFE—GRANDMOTHERS; FLOWERS; FOREIGN LANDS—ASIA—VIETNAM; SEEDS.

459 *Why Ducks Sleep on One Leg*. Ill. by Jean Tseng and Mou-sien Tseng. Scholastic, 1993 (0-590-45697-0). USE LEVEL: M

*Asian—Vietnam*

Three ducks who have only one leg each travel to the Jade Emperor to ask for legs. They end up with golden legs, which they keep hidden while they sleep.

BIRDS—DUCKS; FOLKTALES—ASIA—VIETNAM; POURQUOI TALES.

**GARNE, S. T.**

460 *One White Sail*. Ill. by Lisa Etre. Simon & Schuster, 1992 (0-671-75579-X). USE LEVEL: P

*Caribbean*

Familiar Caribbean island items illustrate the numbers from one to ten, like one white sail and nine steel drums. The book has a rhyming text.

COUNTING, NUMBERS; FOREIGN LANDS—CARIBBEAN ISLANDS; POETRY, RHYME.

**GATES, FRIEDA**

461 *Owl Eyes*. Ill. by Yoshi Miyake. Lothrop, 1994 (0-688-12472-0); LB (0-688-12473-9). USE LEVEL: M

*Native American—Kanienkehaka [Mohawk]*

While Raweno works to create the world and its creatures, he is distracted by Owl's suggestions. Raweno makes owl a nocturnal bird so he can finish his work in the daytime.

BIRDS—OWLS; CREATION; FOLKTALES—NATIVE AMERICAN—KANIENKEHAKA (MOHAWK); POURQUOI TALES.

**GEORGE, JEAN CRAIGHEAD**

462    *The First Thanksgiving.* Ill. by Thomas Locker. Putnam, 1993,
LB (0-399-21991-9). USE LEVEL: P
*Native American*
A retelling of the landing of the Pilgrims and their settlement at
Plymouth. Details about the Native Americans and their role in
helping the Pilgrims are featured.
CELEBRATIONS; CHARACTER TRAITS—HELPFULNESS; HOLIDAYS—
THANKSGIVING; U.S. HISTORY—PILGRIMS.

463    *Julie.* Ill. by Wendell Minor. HarperCollins, 1994 (0-06-
023528-4); LB (0-06-023529-2). USE LEVEL: U
*Native American—Inuit*
After living on the tundra with wolves, Julie returns to live in
the village with her father, Kapugen. She must reconcile her values and cultural beliefs with those of others in her community.
ANIMALS—WOLVES; ARCTIC LANDS; ECOLOGY; ENVIRONMENT.

464    *Julie of the Wolves.* Ill. by John Schoenherr. HarperCollins, 1972
(0-06-021943-2); LB (0-06-021944-0); pap. (0-06-440058-1).
USE LEVEL: U
*Native American—Inuit*
With the help of a pack of Arctic wolves, Miyax, 13, survives
being lost in the Alaskan wilderness.
ANIMALS—WOLVES; ARCTIC LANDS; NEWBERY AWARD; SURVIVAL.

465    *Shark Beneath the Reef.* HarperCollins, 1989 (0-06-021992-0);
LB (0-06-021993-9); pap. (0-06-440308-4). USE LEVEL: U
*Mexican*
Tomás Torres is facing a choice: Should he stay and be a fisher-
man in the Sea of Cortez or should he continue his education?
After an encounter with a shark, Tomás thinks he knows what
to do.
BEHAVIOR—GROWING UP; FOREIGN LANDS—MEXICO; FISH—SHARKS;
ISLANDS; SEA AND SEASHORE; SPORTS—FISHING.

466    *The Talking Earth.* HarperCollins, 1983 (0-06-021975-0); LB
(0-06-021976-9); pap. (0-06-440212-6). USE LEVEL: U
*Native American—Seminole*
Billie Wind, a Seminole Indian girl, is skeptical of the legends
and beliefs of her people. She is sent out alone into the
Everglades, where her belief in science encounters the power of
nature.
BEHAVIOR—GROWING UP; CHARACTER TRAITS—OSTRACISM;
EVERGLADES; NATURE.

467     *Water Sky*. HarperCollins, 1987 (0-06-022198-4); LB (0-06-022199-2); pap. (0-06-440202-9). USE LEVEL: U
**Native American—Inuit**
When Lincoln visits Alaska, he is fascinated by cultural traditions of the Eskimo people and by the beauty of the land.
ANIMALS—WHALES; ARCTIC LANDS; NATURE.

**GERAGHTY, PAUL**
468     *The Hunter*. Ill. by the author. Crown, 1994 (0-517-59692-X); LB (0-517-59693-8). USE LEVEL: P
**African**
Jamina thinks she would like to be a hunter until she finds a young elephant near an adult elephant that has been killed by hunters.
ANIMALS—ELEPHANTS; ECOLOGY; FOREIGN LANDS—AFRICA; SPORTS—HUNTING.

**GERSHATOR, PHILLIS, RETELLER**
469     *The Iroko-man: A Yoruba Folktale*. Ill. by Holly C. Kim. Orchard, 1994 (0-531-06810-2); LB (0-531-08660-7). USE LEVEL: M
**African—Yoruba**
The Iroko-man lives in the iroko tree. When the village women wish to have children, he grants their wish, but Oluronbi must pay with her child. When she does not, she becomes a bird. Her husband carves a child to give to the Iroko-man.
ACTIVITIES—CARVING; FOLKTALES—AFRICA—YORUBA; MAGIC.

470     *Rata-pata-scata-fata: A Caribbean Story*. Ill. by Holly Meade. Little, Brown, 1994 (0-316-30470-0). USE LEVEL: M
**Caribbean**
Even though there is work to do, Junjun likes to dream. When his mother gives him several jobs to do, he says some magic words—and they seem to work.
FOREIGN LANDS—CARIBBEAN ISLANDS; IMAGINATION; MAGIC.

471     *Tukama Tootles the Flute: A Tale from the Antilles*. Ill. by Synthia Saint James. Orchard, 1994 (0-531-06811-0); LB (0-531-08661-5). USE LEVEL: M
**Caribbean—West Indies**
Tukama does not listen to his grandmother and is captured by the two-headed giant. He must use his wits, and his music, to escape.
FOLKTALES—CARIBBEAN ISLANDS—WEST INDIES; GIANTS; MUSIC.

**GERSON, MARY-JOAN, RETELLER**

472 *How Night Came from the Sea: A Story from Brazil.* Ill. by Carla Golembe. Little, Brown, 1994 (0-316-30855-2). USE LEVEL: M
*South American—Brazil*
The African sea goddess Iemanjà has a daughter who chooses to marry a man on earth. The daughter misses the cool darkness of the sea, so Iemanjà sends a bag of night to her.
FOLKTALES—SOUTH AMERICA—BRAZIL; NIGHT.

473 *Why the Sky Is Far Away: A Nigerian Folktale.* Ill. by Carla Golembe. Little, Brown, 1992 (0-316-30852-8). USE LEVEL: M
*African—Nigeria*
The people on the Earth took too many pieces from the sky, until it moved far away. Now people must sow and harvest their own crops.
BEHAVIOR—GREED; FOLKTALES—AFRICA—NIGERIA; POURQUOI TALES; SKY.

**GILCRIST, JAN SPIVEY**

474 *Indigo and Moonlight Gold.* Ill. by the author. Black Butterfly Children's Books, 1993 (0-86316-210-X). USE LEVEL: P
*African American*
Autrie loves her Mama, but she knows their relationship will change with time and that one day she may be a mother watching her own daughter.
FAMILY LIFE—MOTHERS; IMAGINATION; SELF-CONCEPT.

**GILSON, JAMIE**

475 *Hello, My Name Is Scrambled Eggs.* Ill. by John Wallner. Lothrop, 1985 (0-688-04095-0); Pocket, pap. (0-671-74104-7). USE LEVEL: M
*Asian American—Vietnam*
Harvey's family is hosting a Vietnamese family, which includes a boy about his own age, Tuan. Harvey plans to introduce Tuan to American behaviors, but Harvey learns a lot about himself and his country, too.
FAMILY LIFE; FRIENDSHIP; HUMOR.

**GINSBURG, MIRRA, ADAPTER**

476 *The Chinese Mirror: Adapted from a Korean Folktale.* Ill. by Margot Zemach. Harcourt, 1988 (0-15-200420-3). USE LEVEL: M
*Asian—Korea*
A man brings a mirror home from China. The foolish people have never seen their reflections and they are confused by the images.

CHARACTER TRAITS—APPEARANCE; CHARACTER TRAITS—CURIOSITY; CHARACTER TRAITS—FOOLISHNESS; FOLKTALES—ASIA—KOREA.

477    *The Proud Maiden, Tungak, and the Sun: A Russian Eskimo Tale.* Ill. by Igor Galanin. Macmillan, 1974, o.p. USE LEVEL: M
*Native People—Russian Eskimo*
Tungak, the evil spirit of the tundra, chooses the proud daughter of a hunter for his bride. She runs away from him and when he follows, he is destroyed. The maiden marries the Sun and brings light to the tundra.
CHARACTER TRAITS—PRIDE; FOLKTALES—NATIVE PEOPLE—RUSSIAN ESKIMO; MONSTERS; POURQUOI TALES.

**GIOVANNI, NIKKI**
478    *Ego-Tripping: And Other Poems for Young People.* Ill. by George Ford. Lawrence Hill Books, 1993 (1-55652-188-X); pap. (1-55652-189-8). USE LEVEL: U
*African American*
Many of these poems are written as if for specific people, like "A Poem for My Nephew" and "A Poem (for Langston Hughes)." Others deal with emotional issues and concerns, like "Black Power," "Revolutionary Dreams," and "Dreams."
CHARACTER TRAITS—PRIDE; EMOTIONS; POETRY, RHYME; SELF-CONCEPT.

479    *Knoxville, Tennessee.* Ill. by Larry Johnson. Scholastic, 1994 (0-590-47074-4). USE LEVEL: P
*African American*
Nikki Giovanni's free-verse poem celebrates summertime and family togetherness in this rural area.
FAMILY LIFE; POETRY, RHYME; RURAL LIFE; SEASONS—SUMMER.

480    *Spin a Soft Black Song: Poems for Children.* Ill. by George Martins. Hill & Wang, 1985 (0-8090-8796-0); pap. (0-374-46469-3). USE LEVEL: M/U
*African American*
The poems in this collection reflect on the experiences of black children.
BEHAVIOR—GROWING UP; COMMUNITIES, NEIGHBORHOODS; EMOTIONS; POETRY, RHYME.

**GLASER, LINDA**
481    *Tanya's Big Green Dream.* Ill. by Susan McGinnis. Macmillan, 1994 (0-02-735994-8). USE LEVEL: M
*Multicultural*
Tanya and her fourth-grade classmates are preparing for Earth

Day. Although Tanya wants to do her project all by herself, she finds that teamwork is very important.

ECOLOGY; ENVIRONMENT; SCHOOL; TREES.

### GLEESON, BRIAN
482 *Koi and the Kola Nuts.* Ill. by Reynold Ruffins. Picture Book, 1992 (0-88708-281-5). USE LEVEL: M
*African*
When his father, Chief Sadaka, dies, Koi receives only a kola tree. He helps a snake, some ants, and an alligator. Later, when he is being threatened by the villagers, the creatures come to his aid.

ANIMALS; FOLKTALES—AFRICA.

483 *The Tiger and the Brahmin.* Ill. by Kurt Vargö. Picture Book, 1992 (0-88708-232-7). USE LEVEL: M
*Asian—India*
A kind Brahmin frees a captured tiger, but the tiger pounces on the Brahmin, planning to eat him. A jackal helps the Brahmin escape.

ANIMALS—JACKALS; ANIMALS—TIGERS; BEHAVIOR—TRICKERY;
CHARACTER TRAITS—KINDNESS; FOLKTALES—ASIA—INDIA.

### GOBLE, PAUL
484 *Adopted by the Eagles: A Plains Indian Story of Friendship and Treachery.* Ill. by the author. Macmillan, 1994 (0-02-736575-1). USE LEVEL: M
*Native American—Plains Indians*
Two friends, White Hawk and Tall Bear, go to take horses from their enemies. Because White Hawk wants a woman for himself, he betrays his friend.

BEHAVIOR—GREED; BIRDS—EAGLES; FOLKTALES—NATIVE AMERICAN—
PLAINS INDIANS; FOREIGN LANGUAGES; FRIENDSHIP.

485 *Beyond the Ridge.* Ill. by the author. Macmillan, 1989 (0-02-736581-6); pap. (0-689-71731-8). USE LEVEL: M
*Native American—Plains Indians*
As an old woman prepares to die, she seems to travel toward a high pine-covered ridge. Her spirit finds beauty beyond the ridge while her family returns her body to the earth.

CUSTOMS; DEATH; FOLKTALES—NATIVE AMERICAN—PLAINS INDIANS.

486 *Buffalo Woman.* Ill. by the author. Macmillan, 1984 (0-02-737720-2); pap. (0-689-71109-3). USE LEVEL: M
*Native American—Plains Indians*
A young man, who is a great hunter, knows the way of the buffalo. He marries a woman from the Buffalo Nation. When she

takes their son and returns to her people, the young man must find them.

ANIMALS—BUFFALOES; BEHAVIOR—FACING CHALLENGES; CHARACTER TRAITS—BRAVERY; FOLKTALES—NATIVE AMERICAN—PLAINS INDIANS; NATURE.

487    *Crow Chief: A Plains Indian Story.* Ill. by the author. Orchard, 1992 (0-531-05947-2); LB (0-531-08547-3). USE LEVEL: M
*Native American—Plains Indians*
Long ago, crows were white and the Crow Chief warned the buffaloes when hunters were coming. Falling Star came to help the hunters.

BEHAVIOR—TRICKERY; BIRDS—CROWS; FOLKTALES—NATIVE AMERICAN—PLAINS INDIANS; POURQUOI TALES.

488    *Death of the Iron Horse.* Ill. by the author. Macmillan, 1987 (0-02-737830-6); pap. (0-689-71686-9). USE LEVEL: M
*Native American—Cheyenne*
This description of the Cheyenne attack on a freight train in 1867 explores the viewpoint of the Cheyenne people, who see the train and the people on it as a threat to their way of life.

TRAINS; U.S. HISTORY; WAR.

489    *Dream Wolf.* Ill. by the author. Macmillan, 1990 (0-02-736585-9). USE LEVEL: M
*Native American—Plains Indians*
Two children are lost and a wolf finds them and cares for them. This is a revised edition of *The Friendly Wolf* (see main entry).

ANIMALS—WOLVES; BEHAVIOR—LOST; FOLKTALES—NATIVE AMERICAN—PLAINS INDIANS.

490    *The Gift of the Sacred Dog.* Ill. by the author. Macmillan, 1980 (0-02-736560-3); pap. (0-02-043280-1). USE LEVEL: M
*Native American—Plains Indians*
A boy goes to the Great Spirit to get help for his hungry people. Because of his bravery, his people are given horses, "Sacred Dogs," to help them capture animals for food.

ANIMALS—HORSES; BEHAVIOR—FACING CHALLENGES; CHARACTER TRAITS—BRAVERY; FOLKTALES—NATIVE AMERICAN—PLAINS INDIANS.

491    *The Girl Who Loved Wild Horses.* Ill. by the author. Macmillan, 1978 (0-02-736570-0); pap. (0-689-71696-6). USE LEVEL: M
*Native American*
In this original story, a girl who has lived with the wild horses is eventually transformed into a beautiful mare, and her tribe rejoices in her kinship with the Horse People.

ANIMALS—HORSES; BEHAVIOR—LOST; CALDECOTT AWARD.

492 *The Great Race of the Birds and Animals.* Ill. by the author. Macmillan, 1985 (0-02-736950-1); pap. (0-689-71452-1). USE LEVEL: M

*Native American*

The Creator holds a contest to decide who shall be supreme—man or buffalo.

ANIMALS; ANIMALS—BUFFALOES; BIRDS; FOLKTALES—NATIVE AMERICAN.

493 *Her Seven Brothers.* Ill. by the author. Macmillan, 1988 (0-02-737960-4); pap. (0-689-71730-X). USE LEVEL: M

*Native American—Cheyenne*

This Cheyenne legend tells of the stars in the Big Dipper. The illustrations incorporate colors and designs of the Cheyenne.

ANIMALS—BUFFALOES; FOLKTALES—NATIVE AMERICAN—CHEYENNE; POURQUOI TALES; STARS.

494 *Iktomi and the Berries: A Plains Indian Story.* Ill. by the author. Orchard, 1989 (0-531-05819-0); LB (0-531-08419-1); pap. (0-531-07029-8). USE LEVEL: M

*Native American—Plains Indians*

In this story, Iktomi tries to pick berries from their reflection. Iktomi almost drowns because of his own foolishness.

BEHAVIOR—TRICKERY; CHARACTER TRAITS—FOOLISHNESS; FOLKTALES—NATIVE AMERICAN—PLAINS INDIANS.

495 *Iktomi and the Boulder: A Plains Indian Story.* Ill. by the author. Orchard, 1988 (0-531-05760-7); LB (0-531-08360-8); pap. (0-531-07023-9). USE LEVEL: M

*Native American—Plains Indians*

Iktomi is going for a visit, dressed in his very best. Along the way, he gives his blanket to a boulder, only to take it back.

ANIMALS; BEHAVIOR—TRICKERY; FOLKTALES—NATIVE AMERICAN—PLAINS INDIANS; POURQUOI TALES.

496 *Iktomi and the Buffalo Skull: A Plains Indian Story.* Ill. by the author. Orchard, 1991 (0-531-05911-1); LB (0-531-08511-2). USE LEVEL: M

*Native American—Plains Indians*

When Iktomi gets his head stuck in a buffalo skull, the people think he is a spirit. His wife knows he is Iktomi, and she uses her stone hammer to remove the skull from her foolish husband's head.

BEHAVIOR—TRICKERY; CHARACTER TRAITS—FOOLISHNESS; FOLKTALES—NATIVE AMERICAN—PLAINS INDIANS.

497 *Iktomi and the Buzzard: A Plains Indian Story.* Ill. by the author. Orchard, 1994 (0-531-06812-9); LB (0-531-08662-3). USE LEVEL: M
*Native American—Plains Indians*
Iktomi tricks Buzzard into carrying him into the sky, but then he is rude to Buzzard. When Buzzard drops him into a hollow tree, Iktomi tricks two girls into chopping the tree down and releasing him.
BEHAVIOR—TRICKERY; BIRDS—BUZZARDS; CHARACTER TRAITS—FOOL ISHNESS; FOLKTALES—NATIVE AMERICAN—PLAINS INDIANS.

498 *Iktomi and the Ducks: A Plains Indian Story.* Ill. by the author. Orchard, 1990 (0-531-05883-2); LB (0-531-08483-3); pap. (0-531-07044-1). USE LEVEL: M
*Native American—Plains Indians*
Iktomi tricks some ducks and prepares to eat them. While they are cooking, he gets stuck in a tree. Coyote eats the roasted ducks, but he leaves a surprise for Iktomi.
ANIMALS—COYOTES; BEHAVIOR—TRICKERY; FOLKTALES—NATIVE AMERICAN—PLAINS INDIANS.

499 *The Lost Children: The Boys Who Were Neglected.* Ill. by the author. Macmillan, 1993 (0-02-736555-7). USE LEVEL: M
*Native American—Blackfoot*
After they are orphaned, six boys are not cared for by their people. They leave and travel to the sky, becoming a constellation.
FOLKTALES—NATIVE AMERICAN—BLACKFOOT; STARS.

500 *Love Flute.* Ill. by the author. Macmillan, 1992 (0-02-736261-2). USE LEVEL: M
*Native American—Plains Indians*
A young man is too shy to speak to the girl he loves. The Elk Men give him a flute, which, when he plays it, tells the girl of his love.
EMOTIONS—LOVE; FOLKTALES—NATIVE AMERICAN—PLAINS INDIANS; MUSIC; MUSICAL INSTRUMENTS.

501 *Star Boy.* Ill. by the author. Macmillan, 1983 (0-02-722660-3); pap. (0-689-71499-8). USE LEVEL: M
*Native American—Blackfoot*
A girl leaves her people to live in the Sky World with her husband, Morning Star. When she disobeys, she is sent back to Earth with her son, Star Boy, who is poor and ugly. After his mother's death, Star Boy must find a way to reach the sun.
ACTIVITIES—DANCING; FOLKTALES—NATIVE AMERICAN—BLACKFOOT; SKY; STARS.

**GOBLE, PAUL, AND DOROTHY GOBLE**

502　*The Friendly Wolf.* Ill. by Paul Goble. Macmillan, 1974, o.p. USE LEVEL: M

*Native American—Plains Indians*

Little Cloud and his sister, Bright Eyes, wander away from the camp, become lost on the mountain, and are befriended by a wolf, who helps them find their way home. This has been revised as *Dream Wolf* (Macmillan, 1990; see main entry).

ANIMALS—WOLVES; BEHAVIOR—LOST; FOLKTALES—NATIVE AMERICAN— PLAINS INDIANS.

**GODDEN, RUMER**

503　*The Valiant Chatti-Maker.* Ill. by Jeroo Roy. Viking, 1983, o.p. USE LEVEL: M

*Asian—India*

When their village is threatened by a tiger, the Chatti-Maker, helped by his wife, captures the beast.

ANIMALS—TIGERS; CHARACTER TRAITS—LUCK; FOLKTALES—ASIA—INDIA.

**GOLDBERG, WHOOPI**

504　*Alice.* Ill. by John Rocco. Bantam, 1992 (0-553-08990-0). USE LEVEL: M

*African American*

This version of *Alice in Wonderland* has an urban setting and contemporary events. After Alice wins a Sweepstakes prize, she encounters many unusual characters, many of whom want to take her prize.

FANTASY; URBAN LIFE.

**GOLDIN, BARBARA DIAMOND**

505　*Red Means Good Fortune: A Story of San Francisco's Chinatown.* Ill. by Wenhai Ma. Viking, 1994, LB (0-670-85352-6). USE LEVEL: M

*Asian American—China*

Chin Jin Mun lives in Chinatown and is excited about the New Year. He sees America as a land of opportunity until he encounters Wai Hing, a poor slave girl.

HOLIDAYS—CHINESE NEW YEAR; IMMIGRATION; SLAVERY; U.S. HISTORY.

**GOLLUB, MATTHEW**

506　*The Moon Was at a Fiesta.* Ill. by Leovigildo Martinez. Morrow, 1994 (0-688-11637-X); LB (0-688-11638-8). USE LEVEL: P

*Mexican*

The moon realizes that many exciting things happen for the sun during the day, so she decides to have her own fiesta.

CELEBRATIONS; FESTIVALS; FOREIGN LANDS—MEXICO; MOON.

507    *The Twenty-five Mixtec Cats.* Ill. by Leovigildo Martinez.
Morrow, 1993 (0-688-11639-6); LB (0-688-11640-X). USE
LEVEL: M
*Mexican*
When the healer brings 25 kittens to the village, the people are
apprehensive. The butcher asks an evil healer to get rid of the
cats, but she casts a spell on him. The 25 cats help save him.
ANIMALS—CATS; FOREIGN LANDS—MEXICO; MAGIC.

GOMI, TARO
508    *First Comes Harry.* Ill. by the author. Morrow, 1984, o.p. USE
LEVEL: PS/P
*Asian—Japan*
Originally published in Japan, this book features a young boy
who likes to be first: at breakfast, at play, in the bathtub, and in
bed.
ACTIVITIES—PLAYING; FAMILY LIFE; FOREIGN LANDS—ASIA—JAPAN.

GONZÁLEZ, LUCÍA M., RETELLER
509    *The Bossy Gallito/El Gallo de Bodas: A Traditional Cuban
Folktale.* Ill. by Lulu Delacre. Scholastic, 1994 (0-590-46843-
X). USE LEVEL: M
*Caribbean—Cuba*
On his way to his uncle's wedding, a bossy rooster stops to eat a
kernel of corn and he dirties his beak. He orders other charac-
ters to clean his beak and they refuse. Finally the sun helps him,
setting off a chain of events.
BIRDS—ROOSTERS; CUMULATIVE TALES; FOLKTALES—CARIBBEAN
ISLANDS—CUBA; FOREIGN LANGUAGES.

GORDON, GINGER
510    *My Two Worlds.* Photos by Martha Cooper. Houghton, 1993
(0-395-58704-2). USE LEVEL: P
*Hispanic American*
Kirsy Rodriguez, who lives in New York City, describes what it
is like to spend Christmas with her grandparents in the
Dominican Republic. Kirsy will also celebrate her birthday
there.
BIRTHDAYS; FAMILY LIFE—GRANDPARENTS; FOREIGN LANDS—
DOMINICAN REPUBLIC; HOLIDAYS—CHRISTMAS.

GORDON, SHEILA
511    *The Middle of Somewhere: A Story of South Africa.* Orchard,
1990 (0-531-05908-1); LB (0-531-08508-2); Bantam, pap. (0-
553-15991-7). USE LEVEL: U
*African—South Africa*

In South Africa, a new suburb for whites is being planned and the black families in one village face relocation to a distant area. Rebecca, nine, and her family challenge the government's decision. As the story evolves, Nelson Mandela is released.

FOREIGN LANDS—AFRICA—SOUTH AFRICA; PREJUDICE; RACE RELATIONS.

512    *Waiting for the Rain: A Novel of South Africa.* Orchard, 1987 (0-531-05726-7); LB (0-531-08326-8); Bantam, pap. (0-553-27911-4). USE LEVEL: U
*African—South Africa*
As a boy, Tengo worked on a farm and was a friend of the owner's nephew. After leaving the farm, Tengo becomes involved in political and social activities in Soweto, and he encounters prejudice and hatred.

EMOTIONS—ANGER; FOREIGN LANDS—AFRICA—SOUTH AFRICA; PREJUDICE; RACE RELATIONS.

**GRAHAM, LORENZ**
513    *Song of the Boat.* Ill. by Leo Dillon and Diane Dillon. HarperCollins, 1975, LB (0-690-75232-6). USE LEVEL: M
*African—West Africa*
In West Africa, Flumbo searches for the right tree for his new canoe.

BOATS, SHIPS; FOREIGN LANDS—AFRICA; TREES.

**GRAY, LIBBA MOORE**
514    *Dear Willie Rudd.* Ill. by Peter M. Fiore. Simon & Schuster, 1993 (0-671-79774-3). USE LEVEL: P
*African American*
Miss Elizabeth remembers her family's black housekeeper, Willie Rudd, and the deep affection that she had for her. Miss Elizabeth regrets accepting the conventions that separated them and that she never shared her feelings.

ACTIVITIES—REMINISCING; EMOTIONS—SADNESS; RACE RELATIONS.

**GRAY, NIGEL**
515    *A Country Far Away.* Ill. by Philippe Dupasquier. Orchard, 1988 (0-531-05792-5); LB (0-531-08392-6); pap. (0-531-07024-7). USE LEVEL: P
*African*
Two boys, one from rural Africa and one from a developed area in the western world, are depicted in their daily activities, including going to school, reading, and helping at home. The pictures on each page show the two locations.

COMMUNITIES, NEIGHBORHOODS; FAMILY LIFE; FOREIGN LANDS—
AFRICA; WORLD.

**GREENBERG, MELANIE HOPE**

516    *Aunt Lilly's Laundromat.* Ill. by the author. Dutton, 1994 (0-
525-45211-7). USE LEVEL: P
*Caribbean—Haiti*
Long ago, Aunt Lilly left Haiti to come to work in America. She
operates a laundromat, but she remembers her island home.
CAREERS; FOREIGN LANDS—CARIBBEAN ISLANDS—HAITI; LAUNDRY.

**GREENE, BETTE**

517    *Get On Out of Here, Philip Hall.* Dial, 1981 (0-8037-2871-9);
LB (0-8037-2872-7); Dell, pap. (0-440-43038-0). USE LEVEL:
M
*African American*
This is a continuation of the adventures of Beth Lambert and
Philip Hall and their on again/off again friendship.
FRIENDSHIP; RURAL LIFE.

518    *Philip Hall Likes Me, I Reckon Maybe.* Ill. by Charles Lilly. Dial,
1974 (0-8037-6098-1); LB (0-8037-6096-5); Dell, pap. (0-
440-45755-6). USE LEVEL: M
*African American*
Beth Lambert lives in a small community in Arkansas. This
book describes her daily activities, including her attraction to
Philip Hall.
FRIENDSHIP; NEWBERY AWARD; RURAL LIFE.

**GREENE, CAROL**

519    *Hi, Clouds.* Ill. by Gene Sharp. Childrens Pr., 1983, LB (0-516-
02036-6); pap. (0-516-42036-4). USE LEVEL: PS/P
*African American*
Two children look at clouds, often seeing shapes in them. The
slight rhyming pattern helps make this a simple, predictable
reader.
IMAGINATION; POETRY, RHYME; PREDICTABLE TEXT; WEATHER—
CLOUDS.

520    *Please, Wind.* Ill. by Gene Sharp. Childrens Pr., 1982, LB (0-
516-02033-1); pap. (0-516-42033-X). USE LEVEL: PS/P
*African American*

A little girl wants the wind to blow so she can fly her kite. The simple text uses a controlled vocabulary to be predictable.

ACTIVITIES—PLAYING; KITES; PREDICTABLE TEXT; WEATHER—WIND.

### GREENE, ELLIN

521    *The Legend of the Cranberry: A Paleo-Indian Tale.* Ill. by Brad Sneed. Simon & Schuster, 1993 (0-671-75975-2). USE LEVEL: M

*Native American*

Long ago, mastodons helped the People. When the creatures rebelled, there was a battle and many were killed. In the bog where many died, the Great Spirit allowed a plant to grow, the cranberry.

ANIMALS; FOLKTALES—NATIVE AMERICAN; FOOD.

### GREENE, JACQUELINE DEMBAR, RETELLER

522    *Manabozho's Gifts: Three Chippewa Tales.* Ill. by Jennifer Hewitson. Houghton, 1994 (0-395-69251-2). USE LEVEL: M

*Native American—Chippewa*

Manabozho is a legendary figure to many native peoples. He has the ability to change into any shape, and he uses it in these stories, each of which describes an accomplishment—stealing fire, finding rice, and saving the rose.

BEHAVIOR—TRICKERY; FOLKTALES—NATIVE AMERICAN—CHIPPEWA; MAGIC; POURQUOI TALES; SHORT STORIES.

### GREENFIELD, ELOISE

523    *Aaron and Gayla's Alphabet Book.* Ill. by Jan Spivey Gilcrist. Black Butterfly Children's Books, 1993 (0-86316-208-8); LB (0-86316-213-4). USE LEVEL: PS/P

*African American*

Sentences describe the activities of two children, Aaron and Gayla. Within the sentences are words that begin with different letters of the alphabet, from A to Z.

ABC BOOKS; ACTIVITIES; FRIENDSHIP.

524    *Aaron and Gayla's Counting Book.* Ill. by Jan Spivey Gilcrist. Black Butterfly Children's Books, 1993 (0-86316-209-6); LB (0-86316-214-2). USE LEVEL: PS/P

*African American*

Words and sentences depict items from one to 20 as Aaron and Gayla explore their neighborhood on a rainy day.

COUNTING, NUMBERS; FRIENDSHIP; WEATHER—RAIN.

525    *Africa Dream.* Ill. by Carole Byard. HarperCollins, 1977, LB

(0-690-04776-2); pap. (0-06-443277-7). USE LEVEL: P
*African American*
In her dream, a young girl travels to Africa and sees the village of her ancestors.
CORETTA SCOTT KING AWARD; DREAMS; FOREIGN LANDS—AFRICA.

526 *Big Friend, Little Friend.* Ill. by Jan Spivey Gilcrist. Black Butterfly Children's Books, 1991 (0-86316-204-5). USE LEVEL: PS
*African American*
In this sturdy board book a young boy has a big friend who helps him and a little friend whom he helps.
ACTIVITIES—PLAYING; CHARACTER TRAITS—HELPFULNESS; FORMAT, UNUSUAL—BOARD BOOKS; FRIENDSHIP.

527 *Daddy and I.* Ill. by Jan Spivey Gilcrist. Black Butterfly Children's Books, 1991 (0-86316-206-1). USE LEVEL: PS
*African American*
A young boy describes the activities he enjoys with his father. This sturdy board book has a rhyming text.
FAMILY LIFE—FATHERS; FORMAT, UNUSUAL—BOARD BOOKS; POETRY, RHYME.

528 *Darlene.* Ill. by George Ford. Routledge, 1980, o.p. USE LEVEL: P
*African American*
Darlene is in a wheelchair. She is worried when she has to spend the day with her uncle and her cousin, Joanne. But then she does not want to leave.
FAMILY LIFE; HANDICAPS—PHYSICAL.

529 *Daydreamers.* Ill. by Tom Feelings. Dial, 1981 (0-8037-2137-4); LB (0-8037-2134-X); pap. (0-8037-0167-5). USE LEVEL: M/U
*African American*
Poetic language celebrates those who think, plan, reflect, observe, feel, reach, and dream.
BEHAVIOR—SOLITUDE; CORETTA SCOTT KING AWARD; DREAMS; EMOTIONS; POETRY, RHYME.

530 *First Pink Light.* Ill. by Moneta Barnett. HarperCollins, 1976 (0-690-01087-7). USE LEVEL: P
*African American*
Tyree wants to stay awake and surprise his Daddy.
BEDTIME; EMOTIONS—LOVE; FAMILY LIFE—FATHERS; NIGHT.

531 *First Pink Light*. Ill. by Jan Spivey Gilcrist. Black Butterfly Children's Books, 1991 (0-86316-207-X); pap. (0-86316-212-6). USE LEVEL: P
*African American*
Daddy is coming home and Tyree wants to surprise him. He tries to stay awake, but at dawn, when his Daddy does get home, Tyree is sleeping and his Daddy carries him to his bed. This is a newly illustrated version.
BEDTIME; EMOTIONS—LOVE; FAMILY LIFE—FATHERS; NIGHT.

532 *Grandmama's Joy*. Ill. by Carole Byard. Putnam, 1980 (0-399-21064-4). USE LEVEL: P
*African American*
Rhondy lives with her grandmother and they share good times and bad, including moving to a less expensive home.
CORETTA SCOTT KING AWARD; EMOTIONS—LOVE; FAMILY LIFE—GRANDMOTHERS; MOVING.

533 *Grandpa's Face*. Ill. by Floyd Cooper. Putnam, 1988 (0-399-21525-5); pap. (0-399-22106-9). USE LEVEL: P
*African American*
Tamika and her grandpa share some special times together. When Grandpa prepares for a theater performance, his scary face frightens Tamika. Grandpa and Tamika discuss her fear and Grandpa reassures Tamika that he will always love her.
ACTIVITIES—ACTING; EMOTIONS—FEAR; FAMILY LIFE—GRANDFATHERS; OLDER ADULTS; THEATER.

534 *Honey, I Love*. Ill. by Jan Spivey Gilcrist. HarperCollins, 1995 (0-694-00579-7). USE LEVEL: PS/P
*African American*
This is an illustrated picture book of Greenfield's poem.
EMOTIONS—LOVE; POETRY, RHYME; SELF-CONCEPT.

535 *Honey, I Love: And Other Love Poems*. Ill. by Leo Dillon and Diane Dillon. HarperCollins, 1972 (0-690-01344-5); LB (0-690-03845-3); pap. (0-06-443097-9). USE LEVEL: P/M
*African American*
Jumping rope, dressing up, and other familiar experiences are presented in these poems.
ACTIVITIES—PLAYING; EMOTIONS—LOVE; IMAGINATION; POETRY, RHYME.

536 *I Make Music*. Ill. by Jan Spivey Gilcrist. Black Butterfly Children's Books, 1991 (0-86316-205-3). USE LEVEL: PS
*African American*

In this sturdy board book, a child enjoys making different sounds with musical instruments.

FORMAT, UNUSUAL—BOARD BOOKS; MUSIC; POETRY, RHYME.

537 *Koya DeLaney and the Good Girl Blues.* Scholastic, 1992 (0-590-43300-8); pap. (0-590-43299 0). USE LEVEL: U
*African American*
Koya DeLaney enjoys being with her friends, Dawn and Loritha. They work on their double-dutch jumping and they enjoy the music of Koya's cousin, Del. Sometimes, though, Koya does not tell her friends when she is angry or upset.

ACTIVITIES—JUMPING ROPE; EMOTIONS—ANGER; FAMILY LIFE; FRIENDSHIP.

538 *Me and Neesie.* Ill. by Moneta Barnett. HarperCollins, 1975, LB (0-690-00715-9); pap. (0-06-443057-X). USE LEVEL: P
*African American*
Janell has an imaginary friend who stays with her until she makes new friends at school.

FAMILY LIFE; IMAGINATION—IMAGINARY FRIENDS; SCHOOL.

539 *My Doll, Keshia.* Ill. by Jan Spivey Gilcrist. Black Butterfly Children's Books, 1991 (0-86316-203-7). USE LEVEL: PS
*African American*
In a simple, rhyming text, a little girl tells how she plays with her doll. This is a sturdy board book for young children.

FORMAT, UNUSUAL—BOARD BOOKS; POETRY, RHYME; TOYS—DOLLS.

540 *Nathaniel Talking.* Ill. by Jan Spivey Gilcrist. Black Butterfly Children's Books, 1988 (0-86316-200-2); pap. (0-86316-210-0). USE LEVEL: P/M
*African American*
Nathaniel is nine, and he raps and rhymes about his life, telling about some people who are important to him.

COMMUNITIES, NEIGHBORHOODS; CORETTA SCOTT KING AWARD; POETRY, RHYME; URBAN LIFE.

541 *Night on Neighborhood Street.* Ill. by Jan Spivey Gilcrist. Dial, 1991 (0-8037-0777-0); LB (0-8037-0778-9). USE LEVEL: M
*African American*
Seventeen poems describe life on Neighborhood Street during the evening and night.

CHARACTER TRAITS—BRAVERY; COMMUNITIES, NEIGHBORHOODS; CORETTA SCOTT KING AWARD; NIGHT; POETRY, RHYME; URBAN LIFE.

542    *On My Horse.* Ill. by Jan Spivey Gilcrist. HarperCollins, 1995
       (0-694-00583-5). USE LEVEL: PS/P
       *African American*
       A young boy enjoys riding his horse, which is carefully led by
       the owner. The boy, however, imagines he is really riding the
       horse on his own.
       ANIMALS—HORSES; IMAGINATION; POETRY, RHYME.

543    *She Come Bringin Me That Little Baby Girl.* Ill. by John Steptoe.
       HarperCollins, 1974 (0-397-31586-4); LB (0-397-32478-2);
       pap. (0-06-443296-3). USE LEVEL: P
       *African American*
       Kevin has been hoping for a baby brother. He must adjust to
       having a new sister.
       BABIES, TODDLERS; EMOTIONS—ENVY, JEALOUSY; FAMILY LIFE—
       SIBLINGS; SIBLING RIVALRY.

544    *Sister.* Ill. by Moneta Barnett. HarperCollins, 1974 (0-690-
       00497-4); pap. (0-06-440199-5). USE LEVEL: M
       *African American*
       Dorothea Freeman, 13, wants there to be peace between her
       mother and her sister Alberta. Since the death of her father, the
       two have grown apart.
       BEHAVIOR –GROWING UP; DEATH; FAMILY LIFE—SIBLINGS.

545    *Talk about a Family.* Ill. by James Calvin. HarperCollins, 1978
       (0-397-31789-1); LB (0-397-32504-5); pap. (0-06-440444-7).
       USE LEVEL: M
       *African American*
       Genny worries about the problems in her family, especially the
       way her parents argue. She hopes that when her brother, Larry,
       comes home from the army, he will be able to help.
       BEHAVIOR—WORRYING; DIVORCE, SEPARATION; EMOTIONS—ANGER;
       FAMILY LIFE.

546    *Under the Sunday Tree: Poems.* Ill. by Amos Ferguson.
       HarperCollins, 1988 (0-06-022254-9); LB (0-06-022257-3);
       pap. (0-06-443257-2). USE LEVEL: M
       *Caribbean*
       There are 20 poems focusing on different experiences in the
       Bahamas, including fishing and watching the tourists.
       CORETTA SCOTT KING AWARD; FOREIGN LANDS—CARIBBEAN ISLANDS;
       ISLANDS; POETRY, RHYME.

547    *William and the Good Old Days.* Ill. by Jan Spivey Gilcrist.

HarperCollins, 1993 (0-06-021093-1); LB (0-06-021094-X).
USE LEVEL: P
*African American*
When his grandmother is ill, William thinks about the wonderful times that they have shared. He is eager for her to be better.
FAMILY LIFE- GRANDMOTHERS; ILLNESS.

**GREENFIELD, ELOISE, AND LESSIE JONES LITTLE**
548    *Childtimes: A Three-Generation Memoir.* Ill. by Jerry Pinkney.
HarperCollins, 1979 (0-690-03874-7); LB (0-690-03875-5);
pap. (0-06-446134-3). USE LEVEL: M/U
*African American*
Eloise Greenfield and her mother, Lessie Jones Little, reflect on their childhood and on that of Pattie Ridley Jones, the grandmother of Eloise Greenfield. Details of the historical era of the time of their childhoods provide a frame of reference.
ACTIVITIES—REMINISCING; BIOGRAPHY; CORETTA SCOTT KING AWARD; FAMILY LIFE.

**GREENFIELD, ELOISE, AND ALESIA REVIS**
549    *Alesia.* Ill. by George Ford. Photos by Sandra Turner Bond.
Putnam, 1981, o.p. USE LEVEL: M/U
*African American*
In a diary format covering seven months, Alesia, who is wheelchair-bound, describes her life.
FAMILY LIFE; HANDICAPS—PHYSICAL.

**GREGER, SHANA, RETELLER**
550    *The Fifth and Final Sun: An Ancient Aztec Myth of the Sun's Origin.* Ill. by the reteller. Houghton, 1994 (0-395-67438-7).
USE LEVEL: M
*Mexican—Aztec*
In five brief stories, an explanation is given about how there came to be one sun. A final vignette describes the origin of the moon.
CREATION; FOLKTALES—MEXICO—AZTEC; MOON; SUN.

**GRIEGO, MARGOT C., ET AL., SELECTORS**
551    *Tortillitas Para Mamá: And Other Nursery Rhymes.* Ill. by Barbara Cooney. Henry Holt, 1981 (0-8050-0285-5); pap. (0-8050-0317-7). USE LEVEL: P
*Latin American*
The 13 rhymes in this collection are popular in Latin America. The rhymes are written in Spanish and English.
FOREIGN LANDS—LATIN AMERICA; FOREIGN LANGUAGES; NURSERY RHYMES; POETRY, RHYME.

**GRIFALCONI, ANN**

552    *The Bravest Flute: A Story of Courage in the Mayan Tradition.* Ill. by the author. Little, Brown, 1994 (0-316-32878-2). USE LEVEL: M

*Central American—Mayan*

On New Year's Day, a poor young boy finds the strength to lead the parade to town. Playing his flute and carrying a drum, he overcomes his weariness and reaches the cathedral.

CHARACTER TRAITS—PERSEVERANCE; FOREIGN LANDS—CENTRAL AMERICA; HOLIDAYS—NEW YEAR'S; MUSIC.

553    *Darkness and the Butterfly.* Ill. by the author. Little, Brown, 1987 (0-316-32863-4). USE LEVEL: P

*African*

In this African village, the Wise Woman helps Osa learn to overcome her fear of the dark.

EMOTIONS—FEAR; FOREIGN LANDS—AFRICA; INSECTS—BUTTERFLIES, CATERPILLARS; NIGHT.

554    *Flyaway Girl.* Ill. by the author. Little, Brown, 1992 (0-316-32866-9). USE LEVEL: M

*African*

Nsia is a young girl who has not yet begun to do her work helping her mother. Nsia's mother wants her to be a "flyaway girl" a little longer and enjoy her freedom and her childhood.

BEHAVIOR—GROWING UP; CUSTOMS; FOREIGN LANDS—AFRICA; RIVERS.

555    *Kinda Blue.* Ill. by the author. Little, Brown, 1993 (0-316-32869-3). USE LEVEL: P

*African American*

When Sissy feels lonely and "kinda blue," Uncle Dan gives her some extra attention and reminds her how much she is loved.

EMOTIONS—LOVE; EMOTIONS—SADNESS; FAMILY LIFE—AUNTS, UNCLES; RURAL LIFE.

556    *Not Home: A Novel.* Little, Brown, 1995 (0-316-32905-3). USE LEVEL: U

*African American*

Tom's mother is ill and must be hospitalized. Tom and his little brother, Dicky, are placed in a children's home where they meet Jimmy, a boy who is dying of tuberculosis.

DEATH; FAMILY LIFE—FOSTER FAMILY; FAMILY LIFE—SIBLINGS; FRIENDSHIP; ILLNESS.

557     *Osa's Pride.* Ill. by the author. Little, Brown, 1990 (0-316-32865-0). USE LEVEL: P
*African*
Osa's father went to fight in a war and did not come back. In her African village, Osa hides her feelings of sadness and loss by boasting. Osa's grandmother uses a story cloth to teach Osa a lesson about pride.
BEHAVIOR—BOASTING; CHARACTER TRAITS—PRIDE; EMOTIONS—SADNESS; FOREIGN LANDS—AFRICA; STORYTELLING.

558     *The Village of Round and Square Houses.* Ill. by the author. Little, Brown, 1986, LB (0-316-32862-6). USE LEVEL: M
*African*
Based on an African folktale, this story describes the volcanic explosion that led to men living in square houses and women in round ones.
CALDECOTT AWARD; FOLKTALES—AFRICA; HOUSES; POURQUOI TALES; VOLCANOES.

**GRIMES, NIKKI**
559     *From a Child's Heart: Poems.* Ill. by Brenda Joysmith. Just Us, 1993, LB (0-940975-44-0); pap. (0-940975-43-2). USE LEVEL: P
*African American*
The 13 poems in this collection deal with everyday concerns of children with many emphasizing children's communication with God. Some of the poems are like prayers asking for guidance and support, while others feature family members.
EMOTIONS; FAMILY LIFE; POETRY, RHYME; RELIGION.

560     *Meet Danitra Brown.* Ill. by Floyd Cooper. Lothrop, 1994 (0-688-12073-3); LB (0-688-12074-1). USE LEVEL: P/M
*African American*
These poems celebrate the fun and friendship between Danitra Brown and Zuri Jackson.
COMMUNITIES, NEIGHBORHOODS; CORETTA SCOTT KING AWARD; FRIENDSHIP; POETRY, RHYME.

561     *Something on My Mind.* Ill. by Tom Feelings. Dial, 1978, pap. (0-8037-0273-6). USE LEVEL: M/U
*African American*
These free-verse poems were inspired by the illustrations. They convey feelings of wistfulness, confusion, and apprehension. Several poems present children who are waiting—for school, for friends, and to grow up.

BEHAVIOR—GROWING UP; CORETTA SCOTT KING AWARD; EMOTIONS; POETRY, RHYME.

**GROSSMAN, PATRICIA**

562    *Saturday Market.* Ill. by Enrique O. Sánchez. Lothrop, 1994 (0-688-12176-4); LB (0-688-12177-2). USE LEVEL: P
*Mexican*
At the market, everyone has something to sell. One family has rugs; Rosa brings "huaraches"; Paco has a rooster.
FOREIGN LANDS—MEXICO; FOREIGN LANGUAGES; MARKETS.

**GROSSMAN, VIRGINIA**

563    *Ten Little Rabbits.* Ill. by Sylvia Long. Chronicle, 1991 (0-87701-552-X). USE LEVEL: P
*Native American*
Rabbits count from one to ten while demonstrating customs from Native American cultures. A list describing some of the customs is included.
ANIMALS—RABBITS; COUNTING, NUMBERS; POETRY, RHYME.

**GRYSKI, CAMILLA**

564    *Cat's Cradle, Owl's Eyes: A Book of String Games.* Ill. by Tom Sankey. Morrow, 1984, LB (0-688-03940-5); pap. (0-688-03941-3). USE LEVEL: M/U
*Multicultural*
Children enjoy learning these string games and finding out about the cultural origins. Included are games from Japan and the Philippines as well as the Navaho and Inuit peoples.
ACTIVITIES; GAMES; STRING.

565    *Many Stars & More String Games.* Ill. by Tom Sankey. Morrow, 1985, LB (0-688-05793-4); pap. (0-688-05792-6). USE LEVEL: M
*Multicultural*
This is the second book of string games. Central Africa, New Guinea, and Hawaii are the locations for some of these games. Activities from many native peoples are also included.
ACTIVITIES; GAMES; STRING.

566    *Super String Games.* Ill. by Tom Sankey. Morrow, 1987, LB (0-688-07685-8); pap. (0-688-07684-X). USE LEVEL: M
*Multicultural*
This is the third collection of string games and includes games from South America, Fiji, British Columbia, Tonga, and other locations. A brief source note accompanies each activity.
ACTIVITIES; GAMES; STRING.

**GUBACK, GEORGIA**

567    *Luka's Quilt*. Ill. by the author. Greenwillow, 1994 (0-688-12154-3); LB (0-688-12155-1). USE LEVEL: P
*Hawaiian*
Luka's "Tutu"—her grandmother—lives with her and her family. Tutu makes Luka a traditional Hawaiian quilt, and then makes a quilted lei to add more colors.
ACTIVITIES—SEWING; FAMILY LIFE—GRANDMOTHERS; HAWAII; QUILTS.

**GUNNING, MONICA**

568    *Not a Copper Penny in Me House: Poems from the Caribbean*. Ill. by Frané Lessac. Boyds Mills, 1993 (1-56397-050-3). USE LEVEL: M
*Caribbean*
Everyday activities of families as well as experiences in the city and at the beach are featured in these poems.
COMMUNITIES, NEIGHBORHOODS; FOREIGN LANDS—CARIBBEAN ISLANDS; ISLANDS; POETRY, RHYME.

**GUTHRIE, DONNA W.**

569    *Nobiah's Well: A Modern African Folktale*. Ill. by Rob Roth. Ideals, 1993 (0-8249-8622-9); LB (0-8249-8631-8). USE LEVEL: M
*African*
During a drought, Nobiah's mother sends him to the well for water. On his trip home, he shares his water with a hedgehog, a hyena, and an ant bear. For his kindness, the animals help him dig a well.
ANIMALS; CHARACTER TRAITS—KINDNESS; FOREIGN LANDS—AFRICA; WEATHER—DROUGHTS.

**GUY, ROSA**

570    *Billy the Great*. Ill. by Caroline Binch. Dell, 1991, pap. (0-440-40920-9). USE LEVEL: P
*African American*
Billy's parents dote on him, planning for his future. When an older boy, Rod, moves in next door, Mom discourages the friendship, but Billy likes Rod. He likes learning what the older boy can teach him, and Mom accepts his choice.
BEHAVIOR—GROWING UP; CHARACTER TRAITS—INDIVIDUALITY; FAMILY LIFE; FRIENDSHIP.

571    *Mother Crocodile*. Ill. by John Steptoe. Delacorte, 1981 (0-385-28455-1). USE LEVEL: M
*African*
Uncle Amadou tells stories of Mother Crocodile and Golo the

monkey. When men come to the river to fight their war, Mother Crocodile's children do not listen to her.

ANIMALS—MONKEYS; CORETTA SCOTT KING AWARD; FOLKTALES—AFRICA; REPTILES—ALLIGATORS, CROCODILES; WAR.

### HAARHOFF, DORIAN

572 *Desert December.* Ill. by Leon Vermeulen. Houghton, 1992 (0-395-61300-0). USE LEVEL: P

*African—Namibia*

In Namibia, Seth journeys across the Kuiseb Canyon to join his parents in town for Christmas. Along the way, he helps people. He reaches town just in time for the birth of a baby sister.

FAMILY LIFE; FOREIGN LANDS—AFRICA—NAMIBIA; HOLIDAYS—CHRISTMAS.

### HALE, SARAH JOSEPHA

573 *Mary Had a Little Lamb.* Photos by Bruce McMillan. Scholastic, 1990 (0-590-43773-9); pap. (0-590-43774-7). USE LEVEL: PS/P

*African American*

This version of "Mary Had a Little Lamb" is illustrated with color photographs showing Mary as a contemporary African American child attending a small school in Maine.

ANIMALS—SHEEP; NURSERY RHYMES; POETRY, RHYME; SCHOOL.

### HALEY, GAIL E., RETELLER

574 *A Story, a Story.* Ill. by the reteller. Macmillan, 1970, pap. (0-689-71201-4). USE LEVEL: M

*African*

Ananse, a storyteller, tells a story about how he won his stories from the Sky God.

BEHAVIOR—TRICKERY; CALDECOTT AWARD; FOLKTALES—AFRICA; POURQUOI TALES; STORYTELLING.

### HAMADA, CHERYL, RETELLER

575 *The Farmer, the Buffalo, and the Tiger: A Folktale from Vietnam.* Ill. by Rick Regan. Childrens Pr., 1993, LB (0-516-05143-1). USE LEVEL: M

*Asian—Vietnam*

The illustrations appear without words to encourage children to learn the story and retell it. A tiger tells a water buffalo that he can outwit the farmer, but the farmer tricks the tiger and ties him to a tree. The text follows the illustrations.

ANIMALS—BUFFALOES; ANIMALS—TIGERS; FOLKTALES—ASIA—VIETNAM; STORYTELLING.

576     *The Fourth Question: A Chinese Folktale*. Ill. by Janice
Skivington. Childrens Pr., 1993 (0-516-07091-6); LB (0-516-
05144-X). USE LEVEL: M
*Asian—China*
The illustrations appear separate from the text encouraging
readers to learn the story and then tell it aloud. This Chinese
folktale tells of Yee Lee who journeys to the wise man of Kun-
lun to ask for advice.
CHARACTER TRAITS—GENEROSITY; CHARACTER TRAITS—KINDNESS;
CHARACTER TRAITS—QUESTIONING; FOLKTALES—ASIA—CHINA;
STORYTELLING.

577     *Kao and the Golden Fish: A Folktale from Thailand*. Ill. by
Monica Liu. Childrens Pr., 1993 (0-516-07093-2); LB (0-516-
05145-8); pap. (0-51645145-6). USE LEVEL: M
*Asian--Thailand*
Kao's stepmother and stepsister are cruel. She is befriended by a
fish, who has her mother's spirit. After the fish is killed, Kao
plants some trees, which the prince wants. Kao gives him the
trees and they marry. The format promotes storytelling.
CHARACTER TRAITS—KINDNESS; FISH; FOLKTALES—ASIA—THAILAND;
MAGIC; STORYTELLING; TREES.

578     *The White Hare of Inaba: A Japanese Folktale*. Ill. by Lydia G.
Halverson. Childrens Pr., 1993, LB (0-516-05147-4). USE
LEVEL: M
*Asian—Japan*
A hare tricks the crocodiles into making a bridge for him. He
boasts about his cleverness and the crocodiles turn on him.
Later, a young prince is kind to the hare, who tells the prince to
seek the hand of a princess. The format promotes storytelling.
ANIMALS—RABBITS; CHARACTER TRAITS—KINDNESS; FOLKTALES—ASIA—
JAPAN; REPTILES—ALLIGATORS, CROCODILES; STORYTELLING.

**HAMANAKA, SHEILA**
579     *All the Colors of the Earth*. Ill. by the author. Morrow, 1994 (0-
688-11131-9); LB (0-688-11132-7). USE LEVEL: PS/P
*Multicultural*
In lyrical language, this book celebrates the diversity of children
while it emphasizes that children are bound together by love for
each other.
BEHAVIOR—ACCEPTING DIFFERENCES; CHARACTER TRAITS—
APPEARANCE; EMOTIONS—LOVE; POETRY, RHYME; WORLD.

580 *Screen of Frogs: An Old Tale.* Ill. by the author. Orchard, 1993 (0-531-05464-0); LB (0-531-08614-3). USE LEVEL: M
*Asian—Japan*
Koji is too lazy to care for his land and possessions. A frog asks Koji to save the mountain for the forest creatures and Koji is rewarded with a beautiful screen and with a new appreciation for his land.
CHARACTER TRAITS—LAZINESS; FOLKTALES—ASIA—JAPAN; FROGS AND TOADS.

**HAMILTON, VIRGINIA**
581 *The All Jahdu Storybook.* Ill. by Barry Moser. Harcourt, 1991 (0-15-239498-2). USE LEVEL: M
*African American*
Jahdu is a trickster who is able to change his shape. This collection includes revised stories from earlier books about Jahdu.
BEHAVIOR—TRICKERY; CHARACTER TRAITS—SMALLNESS; ELVES AND LITTLE PEOPLE; FOREIGN LANDS—AFRICA; MAGIC; SHORT STORIES.

582 *The Bells of Christmas.* Ill. by Lambert Davis. Harcourt, 1989 (0-15-206450-8). USE LEVEL: M
*African American*
In 1803, a family travels along the National Road in Ohio to spend the holiday with friends.
CORETTA SCOTT KING AWARD; FAMILY LIFE; HOLIDAYS—CHRISTMAS; U.S. HISTORY.

583 *Cousins.* Putnam, 1990 (0-399-22164-6); Scholastic, pap. (0-509-45436-6). USE LEVEL: M
*African American*
Cammy is jealous of her cousin, Patty Ann. When Patty Ann drowns, Cammy must cope with her grief and her guilt. With the help of her grandmother, Cammy comes to accept her feelings.
DEATH; EMOTIONS—ENVY, JEALOUSY; FAMILY LIFE—COUSINS; FAMILY LIFE—GRANDMOTHERS.

584 *The Dark Way: Stories from the Spirit World.* Ill. by Lambert Davis. Harcourt, 1990 (0-15-222340-1); LB (0-15-222341-X). USE LEVEL: U
*Multicultural*
Includes 25 folktales from many countries and cultures, including Japan, India, Native American peoples, and African heritage.
FOLKTALES; SCARY STORIES; SHORT STORIES; SUPERNATURAL.

585     *Drylongso.* Ill. by Jerry Pinkney. Harcourt, 1992 (0-15-224241-
        4). USE LEVEL: M
        *African American*
        During a drought, Lindy and her family try to survive the heat
        and the dust. They also want to salvage some of their crops. A
        strange young boy, Drylongso, appears with a divining rod and
        the hope of finding water.
        FAMILY LIFE; FARMS; WEATHER—DROUGHTS; WEATHER—WIND.

586     *Her Stories: African American Folktales, Fairy Tales, and True
        Tales.* Ill. by Leo Dillon and Diane Dillon. Scholastic, 1995 (0-
        590-47370-0). USE LEVEL: U
        *African American*
        The stories in this collection feature females, who are often
        brave and resourceful. There are stories of the supernatural, of
        transformations, and of magic. "Catskinella," "Lonna and Cat
        Woman," and "Annie Christmas" are three of the stories.
        FOLKTALES—UNITED STATES; SHORT STORIES; SUPERNATURAL.

587     *The House of Dies Drear.* Ill. by Eros Keith. Macmillan, 1968 (0-
        02-742500-2); pap. (0-02-043520-7). USE LEVEL: M
        *African American*
        Thomas is both fascinated and frightened by the mysterious
        occurrences at his family's new home, a former stop on the
        Underground Railroad.
        FAMILY LIFE; MYSTERY AND DETECTIVE STORIES; UNDERGROUND RAIL-
        ROAD.

588     *In the Beginning: Creation Stories from Around the World.* Ill. by
        Barry Moser. Harcourt, 1988 (0-15-238740-4); pap. (0-15-
        238742-0). USE LEVEL: M
        *Multicultural*
        These 25 myths present the beliefs about creation from many
        different peoples including Chinese, Zambian, Guatemalan,
        Egyptian, Greek, and Indian. Familiar characters like Ananse,
        Raven, and Turtle are included as is a retelling from Genesis.
        CREATION; FOLKTALES; NEWBERY AWARD; RELIGION; SHORT STORIES.

589     *Jahdu.* Ill. by Jerry Pinkney. Greenwillow, 1980, o.p. USE LEVEL:
        M
        *African American*
        Jahdu's shadow takes his magic and the trickster must figure out
        how to get his shadow and his Jahdu dust back.
        BEHAVIOR—TRICKERY; CHARACTER TRAITS—SMALLNESS; ELVES AND LIT-
        TLE PEOPLE; FOREIGN LANDS—AFRICA; MAGIC; SHADOWS.

590    *M. C. Higgins the Great.* Macmillan, 1974 (0-02-742480-4);
       pap. (0-02-043490-1). USE LEVEL: U
       *African American*
       Mayo Cornelius Higgins sits on a pole and thinks about a dif-
       ferent life for himself and his family. In the hills around the
       Ohio River, he observes strip mining and the damage it has
       caused to the land.
       BEHAVIOR—SEEKING BETTER THINGS; ECOLOGY; FAMILY LIFE; NEWBERY
       AWARD.

591    *The Magical Adventures of Pretty Pearl.* HarperCollins, 1983 (0-
       06-022186-0); LB (0-06-022187-9); pap. (0-06-440178-2).
       USE LEVEL: U
       *African heritage*
       Pretty Pearl leaves her home on Mount Kenya and comes to live
       among the humankind. She is a god child eager to test her pow-
       ers. With her brother, John de Conquer, she travels to America
       and encounters spirits, slaves, and legendary characters.
       CORETTA SCOTT KING AWARD; FANTASY; MAGIC.

592    *The Mystery of Drear House: The Conclusion of the Dies Drear
       Chronicle.* Greenwillow, 1987 (0-688-04026-8); Macmillan,
       pap. (0-02-043480-4). USE LEVEL: M
       *African American*
       In this continuation of *The House of Dies Drear*, Thomas Small
       and his family are organizing the items they have found hidden
       in their house, while a neighboring family is interested in selling
       the treasures.
       MYSTERY AND DETECTIVE STORIES; TREASURE; UNDERGROUND RAIL-
       ROAD.

593    *The People Could Fly: American Black Folktales.* Ill. by Leo
       Dillon and Diane Dillon. Knopf, 1985 (0-394-86925-7); LB
       (0-394-96925-1). USE LEVEL: M/U
       *African American*
       This collection of folktales features animals; the supernatural;
       the real, extravagant, and fanciful; and freedom tales.
       CORETTA SCOTT KING AWARD; FOLKTALES—UNITED STATES; SCARY STO-
       RIES; SHORT STORIES.

594    *The Planet of Junior Brown.* Macmillan, 1971 (0-02-742510-X);
       pap. (0-02 043540-1). USE LEVEL: U
       *African American*
       Buddy and Junior have dropped out from the eighth grade and

are spending time with the school janitor. Although they are outcasts, they learn to survive.

BEHAVIOR—RUNNING AWAY; FRIENDSHIP; NEWBERY AWARD.

595    *The Time-Ago Tales of Jahdu.* Ill. by Nonny Hogrogian.
Macmillan, 1969, o.p. USE LEVEL: M
*African American*
The four stories in this collection feature Jahdu, the trickster. In one story, Jahdu, who is two feet tall, finds that he can put things to sleep.

BEHAVIOR—TRICKERY; CHARACTER TRAITS—SMALLNESS; ELVES AND LIT-
TLE PEOPLE; FOREIGN LANDS—AFRICA; MAGIC; SHORT STORIES.

596    *Willie Bea and the Time the Martians Landed.* Greenwillow,
1983 (0-688-02390-8); Macmillan, pap. (0-689-71328-2). USE
LEVEL: U
*African American*
It is 1938 and Willie Bea is looking forward to Halloween with her family and friends. After Aunt Leah hears Orson Welles's "The Martians Have Landed" broadcast, everyone becomes caught up in the fear and hysteria.

FAMILY LIFE; HOLIDAYS—HALLOWEEN.

597    *Zeely.* Ill. by Symeon Shimin. Macmillan, 1967 (0-02-742470-
7); pap. (0-689-71695-8). USE LEVEL: M
*African American*
Elizabeth Perry and her brother John are spending the summer on Uncle Ross's farm. They give themselves nicknames and have several adventures including one with a "night traveller" and an encounter with Miss Zeely Taylor.

FAMILY LIFE; FRIENDSHIP; RURAL LIFE.

**HAMMOND, ANNA, AND JOE MATUNIS**
598    *This Home We Have Made/Esta Casa Que Hemos Hecho.* Crown,
1993 (0-517-59339-4). USE LEVEL: M
*Multicultural*
Illustrated with images from a community mural in the Bronx, this book is an imaginative fantasy. A homeless child joins a parade that ends at a new home.

ART; HOMELESSNESS; IMAGINATION; URBAN LIFE.

**HAMSA, BOBBIE**
599    *Polly Wants a Cracker.* Ill. by Jerry Warshaw. Childrens Pr.,
1986, LB (0-516-02071-4). USE LEVEL: P
*African American*

Three children feed Polly the parrot crackers, counting from one to ten. The rhyming text is predictable.

BIRDS—PARROTS; COUNTING, NUMBERS; POETRY, RHYME; PREDICTABLE TEXT.

### HAN, OKI S., ADAPTER

600 *Sir Whong and the Golden Pig.* Edited by Stephanie Haboush Plunkett. Ill. by the adapter. Dial, 1993 (0-8037-1344-4); LB (0-8037-1345-2). USE LEVEL: M

*Asian—Korea*

Mr. Oh tricks Sir Whong out of some money, but Sir Whong finds a way to get even.

BEHAVIOR—GREED; BEHAVIOR—STEALING; BEHAVIOR—TRICKERY; CHARACTER TRAITS—CLEVERNESS; FOLKTALES—ASIA—KOREA.

### HAN, SUZANNE CROWDER

601 *The Rabbit's Escape.* Ill. by Yumi Heo. Henry Holt, 1995 (0-8050-2675-4). USE LEVEL: M

*Asian—Korea*

When the Dragon King of the East Sea is ill, the turtle looks for a rabbit to provide the raw liver to save him. When rabbit realizes what is needed, he uses his wits to survive.

ANIMALS—RABBITS; CHARACTER TRAITS—CLEVERNESS; FOLKTALES—ASIA—KOREA; FOREIGN LANGUAGES; ILLNESS.

602 *The Rabbit's Judgment.* Ill. by Yumi Heo. Henry Holt, 1994 (0-8050-2674-6). USE LEVEL: M

*Asian—Korea*

A tiger becomes trapped in a pit and convinces a man to help him out, promising not to eat him. After he is free, the tiger reconsiders. The text is printed in English and Korean.

ANIMALS; BEHAVIOR—TRICKERY; CHARACTER TRAITS—KINDNESS; FOLKTALES—ASIA— KOREA; FOREIGN LANGUAGES.

### HANDFORTH, THOMAS

603 *Mei Li.* Ill. by the author. Doubleday, 1938 (0-385-07401-8). USE LEVEL: P

*Asian—China*

On the day before the New Year, Mei Li and her brother enjoy themselves at the fair.

CALDECOTT AWARD; FAIRS; FOREIGN LANDS—ASIA—CHINA; HOLIDAYS—CHINESE NEW YEAR.

### HANSEN, JOYCE

604 *The Captive.* Scholastic, 1994 (0-590-41625-1); pap. (0-590-41624-3). USE LEVEL: U

*African*

In the 1780s, Kofi is taken by force from his home in West Africa and loaded onto a slave ship. His memories of his family and the customs of his people are replaced by cruelty and deprivation. In Massachusetts, he is sold into slavery.

CORETTA SCOTT KING AWARD; FOREIGN LANDS—AFRICA; SLAVERY; U.S. HISTORY.

605     *The Gift-Giver.* Houghton, 1980, pap. (0-89919-852-X). USE LEVEL: M/U

*African American*

In this urban neighborhood, Doris and her friends meet Amir, who teaches them about helping each other. When Amir leaves the neighborhood, Doris, Sherman, and their friends are able to build on what he has taught them.

COMMUNITIES, NEIGHBORHOODS; FRIENDSHIP; URBAN LIFE.

606     *Which Way Freedom?* Avon, pap. (0-380-71408-6). USE LEVEL: U

*African American*

Obi escapes from slavery and fights with a black Union regiment in the Civil War. He is one of the few to escape the massacre of a fort in Tennessee. Each chapter of this book begins with a quote from an original source about the Civil War.

CORETTA SCOTT KING AWARD; SLAVERY; U.S. HISTORY—CIVIL WAR.

607     *Yellow Bird and Me.* Houghton, 1986, pap. (0-395-55388-1). USE LEVEL: M/U

*African American*

Now that Amir is not in their neighborhood, Doris tries to continue helping her friends. She works with James, whose nickname is Yellow Bird, and she is able to help him deal with his problems. This is a sequel to *The Gift-Giver*.

ACTIVITIES—ACTING; COMMUNITIES, NEIGHBORHOODS; FRIENDSHIP; URBAN LIFE.

**HARRELL, BEATRICE ORCUTT**

608     *How Thunder and Lightning Came to Be: A Choctaw Legend.* Ill. by Susan L. Roth. Dial, 1995 (0-8037-1748-2). USE LEVEL: M

*Native American—Choctaw*

The Great Sun Father wants to find a way to warn the Choctaw that a storm is coming. Two silly birds try to help and they create thunder and lightning.

BIRDS; FOLKTALES—NATIVE AMERICAN—CHOCTAW; POURQUOI TALES; WEATHER—THUNDER.

**HARRIS, CHRISTIE**

609   *Mouse Woman and the Mischief-Makers.* Ill. by Douglas Tait. Macmillan, 1977, o.p. USE LEVEL: U
*Native American—Northwest Coast*
Mouse Woman is a narnuck, a creature with supernatural powers. In these seven stories, she tries to keep order between her people and humans.
FOLKTALES—NATIVE AMERICAN—NORTHWEST COAST; SHORT STORIES; SUPERNATURAL.

610   *Mouse Woman and the Muddleheads.* Ill. by Douglas Tait. Macmillan, 1979, o.p. USE LEVEL: U
*Native American—Northwest Coast*
The Northwest Coast people told many stories about Mouse Woman, a small creature with supernatural powers. This collection contains seven stories.
ANIMALS; FOLKTALES—NATIVE AMERICAN—NORTHWEST COAST; MAGIC; SHORT STORIES.

611   *Mouse Woman and the Vanished Princesses.* Ill. by Douglas Tait. Macmillan, 1976, o.p. USE LEVEL: U
*Native American—Northwest Coast*
The princesses of the Northwest Coast people are often captured by the narnucks, supernatural beings. In these six stories, Mouse Woman aids the princesses.
FOLKTALES—NATIVE AMERICAN—NORTHWEST COAST; SHORT STORIES; SUPERNATURAL.

612   *Once More Upon a Totem.* Ill. by Douglas Tait. Macmillan, 1973, o.p. USE LEVEL: U
*Native American—Northwest Coast*
There are three stories in this collection. Accompanying the stories are chapters providing background on the setting, illustrations, and people associated with these stories.
FOLKTALES—NATIVE AMERICAN—NORTHWEST COAST; SHORT STORIES.

613   *Once Upon a Totem.* Ill. by John Frazer Mills. Macmillan, 1963, o.p. USE LEVEL: U
*Native American—Northwest Coast*
Five stories feature unusual creatures like "The Giant Ogre, Kloo-Teekl" and "The Wise Woman of the Woods."
FOLKTALES—NATIVE AMERICAN- NORTHWEST COAST; SHORT STORIES.

**HARRIS, JOEL CHANDLER**

614   *Jump Again! More Adventures of Brer Rabbit.* Adapted by Van

Dyke Parks. Ill. by Barry Moser. Harcourt, 1987 (0-15-241352-9). USE LEVEL: M/U
*African American*
More Brer Rabbit stories and a song are included in this collection.
ANIMALS—RABBITS; BEHAVIOR—TRICKERY; FOLKTALES—UNITED STATES; SHORT STORIES; SONGS.

615 *Jump on Over! The Adventures of Brer Rabbit and His Family.* Adapted by Van Dyke Parks. Ill. by Barry Moser. Harcourt, 1989 (0-15-241354-5). USE LEVEL: M/U
*African American*
These five stories feature Brer Rabbit, Brer Fox, Brer Wolf, and Brer Bear.
ANIMALS; ANIMALS—RABBITS; BEHAVIOR—TRICKERY; FOLKTALES—UNITED STATES; SHORT STORIES; SONGS.

**HARRIS, JOEL CHANDLER, AND MALCOLM JONES**
616 *Jump! The Adventures of Brer Rabbit.* Adapted by Van Dyke Parks. Ill. by Barry Moser. Harcourt, 1986 (0-15-241350-2). USE LEVEL: M/U
*African American*
This collection of five Brer Rabbit stories introduces this well-known trickster.
ANIMALS—RABBITS; BEHAVIOR—TRICKERY; FOLKTALES—UNITED STATES; SHORT STORIES.

**HASKINS, FRANCINE**
617 *I Remember "121."* Ill. by the author. Children's Book Pr., 1991 (0-89239-100-6). USE LEVEL: M
*African American*
The author remembers the family house in Washington, D.C. She thinks of the birth of her brother when she was three, the family meals and celebrations, and moving day in 1956 when she was nine.
ACTIVITIES—REMINISCING; BEHAVIOR—GROWING UP; FAMILY LIFE; MOVING.

**HASKINS, JAMES**
618 *The Headless Haunt: And Other African-American Ghost Stories.* Ill. by Ben Otero. HarperCollins, 1994 (0-06-022994-2); LB (0-06-022997-7); pap. (0-06-440602-4). USE LEVEL: U
*African American*
More than 30 stories and vignettes appear in this collection, including "The Ghost Log Cabin," "Daddy and the Plat-Eye

Ghost," "The Saturday-Night Fiddler," and "The Ghost of a Man the Yankees Killed." It includes notes on collecting stories.
FOLKTALES—UNITED STATES; GHOSTS; SHORT STORIES; SUPERNATURAL.

**HASKINS, JIM**

619   *Count Your Way Through Africa*. Ill. by Barbara Knutson.
Carolrhoda, 1989 (0-87614-347-8); pap. (0-87614-514-4).
USE LEVEL: P
*African*
Swahili numbers from one to ten are presented in numerals and words. Details about African life accompany each number.
COUNTING, NUMBERS; FOREIGN LANDS—AFRICA; FOREIGN LANGUAGES.

620   *Count Your Way Through China*. Ill. by Dennis Hockerman.
Carolrhoda, 1987 (0-87614-302-8); pap. (0-87614-486-5).
USE LEVEL: P
*Asian—China*
Arabic numerals and Chinese words and symbols present the numbers from one to ten. Information about China is then included, like "All Chinese music is based on a musical scale of five tones."
COUNTING, NUMBERS; FOREIGN LANDS—ASIA—CHINA; FOREIGN LANGUAGES.

621   *Count Your Way Through India*. Ill. by Liz Brenner Dodson.
Carolrhoda, 1990, LB (0-87614-414-8); pap. (0-87164-577-2). USE LEVEL: P
*Asian—India*
Indian words and symbols are used for the numbers from one to ten. Information about India is included, like "One banyan tree can grow to look like a whole forest."
COUNTING, NUMBERS; FOREIGN LANDS—ASIA—INDIA; FOREIGN LANGUAGES.

622   *Count Your Way Through Japan*. Ill. by Martin Skoro.
Carolrhoda, 1987 (0-87614-301-X); pap. (0-87614-485-7).
USE LEVEL: P
*Asian—Japan*
The numbers from one to ten are accompanied by a brief descriptive text about Japanese culture and life, like "Two chopsticks are the traditional Japanese eating utensils."
COUNTING, NUMBERS; FOREIGN LANDS—ASIA—JAPAN; FOREIGN LANGUAGES.

623   *Count Your Way Through Korea*. Ill. by Dennis Hockerman.

Carolrhoda, 1989 (0-87614-348-6); pap. (0-87614-516-0).
USE LEVEL: P
*Asian—Korea*
Arabic numerals and Korean words and symbols present the numbers from one to ten. Descriptive information about Korea is included, like "Three people are required for Korean seesaw."
COUNTING, NUMBERS; FOREIGN LANDS—ASIA—KOREA; FOREIGN LANGUAGES.

624     *Count Your Way Through Mexico.* Ill. by Helen Byers. Carolrhoda, 1989 (0-87614-349-4); pap. (0-87614-517-9).
USE LEVEL: P
*Mexican*
Numbers from one to ten are presented with the Arabic numeral and the Spanish word. Information about Mexico accompanies each number, for example, "There are four sides to a pyramid" is followed by details about pyramids in Mexico.
COUNTING, NUMBERS; FOREIGN LANDS—MEXICO; FOREIGN LANGUAGES.

625     *Count Your Way Through the Arab World.* Ill. by Dana Gustafson. Carolrhoda, 1987, LB (0-87614-304-4); pap. (0-87614-487-3). USE LEVEL: P
*Middle Eastern—Arabia*
Arabic numerals from one to ten are introduced, along with details about life in the Arab world.
COUNTING, NUMBERS; FOREIGN LANDS—MIDDLE EAST—ARABIA; FOREIGN LANGUAGES.

HAUSMAN, GERALD, RETELLER
626     *Coyote Walks on Two Legs: A Book of Navaho Myths and Legends.* Ill. by Floyd Cooper. Putnam, 1995 (0-399-22018-6). USE LEVEL: M
*Native American—Navajo*
First Man gives Coyote the name "He Who Minds Everybody's Business" but Coyote asks to have it changed to "First Angry." Coyote causes mischief in Navajoland.
ANIMALS—COYOTES; BEHAVIOR—TRICKERY; FOLKTALES—NATIVE AMERICAN—NAVAJO.

627     *Duppy Talk: West Indian Tales of Mystery and Magic.* Simon & Schuster, 1994 (0-671-89000-X). USE LEVEL: U
*Caribbean—West Indies*
Six stories of "duppies" (ghosts), spirits, the "obeah man" (witch doctor), and other supernatural elements are presented. Also, there is an explanation of "The Proverbs of Duppy Talk."

FOLKTALES—CARIBBEAN ISLANDS—WEST INDIES; GHOSTS; MAGIC; SHORT STORIES; SUPERNATURAL.

628    *Turtle Island ABC: A Gathering of Native American Symbols.*
Ill. by Cara Moser and Barry Moser. HarperCollins, 1994 (0-06-021307-8); LB (0-06-021308-6). USE LEVEL: M
*Native American*
This alphabet book highlights items and images associated with various native peoples, like "A—Arrow," "C—Corn," "K—Kachina," and "W—Wolf."
ABC BOOKS; CONCEPTS.

**HAVILL, JUANITA**
629    *Jamaica and Brianna.* Ill. by Anne Sibley O'Brien. Houghton, 1993 (0-395-64489-5). USE LEVEL: P
*African American*
Jamaica and her friend Brianna, who is Asian American, hurt each other's feelings when each has to wear hand-me-down boots.
BEHAVIOR—FIGHTING, ARGUING; CLOTHING—BOOTS; EMOTIONS—ENVY, JEALOUSY; FRIENDSHIP.

630    *Jamaica Tag-Along.* Ill. by Anne Sibley O'Brien. Houghton, 1989 (0-395-49602-0); pap. (0-395-54949-3). USE LEVEL: P
*African American*
When Ossie goes to the park to play basketball, his sister Jamaica follows him. Later, when Jamaica is playing, she is bothered by a toddler named Berto. Jamaica lets Berto play with her and later they let Ossie join them.
ACTIVITIES—PLAYING; BEHAVIOR—GETTING ALONG WITH OTHERS; BEHAVIOR—SHARING; FAMILY LIFE—SIBLINGS; FRIENDSHIP.

631    *Jamaica's Find.* Ill. by Anne Sibley O'Brien. Houghton, 1986 (0-395-39376-0); pap. (0-395-45357-7). USE LEVEL: P
*African American*
When Jamaica finds a stuffed toy at the park, she wants to keep it. When she returns it to the lost and found, she makes a new friend.
BEHAVIOR—LOSING THINGS; CHARACTER TRAITS—HONESTY; FRIENDSHIP.

632    *Sato and the Elephants.* Ill. by Jean Tseng and Mou sien Tseng. Lothrop, 1993 (0-688-11155-6); LB (0-688-11156-4). USE LEVEL: M
*Asian—Japan*
Sato learned to carve ivory from his father, but he realized the harm that came to elephants from his use of ivory.

ANIMALS—ELEPHANTS; ANIMALS—ENDANGERED ANIMALS; CAREERS—
ARTISTS; FOREIGN LANDS—ASIA—JAPAN.

### HAYES, SARAH
633　*Eat Up, Gemma.* Ill. by Jan Ormerod. Lothrop, 1988 (0-688-
08149-5); pap. (0-688-13638-9). USE LEVEL: PS
*African American*
Baby Gemma's brother finds the way to get her to eat.
BABIES, TODDLERS; FAMILY LIFE –SIBLINGS; FOOD.

634　*Happy Christmas, Gemma.* Ill. by Jan Ormerod. Lothrop, 1986
(0-688-06508-2); pap. (0-688-11702-3). USE LEVEL: PS
*African American*
Gemma is a toddler and she creates some mischief for her older
brother while the family prepares for Christmas.
BABIES, TODDLERS; FAMILY LIFE—SIBLINGS; HOLIDAYS—CHRISTMAS.

### HEARN, LAFCADIO
635　*The Voice of the Great Bell.* Retold by Margaret Hodges. Ill. by
Ed Young. Little, Brown, 1989, o.p. USE LEVEL: M
*Asian—China*
The emperor has commanded that Kouan-Yu have a special bell
made. Kousn-Yu tries, but he fails, until his daughter, Ko-Ngai,
sacrifices herself for him.
CHARACTER TRAITS—BRAVERY; DEATH; FOLKTALES—ASIA—CHINA.

### HEATH, AMY
636　*Sofie's Role.* Ill. by Sheila Hamanaka. Macmillan, 1992 (0-02-
743505-9). USE LEVEL: P
*African American*
On the day before Christmas, Sofie helps out at her family's
bakery. She sweeps up, waits on customers, and takes orders.
She is proud to be part of the activity.
ACTIVITIES—COOKING; CAREERS—BAKERS; CHARACTER TRAITS—HELP-
FULNESS; FAMILY LIFE; HOLIDAYS—CHRISTMAS.

### HEIDE, FLORENCE PARRY, AND JUDITH HEIDE GILLILAND
637　*The Day of Ahmed's Secret.* Ill. by Ted Lewin. Lothrop, 1990 (0-
688-08894-5); LB (0-688-08895-3); pap. (0-318-72966-0).
USE LEVEL: P/M
*African—Egypt*
Ahmed must do his job delivering cooking gas in Cairo. When
he finishes, he can share his accomplishment with his family and
show them he can write his name in Arabic.
ACTIVITIES—WORKING; ACTIVITIES—WRITING; BEHAVIOR—SECRETS;
CHARACTER TRAITS—PRIDE; FOREIGN LANDS—AFRICA—EGYPT.

638　*Sami and the Time of the Troubles.* Ill. by Ted Lewin. Houghton, 1992 (0-395-55964-2). USE LEVEL: M
*Middle Eastern—Lebanon*
Sami, ten, lives in Beirut. He enjoys everyday activities with his family but his daily life also includes guns and bombs and living in the basement of his uncle's house.
FAMILY LIFE; FOREIGN LANDS—MIDDLE EAST—LEBANON; WAR.

HEO, YUMI
639　*One Afternoon.* Ill. by the author. Orchard, 1994 (0-531-06845-5); LB (0-531-08695-X). USE LEVEL: P
*Asian American—Korea*
Minho and his mother travel through their neighborhood running errands.
ACTIVITIES; COMMUNITIES, NEIGHBORHOODS; FAMILY LIFE; SHOPPING.

HEST, AMY
640　*Ruby's Storm.* Ill. by Nancy Cote. Macmillan, 1994 (0-02-743160-6). USE LEVEL: P
*Hispanic American*
Ruby walks through a rain storm to visit her grandfather and play checkers with him.
CHARACTER TRAITS—BRAVERY; FAMILY LIFE—GRANDPARENTS; WEATHER—STORMS.

HEWETT, JOAN
641　*Laura Loves Horses.* Photos by Richard Hewett. Houghton, 1990 (0-89919-844-9). USE LEVEL: M
*Hispanic American*
Describes the activities of Laura Santana, a Hispanic girl growing up in California. Her father works on the grounds and in the stables of a ranch and her family lives near the stables. Laura takes riding lessons and competes.
ANIMALS—HORSES; FAMILY LIFE; SPORTS—HORSEBACK RIDING.

HEYER, MARILEE, RETELLER
642　*The Weaving of a Dream: A Chinese Folktale.* Ill. by the reteller. Viking, 1986 (0-670-80555-6); Puffin, pap. (0-14-050528-8). USE LEVEL: M
*Asian—China*
A woman who weaves beautiful tapestries buys a picture of a lovely palace and takes it home to her three sons. She weaves a tapestry of the picture and it is blown away. Each son must search for it.
ACTIVITIES—WEAVING; CHARACTER TRAITS—BRAVERY; FOLKTALES—ASIA—CHINA.

**HIGHWATER, JAMAKE**

643 *Anpao: An American Indian Odyssey.* Ill. by Fritz Scholder. HarperCollins, 1977 (0-397-31750-6); LB (0-06-022878-4); pap. (0-06-440437-4). USE LEVEL: U
*Native American*
Wasicong tells of Anpao, a boy whose search for his destiny brings him many adventures. Woven into the story of Anpao are traditional tales of native peoples, some featuring Coyote, Raven, and the Mouse People.
CHARACTER TRAITS—BRAVERY; FOLKTALES—NATIVE AMERICAN; NEWBERY AWARD.

644 *Moonsong Lullaby.* Photos by Marcia Keegan. Lothrop, 1981, o.p. USE LEVEL: P/M
*Native American*
As the moon moves across the sky there are many activities on earth.
BEDTIME; LULLABIES; MOON; NIGHT; POETRY, RHYME.

**HILBERT, VI**

645 *Loon and Deer Were Traveling: A Story of the Upper Skagit of Puget Sound.* Ill. by Anita Nelson. Childrens Pr., 1992, LB (0-516-05140-7); pap. (0-516-45140-5). USE LEVEL: M
*Native American—Skagit*
Illustrations depict the story of loon and deer, who are together on the water. Deer is captured and eaten by the wolf brothers, but loon escapes. The brief text follows the wordless pages, encouraging readers to learn the story and retell it.
ANIMALS; FOLKTALES—NATIVE AMERICAN—SKAGIT; STORYTELLING.

**HILL, ELIZABETH STARR**

646 *Evan's Corner.* Ill. by Nancy Grossman. Holt, 1967, o.p. USE LEVEL: P/M
*African American*
Evan's home is a very crowded, busy place, but he finds a place of his own.
CHARACTER TRAITS—HELPFULNESS; FAMILY LIFE; SELF-CONCEPT; URBAN LIFE.

647 *Evan's Corner.* Ill. by Sandra Speidel. Viking, 1991 (0-670-82830-0); Puffin, pap. (0-14-054406-2). USE LEVEL: P/M
*African American*
This is a revised version of the 1967 edition. The full-color illustrations update the story.
CHARACTER TRAITS—HELPFULNESS; FAMILY LIFE; SELF-CONCEPT; URBAN LIFE.

**HILL, KIRKPATRICK**
648  *Winter Camp.* Macmillan, 1993 (0-689-50588-4); Puffin, pap. (0-14-037076-5). USE LEVEL: U
*Native American—Athabascan*
Toughboy, 11, and Sister, 9, have gone to live with Natasha, an elderly Athabascan woman, following the death of their parents. Natasha takes pride in the ways of the Athabascan people and she takes the children to a winter camp to learn about their culture and traditions.
CAMPS, CAMPING; FAMILY LIFE; SURVIVAL.

**HILLMAN, ELIZABETH**
649  *Min-Yo and the Moon Dragon.* Ill. by John Wallner. Harcourt, 1992 (0-15-254230-2). USE LEVEL: M
*Asian—China*
Believing that the moon is falling, the emperor sends a child, Min-Yo, to climb the cobweb staircase to the moon dragon. Taking the moon dragon's diamonds, which are weighing down the moon, Min-Yo and the dragon throw them up into the sky, where they become stars.
DRAGONS; FOLKTALES—ASIA—CHINA; MOON; PROBLEM SOLVING; STARS.

**HINTON, LEANNE, TRANSLATOR**
650  *Ishi's Tale of Lizard.* Ill. by Susan L. Roth. Farrar, 1992 (0-374-33643-1). USE LEVEL: M
*Native American—Yahi*
Ishi, a member of the Yahi people, told this story of Lizard, who made arrows and who rescued Long-Tailed Lizard from the belly of the Grizzly Bear.
ANIMALS—BEARS; FOLKTALES—NATIVE AMERICAN—YAHI; REPTILES—LIZARDS.

**HIRSCHFELDER, ARLENE B., AND BEVERLY R. SINGER, SELECTORS**
651  *Rising Voices: Writings of Young Native Americans.* Macmillan, 1992 (0-684-19207-1); Ivy, pap. (0-8041-1167-7). USE LEVEL: U
*Native American*
These writings of young Native Americans describe their lives, feelings, and families. The writings are divided into themes: "Identity," "Family," "Rituals and Ceremony," "Education," "Homelands," and "Harsh Realities."
COMMUNITIES, NEIGHBORHOODS; FAMILY LIFE; POETRY, RHYME; SELF-CONCEPT.

Ho, Minfong

652    *The Clay Marble.* Farrar, 1991 (0-374-31340-7); pap. (0-374-41229-4). USE LEVEL: U
*Asian—Cambodia*
In Cambodia, Dara, 12, her mother, and her older brother leave their village and travel to Nong Chan, a refugee camp. At first it is peaceful there, but the fighting comes and Dara is separated from her family and her friend, Jantu, is killed.
DEATH; FOREIGN LANDS—ASIA—CAMBODIA; REFUGEES; WAR.

Ho, Minfong, and Saphan Ros

653    *The Two Brothers.* Ill. by Jean Tseng and Mou-Sien Tseng. Lothrop, 1995 (0-688-12550-6); LB (0-688-12551-4). USE LEVEL: M
*Asian—Cambodia*
When two brothers leave the temple to find out about the world outside, the abbot gives each some advice. Kem follows the advice and gains his fortune, but Sem does not listen, so his life is a struggle.
CHARACTER TRAITS—WILLFULNESS; FAMILY LIFE—SIBLINGS; FOLKTALES—ASIA—CAMBODIA.

Hoberman, Mary Ann, selector

654    *My Song Is Beautiful: A Celebration of Multicultural Poems and Pictures.* Little, Brown, 1994 (0-316-36738-9). USE LEVEL: P/M
*Multicultural*
Poets and artists from many cultures present images celebrating the power of childhood. Poets include Nikki Giovanni and Toni DeGerez; artists include Yoriko Ito and David Diaz.
POETRY, RHYME; SELF-CONCEPT; WORLD.

Hodges, Margaret, reteller

655    *The Golden Deer.* Ill. by Daniel San Souci. Macmillan, 1992 (0-684-19219-7). USE LEVEL: M
*Asian—India*
Buddha, the holy one, comes to Earth as a golden deer to stop the king of Benares from killing all the deer. The king learns a lesson from the Banyan Deer and agrees to protect the creatures of the earth.
ANIMALS—DEER; FOLKTALES—ASIA—INDIA; SPORTS—HUNTING.

656     *Hauntings: Ghosts and Ghouls from Around the World.* Ill. by David Wenzel. Little, Brown, 1991 (0-316-36796-6). USE LEVEL: M
*Multicultural*
These 16 stories include ghost stories from the American South, a Hansel and Gretel variant from South America, a Hindu story of the "Lord of the Dead," an African story of "The Kindly Ghost," and a Japanese story about taboos.
FOLKTALES; SCARY STORIES; SHORT STORIES; SUPERNATURAL.

657     *The Wave.* Ill. by Blair Lent. Houghton, 1964 (0-395-06817-7). USE LEVEL: M
*Asian—Japan*
Ojiisan, a wise old man, lives on a mountain with his grandson Tada. When Ojiisan sees that a tidal wave is forming, he sets fire to his harvest of rice so that all the villagers will come to his aid and be saved from the wave.
CALDECOTT AWARD; FOLKTALES—ASIA—JAPAN; WEATHER—TIDAL WAVES.

**HOFFMAN, MARY**
658     *Amazing Grace.* Ill. by Caroline Binch. Dial, 1991 (0-8037-1040-2). USE LEVEL: P
*African American*
Grace loves to listen to and read stories, and she loves to act them out. At school, Grace wants to play Peter Pan. Even though she is not encouraged by her classmates, Grace auditions and succeeds.
ACTIVITIES—ACTING; CHARACTER TRAITS—PERSISTENCE; CHARACTER TRAITS—PRIDE; SCHOOL; SELF-CONCEPT.

659     *Boundless Grace.* Ill. by Caroline Binch. Dial, 1995 (0-8037-1715-6). USE LEVEL: P
*African American*
Grace's father lives with his new wife and children in Africa. He sends money for Grace and Nana to come visit him. It takes a while for Grace to accept this other family, but her spirit asserts itself and she embraces her opportunities.
CHARACTER TRAITS—PRIDE; FAMILY LIFE; FOREIGN LANDS—AFRICA; SELF-CONCEPT.

**HONG, LILY TOY, RETELLER**
660     *How the Ox Star Fell from Heaven.* Ill. by the reteller. Whitman, 1991 (0-8075-3428-5). USE LEVEL: M
*Asian—China*
At one time, oxen lived in the Imperial Palace with the Emperor of All Heavens. When the Ox Star makes an error delivering the

emperor's message, he and all oxen are punished by being made beasts of burden on earth.

ANIMALS—OXEN; FOLKTALES—ASIA—CHINA; POURQUOI TALES.

661    *Two of Everything: A Chinese Folktale.* Ill. by the reteller. Whitman, 1993 (0-8075-8157-7). USE LEVEL: M
*Asian—China*
The brass pot that Mr. Haktak finds has the magic ability to double whatever is placed into it, hence when his wife falls into the pot, there are two Mrs. Haktaks.

FAMILY LIFE; FOLKTALES—ASIA—CHINA; MAGIC; OLDER ADULTS.

**HOOBLER, DOROTHY, AND THOMAS HOOBLER**
662    *Next Stop, Freedom: The Story of a Slave Girl.* Ill. by Cheryl Hanna. Silver Burdett, 1991, LB (0-382-24145-2); pap. (0-382-24152-5). USE LEVEL: M
*African American*
Emily, ten, is a slave who dreams of learning to read and being free. With the help of Harriet Tubman, "Moses," Emily escapes to the North.

CHARACTER TRAITS—FREEDOM; SLAVERY; U.S. HISTORY; UNDERGROUND RAILROAD.

**HOOKS, WILLIAM H.**
663    *The Ballad of Belle Dorcas.* Ill. by Brian Pinkney. Knopf, 1990 (0-394-84645-1); LB (0-394-94645-6). USE LEVEL: M
*African American*
Belle Dorcas, a free black woman, loves and marries Joshua, a slave. When Joshua is to be sold, Belle seeks the advice of Granny Lizard, a woman famous for spells and conjuring.

CHARACTER TRAITS—BRAVERY; MAGIC; SLAVERY.

664    *Circle of Fire.* Macmillan, 1982 (0-689-50241-9). USE LEVEL: U
*African American*
In 1936, two boys—Harrison Hawkins, who is white, and Kitty Fisher, who is black—try to prevent a tragedy in their rural North Carolina community. A group of gypsies have a camp and there may be a confrontation between them and the Klan.

GYPSIES; KU KLUX KLAN; PREJUDICE; RACE RELATIONS.

665    *Peach Boy.* Ill. by June Otani. Bantam, 1992, LB (0-553-07621-3); pap. (0-553-35429-9). USE LEVEL: P
*Asian—Japan*
An elderly couple wish for a child. When the old woman finds a large peach, there is a baby inside it. Named Momotaro, the

boy, now 15, meets a dog, a monkey, and a hawk and they defeat the oni.

ANIMALS; CHARACTER TRAITS—BRAVERY; FOLKTALES—ASIA—JAPAN; MONSTERS.

### HOPKINSON, DEBORAH

666 *Sweet Clara and the Freedom Quilt*. Ill. by James Ransome. Knopf, 1993 (0-679-82311-5); LB (0-679-92311-X). USE LEVEL: P/M

*African American*

Clara studies the land around the Home Plantation. Using her knowledge, she sews a quilt that is used as a map by escaping slaves.

ACTIVITIES—SEWING; QUILTS; SLAVERY; U.S. HISTORY.

### HORT, LENNY

667 *How Many Stars in the Sky?* Ill. by James Ransome. Morrow, 1991 (0-688-10103-8); LB (0-688-10104-6). USE LEVEL: P

*African American*

When Mama is away, a boy cannot sleep. He decides to count the stars and he finds that his father is awake, too, and they count the stars together.

EMOTIONS—LOVE; FAMILY LIFE—FATHERS; STARS.

668 *The Tale of the Caliph Stork*. Ill. by Friso Henstra. Dial, 1989 (0-8037-0525-5); LB (0-8037-0526-3). USE LEVEL: M

*Middle Eastern—Iraq*

The Caliph Chasid of Baghdad and his Grand Vizier are turned into storks. They need to find the magic word to become human again.

BIRDS—STORKS; CHARACTER TRAITS—CLEVERNESS; FOLKTALES—MIDDLE EAST—IRAQ; MAGIC.

### HOUSTON, JAMES

669 *The Falcon Bow: An Arctic Legend*. Ill. by the author. Puffin, pap. (0-14-036078-6). USE LEVEL: U

*Native American—Inuit*

After a poor year of fishing and hunting, Kungo, a young Inuit, and his people on the coast face starvation. They distrust the inland people and feel that these people are putting them at risk.

FOREIGN LANDS—CANADA; SURVIVAL.

670 *Frozen Fire: A Tale of Courage*. Ill. by the author. Macmillan, 1977 (0-689-50083-1); pap. (0-689-71612-5). USE LEVEL: M

*Native American—Inuit*

After the death of his mother, Matthew goes with his father to the Canadian Arctic. When his father is lost in a storm, Matthew and his friend, Kayak, embark on a rescue effort that becomes a survival adventure in the Arctic.

ARCTIC LANDS; FOREIGN LANDS—CANADA; SURVIVAL.

### HOW ANANSI OBTAINED THE SKY GOD'S STORIES

671    *How Anansi Obtained the Sky God's Stories: An African Folktale from the Ashanti Tribe.* Ill. by Janice Skivington. Childrens Pr., 1991, LB (0-516-05134-2); pap. (0-516-45134-0). USE LEVEL: M

*African—Ashanti*

This book is designed to encourage storytelling. The story text, about Anansi tricking three animals to pay Nyami for his stories, follows the wordless illustrations. After learning the text, children can retell the story using the pictures.

ANIMALS; BEHAVIOR—TRICKERY; FOLKTALES—AFRICA—ASHANTI; SPIDERS; STORYTELLING.

### HOWARD, ELIZABETH FITZGERALD

672    *Aunt Flossie's Hats (and Crab Cakes Later).* Ill. by James Ransome. Houghton, 1991 (0-395-54682-6); pap. (0-395-72077-X). USE LEVEL: P

*African American*

In Baltimore, Sarah and Susan visit their Great-Great-Aunt Flossie for tea and stories.

CLOTHING—HATS; FAMILY LIFE—AUNTS, UNCLES; OLDER ADULTS; STORYTELLING.

673    *Chita's Christmas Tree.* Ill. by Floyd Cooper. Macmillan, 1989 (0-02-744621-2); pap. (0-689-71739-3). USE LEVEL: P

*African American*

In Baltimore, Chita and Papa take the buggy and go out into the country to select a Christmas tree.

FAMILY LIFE; HOLIDAYS—CHRISTMAS; TREES.

674    *Mac & Marie & the Train Toss Surprise.* Ill. by Gail Gordon Carter. Macmillan, 1993 (0-02-744640-9). USE LEVEL: P

*African American*

Uncle Clem works in the dining car of a train. He promises to toss a surprise from the train to his nephew and niece as it passes them. This story is based on a family experience of the author.

FAMILY LIFE—AUNTS, UNCLES; RURAL LIFE; SHELLS; TRAINS.

675    *Papa Tells Chita a Story.* Ill. by Floyd Cooper. Macmillan, 1995
       (0-02-744623-9). USE LEVEL: P
       *African American*
       After dinner is Chita's special time with Papa. He tells her sto-
       ries, often about his time in the Spanish-American War. Some
       parts of his story are exaggerated, but he does tell about how
       truly brave he was to take a message to the troops.
       FAMILY LIFE—FATHERS; STORYTELLING; U.S. HISTORY; WAR.

676    *The Train to Lulu's.* Ill. by Robert Casilla. Macmillan, 1988 (0-
       02-744620-4); pap. (0-689-71797-0). USE LEVEL: P
       *African American*
       Beppy and Babs are taking the train to visit their Great-Aunt
       Lulu. This book is based on an experience from the author's
       childhood.
       ACTIVITIES—TRAVELING; FAMILY LIFE—SIBLINGS; TRAINS.

## HOYT-GOLDSMITH, DIANE

677    *Arctic Hunter.* Photos by Lawrence Migdale. Holiday, 1992 (0-
       8234-0972-4); pap. (0-8234-1124-9). USE LEVEL: M
       *Native American—Inupiat*
       Reggie, ten, is an Inupiat boy who lives above the Arctic Circle
       in Alaska. He describes his activities, like traveling out to wilder-
       ness camp and hunting seals. These are balanced with going to
       school and the supermarket and eating pizza.
       ARCTIC LANDS; BEHAVIOR—GROWING UP; FAMILY LIFE.

678    *Celebrating Kwanzaa.* Photos by Lawrence Migdale. Holiday,
       1993 (0-8234-1048-X); pap. (0-8234-1130-3). USE LEVEL: M
       *African American*
       Focusing on two children, Andiey and Max, and their parents,
       this book describes the symbols, meaning, history, and celebra-
       tions of Kwanzaa.
       FAMILY LIFE; FOREIGN LANGUAGES; HOLIDAYS—KWANZAA.

679    *Cherokee Summer.* Photos by Lawrence Migdale. Holiday, 1993
       (0-8234-0995-3). USE LEVEL: M
       *Native American—Cherokee*
       Bridget lives in Oklahoma and is a member of the Cherokee
       Nation. She tells of the history of the Cherokee, including the
       Trail of Tears, and of their culture and heritage. Especially
       important are family traditions, like weaving baskets.
       BEHAVIOR—GROWING UP; FAMILY LIFE; FOLKTALES—NATIVE AMERICAN—
       CHEROKEE; RELOCATION.

680 *Hoang Anh: A Vietnamese American Boy.* Photos by Lawrence Migdale. Holiday, 1992 (0-8234-0948-1). USE LEVEL: M
*Asian American—Vietnam*
Hoang Anh enjoys everyday activities similar to those of many children, such as playing football, but he also learns and appreciates the customs from his Vietnamese heritage.
BEHAVIOR—GROWING UP; FAMILY LIFE.

681 *Pueblo Storyteller.* Photos by Lawrence Migdale. Holiday, 1991 (0-8234-0864-7); pap. (0-8234-1080-3). USE LEVEL: M
*Native American—Cochiti Pueblo*
April Trujillo and her family respect the traditions of the Pueblo people. Incorporated in this look at modern native people is a folktale, "How the People Came to Earth: A Pueblo Legend."
BEHAVIOR—GROWING UP; DESERT; FAMILY LIFE; FOLKTALES—NATIVE AMERICAN—COCHITI PUEBLO.

682 *Totem Pole.* Photos by Lawrence Migdale. Holiday, 1990 (0-8234-0809-4); pap. (0-8234-1135-4). USE LEVEL: M
*Native American—Tsimshian*
David's family belongs to the Eagle Clan of the Tsimshian tribe. His father is a wood-carver. David describes the traditions of his people, as well as his step-by-step work with his father, carving the totem pole. A folktale is included in the text.
ART; BEHAVIOR—GROWING UP; FAMILY LIFE; FOLKTALES—NATIVE AMERICAN—TSIMSHIAN; TOTEMS.

**HRU, DAKARI**
683 *Joshua's Masai Mask.* Ill. by Anna Rich. Lee & Low, 1993 (1-880000-02-4). USE LEVEL: M
*African American*
Joshua thinks about being in the school talent show. When his uncle gives him a magical Masai mask, he develops self-confidence.
FAMILY LIFE; FOREIGN LANDS—AFRICA—MASAI; MAGIC; MUSIC; SCHOOL.

**HUDSON, CHERYL WILLIS**
684 *Afro-Bets ABC Book.* Ill. by the author. Just Us, 1987, pap. (0-940975-00-9). USE LEVEL: PS
*African American*
Words for the letters of the alphabet are presented, including some that reflect African traditions, like cornrows and Africa.
ABC BOOKS.

685    *Afro-Bets 123 Book*. Ill. by the author. Just Us, 1987, pap. (0-940975-01-7). USE LEVEL: PS
*African American*
Counting objects from one to ten is accomplished by six young children in this book.
CONCEPTS; COUNTING, NUMBERS.

686    *Animal Sounds for Baby*. Ill. by George Ford. Scholastic, 1995 (0-590-48029-4). USE LEVEL: PS
*African American*
A rhyming text introduces farm animals including cow, horse, lamb, and pig.
ANIMALS; BABIES, TODDLERS; FARMS; FORMAT, UNUSUAL—BOARD BOOKS; POETRY, RHYME.

687    *Good Morning, Baby*. Ill. by George Ford. Scholastic, 1992 (0-590-45760-8). USE LEVEL: PS
*African American*
Waking up, getting dressed, and eating breakfast are some of the things this baby does to get ready for the day.
BABIES, TODDLERS; FORMAT, UNUSUAL—BOARD BOOKS; POETRY, RHYME.

688    *Good Night, Baby*. Ill by George Ford. Scholastic, 1992 (0-590-45761-6). USE LEVEL: PS
*African American*
This board book describes the routine activities as a baby prepares for bed.
BABIES, TODDLERS; BEDTIME; FORMAT, UNUSUAL—BOARD BOOKS; POETRY, RHYME.

689    *Let's Count Baby*. Ill. by George Ford. Scholastic, 1995 (0-590-48028-6). USE LEVEL: PS
*African American*
In this rhyming text, baby counts from one to ten. This book has sturdy board pages for young children.
BABIES, TODDLERS; COUNTING, NUMBERS; FORMAT, UNUSUAL—BOARD BOOKS; POETRY, RHYME.

**HUDSON, CHERYL WILLIS, AND BERNETTE G. FORD**
690    *Bright Eyes, Brown Skin*. Ill. by George Ford. Just Us, 1990, LB (0-940975-10-6); pap. (0-940975-23-8). USE LEVEL: PS
*African American*
The rhyming text celebrates the joyful feelings preschoolers have about themselves.
POETRY, RHYME; SCHOOL; SELF-CONCEPT.

**HUDSON, WADE**

691    *I Love My Family.* Ill. by Cal Massey. Scholastic, 1993 (0-590-45763-2). USE LEVEL: P
*African American*
Every summer, the whole family gathers for a reunion in North Carolina. They dance, tell stories, and take photographs.
ACTIVITIES; EMOTIONS—LOVE; FAMILY LIFE.

692    *I'm Gonna Be!* Ill. by Culverson Blair. Just Us, 1992, pap. (0-940975-40-8). USE LEVEL: P
*African American*
A group of friends talk about the possibilities for future careers by naming famous African Americans like Spike Lee, Ralph Bunche, Elizabeth Catlett, and Jesse Jackson.
CAREERS; SELF-CONCEPT.

693    *Jamal's Busy Day.* Ill. by George Ford. Just Us, 1991, LB (0-940975-21-1); pap. (0-940975-24-6). USE LEVEL: P
*African American*
Jamal describes the activities at home and at school that keep him very busy.
ACTIVITIES; FAMILY LIFE; SCHOOL.

694    *Pass It On: African-American Poetry for Children.* Ill. by Floyd Cooper. Scholastic, 1993 (0-590-45770-5). USE LEVEL: P/M
*African American*
The poems in this collection provide images of African American life. Langston Hughes, Nikki Giovanni, and Eloise Greenfield are among the poets included.
POETRY, RHYME; SELF-CONCEPT.

**HUGHES, LANGSTON**

695    *The Dream Keeper: And Other Poems.* Ill. by Helen Sewell. Knopf, 1986, c1932, o.p. USE LEVEL: M/U
*African American*
There are 59 poems in this collection, including some of Langston Hughes's best-known poems for young people, like "Dream Variation" and "Dreams."
DREAMS; EMOTIONS; POETRY, RHYME.

696    *The Dream Keeper: And Other Poems.* Ill. by Brian Pinkney. Knopf, 1994 (0-679-84421-X); LB (0-679-94421-4). USE LEVEL: M/U
*African American*
There are seven additional poems in this newly illustrated ver-

sion. Themes include dreaming, the sea, and everyday experiences.

DREAMS; EMOTIONS; POETRY, RHYME.

### HUGHES, MONICA, RETELLER

697 *Little Fingerling*. Ill. by Brenda Clark. Ideals, 1989 (0-8249-8553-2). USE LEVEL: M

*Asian—Japan*

Issun Boshi, "Little Fingerling," is only as tall as his father's finger, but he is clever and brave. When Plum Blossom goes to visit the temple, Issun Boshi protects her and he grows to full size.

CHARACTER TRAITS—BRAVERY; CHARACTER TRAITS—SMALLNESS; ELVES AND LITTLE PEOPLE; FOLKTALES—ASIA—JAPAN.

### HULL, ROBERT, RETELLER

698 *African Stories*. Ill. by Peter Kettle. Thomson Learning, 1992 (1-56847-004-5). USE LEVEL: M

*African*

There are eight stories in this collection including "Two Sisters," "Chameleon and Hare," and "The Kid Goat." Cultures from different regions of Africa are represented.

FOLKTALES—AFRICA; SHORT STORIES.

699 *Caribbean Stories*. Ill. by Colin Williams and Joanne Makin. Thomson Learning, 1994, LB (1-56847-190-4). USE LEVEL: M

*Caribbean*

The eight stories in this collection include several about Anancy, the well-known trickster. An introduction provides background information about Caribbean folktale traditions.

BEHAVIOR—TRICKERY; FOLKTALES—CARIBBEAN ISLANDS; SHORT STORIES.

700 *Indian Stories*. Ill. by Noël Bateman and Claire Robinson. Thomson Learning, 1994, LB (1-56847-189-0). USE LEVEL: M

*Asian—India*

There are seven stories in this collection including "The Rain God and the Drought Demon" and "Shiva Goes Fishing." An introduction provides an overview of the traditions of folktales in India.

FOLKTALES—ASIA—INDIA; SHORT STORIES.

701 *Native North American Stories*. Ill. by Richard Hook and Claire Robinson. Thomson Learning, 1992 (1-56847-005-3). USE LEVEL: M

*Native American*

Featured in some of the eight stories in this collection are familiar animal characters like Raven, Coyote, and Thunderbird. Creation stories and stories explaining natural phenomena are also included.

ANIMALS; CREATION; FOLKTALES—NATIVE AMERICAN; POURQUOI TALES; SHORT STORIES.

### HUNTER, KRISTIN

702 *Boss Cat.* Ill. by Harold Franklin. Macmillan, 1971, o.p. USE LEVEL: M

*African American*

When Daddy brings home a stray black cat, the children are happy but Mom is not. Tyrone and his sisters hope they can keep Pharaoh.

ANIMALS—CATS; FAMILY LIFE; PETS; URBAN LIFE.

### HURMENCE, BELINDA

703 *Dixie in the Big Pasture.* Houghton, 1994 (0-395-52022-9). USE LEVEL: U

*Native American*

In the early 1900s, Daisy and her family move to Oklahoma territory. Adjusting to the move is a struggle for Daisy, including adjusting to the attitudes toward the Kiowa people and her relationship with a Kiowa boy.

ANIMALS—HORSES; FRONTIER AND PIONEER LIFE; PREJUDICE; RACE RELATIONS; U.S. HISTORY.

704 *A Girl Called Boy.* Houghton, 1982 (0-395-31022-9); pap. (0-395-55698-8). USE LEVEL: U

*African American*

"Boy" is Blanche Overtha Yancey. She is 11 and she feels alienated from her family. After becoming lost in the woods in North Carolina, Boy realizes that she has been transported back to the 1850s and the era of slavery.

FAMILY LIFE; FANTASY; SLAVERY; U.S. HISTORY.

705 *Tough Tiffany.* Doubleday, 1980, o.p. USE LEVEL: M/U

*African American*

Tiffany, 11, has a lot to deal with as she grows up in rural North Carolina. With six children in the family, there is not much money and Tiffany must deal with problems at home and at school.

FAMILY LIFE; POVERTY; RURAL LIFE; SCHOOL.

HURWITZ, JOHANNA

706 *Class President*. Ill. by Sheila Hamanaka. Morrow, 1990 (0-688-09114-8); Scholastic, pap. (0-590-44064-0). USE LEVEL: M
*Hispanic American—Puerto Rico*
Julio Sanchez is surprised when his new teacher for fifth grade is a man, Mr. Ernesto Flores. Julio is also surprised when his classmates realize how helpful he is and they elect him class president.
CHARACTER TRAITS—HELPFULNESS; ELECTIONS; FRIENDSHIP; SCHOOL.

707 *New Shoes for Silvia*. Ill. by Jerry Pinkney. Morrow, 1993 (0-688-05286-X); LB (0-688-05287-8). USE LEVEL: P
*Latin American*
Silvia's new shoes, a gift from Tía Rosita, do not fit her yet, so she finds different ways to use them until she can wear them.
BEHAVIOR—GROWING UP; CLOTHING—SHOES; FAMILY LIFE; FOREIGN LANDS—LATIN AMERICA; GIFTS.

708 *School Spirit*. Ill. by Karen Dugan. Morrow, 1994 (0-688-12825-4). USE LEVEL: M
*Hispanic American—Puerto Rico*
Julio Sanchez, who is the fifth-grade class president, gets his friends involved in stopping the school board from closing their school.
FRIENDSHIP; SCHOOL.

HUTCHINS, PAT

709 *My Best Friend*. Ill. by the author. Greenwillow, 1993 (0-688-11485-7); LB (0-688-11486-5). USE LEVEL: P
*African American*
Although the younger girl recognizes there are many things that her friend can do that she cannot, they are still best friends.
BEHAVIOR—GROWING UP; FRIENDSHIP.

HYPPOLITE, JOANNE

710 *Seth and Samona*. Ill. by Colin Bootman. Delacorte, 1995 (0-385-32093-0). USE LEVEL: U
*Caribbean American—Haiti*
Seth Michelin and his family, originally from Haiti, are now living in Boston. Samona Gemini is a fifth-grade classmate who often involves Seth in her escapades, including visiting Mrs. Fabiyi, who might be a witch.
FAMILY LIFE; FRIENDSHIP; SELF-CONCEPT.

**IGUS, TOYOMI**

711     *When I Was Little.* Ill. by Higgins Bond. Just Us, 1992 (0-940975-32-7); pap. (0-940975-33-5). USE LEVEL: P
*African American*
Noel loves to visit his grandfather during the summer. While they are fishing, Grandpa tells Noel about how times have changed and what it was like growing up in the country when he was little.
ACTIVITIES—REMINISCING; FAMILY LIFE—GRANDFATHERS; RURAL LIFE; SPORTS—FISHING.

**INGPEN, ROBERT, AND BARBARA HAYES**

712     *Folk Tales and Fables of Asia and Australia.* Chelsea House, 1994 (0-7910-2757-0). USE LEVEL: U
*Multicultural*
Nine stories from Asia (including two Baba Yaga tales and one about Momotaro) and eight from Australia and New Zealand provide insight into the traditions of these areas.
FOLKTALES—ASIA; FOLKTALES—AUSTRALIA; FOLKTALES—NEW ZEALAND; SHORT STORIES.

713     *Folk Tales and Fables of the Americas and the Pacific.* Chelsea House, 1994 (0-7910-2759-7). USE LEVEL: U
*Multicultural*
Legends of native peoples of North and South America, including stories featuring animals like Crow and Nanook the Bear are included along with five stories from the Pacific, including Fiji and New Guinea.
ANIMALS; FOLKTALES; POURQUOI TALES; SHORT STORIES.

714     *Folk Tales and Fables of the Middle East and Africa.* Chelsea House, 1994, LB (0-7910-2758-9). USE LEVEL: U
*Multicultural*
Four stories from the Middle East, including one about Aladdin, and seven stories from Africa, including a trickster story with Rabbit, are featured in this collection.
FOLKTALES—AFRICA; FOLKTALES—MIDDLE EAST; SHORT STORIES.

**ISADORA, RACHEL**

715     *At the Crossroads.* Ill. by the author. Greenwillow, 1991 (0-688-05270-3); LB (0-688-05271-1); pap. (0-688-13103-4). USE LEVEL: P
*African—South Africa*

The fathers have been away working in the mines. Now they are coming home. The children celebrate and then wait at the crossroads for their fathers.

CAREERS—MINERS; FAMILY LIFE—FATHERS; FOREIGN LANDS—AFRICA—SOUTH AFRICA.

716　*Ben's Trumpet.* Ill. by the author. Greenwillow, 1979 (0-688-80194-3); pap. (0-688-10988-8). USE LEVEL: P
**African American**
A musician remembers his own childhood dream as he helps Ben achieve his dream.

CALDECOTT AWARD; CAREERS—MUSICIANS; DREAMS; MUSIC.

717　*Over the Green Hills.* Ill. by the author. Greenwillow, 1992 (0-688-10509-2); LB (0-688-10510-6). USE LEVEL: P
**African—South Africa**
Zolani lives in a village by the sea on the east coast of South Africa. He and his mother travel inland to visit Zolani's grandmother. Included are details about the Transkei homeland of South Africa.

ACTIVITIES—TRAVELING; COMMUNITIES, NEIGHBORHOODS; FAMILY LIFE; FOREIGN LANDS—AFRICA—SOUTH AFRICA.

**ISHII, MOMOKO, RETELLER**
718　*The Tongue-cut Sparrow.* Translated by Katherine Paterson. Ill. by Suekichi Akaba. Dutton, 1987 (0-525-67199-4). USE LEVEL: M
**Asian—Japan**
When the sparrow drinks her starch, the old woman snips the sparrow's tongue. The old man goes to apologize to the sparrow and is given a box of treasures. The old woman goes to the sparrow but, because of her greed, she receives a snake and a toad.

BEHAVIOR—GREED; BIRDS—SPARROWS; CHARACTER TRAITS—KINDNESS; FOLKTALES—ASIA—JAPAN.

**IZUKI, STEVEN**
719　*Believers in America: Poems about Americans of Asian and Pacific Islander Descent.* Ill. by Bill Fukuda McCoy. Childrens Pr., 1994, LB ( 0-516-05152-0); pap. (0-516-45152-9). USE LEVEL: M/U
**Asian American**
The experiences of Asian migrant workers, refugees, and railroad workers are among the topics of these poems. Well-known

people like Bruce Lee, Daniel Inouye, and Kristi Yamaguchi are also featured.

BIOGRAPHY; POETRY, RHYME; SELF-CONCEPT.

### JACOBS, SHANNON K.

720 *The Boy Who Loved Morning.* Ill. by Michael Hays. Little, Brown, 1993 (0-316-45556-3). USE LEVEL: M
*Native American*
The boy loves to welcome morning, playing his flute and celebrating with the animals. He is proud of his ability to bring the morning, and he shows off before his people. Grandfather helps him overcome his pride and earn his name, Morning Song.

CHARACTER TRAITS—PRIDE; FAMILY LIFE—GRANDFATHERS; MORNING; NAMES.

721 *Song of the Giraffe.* Ill. by Pamela Johnson. Little, Brown, 1991 (0-316-45555-5). USE LEVEL: M
*African*
Kisana feels that she is an outsider among her people. She is small and light-skinned while the villagers are tall with darker skin tones. She travels a long way to find a gift for her ancestors, only to find the best gift within herself.

ANIMALS—GIRAFFES; CELEBRATIONS; DREAMS; FOREIGN LANDS—AFRICA; SONGS; WEATHER—DROUGHTS.

### JAFFE, NINA, RETELLER

722 *Older Brother, Younger Brother: A Korean Folktale.* Ill. by Wenhai Ma. Viking, 1995 (0-670-85645-2). USE LEVEL: M
*Asian—Korea*
Nolbu, the older brother, is greedy and lazy while Hungbu is kind and hard-working. When he befriends a sparrow, Hungbu is rewarded with wealth. Nolbu tries to get riches in a similar way, but he is given manure, snakes, and evil spirits.

BIRDS—SPARROWS; CHARACTER TRAITS—KINDNESS; FAMILY LIFE—SIBLINGS; FOLKTALES—ASIA—KOREA.

### JAFFREY, MADHUR

723 *Seasons of Splendour: Tales, Myths, and Legends of India.* Ill. by Michael Foreman. Puffin, pap. (0-14-031854-2). USE LEVEL: U
*Asian—India*
King Ram, the great god Krishna, the demon king Ravan, and the monkey god Hanuman are among the extraordinary characters in this collection of Hindi stories.

FOLKTALES—ASIA—INDIA; MAGIC; SHORT STORIES.

**JAMES, BETSY**

724 *The Mud Family.* Ill. by Paul Morin. Putnam, 1994 (0-399-22549-8). USE LEVEL: M
*Native American—Anasazi*
During a drought, the crops wither. Sosi and her family may have to leave their home. Everyone is too worried and busy tothink about how Sosi feels. She shares her concerns with some mud dolls she has made. Her wish for rain is fulfilled.
BEHAVIOR—WORRYING; DESERT; WEATHER—DROUGHTS.

**JAMESON, CYNTHIA, RETELLER**

725 *One for the Price of Two.* Ill. by Anita Lobel. Parents Magazine Pr., 1972, o.p. USE LEVEL: M
*Asian—Japan*
Kichei's boasting bothers his friends, who decide to teach him a lesson. They take his new heifer and then sell her back to him.
ANIMALS—COWS; BEHAVIOR—BOASTING; CHARACTER TRAITS—FOOLISHNESS; FOLKTALES—ASIA—JAPAN.

**JAVERNICK, ELLEN**

726 *Where's Brooke?* Ill. by Rick Hackney. Childrens Pr., 1992, LB (0-516-02012-9); pap. (0-516-42012-7). USE LEVEL: PS/P
*Asian American*
A father seems to look for his daughter, who is right in the room with him. This book has a predictable rhyming text.
BABIES, TODDLERS; POETRY, RHYME; PREDICTABLE TEXT.

**JEKYLL, WALTER, COLLECTOR**

727 *I Have a News: Rhymes from the Caribbean.* Ill. by Jacqueline Mair. Lothrop, 1994 (0-688-13367-3). USE LEVEL: M
*Caribbean*
Fifteen poems capture the rhythms and spirit of the Caribbean. Lilting language spiced with dialect make this a lively collection.
FOREIGN LANDS—CARIBBEAN ISLANDS; POETRY, RHYME.

**JENKINS, JESSICA**

728 *Thinking about Colors.* Ill. by the author. Dutton, 1992 (0-525-44908-6). USE LEVEL: P
*Multicultural*
A group of children from diverse backgrounds present information and feelings about colors—red, yellow and orange, green, blue, pink, and black and white.
CONCEPTS—COLOR; EMOTIONS.

**JENSEN, PATSY**

729 *John Henry and His Mighty Hammer.* Ill. by Roseanne Litzinger. Troll, 1994, LB (0-8167-3156-X); pap. (0-8167-5157-8). USE LEVEL: P

*African American*

This is a simplified retelling of the legend of John Henry, who challenged the steam drill and won.

CHARACTER TRAITS—PERSEVERANCE; CHARACTER TRAITS—PRIDE; FOLKTALES—UNITED STATES; TRAINS.

**JOHNSON, ANGELA**

730 *Do Like Kyla.* Ill. by James Ransome. Orchard, 1990 (0-531-05852-2); LB (0-531-08452-3); pap. (0-531-07040-9). USE LEVEL: PS/P

*African American*

All day long, a little girl follows her older sister, Kyla, and imitates her behavior.

ACTIVITIES—PLAYING; BEHAVIOR—IMITATION; BEHAVIOR—SHARING; FAMILY LIFE—SIBLINGS.

731 *The Girl Who Wore Snakes.* Ill. by James E. Ransome. Orchard, 1993 (0-531-05491-8); LB (0-531-08641-0). USE LEVEL: P

*African American*

Ali finds that she loves snakes. Others are less enchanted with them, but one of her aunts shares her appreciation.

FAMILY LIFE—AUNTS, UNCLES; PETS; REPTILES—SNAKES; SELF-CONCEPT.

732 *Joshua by the Sea.* Ill. by Rhonda Mitchell. Orchard, 1994 (0-531-06846-3). USE LEVEL: PS

*African American*

Joshua tells of the activities he enjoys with his family on a trip to the sea. This is a sturdy board book.

FAMILY LIFE; FORMAT, UNUSUAL—BOARD BOOKS; POETRY, RHYME; SEA AND SEASHORE.

733 *Joshua's Night Whispers.* Ill. by Rhonda Mitchell. Orchard, 1994 (0-531-06847-1). USE LEVEL: PS

*African American*

When he is worried by the noises at night, Joshua is comforted by his father. This is a sturdy board book.

BEDTIME; FAMILY LIFE—FATHERS; FORMAT, UNUSUAL—BOARD BOOKS; NIGHT.

734 *Julius.* Ill. by Dav Pilkey. Orchard, 1993 (0-531-05465-9); LB (0-531-08615-1). USE LEVEL: P
*African American*
Maya's uncle has given her a gift—a big Alaskan pig named Julius. Improbably, Julius becomes involved in all the activities in the house.
ANIMALS—PIGS; FAMILY LIFE; FRIENDSHIP; IMAGINATION.

735 *The Leaving Morning.* Ill. by David Soman. Orchard, 1992 (0-531-05992-8); LB (0-531-08592-9). USE LEVEL: P
*African American*
Two children, a brother and sister, are moving from their apartment and are saying good-bye to their friends and neighbors.
BEHAVIOR—SEEKING BETTER THINGS; COMMUNITIES, NEIGHBORHOODS; EMOTIONS—APPREHENSION; FAMILY LIFE; MOVING; URBAN LIFE.

736 *Mama Bird, Baby Birds.* Ill. by Rhonda Mitchell. Orchard, 1994 (0-531-06848-X). USE LEVEL: PS
*African American*
Joshua watches a mother robin care for her baby birds, just like his mother cares for him.
BIRDS—ROBINS; EMOTIONS—LOVE; FAMILY LIFE—MOTHERS; FORMAT, UNUSUAL—BOARD BOOKS; POETRY, RHYME.

737 *One of Three.* Ill. by David Soman. Orchard, 1991 (0-531-05955-3); LB (0-531-08555-4); pap. (0-531-07061-1). USE LEVEL: P
*African American*
A little girl enjoys doing things with her older sisters, Eva and Nikki. Sometimes, though, she feels left out because she is the youngest.
EMOTIONS—LOVE; FAMILY LIFE—SIBLINGS; URBAN LIFE.

738 *Rain Feet.* Ill. by Rhonda Mitchell. Orchard, 1994 (0-531-06849-8). USE LEVEL: PS
*African American*
Whether in bare feet or boots, this young boy enjoys the rain. There is a simple, rhyming pattern in this board book.
FORMAT, UNUSUAL—BOARD BOOKS; POETRY, RHYME; WEATHER—RAIN.

739 *Shoes like Miss Alice's.* Ill. by Ken Page. Orchard, 1995 (0-531-06814-5); LB (0-531-08664-X). USE LEVEL: P
*African American*
When Miss Alice comes to baby-sit, Sara is apprehensive. But Miss Alice is lively and caring and together they dance and go

for a walk. Miss Alice has special shoes for different activities, including fuzzy blue shoes for when Sara naps.

ACTIVITIES—BABY-SITTING; CLOTHING—SHOES.

740 *Tell Me a Story, Mama.* Ill. by David Soman. Orchard, 1989 (0-531-05794-1); LB (0-531-08394-2); pap. (0-531-07032-8).
USE LEVEL: P
*African American*
A girl wants to hear stories about when her mother was young, including a story about a mean old lady and a story about finding a puppy.

ACTIVITIES—REMINISCING; FAMILY LIFE—MOTHERS; STORYTELLING.

741 *Toning the Sweep.* Orchard, 1993 (0-531-05476-4); LB (0-531-08626-7); Scholastic, pap. (0-590-48142-8). USE LEVEL: U
*African American*
For many summers, Emmie and her mother have gone to the desert to visit Grandmama Ola. This year it is different. Grandmama Ola is ill and will return with them to Ohio. Emmie, 14, sees some of the difficult issues that come with growing up.

BEHAVIOR—GROWING UP; CORETTA SCOTT KING AWARD; DESERT; FAMILY LIFE—GRANDMOTHERS; ILLNESS.

742 *When I Am Old with You.* Ill. by David Soman. Orchard, 1990 (0-531-05884-0); LB (0-531-08484-1); pap. (0-531-07035-2).
USE LEVEL: P
*African American*
A young boy tells about the times he will share with his grandfather, imagining they are both old.

CORETTA SCOTT KING AWARD; FAMILY LIFE—GRANDFATHERS; IMAGINATION; OLDER ADULTS.

**JOHNSON, DOLORES**
743 *The Best Bug to Be.* Ill. by the author. Macmillan, 1992 (0-02-747842-4). USE LEVEL: P
*African American*
In the school play, Kelly wants the lead, but she is chosen to be a bumblebee.

ACTIVITIES—ACTING; CHARACTER TRAITS—PRIDE; INSECTS—BEES; SCHOOL; SELF-CONCEPT.

744 *Now Let Me Fly: The Story of a Slave Family.* Ill. by the author. Macmillan, 1993 (0-02-747699-5). USE LEVEL: M
*African American*

In the early 1800s, a young girl is kidnapped from her home in Africa, transported to America, and sold into slavery.
SLAVERY; U.S. HISTORY.

745    *Papa's Stories.* Ill. by the author. Macmillan, 1994 (0-02-747847-5). USE LEVEL: P
*African American*
While Mama cooks supper, Kari and Papa share stories. As Kari gets a little older, she realizes that Papa cannot read.
ACTIVITIES—READING; BEHAVIOR—SEEKING BETTER THINGS; FAMILY LIFE; SELF-CONCEPT.

746    *Seminole Diary.* Ill. by the author. Macmillan, 1994 (0-02-747848-3). USE LEVEL: M
*African American*
Gina and her mother read the diary of Libbie, an ancestor who was a slave. She escaped from the plantation with her family and reached South Florida, where they lived as slaves of the Seminoles, who were later forced to move to Oklahoma territory.
FAMILY LIFE; RELOCATION; SLAVERY; U.S. HISTORY.

747    *What Kind of Baby-Sitter Is This?* Ill. by the author. Macmillan, 1991 (0-02-747846-7). USE LEVEL: P
*African American*
Kevin does not want his mother to leave, and he does not want to like Mrs. Lovey Pritchard, his baby-sitter. Mrs. Pritchard's love of baseball wins Kevin's friendship.
ACTIVITIES—BABY-SITTING; FRIENDSHIP; SPORTS—BASEBALL.

748    *What Will Mommy Do When I'm at School?* Ill. by the author. Macmillan, 1990 (0-02-747845-9). USE LEVEL: PS/P
*African American*
As a little girl prepares to begin school, she wonders how her mother will spend the day without her.
BEHAVIOR—GROWING UP; EMOTIONS—APPREHENSION; FAMILY LIFE—MOTHERS.

749    *Your Dad Was Just Like You.* Ill. by the author. Macmillan, 1993 (0-02-747838-6). USE LEVEL: P
*African American*
When Peter has a fight with his father, his grandfather helps him understand why his dad is sometimes strict with him.
BEHAVIOR—FIGHTING, ARGUING; BEHAVIOR—GROWING UP; EMOTIONS—LOVE; FAMILY LIFE—FATHERS; FAMILY LIFE—GRANDFATHERS.

**JOHNSON, HERSCHEL**

750     *A Visit to the Country.* Ill. by Romare Bearden. HarperCollins, 1989 (0-06-022849-0); LB (0-06-022854-7). USE LEVEL: P
*African American*
On a visit to his grandparents' farm, Mike finds a baby cardinal and takes care of it. Mike names the bird Max and enjoys watching Max grow and learn to fly. Mike comes to realize that Max needs to be set free.
BIRDS—CARDINALS; CHARACTER TRAITS—KINDNESS; FAMILY LIFE—GRANDPARENTS.

**JOHNSON, JAMES WELDON**

751     *The Creation.* Ill. by James Ransome. Holiday, 1994 (0-8234-1069-2). USE LEVEL: P/M
*African American*
A well-known poem about God creating the earth is illustrated with dramatic paintings of the events. Extending the mood of the poem are scenes showing children listening to a storyteller
CORETTA SCOTT KING AWARD; CREATION; POETRY, RHYME; RELIGION; STORYTELLING.

752     *The Creation: A Poem.* Ill. by Carla Golembe. Little, Brown, 1993 (0-316-46744-8). USE LEVEL: P/M
*African American*
An illustrated version of a well-known poem about God creating the earth.
CREATION; POETRY, RHYME; RELIGION.

753     *Lift Every Voice and Sing.* Introduction by Jim Haskins. Ill. by Elizabeth Catlett. Walker, 1993 (0-8027-8250-7); LB (0-8027-9251-5). USE LEVEL: P/M
*African American*
The "Negro National Anthem" is illustrated with linocuts, many depicting hardships that African Americans have endured.
MUSIC; POETRY, RHYME; SONGS.

754     *Lift Ev'ry Voice and Sing.* Ill. by Jan Spivey Gilcrist. Scholastic, 1994 (0-590-46982-7). USE LEVEL: M
*African American*
This is an illustrated version of the African American national anthem. The illustrations link modern African Americans with their African heritage.
MUSIC; POETRY, RHYME; SONGS.

**JOHNSON, MILDRED D.**

755   *Wait, Skates!* Ill. by Tom Dunnington. Childrens Pr., 1983, LB (0-516-02039-0); pap. (0-516-42039-9). USE LEVEL: PS/P
*African American*
A boy learns to use his roller skates. This book has a simple, predictable text.
PREDICTABLE TEXT; SPORTS—ROLLER SKATING.

**JOHNSON, RYERSON**

756   *Kenji and the Magic Geese.* Ill. by Jean Tseng and Mou-Sien Tseng. Simon & Schuster, 1992 (0-671-75974-4). USE LEVEL: M
*Asian—Japan*
Although they are poor, Kenji and his family have one treasure—a picture of flying geese. An art collector agrees to buy it, but the picture changes as one goose leaves the picture, then returns with two eggs, which hatch.
ART; BIRDS—GEESE; FOREIGN LANDS—ASIA—JAPAN; MAGIC.

**JOHNSTON, TONY, ADAPTER**

757   *The Badger and the Magic Fan: A Japanese Folktale.* Ill. by Tomie dePaola. Putnam, 1990 (0-399-21945-5). USE LEVEL: M
*Asian—Japan*
The badger steals a fan from the tengu children and uses it to make his fortune. The tengu children get their fan back and make the badger's nose grow.
ANATOMY—NOSES; ANIMALS—BADGERS; BEHAVIOR—TRICKERY; FOLKTALES—ASIA—JAPAN; MAGIC.

758   *The Old Lady and the Birds.* Ill. by Stephanie Garcia. Harcourt, 1994 (0-15-257769-6). USE LEVEL: P
*Mexican*
An old lady spends a day in her garden enjoying the sun and the flowers and sharing tortillas and seeds with the birds.
BEHAVIOR—SHARING; BIRDS; FOREIGN LANDS—MEXICO; FOREIGN LANGUAGES.

759   *The Tale of Rabbit and Coyote.* Ill. by Tomie dePaola. Putnam, 1994 (0-399-22258-8). USE LEVEL: M
*Native American—Zapotec*
When Rabbit is caught by the farmer, he tricks Coyote into taking his place. When Coyote tries to get even, Rabbit continues to trick him, until Rabbit goes to the moon and Coyote sits and howls at it.

ANIMALS—COYOTES; ANIMALS—RABBITS; BEHAVIOR—TRICKERY;
FOLKTALES—NATIVE AMERICAN—ZAPOTEC; POURQUOI TALES.

**JONAS, ANN**

760    *Color Dance.* Ill. by the author. Greenwillow, 1989 (0-688-05990-2); LB (0-688-05991-0). USE LEVEL: PS/P
*Multicultural*
Three girls, one of whom is African American, and a boy dance
to combine colors to create different colors.
ACTIVITIES—DANCING; CONCEPTS—COLOR.

761    *Holes and Peeks.* Ill. by the author. Greenwillow, 1984 (0-688-02537-4); LB (0-688-02538-2). USE LEVEL: PS
*African American*
A little girl looks around her bathroom and describes the holes
that she is afraid of.
ACTIVITIES—PLAYING; EMOTIONS—FEAR; PROBLEM SOLVING.

762    *The Quilt.* Ill. by the author. Greenwillow, 1984 (0-688-03825-5); LB (0-688-03826-3); Puffin, pap. (0-14-055308-8). USE
LEVEL: PS/P
*African American*
As a little girl sleeps, she dreams that the patches on her quilt
are places she can visit. She imagines she is looking for her miss-
ing stuffed dog, only to wake up and find the dog on the floor.
BEDTIME; DREAMS; QUILTS.

763    *The Trek.* Ill. by the author. Greenwillow, 1985 (0-688-04799-8); LB (0-688-04800-5); pap. (0-688-08742-6). USE LEVEL:
PS/P
*African American*
Walking to school, a little girl imagines that she sees animals all
around her.
ACTIVITIES—WALKING; ANIMALS; GAMES; IMAGINATION.

764    *When You Were a Baby.* Ill. by the author. Greenwillow, 1982
(0-688-00863-1); LB (0-688-00864-X). USE LEVEL: PS
*African American*
A preschooler describes all the things that could not be done by
a baby.
ACTIVITIES; BABIES, TODDLERS; BEHAVIOR—GROWING UP.

**JONES, HETTIE, SELECTOR**

765    *The Trees Stand Shining: Poetry of the North American Indians.*

Ill. by Robert Andrew Parker. Dial, 1971 (0-8037-9083-X); LB (0-8037-9084-8). USE LEVEL: M

*Native American*

These poems, collected from many Native American peoples, have the recurring theme of respect for the natural world.

ECOLOGY; NATURE; POETRY, RHYME.

**JONES, REBECCA C.**

766    *Matthew and Tilly.* Ill. by Beth Peck. Dutton, 1991 (0-525-44684-2). USE LEVEL: P

*African American*

These two friends enjoy the time they spend together in their urban neighborhood, even though they sometimes disagree.

BEHAVIOR—GETTING ALONG WITH OTHERS; COMMUNITIES, NEIGHBOR-HOODS; FRIENDSHIP; URBAN LIFE.

**JOOSSE, BARBARA**

767    *Mama, Do You Love Me?* Ill. by Barbara Lavallee. Chronicle, 1991 (0-87701-759-X). USE LEVEL: PS/P

*Native American—Inuit*

An Inuit mother reassures her daughter that she is loved. Cultural information about the Inuit follows the text.

ARCTIC LANDS; EMOTIONS—LOVE; FAMILY LIFE—MOTHERS.

**JORDAN, JUNE**

768    *Kimako's Story.* Ill. by Kay Burford. Houghton, 1981 pap. (0-395-60338-2). USE LEVEL: P

*African American*

Kimako is seven and she lives in an urban neighborhood. She is often left without adult supervision, and she describes how she passes the time—watching TV, reading, and writing poetry. What she really likes is watching Bobby's dog, Bucks.

ANIMALS—DOGS; COMMUNITIES, NEIGHBORHOODS; FAMILY LIFE; PETS; URBAN LIFE.

769    *New Life: New Room.* Ill. by Ray Cruz. HarperCollins, 1975 (0-690-00211-4); LB (0-690-00212-2). USE LEVEL: M

*African American*

With a new baby coming, the Robinsons must rearrange the living space and the three children, Rudy, Tyrone, and Linda, must share a room.

BEHAVIOR—SHARING; FAMILY LIFE; URBAN LIFE.

**JOSEPH, LYNN**

770   *Coconut Kind of Day: Island Poems*. Ill. by Sandra Speidel.
Lothrop, 1990 (0-688-09119-9); LB (0-688-09120-2). USE
LEVEL: M
*Caribbean*
Tropical colors and rhythmic poems describe the experiences of
a young girl in Trinidad.
FOREIGN LANDS—CARIBBEAN ISLANDS; ISLANDS; POETRY, RHYME.

771   *An Island Christmas*. Ill. by Catherine Stock. Houghton, 1992
(0-395-58761-1). USE LEVEL: P
*Caribbean*
Preparing for Christmas includes many traditional activities, like
making black currant cake and soursop ice cream as well as dec-
orating a tree, singing, and giving gifts.
FAMILY LIFE; FOREIGN LANDS—CARIBBEAN ISLANDS; HOLIDAYS—
CHRISTMAS.

772   *Jasmine's Parlour Day*. Ill. by Ann Grifalconi. Lothrop, 1994
(0-688-11487-3); LB (0-688-11488-1). USE LEVEL: P
*Caribbean—Trinidad*
Parlour day is when Mama and Jasmine go to a wooden parlour
stall at the market to sell fish and sugar cakes. Language and
colors capture the images of Trinidad.
FAMILY LIFE—MOTHERS; FOREIGN LANDS—CARIBBEAN ISLANDS—
TRINIDAD; ISLANDS; MARKETS.

773   *The Mermaid's Twin Sister: More Stories from Trinidad*. Ill. by
Donna Perrone. Houghton, 1994 (0-395-64365-1). USE LEVEL:
M
*Caribbean*
Six stories present images of spirits and magical beings, of island
life and storytelling traditions.
FOLKTALES—CARIBBEAN ISLANDS; SHORT STORIES; STORYTELLING.

774   *A Wave in Her Pocket: Stories from Trinidad*. Ill. by Brian
Pinkney. Houghton, 1991 (0-395-54432-7). USE LEVEL: M/U
*Caribbean*
Six stories are related here, some from the folklore of Trinidad,
some reflecting the heritage of Africa.
FOLKTALES—CARIBBEAN ISLANDS; FOREIGN LANDS—CARIBBEAN ISLANDS;
ISLANDS; SHORT STORIES.

**KALMAN, MAIRA**

775 *Sayonora, Mrs. Kackleman.* Ill. by the author. Viking, 1989 (0-670-82945-5); Puffin, pap. (0-14-054159-4). USE LEVEL: P
*Asian—Japan*
Lulu escapes her piano lesson with Mrs. Kackleman by traveling to Japan with her brother, Alexander. With their tour guide, Hiroki, they visit the subway, a school, a noodle restaurant, and other sites before going home.
ACTIVITIES—TRAVELING; FAMILY LIFE—SIBLINGS; FOREIGN LANDS—ASIA—JAPAN; FOREIGN LANGUAGES.

**KAMAL, ALEPH**

776 *The Bird Who Was an Elephant.* Ill. by Frané Lessac. HarperCollins, 1990 (0-397-32445-6); LB (0-397-32446-4). USE LEVEL: M
*Asian—India*
The bird flies into the village and visits the river, the shops, a chai shop for a tiffin (tea break), even a palmist. The palmist tells the bird that it was an elephant in a former life and next would be a fish.
BIRDS; FOREIGN LANDS—ASIA—INDIA; FOREIGN LANGUAGES.

**KEATS, EZRA JACK**

777 *Dreams.* Ill. by the author. Macmillan, 1974 (0-02-749611-2); pap. (0-689-71599-4). USE LEVEL: PS/P
*Hispanic American*
Everyone is asleep and dreaming but Roberto. When his paper mouse falls out of his window, the eerie shadows that are cast save his friend Archie's cat from a threatening dog.
DREAMS; IMAGINATION; NIGHT; SHADOWS; SLEEP.

778 *Goggles.* Ill. by the author. Macmillan, 1969, pap. (0-689-71157-3). USE LEVEL: P
*African American*
Peter and Archie find some goggles and get chased by some older boys.
BEHAVIOR—BULLYING; CALDECOTT AWARD; GLASSES; PROBLEM SOLVING; URBAN LIFE.

779 *Hi, Cat!* Ill. by the author. Macmillan, 1970, pap. (0-689-71258-8). USE LEVEL: PS/P
*African American*
Does Archie pick his own pet or does the pet pick Archie? A cat follows Archie and Peter around their neighborhood.
ANIMALS—CATS; PETS; URBAN LIFE.

780     *John Henry: An American Legend.* Ill. by the author. Knopf,
        1987, LB (0-394-99052-8); pap. (0-394-89052-3). USE LEVEL:
        M
        ***African American***
        John Henry's strength made him famous as a worker on the
        railroad.
        CHARACTER TRAITS—PERSEVERANCE; CHARACTER TRAITS—PRIDE;
        FOLKTALES—UNITED STATES; TRAINS.

781     *A Letter to Amy.* Ill. by the author. HarperCollins, 1968 (0-06-
        023108-4); LB (0-06-023109-2); pap. (0-06-443063-4). USE
        LEVEL: P
        ***African American***
        Peter writes an invitation for Amy to come to his birthday party.
        ACTIVITIES—WRITING; BIRTHDAYS; FRIENDSHIP; LETTERS; PARTIES.

782     *Louie.* Ill. by the author. Greenwillow, 1975 (0-688-02383-5).
        USE LEVEL: P
        ***Multicultural***
        When he sees a puppet show, Louie is entranced. Later, he is
        given a puppet.
        CHARACTER TRAITS—SHYNESS; EMOTIONS—LONELINESS; PUPPETS;
        URBAN LIFE.

783     *Louie's Search.* Ill. by the author. Macmillan, 1980 (0-02-
        749700-3); pap. (0-689-71354-1). USE LEVEL: P
        ***Multicultural***
        Louie wants a father, so he looks around his neighborhood. He
        is accused of stealing a music box but is able to explain.
        BEHAVIOR—NEEDING SOMEONE; FAMILY LIFE; URBAN LIFE.

784     *Pet Show!* Ill. by the author. Macmillan, 1972 (0-02-749620);
        pap. (0-689-71159-X). USE LEVEL: PS/P
        ***African American***
        Archie cannot find his cat for the pet show, so he creates a pet—
        a germ.
        ANIMALS; ANIMALS—CATS; PETS; URBAN LIFE.

785     *Peter's Chair.* Ill. by the author. HarperCollins, 1967 (0-06-
        023111-4); LB (0-06-023112-2); pap. (0-06-443040-5). USE
        LEVEL: PS/P
        ***African American***
        Peter sees many of his old things being readied for the new
        baby.
        BABIES, TODDLERS; BEHAVIOR—SHARING; FAMILY LIFE; FURNITURE—
        CHAIRS; SELF-CONCEPT.

786    *The Snowy Day*. Ill. by the author. Viking, 1962 (0-670-65400-0); Puffin, pap. (0-14-050182-7). USE LEVEL: PS/P
*African American*
Peter enjoys his day in the snow, making a snowman and snow angels. He even tries to save some snow for later.
ACTIVITIES—PLAYING; CALDECOTT AWARD; SEASONS—WINTER; WEATHER—SNOW.

787    *The Trip*. Ill. by the author. Greenwillow, 1978, LB (0-688-84123-6); pap. (0-688-07328-X). USE LEVEL: P
*Multicultural*
Louie's family is new in the neighborhood. He misses his old friends and imagines that he flies back to see them.
ACTIVITIES—FLYING; EMOTIONS—LONELINESS; FRIENDSHIP; HOLIDAYS—HALLOWEEN; IMAGINATION; MOVING.

788    *Whistle for Willie*. Ill. by the author. Viking, 1964 (0-670-76240-7); Puffin, pap. (0-14-050202-5). USE LEVEL: PS/P
*African American*
Peter wishes he could whistle so he could surprise his dog, Willie.
ACTIVITIES—WHISTLING; ANIMALS—DOGS; PETS; PROBLEM SOLVING; SELF-CONCEPT.

**KEATS, EZRA JACK, AND PAT CHERR**
789    *My Dog Is Lost!* Ill. by the authors. Harper, 1960, o.p. USE LEVEL: P
*Hispanic American—Puerto Rico*
On his eighth birthday, Juanito and his family arrive in New York from Puerto Rico. Now, Juanito's dog is lost and he is worried. His dog only knows Spanish. Juanito searches the neighborhood and is helped by many people.
ANIMALS—DOGS; BEHAVIOR—LOST; CHARACTER TRAITS—HELPFULNESS; FOREIGN LANGUAGES.

**KEEGAN, MARCIA**
790    *Pueblo Boy: Growing Up in Two Worlds*. Photos by the author. Dutton, 1991 (0-525-65060-1). USE LEVEL: M
*Native American—Pueblo*
Timmy Roybal, ten, is in the fifth grade and lives in New Mexico. He works on math and on a computer, but he also learns about the art and ceremonies of the Pueblo people. He participates in ceremonial activities, including the Corn Dance.
BEHAVIOR—GROWING UP; FAMILY LIFE.

**KELLER, HOLLY**

791   *Grandfather's Dream.* Ill. by the author. Greenwillow, 1994 (0-688-12339-2); LB (0-688-12340-6). USE LEVEL: P

*Asian—Vietnam*

Grandfather wants to restore the wetlands, hoping that the cranes will return. Others in the village want to use the land to grow more rice.

BIRDS—CRANES; ECOLOGY; ENVIRONMENT; FAMILY LIFE—GRANDFA-THERS; FOREIGN LANDS—ASIA—VIETNAM.

792   *Island Baby.* Ill. by the author. Greenwillow, 1992 (0-688-10579-3); LB (0-688-10580-7). USE LEVEL: P

*Caribbean*

Simon's grandfather cares for injured birds. With his grandfather's help, Simon rescues a wounded flamingo and nurses it back to health.

BIRDS—FLAMINGOS; ECOLOGY; FOREIGN LANDS—CARIBBEAN ISLANDS; ISLANDS; NATURE.

**KENDALL, CAROL, AND YAO-WEN LI, RETELLERS**

793   *Sweet and Sour: Tales from China.* Ill. by Shirley Felts. Houghton, 1979, o.p. USE LEVEL: M

*Asian—China*

There are 24 Chinese folktales in this collection, including "The Clever Wife," "Golden Life," and "The Noodle."

FOLKTALES—ASIA—CHINA; SHORT STORIES.

**KENDALL, RUSS**

794   *Eskimo Boy: Life in an Inupiaq Eskimo Village.* Photos by the author. Scholastic, 1992 (0-590-43695-3). USE LEVEL: M

*Native American—Inupiaq*

Norman Kokeok, seven, is an Inupiaq Eskimo boy who lives with his family on the northwest coast of Alaska. He goes ice fishing with his father, but he is not old enough to hunt. He attends school and participates in familiar activities.

ARCTIC LANDS; BEHAVIOR—GROWING UP; FAMILY LIFE.

**KENDALL, SARITA**

795   *Ransom for a River Dolphin.* Lerner, 1992 (0-8225-0735-8). USE LEVEL: U

*South American—Colombia*

In the Amazon River, Carmenza and Ramiro find an injured dolphin. With the help of Ramiro's father, Omar, they care for the dolphin, keeping it hidden in the shallow water. Carmenza realizes that her stepfather is the cause of the dolphin's injury.

ANIMALS—DOLPHINS; ECOLOGY; FOREIGN LANDS—SOUTH AMERICA—
COLOMBIA; NATURE.

### KESEY, KEN

796    *The Sea Lion: A Story of the Sea Cliff People.* Ill. by Neil
Waldman. Viking, 1991 (0-670-83916-7); Puffin, pap. (0-14-
054950-1). USE LEVEL: M
*Native American—Northwest Coast*
Eemook's name means "the broken gift." He was given that
name because of his handicaps and he is demeaned by his peo-
ple. When the Lion of the Sea enchants his people, Eemook
saves them through his bravery and cleverness.
ANIMALS—SEA LIONS; CHARACTER TRAITS—BRAVERY; HANDICAPS—PHYSI-
CAL; MAGIC.

### KESSEL, JOYCE K.

797    *Squanto and the First Thanksgiving.* Ill. by Lisa Donze.
Carolrhoda, 1983 (0-87614-199-8); pap. (0-87614-452-0).
USE LEVEL: P
*Native American—Patuxet*
When the English colonists first came to Plymouth, they cap-
tured Squanto and some other braves, sent them to England,
and sold them as slaves. Squanto learned to speak English. He
returned to Plymouth and helped the Pilgrims.
CELEBRATIONS; CHARACTER TRAITS—HELPFULNESS; HOLIDAYS—
THANKSGIVING; U.S. HISTORY—PILGRIMS.

### KESSLER, CRISTINA

798    *One Night: A Story from the Desert.* Ill. by Ian Schoenherr.
Putnam, 1995 (0-399-22726-1). USE LEVEL: P
*Middle Eastern—Tuareg*
Muhamad has learned about life in the desert from his grand-
mother and his father. When he herds the goats by himself, he
takes the responsibility for helping a mother goat deliver her
kid. His family is proud of his independence.
ANIMALS—GOATS; DESERT; DESERT; FAMILY LIFE; FOREIGN LANDS—
MIDDLE EAST—TUAREG.

### KETTEMAN, HELEN

799    *Not Yet, Yvette.* Ill. by Irene Trivas. Whitman, 1992, LB (0-
8075-5771-4); pap. (0-8075-5772-2). USE LEVEL: PS/P
*African American*
As they straighten up the house, Yvette keeps asking her father if
it is time yet. They buy gifts, bake a cake, and set the table and
finally it is time for Mother's surprise birthday party.
BIRTHDAYS; CHARACTER TRAITS—PATIENCE; CHARACTER TRAITS—QUES-
TIONING; FAMILY LIFE; PARTIES.

**KHERDIAN, DAVID, RETELLER**

800    *Feathers and Tails: Animal Fables from Around the World.* Ill. by
Nonny Hogrogian. Putnam, 1992, LB (0-399-21876-9). USE
LEVEL: M
*Multicultural*
Familiar fables, like those from Aesop, are presented along with
less familiar stories from West Africa, India, and the Muskogee
people, introducing readers to a variety of stories teaching
lessons.
ANIMALS; FABLES; FOLKTALES; SHORT STORIES.

**KIDD, DIANA**

801    *Onion Tears.* Ill. by Lucy Montgomery. Orchard, 1991 (0-531-
05870-1); LB (0-531-08470-1); Morrow, pap. (0-688-11862-
3). USE LEVEL: M
*Asian—Vietnam*
When she settles in Australia, Nam-Huong misses her family
and customs in Vietnam. Her loneliness is captured in letters
she writes to animals she had known in Vietnam.
EMOTIONS—LONELINESS; EMOTIONS—SADNESS; FOREIGN LANDS—ASIA—
VIETNAM; FOREIGN LANDS—AUSTRALIA.

**KIMMEL, ERIC A., RETELLER**

802    *Anansi and the Moss-Covered Rock.* Ill. by Janet Stevens.
Holiday, 1988 (0-8234-0689-X); LB (0-8234-0798-5). USE
LEVEL: M
*African*
Anansi tricks the animals and takes their food until Little Bush
Deer tricks Anansi.
ANIMALS; BEHAVIOR—TRICKERY; CHARACTER TRAITS—LAZINESS;
FOLKTALES—AFRICA; SPIDERS.

803    *Anansi and the Talking Melon.* Ill. by Janet Stevens. Holiday,
1994 (0-8234-1104-4). USE LEVEL: M
*African*
Anansi climbs into a melon and eats so much he cannot get out.
He tricks his animal friends into believing the melon can talk.
ANIMALS; BEHAVIOR—TRICKERY; CHARACTER TRAITS—FOOLISHNESS;
FOLKTALES—AFRICA; SPIDERS.

804    *Anansi Goes Fishing.* Ill. by Janet Stevens. Holiday, 1992 (0-
8234-0918-X); pap. (0-8234-1022-6). USE LEVEL: M
*African*
Anansi wants to eat fish and thinks he can trick Turtle into
doing all the work.
BEHAVIOR—TRICKERY; CHARACTER TRAITS—LAZINESS; FOLKTALES—
AFRICA; REPTILES—TURTLES, TORTOISES; POURQUOI TALES; SPIDERS.

805    *The Greatest of All: A Japanese Folktale.* Ill. by Giora Carmi.
       Holiday, 1991 (0-8234-0885-X). USE LEVEL: M
       *Asian—Japan*
       Father Mouse wants only the very best for his daughter, Chuko.
       After asking many others, Father Mouse chooses another field
       mouse to be Chuko's husband.
       ANIMALS—MICE; CHARACTER TRAITS—PRIDE; FOLKTALES—ASIA—JAPAN;
       WEDDINGS.

806    *The Tale of Aladdin and the Wonderful Lamp: A Story from the
       Arabian Nights.* Ill. by Ju-Hong Chen. Holiday, 1992 (0-8234-
       0938-4). USE LEVEL: M
       *Middle Eastern—Arabia*
       A magician pretends to be Aladdin's uncle and tricks Aladdin
       into entering an underground cavern. Aladdin releases a *djinn*
       from an old lamp he finds there, who grants his wishes and
       helps him win the hand of Princess Shadjarr ad-Darr.
       FOLKTALES—MIDDLE EAST—ARABIA; MAGIC.

807    *The Three Princes: A Tale from the Middle East.* Ill. by Leonard
       Everett Fisher. Holiday, 1994 (0-8234-1115-X). USE LEVEL: M
       *Middle Eastern—Arabia*
       The princess will marry the prince who brings her the greatest
       wonder. When all three princes work to save her life, the
       princess must choose one for her husband.
       DESERT; FOLKTALES—MIDDLE EAST—ARABIA; MAGIC; ROYALTY.

808    *The Witch's Face: A Mexican Tale.* Ill. by Fabricio Vanden
       Broeck. Holiday, 1993 (0-8234-1038-2). USE LEVEL: M
       *Mexican*
       On his way home, Don Aurelio stays in the home of three
       women, two of whom are witches. Don Aurelio is aided by the
       third woman, Emilia, but breaks his promise to her.
       CHARACTER TRAITS—APPEARANCE; FOLKTALES—MEXICO; MAGIC;
       WITCHES.

       **KLINE, SUZY**
809    *Horrible Harry and the Ant Invasion.* Ill. by Frank Remkiewicz.
       Viking, 1989, LB (0-670-82469-0); Puffin, pap. (0-14-
       032914-5). USE LEVEL: M
       *Asian American—Korea*
       Harry loses his job as "ant monitor" when he is bitten by some
       escaped ants. Song Lee, a Korean American girl, is a close friend
       and classmate of Harry's.
       FRIENDSHIP; INSECTS—ANTS; SCHOOL.

810    *Horrible Harry and the Christmas Surprise.* Ill. by Frank
       Remkiewicz. Viking, 1981, LB (0-670-83357-6). USE LEVEL: M
       *Asian American—Korea*
       Horrible Harry, Song Lee, and the kids in Miss Mackle's class
       are upset when Miss Mackle hurts her knee and Mr. Cardini,
       the principal, takes over their class. Song Lee provides some
       details about Christmas in Korea.
       FRIENDSHIP; HOLIDAYS—CHRISTMAS; SCHOOL.

811    *Horrible Harry and the Green Slime.* Ill. by Frank Remkiewicz.
       Viking, 1989, LB (0-670-82468-2); Puffin, pap. (0-14-
       032913-7). USE LEVEL: M
       *Asian American—Korea*
       In this second-grade classroom, Song Lee, a Korean girl now
       living in America, has a featured role. In this book, the class
       sends secret pal gifts and puts on a skit.
       FRIENDSHIP; SCHOOL.

812    *Horrible Harry and the Kickball Wedding.* Ill. by Frank
       Remkiewicz. Viking, 1992, LB (0-670-83358-4); Puffin, pap.
       (0-14-034453-5). USE LEVEL: M
       *Asian American—Korea*
       Harry and Song Lee, a Korean girl in his second-grade class,
       plan a Valentine's Day wedding for fun.
       FRIENDSHIP; HOLIDAYS—VALENTINE'S DAY; SCHOOL; WEDDINGS.

813    *Horrible Harry in Room 2B.* Ill. by Frank Remkiewicz. Viking,
       1988, LB (0-670-82176-4); Puffin, pap. (0-14-032825-4). USE
       LEVEL: M
       *Asian American—Korea*
       This book introduces Harry and his classmates, including Song
       Lee, a Korean girl. Harry likes Song Lee, so he shows her a
       garter snake.
       FRIENDSHIP; SCHOOL.

814    *Horrible Harry's Secret.* Ill. by Frank Remkiewicz. Viking, 1990,
       LB (0-670-82470-4); Puffin, pap. (0-14-032915-3). USE LEVEL:
       M
       *Asian American—Korea*
       Harry falls in love with Song Lee, a Korean girl in his class. He
       is first smitten when she shares her water frog with him and his
       classmates.
       FRIENDSHIP; SCHOOL.

815 *Song Lee and the Hamster Hunt.* Ill. by Frank Remkiewicz. Viking, 1994 (0-670-84773-9). USE LEVEL: M
*Asian American—Korea*
Song Lee, a Korean American student in Horrible Harry's class, is featured in this book in which her hamster, Yi, is being studied as a science project. When Yi escapes, the whole class becomes involved in finding him.
ANIMALS—HAMSTERS; FRIENDSHIP; PETS; SCHOOL.

816 *Song Lee in Room 2B.* Ill. by Frank Remkiewicz. Viking, 1993, LB (0-670-84772-0). USE LEVEL: M
*Asian American—Korea*
Song Lee and her classmates in Room 2B (including Horrible Harry) enjoy the winter weather and being friends, but Song Lee does not like performing in front of the class.
BEHAVIOR—SHYNESS; FRIENDSHIP; SCHOOL.

KNIGHT, MARGY BURNS
817 *Talking Walls.* Ill. by Anne Sibley O'Brien. Tilbury House, 1992 (0-88448-102-6); pap. (0-88448-154-9). USE LEVEL: M
*Multicultural*
This book describes 14 walls around the world, including Aborigine wall art, Muslim walls, the Vietnam Veterans Memorial, and the Berlin Wall.
FOREIGN LANDS; HISTORY; WALLS.

818 *Who Belongs Here? An American Story.* Ill. by Anne Sibley O'Brien. Tilbury House, 1993, pap. (0-88448-111-5). USE LEVEL: M
*Asian American—Cambodia*
Nary lives in the United States with his grandparents. His parents were killed in the civil war in Cambodia. A counterpoint to his story is information about other immigrants in the United States and about the problems and promise for Nary.
PREJUDICE; REFUGEES; WORLD.

KNUTSON, BARBARA, RETELLER
819 *How the Guinea Fowl Got Her Spots: A Swahili Tale of Friendship.* Ill. by the reteller. Carolrhoda, 1990, LB (0-87614-416-4); pap. (0-87614-537-3). USE LEVEL: M
*African—Swahili*
After helping Cow, Guinea Fowl is rewarded by being sprinkled with Cow's milk, which creates spots that allow Guinea Fowl to hide more easily.
ANIMALS; BIRDS—GUINEA FOWL; FOLKTALES—AFRICA—SWAHILI; FRIENDSHIP; POURQUOI TALES.

820     *Sungura and Leopard: A Swahili Trickster Tale.* Ill. by the reteller. Little, Brown, 1993 (0-316-50010-0). USE LEVEL: M
*African—Swahili*
Sungura, the hare, decides to build his house on a hill, but so does Leopard.
ANIMALS—LEOPARDS; ANIMALS—RABBITS; BEHAVIOR—TRICKERY; FOLKTALES—AFRICA—SWAHILI.

821     *Why the Crab Has No Head: An African Tale.* Ill. by the reteller. Carolrhoda, 1987, LB (0-87614-322-2); pap. (0-87614-489-X). USE LEVEL: M
*African—Zaire*
When Nzambi was creating the animals, she was too tired to finish the crab. Crab annoys Nzambi when she wants to sleep, so Nzambi leaves crab without a head. He is so embarrassed, he still walks sideways.
BEHAVIOR—BOASTING; CREATION; CRUSTACEA; FOLKTALES—AFRICA—ZAIRE; POURQUOI TALES.

**KONIGSBURG, E. L.**
822     *Jennifer, Hecate, Macbeth, William McKinley, and Me, Elizabeth.* Ill. by the author. Macmillan, 1967 (0-689-30007-7); Dell, pap. (0-440-44162-5). USE LEVEL: M
*African American*
Elizabeth, who is white, and Jennifer, who is black, become friends and share their interest in witchcraft.
FRIENDSHIP; NEWBERY AWARD; SCHOOL; WITCHCRAFT.

**KRENSKY, STEPHEN**
823     *Children of the Wind and Water: Five Stories about Native American Children.* Ill. by James Watling. Scholastic, 1994, pap. (0-590-46963-0). USE LEVEL: M
*Native American*
In these stories, the daily activities of children are featured. Muskogee, Dakota, Huron, Tlingit, and Nootka peoples are represented. In one story, a girl trades her armband for some deerskins. In another, a boy prepares to paint a totem.
BEHAVIOR—GROWING UP; SHORT STORIES.

824     *The Iron Dragon Never Sleeps.* Ill. by John Fulweiler. Delacorte, 1994 (0-385-31171-0). USE LEVEL: U
*Asian American—China*
Winnie Tucker, ten, has come to live in California in 1867. She befriends a Chinese boy, Lee Cheng, and she learns about the

harsh life of the Chinese immigrants who are building the transcontinental railroad.

PREJUDICE; TRAINS; U.S. HISTORY.

**KROLL, VIRGINIA**

825 *Africa Brothers and Sisters.* Ill. by Vanessa French. Macmillan, 1993 (0-02-751166-9). USE LEVEL: P

*African American*

Jesse and his father discuss their link to the peoples of Africa.

COMMUNITIES, NEIGHBORHOODS; FAMILY LIFE—FATHERS; FOREIGN LANDS—AFRICA.

826 *Jaha and Jamil Went Down the Hill: An African Mother Goose.* Ill. by Katherine Roundtree. Charlesbridge, 1995 (0-88106-866-7); LB (0-88106-867-5); pap. (0-88106-865-9). USE LEVEL: P

*African*

Using well-known Mother Goose rhymes as a pattern, these verses reflect the experiences of children in Africa. African animals, like gazelles, pangolin, and colobus, and activities, like dancing and going to market, are featured.

ACTIVITIES; ANIMALS; FOREIGN LANDS—AFRICA; NURSERY RHYMES; POETRY, RHYME.

827 *Masai and I.* Ill. by Nancy Carpenter. Macmillan, 1992 (0-02-751165-0). USE LEVEL: P

*African—Masai*

While learning about East Africa, Linda develops a feeling of kinship with the Masai.

COMMUNITIES, NEIGHBORHOODS; FAMILY LIFE; FOREIGN LANDS—AFRICA—MASAI.

828 *Pink Paper Swans.* Ill. by Nancy L. Clouse. Eerdmans, 1994 (0-8028-5081-2). USE LEVEL: P

*Multicultural*

One summer, Janetta, who is African American, watches her neighbor from Japan, Mrs. Tsujimoto, create origami figures. The following summer, Mrs. Tsujimoto's arthritis prevents her from doing origami and Janetta learns from her.

ACTIVITIES—PAPERFOLDING; FRIENDSHIP; ILLNESS; OLDER ADULTS.

829 *The Seasons and Someone.* Ill. by Tatsuro Kiuchi. Harcourt, 1994 (0-15-271233-X). USE LEVEL: M

*Native American—Eskimo*

A young Eskimo, who is called "Someone," enjoys the changing seasons. She knows that warmer weather will return and she will pick basketfuls of berries. She also knows that she must thank the beautiful land and plant new seeds.

ARCTIC LANDS; FOLKTALES—NATIVE AMERICAN—ESKIMO; SEASONS.

830   *Wood-hoopoe Willie*. Ill. by Katherine Roundtree. Charlesbridge, 1992 (0-88106-409-2); LB (0-88106-410-6); pap. (0-88106-408-4). USE LEVEL: P
*African American*
Willie is filled with music and rhythm. His activities are often distracting at home, school, and church, but he reminds Grandpa of the wood-hoopoe bird in Africa. When there is no drummer for the Kwanzaa celebration, Willie plays the drums.

BIRDS—WOOD-HOOPOES; FAMILY LIFE—GRANDFATHERS; HOLIDAYS—
KWANZAA; MUSIC; SELF-CONCEPT.

KRULL, KATHLEEN
831   *Maria Molina and the Days of the Dead*. Ill. by Enrique O. Sanchez. Macmillan, 1994 (0-02-750999-0). USE LEVEL: M
*Mexican*
In Mexico, Maria and her family remember their loved ones on the Days of the Dead. Even after her family moves to the United States and Maria celebrates Halloween during the festival time, she is still able to remember.

DEATH; FAMILY LIFE; FOREIGN LANDS—MEXICO; HOLIDAYS.

KUDLINSKI, KATHLEEN V.
832   *Night Bird: A Story of the Seminole Indians*. Ill. by James Watling. Viking, 1993, LB (0-670-83157-3); Puffin, pap. (0-14-034353-9). USE LEVEL: M
*Native American—Seminole*
In 1840, Night Bird and her people, the Seminole, are facing relocation from Florida to Oklahoma.

CHARACTER TRAITS—BRAVERY; EVERGLADES; RELOCATION; U.S.
HISTORY.

KURTZ, JANE
833   *Fire on the Mountain*. Ill. by E. B. Lewis. Simon & Schuster, 1994 (0-671-88268-6). USE LEVEL: M
*African—Ethiopia*
The rich man challenges Alemayu to stay on the mountain with only a thin cloak to keep him warm. When Alemayu succeeds, the greedy man tries to cheat him out of his prize.

BEHAVIOR—GREED; CAREERS—SHEPHERDS; FAMILY LIFE—SIBLINGS;
FOLKTALES—AFRICA—ETHIOPIA.

KWON, HOLLY H., RETELLER

834 *The Moles and the Mireuk: A Korean Folktale*. Ill. by Woodleigh Hubbard. Houghton, 1993 (0-395-64347-3). USE LEVEL: M
*Asian—Korea*
Papa Mole travels to the sky, the sun, the clouds, and the wind searching for the best husband for his daughter. He asks the stone Mireuk to marry her, but finds that it is afraid of moles, so Papa Mole chooses a mole for his daughter to marry.
ANIMALS—MOLES; CHARACTER TRAITS—PRIDE; FOLKTALES—ASIA—KOREA; WEDDINGS.

LACAPA, KATHLEEN, AND MICHAEL LACAPA

835 *Less Than Half, More Than Whole*. Ill. by Michael Lacapa. Northland, 1994 (0-87358-592-5). USE LEVEL: M
*Multicultural*
A young boy questions his family about his heritage, part Anglo and part Indian. He realizes that his differences make him unique and special.
CHARACTER TRAITS—PRIDE; EMOTIONS; FAMILY LIFE; MARRIAGE, INTER-RACIAL; SELF-CONCEPT.

LACAPA, MICHAEL, RETELLER

836 *Antelope Woman: An Apache Folktale*. Ill. by the reteller. Northland, 1992 (0-87358-543-7). USE LEVEL: M
*Native American—Apache*
A beautiful young woman is not interested in the men in her village. When a young man comes and teaches about caring for the earth and honoring its creatures, she follows him. Both are transformed into antelopes, but later return to her people.
ANIMALS—ANTELOPES; FOLKTALES—NATIVE AMERICAN—APACHE; NATURE.

837 *The Flute Player: An Apache Folktale*. Ill. by the reteller. Northland, 1990 (0-87358-500-3). USE LEVEL: M
*Native American—Apache*
A young boy meets a young girl at a social dance. Later when she works in her father's fields, she hears the boy's flute. When he goes on a hunt, she misses his music and becomes ill and dies. He returns and, after learning of her death, he disappears.
DEATH; EMOTIONS—LOVE; FOLKTALES—NATIVE AMERICAN—APACHE; MUSIC.

LANGER, NOLA

838 *Rafiki*. Ill. by the author. Viking, 1977 (0-670-58907-1). USE LEVEL: P
*African*

Even though the lion's advice is foolish, the animals listen to him. A little girl, Rafiki, helps them make their own decisions.
ANIMALS; FOREIGN LANDS—AFRICA.

**LANGSTAFF, JOHN, EDITOR**
839    *Climbing Jacob's Ladder: Heroes of the Bible in African-American Spirituals.* Piano arrangements by John Andrew Ross. Ill. by Ashley Bryan. Macmillan, 1991 (0-689-50494-2). USE LEVEL: P/M
*African American*
The spiritual "Didn't It Rain?" describes the experiences of Noah on the ark. Some other songs are "Rock-a-My Soul," "Go Down, Moses," and "Ezekiel Saw the Wheel."
BIBLE; MUSIC; RELIGION; SONGS.

840    *What a Morning! The Christmas Story in Black Spirituals.* Arrangements for singing and piano by John Andrew Ross. Ill. by Ashley Bryan. Macmillan, 1987 (0-689-50422-5). USE LEVEL: P/M
*African American*
The five songs in this book focus on the Nativity and celebrate the Christmas story.
CORETTA SCOTT KING AWARD; HOLIDAYS—CHRISTMAS; MUSIC; RELIGION; SONGS.

**LANKFORD, MARY D.**
841    *Hopscotch Around the World.* Ill. by Karen Milone. Morrow, 1992 (0-688-08419-2); LB (0-688-08420-6). USE LEVEL: P/M
*Multicultural*
Many versions of hopscotch are played around the world, including Pele, which is played in Aruba, and Ta Galagala, which is played in Nigeria. Nineteen hopscotch games are described and a map of locations is included.
ACTIVITIES—PLAYING; FOREIGN LANDS; GAMES; SPORTS.

**LARRICK, NANCY, SELECTOR**
842    *The Night of the Whippoorwill: Poems.* Ill. by David Ray. Putnam, 1992 (0-399-21874-2). USE LEVEL: M
*Multicultural*
Poems about the night are presented from many poets and cultures, including the Hopi people and the Papago Indians.
NIGHT; POETRY, RHYME.

**LARRY, CHARLES, RETELLER**
843    *Peboan and Seegwun.* Ill. by the reteller. Farrar, 1993 (0-374-35773-0). USE LEVEL: M
*Native American—Ojibway*

Peboan, an old man, sits alone in his hut. Through him, winter comes. A young man, Seegwun, comes to visit with the power of bringing spring.

FOLKTALES—NATIVE AMERICAN—OJIBWAY; SEASONS.

### LASKY, KATHRYN

844 *Cloud Eyes.* Ill. by Barry Moser. Harcourt, 1994 (0-15-219168-2). USE LEVEL: M

*Native American*

The bears take all the honey, angering the bees. Cloud Eyes learns from the bees and finds a way to get honey for his people.

ANIMALS—BEARS; FOOD; INSECTS—BEES; PROBLEM SOLVING.

### LATTIMORE, DEBORAH NOURSE

845 *The Dragon's Robe.* Ill. by the author. HarperCollins, 1990 (0-06-023719-8); LB (0-06-023723-6); Trophy, pap. (0-06-443321-8). USE LEVEL: M

*Asian—China*

Kwan Yin is a weaver on her way to the emperor's palace. She helps the keeper of the royal rain dragon's shrine. When two noblemen do not deliver gifts to the shrine, the dragon brings a drought. Kwan Yin weaves a robe as a gift to the dragon.

ACTIVITIES—WEAVING; CHARACTER TRAITS—GENEROSITY; CHARACTER TRAITS—SELFISHNESS; CLOTHING; DRAGONS; FOLKTALES—ASIA—CHINA; WEATHER—DROUGHTS.

846 *The Flame of Peace: A Tale of the Aztecs.* Ill. by the author. HarperCollins, 1987 (0-06-023708-2); LB (0-06-023709-0); pap. (0-06-443272-6). USE LEVEL: M

*Mexican—Aztec*

The Emperor Itzcoatl and his people are going to battle with Tezozomoc and his army. A boy called Two Flint wants peace, so he travels to Lord Morning Star to get New Fire for the temples.

BEHAVIOR—FIGHTING, ARGUING; CHARACTER TRAITS—BRAVERY; FOLKTALES—MEXICO—AZTEC; WAR.

847 *Punga: The Goddess of Ugly.* Ill. by the author. Harcourt, 1993 (0-15-292862-6). USE LEVEL: M

*New Zealand—Maori*

Kiri and Maraweia must learn the traditional "haka" dance or Punga, the goddess of ugly, may take them to her lodge. Unfortunately, Maraweia is foolish about her dancing and Kiri must rescue her from Punga.

ACTIVITIES—DANCING; FOLKTALES—NEW ZEALAND—MAORI; TWINS.

848    *Why There Is No Arguing in Heaven: A Mayan Myth*. Ill. by the
       author. HarperCollins, 1989 (0-06-023717-1); LB (0-06-
       023718-X). USE LEVEL: M
       *Central American—Mayan*
       Moon Goddess and Lizard House argue about who is greatest
       after Hunab Ku. Maize Goddess creates new beings and ends
       the arguing.
       BEHAVIOR—FIGHTING, ARGUING; CREATION; FOLKTALES—CENTRAL
       AMERICA—MAYAN; POURQUOI TALES.

849    *The Winged Cat: A Tale of Ancient Egypt*. Ill. by the author.
       HarperCollins, 1992 (0-06-023635-3); LB (0-06-023636-1).
       USE LEVEL: M
       *African—Egypt*
       Merit is a young girl who serves in the temple of Bastet, the cat
       goddess. Waha, pharaoh's high priest, kills a cat, but lies about
       it. Merit and Waha journey to the Netherworld to prove who is
       telling the truth.
       ANIMALS—CATS; CHARACTER TRAITS—HONESTY; FOLKTALES—AFRICA—
       EGYPT.

       **LAURIN, ANNE**
850    *Perfect Crane*. Ill. by Charles Mikolaycak. HarperCollins, 1981,
       LB (0-06-023744-9); pap. (0-06-443154-1). USE LEVEL: M
       *Asian—Japan*
       A magician folds a paper crane and then uses his magic to bring
       it to life. Eventually, the crane must leave him to fly with other
       birds.
       ACTIVITIES—PAPERFOLDING; BIRDS—CRANES; FOREIGN LANDS—ASIA—
       JAPAN; MAGIC.

       **LAUTURE, DENIZÉ**
851    *Father and Son*. Ill. by Jonathan Green. Putnam, 1993 (0-399-
       21867-X). USE LEVEL: P
       *African American*
       On the beach, in church, in a boat, flying kites—a father and
       son enjoy being together.
       EMOTIONS—LOVE; FAMILY LIFE—FATHERS; POETRY, RHYME.

       **LAWRENCE, JACOB**
852    *The Great Migration: An American Story*. With a poem in
       appreciation by Walter Dean Myers. Ill. by the author.
       HarperCollins, 1993 (0-06-023037-1); LB (0-06-023038-X).
       USE LEVEL: M/U
       *African American*
       In the 1910s, many blacks left the South in hope of finding jobs

in the industrialized North. Lawrence's paintings dramatically portray this era.

ART; U.S. HISTORY.

853 *Harriet and the Promised Land*. Ill. by the author. Simon & Schuster, 1993 (0-671-86673-7). USE LEVEL: M
*African American*
A poetic text describes the efforts of Harriet Tubman as she risked her life to help slaves escape to freedom.

POETRY, RHYME; SLAVERY; TUBMAN, HARRIET; U.S. HISTORY; UNDERGROUND RAILROAD.

LAWSON, JULIE, RETELLER
854 *The Dragon's Pearl*. Ill. by Paul Morin. Houghton, 1993 (0-395-63623-X). USE LEVEL: M
*Asian—China*
During a drought, Xiao Sheng finds a magic pearl that brings him good fortune, yet he remains kind. When two men try to steal the pearl, Xiao Sheng swallows it and he is transformed into a dragon.

DRAGONS; FOLKTALES—ASIA—CHINA; MAGIC; WEATHER—DROUGHTS.

LEAF, MARGARET
855 *Eyes of the Dragon*. Ill. by Ed Young. Lothrop, 1987 (0-688-06155-9); LB (0-688-06156-7). USE LEVEL: M
*Asian—China*
In a small village in China, the people decide to build a wall to protect them. They hire an artist to decorate the wall, but when they ask him to change his work, their village is threatened by a dragon that comes to life from his painting.

ACTIVITIES—PAINTING; ART; CAREERS—ARTISTS; CHARACTER TRAITS—STUBBORNNESS; DRAGONS; FOREIGN LANDS—ASIA—CHINA.

LEE, HUY VOUN
856 *At the Beach*. Ill. by the author. Henry Holt, 1994 (0-8050-2768-8). USE LEVEL: P
*Asian—China*
Xiao Ming learns to write Chinese by writing in the sand at the beach. His mother helps him see relationships between the Chinese characters and objects around him.

FAMILY LIFE; FOREIGN LANGUAGES; SEA AND SEASHORE.

LEE, JEANNE M., RETELLER
857 *Ba-Nam*. Ill. by the author. Henry Holt, 1987 (0-8050-0169-7). USE LEVEL: P
*Asian—Vietnam*

At the cemetery, Nan is afraid of an old woman, Ba-Nam, who cares for the graves. When she and her brother are lost in a storm, Ba-Nam finds them.

CHARACTER TRAITS—KINDNESS; FOREIGN LANDS—ASIA—VIETNAM; OLDER ADULTS; WEATHER—STORMS.

858 *Legend of the Milky Way.* Ill. by the reteller. Henry Holt, 1982, pap. (0-8050-1361-X). USE LEVEL: M
*Asian—China*
The seventh daughter of the king of the heaven heard the young man's flute and came to earth and married him. Her angry mother placed them as stars in the sky, but kept them separate.

FOLKTALES—ASIA—CHINA; STARS.

859 *Silent Lotus.* Ill. by the author. Farrar, 1991 (0-374-36911-9); pap. (0-374-46646-7). USE LEVEL: M
*Asian—Cambodia*
Lotus cannot hear or speak. She loves the herons, cranes, and egrets near the lake. Other children ignore her, so her parents take her to the temple for help. Lotus learns to dance and to communicate through movements.

ACTIVITIES—DANCING; FOREIGN LANDS—ASIA—CAMBODIA; HANDICAPS— DEAFNESS; HANDICAPS—PHYSICAL.

860 *Toad Is the Uncle of Heaven: A Vietnamese Folk Tale.* Ill. by the author. Henry Holt, 1985 (0-8050-1146-3); pap. (0-8050-1147-1). USE LEVEL: M
*Asian—Vietnam*
When there is a drought on earth, Toad journeys to the King of Heaven to ask for rain. With the help of his friends, he is able to convince the king to send rain.

ACTIVITIES—TRAVELING; CUMULATIVE TALES; FOLKTALES—ASIA— VIETNAM; FROGS AND TOADS; WEATHER—RAIN; WEATHER—DROUGHTS.

**LEE, MARIE G.**
861 *If It Hadn't Been for Yoon Jun.* Houghton, 1993 (0-395-62941-1). USE LEVEL: U
*Asian American—Korea*
When Yoon Jun and his mother arrive from Korea, Alice's adoptive parents, the Larsens, encourage Alice, who is in the seventh grade, to learn about her own Korean heritage as she befriends Yoon Jun.

FAMILY LIFE; FRIENDSHIP; IMMIGRATION; SELF-CONCEPT.

**LEHNE, JUDITH LOGAN**

862 *When the Ragman Sings.* HarperCollins, 1993 (0-06-023316-8); LB (0-06-023317-6). USE LEVEL: U
*African American*
After her mother dies, Dorothea, ten, is lonely and confused. She does not understand her mother's friendship with an old black man who sells rags. When she learns that they both loved poetry, Dorothea comes to care for the ragman too.
DEATH; FAMILY LIFE—MOTHERS; FRIENDSHIP; RACE RELATIONS.

**LEIGH, NILA K.**

863 *Learning to Swim in Swaziland: A Child's-Eye View of a South African Country.* Ill. by the author. Scholastic, 1993 (0-590-45938-4). USE LEVEL: P
*African—Swaziland*
A young girl, who is white, describes the year she spent in Swaziland when she was eight. She describes the customs and activities that she observed, including going to school.
ACTIVITIES—TRAVELING; FOREIGN LANDS—AFRICA—SWAZILAND.

**LEMIEUX, MARGO**

864 *Full Worm Moon.* Ill. by Robert Andrew Parker. Morrow, 1994 (0-688-12105-5); LB (0-688-12106-3). USE LEVEL: M
*Native American—Algonquin*
After hearing their mother tell of a Full Worm Moon, Atuk and Mequin go out with their parents to see if the legend of worms dancing in the moonlight is true.
ANIMALS—WORMS; FAMILY LIFE; NATURE; SEASONS—SPRING.

**LESSAC, FRANÉ**

865 *Caribbean Alphabet.* Ill. by the author. Morrow, 1994 (0-688-12952-8); LB (0-688-12953-6). USE LEVEL: P
*Caribbean*
Each letter of the alphabet is accompanied by several words, many of which describe the customs and way of life on the islands, like "hibiscus," "mangoes," and "reggae."
ABC BOOKS; FOREIGN LANDS—CARIBBEAN ISLANDS; ISLANDS.

866 *Caribbean Canvas.* Ill. by the author. HarperCollins, 1989 (0-397-32367-0); LB (0-397-32368-9). USE LEVEL: M/U
*Caribbean*
Lessac's paintings reflect the activities on several islands in the Caribbean. They are accompanied by poems and sayings from a variety of poets.
ART; FOREIGN LANDS—CARIBBEAN ISLANDS; ISLANDS; POETRY, RHYME.

867    *My Little Island.* Ill. by the author. HarperCollins, 1984 (0-397-32115-5); LB (0-397-32114-7); pap. (0-06-443146-0).
USE LEVEL: P
*Caribbean*
A boy takes his friend to visit the Caribbean island where he was born. Details about everyday life on the island are incorporated into the story.
FOREIGN LANDS—CARIBBEAN ISLANDS; FRIENDSHIP; ISLANDS.

LESTER, JULIUS, RETELLER
868    *Further Tales of Uncle Remus: The Misadventures of Brer Rabbit, Brer Fox, Brer Wolf, the Doodang, and All the Other Creatures.* Ill. by Jerry Pinkney. Dial, 1990 (0-8037-0610-3); LB (0-8037-0611-1). USE LEVEL: M/U
*African American*
Brer Rabbit has a lesser role in these stories as Brer Wolf, Brer Fox, and Brer Bear are featured.
ANIMALS; ANIMALS—RABBITS; BEHAVIOR—TRICKERY; FOLKTALES—UNITED STATES; SHORT STORIES.

869    *How Many Spots Does a Leopard Have? and Other Tales.* Ill. by David Shannon. Scholastic, 1989 (0-590-41973-0); pap. (0-590-41972-2). USE LEVEL: M
*African*
Most of the stories in this collection are African; two are Jewish.
FOLKTALES—AFRICA; SHORT STORIES.

870    *John Henry.* Ill. by Jerry Pinkney. Dial, 1994 (0-8037-1606-0); LB (0-8037-1607-9). USE LEVEL: M
*African American*
An expanded version of the legend of John Henry, who beats the steam drill with his sledgehammer.
CALDECOTT AWARD; CHARACTER TRAITS—PERSEVERANCE; CHARACTER TRAITS—PRIDE; FOLKTALES—UNITED STATES; TRAINS.

871    *The Knee-High Man: And Other Tales.* Ill. by Ralph Pinto. Dial, 1972 (0-8037-4593-1); LB (0-8037-4607-5); pap. (0-8037-0234-5). USE LEVEL: M
*African American*
The six stories in this collection feature animals and often describe humorous events.
ANIMALS; FOLKTALES—UNITED STATES; SHORT STORIES.

872    *The Last Tales of Uncle Remus.* Ill. by Jerry Pinkney. Dial, 1994 (0-8037-1303-7); LB (0-8037-1304-5). USE LEVEL: M
*African American*

There are 39 stories of Brer Rabbit and his friends in this collection.
ANIMALS; BEHAVIOR—TRICKERY; FOLKTALES—UNITED STATES; SHORT STORIES.

873    *The Man Who Knew Too Much: A Moral Tale from the Baila of Zambia*. Ill. by Leonard Jenkins. Houghton, 1994 (0-395-60521-0). USE LEVEL: M
*African—Zambia*
A father does not believe that the eagle will not harm his child. When he tries to kill the eagle, he kills his child.
BIRDS—EAGLES; DEATH; FOLKTALES—AFRICA—ZAMBIA.

874    *More Tales of Uncle Remus: Further Adventures of Brer Rabbit, His Friends, Enemies, and Others*. Ill. by Jerry Pinkney. Dial, 1988 (0-8037-0419-4); LB (0-8037-0420-8). USE LEVEL: M/U
*African American*
This collection features 37 stories of Brer Rabbit and his animal friends.
ANIMALS; ANIMALS—RABBITS; BEHAVIOR—TRICKERY; FOLKTALES—UNITED STATES; SHORT STORIES.

875    *The Tales of Uncle Remus: The Adventures of Brer Rabbit*. Ill. by Jerry Pinkney. Dial, 1987 (0-8037-0271-X); LB (0-8037-0272-8). USE LEVEL: M/U
*African American*
This collection features 48 Brer Rabbit stories.
ANIMALS; ANIMALS—RABBITS; BEHAVIOR—TRICKERY; CORETTA SCOTT KING AWARD; FOLKTALES—UNITED STATES; SHORT STORIES.

**LEVINE, ARTHUR A.,** RETELLER
876    *The Boy Who Drew Cats: A Japanese Folktale*. Ill. by Frédéric Clément. Dial, 1993 (0-8037-1172-7); LB (0-8037-1173-5). USE LEVEL: M
*Asian—Japan*
Kenji loved to draw, especially cats. When he enters the temple of Goblin Rat, Kenji decorates the screens with cats, which destroy the rats.
ACTIVITIES—DRAWING; ANIMALS—CATS; ART; FOLKTALES—ASIA—JAPAN.

**LEVINSON, RIKI**
877    *Our Home Is the Sea*. Ill. by Dennis Luzak. Dutton, 1988 (0-525-44406-8); Puffin, pap. (0-14-054552-2). USE LEVEL: P
*Asian—Hong Kong*
On his last day of school, a boy rushes through the streets of Hong Kong to return to his family's houseboat.

BOATS, SHIPS; FAMILY LIFE; FOREIGN LANDS– ASIA–HONG KONG; HOUSES; URBAN LIFE.

**LEVITIN, SONIA**

878 *The Golem and the Dragon Girl.* Dial, 1993 (0-8037-1280-4); LB (0-8037-1281-2); Fawcett, pap. (0-449-70441-6). USE LEVEL: U

*Multicultural*

Laurel Wang's family has sold their house to Jonathan and his family. She misses her home and the memories of her great-grandfather. Laurel, who is Chinese American, and Jonathan, who is Jewish, become friends, learning about each other's heritage.

FAMILY LIFE; FRIENDSHIP; MOVING.

**LEWIN, HUGH**

879 *Jafta.* Ill. by Lisa Kopper. Carolrhoda, 1981 pap. (0-87614-494-6). USE LEVEL: P

*African—South Africa*

Jafta's lively personality is compared with animals that are a familiar part of his South African home.

COMMUNITIES, NEIGHBORHOODS; EMOTIONS; FAMILY LIFE; FOREIGN LANDS–AFRICA–SOUTH AFRICA.

880 *Jafta and the Wedding.* Ill. by Lisa Kopper. Carolrhoda, 1981 pap. (0-87614-497-0). USE LEVEL: P

*African—South Africa*

Jafta and other village children do a "songololo," a Zulu word for centipede or millipede.

ACTIVITIES–GAMES; COMMUNITIES, NEIGHBORHOODS; FOREIGN LANDS–AFRICA–SOUTH AFRICA; WEDDINGS.

881 *Jafta: The Homecoming.* Ill. by Lisa Kopper. Knopf, 1994 (0-679-84722-7); LB (0-679-94722-1). USE LEVEL: P

*African—South Africa*

Jafta's father has worked in the mines far from the family's home. With the changes in South Africa, he is coming home.

COMMUNITIES, NEIGHBORHOODS; FAMILY LIFE –FATHERS; FOREIGN LANDS–AFRICA–SOUTH AFRICA.

882 *Jafta—The Journey.* Ill. by Lisa Kopper. Carolrhoda, 1983, LB (0-87614-265-X). USE LEVEL: P

*African—South Africa*

Jafta is going to visit his father. It is not an easy trip, but everyone works together and Jafta feels the joy of being held in his father's arms.

ACTIVITIES—TRAVELING; COMMUNITIES, NEIGHBORHOODS; EMOTIONS—
LOVE; FAMILY LIFE—FATHERS; FOREIGN LANDS—AFRICA—SOUTH AFRICA.

883 *Jafta—The Town.* Ill. by Lisa Kopper. Carolrhoda, 1983, LB (0-
87614-266-8). USE LEVEL: P
*African—South Africa*
Jafta and his mother have traveled to town for the funeral of an
uncle. Jafta misses the animals and birds that he is used to, but
he is happy to see his father, who must live in the town in order
to have a job.
ACTIVITIES—TRAVELING; COMMUNITIES, NEIGHBORHOODS; EMOTIONS;
FAMILY LIFE; FOREIGN LANDS—AFRICA—SOUTH AFRICA.

884 *Jafta's Father.* Ill. by Lisa Kopper. Carolrhoda, 1981 pap. (0-
87614-496-2). USE LEVEL: P
*African—South Africa*
Jafta's father lives in town, where there is work. He can only
come home for a visit every few months. Jafta thinks of the joy
he feels when his father is home and how much he misses his
father when he is at work.
COMMUNITIES, NEIGHBORHOODS; EMOTIONS—LOVE; EMOTIONS—SAD-
NESS; FAMILY LIFE—FATHERS; FOREIGN LANDS—AFRICA—SOUTH AFRICA.

885 *Jafta's Mother.* Ill. by Lisa Kopper. Carolrhoda, 1981 pap. (0-
87614-495-4). USE LEVEL: P
*African—South Africa*
Jafta describes his mother and the activities that are part of her
life.
COMMUNITIES, NEIGHBORHOODS; FAMILY LIFE—MOTHERS; FOREIGN
LANDS—AFRICA—SOUTH AFRICA.

**LEWIN, TED**
886 *Amazon Boy.* Ill. by the author. Macmillan. 1993 (0-02-
757383-4). USE LEVEL: P/M
*South American—Brazil*
Paulo, a Brazilian boy, travels up the Amazon River and learns
something about its beauty. Paulo also realizes the importance
of caring for this resource.
ACTIVITIES—TRAVELING; AMAZON RIVER; ECOLOGY; FOREIGN LANDS—
SOUTH AMERICA—BRAZIL; RIVERS.

**LEWIS, ELIZABETH FOREMAN**
887 *Young Fu of the Upper Yangtze.* Introduction by Pearl S. Buck.
Ill. by Ed Young. Henry Holt, 1973, ©1932 (0-8050-0549-8);
Dell, pap. (0-440-49043-X). USE LEVEL: U
*Asian—China*

Young Fu has left his village to travel to Chunking and serve as a coppersmith's apprentice. This Newbery Award-winning novel is full of descriptions of China during the 1920s. Notes in this fortieth anniversary edition add details about modern China.

FOREIGN LANDS—ASIA—CHINA; HISTORY; NEWBERY AWARD.

**LEWIS, RICHARD**

888 *All of You Was Singing*. Ill. by Ed Young. Macmillan, 1991 (0-689-31596-1); pap. (0-689-71853-5). USE LEVEL: M
*Mexican—Aztec*
This creation myth tells how music came to Earth. When two serpents tore the earth in half, the heavens and the earth were created. After the plants and creatures were made, there was music and singing.

CREATION; FOLKTALES—MEXICO—AZTEC; MUSIC; POURQUOI TALES; SINGING.

889 *In a Spring Garden*. Ill. by Ezra Jack Keats. Dial, 1965, o.p. USE LEVEL: M
*Asian—Japan*
Haiku from Issa, Bashō, Onitsura, and other poets introduce children to this poetic form. Nature is the theme of these haiku.

FOREIGN LANDS—ASIA—JAPAN; HAIKU; NATURE; POETRY, RHYME.

890 *In the Night, Still Dark*. Ill. by Ed Young. Macmillan, 1988 (0-689-31310-1). USE LEVEL: M
*Hawaiian*
This poem is based on a Hawaiian chant describing the creation of the world.

CREATION; HAWAII; POETRY, RHYME.

**LEWIS, THOMAS P.**

891 *Hill of Fire*. Ill. by Joan Sandin. HarperCollins, 1971, LB (0-06-023804-6); pap. (0-06-444040-0). USE LEVEL: P
*Mexican*
A farmer feels that his life is not very exciting. One day, while he and his son are working in the fields, a volcanic eruption begins and they must leave their home.

FOREIGN LANDS—MEXICO; VOLCANOES.

**LEXAU, JOAN M.**

892 *Striped Ice Cream*. Ill. by John Wilson. HarperCollins, 1968 (0-397-31406-3); LB (0-397-31407-1); Scholastic, pap. (0-590-45729-2). USE LEVEL: M
*African American*
Becky is the youngest of five children and the family's resources

do not stretch very far. Becky wonders if there will be enough for her to celebrate her birthday.

BIRTHDAYS; FAMILY LIFE; FOOD; GIFTS.

### LICHTVELD, NONI

893 *I Lost My Arrow in a Kankan Tree.* Ill. by the author. Lothrop, 1993 (0-688-12748-7); LB (0-688-12749-5). USE LEVEL: M

*South American—Surinam*

A boy decides to help his family by going to town and getting a job. Along the way, he helps others, and he receives something special in return. When he reaches the town, he helps the king, who rewards him with land to farm.

CHARACTER TRAITS—HELPFULNESS; CUMULATIVE TALES; FOREIGN LANDS—SOUTH AMERICA—SURINAM; TREES.

### LIDDELL, JANICE

894 *Imani and the Flying Africans.* Ill. by Linda Nickens. Africa World, 1994 (0-86543-365-8); LB (0-86543-366-6). USE LEVEL: M

*African American*

Imani and Mama are going south to visit his grandparents for the first time. Mama tells him a story of slavery and magic when slaves flew back to Africa. In a dream, Imani escapes from a man who had caught him. He awakes at his grandparents' home.

ACTIVITIES—TRAVELING; FAMILY LIFE—GRANDPARENTS; MAGIC; SLAVERY; STORYTELLING.

### LIFTON, BETTY JEAN

895 *Joji and the Dragon.* Ill. by Eiichi Mitsui. Shoe String, 1989, ©1957 (0-208-02245-7). USE LEVEL: P

*Asian—Japan*

Joji is a scarecrow whose best friends are crows. Because he is polite to them, the crows do not eat his rice. The farmer still worries, so he gets a dragon, Toho the Terrible, to guard his rice.

BIRDS; DRAGONS; FOREIGN LANDS—ASIA—JAPAN; SCARECROWS.

### LILLIE, PATRICIA

896 *When This Box Is Full.* Photos by Donald Crews. Greenwillow, 1993 (0-688-12016-4); LB (0-688-12017-2). USE LEVEL: P

*African American*

During each month of the year a seasonal item is added to the box. The photos depict African American children.

CONCEPTS—OPPOSITES; DAYS OF THE WEEK, MONTHS OF THE YEAR; SEASONS.

**LINDEN, ANN MARIE**

897 *Emerald Blue.* Ill. by Katherine Doyle. Macmillan, 1994 (0-689-31946-0). USE LEVEL: P
*Caribbean*
A woman remembers her childhood on a Caribbean island, living with Grandma and enjoying activities with her brother.
BEHAVIOR—GROWING UP; FAMILY LIFE; FOREIGN LANDS—CARIBBEAN ISLANDS; ISLANDS.

898 *One Smiling Grandma: A Caribbean Counting Book.* Ill. by Lynne Russell. Dial, 1992 (0-8037-1132-8); Puffin, pap. (0-14-055341-X). USE LEVEL: PS/P
*Caribbean*
Familiar island items, like steel drums and conch shells, are used to depict the numbers from one to ten.
COUNTING, NUMBERS; FOREIGN LANDS—CARIBBEAN ISLANDS; ISLANDS.

**LIPPERT, MARGARET H., ADAPTER**

899 *The Sea Serpent's Daughter: A Brazilian Legend.* Ill. by Felipe Davalos. Troll, 1993, LB (0-8167-3053-9); pap. (0-8167-3054-7). USE LEVEL: M
*South American—Brazil*
Once, there was no night. Bonita, daughter of the Great Sea Serpent, comes to live on earth. She marries the chief, but she misses the darkness from the sea. Her father sends night to her, along with all the creatures of the night.
FOLKTALES—SOUTH AMERICA—BRAZIL; NIGHT.

**LITTLE, LESSIE JONES**

900 *Children of Long Ago.* Ill. by Jan Spivey Gilcrist. Putnam, 1988, o.p. USE LEVEL: M
*African American*
These poems are based on the memories of the author, who grew up in the early 1900s. There are poems about going to church, playing with paper dolls, chopping wood, and going barefoot.
POETRY, RHYME; U.S. HISTORY.

**LITTLE, LESSIE JONES, AND ELOISE GREENFIELD**

901 *I Can Do It by Myself.* Ill. by Carole Byard. HarperCollins, 1978 (0-690-01369-8); LB (0-690-03851-8). USE LEVEL: PS/P
*African American*
Donny wants to buy his mother something special for her birthday, even though it means walking past a scary dog on his way to the plant store.
BIRTHDAYS; CHARACTER TRAITS—BRAVERY; EMOTIONS—FEAR; GIFTS; PLANTS.

LITTLECHILD, GEORGE

902   *This Land Is My Land.* Ill. by the author. Children's Book Pr., 1993 (0-89239-119-7). USE LEVEL: M
*Native American*
A descriptive text accompanies paintings that depict historical events involving Native Americans as well as specific experiences in the author's own life.
CAREERS—ARTISTS; U.S. HISTORY.

LIVINGSTON, MYRA COHN

903   *Keep On Singing: A Ballad of Marian Anderson.* Ill. by Samuel Byrd. Holiday, 1994 (0-8234-1098-6). USE LEVEL: M
*African American*
This ballad presents dramatic images from the life of Marian Anderson, a pioneer for African Americans in music and race relations
ANDERSON, MARIAN; MUSIC; POETRY, RHYME; PREJUDICE; RACE RELATIONS.

904   *Let Freedom Ring: A Ballad of Martin Luther King, Jr.* Ill. by Samuel Byrd. Holiday, 1992 (0-8234-0957-0). USE LEVEL: M
*African American*
The poetic text describes the life and accomplishments of Dr Martin Luther King, Jr.
EMOTIONS; KING, DR. MARTIN LUTHER, JR.; POETRY, RHYME.

LIVO, NORMA J., AND DIA CHA

905   *Folk Stories of the Hmong: Peoples of Laos, Thailand, and Vietnam.* Libraries Unlimited, 1991, LB (0-87287-854-6). USE LEVEL: U
*Asian*
The chapter "The Hmong and Their Culture" precedes the 27 folk stories in this collection. The stories are divided into three groups: "In the Beginning," "How/Why Folk Stories," and "Folk Stories of Love, Magic, and Fun."
FOLKTALES—ASIA; MAGIC; POURQUOI TALES; SHORT STORIES.

LLOYD, ERROL

906   *Nini at Carnival.* Ill. by the author. HarperCollins, 1979 (0-690-03891-7); LB (0-690-03892-5). USE LEVEL: P
*Mexican*
Nini does not have a costume for the carnival, but her friend Betti, disguised as a fairy godmother, finds a costume for Nini.
CHARACTER TRAITS—HELPFULNESS; CLOTHING; FESTIVALS; FOREIGN LANDS—MEXICO; FRIENDSHIP.

**LOBEL, ARNOLD**

907    *Ming Lo Moves the Mountain*. Ill. by the author. Greenwillow, 1982, LB (0-688-00611-6); pap. (0-688-10995-0). USE LEVEL: P

*Asian*

The mountain causes Ming Lo nothing but trouble, so he decides to move the mountain. The wise man gives Ming Lo and his wife many suggestions, but it is a special dance that finally works.

CHARACTER TRAITS—FOOLISHNESS; HOUSES; HUMOR; MOVING.

**LOCKER, THOMAS**

908    *The Land of Gray Wolf*. Ill. by the author. Dial, 1991 (0-8037-0936-6); LB (0-8037-0937-4). USE LEVEL: P

*Native American*

Running Deer, his father Gray Wolf, and their people worry about the coming settlers who hunt and clear the land of the native people. When the men try to stop the settlers, many are killed, including Gray Wolf.

DEATH; U.S. HISTORY.

**LOH, MORAG JEANETTE**

909    *Tucking Mommy In*. Ill. by Donna Rawlins. Orchard, 1988 (0-531-05740-2); LB (0-531-08340-3). USE LEVEL: P

*Multicultural*

When Mommy comes home she is so tired that her two little girls help her relax.

EMOTIONS—LOVE; FAMILY LIFE—MOTHERS; SLEEP.

**LOMAS GARZA, CARMEN**

910    *Family Pictures/Cuadros de Familia*. Spanish version by Rosalma Zubizarreta. Ill. by the author. Children's Book Pr., 1990, LB (0-89239-050-6); pap. (0-89239-108-1). USE LEVEL: P/M

*Hispanic American*

The daily activities of a Hispanic American family are presented, including going to the fair, picking oranges, making tamales, and going to church.

FAMILY LIFE; FOREIGN LANGUAGES.

**LONDON, JONATHAN, RETELLER**

911    *Fire Race: A Karuk Coyote Tale about How Fire Came to the People*. Ill. by Sylvia Long. Chronicle, 1993 (0-8118-0241-8). USE LEVEL: M

*Native American—Karuk*

The Yellow Jacket sisters have fire and the other animals want it. Coyote and the other animals devise a plan to steal the fire. The fire is swallowed by the willow, which is why fires can be started using sticks.

ANIMALS; ANIMALS—COYOTES; FIRE; FOLKTALES—NATIVE AMERICAN— KARUK; POURQUOI TALES.

### LONG, HUA

912   *The Moon Maiden: And Other Asian Folktales.* China Books, 1993 (0-8351-2494-0); pap. (0-8351-2493-2). USE LEVEL: M
*Asian*
There are 12 stories here, each illustrated by a different artist. Included are stories of dragons, serpents, and other animals as well as stories with magic.

FOLKTALES—ASIA; MAGIC; SHORT STORIES.

### LONGFELLOW, HENRY WADSWORTH

913   *Hiawatha.* Ill. by Susan Jeffers. Dial, 1983 (0-8037-0013-X); LB (0-8037-0014-8). USE LEVEL: M
*Native American*
The verses in this book are excerpted from Longfellow's epic poem "The Song of Hiawatha."

ECOLOGY; NATURE; POETRY, RHYME.

914   *Hiawatha's Childhood.* Ill. by Errol Le Cain. Farrar, 1984 (0-374-33065-4); Puffin, pap. (0-14-050562-8). USE LEVEL: M
*Native American*
An illustrated version of selected verses from Longfellow's poem.

ECOLOGY; NATURE; POETRY, RHYME.

### LORD, BETTE BAO

915   *In the Year of the Boar and Jackie Robinson.* Ill. by Marc Simont. HarperCollins, 1984 (0-06-024003-2); LB (0-06-024004-0); pap. (0-06-440175-8). USE LEVEL: M
*Asian American—China*
Bandit, now called Shirley Temple Wong, and her family have moved to Brooklyn. There, she learns about baseball and tries to make friends while trying to maintain a connection with her Chinese heritage and customs.

FRIENDSHIP; IMMIGRATION; SCHOOL; SPORTS—BASEBALL.

**LOTTRIDGE, CELIA BARKER, RETELLER**

916     *The Name of the Tree: A Bantu Folktale.* Ill. by Ian Wallace.
Macmillan, 1989 (0-689-50490-X). USE LEVEL: M
*African—Bantu*
During a long drought, the animals find a tree laden with fruit.
Only by knowing the name of the tree can the fruit be gathered.
FOLKTALES—AFRICA BANTU; NAMES; TREES; WATER; WEATHER—
DROUGHTS.

**LOTZ, KAREN E.**

917     *Can't Sit Still.* Ill. by Colleen Browning. Dutton, 1993 (0-525-
45066-1). USE LEVEL: P
*African American*
A little girl describes the various activities she enjoys in her
urban neighborhood throughout the year.
FAMILY LIFE; POETRY, RHYME; SEASONS; URBAN LIFE.

**LOUIE, AI-LING, RETELLER**

918     *Yeh-Shen: A Cinderella Story from China.* Ill. by Ed Young.
Putnam, 1982 (0-399-20900-X); pap. (0-399-21594-8). USE
LEVEL: M
*Asian—China*
The cruelty of Yeh-Shen's stepmother and stepsister is punished
with death after Yeh-Shen is chosen to marry the king.
CHARACTER TRAITS—KINDNESS; EMOTIONS—ENVY, JEALOUSY; FISH;
FOLKTALES—ASIA—CHINA; MAGIC.

**LOVELACE, MAUD HART**

919     *The Trees Kneel at Christmas.* Ill. by Marie-Claude Monchaux.
Abdo, 1994 (1-56239-999-3). USE LEVEL: M
*Middle Eastern American—Lebanon*
Grandmother tells Afify, seven, and her brother Hanna, five, a
story of how the trees in their homeland, Lebanon, kneel at
Christmas to show respect for the Christ Child. The children
hope to see the trees kneel in Prospect Park in Brooklyn.
FAMILY LIFE; HOLIDAYS—CHRISTMAS; TREES.

**LOVERSEED, AMANDA, RETELLER**

920     *Thunder King: A Peruvian Folk Tale.* Ill. by the reteller.
Bedrick, 1991, o.p. USE LEVEL: M
*South American—Peru*
Twin brothers Tantay and Illanti live on the plains of Peru.
When Thunder sees Tantay working in the field, he takes him to

work in his palace. Aided by Condor, Illanti rescues his brother.
BIRDS—CONDORS; FOLKTALES—SOUTH AMERICA—PERU; WEATHER—
THUNDER.

### LUENN, NANCY

921 *Nessa's Fish.* Ill. by Neil Waldman. Macmillan, 1990 (0-689-
31477-9). USE LEVEL: P
*Native American—Inuit*
Nessa and her grandmother are ice fishing. When her grand-
mother becomes ill, Nessa protects her grandmother and their
fish from a fox, wolves, and a bear.
ARCTIC LANDS; CHARACTER TRAITS—BRAVERY; FAMILY LIFE—GRAND-
MOTHERS; SPORTS—FISHING.

922 *Nessa's Story.* Ill. by Neil Waldman. Macmillan, 1994 (0-689-
31782-4). USE LEVEL: P
*Native American—Inuit*
Nessa loves to listen to her grandmother's stories, and she wish-
es she had a story of her own.
ARCTIC LANDS; FAMILY LIFE; IMAGINATION; STORYTELLING.

### LUM, DARRELL, RETELLER

923 *The Golden Slipper: A Vietnamese Legend.* Ill. by Makiko
Nagano. Troll, 1994, LB (0-8167-3405-4); pap. (0-8167-
3406-2). USE LEVEL: M
*Asian—Vietnam*
In this Cinderella variant, Tam is treated cruelly by her step-
mother and stepsister, Cam. A beautiful woman appears and
reminds her to listen to the animals. The animals help her pre-
pare for the Autumn Festival, where the prince chooses her.
ANIMALS; CHARACTER TRAITS—KINDNESS; CLOTHING—SHOES;
EMOTIONS—ENVY, JEALOUSY; FOLKTALES—ASIA—VIETNAM.

### LUNN, CAROLYN

924 *Bobby's Zoo.* Ill. by Tom Dunnington. Childrens Pr., 1989, LB
(0-516-02089-7); pap. (0-516-42089-5). USE LEVEL: PS/P
*African American*
A boy has a problem—his house is full of animals, so he opens a
zoo. The rhyming text makes this a predictable reader.
ANIMALS; POETRY, RHYME; PREDICTABLE TEXT; PROBLEM SOLVING.

### LYON, GEORGE ELLA

925 *Dreamplace.* Ill. by Peter Catalanotto. Orchard, 1993 (0-531-
05466-7); LB (0-531-08616-X). USE LEVEL: P
*Native American—Pueblo*
On a visit to the pueblos of the Anasazi, visitors feel the pres-

ence of these peoples from the past and envision their way of life.

FAMILY LIFE; PUEBLOS; U.S. HISTORY.

926   *The Outside Inn.* Ill. by Vera Rosenberry. Orchard, 1991 (0-531-05936-7); LB (0-531-08536-8). USE LEVEL: P
*Multicultural*
A group of friends pretend to enjoy unusual foods outdoors, including "caterpillar feet" and "puddle ink."

FOOD; IMAGINATION; NATURE; POETRY, RHYME.

927   *Together.* Ill. by Vera Rosenberry. Orchard, 1989 (0-531-05831-X); LB (0-531-08431-0); pap. (0-531-07047-6). USE LEVEL: P
*Multicultural*
In this rhyming text, friends from diverse cultural backgrounds show ways they share activities.

FRIENDSHIP; POETRY, RHYME.

928   *Who Came Down That Road?* Ill. by Peter Catalanotto. Orchard, 1992 (0-531-05987-1); LB (0-531-08587-2). USE LEVEL: P/M
*Native American*
A boy asks his mother to tell him about the people who have traveled down the old road. She tells him of the farmers, settlers, Native American peoples, and animals that have passed this way before them.

CHARACTER TRAITS—QUESTIONING; FAMILY LIFE; ROADS; U.S. HISTORY.

**LYONS, MARY E., RETELLER**
929   *The Butter Tree: Tales of Bruh Rabbit.* Ill. by Mireille Vautier. Henry Holt, 1995 (0-8050-2673-8). USE LEVEL: M
*African American*
There are six stories about animals like Bruh Bear, Bruh Rabbit, Bruh Wolf, and Bruh Guinea Fowl. Several stories involve cleverness and trickery.

ANIMALS; ANIMALS—RABBITS; BEHAVIOR—TRICKERY; CHARACTER TRAITS—CLEVERNESS; FOLKTALES—UNITED STATES.

930   *Letters from a Slave Girl: The Story of Harriet Jacobs.* Macmillan, 1992 (0-684-19446-5). USE LEVEL: U
*African American*
Harriet Jacobs was a slave in North Carolina. In the 1840s, she escaped to the North. This book is presented as a series of letters from Harriet and is based on her 1861 autobiography.

CHARACTER TRAITS—BRAVERY; CHARACTER TRAITS—FREEDOM; JACOBS, HARRIET A.; SLAVERY.

931     *Raw Head, Bloody Bones: African-American Tales of the Supernatural.* Macmillan, 1991 (0-684-19333-7). USE LEVEL: U
*African American*
There are 15 stories in this collection, most from African American traditions, although there are a few from the Caribbean. Stories are grouped by "Gullah Goblins," "Ghosts," "Monsters," and "Superhumans."
FOLKTALES—CARIBBEAN ISLANDS; FOLKTALES—UNITED STATES; MONSTERS; SCARY STORIES; SHORT STORIES; SUPERNATURAL.

**MAARTENS, MARETHA**

932     *Paper Bird: A Novel of South Africa.* Houghton, 1991 (0-395-56490-5). USE LEVEL: U
*African—South Africa*
In his village, Adam and his family face violence from policemen riding in Casspirs. On the road to the city, there are marauders who attack travelers. Adam must face this violence and his own fear to provide for his family.
FOREIGN LANDS—AFRICA—SOUTH AFRICA; POVERTY; RACE RELATIONS; VIOLENCE.

**MCCOY, KAREN KAWAMOTO, RETELLER**

933     *A Tale of Two Tengu: A Japanese Folktale.* Ill. by Koen Fossey. Whitman, 1993 (0-8075-7748-0). USE LEVEL: M
*Asian—Japan*
Two tengu (goblins with long noses) argue about whose nose is the most wonderful.
ANATOMY—NOSES; BEHAVIOR—FIGHTING, ARGUING; FOLKTALES—ASIA—JAPAN.

**MCDERMOTT, GERALD, ADAPTER**

934     *Anansi the Spider: A Tale from the Ashanti.* Ill. by the adapter. Henry Holt, 1972 (0-8050-0310-X); pap. (0-8050-0311-8). USE LEVEL: P
*African—Ashanti*
After Anansi's sons rescue him, they find a beautiful globe of light. They cannot decide who should have the light, so the god who lives in the sky takes it, and it becomes the moon.
CALDECOTT AWARD; FOLKTALES—AFRICA; MOON; POURQUOI TALES; SPIDERS.

935     *Arrow to the Sun: A Pueblo Indian Tale.* Ill. by the adapter. Viking, 1974 (0-670-13369-8); Puffin, pap. (0-14-050211-4). USE LEVEL: P/M
*Native American—Pueblo*

A boy must survive four tests to prove his identity and find his father.
BEHAVIOR—FACING CHALLENGES; CALDECOTT AWARD; CHARACTER TRAITS BRAVERY; FOLKTALES—NATIVE AMERICAN—PUEBLO.

936 *Coyote: A Trickster Tale from the American Southwest.* Ill. by the author. Harcourt, 1994 (0-15-220724-4). USE LEVEL: M
*Native American*
Coyote is often in trouble. When coyote wants to fly, the crows trick him.
ACTIVITIES—FLYING; ANIMALS—COYOTES; BEHAVIOR—TRICKERY; BIRDS—CROWS; FOLKTALES—NATIVE AMERICAN.

937 *The Magic Tree: A Tale from the Congo.* Ill. by the adapter. Henry Holt, 1994 (0-8050-3080-8). USE LEVEL: M
*African—Zaire*
Lluemba and Mavungu are twins. Scorned by his mother and brother, Mavungu finds a magic tree and releases the people that are enchanted there. He forgets his promise of secrecy and loses all his possessions.
CHARACTER TRAITS—APPEARANCE; FOLKTALES—AFRICA—ZAIRE; MAGIC; TREES.

938 *Raven: A Trickster Tale from the Pacific Northwest.* Ill. by the author. Harcourt, 1993 (0-15-265661-8). USE LEVEL: M
*Native American*
Raven wants to bring light to the people, so he tricks Sky Chief into giving him a ball of light, which becomes the sun.
BEHAVIOR—TRICKERY; BIRDS—RAVENS; CALDECOTT AWARD; FOLKTALES—NATIVE AMERICAN; POURQUOI TALES.

939 *The Stonecutter: A Japanese Folktale.* Ill. by the adapter. Viking, 1975 (0-670-67074-X); Puffin, pap. (0-14-050289-0). USE LEVEL: M
*Asian—Japan*
A stonecutter is transformed into a variety of objects, yet he is not satisfied.
BEHAVIOR—DISSATISFACTION; BEHAVIOR—GREED; FOLKTALES—ASIA—JAPAN.

940 *The Voyage of Osiris: A Myth of Ancient Egypt.* Ill. by the author. Harcourt, 1977 (0-15-200216-2); pap. (0-15-294446-X). USE LEVEL: M
*African—Egypt*
Osiris is the pharaoh. When his evil brother, Set, traps him,

Osiris embarks on a journey. His wife, Isis, tries to release him from Set's evil. With the help of Thor and Anubis, Osiris becomes lord of the underworld.

DEATH; FOLKTALES—AFRICA—EGYPT; RELIGION; ROYALTY.

941 *Zomo the Rabbit: A Trickster Tale from West Africa.* Ill. by the reteller. Harcourt, 1992 (0-15-299967-1). USE LEVEL: M
*African*
Zomo outwits Big Fish, Wild Cow, and Leopard in order to receive wisdom from Sky God.

BEHAVIOR—TRICKERY; CHARACTER TRAITS—CLEVERNESS; FOLKTALES—AFRICA.

## McDONALD, BECKY BRING
942 *Katie Couldn't.* Ill. by Lois Axeman. Childrens Pr., 1985, LB (0-516-02069-2); pap. (0-516-42069-0). USE LEVEL: PS/P
*Asian American*
Katie is the littlest and she sometimes feels left out but Daddy makes her feel special. The simple text makes this a predictable reader.

FAMILY LIFE; PREDICTABLE TEXT.

943 *Larry and the Cookie.* Ill. by Clovis Martin. Childrens Pr., 1993, LB (0-516-02014-5); pap. (0-516-42014-3). USE LEVEL: PS/P
*African American*
Larry puts a cookie in his pocket for later. After he plays, all he has is crumbs. This book has a simple, predictable text.

ACTIVITIES—PLAYING; FOOD; PREDICTABLE TEXT.

## McDONALD, JOYCE
944 *Mail-Order Kid.* Putnam, 1988, o.p. USE LEVEL: M
*Asian American—Korea*
When his parents adopt a six-year-old Korean boy, Flip Doty rebels by ordering a fox from a catalog. He resents his new brother and argues that he should keep his pet, although he comes to realize that the situations are not similar.

ADOPTION; ANIMALS—FOXES; FAMILY LIFE.

## MacDONALD, SUSE
945 *Nanta's Lion: A Search-and-Find Adventure.* Ill. by the author. Morrow, 1995 (0-688-13125-5). USE LEVEL: P
*African—Masai*
Nanta is curious about the lion that the men of her village are

going to hunt. She visits her friends in the next village but she never sees the lion. Die-cut pages build layers that become the lion that readers can see.

ANIMALS—LIONS; CHARACTER TRAITS—CURIOSITY; FOREIGN LANDS—AFRICA—MASAI; SPORTS HUNTING.

### McGee, Charmayne

946 *So Sings the Blue Deer.* Macmillan, 1994 (0-689-31888-X). USE LEVEL: U
*Native American—Huichol*
In the Sierra Madre mountains of Mexico, the Huichol people use the white-tailed deer in their ceremonies, but all the deer are gone from their region. Moon Feather, 13, is chosen to go to Mexico City with some of his people and be given 20 deer.

ADVENTURE; ANIMALS—DEER; ECOLOGY; FOREIGN LANDS—MEXICO; NATURE.

### McKissack, Patricia

947 *The Dark Thirty: Southern Tales of the Supernatural.* Ill. by Brian Pinkney. Knopf, 1992 (0-679-81863-4); LB (0-679-91863-3). USE LEVEL: M/U
*African American*
Black-and-white scratchboard illustrations capture the mood of the ten spooky stories in this collection.

CORETTA SCOTT KING AWARD; FOLKTALES—UNITED STATES; NEWBERY AWARD; SCARY STORIES; SHORT STORIES; SUPERNATURAL.

948 *Flossie and the Fox.* Ill. by Rachel Isadora. Dial, 1986 (0-8037-0250-7); LB (0-8037-0251-5). USE LEVEL: P
*African American*
Flossie's grandmother has sent her to deliver a basket of eggs to Miz Viola. Walking through the woods, Flossie meets a sly fox. She outwits the fox and completes her journey.

ANIMALS—FOXES; BEHAVIOR—TRICKERY; CHARACTER TRAITS—CLEVERNESS; RURAL LIFE.

949 *A Million Fish . . . More or Less.* Ill. by Dena Schutzer. Knopf, 1992 (0-679-80692-X); LB (0-679-90692-4). USE LEVEL: M
*African American*
On the Bayou Clapateaux, young Hugh Thomas is fishing. After hearing some wild stories from some men, Hugh has his own adventure, which becomes a tall tale for him to tell.

IMAGINATION; SPORTS—FISHING; STORYTELLING.

950     *Mirandy and Brother Wind.* Ill. by Jerry Pinkney. Knopf, 1988
        (0-394-88765-4); LB (0-394-98765-9). USE LEVEL: P
        *African American*
        Mirandy wants the best partner for the cake walk, so she tries to
        catch Brother Wind.
        ACTIVITIES—DANCING; CALDECOTT AWARD; CHARACTER TRAITS—CLEV-
        ERNESS; CORETTA SCOTT KING AWARD; WEATHER—WIND.

951     *Monkey-Monkey's Trick.* Ill. by Paul Meisel. Random, 1988, LB
        (0-394-99173-7); pap. (0-394-89173-2). USE LEVEL: P
        *African*
        When Monkey-Monkey is tricked out of his food by Hyena,
        Monkey-Monkey must be clever to get even. He tricks Hyena
        into building him a house.
        ANIMALS—HYENAS; ANIMALS—MONKEYS; BEHAVIOR—TRICKERY;
        CHARACTER TRAITS—CLEVERNESS; FOLKTALES—AFRICA.

952     *Nettie Jo's Friends.* Ill. by Scott Cook. Knopf, 1988 (0-394-
        89158-9); LB (0-394-99158-3); pap. (0-679-86573-X). USE
        LEVEL: P
        *African American*
        Nettie Jo is helped by three animals as she searches for a needle
        to sew a dress for her doll.
        ACTIVITIES—SEWING; CLOTHING; FAMILY LIFE; TOYS—DOLLS.

        **McKissack, Patricia, and Fredrick McKissack**
953     *Bugs!* Ill. by Clovis Martin. Childrens Press, 1988, LB (0-516-
        02088-9); pap. (0-516-42088-7). USE LEVEL: P
        *African American*
        Two children look for bugs and, as they find them, they count
        from one to five.
        COUNTING, NUMBERS; INSECTS; PREDICTABLE TEXT.

954     *Christmas in the Big House, Christmas in the Quarters.* Ill. by
        John Thompson. Scholastic, 1994 (0-590-43027-0). USE LEVEL:
        M
        *African American*
        This book tells about the preparations for Christmas on a plan-
        tation in Virginia just before the Civil War.
        CORETTA SCOTT KING AWARD; HOLIDAYS—CHRISTMAS; SLAVERY; U.S.
        HISTORY.

955     *Constance Stumbles.* Ill. by Tom Dunnington. Childrens Pr.,
        1988, LB (0-516-02086-2); pap. (0-516-42086-0). USE LEVEL:
        P
        *African American*

Even though she is not well coordinated, Constance learns to ride a bike. This beginning reader has a simple, predictable text.

BEHAVIOR—GROWING UP; PREDICTABLE TEXT; SPORTS—BICYCLING.

956   *Messy Bessey.* Ill. by Richard Hackney. Childrens Pr., 1987, LB (0-516-02083 8); pap (0-516-42083-6). USE LEVEL: P
*African American*
Bessey's room is a mess, so she picks up her toys, books, games, clothes, paints, and other debris and puts them all in the closet. The rhyming text is predictable for beginning readers.

ACTIVITIES—CLEANING; BEHAVIOR—MESSY; CHARACTER TRAITS—CLEAN-LINESS; POETRY, RHYME; PREDICTABLE TEXT.

957   *Messy Bessey's Closet.* Ill. by Richard Hackney. Childrens Pr., 1989, LB (0-516-02091-9); pap. (0-516-42091-7). USE LEVEL: P
*African American*
When Bessey opens the door to her closet, everything falls out. She decides to give away the things she does not use. This beginning reader has a predictable, rhyming text.

BEHAVIOR—MESSY; BEHAVIOR—SHARING; CHARACTER TRAITS—CLEANLI-NESS; POETRY, RHYME; PREDICTABLE TEXT.

958   *Messy Bessey's Garden.* Ill. by Richard Hackney. Childrens Pr., 1991, LB (0-516-02008-0); pap. (0-516-42008-9). USE LEVEL: P
*African American*
In the spring, Bessey plants a garden. During the summer she finds she must work hard to care for it, but in the fall, her plants have grown. This beginning reader has a predictable, rhyming text.

GARDENS, GARDENING; POETRY, RHYME; PREDICTABLE TEXT.

McMILLAN, BRUCE
959   *Eating Fractions.* Photos by the author. Scholastic, 1991 (0-590-43770-4); pap. (0-590-72732-X). USE LEVEL: P
*Multicultural*
Color photographs show children from diverse backgrounds sharing food. Fractions including halves, thirds, and fourths are depicted.

ACTIVITIES—SHARING; COUNTING, NUMBERS; FRACTIONS; MATHEMATICS.

960   *Sense Suspense: A Guessing Game for the Five Senses.* Photos by the author. Scholastic, 1994 (0-590-47904-0). USE LEVEL: P
*Multicultural*

Two children from diverse backgrounds demonstrate activities that involve the senses. The brief text is written in Spanish and English.

ACTIVITIES; FOREIGN LANGUAGES; SENSES.

### MADDERN, ERIC, RETELLER
961    *The Fire Children: A West African Creation Tale.* Ill. by Frané Lessac. Dial, 1993 (0-8037-1477-7). USE LEVEL: M

*African*

Aso Yaa and Kwaku Ananse create children from clay, hide them in the fire, and then give them life, thus creating people of various skin tones.

CHARACTER TRAITS—APPEARANCE; CREATION; FOLKTALES—AFRICA.

962    *Rainbow Bird: An Aboriginal Folktale from Northern Australia.* Ill. by Adrienne Kennaway. Little, Brown, 1993 (0-316-54314-4). USE LEVEL: M

*Australian—Aborigine*

The people are given fire when Bird Woman takes it from Crocodile Man. After she shares the fire, Bird Woman uses the firesticks to change her appearance, becoming Rainbow Bird.

BIRDS; FIRE; FOLKTALES—AUSTRALIA—ABORIGINE; POURQUOI TALES; REPTILES—ALLIGATORS, CROCODILES.

### MADO, MICHIO
963    *The Animals: Selected Poems.* Translated by the Empress Michiko of Japan. Ill. by Mitsumasa Anno. Macmillan, 1992 (0-689-50574-4). USE LEVEL: M/U

*Asian—Japan*

There are 20 poems in this collection, each featuring animals, like "A Little Bird," "Zebra," "Giraffe," and "An Ant." The poems are printed in both Japanese and English.

ANIMALS; FOREIGN LANDS—ASIA—JAPAN; FOREIGN LANGUAGES; POETRY, RHYME.

### MAHER, RAMONA
964    *Alice Yazzie's Year: Poems.* Ill. by Stephen Gammell. Putnam, 1977, o.p. USE LEVEL: M

*Native American—Navajo*

For each month of the year, a free-verse poem describes Alice Yazzie's life in the desert. The traditions of the Navajo people are contrasted with the modern world of Mickey Mouse and Halloween.

DAYS OF THE WEEK, MONTHS OF THE YEAR; DESERT; POETRY, RHYME.

**MAHY, MARGARET**

965 *The Seven Chinese Brothers.* Ill. by Jean Tseng and Mou-Sien Tseng. Scholastic, 1990 (0-590-42055-0); pap. (0-590-42057-7). USE LEVEL: M

*Asian—China*

When these brothers offend the emperor, they each avoid death because of a special attribute.

CHARACTER TRAITS—CLEVERNESS; FAMILY LIFE; FOLKTALES—ASIA—CHINA.

**MAIORANO, ROBERT**

966 *Francisco.* Ill. by Rachel Isadora. Macmillan, 1978, o.p. USE LEVEL: P

*West Indian*

Francisco must provide for his family while his father is away. His family faces many hardships, yet Francisco finds a way to support them.

FAMILY LIFE; FOREIGN LANDS—DOMINICAN REPUBLIC; POVERTY; PROBLEM SOLVING.

967 *A Little Interlude.* Ill. by Rachel Isadora. Putnam, 1980, o.p. USE LEVEL: P

*African American*

Bobby, who is white, is looking forward to dancing the Nutcracker Ballet. He meets Jiminy Cricket, a black pianist, and they share their love of music and dance. Jiminy returns to his work as a stagehand while Bobby prepares to dance.

ACTIVITIES—DANCING; FRIENDSHIP; MUSIC.

**MAJOR, BEVERLY**

968 *Over Back.* Ill. by Thomas B. Allen. HarperCollins, 1993 (0-06-020286-6); LB (0-06-020287-4). USE LEVEL: M

*African American*

"Over Back" is "over across the fields, back behind the barn." It is a place to see and appreciate nature and the beauty of the countryside.

NATURE; RURAL LIFE.

**MAKHANLALL, DAVID**

969 *Brer Anansi and the Boat Race: A Caribbean Folk Tale.* Ill. by Amelia Rosato. Bedricks, 1988 (0-87226-184-0). USE LEVEL: M

*Caribbean*

Brer Anansi tricks Brer Rabbit and Brer Bear into leaving their supplies so they can compete in a boat race. Of course, Brer Anansi takes the supplies.

ANIMALS; BEHAVIOR—TRICKERY; FOLKTALES—CARIBBEAN ISLANDS; SPIDERS.

### MANDELBAUM, PILI

970 *You Be Me, I'll Be You.* Ill. by the author. Kane-Miller, 1990 (0-916291-27-8); pap. (0-916291-47-2). USE LEVEL: P
*Multicultural*
Anna, who has brown skin, tells her father, who is white, that she is not happy with her appearance. They trade places and Anna learns to appreciate differences and be satisfied with herself.
CHARACTER TRAITS—APPEARANCE; FAMILY LIFE—FATHERS; MARRIAGE, INTERRACIAL; SELF-CONCEPT.

### MANITONQUAT (MEDICINE STORY)

971 *The Children of the Morning Light: Wampanoag Tales.* Ill. by Mary F. Arquette. Macmillan, 1994 (0-02-765905-4). USE LEVEL: U
*Native American—Wampanoag*
An elder of the Assonet Wampanoag people tells 11 stories of his people including creation myths and pourquoi tales. Several stories feature Maushop, who helped the creator.
CREATION; FOLKTALES—NATIVE AMERICAN—WAMPANOAG; POURQUOI TALES; SHORT STORIES.

### MANN, KENNY

972 *"I Am Not Afraid!": Based on a Masai Tale.* Ill. by Richard Leonard and Alfredo Alcala. Bantam, 1993, LB (0-553-09119-0); pap. (0-513-37108-8). USE LEVEL: P
*African—Masai*
Leyo, the younger brother, is afraid of many things. His older brother, Tipilit, shows him how to be brave, even when they face the nine-headed demon.
CHARACTER TRAITS—BRAVERY; EMOTIONS—FEAR; FOLKTALES—AFRICA—MASAI; MONSTERS.

### MANNICHE, LISE, TRANSLATOR

973 *The Prince Who Knew His Fate: An Ancient Egyptian Tale.* Ill. by the translator. Metropolitan Museum of Art, 1981 (0-87099-278-3). USE LEVEL: M
*African—Egypt*
The king's son is destined to be killed by a crocodile or a snake or a dog. Knowing his fate, the prince chooses not to hide from life. This tale was translated from hieroglyphs.
FOLKTALES—AFRICA—EGYPT; HIEROGLYPHICS; MAGIC; ROYALTY—PRINCES.

**MARIE, D.**

974    *Tears for Ashan*. Ill. by Norman Childers. Creative Press Works, 1989 (0-9621681-0-6). USE LEVEL: M
*African*
In Africa, two boys are friends. When Ashan is taken by slave traders, Kumasi remembers his friend with sadness.
CRUELTY; EMOTIONS—SADNESS; FOREIGN LANDS—AFRICA; SLAVERY.

**MARKEL, MICHELLE**

975    *Gracias, Rosa*. Ill. by Diane Paterson. Whitman, 1995 (0-8075-3024-7). USE LEVEL: P
*Central American— Guatemala*
Rosa is from Guatemala and she baby-sits for Kate. Kate learns about the poverty of Rosa's family and of the husband and daughter, Juana, who still live in Guatemala. When Rosa goes back home, Kate gives her her favorite doll for Juana.
ACTIVITIES—BABY-SITTING; FOREIGN LANDS—CENTRAL AMERICA—
GUATEMALA; FOREIGN LANGUAGES; GIFTS; POVERTY.

**MARKUN, PATRICIA MALONEY**

976    *The Little Painter of Sabana Grande*. Ill. by Robert Casilla. Macmillan, 1993 (0-02-762205-3). USE LEVEL: M
*Central American—Panama*
At school, Fernando has learned to make his own paints. Now that he has paint, he wants to create pictures, so he uses the adobe walls of his family's house. The whole village enjoys his art and he creates paintings on all the houses.
ART; CHARACTER TRAITS—PERSEVERANCE; FOREIGN LANDS—CENTRAL
AMERICA—PANAMA; SELF-CONCEPT.

**MARTEL, CRUZ**

977    *Yagua Days*. Ill. by Jerry Pinkney. Dial, 1976, LB (0-8037-9766-4); pap. (0-8037-0457-7). USE LEVEL: M
*Hispanic American—Puerto Rico*
Adan's parents own a small store, a "bodega." On a rainy day, Adan is upset because he cannot play. On a visit to his family's home in Puerto Rico, he enjoys a yagua day, when everyone uses palm fronds, "yaguas," to slide in the rain.
COMMUNITIES, NEIGHBORHOODS; FAMILY LIFE; FOREIGN LANDS—
CARIBBEAN ISLANDS—PUERTO RICO; STORES; WEATHER—RAIN.

**MARTIN, BILL, JR., AND JOHN ARCHAMBAULT**

978    *Knots on a Counting Rope*. Ill. by Ted Rand. Henry Holt, 1987 (0-8050-0571-4); pap. (0-8050-2955-9). USE LEVEL: P/M
*Native American*

A young Native American boy and his grandfather share the story of the boy's courage. As the story is completed, the grandfather adds a knot to the counting rope.

CHARACTER TRAITS—BRAVERY; FAMILY LIFE—GRANDFATHERS; HANDICAPS—BLINDNESS; STORYTELLING.

### MARTIN, FRAN, RETELLER

979 *Raven-Who-Sets-Things-Right: Indian Tales of the Northwest Coast*. Ill. by Dorothy McEntee. Harper & Row, 1975, o.p. USE LEVEL: M

*Native American—Northwest Coast*

In the Northwest, near the Pacific Ocean, many native peoples tell of Raven, who can be a trickster as well as helpful.

ANIMALS; BEHAVIOR—TRICKERY; BIRDS—RAVENS; CHARACTER TRAITS— HELPFULNESS; FOLKTALES—NATIVE AMERICAN—NORTHWEST COAST.

### MARTIN, FRANCESCA

980 *The Honey Hunters: A Traditional African Tale*. Ill. by the author. Candlewick, 1992 (1-56402-086-X); pap. (1-56402-276-5). USE LEVEL: M

*African*

A boy follows the honey guide bird and is joined by other animals. When they find the honey, the once friendly animals begin to fight.

ANIMALS; BEHAVIOR—FIGHTING, ARGUING; FOLKTALES—AFRICA.

### MARTIN, RAFE

981 *The Boy Who Lived with the Seals*. Ill. by David Shannon. Putnam, 1993 (0-399-22413-0). USE LEVEL: M

*Native American—Chinook*

A boy wanders away from his people and is raised by seals. Years later, his people find him and bring him home. He seems to adjust, but then he returns to live with the seals.

ANIMALS—SEALS; FOLKTALES—NATIVE AMERICAN—CHINOOK.

982 *Foolish Rabbit's Big Mistake*. Ill. by Ed Young. Putnam, 1985 (0-399-21178-4); pap. (0-685-73728-4). USE LEVEL: M

*Asian—India*

A foolish rabbit hears an apple fall and thinks the earth may be breaking up. He convinces the other animals to panic and run with him.

ANIMALS—RABBITS; BEHAVIOR—MISTAKES; CHARACTER TRAITS—FOOL-ISHNESS; CUMULATIVE TALES; FOLKTALES—ASIA—INDIA.

983 *The Rough-Face Girl*. Ill. by David Shannon. Putnam, 1992 (0-399-21859-9). USE LEVEL: M

*Native American—Algonquian*

A girl who is scarred from tending the fire is the only one who is able to see the invisible being, and becomes his bride. This folktale has links to other Cinderella stories.

CHARACTER TRAITS—APPEARANCE; CHARACTER TRAITS—KINDNESS; FAMILY LIFE—SIBLINGS; FOLKTALES—NATIVE AMERICAN—ALGONQUIAN.

MARZOLLO, JEAN

984     *Pretend You're a Cat*. Ill. by Jerry Pinkney. Dial, 1990 (0-8037-0773-8); LB (0-8037-0774-6). USE LEVEL: PS/P
*Multicultural*
Animal activities are described in these poems, which encourage children to participate as they imitate each animal.

ACTIVITIES—PLAYING; ANIMALS; BEHAVIOR—IMITATION; IMAGINATION; POETRY, RHYME.

MATHIS, SHARON BELL

985     *The Hundred Penny Box*. Ill. by Leo Dillon and Diane Dillon. Viking, 1975 (0-670-38787-8); Puffin, pap. (0-14-032169-1).
USE LEVEL: M
*African American*
Michael's Great-Great-Aunt Dew keeps a box with a penny for every year of her life—one hundred pennies.

ACTIVITIES—REMINISCING; FAMILY LIFE—AUNTS, UNCLES; NEWBERY AWARD; OLDER ADULTS.

986     *Red Dog, Blue Fly: Football Poems*. Ill. by Jan Spivey Gilcrist. Viking, 1991 (0-670-83623-0). USE LEVEL: M
*African American*
Poems celebrate the joy and frustration of playing football. Listening to the coach, sacking the quarterback, and scoring a touchdown are some of the images presented.

POETRY, RHYME; SPORTS—FOOTBALL.

987     *Sidewalk Story*. Ill. by Leo Carty. Viking, 1971 Puffin, pap. (0-14-032165-9). USE LEVEL: M
*African American*
When Tanya and her family are evicted, Lilly Etta wants to help them. Lilly Etta finds a way to bring attention to her friend's situation and people in the community offer to help.

FRIENDSHIP; POVERTY; URBAN LIFE.

MATSUTANI, MIYOKO

988     *The Crane Maiden*. Ill. by Chihiro Iwasaki. Parents Magazine Pr., 1968, o.p. USE LEVEL: M
*Asian—Japan*
A poor old man rescues a crane. Later, he and his wife meet a

lovely maiden who weaves them a beautiful cloth. The wife's curiosity forces the maiden to become a crane again and leave them.

ACTIVITIES—WEAVING; BIRDS—CRANES; CHARACTER TRAITS—CURIOSITY; FOLKTALES—ASIA—JAPAN; MAGIC.

### MATTINGLY, CHRISTOBEL

989 *The Miracle Tree*. Ill. by Marianne Yamaguchi. Harcourt, 1985 (0-15-200530-7). USE LEVEL: M

*Asian—Japan*

Three people who were separated by the bombing of Nagasaki live for 20 years without knowing each is still living. They are all aware of one special tree, planted after the war. One Christmas, they are reunited.

FOREIGN LANDS—ASIA—JAPAN; HOLIDAYS—CHRISTMAS; TREES; WAR; WORLD WAR II.

### MATTOX, CHERYL WARREN, COLLECTOR AND ADAPTER

990 *Shake It to the One That You Love the Best: Play Songs and Lullabies from Black Musical Traditions*. Ill. by Varnette P. Honeywood and Brenda Joysmith. Warren-Mattox Productions, 1989, pap. (0-9623381-0-9). USE LEVEL: M/U

*African American*

A collection of songs that encourage participation. A cultural notation accompanies each song; for example, "Loop De Loo" is an African American ring game.

ACTIVITIES—PLAYING; GAMES; POETRY, RHYME.

### MAYER, MARIANNA, RETELLER

991 *Aladdin and the Enchanted Lamp*. Ill. by Gerald McDermott. Macmillan, 1985, o.p. USE LEVEL: M

*Middle Eastern—Arabia*

This is an expanded retelling of the traditional story of Aladdin. After finding the magic lamp, Aladdin uses it to win the love of Badoura, but there is always danger from the evil sorcerer.

FOLKTALES—MIDDLE EAST—ARABIA; MAGIC.

992 *The Golden Swan: An East Indian Tale of Love from the Mahabharata*. Ill. by Robert Sauber. Bantam, 1990 (0-553-07054-1). USE LEVEL: M

*Asian—India*

King Nala falls in love with a beautiful princess and Kali, the god of misfortune, tries to separate them.

EMOTIONS—LOVE; FOLKTALES—ASIA—INDIA; ROYALTY.

**MAYER, MERCER**

993     *Liza Lou and the Yeller Belly Swamp*. Ill. by the author. Macmillan, 1976 (0-02-765220-3). USE LEVEL: P

*African American*

Liza Lou must use her wits to escape the creatures in the Yeller Belly Swamp.

CHARACTER TRAITS—BRAVERY; CHARACTER TRAITS—CLEVERNESS; MONSTERS.

**MAYO, GRETCHEN WILL, RETELLER**

994     *Big Trouble for Tricky Rabbit!* Ill. by the reteller. Walker, 1994 (0-8027-8275-2); LB (0-8027-8276-0). USE LEVEL: M

*Native American*

This collection features Rabbit as a trickster in stories from different Native American peoples.

ANIMALS—RABBITS; BEHAVIOR—TRICKERY; FOLKTALES—NATIVE AMERICAN; SHORT STORIES.

995     *Here Comes Tricky Rabbit!* Ill. by the reteller. Walker, 1994 (0-8027-8273-6); LB (0-8027-8274-4). USE LEVEL: M

*Native American*

There are five stories about Rabbit from different native traditions.

ANIMALS—RABBITS; BEHAVIOR—TRICKERY; FOLKTALES—NATIVE AMERICAN; SHORT STORIES.

996     *Meet Tricky Coyote!* Ill. by the reteller. Walker, 1993 (0-8027-8198-5); LB (0-8027-8199-3). USE LEVEL: M

*Native American*

This collection features Coyote as a trickster in the stories of different Native American peoples.

ANIMALS—COYOTES; BEHAVIOR—TRICKERY; FOLKTALES—NATIVE AMERICAN; SHORT STORIES.

997     *Star Tales: North American Indian Stories about the Stars*. Ill. by the author. Walker, 1987 (0-8027-6672-2); LB (0-8027-6673-0). USE LEVEL: M/U

*Native American*

Many of these stories are "pourquoi tales" — they describe natural phenomena. These legends represent a variety of peoples, including the Wasco, the Shoshoni, the Ojibwa, and the Cherokee.

ASTRONOMY; FOLKTALES—NATIVE AMERICAN; POURQUOI TALES; SHORT STORIES; STARS.

998 *That Tricky Coyote!* Ill. by the reteller. Walker, 1993 (0-8027-8200-0); LB (0-8027-8201-9). USE LEVEL: M
*Native American*
There are six stories about Coyote from different Native American peoples.
ANIMALS—COYOTES; BEHAVIOR—TRICKERY; FOLKTALES—NATIVE AMERICAN; SHORT STORIES.

MAYO, MARGARET, RETELLER
999 *Magical Tales from Many Lands.* Ill. by Jane Ray. Dutton, 1993 (0-525-45017-3). USE LEVEL: M
*Multicultural*
The 14 stories in this collection are from diverse cultures, including Native Americans and Aborigines. Locations include Japan, West Africa, and China.
FOLKTALES; SHORT STORIES.

MEAD, ALICE
1000 *Crossing the Starlight Bridge.* Macmillan, 1994 (0-02-765950-X). USE LEVEL: M
*Native American—Penobscot*
When her father leaves them, Rayanne, nine, and her mother leave Two River Island, home of the Penobscot people, and move into town with Gram.
BEHAVIOR—GROWING UP; COMMUNITIES, NEIGHBORHOODS; DIVORCE, SEPARATION; FAMILY LIFE; MOVING.

MEDEARIS, ANGELA SHELF
1001 *Dancing with the Indians.* Ill. by Samuel Byrd. Holiday, 1991 (0-8234-0893-0); pap. (0-8234-1023-4). USE LEVEL: P
*Multicultural*
Traveling by wagon, an African American family visits the Seminole people who helped their grandfather when he was an escaping slave.
ACTIVITIES—DANCING; POETRY, RHYME; SLAVERY.

1002 *Our People.* Ill. by Michael Bryant. Macmillan, 1994 (0-689-31826-X). USE LEVEL: P
*African American*
A father tells his daughter of the contributions of many people of African heritage, including working on the pyramids and creating inventions. She realizes that she has a wonderful past and a future full of possibilities.
CHARACTER TRAITS—PRIDE; FAMILY LIFE—FATHERS; SELF-CONCEPT.

1003    *Poppa's New Pants.* Ill. by John Ward. Holiday, 1995 (0-8234-1155-9). USE LEVEL: P
*African American*
Poppa buys new pants that are too long. Grandma Tiny, Big Mama, and Aunt Viney are too tired to shorten them. In the night, George thinks he sees ghosts, but it turns out to be the three women coming to fix the pants. Now they are very short.
CLOTHING—PANTS; FAMILY LIFE; OLDER ADULTS; RURAL LIFE.

1004    *The Singing Man: A West African Folktale.* Ill. by Terea Shaffer. Holiday, 1994 (0-8234-1103-6). USE LEVEL: M
*African*
Banzar, the third son, is interested in music, but his family feels that he must make a better choice. Banzar leaves his village, becomes a praise singer, and is chosen to be the king's musician. He returns to his village to share his good fortune.
ACTIVITIES—SINGING; CORETTA SCOTT KING AWARD; FOLKTALES—AFRICA; MUSIC; SELF-CONCEPT.

1005    *Skin Deep: And Other Teenage Reflections.* Ill. by Michael Bryant. Macmillan, 1995 (0-02-765980-1). USE LEVEL: U
*African American*
These poems look at specific concerns of young teens, like dating, self-image, family issues, grades, and other anxieties. There are poems that capture the confidence and promise of teens who feel invincible and poems of hopelessness and despair.
BEHAVIOR—GROWING UP; EMOTIONS; POETRY, RHYME; SELF-CONCEPT.

**MEEKER, CLARE HODGSON, ADAPTER**
1006    *A Tale of Two Rice Birds: A Folktale from Thailand.* Ill. by Christine Lamb. Sasquatch, 1994 (1-57061-008-8). USE LEVEL: M
*Asian—Thailand*
While the father rice bird is caught in a lotus blossom, a fire kills the baby birds. The mother rice bird blames him for not returning. Later, when she returns as a princess and the father bird is a farmer, he proves the strength of his love.
BIRDS; EMOTIONS—LOVE; FOLKTALES—ASIA—THAILAND.

**MELMED, LAURA KRAUSS**
1007    *The First Song Ever Sung.* Ill. by Ed Young. Lothrop, 1993 (0-688-08230-0); LB (0-688-08231-9). USE LEVEL: P
*Asian—Japan*
A child asks members of the family about the first song. Some

answers are energetic, others are reflective, like the mother's lullaby that puts the child to sleep.

BEDTIME; FOREIGN LANDS—ASIA—JAPAN; SONGS.

### MENDEZ, PHIL

1008   *The Black Snowman*. Ill. by Carole Byard. Scholastic, 1989 (0-590-40552-7); pap. (0-590-44873-0). USE LEVEL: P/M
*African American*
With the help of a black snowman, who magically comes to life, Jacob learns about his past and develops a feeling of pride in himself and his heritage.

CHARACTER TRAITS—PRIDE; HOLIDAYS—CHRISTMAS; SELF-CONCEPT.

### MENNEN, INGRID

1009   *One Round Moon and a Star for Me*. Ill. by Niki Daly. Orchard, 1994 (0-531-06804-8); LB (0-531-08654-2). USE LEVEL: P
*African*
When the new baby is born, Papa hugs and reassures the baby's slightly older brother.

BABIES, TODDLERS; FOREIGN LANDS—AFRICA; NIGHT.

### MENNEN, INGRID, AND NIKI DALY

1010   *Somewhere in Africa*. Ill. by Nicholaas Maritz. Dutton, 1992 (0-525-44848-9). USE LEVEL: P
*African*
Ashraf lives in an urban center in Africa and he reads about the more open areas of his continent in a book borrowed from the library.

ACTIVITIES—READING; FOREIGN LANDS—AFRICA; LIBRARIES; URBAN LIFE.

### MERRILL, JEAN, ADAPTER

1011   *The Girl Who Loved Caterpillars: A Twelfth Century Tale from Japan*. Ill. by Floyd Cooper. Putnam, 1992 (0-399-21871-8). USE LEVEL: M
*Asian—Japan*
In the society of twelfth-century Japan, Izumi must conform or be rejected by her community and by possible suitors. Izumi chooses to be independent in thought and appearance.

CHARACTER TRAITS—INDIVIDUALITY; FOLKTALES—ASIA—JAPAN; INSECTS—BUTTERFLIES, CATERPILLARS; SELF-CONCEPT.

1012   *The Toothpaste Millionaire*. Ill. by Jan Palmer. Houghton, 1972 (0-395-18511-4); pap. (0-395-66954-5). USE LEVEL: M
*African American*

Rufus Mayflower, 12, has many creative ideas. He figures out how to make nylon saddlebags, including all the materials needed. Then he organizes a business to make toothpaste.
ACTIVITIES; CAREERS; FRIENDSHIP.

**MEYER, CAROLYN**
1013   *Rio Grande Stories.* Harcourt, 1994 (0-12-200548-X); pap. (0-15-200066-6). USE LEVEL: U
*Multicultural*
The students at Rio Grande Middle School in Albuquerque come from all over the city. One group of seventh graders is participating in the Heritage Project, collecting stories about the important contributions of their ancestors.
ACTIVITIES—REMINISCING; FAMILY LIFE; SCHOOL; SHORT STORIES; STORYTELLING.

1014   *White Lilacs.* Harcourt, 1993 (0-15-200641-9); pap. (0-15-295876-2). USE LEVEL: U
*African American*
In Dillon, Texas, in the 1920s there are plans to build a new park on land currently owned by blacks. Despite protests, families are relocated and their homes destroyed. Rose, 12, describes the events and their impact, especially on her grandfather.
FAMILY LIFE; KU KLUX KLAN; PREJUDICE; RACE RELATIONS; RELOCATION.

**MIKE, JAN M., RETELLER**
1015   *Gift of the Nile: An Ancient Egyptian Legend.* Ill. by Charles Reasoner. Troll, 1993, LB (0-8167-2813-5); pap. (0-8167-2814-3). USE LEVEL: M
*African—Egypt*
When Senefru was pharaoh, he was given Mutemwia as a gift. She became his friend, always telling him the truth, but she missed being free. With the help of his magician, Senefru gave Mutemwia her freedom.
CHARACTER TRAITS—FREEDOM; FOLKTALES—AFRICA—EGYPT.

1016   *Opossum and the Great Firemaker: A Mexican Legend.* Ill. by Charles Reasoner. Troll, 1993, LB (0-8167-3055-4); pap. (0-8167-3056-3). USE LEVEL: M
*Mexican*
Iguana, the Great Firemaker, takes his fire away from the people. Opossum tricks Iguana and steals the fire. Now, Opossum has a hairless tail and can pretend to be dead.
ANIMALS—OPOSSUMS; BEHAVIOR—TRICKERY; FOLKTALES—MEXICO; POURQUOI TALES; REPTILES—IGUANAS.

**MILES, BETTY**

1017    *Sink or Swim*. Knopf, 1986 (0-394-85515-9); Avon, pap. (0-380-69913-3). USE LEVEL: M

*African American*

B.J. is an urban child, 11 years old, who is spending two weeks in rural New Hampshire. It is an adjustment for him to fit in with the white host family, but he succeeds and enjoys the rural experience.

COMMUNITIES, NEIGHBORHOODS; FRIENDSHIP; RURAL LIFE; URBAN LIFE.

**MILES, MISKA**

1018    *Annie and the Old One*. Ill. by Peter Parnall. Little, Brown, 1971 (0-316-57117-2); pap. (0-316-57120-2). USE LEVEL: M

*Native American—Navajo*

Annie realizes that her grandmother is nearing the end of her life. Annie learns about the beliefs and traditions of her people.

CUSTOMS; DEATH; FAMILY LIFE—GRANDMOTHERS; NEWBERY AWARD; OLDER ADULTS.

**MILICH, MELISSA**

1019    *Can't Scare Me!* Ill. by Tyrone Geter. Doubleday, 1995 (0-385-31052-8). USE LEVEL: M

*African American*

Eugenia listens to her father, Mr. Hayman, tell ghost stories to his friend, Mr. Munroe, even though they scare Mr. Munroe so much he is afraid to walk home.

EMOTIONS—FEAR; GHOSTS; SCARY STORIES; STORYTELLING.

**MILIOS, RITA**

1020    *Sneaky Pete*. Ill. by Clovis Martin. Childrens Pr., 1989, LB (0-516-02092-7); pap. (0-516-42092-5). USE LEVEL: PS/P

*African American*

When his family looks for him to do chores or help out, Sneaky Pete cannot be found. The rhyming text is predictable and easy to read.

BEHAVIOR—HIDING; POETRY, RHYME; PREDICTABLE TEXT.

**MILLER, MARGARET**

1021    *Can You Guess?* Photos by the author. Greenwillow, 1993 (0-688-11180-7); LB (0-688-11181-5). USE LEVEL: PS/P

*Multicultural*

Children from diverse backgrounds are depicted answering questions about everyday activities, like combing hair, sending a letter, and wearing a hat.

ACTIVITIES; LANGUAGE.

1022    *Whose Hat?* Photos by the author. Greenwillow, 1988 (0-688-06906-1); LB (0-688-06907-X). USE LEVEL: PS/P
*Multicultural*
Photos of different hats are accompanied by the question "Whose Hat?" People from diverse backgrounds are depicted in the photos.
CAREERS; CLOTHING—HATS.

1023    *Whose Shoe?* Photos by the author. Greenwillow, 1991 (0-688-10008-2); LB (0-688-10009-0). USE LEVEL: PS/P
*Multicultural*
Photos show different types of footwear and who would wear them. Cultural diversity is presented in the photos.
CLOTHING—SHOES.

**MILLER, MOIRA**
1024    *The Moon Dragon.* Ill. by Ian Deuchar. Dial, 1989 (0-8037-0566-2). USE LEVEL: M
*Asian—China*
Ling Pao is always boasting. When he boasts that his kite could reach the moon, the emperor decides to come to the Kite Flying Festival.
BEHAVIOR—BOASTING; FOLKTALES—ASIA—CHINA; KITES.

**MILLER, MONTZALEE**
1025    *My Grandmother's Cookie Jar.* Ill. by Katherine Potter. Price/Stern/Sloan, 1987, o.p. USE LEVEL: P
*Native American*
A little girl loves eating cookies and listening to her grandmother's stories about their people. When her grandmother dies, the girl is given grandmother's cookie jar and she is reminded of the importance of remembering her heritage.
DEATH; FAMILY LIFE—GRANDMOTHERS; STORYTELLING.

**MILLS, CLAUDIA**
1026    *A Visit to Amy-Claire.* Ill. by Sheila Hamanaka. Macmillan, 1992 (0-02-766991-2). USE LEVEL: PS/P
*Asian American*
Tired of playing with Jessie, her two-year-old sister, Rachel, who is five, looks forward to visiting with her cousin Amy-Claire, who is two years older. On this trip, Amy-Claire seems to like playing with Jessie more than with Rachel.
ACTIVITIES—PLAYING; EMOTIONS—ENVY, JEALOUSY; FAMILY LIFE; SIBLING RIVALRY.

**MILSTEIN, LINDA**

1027 *Coconut Mon.* Ill. by Cheryl Munro Taylor. Morrow, 1995 (0-688-12862-9); LB (0-688-12863-7). USE LEVEL: P

*Caribbean*

The coconut mon has ten coconuts to sell. Counting backward from ten, he sells them all, except for the last one, which he gives to a young mon to eat.

COUNTING, NUMBERS; FOOD; FOREIGN LANDS—CARIBBEAN ISLANDS.

**MITCHELL, MARGARET KING**

1028 *Uncle Jed's Barbershop.* Ill. by James Ransome. Simon & Schuster, 1993 (0-671-76969-3). USE LEVEL: P/M

*African American*

A woman remembers her favorite uncle and the hardships her family endured in the segregated South in the 1920s.

ACTIVITIES—REMINISCING; CAREERS—BARBERS; CORETTA SCOTT KING AWARD; FAMILY LIFE—AUNTS, UNCLES; RACE RELATIONS; U.S. HISTORY.

**MITCHELL, RITA PHILLIPS**

1029 *Hue Boy.* Ill. by Caroline Binch. Dial, 1993 (0-8037-1448-3). USE LEVEL: P/M

*Caribbean*

Hue Boy is the smallest in his village and everyone has an idea to help him grow. When his father returns to the Caribbean island, Hue Boy stands tall.

COMMUNITIES, NEIGHBORHOODS; CONCEPTS—SIZE; EMOTIONS—LOVE; FAMILY LIFE—FATHERS; FOREIGN LANDS—CARIBBEAN ISLANDS.

**MOBLEY, JANE**

1030 *The Star Husband.* Ill. by Anna Bojtech. Doubleday, 1979, o.p. USE LEVEL: M

*Native American*

A woman wishes for a star to be her husband. Her wish is granted and she lives in the sky world and has a son, the Moon. She misses her old life and her people, and she returns to her village to complete the cycle of her life.

DEATH; FOLKTALES—NATIVE AMERICAN; STARS.

**MOCHIZUKI, KEN**

1031 *Baseball Saved Us.* Ill. by Dom Lee. Lee & Low, 1993 (1-880000-01-6). USE LEVEL: M

*Asian American—Japan*

During World War II, many Americans of Japanese descent were sent to internment camps. This book describes the emotions and activities in one camp, including how focusing on baseball provided a diversion from some of the hardships.

PREJUDICE; RACE RELATIONS; SPORTS—BASEBALL; U.S. HISTORY—WORLD WAR II.

### MOGENSEN, JAN

1032    *Kakalambalala*. Ill. by the author. Crocodile Books, 1993 (1-56656-136-1). USE LEVEL: M
*African*
During a drought, the animals go to a magic tree. If they can learn the name of the tree, they will get all the fruit they can eat. Although slow, the turtle travels to the mountain spirit and remembers the name—Kakalambalala.

FOLKTALES—AFRICA; NAMES; TREES; WATER; WEATHER—DROUGHTS.

### MOHR, NICHOLASA

1033    *Felita*. Ill. by Ray Cruz. Dial, 1979 (0-8037-3143-4); LB (0-8037-3144-2); Bantam, pap. (0-553-15792-2). USE LEVEL: M
*Hispanic American—Puerto Rico*
Felita, nine, learns about prejudice when her family leaves their city neighborhood.

FAMILY LIFE; MOVING; PREJUDICE; URBAN LIFE.

1034    *Going Home*. Dial, 1986 (0-8037-0269-8); LB (0-8037-0338-4); Bantam, pap. (0-553-15699-3). USE LEVEL: M
*Hispanic American—Puerto Rico*
Felita and her family travel together to visit their family and former home in Puerto Rico. When she finds that she will stay the summer there, Felita is happy at first, but she finds that she is an outsider and must learn to adjust.

ACTIVITIES—TRAVELING; BEHAVIOR—ACCEPTING DIFFERENCES; FAMILY LIFE; FOREIGN LANDS—CARIBBEAN ISLANDS—PUERTO RICO.

### MOLLEL, TOLOLWA M.

1035    *Big Boy*. Ill. by E. B. Lewis. Houghton, 1995 (0-395-67403-4). USE LEVEL: P
*African*
In Africa, Oli wants to go to the woods with his brother Mbachu. When he is supposed to be napping, Oli goes to the woods. He sees Tunukia-zawadi, a magical bird, who grants his wish to be big. But being big is hard when you are still a little boy.

BEHAVIOR—WISHING; CONCEPTS—SIZE; FAMILY LIFE; FOREIGN LANDS—AFRICA.

1036 *The Flying Tortoise: An Igbo Tale*. Ill. by Barbara Spurll.
Houghton, 1994 (0-395-68845-0). USE LEVEL: M
*African—Igbo*
At one time, Mbeku the tortoise has a smooth shell. He goes
with the birds to Skyland and eats all the banquet food himself.
When the birds realize they have been tricked, they leave
Mbeku to jump back to earth, and he cracks his shell.
BEHAVIOR—GREED; FOLKTALES—AFRICA—IGBO; POURQUOI TALES;
REPTILES—TURTLES, TORTOISES.

1037 *The King and the Tortoise*. Ill. by Kathy Blankley. Houghton,
1993 (0-395-64480-1). USE LEVEL: M
*African—Cameroon*
The king believes that no one is more clever than he, so he challenges all the creatures in his kingdom. Hare, fox, leopard, and
elephant fail to make a robe of smoke. Tortoise does not make a
robe either, but he does outwit the king.
ANIMALS; BEHAVIOR—TRICKERY; CHARACTER TRAITS—CLEVERNESS;
FOLKTALES—AFRICA—CAMEROON; REPTILES—TURTLES, TORTOISES.

1038 *The Orphan Boy: A Masai Story*. Ill. by Paul Morin. Houghton,
1990 (0-685-53587-8); pap. (0-395-72079-6). USE LEVEL: M
*African—Masai*
An old man finds an orphan boy, Kileken, and takes him into his
home. Kileken possesses special powers, but they must remain a
secret. When the old man learns the secret, Kileken returns to
his home as a star in the sky.
CHARACTER TRAITS—CURIOSITY; FOLKTALES—AFRICA—MASAI; STARS.

1039 *The Princess Who Lost Her Hair: An Akamba Legend*. Ill. by
Charles Reasoner. Troll, 1993, LB (0-8167-2815-1); pap. (0-
8167-2816-X). USE LEVEL: M
*African—Akamba*
The vain princess will not share her hair with the bird, so during
the dry season, she loses her hair. Muoma, the beggar boy, is
kind to the bird and is able to restore the princess's hair.
BIRDS; CHARACTER TRAITS—APPEARANCE; CHARACTER TRAITS—KIND-
NESS; FOLKTALES—AFRICA—AKAMBA; HAIR.

1040 *A Promise to the Sun: An African Story*. Ill. by Beatriz Vidal.
Little, Brown, 1992 (0-316-57813-4). USE LEVEL: M
*African*
During a drought, the birds send Bat to search for rain. Bat
promises that the birds will build a nest for the Sun, so the Sun

sends rain. The birds do not honor their promise, so now bats must hide in caves and stay hidden from the sun.

ANIMALS—BATS; BIRDS; FOLKTALES—AFRICA; POURQUOI TALES; WEATHER—DROUGHTS.

1041    *Rhinos for Lunch and Elephants for Supper! A Masai Tale*. Ill. by Barbara Spurll. Houghton, 1991 (0-395-60734-5). USE LEVEL: M

*African—Masai*

There is a monster in rabbit's cave. A fox, a leopard, a rhino, and an elephant try to help, but a frog scares the caterpillar out of the cave.

ANIMALS; CUMULATIVE TALES; EMOTIONS—FEAR; FOLKTALES—AFRICA—MASAI; INSECTS—BUTTERFLIES, CATERPILLARS.

**MONJO, F. N.**

1042    *The Drinking Gourd*. Ill. by Fred Brenner. HarperCollins, 1970 (0-06-024329-5); LB (0-06-024330-9); pap. (0-06-444042-7). USE LEVEL: P/M

*African American*

Tommy and his family become involved in helping runaway slaves escape to Canada.

SLAVERY; STARS; U.S. HISTORY; UNDERGROUND RAILROAD.

**MONROE, JEAN GUARD, AND RAY A. WILLIAMSON**

1043    *They Dance in the Sky: Native American Star Myths*. Ill. by Edgar Stewart. Houghton, 1987 (0-395-39970-X). USE LEVEL: M/U

*Native American*

Two chapters in this book present stories from different native peoples about the Pleiades and the Big Dipper. Six remaining chapters are organized by regions and peoples, like the Southwest and the Plains Indians.

ASTRONOMY; FOLKTALES—NATIVE AMERICAN; POURQUOI TALES; SHORT STORIES; STARS.

**MOORE, DESSIE**

1044    *Getting Dressed*. Ill. by Chevelle Moore. HarperCollins, 1994 (0-694-00590-8). USE LEVEL: PS

*African American*

A little boy tells of his routine for getting dressed. This book has a sturdy board format.

ACTIVITIES—GETTING DRESSED; CLOTHING; FORMAT, UNUSUAL—BOARD BOOKS; PREDICTABLE TEXT.

1045 *Good Morning.* Ill. by Chevelle Moore. HarperCollins, 1994 (0-694-00593-2). USE LEVEL: PS
*African American*
A little boy describes his activities as he is waking up. The heavy board format makes this appropriate for young children.
FORMAT, UNUSUAL—BOARD BOOKS; MORNING; PREDICTABLE TEXT.

1046 *Good Night.* Ill. by Chevelle Moore. HarperCollins, 1994 (0-694-00592-4). USE LEVEL: PS
*African American*
Taking a bath and hearing a story are part of this little girl's bedtime routine. The sturdy board format makes this a good choice for preschoolers.
BEDTIME; FORMAT, UNUSUAL—BOARD BOOKS; PREDICTABLE TEXT.

1047 *Let's Pretend.* Ill. by Chevelle Moore. HarperCollins, 1994 (0-694-00591-6). USE LEVEL: PS
*African American*
This little girl pretends to run a store, bake a cake, and be an adult. This book has a sturdy board format.
FORMAT, UNUSUAL—BOARD BOOKS; IMAGINATION; POETRY, RHYME; PREDICTABLE TEXT.

MOORE, EMILY
1048 *Just My Luck.* Puffin, pap. (0-14-034790-9). USE LEVEL: M
*African American*
Olivia, ten, wants a puppy but her parents feel they are too busy to help her care for one. Also, money will be scarce now that her father is taking time off to write.
FAMILY LIFE; FRIENDSHIP.

1049 *Something to Count On.* Puffin, pap. (0-14-034791-7). USE LEVEL: M
*African American*
When Lorraine's parents split up and her father moves out, Lorraine has problems at home, at school, and with her friends. She does not understand why her father keeps breaking his promises to her.
DIVORCE, SEPARATION; FAMILY LIFE; FRIENDSHIP; SCHOOL.

1050 *Whose Side Are You On?* Farrar, 1988 (0-374-38409-6); pap. (0-374-48373-6). USE LEVEL: M
*African American*
After she fails math, Barbra is told to let T.J. be her tutor. At

first, Barbra resents his help, but she comes to understand math, and to like T.J.

COMMUNITIES, NEIGHBORHOODS; FRIENDSHIP; SCHOOL; URBAN LIFE.

**MOORE, YVETTE**

1051    *Freedom Songs.* Orchard, 1991 (0-531-05812-3); LB (0-531-08412-4). USE LEVEL: U
*African American*
In 1963, Sheryl, 14, becomes more aware of the prejudice and injustice that she and other African Americans face. To help her uncle, who is a civil rights worker in the South, Sheryl organizes the Freedom Rider Benefit Concert.

CIVIL RIGHTS; MUSIC; PREJUDICE; RACE RELATIONS.

**MORA, FRANCISCO X.**

1052    *Juan Tuza and the Magic Pouch.* Ill. by the author. Highsmith, 1993, LB (0-917846-24-9). USE LEVEL: M
*Mexican*
In the desert, Juan Tuza, the prairie dog, and Pepe, the armadillo, need money for their rent. Juan Tuza helps a coyote, who is really the Great Spirit, and is rewarded with a magic pouch.

ANIMALS; DESERT; FOREIGN LANDS—MEXICO; FOREIGN LANGUAGES; MAGIC.

1053    *The Legend of the Two Moons.* Ill. by the author. Highsmith, 1992 (0-917846-15-X). USE LEVEL: M
*Mexican*
Chucho, the dog, sees two moons in the sky and Perico, the parrot, wants one of them. Perico drops the moon into the water, where we now see it as the reflection.

ANIMALS—DOGS; BIRDS—PARROTS; FOLKTALES—MEXICO; FOREIGN LANGUAGES; MOON.

1054    *The Tiger and the Rabbit: A Puerto Rican Folktale.* Ill. by the author. Childrens Pr., 1991, LB (0-516-05137-7); pap. (0-516-45137-5). USE LEVEL: M
*Caribbean—Puerto Rico*
To encourage storytelling, the illustrations are presented without the text. In the story (which follows the text), three times Señor Rabbit tricks Señor Tiger out of eating him. Finally, Señor Tiger realizes he will never outwit the rabbit.

ANIMALS—RABBITS; ANIMALS—TIGERS; BEHAVIOR—TRICKERY; CHARACTER TRAITS—FOOLISHNESS; FOLKTALES—CARIBBEAN ISLANDS—PUERTO RICO; STORYTELLING.

**MORA, PAT**

1055 *A Birthday Basket for Tia*. Ill. by Cecily Lang. Macmillan, 1992 (0-02-767400-2); LB (0-695-64816-8). USE LEVEL: P
*Mexican American*
Cecilia is excited about her great-aunt's ninetieth birthday, but she is worried about finding a gift.
BIRTHDAYS; FAMILY LIFE—AUNTS, UNCLES; GIFTS.

1056 *Pablo's Tree*. Ill. by Cecily Lang. Macmillan, 1994 (0-02-767401-0). USE LEVEL: P
*Mexican American*
On his birthday Pablo visits his grandfather, Lito. He wants to see the tree Lito planted on the day he was adopted. His grandfather decorates the tree for Pablo's birthday.
ADOPTION; BIRTHDAYS; FAMILY LIFE—GRANDFATHERS; TREES.

**MORGAN, PIERR, RETELLER**

1057 *Supper for Crow: A Northwest Coast Indian Tale*. Ill. by the reteller. Crown, 1995 (0-517-59378-5); LB (0-517-59379-3). USE LEVEL: M
*Native American—Northwest Coast*
Mama Crow and her babies are hungry, but Raven tricks them out of their food.
BEHAVIOR—TRICKERY; BIRDS—CROWS; BIRDS—RAVENS; FOLKTALES— NATIVE AMERICAN—NORTHWEST COAST.

**MORGAN, SALLY**

1058 *The Flying Emu: And Other Australian Stories*. Ill. by the author. Knopf, 1992 (0-679-84705-7). USE LEVEL: U
*Australian—Aborigine*
There are 20 stories in this collection, including stories of creation and of creatures like the emu, crocodile, kangaroo, wombat, and dingo.
ANIMALS; CREATION; FOLKTALES—AUSTRALIA—ABORIGINE; SHORT STORIES.

**MORIMOTO, JUNKO**

1059 *The Inch Boy*. Ill. by the author. Puffin, pap. (0-14-050677-2). USE LEVEL: M
*Asian—Japan*
An elderly couple is blessed with a child who is only one inch long. Issunboshi is brave and clever and eventually grows to full size.
CHARACTER TRAITS—BRAVERY; CHARACTER TRAITS—SMALLNESS; ELVES AND LITTLE PEOPLE; FOLKTALES—ASIA—JAPAN; MONSTERS.

MORONEY, LYNN, RETELLER

1060   *The Boy Who Loved Bears: A Pawnee Tale.* Ill. by Charles W. Chapman. Childrens Pr., 1994, LB (0-516-05142-3); pap. (0-516-45142-1). USE LEVEL: M
*Native American—Pawnee*
A Pawnee hunter saves the life of a bear cub. Later, the hunter's son, who is named Little Bear, is killed by enemies. A bear uses his magic to restore life to Little Bear, who comes to be called Bear Man. Unlike earlier books in this series, the text and pictures are together.
ANIMALS—BEARS; CHARACTER TRAITS—KINDNESS; FOLKTALES—NATIVE AMERICAN—PAWNEE; STORYTELLING.

MORRIS, ANN

1061   *Bread, Bread, Bread.* Photos by Ken Heyman. Lothrop, 1989 (0-688-06334-9); LB (0-688-06335-7); pap. (0-688-12275-2). USE LEVEL: PS/P
*Multicultural*
Throughout the world, people make, share, and enjoy bread. Different shapes and kinds of bread are described and the importance of bread in many cultures is shown.
FOOD; FOREIGN LANDS.

1062   *Hats, Hats, Hats.* Photos by Ken Heyman. Lothrop, 1989 (0-688-06338-1); LB (0-688-06339-X); pap. (0-688-12274-4). USE LEVEL: PS/P
*Multicultural*
This book depicts many cultures, focusing on different varieties of hats. An index of the locations is included.
CLOTHING—HATS; FOREIGN LANDS.

1063   *Houses and Homes.* Photos by Ken Heyman. Lothrop, 1992 (0-688-10168-2); LB (0-688-10169-0); pap. (0-688-13578-1). USE LEVEL: PS/P
*Multicultural*
Color photos show a variety of homes around the world, including tents, mud huts, and cabins.
FAMILY LIFE; FOREIGN LANDS; HOUSES.

1064   *Loving.* Photos by Ken Heyman. Lothrop, 1990 (0-688-06340-3); LB (0-688-06341-1); pap. (0-688-13613-3). USE LEVEL: PS/P
*Multicultural*
This book focuses on caring relationships in families around the world. A map and an index of locations are included.
EMOTIONS—LOVE; FAMILY LIFE; FOREIGN LANDS.

1065   *On the Go.* Photos by Ken Heyman. Lothrop, 1990, pap. (0-688-13637-0). USE LEVEL: PS/P
*Multicultural*
Different methods of travel are described and pictured, including vehicles powered by animals and by engines.
FOREIGN LANDS; TRANSPORTATION.

1066   *Tools.* Photos by Ken Heyman. Lothrop, 1992 (0-688-10170-4); LB (0-688-10171-2); Hampton-Brown, pap. (1-56334-301-0). USE LEVEL: PS/P
*Multicultural*
The use of tools around the world is described. Locations include Egypt, Hong Kong, Peru, Bali, and El Salvador.
FOREIGN LANDS; TOOLS.

**MORRIS, WINIFRED**

1067   *The Future of Yen-Tzu.* Ill. by Friso Henstra. Macmillan, 1992 (0-689-31501-5). USE LEVEL: M
*Asian—China*
Yen-tzu is a farmer's son who wants a different future, so he leaves the farm. He meets the emperor, who believes Yen-tzu speaks in riddles and can predict the future.
BEHAVIOR—SEEKING BETTER THINGS; FOLKTALES—ASIA—CHINA; ROYALTY—EMPERORS.

1068   *The Magic Leaf.* Ill. by Ju-Hong Chen. Macmillan, 1987, o.p. USE LEVEL: M
*Asian—China*
Lee Foo believes that he is a very smart man. When he loses his sword, he marks the side of the boat so he can return and find the spot. When he reads about a magic leaf, he searches for it until he thinks he has found it.
CHARACTER TRAITS—FOOLISHNESS; FOLKTALES—ASIA—CHINA.

**MOSEL, ARLENE, RETELLER**

1069   *The Funny Little Woman.* Ill. by Blair Lent. Dutton, 1972 (0-525-30265-4); pap. (0-525-45036-X). USE LEVEL: M
*Asian—Japan*
A woman makes a rice dumpling that rolls away from her. When she chases it, she becomes a prisoner of the oni and is given a magic rice paddle.
CALDECOTT AWARD; FOLKTALES—ASIA—JAPAN; FOOD; MAGIC; MONSTERS.

1070    *Tikki Tikki Tembo*. Ill. by Blair Lent. Henry Holt, 1968 (0-
        8050-0662-1); pap. (0-8050-1166-8). USE LEVEL: M
        *Asian—China*
        When Chang's brother falls into the well, it takes so long to say
        his name that he is nearly drowned.
        FOLKTALES—ASIA—CHINA; NAMES.

        **MOSES, AMY**
1071    *I Am an Explorer.* Ill. by Rick Hackney. Childrens Pr., 1990, LB
        (0-516-02059-5); pap. (0-516-42059-3). USE LEVEL: P
        *African American*
        A little boy has fantastic adventures as he explores in his neigh-
        borhood. Opposites like up/down and above/under are pre-
        sented in the simple, predictable text.
        ACTIVITIES—EXPLORING; CONCEPTS—OPPOSITES; IMAGINATION;
        PREDICTABLE TEXT.

        **MOSS, MARISSA**
1072    *Mel's Diner.* Ill. by the author. BridgeWater, 1994 (0-8167-
        3460-7); pap. (0-8167-3461-5). USE LEVEL: P
        *African American*
        A young girl, Mabel, helps her parents work at the family busi-
        ness—a diner. She passes out menus and talks with customers.
        She likes knowing that she helps her family.
        CAREERS; FAMILY LIFE; RESTAURANTS.

1073    *Regina's Big Mistake.* Ill. by the author. Houghton, 1990 (0-
        395-55330-X); pap. (0-395-70093-0). USE LEVEL: P
        *African American*
        Regina is not happy with her artwork, which does not convey
        her ideas.
        ACTIVITIES—DRAWING; CAREERS—ARTISTS; EMOTIONS; SCHOOL; SELF-
        CONCEPT.

        **MOSS, THYLIAS**
1074    *I Want to Be.* Ill. by Jerry Pinkney. Dial, 1993 (0-8037-1286-
        3); LB (0-8037-1287-1). USE LEVEL: P/M
        *African American*
        A girl uses her imagination to think about her future. She
        believes that she can be anything and accomplish anything.
        DREAMS; EMOTIONS—HAPPINESS; IMAGINATION; SELF-CONCEPT.

### MUNSCH, ROBERT

1075　*Where is Gah-Ning?* Ill. by Hélène Desputeaux. Annick, 1994, LB (1-55037-983-6); pap. (1-55037-98208). USE LEVEL: P
*Asian American—China*
In Canada, a girl wants to go shopping in Kapuskasing but her father, who has a Chinese restaurant, says no. She tries several methods of travel on her own, finally using 300 balloons.
ACTIVITIES—SHOPPING; BEHAVIOR—MISBEHAVIOR; FAMILY LIFE; TRANSPORTATION.

### MUNSCH, ROBERT, AND MICHAEL KUSUGAK

1076　*A Promise Is a Promise.* Ill. by Vladyana Krykorka. Annick, 1988 (1-55037-009-X); pap. (1-55037-008-1). USE LEVEL: P
*Native American—Inuit*
When Allashua disobeys her family's warnings and goes to the ocean to fish, she is caught by the Qallupilluit. She promises these monsters that she will bring them her brothers and sisters in exchange for saving herself.
FOLKTALES—NATIVE AMERICAN—INUIT; FOREIGN LANDS—CANADA; MONSTERS; SEA AND SEASHORE.

### MUSGROVE, MARGARET

1077　*Ashanti to Zulu: African Traditions.* Ill. by Leo Dillon and Diane Dillon. Dial, 1976 (0-8037-0357-0); LB (0-8037-0358-9); pap. (0-8037-0308-2). USE LEVEL: M
*African*
Each letter of the alphabet introduces another group of African people. Information about their customs and location is included in the brief description.
ABC BOOKS; CALDECOTT AWARD; CUSTOMS; FOREIGN LANDS—AFRICA.

### MWALIMU, AND ADRIENNE KENNAWAY

1078　*Awful Aardvark.* Ill. by Adrienne Kennaway. Little, Brown, 1989 (0-316-59218-8). USE LEVEL: M
*African*
At night, Aardvark's snoring keeps Mongoose awake. Mongoose and the other animals devise a plan that results in all aardvarks staying awake at night.
ANIMALS—AARDVARKS; ANIMALS—MONGOOSES; FOLKTALES—AFRICA; NIGHT; POURQUOI TALES; SLEEP.

### MYERS, CHRISTOPHER A., AND LYNNE BORN MYERS

1079　*Forest of the Clouded Leopard.* Houghton, 1994 (0-395-67408-5). USE LEVEL: U
*African—Iban*

Kenchendai hunts along the Batang Ai River in Borneo. After Grandfather dies, Kenchendai's father, Ribai, listens to a dream and travels alone to the land of the dead. Kenchendai must follow. He feels conflict between traditions and modern life.
DEATH; FAMILY LIFE—FATHERS; FOREIGN LANDS—AFRICA—IBAN.

### MYERS, LAURIE

1080    *Garage Sale Fever.* Ill. by Kathleen Collins Howell. HarperCollins, 1993 (0-06-022905-5); LB (0-06-022980-X).
USE LEVEL: M
*African American*
Will and his best friend, Pete, plan a garage sale and their friends join in.
BIRTHDAYS; FRIENDSHIP; GIFTS; MONEY; SCHOOL.

### MYERS, WALTER DEAN

1081    *Brown Angels: An Album of Pictures and Verse.* Photos selected by the author. HarperCollins, 1993 (0-06-022917-9); LB (0-06-022918-7). USE LEVEL: M
*African American*
Illustrated with photographs of African American children from the turn of the century, these poems celebrate the joys of childhood and the beauty of being black.
CHARACTER TRAITS—PRIDE; POETRY, RHYME; SELF-CONCEPT.

1082    *Darnell Rock Reporting.* Delacorte, 1994 (0-385-32096-5). USE LEVEL: U
*African American*
Darnell Rock gets involved in the school newspaper. When he decides to interview a homeless man, he gains insight into his own attitude about school and thinks about opportunities. His family and friends provide support as well as some distractions.
FAMILY LIFE; HOMELESSNESS; SCHOOL; SELF-CONCEPT.

1083    *Fast Sam, Cool Clyde, and Stuff.* Puffin, pap. (0-14-032613-8). USE LEVEL: U
*African American*
In his new neighborhood, Stuff, who is almost 13, begins to make new friends including Clyde, Gloria, BB, and Fast Sam. They help each other, as when Clyde's father dies and when Stuff falls in love with Kitty and then Susan and then Kitty again.
CORETTA SCOTT KING AWARD; FRIENDSHIP; URBAN LIFE.

1084    *Me, Mop, and the Moondance Kid.* Delacorte, 1988 (0-440-50065-6). USE LEVEL: M/U
*African American*
Even after he and his brother have been adopted, Moondance stays friends with Mop, a girl in the orphanage. Together, they play baseball and hatch plans to get Mop adopted.
ADOPTION; FAMILY LIFE; FRIENDSHIP; SPORTS—BASEBALL.

1085    *Mop, Moondance, and the Nagasaki Knights.* Delacorte, 1992 (0-385-30687-3); Dell, pap. (0-440-40914-4). USE LEVEL: M/U
*African American*
Having been adopted, T. J. and his brother enjoy their new situation and get involved in an important baseball game and helping a homeless friend.
ADOPTION; FAMILY LIFE; HOMELESSNESS; SPORTS—BASEBALL.

1086    *The Mouse Rap.* HarperCollins, 1990 (0-06-024343-0); LB (0-06-024344-9); pap. (0-06-440356-4). USE LEVEL: U
*African American*
Mouse is 14 and he enjoys hanging out with his friends, especially Styx and a new girl, Beverly. During the summer, the friends participate in a dance contest and investigate a mystery.
FRIENDSHIP; MYSTERY AND DETECTIVE STORIES; TREASURE; URBAN LIFE.

1087    *The Righteous Revenge of Artemis Bonner.* HarperCollins, 1992 (0-06-020844-9); LB (0-06-020846-5); pap. (0-06-440462-5). USE LEVEL: U
*African American*
When Artemis Bonner's uncle is killed, Artemis, 15, makes a round-about trip from New York City to the Southwest to avenge his death and to find his treasure. Finally, in Tombstone, Arizona, Artemis and his friend Frolic confront Catfish Grimes.
ADVENTURE; HUMOR; TREASURE; U.S. HISTORY.

1088    *Scorpions.* HarperCollins, 1988 (0-06-024364-3); LB (0-06-024365-1); pap. (0-06-447066-0). USE LEVEL: U
*African American*
While his older brother is in jail, Jamal, 12, takes over the leadership of the gang. For a while, the gang accepts Jamal as the leader, because he has a gun. Later, they confront him, causing a dangerous situation for Jamal and his friend, Tito.
FAMILY LIFE—SIBLINGS; GANGS; NEWBERY AWARD; URBAN LIFE; VIOLENCE.

1089    *The Young Landlords.* Viking, 1979, pap. (0-14-034244-3). USE
LEVEL: U
*African American*
Paul and his Action Group friends want to improve their
Harlem neighborhood. When they become the landlords of an
apartment building, they find that responsibility and change are
hard work.
CORETTA SCOTT KING AWARD; FRIENDSHIP; URBAN LIFE.

NAIDOO, BEVERLEY
1090    *Chain of Fire.* Ill. by Eric Velasquez. HarperCollins, 1990 (0-
397-32426-X); LB (0-397-32427-8); pap. (0-06-440468-4).
USE LEVEL: U
*African—South Africa*
Naledi, 15, and her family are removed from their homes and
exiled to "homelands" in South Africa. Naledi becomes
involved in the political and social unrest in South Africa.
FOREIGN LANDS—AFRICA—SOUTH AFRICA; PREJUDICE; RACE RELATIONS;
RELOCATION.

1091    *Journey to Jo'burg: A South African Story.* Ill. by Eric Velasquez.
HarperCollins, 1986 (0-397-32168-6); LB (0-397-32169-4);
pap. (0-06-440237-1). USE LEVEL: U
*African—South Africa*
Naledi, 13, and Tiro, 9, travel to Johannesburg to bring their
mother back to their village. When all three return, they take
the baby, Dineo, to the hospital. Throughout these events, the
children experience prejudice and inequity.
FAMILY LIFE; FOREIGN LANDS—AFRICA—SOUTH AFRICA; PREJUDICE;
RACE RELATIONS.

NAMIOKA, LENSEY
1092    *The Coming of the Bear.* HarperCollins, 1992 (0-06-020288-2);
LB (0-06-020289-0). USE LEVEL: U
*Asian—Japan*
In sixteenth century Japan, Zenta and Matsuzo are ronin
(unemployed samurai) whose boat has crashed. The Ainu peo-
ple aid them but the men escape when they realize that a war
may begin between the Ainu and the Japanese.
BEHAVIOR—FIGHTING, ARGUING; CHARACTER TRAITS—BRAVERY;
FOREIGN LANDS—ASIA—JAPAN; HISTORY.

1093    *Island of Ogres.* HarperCollins, 1989 (0-06-024372-4); LB (0-
06-024373-2). USE LEVEL: U
*Asian—Japan*

Kajiro is a ronin (an unemployed samurai) in sixteenth century Japan. He has landed on an island where the villagers are bothered by ogres. Kajiro is mistaken for a warrior and becomes involved with the villagers and their problems—and with Lady Yuri.

CHARACTER TRAITS—BRAVERY; FOREIGN LANDS—ASIA—JAPAN; HISTORY; MONSTERS.

1094 *Yang the Third and Her Impossible Family.* Ill. by Kees de Kiefte. Little, Brown, 1995 (0-316-59726-0). USE LEVEL: M
*Asian American—China*
Yingmei Yang is trying to adjust to life in America, but she is often embarrassed by the actions of her family and their Chinese background. She calls herself Mary and hopes to be Holly's friend, and she wishes she could have a kitten.

EMOTIONS—EMBARRASSMENT; FAMILY LIFE; FRIENDSHIP; PETS.

1095 *Yang the Youngest and His Terrible Ear.* Ill. by Kees de Kiefte. Little, Brown, 1992 (0-316-59701-5); Dell, pap. (0-440-40917-9). USE LEVEL: M
*Asian American—China*
Yingtao Yang is the youngest in his musical family, but he is not musical. As his family adjusts to life in Seattle, Yingtao learns English and baseball.

FAMILY LIFE; FRIENDSHIP; MUSIC; SELF-CONCEPT; SPORTS—BASEBALL.

NARAHASHI, KEIKO
1096 *Is That Josie?* Ill. by the author. Macmillan, 1994 (0-689-50606-6). USE LEVEL: PS/P
*Asian American*
As Josie plays, she imagines that she can be different animals like a turtle, a possum, and a cheetah. After a busy day, she is ready for a hug from Mommy and her bed.

ACTIVITIES—PLAYING; BABIES, TODDLERS; IMAGINATION.

NAVASKY, BRUNO, SELECTOR AND TRANSLATOR
1097 *Festival in My Heart: Poems by Japanese Children.* Abrams, 1993 (0-8109-3314-4). USE LEVEL: U
*Asian—Japan*
These poems by Japanese elementary school children include details about life in Japan and reflect the concerns of children everywhere, like their hopes and dreams for the future. The illustrations are reproductions of classic art from Japan.

EMOTIONS; FOREIGN LANDS—ASIA—JAPAN; POETRY, RHYME.

**NEASI, BARBARA J.**

1098 *Listen to Me.* Ill. by Gene Sharp. Childrens Pr., 1986, LB (0-516-02072-2); pap. (0-516-42072-0). USE LEVEL: PS/P
*African American*
A little boy feels that his parents are sometimes too busy for him but his Grandma has time for him. This book has a simple, predictable text.
FAMILY LIFE; PREDICTABLE TEXT.

**NELSON, VAUNDA MICHEAUX**

1099 *Mayfield Crossing.* Ill. by Leonard Jenkins. Putnam, 1993 (0-399-2231-2); Avon, pap. (0-380-72179-1). USE LEVEL: U
*African American*
In 1960, the school at Mayfield Crossing is closing and the students from that school will integrate Parkview Elementary. Meg and her friends encounter prejudice but they also find some support, especially in a baseball game.
FRIENDSHIP; PREJUDICE; RACE RELATIONS; SCHOOL; SPORTS—BASEBALL.

**NEVILLE, EMILY CHENEY**

1100 *The China Year: A Novel.* HarperCollins, 1991 (0-06-024383-X); LB (0-06-024384-8). USE LEVEL: U
*Asian—China*
Henrietta spends the year in China learning about her own way of life and that of the Chinese. When her mother becomes ill and must be flown home, Henri's friendship with Minyuan is ended. At home, she watches the events in Tiananmen Square on television.
FAMILY LIFE; FOREIGN LANDS—ASIA—CHINA; PROTEST; SCHOOL.

**NEWTON, PAM, RETELLER**

1101 *The Stonecutter: An Indian Folktale.* Ill. by the reteller. Putnam, 1990 (0-399-22187-5). USE LEVEL: M
*Asian—India*
The stonecutter becomes dissatisfied with his life and makes several wishes, only to realize that being a stonecutter is what he really wants.
BEHAVIOR—GREED; BEHAVIOR—WISHING; EMOTIONS—ENVY, JEALOUSY; FOLKTALES—ASIA—INDIA.

**NEWTON, PATRICIA MONTGOMERY, ADAPTER**

1102 *The Five Sparrows: A Japanese Folktale.* Ill. by the adapter. Macmillan, 1982, o.p. USE LEVEL: M
*Asian—Japan*

After children throw stones and hurt a sparrow, an old woman nurses it back to health. She is rewarded with a seed that grows to be gourds that are always filled with rice. A jealous neighbor wounds four sparrows, but her gourds are filled with flies.

BIRDS—SPARROWS; CHARACTER TRAITS—KINDNESS; FOLKTALES—ASIA—JAPAN.

### NIKOLA-LISA, W.

1103   *Bein' With You This Way.* Ill. by Michael Bryant. Lee & Low, 1994 (1-880000-05-9). USE LEVEL: P
*Multicultural*
The rhyming text celebrates the diversity of children playing at a neighborhood playground. The variety of skin, legs, arms, eyes, noses, and hair is highlighted.

ACTIVITIES—PLAYING; ANATOMY; COMMUNITIES, NEIGHBORHOODS; POETRY, RHYME.

### NODAR, CARMEN SANTIAGO

1104   *Abuelita's Paradise.* Ill. by Diane Paterson. Whitman, 1992 (0-8075-0129-8). USE LEVEL: P
*Caribbean—Puerto Rico*
A young girl, Marita, remembers the stories her grandmother would tell her about Puerto Rico. Now that Abuelita has died, Marita is sad, but she knows that she has her memories and she plans to visit Puerto Rico someday.

DEATH; EMOTIONS—SADNESS; FAMILY LIFE—GRANDMOTHERS; FOREIGN LANDS—CARIBBEAN ISLANDS—PUERTO RICO.

### NORMAN, HOWARD

1105   *How Glooskap Outwits the Ice Giants: And Other Tales of the Maritime Indians.* Ill. by Michael McCurdy. Little, Brown, 1989 (0-316-61181-6). USE LEVEL: M
*Native American*
The six stories in this collection feature the familiar giant, Glooskap, and describe how he protects the native peoples.

FOLKTALES—NATIVE AMERICAN; GIANTS; SHORT STORIES.

### NUNES, SUSAN

1106   *The Last Dragon.* Ill. by Chris K. Soentpiet. Houghton, 1995 (0-395-67020-9). USE LEVEL: P
*Asian American—China*
Peter Chang visits his great-aunt in Chinatown. He finds an old dragon in a store and becomes involved in getting people in the neighborhood to help restore it. On the last night of his visit, the Last Dragon is paraded through the streets.

ACTIVITIES; CHARACTER TRAITS—HELPFULNESS; COMMUNITIES, NEIGH-
BORHOODS; DRAGONS; FAMILY LIFE—AUNTS, UNCLES.

1107　*Tiddalick the Frog.* Ill. by Ju-Hong Chen. Macmillan, 1989 (0-
689-31502-3). USE LEVEL: M
*Australian—Aborigine*
After Tiddalick the frog swallows all the fresh water in the
world, the animals try to make Tiddalick laugh. Noyang, the
eel, dances, tying himself in a knot, and Tiddalick laughs,
spilling all the water out.
ANIMALS; FOLKTALES—AUSTRALIA—ABORIGINE; FROGS AND TOADS;
WATER.

1108　*To Find the Way.* Ill. by Cissy Gray. Univ. of Hawaii Pr., 1992
(0-8248-1376-6). USE LEVEL: M
*Tahitian*
In ancient times, a group of Polynesians left Tahiti to voyage to
islands to the north. Teva and his grandfather leave family
behind to make the dangerous sea journey.
CHARACTER TRAITS—BRAVERY; FOREIGN LANDS—TAHITI; SEA AND
SEASHORE.

NYE, NAOMI SHIHAB
1109　*Sitti's Secrets.* Ill. by Nancy Carpenter. Macmillan, 1994 (0-02-
768460-1). USE LEVEL: P
*Middle Eastern American—Arab*
Sitti visits her grandmother, who lives in a Palestinian village on
the West Bank. There, she learns about the way of life and customs of this region, as well as the political situation.
COMMUNITIES, NEIGHBORHOODS; CUSTOMS; FAMILY LIFE—GRAND-
MOTHERS; FOREIGN LANDS—MIDDLE EAST—PALESTINE.

OBER, HAL, RETELLER
1110　*How Music Came to the World: An Ancient Mexican Myth.* Ill. by
Carol Ober. Houghton, 1994 (0-395-67523-5). USE LEVEL: M
*Mexican—Aztec*
The sky god sends the wind god to the House of the Sun to get
singers and musicians and bring them to earth.
FOLKTALES—MEXICO—AZTEC; MUSIC; POURQUOI TALES.

O'BRIEN, ANNE SIBLEY, ADAPTER
1111　*The Princess and the Beggar: A Korean Folktale.* Ill. by the
adapter. Scholastic, 1993 (0-590-46092-7). USE LEVEL: M
*Asian—Korea*
Since she will not agree to an arranged marriage, the princess is

banished and sent to marry the beggar, Pabo Ondal. She comes to love him and they live happily.

CHARACTER TRAITS—KINDNESS; EMOTIONS—LOVE; FOLKTALES—ASIA— KOREA.

## OCHS, CAROL PARTRIDGE

1112 *When I'm Alone*. Ill. by Vicki Jo Redenbaugh. Carolrhoda, 1993 (0-87614-752-X); pap. (0-87614-620-5). USE LEVEL: P
*African American*

A little girl pretends that there are animals that come into her house and mess up her room. She counts backward from ten to one as she describes what the animals do. When her mother comes, there is only one kitten, and a big mess.

ANIMALS; BEHAVIOR—MESSY; COUNTING, NUMBERS; IMAGINATION; POETRY, RHYME.

## O'CONNOR, JANE

1113 *Molly the Brave and Me*. Ill. by Sheila Hamanaka. Random, 1990, LB (0-394-94175-6); pap. (0-394-84175-1). USE LEVEL: P
*African American*

Molly always seems so brave, but on a trip to the country, Beth finds she can be brave, too.

CHARACTER TRAITS—BRAVERY; FRIENDSHIP.

## O'DELL, SCOTT

1114 *The Black Pearl*. Ill. by Milton Johnson. Houghton, 1967 (0-395-06961-0); Dell, pap. (0-440-90803-5). USE LEVEL: U
*Mexican*

Ramón Salazar, 16, describes diving for pearls in the waters off Baja California. He finds a large pearl the color of smoke, but it seems cursed. His father and the fleet are lost in a storm and Ramón and the Sevillano face the Manta Diablo.

ADVENTURE; BEHAVIOR—GROWING UP; FOREIGN LANDS—MEXICO; NEWBERY AWARD; SEA AND SEASHORE.

1115 *Black Star, Bright Dawn*. Houghton, 1988 (0-395-47778-6); Fawcett, pap. (0-449-70340-1). USE LEVEL: U
*Native American—Eskimo*

Bright Dawn's father goes out hunting and is stranded in the blizzard. He is found but he is injured, so Bright Dawn takes his place in the Iditarod dogsled race. She learns to depend on her lead dog, Black Star, and on herself.

ANIMALS—DOGS; ARCTIC LANDS; CHARACTER TRAITS—BRAVERY; SPORTS—SLED RACING; SURVIVAL.

1116　*The Captive.* Houghton, 1979 (0-395-27811-2). USE LEVEL: U
**Central American—Mayan**
A Jesuit seminarian, Julián Escobar deplores the use of Mayan Indians as slaves. On a slave ship, Julián becomes involved in their plight and in their culture.
FOREIGN LANDS—CENTRAL AMERICA; HISTORY; SEA AND SEASHORE; SLAVERY.

1117　*Child of Fire.* Houghton, 1974, o.p. USE LEVEL: U
**Mexican American**
Delaney, the parole officer, first encounters Manuel Castillo when Manuel faces a bull in the bullring in Mexico. Later, their paths cross when Manuel leads a gang and then protests the use of a mechanical grape picker, which kills him.
CHARACTER TRAITS—BRAVERY; DEATH; FOREIGN LANDS—MEXICO; GANGS.

1118　*Island of the Blue Dolphins.* Ill. by Ted Lewin. Houghton, 1990 (0-395-53680-4); Dell, pap. (0-440-43988-4). USE LEVEL: U
**Native American**
When the villagers flee their island, Karana's brother, Ramo, is left behind. Karana leaves the ship to be with him. When Ramo is killed by wild dogs, Karana survives on the island alone. This is a newly illustrated reissue of the 1960 title.
ADVENTURE; ANIMALS—DOGS; ISLANDS; NEWBERY AWARD; SURVIVAL.

1119　*The King's Fifth.* Ill. by Samuel Bryant. Houghton, 1966 (0-395-06963-7). USE LEVEL: U
**Mexican**
Esteban de Sandoval travels with Captain Mendoza, one of Coronado's officers, searching for gold. Esteban draws maps and witnesses the greed and cruelty that surface as the group struggles to survive and find the gold.
ADVENTURE; FOREIGN LANDS—MEXICO; HISTORY; NEWBERY AWARD; SURVIVAL.

1120　*My Name Is Not Angelica.* Houghton, 1989 (0-395-51061-9); Dell, pap. (0-440-40379-0). USE LEVEL: U
**Caribbean**
Raisha is taken by force from her home in Africa and sold into slavery on St. John in the West Indies. Renamed Angelica, she and the other slaves organize a revolt that ends in the slaves leaping from a cliff to their deaths rather than submit.
CRUELTY; FOREIGN LANDS—CARIBBEAN ISLANDS; HISTORY; SLAVERY.

1121    *Sing Down the Moon.* Houghton, 1970 (0-395-10919-1); Dell, pap. (0-440-97975-7). USE LEVEL: U
*Native American*
Bright Morning, 15, is a Navajo in the Canyon de Chelly. In the 1860s, she and her friend, Running Bird, are taken by Spanish slave traders. They escape and return home only to have U.S. soldiers destroy their community and force their relocation.
NEWBERY AWARD; RELOCATION; SLAVERY; U.S. HISTORY.

1122    *Streams to the River, River to the Sea: A Novel of Sacagawea.* Houghton, 1986 (0-395-40430-4); Fawcett, pap. (0-449-70244-8). USE LEVEL: U
*Native American*
Sacagawea was a Shoshone who traveled with Lewis and Clark through the vast lands of the Louisiana Purchase. This book, although based on journals and historical texts, is a fictionalized account of her experiences.
FRONTIER AND PIONEER LIFE; HISTORY—EXPLORERS; SACAGAWEA; U.S. HISTORY.

1123    *Zia.* Houghton, 1976 (0-395-24393-9); Dell, pap. (0-440-99904-9). USE LEVEL: U
*Native American*
Zia and her brother try to travel to the Island of the Blue Dolphins but are captured by a whaling ship. After they escape and return to the Mission, Zia's aunt, Karana, comes from the island to see her.
ADVENTURE; FAMILY LIFE—AUNTS, UNCLES; SEA AND SEASHORE.

O'DELL, SCOTT, AND ELIZABETH HALL
1124    *Thunder Rolling in the Mountains.* Houghton, 1992 (0-395-59966-0); Dell, pap. (0-440-40879-2). USE LEVEL: U
*Native American—Nez Perce*
In 1877, Sound of Running Feet and her people, the Nez Perce, are led by her father, Chief Joseph, into leaving their land. Forced by soldiers, they are relocated and their resources taken from them.
CHARACTER TRAITS—BRAVERY; CRUELTY; RELOCATION; U.S. HISTORY.

OLALEYE, ISAAC
1125    *The Distant Talking Drum: Poems from Nigeria.* Ill. by Frané Lessac. Boyds Mills, 1995 (1-56397-095-3). USE LEVEL: M
*African—Nigeria*

Poems describe everyday life in Nigeria, including working on the farm, listening to stories, weaving, going to the market, and doing laundry in the stream.

ACTIVITIES; FOREIGN LANDS—AFRICA—NIGERIA; POETRY, RHYME.

**OLIVIERO, JAMIE**

1126 *The Fish Skin.* Ill. by Brent Morrisseau. Hyperion, 1993 (1-56282-401-5); LB (1-56282-402-3). USE LEVEL: M
*Native American*
Even though he is afraid, a boy journeys to Wisahkecàhk, the Great Spirit, to ask for rain. The spirit gives the boy a magic fish skin.

CHARACTER TRAITS—BRAVERY; FOLKTALES—NATIVE AMERICAN; MAGIC; POURQUOI TALES; WEATHER—DROUGHTS; WEATHER—RAIN.

1127 *Som See and the Magic Elephant.* Ill. by Jo'Anne Kelly. Hyperion, 1995 (0-7868-0025-9); LB (0-7868-2020-9). USE LEVEL: M
*Asian—Thailand*
Pa Nang (great-aunt) lives with Som See and her family. She knows that she will begin her final journey and she wishes to touch Chang, a white elephant who brings good fortune. In a fantasy, Som See enters the jungle and finds Chang.

ANIMALS—ELEPHANTS; DEATH; FAMILY LIFE—AUNTS, UNCLES; FOREIGN LANDS—ASIA—THAILAND.

**ONYEFULU, IFEOMA**

1128 *A Is for Africa.* Photos by the author. Dutton, 1993 (0-525-65147-0). USE LEVEL: P/M
*African*
Each letter of the alphabet correlates with an aspect of African life and culture.

ABC BOOKS; CUSTOMS; FOREIGN LANDS—AFRICA.

1129 *Emeka's Gift: An African Counting Story.* Photos by the author. Dutton, 1995 (0-525-65205-1). USE LEVEL: P
*African*
Emeka leaves his village to visit his grandmother. Along the way, he counts items that are a familiar part of his everyday life, including three women going to market and seven musical instruments called "ishaka."

COUNTING, NUMBERS; FAMILY LIFE; FOREIGN LANDS—AFRICA; FOREIGN LANGUAGES.

**ONYEFULU, OBI, RETELLER**

1130    *Chinye: A West African Folk Tale*. Ill. by Evie Safarewicz.
Viking, 1994 (0-670-85115-9). USE LEVEL: M
*African*
Chinye is mistreated by her stepmother and stepsister. She must
do all the work but she is always kind, and her kindness is
rewarded.
ANIMALS; CHARACTER TRAITS—KINDNESS; FOLKTALES—AFRICA; MAGIC.

**OODGEROO**

1131    *Dreamtime: Aboriginal Stories*. Ill. by Bronwyn Bancroft.
Lothrop, 1993 (0-688-13296-0). USE LEVEL: M
*Australian—Aborigine*
Family stories and some retellings of aboriginal folktales are pre-
sented in this collection.
FAMILY LIFE; FOLKTALES—AUSTRALIA—ABORIGINE; SHORT STORIES.

**OPPENHEIM, SHULAMITH LEVEY**

1132    *Fireflies for Nathan*. Ill. by John Ward. Morrow, 1994 (0-688-
12147-0); LB (0-688-12148-9). USE LEVEL: P
*African American*
On a visit to his grandparents, Nathan, six, enjoys catching fire-
flies just as his father did when he was little.
FAMILY LIFE—GRANDPARENTS; INSECTS—FIREFLIES; NIGHT; RURAL LIFE.

**ORMEROD, JAN**

1133    *Joe Can Count*. Ill. by the author. Morrow, 1986, pap. (0-688-
04588-X). USE LEVEL: PS
*African American*
Joe can count from one to ten. After counting ten puppies, he
chooses one to keep.
ANIMALS—DOGS; COUNTING, NUMBERS.

**OROZCO, JOSÉ-LUIS, SELECTOR, ARRANGER, AND TRANSLATOR**

1134    *De Colores: And Other Latin-American Folk Songs for Children*.
Ill. by Elisa Kleven. Dutton, 1994 (0-525-45260-5). USE LEVEL:
M/U
*Latin American*
There are 27 songs in this collection, presented in Spanish and
English and accompanied by musical notations. Songs include
"Al tambor/The Drum Song," "La villa/The Village," and
"Caballito blanco/My Little White Horse."
FOREIGN LANDS—LATIN AMERICA; FOREIGN LANGUAGES; MUSIC; SONGS.

**ORR, KATHERINE**

1135    *My Grandpa and the Sea.* Ill. by the author. Carolrhoda, 1990,
        LB (0-87614-409-1). USE LEVEL: M
        *Caribbean*
        Lila recalls her grandfather, who was a fisherman in the waters
        around St. Lucia. When larger fishing boats took his business,
        Lila's grandfather found a way to enjoy the sea and survive.
        CAREERS—FISHERMEN; FAMILY LIFE—GRANDFATHERS; FOREIGN LANDS—
        CARIBBEAN ISLANDS; SEA AND SEASHORE; SPORTS—FISHING.

1136    *Story of a Dolphin.* Ill. by the author. Carolrhoda, 1993 (0-
        87614-777-5); pap. (0-87614-951-4). USE LEVEL: P
        *Caribbean*
        Laura and her father live on an island in the Caribbean. A dol-
        phin befriends her father, but a problem develops when the
        people and the dolphin do not understand how to treat each
        other. A scientist helps explain the needs of the dolphin.
        ANIMALS—DOLPHINS; FOREIGN LANDS—CARIBBEAN ISLANDS; ISLANDS;
        SEA AND SEASHORE.

**OSBORNE, MARY POPE, RETELLER**

1137    *Mermaid Tales from Around the World.* Ill. by Troy Howell.
        Scholastic, 1993 (0-590-44377-1). USE LEVEL: M
        *Multicultural*
        The 12 stories in this collection feature mermaids and come
        from diverse peoples, including the Yoruba, the Ottawa, and the
        Chinese.
        FOLKTALES; MYTHICAL CREATURES—MERMAIDS; SHORT STORIES.

**OSOFSKY, AUDREY**

1138    *Dreamcatcher.* Ill. by Ed Young. Orchard, 1992 (0-531-05988-
        X); LB (0-531-08588-0). USE LEVEL: M
        *Native American—Ojibway*
        The baby sleeps dreaming good dreams and protected from bad
        dreams by the net of the dreamcatcher.
        BABIES, TODDLERS; DREAMS; FAMILY LIFE; FOLKTALES—NATIVE
        AMERICAN—OJIBWAY.

**OTSUKA, YUZO**

1139    *Suho and the White Horse: A Legend of Mongolia.* Ill. by Suekichi
        Akaba. Macmillan, 1967, o.p. USE LEVEL: M
        *Asian—Mongolia*

Suho, a poor shepherd boy, finds a newborn foal. When Suho and his horse are grown, they race and win. The governor takes Suho's horse and Suho is beaten, but they cannot break the spirit and love of Suho and his horse.

ANIMALS—HORSES; DEATH; FOLKTALES—ASIA—MONGOLIA.

**OUGHTON, JERRIE**

1140 *How the Stars Fell into the Sky: A Navajo Legend.* Ill. by Lisa Desimini. Houghton, 1992 (0-395-58798-0). USE LEVEL: M
*Native American—Navajo*
First Woman tries to place the stars in the sky, but Coyote becomes impatient and throws them into the sky.

ANIMALS—COYOTES; FOLKTALES—NATIVE AMERICAN—NAVAJO;
POURQUOI TALES; STARS.

1141 *The Magic Weaver of Rugs: A Tale of the Navaho.* Ill. by Lisa Desimini. Houghton, 1994 (0-395-66140-4). USE LEVEL: M
*Native American—Navajo*
Because their people are often cold and hungry, two women search for a way to help them. Spider Woman teaches the women how to weave and, with that skill, they use their weavings to keep warm and to sell for food.

ACTIVITIES—WEAVING; CHARACTER TRAITS—HELPFULNESS; FOLKTALES—
NATIVE AMERICAN—NAVAJO.

**OWEN, ROY**

1142 *My Night Forest.* Ill. by Amy Córdova. Macmillan, 1994 (0-02-769005-9). USE LEVEL: PS/P
*Hispanic American*
As she prepares for bed, a young child, who is depicted as Hispanic, imagines five animals, each exploring a different sensory area.

BEDTIME; IMAGINATION; SENSES.

**OXENBURY, HELEN**

1143 *All Fall Down.* Ill. by the author. Macmillan, 1987 (0-02-769040-7). USE LEVEL: PS
*Multicultural*
The babies in these pictures are from diverse backgrounds and are enjoying simple games.

ACTIVITIES—PLAYING; BABIES, TODDLERS; FORMAT, UNUSUAL—BOARD
BOOKS; GAMES.

1144 *Clap Hands.* Ill. by the author. Macmillan, 1987 (0-02-769030-X). USE LEVEL: PS
*Multicultural*

Babies from diverse backgrounds enjoy movement activities.

ACTIVITIES—PLAYING; BABIES, TODDLERS; FORMAT, UNUSUAL—BOARD BOOKS.

1145 *Say Goodnight.* Ill. by the author. Macmillan, 1987 (0-02-769010-5). USE LEVEL: PS

*Multicultural*

The illustrations show babies from diverse backgrounds in playful moments as they get ready for bed.

ACTIVITIES—PLAYING; BABIES, TODDLERS; BEDTIME; FORMAT, UNUSUAL—BOARD BOOKS; SLEEP.

1146 *Tickle, Tickle.* Ill. by the author. Macmillan, 1987 (0-02-769020-2). USE LEVEL: PS

*Multicultural*

Babies from diverse backgrounds participate in everyday activities, like taking a bath and being tickled.

ACTIVITIES—PLAYING; BABIES, TODDLERS; FORMAT, UNUSUAL—BOARD BOOKS.

**PALACIOS, ARGENTINA**

1147 *A Christmas Surprise for Chabelita.* Ill. by Lori Lohstoeter. BridgeWater, 1993 (0-8167-3131-4); pap. (0-8167-3132-2). USE LEVEL: M

*Central American—Panama*

Chabelita is staying with her grandparents. Although she is happy there, she misses her mother, who has moved to be closer to her job. At Christmas, Chabelita says a special poem at the holiday program, and her mother is there to see her.

FAMILY LIFE; FOREIGN LANDS—CENTRAL AMERICA—PANAMA; HOLIDAYS—CHRISTMAS.

1148 *The Hummingbird King: A Guatemalan Legend.* Ill. by Felipe Davalos. Troll, 1993, LB (0-8167-3051-2); pap. (0-8167-3052-0). USE LEVEL: M

*Central American—Guatemala—Mayan*

Kukul is protected by the hummingbird. When his father dies, Kukul becomes the leader of his people. Chirumá steals Kukul's charm and then kills him, but Kukul is transformed into a quetzal.

BIRDS—HUMMINGBIRDS; BIRDS—QUETZALS; FOLKTALES—CENTRAL AMERICA—GUATEMALA—MAYAN.

1149 *The Llama's Secret: A Peruvian Legend.* Ill. by Charles Reasoner. Troll, 1993, LB (0-8167-3049-0); pap. (0-8167-3050-4). USE LEVEL: M
*South American—Peru*
A llama warns his master of the coming of a flood and they seek refuge on Huillcacoto, a mountain peak in the Andes.
ANIMALS—LLAMAS; FOLKTALES—SOUTH AMERICA—PERU; WEATHER—FLOODS.

**PARKISON, JAMI**
1150 *Pequeña the Burro.* Ill. by Itoko Maeno. MarshMedia, 1994 (1-55942-055-3). USE LEVEL: M
*Mexican*
Pequeña the burro feels apprehensive about going to the birthday party for Captain Alvarez's daughter, Maria. He is not as grand as horses the captain rides. When there is an accident at the party, Pequeña rescues Maria.
ANIMALS—DONKEYS; BIRTHDAYS; FOREIGN LANDS—MEXICO; SELF-CONCEPT.

**PATERSON, KATHERINE**
1151 *Park's Quest.* Dutton, 1988 (0-525-67258-3); Puffin, pap. (0-14-034262-1). USE LEVEL: U
*Asian American—Vietnam*
Park, 11, is the son of an American soldier and a Vietnamese woman. Living with his father's family in America, Park seeks to learn more about his father and about his heritage.
BEHAVIOR—FACING CHALLENGES; BEHAVIOR—GROWING UP; FAMILY LIFE; SELF-CONCEPT.

1152 *The Tale of the Mandarin Ducks.* Ill. by Leo Dillon and Diane Dillon. Dutton, 1989 (0-525-67283-4). USE LEVEL: M
*Asian—Japan*
A Mandarin duck is separated from his mate and held captive, but a servant sets him free. Later, the servant is rewarded for her kindness.
BIRDS—DUCKS; CHARACTER TRAITS—KINDNESS; FOLKTALES—ASIA—JAPAN.

**PATRICK, DENISE LEWIS**
1153 *The Car Washing Street.* Ill. by John Ward. Morrow, 1993 (0-688-11452-0), LB (0-688-11453-9). USE LEVEL: P
*African American*
In this urban neighborhood, people get together on Saturday mornings to wash their cars, talk, and have fun.

AUTOMOBILES; COMMUNITIES, NEIGHBORHOODS; FAMILY LIFE—
FATHERS; URBAN LIFE.

1154  *Red Dancing Shoes.* Ill. by James Ransome. Morrow, 1993 (0-
688-10392-8); LB (0-688-19393-6). USE LEVEL: P
*African American*
Grandma returns from her trip with gifts for everyone, includ-
ing shiny red shoes just perfect for dancing. When the little girl
gets the shoes dirty, her great-aunt fixes them.
ACTIVITIES—DANCING; CLOTHING—SHOES; FAMILY LIFE—GRANDMOTH-
ERS; GIFTS.

**PATTISON, DARCY**
1155  *The River Dragon.* Ill. by Jean Tseng and Mou-Sien Tseng.
Lothrop, 1991 (0-688-10426-6); LB (0-688-10427-4). USE
LEVEL: M
*Asian—China*
Ying Shao is a blacksmith who lives on the banks of the river.
Three times the goldsmith tries to keep Ying Shao from marry-
ing his daughter, but Ying Shao outwits him and makes it home
safely past the River Dragon.
CHARACTER TRAITS—CLEVERNESS; DRAGONS; FOREIGN LANDS—ASIA—
CHINA.

**PAULSEN, GARY**
1156  *Canyons.* Delacorte, 1990 (0-385-30153-7); Dell, pap. (0-440-
21023-2). USE LEVEL: U
*Native American—Apache*
After he finds a skull in the canyons near El Paso, Texas,
Brennan Cole, 15, studies the life of a young Apache. Coyote
Runs was executed by soldiers in the 1860s. Brennan's research
helps release the spirit of Coyote Runs.
DESERT; FANTASY; U.S. HISTORY.

1157  *Dogsong.* Macmillan, 1985 (0-02-770180-8); Puffin, pap. (0-
14-032235-3). USE LEVEL: U
*Native American—Inuit*
Russel Susskit, 14, lives in an Arctic village. After learning about
Eskimo traditions from Oogruk, Russel takes Oogruk's sled and
dogs on a journey that becomes a search for himself and a test
of his survival skills.
ANIMALS—DOGS; ARCTIC LANDS; NEWBERY AWARD; SURVIVAL.

1158  *The Tortilla Factory.* Ill. by Ruth Wright Paulsen. Harcourt,
1995 (0-15-292876-6). USE LEVEL: P
*Mexican*

Simple language describes the process of growing corn and then making tortillas. Colors, like black earth, brown hands, green plants, add details to the description.

FOOD; FOREIGN LANDS—MEXICO.

PELLOWSKI, ANNE

1159    *The Family Storytelling Handbook: How to Use Stories, Anecdotes, Rhymes, Handkerchiefs, Paper, and Other Objects to Enrich Your Family Traditions.* Ill. by Lynn Sweat. Macmillan, 1987 (0-02-770610-9). USE LEVEL: M/U
*Multicultural*
This collection includes stories from around the world along with suggestions for telling them, using props and movement. Included are stories from Europe, Asia, and the Americas.

ACTIVITIES; STORYTELLING.

1160    *Hidden Stories in Plants: Unusual and Easy-to-Tell Stories from Around the World Together with Creative Things to Do While Telling Them.* Ill. by Lynn Sweat. Macmillan, 1990 (0-02-770611-7). USE LEVEL: M/U
*Multicultural*
Ideas are given for using plants to make ornaments, disguises, playthings, dolls, and musical instruments. Stories from many cultures, including Guatemala, Mexico, and Japan, accompany the projects.

ACTIVITIES; FOLKTALES; NATURE; PLANTS; STORYTELLING.

1161    *The Story Vine: A Source Book of Unusual and Easy-to-Tell Stories from Around the World.* Ill. by Lynn Sweat. Macmillan, 1984 (0-02-770590-0); pap. (0-02-044690-X). USE LEVEL: M/U
*Multicultural*
As the subtitle states, children will find these stories easy to tell and will enjoy the activities that correlate with the telling. Among the continents represented are Africa, Europe, and North America.

ACTIVITIES; STORYTELLING.

PENNINGTON, DANIEL

1162    *Itse Selu: Cherokee Harvest Festival.* Ill. by Don Stewart. Charlesbridge, 1994 (0-88106-851-9); LB (0-88106-852-7); pap. (0-88106-850-0). USE LEVEL: M
*Native American—Cherokee*
Little Wolf is looking forward to the Green Corn Festival, "Itse Selu," a time of celebration and thanksgiving that marks the

beginning of the new year. With his sister, Skye, and his friend, Little Buffalo, they prepare for the events.
CELEBRATIONS; FESTIVALS; HOLIDAYS.

**PERKINS, MITALI**

1163    *The Sunita Experiment.* Little, Brown, 1993 (0-316-69943-8); Hyperion, pap. (1-56282-671-9). USE LEVEL: U
*Asian American—India*
Sunita Sen, 13, is in the eighth grade and she worries about friends, school, and boys. Now that her grandparents are visiting from India, Sunni also worries about being different, especially when her teacher assigns a family heritage project.
BEHAVIOR—ACCEPTING DIFFERENCES; FAMILY LIFE—GRANDPARENTS; FRIENDSHIP; SCHOOL.

**PETERS, JULIE ANNE**

1164    *The Stinky Sneakers Contest.* Ill. by Cat Bowman Smith. Little, Brown, 1992 (0-316-70214-5); Camelot, pap. (0-380-72278-X). USE LEVEL: M
*African American*
Earl Cutter hopes to win the Stinky Sneakers Contest sponsored by a local shoe company. He also hopes he can finally beat Damian Stillwell at something. Earl is surprised to learn that Damian is cheating so that Earl will win!
CHARACTER TRAITS—HONESTY; CLOTHING—SHOES; CONTESTS; FRIENDSHIP.

**PETERSON, JEANNE WHITEHOUSE**

1165    *My Mama Sings.* Ill. by Sandra Speidel. HarperCollins, 1994 (0-06-023854-2); LB (0-06-023859-3). USE LEVEL: P
*African American*
A little boy describes how his mother sings to him throughout the year. One day, when there are some problems, the boy makes a song for his mother.
ACTIVITIES—SINGING; EMOTIONS—LOVE; FAMILY LIFE—MOTHERS; MUSIC.

**PETRIE, CATHERINE**

1166    *Joshua James Likes Trucks.* Ill. by Jerry Warshaw. Childrens Pr., 1982, LB (0-516-03525-8); pap. (0-516-43525-6). USE LEVEL: P
*African American*
Joshua James enjoys playing with his toy trucks and looking at real trucks. This beginning reader has a simple, predictable text.
ACTIVITIES—PLAYING; PREDICTABLE TEXT; TOYS; TRUCKS.

**PETTIT, JAYNE**

1167    *My Name Is San Ho.* Scholastic, 1992 (0-590-44172-8). USE
LEVEL: U
*Asian American—Vietnam*
During the war in Vietnam, San Ho's mother sends him to
Saigon to escape some of the brutality in his village. After she
marries an American soldier, San Ho comes to America and
must adjust to a new father and a new culture.
BEHAVIOR—ACCEPTING DIFFERENCES; BEHAVIOR—GROWING UP; FAMILY
LIFE; MOVING; U.S. HISTORY—VIETNAM WAR.

**PFEFFER, SUSAN BETH**

1168    *The Riddle Streak.* Ill. by Michael Chesworth. Henry Holt,
1993 (0-8050-2147-7). USE LEVEL: M
*African American*
Amy Gale, a third grader, wishes that she could find some way
to beat her older brother, Peter.
CONTESTS; FAMILY LIFE—SIBLINGS; RIDDLES; SIBLING RIVALRY.

**PHILIP, NEIL**

1169    *The Arabian Nights.* Ill. by Sheila Moxley. Orchard, 1994 (0-
531-06868-4). USE LEVEL: U
*Middle Eastern—Arabia*
When King Shahryar marries Sheherazade, she stays alive by
telling stories like "Aladdin" and "Ali Baba and the Forty
Thieves." There are 14 other stories in this collection.
FOLKTALES—MIDDLE EAST—ARABIA; MAGIC; SHORT STORIES.

1170    *Songs Are Thoughts: Poems of the Inuit.* Ill. by Maryclare Foa.
Orchard, 1995 (0-531-06893-5). USE LEVEL: M
*Native American—Inuit*
Arctic animals are featured in several of these poems, like musk
oxen, caribou, the gull, and bears. The poems express the emo-
tions of the young, looking forward to the hunt, and the elderly,
remembering life.
ARCTIC LANDS; POETRY, RHYME.

**PICÓ, FERNANDO**

1171    *The Red Comb.* Ill. by María Antonia Ordóñez. BridgeWater,
1991, LB (0-8167-3539-5). USE LEVEL: M
*Caribbean—Puerto Rico*
In nineteenth century Puerto Rico, escaping slaves were often
caught by villagers and returned for the reward. Greedy Pedro
Calderón had caught four runaways. With the help of a wise
neighbor woman, *siña* Rosa, Vitita hides a female slave.

BEHAVIOR—GREED; CHARACTER TRAITS—CLEVERNESS; CHARACTER TRAITS—KINDNESS; FOREIGN LANDS—CARIBBEAN ISLANDS—PUERTO RICO; SLAVERY.

**PINKNEY, ANDREA DAVIS**

1172    *Hold Fast to Dreams.* Morrow, 1995 (0-688-12832-7). USE LEVEL: U
*African American*
Deirdre Willis, 12, and her family move to Connecticut after her father is promoted. Deirdre must adjust to being the only black girl in her class. She uses her talent as a photographer and her love of Langston Hughes's poetry to be true to herself.
ACTIVITIES—PHOTOGRAPHY, FAMILY LIFE; MOVING; PREJUDICE; SELF-CONCEPT.

1173    *Seven Candles for Kwanzaa.* Ill. by Brian Pinkney. Dial, 1993 (0-8037-1292-8); LB (0-8037-1293-6). USE LEVEL: P/M
*African American*
Focusing on one family, this book presents information about the African American celebration of the harvest, Kwanzaa. Seven candles, symbolizing special principles, are part of the weeklong activities.
FAMILY LIFE; FOREIGN LANGUAGES; HOLIDAYS—KWANZAA.

**PINKNEY, BRIAN**

1174    *Max Found Two Sticks.* Ill. by the author. Simon & Schuster, 1994 (0-671-78776-4). USE LEVEL: P
*African American*
When two sticks fall from a tree, Max, who doesn't feel like talking, communicates with rhythms and beats.
ACTIVITIES; IMAGINATION; MUSIC; MUSICAL INSTRUMENTS.

**PINKNEY, GLORIA JEAN**

1175    *Back Home.* Ill. by Jerry Pinkney. Dial, 1992 (0-8037-1168-9); LB (0-8037-1169-7). USE LEVEL: P/M
*African American*
Ernestine, who is eight, has traveled by train to visit her relatives in North Carolina. She is worried about meeting them and making friends.
ACTIVITIES—TRAVELING; BEHAVIOR—GETTING ALONG WITH OTHERS; EMOTIONS—APPREHENSION; FAMILY LIFE; FRIENDSHIP; RURAL LIFE.

1176    *The Sunday Outing.* Ill. by Jerry Pinkney. Dial, 1994 (0-8037-1198-0); LB (0-8037-1199-9). USE LEVEL: P/M
*African American*

Ernestine and her Aunt Odessa enjoy going to the railroad station and watching the trains. Ernestine hopes she will be allowed to take the train to visit her relatives. This story continues in *Back Home*.

FAMILY LIFE—AUNTS, UNCLES; TRAINS.

### PITRE, FELIX, RETELLER

1177    *Juan Bobo and the Pig: A Puerto Rican Folktale*. Ill. by Christy Hale. Dutton, 1993 (0-525-67429-2). USE LEVEL: M
*Caribbean—Puerto Rico*
Juan Bobo is a foolish character. He dresses the pig in his mother's clothes because he thinks the pig wants to go to church.

ANIMALS—PIGS; CHARACTER TRAITS—FOOLISHNESS; FOLKTALES—CARIBBEAN ISLANDS—PUERTO RICO.

1178    *Paco and the Witch: A Puerto Rican Folktale*. Ill. by Christy Hale. Dutton, 1995 (0-525-67501-9). USE LEVEL: M
*Caribbean—Puerto Rico*
Paco has been warned about the witch who lives in the woods, yet he still goes with the old woman to her house. She catches him and to escape he must guess her name. He gets help from the crab, who now always hides when he sees people.

CRUSTACEA; FOLKTALES—CARIBBEAN ISLANDS—PUERTO RICO; NAMES; POURQUOI TALES; WITCHES.

### POLACCO, PATRICIA

1179    *Chicken Sunday*. Ill. by the author. Putnam, 1992 (0-399-22133-6). USE LEVEL: M
*African American*
A little girl loves her neighbors, brothers Stewart and Winston, and is especially fond of their gramma, Eula Mae Walker. They want to buy her a special hat for Easter. They decorate Easter eggs and they make a friend of the owner of the hat shop, Mr. Kodinski.

CLOTHING—HATS; FAMILY LIFE—GRANDMOTHERS; FOOD; FRIENDSHIP; HOLIDAYS—EASTER.

1180    *Mrs. Katz and Tush*. Ill. by the author. Bantam, 1992 (0-553-08122-5); Dell, pap. (0-440-40936-5). USE LEVEL: M
*African American*
Mrs. Katz is lonely and Larnel befriends her by giving her a kitten, Tush, which Larnel helps care for. Mrs. Katz and Larnel share a Passover celebration and then celebrate the birth of Tush's kittens.

ANIMALS—CATS; FRIENDSHIP; HOLIDAYS—PASSOVER.

1181    *Pink and Say*. Ill. by the author. Putnam, 1994 (0-399-22671-0). USE LEVEL: M
*African American*
Pinkus Aylee helps Sheldon Curtis when he is wounded, taking him to his mother's until he is well. Later, when the two try to rejoin their Union outfits, they are captured by the Confederates and Pinkus is killed.
CHARACTER TRAITS—BRAVERY; DEATH; FRIENDSHIP; RACE RELATIONS; U.S. HISTORY—CIVIL WAR.

POLITI, LEO
1182    *Juanita*. Ill. by the author. Macmillan, 1948, o.p. USE LEVEL: M
*Mexican American*
The Gonzalez family has a little shop in the old Los Angeles section of town. Juanita Gonzalez enjoys her everyday activities. She often celebrates holidays and traditions from her Mexican heritage. Three simple songs are included.
CALDECOTT AWARD; FAMILY LIFE; FOREIGN LANGUAGES; MUSIC; SONGS.

1183    *Song of the Swallows*. Ill. by the author. Macmillan 1987, ©1949 (0-684-18831-7); pap. (0-689-71140-9). USE LEVEL: M
*Mexican American*
Old Julian tells Juan the story of the Mission in the village of Capistrano. When the swallows return to the Mission, Julian lets Juan help him ring the bells to welcome them. Two songs are included.
BIRDS—SWALLOWS; CALDECOTT AWARD; MISSIONS; SONGS.

1184    *Three Stalks of Corn*. Ill. by the author. Macmillan, 1993, ©1976 (0-684-19538-0); pap. (0-689-71782-2). USE LEVEL: M
*Mexican American*
Angelica and her grandmother make tortillas and Angelica learns about the importance of corn to the people of Mexico. After a fiesta in their neighborhood in California, Angelica's grandmother teaches other children how to cook favorite foods.
ACTIVITIES—COOKING; FAMILY LIFE; FOOD; FOREIGN LANGUAGES.

POMERANTZ, CHARLOTTE
1185    *The Chalk Doll*. Ill. by Frané Lessac. HarperCollins, 1989 (0-397-32318-2); LB (0-397-32319-0); pap. (0-06-44333-1). USE LEVEL: P
*Caribbean—Jamaica*
Rose's mother tells her about growing up in Jamaica. One cherished memory from her childhood is a simple doll.
ACTIVITIES—REMINISCING; FAMILY LIFE—MOTHERS; FOREIGN LANDS—CARIBBEAN ISLANDS—JAMAICA; TOYS—DOLLS.

1186    *The Outside Dog.* Ill. by Jennifer Plecas. HarperCollins, 1993 (0-06-024782-7); LB (0-06-024783-5); pap. (0-06-444187-3). USE LEVEL: P
*Caribbean—Puerto Rico*
Marisol wants a dog, but her grandfather does not.
ANIMALS—DOGS; FAMILY LIFE—GRANDFATHERS; FOREIGN LANDS—CARIBBEAN ISLANDS—PUERTO RICO.

1187    *The Tamarindo Puppy: And Other Poems.* Ill. by Byron Barton. Greenwillow, 1980 (0-688-11902-6); LB (0-688-11903-4); pap. (0-688-11514-4). USE LEVEL: M
*Hispanic*
Poems about everyday experiences, including going to the bakery and singing a lullaby, are presented in both English and Spanish.
FOREIGN LANGUAGES; POETRY, RHYME.

**PORTE, BARBARA ANN**
1188    *"Leave That Cricket Be, Alan Lee."* Ill. by Donna Ruff. Greenwillow, 1993 (0-688-11793-7); LB (0-688-11794-5). USE LEVEL: P
*Asian American—China*
Just as he drifts off to sleep, Alan Lee hears a cricket and he is determined to find it. When he catches the cricket, it will not sing, so he decides to let it go.
FAMILY LIFE; INSECTS—CRICKETS.

**PORTER, CONNIE**
1189    *Addy Learns a Lesson: A School Story.* Ill. by Melodye Rosales. Pleasant Company, 1993, LB (1-56247-078-7); pap. (1-56247-077-9). USE LEVEL: M
*African American*
Free from slavery with her mother in Philadelphia, Addy begins to attend school, where she learns to read and write. She also learns that Sarah is a true friend, even though she is not as wealthy as others in the class.
FRIENDSHIP; SCHOOL; U.S. HISTORY—CIVIL WAR.

1190    *Addy Saves the Day: A Summer Story.* Ill. by Bradford Brown. Pleasant Company, 1994, LB (1-56247-084-1); pap. (1-56247-083-3). USE LEVEL: M
*African American*
Following the Civil War, Addy and her friends help at the church fund-raising fair. The money will be used to help find family members separated by slavery and by the war.
CHARACTER TRAITS—HELPFULNESS; DEATH; FAMILY LIFE; FRIENDSHIP.

1191   *Addy's Surprise: A Christmas Story.* Ill. by Melodye Rosales.
       Pleasant Company, 1993 (1-56247-080-9); pap. (1-56247-
       079-5). USE LEVEL: M
       *African American*
       In Philadelphia, Addy learns that being free is very costly. She
       and her mother both work to pay their bills and to help other
       escaping slaves. At Christmas, they are reunited with Poppa.
       CHARACTER TRAITS—FREEDOM; CHARACTER TRAITS—HELPFULNESS;
       FAMILY LIFE; HOLIDAYS—CHRISTMAS; U.S. HISTORY—CIVIL WAR.

1192   *Changes for Addy: A Winter Story.* Ill. by Bradford Brown.
       Pleasant Company, 1994, LB (1-56247-086-8); pap. (1-56247-
       085-X). USE LEVEL: M
       *African American*
       At the end of the Civil War, Addy and her mother have been
       reunited with her father and brother. Together, they look for
       Baby Esther, who was left on the plantation with Auntie Lula
       and Uncle Solomon.
       CHARACTER TRAITS—FREEDOM; FAMILY LIFE; SLAVERY; U.S. HISTORY—
       CIVIL WAR.

1193   *Happy Birthday, Addy: A Springtime Story.* Ill. by Bradford
       Brown. Pleasant Company, 1994 (1-56247-082-5); pap. (1-
       56247-081-7). USE LEVEL: M
       *African American*
       As the Civil War ends, Addy lives with her parents in Philadel-
       phia, hoping to be reunited with her brother and sister. Addy is
       befriended by an elderly blind woman who helps her choose and
       celebrate a birthday.
       BIRTHDAYS; FRIENDSHIP; HANDICAPS—BLINDNESS; OLDER ADULTS;
       PREJUDICE; U.S. HISTORY—CIVIL WAR.

1194   *Meet Addy: An American Girl.* Ill. by Melodye Rosales. Pleasant
       Company, 1993, LB (1-56247-076-0); pap. (1-56247-075-2).
       USE LEVEL: M
       *African American*
       Addy and her family are slaves in North Carolina. When her
       father, Poppa, and brother, Sam, are sold, Addy and her mother
       leave Baby Esther on the plantation and escape to Philadelphia.
       CHARACTER TRAITS—BRAVERY; CHARACTER TRAITS—FREEDOM; FAMILY
       LIFE; SLAVERY; U.S. HISTORY—CIVIL WAR.

       **POWELL, MARY, EDITOR**
1195   *Wolf Tales: Native American Children's Stories.* Ill. by Deborah
       Reade. Ancient City Pr., 1992, pap. (0-941270-73-4). USE
       LEVEL: M
       *Native American*

The seven stories in this collection feature the special bond between native peoples and the wolf. Included are "The Wolf and the Turtle" (Cherokee), "Medicine Wolves and Coyotes" (Pawnee), and "The Tired Wolf" (Tlingit).

ANIMALS—WOLVES; FOLKTALES—NATIVE AMERICAN; SHORT STORIES.

### POYDAR, NANCY

1196 *Busy Bea*. Ill. by the author. Macmillan, 1994 (0-689-50592-2). USE LEVEL: P

*African American*

Bea is so busy that she often misplaces things like her lunch box, her raincoat, and her jacket. Bea always helps Grandma find her things.

BEHAVIOR—LOSING THINGS; FAMILY LIFE.

### PRATHER, RAY

1197 *Fish and Bones*. HarperCollins, 1992 (0-06-025121-2); LB (0-06-025122-0). USE LEVEL: U

*African American*

It is 1971. Bones is involved in a mystery after the Sun City bank is robbed. He learns some town secrets, including that Mose Baker's father was lynched and that Fish (Mose's brain-injured son) is often duped into accepting the blame for others.

DEATH; MYSTERY AND DETECTIVE STORIES; PREJUDICE; RACE RELATIONS; RURAL LIFE.

### PRICE, LEONTYNE, RETELLER

1198 *Aïda*. Ill. by Leo Dillon and Diane Dillon. Harcourt, 1990 (0-15-200405-X). USE LEVEL: U

*African*

Aïda, an Ethiopian princess, is captured by Egyptian soldiers and forced to be a slave. She comes to love an Egyptian leader, Radames, and both are punished.

CORETTA SCOTT KING AWARD; DEATH; FOREIGN LANDS—AFRICA; MUSIC; SLAVERY.

### PRINGLE, LAURENCE

1199 *Octopus Hug*. Ill. by Kate Salley Palmer. Boyds Mills, 1993 (1-56397-034-1). USE LEVEL: PS/P

*African American*

While Mom is away, Dad watches Becky and Jesse. He invents games for them involving hugging, falling, riding, and scampering.

ACTIVITIES—PLAYING; FAMILY LIFE—FATHERS; GAMES.

**PRUSSKI, JEFFREY**

1200  *Bring Back the Deer.* Ill. by Neil Waldman. Harcourt, 1988 (0-15-200418-1). USE LEVEL: P

*Native American*

After his sister is born, the boy hunts to feed his family. As he stalks the deer, the boy encounters a wolf and begins to feel a kinship with the natural world.

ANIMALS; FAMILY LIFE; FOREST, WOODS; SELF-CONCEPT; SPORTS—HUNTING.

**QUALE, ERIC**

1201  *The Shining Princess: And Other Japanese Legends.* Ill. by Michael Foreman. Arcade, 1989 (1-55970-039-4). USE LEVEL: M/U

*Asian—Japan*

There are ten stories in this collection, each reflecting the cultural heritage of Japan. Familiar stories include "The Tongue-Cut Sparrow" and "Momotaro—the Peach Warrior."

FOLKTALES—ASIA—JAPAN; SHORT STORIES.

**QUATTLEBAUM, MARY**

1202  *Jackson Jones and the Puddle of Thorns.* Ill. by Melodye Rosales. Delacorte, 1994 (0-385-31165-6); Dell, pap. (0-440-41066-5). USE LEVEL: M

*African American*

Jackson wants a basketball for his birthday. Instead, his mother gives him a plot in the community garden. Now Jackson plans to grow flowers to sell so he can buy a basketball.

COMMUNITIES, NEIGHBORHOODS; FAMILY LIFE; FRIENDSHIP; GARDENS, GARDENING; URBAN LIFE.

**RAM, GOVINDER**

1203  *Rama and Sita: An Indian Folk Tale.* Ill. by the author. Bedrick, 1987, LB (0-87226-171-9). USE LEVEL: M

*Asian—India*

Rama, his wife, Sita, and his brother, Lakshman, are exiled to the forest. Ravana, the king of demons, captures Sita and she must be rescued.

CHARACTER TRAITS—BRAVERY; FOLKTALES—ASIA—INDIA.

**RANKIN, LAURA**

1204  *The Handmade Alphabet.* Ill. by the author. Dial, 1991 (0-8037-0974-9); LB (0-8037-0975-7). USE LEVEL: P/M

*Multicultural*

The alphabet is shown as capital letters and by hands forming the letter through the manual alphabet of American Sign Language. An item that depicts the letter is also shown. The hands that shape the letters are multicultural and multigenerational.

ABC BOOKS; HANDICAPS; SIGN LANGUAGE.

**RAPPAPORT, DOREEN, RETELLER**

1205    *The Journey of Meng: A Chinese Legend.* Ill. by Yang Ming-Yi. Dial, 1991 (0-8037-0895-5); LB (0-8037-0896-3). USE LEVEL: M

*Asian—China*

After her husband is taken by the emperor's soldiers to work on the Great Wall, Meng searches for him, only to find he has died. Meng leaps into the sea to avoid being taken by the emperor.

CHARACTER TRAITS—BRAVERY; DEATH; FOLKTALES—ASIA—CHINA.

1206    *The Long-Haired Girl: A Chinese Legend.* Ill. by Yang Ming-Yi. Dial, 1995 (0-8037-1411-4); LB (0-8037-1412-2). USE LEVEL: M

*Asian—China*

During a drought, Ah-mei discovers the God of Thunder's hidden spring. Ah-mei shows the spring to the villagers and faces punishment. An old man she has been kind to helps her escape the God of Thunder.

CHARACTER TRAITS—BRAVERY; CHARACTER TRAITS—KINDNESS; FOLKTALES—ASIA—CHINA; WEATHER—DROUGHTS.

1207    *The New King: A Madagascan Legend.* Ill. by E. B. Lewis. Dial, 1995 (0-8037-1460-2); LB (0-8037-1461-0). USE LEVEL: M

*African—Madagascar*

Prince Rakoto is frightened by the news that his father is dead. Now, he is to be the king. Rakoto commands his leaders to use their powers to restore his father to life. The Wise Woman teaches him about the cycle of life.

DEATH; FOLKTALES—AFRICA—MADAGASCAR; ROYALTY.

**RASCHKA, CHRIS**

1208    *Charlie Parker Played Be Bop.* Ill. by the author. Orchard, 1992 (0-531-05999-5); LB (0-531-08599-6). USE LEVEL: P

*African American*

In a rhyming text, the music of jazz great Charlie Parker is described. Repetition and nonsense words create a beat that slides, snaps, and pops.

CAREERS—MUSICIANS; MUSIC; POETRY, RHYME.

1209   *Yo! Yes?* Ill. by the author. Orchard, 1993 (0-531-05469-1); LB (0-531-08619-4). USE LEVEL: P/M
*Multicultural*
Two boys from different cultural backgrounds meet and are apprehensive of each other. They overcome their initial concerns and become friends.
CALDECOTT AWARD; EMOTIONS—HAPPINESS; FRIENDSHIP; RACE RELATIONS.

**RATTIGAN, JAMA KIM**
1210   *Dumpling Soup.* Ill. by Lillian Hsu-Flanders. Little, Brown, 1993 (0-316-73445-4). USE LEVEL: P
*Hawaiian*
Marisa helps make the dumplings for her family's New Year's Eve celebration.
FAMILY LIFE; FOOD; HOLIDAYS—NEW YEAR'S.

**REASONER, CHARLES, RETELLER**
1211   *The Magic Amber: A Korean Legend.* Ill. by the reteller. Troll, 1994, LB (0-8167-3407-0); pap. (0-8167-3408-9). USE LEVEL: M
*Asian—Korea*
A poor elderly couple share their meager meal with a stranger. They are rewarded with a magic amber stone. The stone brings them wealth, but they are kind to those in need. Their landlord steals the stone but loses it. It is returned to the couple.
BEHAVIOR—GREED; CHARACTER TRAITS—KINDNESS; FOLKTALES—ASIA—KOREA; MAGIC.

**REED, LYNN ROWE**
1212   *Pedro, His Perro, and the Alphabet Sombrero.* Ill. by the author. Hyperion, 1995 (0-7868-0071-2); LB (0-7868-2058-6). USE LEVEL: P
*Hispanic*
When Pedro receives a dog and a sombrero for his birthday, he decides to decorate his sombrero using alphabetical items, from avión (airplane) to zorrillo (skunk).
ABC BOOKS; CLOTHING—HATS; FOREIGN LANGUAGES.

**REES, ENNIS**
1213   *Brer Rabbit and His Tricks.* Ill. by Edward Gorey. Hyperion, 1992, ©1967 (1-56282-215-2); pap. (1-56282-577-1). USE LEVEL: M
*African American*

The three stories in this book are "Brer Rabbit and the Tar Baby," "Hello, House!" and "Winnianimus Grass and Whipmewhompme Cake." They feature Brer Rabbit as a trickster who outwits animals like Brer Wolf and Brer Fox. The text is written in verse.

ANIMALS; ANIMALS—RABBITS; BEHAVIOR—TRICKERY; FOLKTALES—
UNITED STATES; POETRY, RHYME; SHORT STORIES.

1214    *More of Brer Rabbit's Tricks.* Ill. by Edward Gorey. Hyperion, 1992, ©1968 (1-56282-217-9); pap. (1-56282-578-X). USE LEVEL: M
*African American*
"Brer Fox Bags a Lesson," "Fishing for Suckers," and "Brer Rabbit's Visit to Aunt Mammy-Bammy" are the three stories in this collection. The text is presented in verse.

ANIMALS; ANIMALS—RABBITS; BEHAVIOR—TRICKERY; FOLKTALES—
UNITED STATES; POETRY, RHYME; SHORT STORIES.

### REISER, LYNN

1215    *Margaret and Margarita/Margarita y Margaret.* Ill. by the author. Greenwillow, 1993 (0-688-12239-6); LB (0-688-12240-X). USE LEVEL: P
*Hispanic American*
Two girls, one who speaks only English, one who speaks only Spanish, tell the same story about going to the park. When they meet, they begin to build a friendship and to learn each other's language.

ACTIVITIES—PLAYING; FOREIGN LANGUAGES; FRIENDSHIP.

### RHEE, NAMI, RETELLER

1216    *Magic Spring: A Korean Folktale.* Ill. by the reteller. Putnam, 1993 (0-399-22420-3). USE LEVEL: M
*Asian—Korea*
An old man and an old woman find a spring that makes them young again, but their greedy neighbor drinks so much water from the spring that he becomes a baby.

BEHAVIOR—GREED; FOLKTALES—ASIA—KOREA; MAGIC; WISHES.

### RICHARD, FRANÇOISE

1217    *On Cat Mountain.* Ill. by Anne Buguet. Putnam, 1993 (0-399-22608-7). USE LEVEL: M
*Asian—Japan*
Young Sho has a cat she calls Secret. Her mistress, who dislikes cats and children, frightens the cat away. Sho travels to Cat

Mountain and is rewarded with riches. Her mistress goes there and is devoured.

ANIMALS—CATS; BEHAVIOR—GREED; FOLKTALES—ASIA—JAPAN.

### RICHARDSON, JEAN

1218    *The Courage Seed*. Ill. by Pat Finney. Sunbelt Media/Eakin Press, 1993 (0-89015-902-5). USE LEVEL: M
*Native American*
After her family is killed in an accident, Mary Manygoats moves to Texas to live with her Aunt Betsy. As the only Navajo in her class, she is apprehensive about school until her schoolmates share their diverse backgrounds.

EMOTIONS—APPREHENSION; EMOTIONS—SADNESS; MOVING; SCHOOL.

### RICHEMONT, ENID

1219    *The Magic Skateboard*. Ill. by Jan Ormerod. Candlewick, 1991 (1-56402-132-7); pap. (1-56402-449-0). USE LEVEL: M
*African heritage*
Just before Christmas, Danny encounters a strange, elderly woman whose magic makes his skateboard able to transport him to unusual locations, including the bathroom of the queen.

FANTASY; FOREIGN LANDS—ENGLAND; HOLIDAYS—CHRISTMAS; MAGIC; SPORTS—SKATEBOARDING.

### RINGGOLD, FAITH

1220    *Aunt Harriet's Underground Railroad in the Sky*. Ill. by the author. Crown, 1992 (0-517-58767-X); LB (0-517-58768-8). USE LEVEL: P/M
*African American*
While flying, Cassie and Be Be meet Harriet Tubman. Be Be rides on the train in the sky, and Cassie follows the route to freedom on the ground.

ACTIVITIES—FLYING; FAMILY LIFE; IMAGINATION; SLAVERY; U.S. HISTORY; UNDERGROUND RAILROAD.

1221    *Dinner at Aunt Connie's House*. Ill. by the author. Hyperion, 1993 (1-56282-425-2); LB (1-56282-426-0). USE LEVEL: P/M
*African American*
Melody and her newly adopted cousin, Lonnie, get to know each other and learn about the past of their people. In a fantasy sequence, pictures of famous women seem to come to life and tell about their contributions.

BIOGRAPHY; FAMILY LIFE; IMAGINATION; U.S. HISTORY.

1222    *Tar Beach.* Ill. by the author. Crown, 1991 (0-517-58030-6);
         LB (0-517-58031-4). USE LEVEL: P/M
         *African American*
         Eight-year-old Cassie Louise Lightfoot thinks about the hot
         summer nights when her family and friends go up to the roof of
         their apartment building in Harlem. Cassie imagines she can fly
         over the city.
         ACTIVITIES—FLYING; CALDECOTT AWARD; CORETTA SCOTT KING AWARD;
         FAMILY LIFE; IMAGINATION; URBAN LIFE.

**RIORDAN, JAMES**
1223    *The Woman in the Moon: And Other Tales of Forgotten Heroines.*
         Ill. by Angela Barrett. Dial, 1984 (0-8037-0194-2); LB (0-
         8037-0196-9). USE LEVEL: M/U
         *Multicultural*
         This collection of 13 folktales features women who accomplish
         tasks and succeed against the odds. Included are stories from
         many cultures including Native American, Ghanaian, Japanese,
         and Vietnamese.
         FOLKTALES; SHORT STORIES; WOMEN.

**ROBINET, HARRIETTE GILLEM**
1224    *If You Please, President Lincoln.* Macmillan, 1995 (0-915793-
         86-5). USE LEVEL: U
         *African American*
         In 1864, a group of freed slaves (and some runaways) partici-
         pate in a plan to colonize a small island in "Hayti." Moses
         Lincoln Christmas, 14, and 400 others endured horrible condi-
         tions, with many dying. Moses returns to America to tell this story.
         FOREIGN LANDS—CARIBBEAN ISLANDS—HAITI; SLAVERY; SURVIVAL; U.S.
         HISTORY.

1225    *Mississippi Chariot.* Macmillan, 1994 (0-689-31960-6). USE
         LEVEL: U
         *African American*
         In 1936, Shortning Bread Jackson, 12, faces prejudice and dis-
         crimination in Mississippi. He tries to help free his father, who
         has been wrongly convicted and sent to work on a chain gang.
         PREJUDICE; RACE RELATIONS; U.S. HISTORY.

1226    *Ride the Red Cycle.* Ill. by David Brown. Houghton, 1980, o.p.
         USE LEVEL: M
         *African American*
         Jerome, 11, has been handicapped since he had a viral infection

when he was 2. He wants to be more independent and becomes committed to leaving his wheelchair and riding a shiny red cycle. He accomplishes that—and more.
CHARACTER TRAITS—PERSEVERANCE; CHARACTER TRAITS—PRIDE; HANDICAPS; SELF-CONCEPT.

### ROBINSON, ADJAI
1227 *Three African Tales.* Ill. by Carole Byard. Putnam, 1979, o.p.
USE LEVEL: M
*African*
"The Hunter's Dilemma," "Kefala's Secret Something," and "The King's Rival" are the three stories that provide insight into the customs and beliefs in several African communities. Traditions of honor and respect are featured.
FOREIGN LANDS—AFRICA; SHORT STORIES; STORYTELLING.

### ROBINSON, GAIL, RETELLER
1228 *Raven the Trickster: Legends of the North American Indians.* Introduction by Douglas Hill. Ill. by Joanna Troughton. Macmillan, 1981, o.p. USE LEVEL: U
*Native American—Pacific Northwest*
Included among these nine tales from the Pacific Northwest are "Raven Brings Fire" and "How Raven Brought the Salmon."
BEHAVIOR—TRICKERY; BIRDS—RAVENS; FOLKTALES—NATIVE AMERICAN; POURQUOI TALES.

### ROCHELLE, BELINDA
1229 *When Jo Louis Won the Title.* Ill. by Larry Johnson. Houghton, 1994 (0-395-66614-7). USE LEVEL: P/M
*African American*
Jo Louis dreads the first day in her new school. Her grandfather, who is named John Henry, explains why she has such a special name.
FAMILY LIFE—GRANDFATHERS; MOVING; NAMES.

### ROCKWELL, ANNE
1230 *Tuhurahura and the Whale.* Ill. by the author. Parents Magazine Pr., 1971, o.p. USE LEVEL: M
*New Zealand—Maori*
Tuhurahura builds a canoe and Kiki, the wicked sorcerer, wants to punish Tuhurahura for using one of his trees. Tutunai, the whale, helps Tuhurahura.
ANIMALS—WHALES; FOLKTALES—NEW ZEALAND—MAORI; ISLANDS.

**RODANAS, KRISTINA, ADAPTER**

1231 *Dance of the Sacred Circle: A Native American Tale.* Ill. by the adapter. Little, Brown, 1994 (0-316-75358-0). USE LEVEL: M
*Native American—Blackfoot*
When his people are hungry, a young boy leaves them to ask for the help of the Great Chief in the Sky. His courage is rewarded when the Great Chief and his sacred council create a gift for the boy and his people—the horse.
ANIMALS—HORSES; CHARACTER TRAITS—BRAVERY; FOLKTALES—NATIVE AMERICAN—BLACKFOOT; POURQUOI TALES.

1232 *Dragonfly's Tale.* Ill. by the reteller. Houghton, 1992 (0-395-57003-4); pap. (0-395-72076-1). USE LEVEL: M
*Native American—Zuni*
The people of the tribe take their prosperity for granted so the Corn Maidens bring a drought. Two children succeed in regaining the blessing of the Corn Maidens.
FOLKTALES—NATIVE AMERICAN—ZUNI; FOOD; INSECTS; POURQUOI TALES; WEATHER—DROUGHTS.

1233 *The Story of Wali Dâd.* Ill. by the reteller. Lothrop, 1988 (0-688-07262-3); LB (0-688-07263-1). USE LEVEL: M
*Asian—India*
When his pot is filled with coins, Wali Dâd decides to spend them. He buys a bracelet and then gives it away to a princess. She gives him a gift, which he gives to a prince, thus acting as a go-between.
CHARACTER TRAITS—GENEROSITY; FOLKTALES—ASIA—INDIA; ROYALTY; WEDDINGS.

**RODDY, PATRICIA**

1234 *Api and the Boy Stranger: A Village Creation Tale.* Ill. by Lynne Russell. Dial, 1994 (0-8037-1221-9); LB (0-8037-1222-7). USE LEVEL: M
*African—Ivory Coast*
When a strange boy enters their village, only Api's mother will share food with him. He gives her family a warning, which they follow, and they escape the volcanic eruption.
CHARACTER TRAITS—KINDNESS; FOLKTALES—AFRICA—IVORY COAST; VOLCANOES.

**RODRIGUEZ, ANITA**

1235 *Aunt Martha and the Golden Coin.* Ill. by the author. Crown, 1993 (0-517-59337-8); LB (0-517-59338-6). USE LEVEL: P
*African American*

Aunt Martha tells the neighborhood children about how she found her magic coin. Later, when a robber comes to her apartment, Aunt Martha's magic coin protects her.

CRIME; MAGIC; STORYTELLING; URBAN LIFE.

1236    *Jamal and the Angel.* Ill. by the author. Crown, 1992 (0-517-58601-0); LB (0-517-59115-4). USE LEVEL: P
        ***African American***
        Aunt Martha tells a story about Jamal, a young boy who dreams of being a musician. He does not get a guitar for Christmas, but he is visited by his guardian angel. Jamal works for his dream and finally gets a guitar.

        DREAMS; MUSIC; STORYTELLING; URBAN LIFE.

        ROHMER, HARRIET, ADAPTER
1237    *Uncle Nacho's Hat: El Sombrero del Tio Nacho.* Ill. by Veg Reisberg. Children's Book Pr., 1989 (0-89239-043-3); pap. (0-89239-112-X). USE LEVEL: M
        ***Central American—Nicaragua***
        Uncle Nacho's hat is old and full of holes. His niece, Ambrosia, gives him a new hat but Uncle Nacho worries about his old hat, until his niece gives him some good advice.

        CHARACTER TRAITS—FOOLISHNESS; CLOTHING—HATS; FOLKTALES—CENTRAL AMERICA—NICARAGUA; FOREIGN LANGUAGES.

        ROHMER, HARRIET, AND MARY ANCHONDO, ADAPTERS
1238    *How We Came to the Fifth World/Como vinimos al quinto mundo: A Creation Story from Ancient Mexico.* Ill. by Graciela Carrillo. Children's Book Pr., 1988 (0-89239-024-7). USE LEVEL: M
        ***Mexican—Aztec***
        Because the people became selfish and cruel, the world was destroyed four times before the fifth world was created. From the earlier worlds, fish, animals, and birds were created. In the fifth world, there is peace and happiness.

        CREATION; FOLKTALES—MEXICO—AZTEC; FOREIGN LANGUAGES.

        ROHMER, HARRIET, OCTAVIO CHOW, AND MORRIS VIDAURE
1239    *The Invisible Hunters/Los Cazadores Invisibles: A Legend from the Miskito Indians of Nicaragua/Una Leyenda de los Indios Miskitos de Nicaragua.* Ill. by Joe Sam. Children's Book Pr., 1987, LB (0-89239-031-X). USE LEVEL: M
        ***Central American—Nicaragua***
        Three brothers go hunting for wari, the wild pig. A magic vine

makes the brothers invisible, but they misuse the power. Their punishment is to remain invisible.

BEHAVIOR—GREED; CORETTA SCOTT KING AWARD; FOLKTALES—CENTRAL AMERICA—NICARAGUA; FOREIGN LANGUAGES; MAGIC; SPORTS—HUNTING.

### ROLLINS, CHARLEMAE HILL, COMPILER

1240  *Christmas Gif': An Anthology of Christmas Poems, Songs, and Stories Written by and about Black People*. Ill. by Ashley Bryan. Morrow, 1993, ©1963 (0-688-11667-1); LB (0-688-11668-X). USE LEVEL: M/U

*African American*

Paul Laurence Dunbar, Langston Hughes, Effie Lee Newsom, Frederick Douglass, Lorenz Graham, and Countee Cullen are among the authors whose works are included here. There are also some traditional spirituals as well as some recipes.

HOLIDAYS—CHRISTMAS; POETRY, RHYME; SHORT STORIES; SONGS.

### ROSE, ANNE, RETELLER

1241  *Akimba and the Magic Cow: A Folktale from Africa*. Ill. by Hope Meryman. Macmillan, 1976, o.p. USE LEVEL: M

*African*

When Akimba takes a trip, he leaves his magic cow with his neighbor, Bumba. Bumba gives Akimba an ordinary cow. The same thing happens with Akimba's magic sheep and chicken, but not with his magic stick.

ANIMALS; FOLKTALES—AFRICA; MAGIC.

### ROSE, DEBORAH LEE, ADAPTER

1242  *The People Who Hugged the Trees: An Environmental Folktale*. Ill. by Birgitta Säflund. Roberts Rinehart, 1990 (0-911797-80-7); pap. (1-879373-50-5). USE LEVEL: M

*Asian—India*

Amrita loves the trees for she knows they provide shade from the sun and protection from the wind. When the maharajah orders the trees cut for his fortress, Amrita and the villagers hug the trees to protect them.

ECOLOGY; FOLKTALES—ASIA—INDIA; TREES.

### ROSEN, MICHAEL

1243  *Bonesy and Isabel*. Ill. by James Ransome. Harcourt, 1995 (0-15-209813-5). USE LEVEL: P

*Hispanic American—El Salvador*

Isabel, who is from El Salvador, must adjust to her new home in the United States. She has been adopted and is trying to learn

English as well as new customs. She becomes close to Bonesy, an old dog, and she is filled with sadness when he dies.
ADOPTION; ANIMALS—DOGS; DEATH; EMOTIONS—SADNESS; PETS.

1244    *Crow and Hawk: A Traditional Pueblo Indian Story.* Ill. by John Clementson. Harcourt, 1995 (0-15-200257-X). USE LEVEL: M
*Native American—Pueblo*
Crow leaves a nest filled with eggs and Hawk hatches them and cares for the young crows. When Crow wants the birds back, Eagle, the King of Birds, must decide their fate.
BIRDS—CROWS; BIRDS—HAWKS; FOLKTALES—NATIVE AMERICAN—PUEBLO.

1245    *Elijah's Angel: A Story for Chanukah and Christmas.* Ill. by Aminah Brenda Lynn Robinson. Harcourt, 1992 (0-15-225394-7). USE LEVEL: M
*Multicultural*
After his fourth-grade class visits Elijah's barber shop, Michael, a Jewish boy, continues to visit him. Elijah gives Michael an angel as a Christmas gift and Michael gives Elijah a menorah.
CAREERS—ARTISTS; FRIENDSHIP; HOLIDAYS—CHRISTMAS; HOLIDAYS—HANUKKAH.

1246    *How Giraffe Got Such a Long Neck . . . and Why Rhino Is So Grumpy: A Tale from East Africa.* Ill. by John Clementson. Dial, 1993 (0-8037-1621-4). USE LEVEL: M
*African—East Africa*
During a drought, Giraffe and Rhino find a tree but they cannot reach the leaves. Man gives Giraffe some magic, which he uses all himself, and his neck grows long.
ANIMALS—GIRAFFES; ANIMALS—RHINOCEROS; FOLKTALES—AFRICA—EAST AFRICA; MAGIC; POURQUOI TALES; WEATHER—DROUGHTS.

1247    *How the Animals Got Their Colors: Animal Myths from Around the World.* Ill. by John Clementson. Harcourt, 1992 (0-15-236783-7). USE LEVEL: M
*Multicultural*
Stories about animals, including the coyote, frog, tiger, and peacock, are included in this collection. Origins of the tales include Native American people, Greece, China, and India.
ANIMALS; CONCEPTS—COLOR; FOLKTALES; POURQUOI TALES.

1248    *South and North, East and West: The Oxfam Book of Children's Stories.* Introduction by Whoopi Goldberg. Candlewick, 1992 (1-56402-117-3); pap. (1-56402-396-6). USE LEVEL: M
*Multicultural*

Stories from around the world are illustrated by many artists. In her introduction, Whoopi Goldberg writes that sharing stories helps us "find how much we have in common." Included are stories from Zimbabwe, Nepal, Malta, Botswana, and Bangladesh.

FOLKTALES; SHORT STORIES.

### ROSS, GAYLE, RETELLER

1249 *How Turtle's Back Was Cracked: A Traditional Cherokee Tale.* Ill. by Murv Jacob. Dial, 1995 (0-8037-1728-8); LB (0-8037-1729-6). USE LEVEL: M
*Native American—Cherokee*
Turtle and Possum were once good friends. When Turtle takes credit for killing Wolf, the other wolves are angry with Turtle. He convinces them to throw him into the river. He escapes, but his shell is cracked.

FOLKTALES—NATIVE AMERICAN—CHEROKEE; POURQUOI TALES; REPTILES—TURTLES, TORTOISES.

### ROTH, SUSAN L.

1250 *Fire Came to the Earth People: A Dahomean Folktale.* Ill. by the author. St. Martin's, 1988; Dell, pap. (0-440-40844-X). USE LEVEL: M
*African*
Moon-God Mawu kept Fire for herself. The animals want Fire, and Chameleon and Tortoise work together to get it.

ANIMALS; FIRE; FOLKTALES—AFRICA; POURQUOI TALES.

1251 *Kanahéna: A Cherokee Story.* Ill. by the author. St. Martin's, 1988, o.p. USE LEVEL: M
*Native American—Cherokee*
While cooking Kanahéna (corn meal), an old woman tells a little girl the story of Terrapin and how he outwitted Bad Wolf. When the other wolves came to punish Terrapin, he tricked them too.

ANIMALS—WOLVES; BEHAVIOR—TRICKERY; FOLKTALES—NATIVE AMERICAN—CHEROKEE; REPTILES—TURTLES, TORTOISES.

1252 *The Story of Light.* Ill. by the author. Morrow, 1990 (0-688-08676-4); LB (0-688-08677-2). USE LEVEL: M
*Native American—Cherokee*
The earth is dark and the animals want to take some of the sun for themselves. Possum and Buzzard fail but Spider succeeds.

FOLKTALES—NATIVE AMERICAN—CHEROKEE; POURQUOI TALES; SPIDERS; SUN.

**ROY, RONALD**

1253    *A Thousand Pails of Water.* Ill. by Vo-Dinh Mai. Knopf, 1978, o.p. USE LEVEL: P
*Asian*
In Yukio's village, the people hunt whales. His father's hands are often bloody and Yukio wonders why. When Yukio finds a stranded whale, he tries to save him and the villagers come to help, too.
ANIMALS—WHALES; FAMILY LIFE—FATHERS; FOREIGN LANDS; SPORTS – HUNTING.

**RUBY, LOIS**

1254    *Steal Away Home.* Macmillan, 1994 (0-02-777883-5). USE LEVEL: U
*African American*
Alternating chapters present different time periods and adventures in an old house in Kansas. In present day, a white girl, Dana, 12, finds a skeleton in a secret room. It is of Lizbet Charles, a black woman who helped escaping slaves 130 years ago.
CHARACTER TRAITS—FREEDOM; MYSTERY AND DETECTIVE STORIES; SLAVERY; U.S. HISTORY; UNDERGROUND RAILROAD.

**RUCKI, ANI**

1255    *Turkey's Gift to the People.* Ill. by the author. Northland, 1992 (0-87358-541-0). USE LEVEL: M
*Native American—Navajo*
When a flood comes, the animals hide in hollow reeds. Mr. and Mrs. Turkey come last because they have been gathering the seeds that will be needed after the flood.
ANIMALS; BIRDS—TURKEYS; FOLKTALES—NATIVE AMERICAN—NAVAJO; WEATHER—FLOODS.

**RUPERT, JANET E.**

1256    *The African Mask.* Houghton, 1994 (0-395-67295-3). USE LEVEL: U
*African—Yoruba*
Layo, 12, lives in eleventh century Africa (in the area that is now Nigeria). Her talent for creating pottery will be wasted if she marries into a family of metal workers. She must find a way to escape this arranged marriage and realize her potential.
FOREIGN LANDS—AFRICA—YORUBA; HISTORY; SELF-CONCEPT.

**RUPERT, RONA**

1257    *Straw Sense.* Ill. by Mike Dooling. Simon & Schuster, 1993 (0-671-77047-0). USE LEVEL: P
*African*

Goolam-Habib does not speak. He is fascinated by the straw figures that are made by an older man, Saul, and they begin a friendship.

ACTIVITIES; FOREIGN LANDS—AFRICA; FRIENDSHIP; HANDICAPS; TOYS—DOLLS.

### RYAN, PAM MUÑOZ

1258    *One Hundred Is a Family.* Ill. by Benrei Huang. Hyperion, 1994 (1-56282-672-7); LB (1-56282-673-5). USE LEVEL: PS/P
*Multicultural*
Family groups are counted from 1 to 10, then families are shown by 10s from 20 to 100. Families with diverse backgrounds are enjoying many locations and activities.

ACTIVITIES; COUNTING, NUMBERS; FAMILY LIFE; POETRY, RHYME.

### SABUDA, ROBERT

1259    *Tutankhaman's Gift.* Ill. by the author. Macmillan, 1994 (0-689-31818-9). USE LEVEL: M
*African—Egypt*
Describes the customs and beliefs in Ancient Egypt through the eyes of the child, Tutankhamen.

ANCIENT TIMES; FOREIGN LANDS—AFRICA—EGYPT; HISTORY; ROYALTY.

### SACKS, MARGARET

1260    *Themba.* Ill. by Wil Clay. Dutton, 1992 (0-525-67414-4); Puffin, pap. (0-14-036445-5). USE LEVEL: M
*African—South Africa*
Themba's father has been working in the gold mines. After three years there, he is coming home. When his father does not arrive, Themba goes to look for him.

EMOTIONS—APPREHENSION; FAMILY LIFE—FATHERS; FOREIGN LANDS—AFRICA—SOUTH AFRICA.

### SADLER, CATHERINE EDWARDS, RETELLER

1261    *Heaven's Reward: Fairy Tales from China.* Ill. by Cheng Mung Yun. Macmillan, 1985 (0-689-31127-3). USE LEVEL: M
*Asian—China*
Six stories provide insight into Chinese philosophy and culture. The hierarchy of Confucian society is seen in "Heaven's Reward." The Taoist belief in equality is seen in "The Little Goddess." An introduction gives background information.

FOLKTALES—ASIA—CHINA; SHORT STORIES.

1262    *Treasure Mountain: Folktales from Southern China.* Ill. by Cheng Mung Yun. Atheneum, 1982, o.p. USE LEVEL: M
*Asian—China*

Six stories—two from the Han, two from the Yao, and one each from the Chung and T'ung peoples—are presented in this collection. The stories reflect the customs and beliefs of the peoples of southern China.

FOLKTALES—ASIA—CHINA; MAGIC; SHORT STORIES.

### SAGE, JAMES

1263 *The Little Band.* Ill. by Keiko Narahashi. Macmillan, 1991 (0-689-50516-7). USE LEVEL: P

*Multicultural*

Six children from diverse backgrounds march through town and countryside playing music and delighting all who see and hear them.

MUSIC; PARADES.

### SAINT JAMES, SYNTHIA

1264 *The Gifts of Kwanzaa.* Ill. by the author. Whitman, 1994 (0-8075-2907-9). USE LEVEL: P

*African American*

A young girl describes her family's celebration of this African American festival of the harvest.

CELEBRATIONS; FAMILY LIFE; HOLIDAYS—KWANZAA.

### SAKAI, KIMIKO

1265 *Sachiko Means Happiness.* Ill. by Tomie Arai. Children's Book Pr., 1990 (0-89239-065-4). USE LEVEL: P

*Asian American—Japan*

Grandmother's memory is failing, and she does not recognize Sachiko. Sachiko is worried about Grandmother and she does not like to be with her. On a walk with Grandmother, Sachiko comes to understand her illness and she tries to help her.

FAMILY LIFE—GRANDMOTHERS; ILLNESS—ALZHEIMER'S; OLDER ADULTS.

### SAKURAI, GAIL

1266 *Peach Boy: A Japanese Legend.* Ill. by Makiko Nagano. Troll, 1994, LB (0-8167-3409-7); pap. (0-8167-3410-0). USE LEVEL: M

*Asian—Japan*

An elderly couple wishes for a child. They find a boy in a large peach. The boy, Momotaro, grows to be strong and with a dog, a monkey, and a pheasant, he defeats the ogres.

CHARACTER TRAITS—BRAVERY; CHARACTER TRAITS—KINDNESS; FOLKTALES—ASIA—JAPAN; MONSTERS.

**SAMTON, SHEILA**

1267    *Amazing Aunt Agatha*. Ill. by Yvette Banek. Raintree, 1990 (0-8172-3575-2); pap. (0-8114-6737-6). USE LEVEL: P
*African American*
The letters of the alphabet introduce words that describe the activities of Aunt Agatha. She "entertains elephants," "makes masks," and "understands unicorns."
ABC BOOKS; ACTIVITIES.

**SAMUELS, VYANNE**

1268    *Carry Go Bring Come*. Ill. by Jennifer Northway. Macmillan, 1988 (0-02-778121-6). USE LEVEL: P
*Caribbean—Jamaica*
Leon tries to be helpful as his family prepares for his sister's wedding. He keeps being given new jobs to do.
CHARACTER TRAITS—HELPFULNESS; FAMILY LIFE; FOREIGN LANDS—CARIBBEAN ISLANDS—JAMAICA; WEDDINGS.

**SANFIELD, STEVE**

1269    *The Adventures of High John the Conqueror*. Ill. by John Ward. Orchard, 1988 (0-531-05807-7); LB (0-531-08407-8). USE LEVEL: M/U
*African American*
High John is a trickster and in these 16 stories, he often has to use his wits.
BEHAVIOR—TRICKERY; FOLKTALES—UNITED STATES; SHORT STORIES.

**SAN SOUCI, ROBERT D.**

1270    *The Boy and the Ghost*. Ill. by Brian Pinkney. Simon & Schuster, 1989 (0-671-67176-6); pap. (0-671-79248-2). USE LEVEL: P
*African American*
A boy spends the night in a haunted house, facing the ghost that lives there.
CHARACTER TRAITS—BRAVERY; GHOSTS; HOUSES; SCARY STORIES.

1271    *Cut from the Same Cloth: American Women of Myth, Legend, and Tall Tale*. Introduction by Jane Yolen. Ill. by Brian Pinkney. Putnam, 1993 (0-399-21987-0). USE LEVEL: U
*Multicultural*
Fifteen stories feature women who face challenges and succeed. Included are African American and Native American stories, like "Molly Cottontail" and "The Star Maiden."
FOLKTALES—UNITED STATES; WOMEN.

1272 *The Enchanted Tapestry: A Chinese Folktale*. Ill. by László Gál.
Dial, 1987 (0-8037-0304-X); LB (0-8037-0306-6); pap. (0-
8037-0862-9). USE LEVEL: M
*Asian—China*
A woman weaves beautiful tapestries to support herself and her
three sons. She weaves a special tapestry that is blown away by
the wind and each son must search for it.
ACTIVITIES—WEAVING; BEHAVIOR—GREED; CHARACTER TRAITS—BRAV-
ERY; FOLKTALES—ASIA—CHINA.

1273 *Larger Than Life: The Adventures of American Legendary
Heroes*. Ill. by Andrew Glass. Doubleday, 1991, o.p. USE LEVEL:
M
*Multicultural*
Five stories feature legendary heroes like John Henry, Old
Stormalong, and Paul Bunyan.
FOLKTALES—UNITED STATES; SHORT STORIES.

1274 *The Legend of Scarface: A Blackfeet Indian Tale*. Ill. by Daniel
San Souci. Doubleday, 1978, pap. (0-385-15874-2). USE LEVEL:
M
*Native American—Blackfoot*
Scarface wishes to marry Singing Rains but she has promised
the sun that she will never wed. Scarface travels to the Land of
the Sun and saves Morning Star. As his reward, the Sun releases
Singing Rains from her promise.
CHARACTER TRAITS—APPEARANCE; CHARACTER TRAITS—BRAVERY;
FOLKTALES—NATIVE AMERICAN—BLACKFOOT.

1275 *The Samurai's Daughter: A Japanese Legend*. Ill. by Stephen T.
Johnson. Dial, 1992 (0-8037-1135-2); LB (0-8037-1136-0).
USE LEVEL: M
*Asian—Japan*
Tokoyo journeys to join her father, who has been exiled on an
island. When she reaches the island, she bravely dives to face the
sea serpent, whom she slays.
CHARACTER TRAITS—BRAVERY; FOLKTALES—ASIA—JAPAN; MONSTERS; SEA
AND SEASHORE.

1276 *Short and Shivery: Thirty Chilling Tales*. Ill. by Katherine
Coville. Doubleday, 1987 (0-385-23886-X); pap. (0-385-
26426-7). USE LEVEL: M/U
*Multicultural*

This collection includes stories from around the world, including Japan, Africa, Latin America, and the United States.

FOLKTALES; GHOSTS; SCARY STORIES; SHORT STORIES.

1277    *The Snow Wife.* Ill. by Stephen T. Johnson. Dial, 1992 (0-8037-1409-2); LB (0-8037-1410-6). USE LEVEL: M
*Asian—Japan*
Minokichi promises that he will not reveal his encounter with the Woman of the Snow. When he breaks his promise, he loses his wife and must struggle to be reunited with her.

FOLKTALES—ASIA—JAPAN; MONSTERS; WEATHER—SNOW.

1278    *Song of Sedna.* Ill. by Daniel San Souci. Doubleday, 1981 (0-385-15866-1). USE LEVEL: M
*Native American—Inuit*
Sedna marries Mattack, a hunter, but she finds he is a bird-spirit who has come to her in human form. Her father, Noato, comes to rescue her but he loses his nerve. Sedna becomes goddess of the sea.

ARCTIC LANDS; BIRDS; FOLKTALES—NATIVE AMERICAN—INUIT; SEA AND SEASHORE.

1279    *Sootface: An Ojibwa Cinderella Story.* Ill. by Daniel San Souci. Doubleday, 1994 (0-385-31202-4). USE LEVEL: M
*Native American—Ojibway*
Two sisters make their younger sister dress in rags and do all the work. A hunter who can become invisible decides that he will marry the woman who can see him and only Sootface succeeds.

CHARACTER TRAITS—APPEARANCE; CHARACTER TRAITS—KINDNESS; FAMILY LIFE—SIBLINGS; FOLKTALES—NATIVE AMERICAN—OJIBWAY.

1280    *Sukey and the Mermaid.* Ill. by Brian Pinkney. Macmillan, 1992 (0-02-778141-0). USE LEVEL: M
*African American*
Sukey lives with her mother and her stepfather. Her step-pa, Mr. Jones, is a mean-spirited man who makes Sukey work very hard. Sukey meets a mermaid, who befriends her and who helps her find love and wealth.

CHARACTER TRAITS—BRAVERY; CORETTA SCOTT KING AWARD; FOLKTALES—UNITED STATES; MYTHICAL CREATURES—MERMAIDS.

1281    *The Talking Eggs: A Folktale from the American South.* Ill. by Jerry Pinkney. Dial, 1989 (0-8037-0619-7); LB (0-8037-0620-0). USE LEVEL: M
*African American*

Long ago, in the rural South, a mother lives with her two daughters. Mother and Rose are both lazy and mean; Blanche is sweet-tempered, but she is made to do all the work. Blanche's kindness to an old woman brings her riches.

CALDECOTT AWARD; CHARACTER TRAITS—KINDNESS; CORETTA SCOTT KING AWARD; EGGS; FOLKTALES—UNITED STATES; MAGIC.

### SAY, ALLEN

1282   *The Bicycle Man.* Ill. by the author. Houghton, 1982 (0-395-32254-5); pap. (0-395-50652-2). USE LEVEL: M
*Asian—Japan*
In Japan, two American soldiers visit the Japanese school on Sportsday and add to the fun of that special day.

BEHAVIOR—ACCEPTING DIFFERENCES; FOREIGN LANDS—ASIA—JAPAN; GAMES; SPORTS—BICYCLING.

1283   *Grandfather's Journey.* Ill. by the author. Houghton, 1993 (0-395-57035-2). USE LEVEL: M
*Asian American—Japan*
A man reminisces about his grandfather, who journeyed from Japan to America. While in America, he missed parts of his life in Japan, yet when he returned to Japan, he was lonely for America.

ACTIVITIES—TRAVELING; CALDECOTT AWARD; EMOTIONS—HOMESICK-NESS; FAMILY LIFE—GRANDFATHERS; FOREIGN LANDS—ASIA—JAPAN.

1284   *The Ink-Keeper's Apprentice.* Houghton, 1994, c1979 (0-395-70562-2). USE LEVEL: U
*Asian—Japan*
In this autobiographical novel, the author describes the apprenticeship of Kiyoi, 13, to a cartoonist, Noro Shinpei. In addition to learning about art and illustration, Kiyoi is introduced to people and ideas that help him develop independence.

ART; BEHAVIOR—GROWING UP; CAREERS—ARTISTS; FOREIGN LANDS—ASIA—JAPAN.

1285   *The Lost Lake.* Ill. by the author. Houghton, 1989 (0-395-50933-5); pap. (0-395-63036-3). USE LEVEL: M
*Asian American*
A young boy is spending the summer with his father. Together, they hike to a lake that the father remembers from his childhood, but it is now overcrowded. They continue to hike until they find their own special lake.

ACTIVITIES—HIKING; BEHAVIOR—NEEDING SOMEONE; CAMPS, CAMPING; FAMILY LIFE.

1286    *Once Under the Cherry Blossom Tree: An Old Japanese Tale*. Ill.
by the reteller. Harper & Row, 1974, o.p. USE LEVEL: M
*Asian—Japan*
When a mean-spirited landlord swallows a cherry pit, a cherry
tree grows out of the top of his head. When he uproots the tree,
it leaves a fish pool.
CHARACTER TRAITS—MEANNESS; FOLKTALES—ASIA—JAPAN; TREES.

1287    *A River Dream*. Ill. by the author. Houghton, 1988 (0-395-
48294-2); pap. (0-395-65749-0). USE LEVEL: P
*Asian American*
When he is ill, Mark receives a tackle box from his Uncle Scott.
The gift sparks a memory of a special fishing trip, which
becomes a dream in which Mark, still in his pajamas, is fishing
with his uncle.
DREAMS; FAMILY LIFE—AUNTS, UNCLES; ILLNESS; SPORTS—FISHING.

1288    *Tree of Cranes*. Ill. by the author. Houghton, 1991 pap. (0-395-
52024-X). USE LEVEL: P/M
*Asian American—Japan*
In Japan, a young boy's mother describes the Christmas she
remembers from California.
FAMILY LIFE; FOREIGN LANDS—ASIA—JAPAN; HOLIDAYS—CHRISTMAS;
TREES.

**SCHECTER, ELLEN, RETELLER**
1289    *Sim Chung and the River Dragon: A Folktale from Korea*. Ill. by
June Otani. Bantam, 1993 (0-553-09117-4); pap. (0-553-
37109-6). USE LEVEL: P
*Asian—Korea*
After her mother dies and her father loses his sight, Sim Chung
agrees to marry the River Dragon to pay the priest so her father
can see again. She bravely honors her promise and is later
returned to her home.
CHARACTER TRAITS—BRAVERY; DRAGONS; FOLKTALES—ASIA—KOREA;
HANDICAPS—BLINDNESS.

1290    *The Warrior Maiden: A Hopi Legend*. Ill. by Laura Kelly.
Bantam, 1992, LB (0-553-08949-8); pap. (0-553-37022-7).
USE LEVEL: P
*Native American—Hopi*
Huh-áy-ay lives in the Hopi pueblo. When the men go to work
in the fields, some Apache warriors come to the pueblo. Huh-
áy-ay runs to bring the men back to the pueblo.
CHARACTER TRAITS—BRAVERY; FOLKTALES—NATIVE AMERICAN—HOPI.

**SCHERMBRUCKER, REVIVA**

1291 *Charlie's House.* Ill. by Niki Daly. Viking, 1991 (0-670-84024-6). USE LEVEL: P/M

*African—South Africa*

Charlie lives in a shelter made of sheets of iron. Charlie's imagination lets him dream about leaving the shelter home one day.

FAMILY LIFE; FOREIGN LANDS—AFRICA—SOUTH AFRICA; HOUSES; IMAGINATION; POVERTY.

**SCHLEIN, MIRIAM**

1292 *The Year of the Panda.* Ill. by Kam Mak. HarperCollins, 1990 (0-690-04864-5); LB (0-690-04866-1); pap. (0-06-440366-1). USE LEVEL: M

*Asian—China*

Yu Li and his family have farmed this land for generations. Suddenly some men from the Chinese government want his family to relocate; then Yu Li finds an orphaned baby panda.

ANIMALS—ENDANGERED ANIMALS; ANIMALS—PANDAS; CONSERVATION; FOREIGN LANDS—ASIA—CHINA.

**SCHOTTER, RONI**

1293 *A Fruit and Vegetable Man.* Ill. by Jeanette Winter. Little, Brown, 1993 (0-316-77467-7). USE LEVEL: P

*Asian American*

Sun Ho forms a friendship with Ruby Rubenstein, an elderly man who has a store. When Ruby becomes ill, Sun Ho and his family help out in the store.

CAREERS—STOREKEEPERS; CHARACTER TRAITS—HELPFULNESS; CHARACTER TRAITS—KINDNESS; FOOD; STORES.

**SCHROEDER, ALAN**

1294 *Lily and the Wooden Bowl.* Ill. by Yoriko Ito. Doubleday, 1994 (0-385-30792-6). USE LEVEL: M

*Asian—Japan*

Lily hides her beauty by wearing a wooden bowl on her head. Kumaso falls in love with Lily but his mother tries to keep them apart.

CHARACTER TRAITS—APPEARANCE; FOLKTALES—ASIA—JAPAN; MAGIC.

1295 *The Stone Lion.* Ill. by Todd L. W. Doney. Macmillan, 1994 (0-684-19578-X). USE LEVEL: M

*Asian—Tibet*

A widow lives in Tibet with her two sons, Jarlo and Drashi. Jarlo is cruel and greedy while Drashi is kind. Drashi's kindness is rewarded while Jarlo learns humility when each faces a stone lion in the mountains.

ANIMALS—LIONS; CHARACTER TRAITS—KINDNESS; FAMILY LIFE—SIB-
LINGS; FOLKTALES—ASIA—TIBET.

### SCOTT, ANN HERBERT

1296    *Hi*. Ill. by Glo Coalson. Putnam, 1994 (0-399-21964-1). USE
LEVEL: P
*Hispanic American*
Margarita says "Hi" to everyone she sees, but it seems that no
one notices her.
EMOTIONS—HAPPINESS; FRIENDSHIP; POST OFFICE.

1297    *On Mother's Lap*. Ill. by Glo Coalson. Houghton, 1972 (0-395-
58920-7); pap. (0-395-62976-4). USE LEVEL: P
*Native American—Eskimo*
Mother's lap is a special place with room for everyone and
everything.
ACTIVITIES—REMINISCING; EMOTIONS—LOVE; FAMILY LIFE—MOTHERS.

1298    *Sam*. Ill. by Symeon Shimin. Putnam, 1967, LB (0-399-22104-
2). USE LEVEL: P
*African American*
Everyone in Sam's family is so busy, they do not seem to have
time for him.
EMOTIONS—LONELINESS; FAMILY LIFE.

### SEATTLE, CHIEF

1299    *Brother Eagle, Sister Sky: A Message from Chief Seattle*. Ill. by
Susan Jeffers. Dial, 1991 (0-8037-0969-2); LB (0-8037-0963-
3). USE LEVEL: M
*Native American*
A powerful message about caring for the earth and for each
other is presented in this book.
ECOLOGY; ENVIRONMENT; NATURE; U.S. HISTORY.

### SEBESTYEN, OUIDA

1300    *Words by Heart*. Little, Brown, 1979 (0-316-77931-8); Bantam,
pap. (0-553-27179-2). USE LEVEL: U
*African American*
It is the early 1900s and Lena and her family are the first black
family in Bethel Springs, where they face resentment and prejudice. When Lena wins the scripture-reading contest, there is an
even greater threat of violence.
FAMILY LIFE; PREJUDICE; RACE RELATIONS.

SEED, JENNY
1301    *Ntombi's Song.* Ill. by Anno Berry. Beacon, 1989 (0-8070-8318-6). USE LEVEL: PS/P
*African—South Africa*
Ntombi, a young Zulu girl, spills the sugar she is carrying home. She must find a way to buy more sugar. She picks plums, but no one buys them. When she sings and dances, tourists give her money.
FAMILY LIFE; FOREIGN LANDS—AFRICA—SOUTH AFRICA; PROBLEM SOLVING.

SEEGER, PETE
1302    *Abiyoyo: Based on a South African Lullaby and Folk Song.* Ill. by Michael Hays. Macmillan, 1986 (0-02-781490-4); pap. (0-689-71810-1). USE LEVEL: M
*African—South Africa*
A boy and his father are outcasts until they find the way to trick Abiyoyo, the giant.
FOREIGN LANDS—AFRICA—SOUTH AFRICA; GIANTS; MAGIC; SONGS.

SELTZER, ISADORE
1303    *The House I Live In: At Home in America.* Ill. by the author. Macmillan, 1992 (0-02-781801-2). USE LEVEL: P
*Multicultural*
Twelve houses are featured along with information about the people who live in them. The influences of geography and history are reflected in many of the houses.
FAMILY LIFE; FOREIGN LANDS; HOUSES.

SERWADDA, W. MOSES
1304    *Songs and Stories from Uganda.* Transcribed and edited by Hewitt Pantaleoni. Ill. by Leo Dillon and Diane Dillon. HarperCollins, 1974 (0-690-75240-7); LB (0-690-75241-5); pap. (0-937203-17-3). USE LEVEL: M
*African—Uganda*
Within the 13 stories in this book are songs and lullabies that connect to the culture. A pronunciation guide helps readers sing the words in Luganda, the language of the Baganda people.
FOLKTALES—AFRICA—UGANDA; FOREIGN LANGUAGES; MUSIC; SONGS.

SEWELL, MARCIA
1305    *People of the Breaking Day.* Ill. by the author. Macmillan, 1990 (0-689-31407-8). USE LEVEL: M
*Native American—Wampanoag*
The Wampanoag people lived in southeastern Massachusetts at

the time of the Pilgrims. The men and boys would hunt, fish, and prepare for battle, making arrows. Women and girls would garden, preserve food, make clothes, and make pots.

FAMILY LIFE; U.S. HISTORY.

## SHANGE, NTOZAKE

1306   *I Live in Music.* Ill. by Romare Bearden. Welcome Enterprise, 1994 (1-55670-372-4). USE LEVEL: M
*African American*
This poem celebrates the emotions that come from truly feeling music. The illustrations are collages from the well-known African American artist Romare Bearden.

ART; MUSIC; POETRY, RHYME.

## SHANNON, GEORGE, RETELLER

1307   *More Stories to Solve: Fifteen Folktales from Around the World.* Ill. by Peter Sis. Greenwillow, 1991 (0-688-09161-X); pap. (0-688-12947-1). USE LEVEL: M
*Multicultural*
These 15 stories follow the same format as *Stories to Solve.* Among the locations for these stories are Ethiopia, Mexico, Chile, and the Philippines.

FOLKTALES; RIDDLES; SHORT STORIES.

1308   *Still More Stories to Solve: Fourteen Folktales from Around the World.* Ill. by Peter Sis. Greenwillow, 1994 (0-688-04619-3). USE LEVEL: M
*Multicultural*
Each of these stories ends with a query and then is followed by the solution. Among the locations for these stories are India, Nepal, China, and the West Indies.

FOLKTALES; RIDDLES; SHORT STORIES.

1309   *Stories to Solve: Folktales from Around the World.* Ill. by Peter Sis. Greenwillow, 1985 (0-688-04303-8); LB (0-688-04304-6); pap. (0-688-10496-7). USE LEVEL: M
*Multicultural*
In each of these 14 stories, there is a problem to be solved, and readers are invited to propose solutions before they are revealed. Included are stories from Japan, China, Tibet, Ethiopia, and other countries and peoples.

FOLKTALES; RIDDLES; SHORT STORIES.

**SHEFELMAN, JANICE**

1310 *A Mare for Young Wolf.* Ill. by Tom Shefelman. Random, 1993, LB (0-679-93445-6); pap. (0-679-83445-1). USE LEVEL: P
*Native American*
Young Wolf is mocked for choosing a mare, Red Wind, for his horse. When Apaches come to their camp, Young Wolf and Red Wind sound the alarm.
ANIMALS—HORSES; BEHAVIOR—GROWING UP; SELF-CONCEPT.

**SHELBY, ANNE**

1311 *Potluck.* Ill. by Irene Trivas. Orchard, 1991 (0-531-05919-7); LB (0-531-08519-8); pap. (0-531-07045-X). USE LEVEL: P
*Multicultural*
When Alpha and Betty decide to have a party, their friends bring items from A to Z. Children and foods from diverse cultures are included.
ABC BOOKS; CELEBRATIONS; FOOD.

1312 *We Keep a Store.* Ill. by John Ward. Orchard, 1990 (0-531-05856-5); LB (0-531-08456-6). USE LEVEL: P
*African American*
A family runs a small store in a rural community. Children play in the store, and adults gather there and share stories.
CAREERS—STOREKEEPERS; FAMILY LIFE; RURAL LIFE; STORES.

**SHEPARD, AARON, RETELLER**

1313 *The Gifts of Wali Dad: A Tale of India and Pakistan.* Ill. by Daniel San Souci. Macmillan, 1995 (0-684-19445-7). USE LEVEL: M
*Asian—India/Pakistan*
Wali Dad is a old man who makes money by selling grass. When he has enough money, he buys a bracelet for the young queen. She sends a gift to him, which he passes on to a young king. Through giving gifts, Wali Dad brings the queen and king together.
CHARACTER TRAITS—GENEROSITY; FOLKTALES—ASIA—INDIA; FOLKTALES—ASIA—PAKISTAN; ROYALTY; WEDDINGS.

**SHEPHERD, SANDY**

1314 *Myths and Legends from Around the World.* Ill. by Tudor Humphries. Macmillan, 1995 (0-02-762355-6). USE LEVEL: M
*Multicultural*

This collection links familiar myths, like those from Greece and Rome, to similar stories from other peoples, like creation myths from Japan, Tahiti, and Guatemala and sky stories from Africa, China, and the Hindu people.

CREATION; FOLKTALES; MYTHICAL CREATURES; SHORT STORIES; SKY; WORLD.

### SHERLOCK, PHILIP, RETELLER

1315 *Anansi, the Spider Man: Jamaican Folk Tales.* Ill. by Marcia Brown. HarperCollins, 1954 (0-690-08905-8). USE LEVEL: M *Caribbean—Jamaica*
In these 15 stories, Anansi appears as both a man and a spider, and he often uses his wits to survive.

BEHAVIOR—TRICKERY; FOLKTALES—CARIBBEAN ISLANDS—JAMAICA; SHORT STORIES; SPIDERS.

1316 *West Indian Folk-Tales.* Ill. by Joan Kiddell-Monroe. Oxford Univ. Pr., 1966 (0-19-274116-0). USE LEVEL: M/U *Caribbean—West Indies*
These 21 stories include a variety of types and characters, including stories that explain natural events and stories with the trickster Anansi.

BEHAVIOR—TRICKERY; FOLKTALES—CARIBBEAN ISLANDS—WEST INDIES; POURQUOI TALES; SHORT STORIES; SPIDERS.

### SHETTERLY, SUSAN HAND, RETELLER

1317 *The Dwarf-Wizard of Uxmal.* Ill. by Robert Shetterly. Macmillan, 1990 (0-689-31455-8). USE LEVEL: M *Central American—Mayan*
An old woman is given eggs by the water carriers and a boy hatches from one. He is Tol, the dwarf-wizard. When he is older, Tol challenges the governor and wins, eventually becoming the ruler of Uxmal.

CHARACTER TRAITS—BRAVERY; CHARACTER TRAITS—SMALLNESS; ELVES AND LITTLE PEOPLE; FOLKTALES—CENTRAL AMERICA—MAYAN; MAGIC.

1318 *Muwin and the Magic Hare.* Ill. by Robert Shetterly. Macmillan, 1993 (0-689-31699-2). USE LEVEL: M *Native American—Passamaquoddy*
Just before winter comes, Muwin the bear follows the scent of a hare and encounters three native people, each of whom tells him a story to teach a lesson. The hare he chases is the Great Magic Hare of the Woods.

ANIMALS—BEARS; ANIMALS—RABBITS; FOLKTALES—NATIVE AMERICAN—PASSAMAQUODDY; HIBERNATION; SEASONS—WINTER.

1319    *Raven's Light: A Myth from the People of the Northwest Coast.* Ill.
        by Robert Shetterly. Macmillan, 1991 (0-689-31629-1). USE
        LEVEL: M
        **Native American**
        When Raven drops a stone, it grows to be the earth. He fills it
        with plants and creatures. Raven transforms himself into a child
        and steals Day from the Great Chief.
        BEHAVIOR—TRICKERY; BIRDS—RAVENS; FOLKTALES—NATIVE AMERICAN;
        POURQUOI TALES.

        SHIGEKAWA, MARLENE
1320    *Blue Jay in the Desert.* Ill. by Isao Kikuchi. Polychrome, 1993
        (1-879965-04-6). USE LEVEL: M
        **Asian American—Japan**
        In an internment camp in Arizona during World War II, Junior
        and his family try to adjust. They miss their home in California.
        Grandpa spends his time carving, making a blue jay for Junior.
        ACTIVITIES—CARVING; BIRDS—BLUE JAYS; FAMILY LIFE—GRANDFATHERS;
        RELOCATION; U.S. HISTORY—WORLD WAR II.

        SHOR, PEKAY, RETELLER
1321    *When the Corn Is Red.* Ill. by Gary Von Ilg. Abingdon, 1973,
        o.p. USE LEVEL: M
        **Native American—Tuscaroran**
        When the Tuscaroras honored the Great Spirit, they received
        the gift of red corn. When they began to quarrel and fight, they
        lost their land to white settlers and their corn changed from red
        to white.
        BEHAVIOR—FIGHTING, ARGUING; FOLKTALES—NATIVE AMERICAN—
        TUSCARORAN; FOOD; U.S. HISTORY.

        SHUTE, LINDA, RETELLER
1322    *Momotaro the Peach Boy: A Traditional Japanese Tale.* Ill. by the
        reteller. Lothrop, 1986 (0-688-05863-9); LB (0-688-05864-
        7). USE LEVEL: M
        **Asian—Japan**
        An old woodcutter and his wife wish for a child. They find a
        boy inside a peach. Momotaro is kind to three animals and they
        help him fight the greedy oni.
        CHARACTER TRAITS—BRAVERY; CHARACTER TRAITS—KINDNESS;
        CHARACTER TRAITS—SMALLNESS; ELVES AND LITTLE PEOPLE;
        FOLKTALES—ASIA—JAPAN; MONSTERS.

        SIBERELL, ANNE
1323    *A Journey to Paradise.* Ill. by the author. Henry Holt, 1990,
        o.p. USE LEVEL: M
        **Asian—India**

Guba cares for the garden with the help of his pet monkey, Kaloo. Together, they search for Paradise, accompanied by the potter, the spice seller, and the weaver.
BEHAVIOR—SEEKING BETTER THINGS; FOREIGN LANDS—ASIA— INDIA; MAGIC.

1324    *Whale in the Sky.* Ill. by the author. Dutton, 1982 (0-525-44021-6); pap. (0-525-44197-2). USE LEVEL: M
*Native American—Northwest Coast*
This legend from the Northwest Coast Indians uses woodcuts to tell the story of how Thunderbird saved the salmon from Whale. The people had the story carved into a totem pole.
ANIMALS; ANIMALS—WHALES; BIRDS; FOLKTALES—NATIVE AMERICAN— NORTHWEST COAST; TOTEMS.

SIERRA, JUDY
1325    *The Elephant's Wrestling Match.* Ill. by Brian Pinkney. Dutton, 1992 (0-525-67366-0). USE LEVEL: M
*African*
Believing in his own strength, the elephant challenges the other animals to a wrestling match. After larger animals fail, the bat flies in the elephant's ear and brings the elephant to the ground.
ANIMALS; ANIMALS—ELEPHANTS; CHARACTER TRAITS—PRIDE; CHARACTER TRAITS—VANITY; FOLKTALES—AFRICA.

SINGER, MARILYN
1326    *Nine O'Clock Lullaby.* Ill. by Frané Lessac. HarperCollins, 1991 (0-06-025647-8); LB (0-06-025648-6); pap. (0-06-443319-6). USE LEVEL: P
*Multicultural*
When it is 9:00 P.M. in Brooklyn, New York, it is time for a bedtime story. Around the world, the times and activities are different—people are waking up in Moscow and having lunch in Australia.
FOREIGN LANDS; TIME.

1327    *The Painted Fan.* Ill. by Wenhai Ma. Morrow, 1994 (0-688-11742-2); LB (0-688-11743-0). USE LEVEL: M
*Asian—China*
After the soothsayer warns Lord Shang of the Painted Fan, Lord Shang orders all fans be destroyed. When he falls in love with Bright Willow, she brings the Painted Fan that destroys him.
FANS; FANTASY; FOREIGN LANDS—ASIA—CHINA.

**SINGH, JACQUELIN**

1328    *Fat Gopal.* Ill. by Demi. Harcourt, 1984, o.p. USE LEVEL: M
*Asian—India*
A maharajah decides to visit the Nawab, taking presents for the
Nawab and his jester, Fat Gopal, whose job is to make every-
body laugh. The Nawab sets an impossible group of tasks,
which Gopal, by using his wits, is able to complete.
CHARACTER TRAITS—CLEVERNESS; FOREIGN LANDS—ASIA—INDIA;
PROBLEM SOLVING; ROYALTY.

**SIS, PETER**

1329    *Komodo!* Ill. by the author. Greenwillow, 1993 (0-688-11583-
7); LB (0-688-11584-5). USE LEVEL: P
*Indonesian*
A young boy travels to Indonesia to see Komodo dragons.
ACTIVITIES—TRAVELING; FOREIGN LANDS—INDONESIA; REPTILES—
KOMODO DRAGONS.

1330    *A Small, Tall Tale from the Far, Far North.* Ill. by the author.
Knopf, 1993 (0-679-84345-0); LB (0-679-94345-5). USE
LEVEL: M
*Native American—Inuit*
Jan Welzl travels to the Arctic and meets and receives help from
the Eskimos.
ARCTIC LANDS; HISTORY—EXPLORERS.

**SLEATOR, WILLIAM**

1331    *The Angry Moon.* Ill. by Blair Lent. Little, Brown, 1970, o.p.
USE LEVEL: M
*Native American—Tlingit*
When Lapowinsa makes fun of the moon, a rainbow covers her
and takes her to be the moon's prisoner. Lupan travels to the
sky where he is befriended by an old woman. She gives him four
enchanted objects that help him rescue Lapowinsa.
CALDECOTT AWARD; FOLKTALES—NATIVE AMERICAN—TLINGIT; MAGIC;
MOON.

**SLIER, DEBORAH, EDITOR**

1332    *Make a Joyful Sound: Poems for Children by African-American
Poets.* Ill. by Cornelius Van Wright and Ying-Hwa Hu.
Checkerboard, 1991 (1-56288-000-4). USE LEVEL: M
*African American*
Poetry from well-known poets like Langston Hughes and Eloise

Greenfield are included in the collection as are some poems from less well-known poets like Quincy Troupe and Mari Evans.

POETRY, RHYME; SELF-CONCEPT.

SLOAT, TERI, RETELLER

1333 *The Eye of the Needle: Based on a Yupik Tale as Told by Betty Huffman*. Ill. by the reteller. Dutton, 1990 (0-525-44623-0); Puffin, pap. (0-14-054933-1). USE LEVEL: M
*Native American—Yupik*
Amik is sent out to find food. While he hunts, he is hungry, so when he catches something, he eats it, planning to catch something larger. By the time he eats a whale, Amik is too large for his grandmother's house.

BEHAVIOR—GREED; FAMILY LIFE—GRANDMOTHERS; FOLKTALES—NATIVE AMERICAN—YUPIK.

1334 *The Hungry Giant of the Tundra*. Ill. by Robert Sloat and Teri Sloat. Dutton, 1993 (0-525-45126-9). USE LEVEL: M
*Native American—Yupik*
The children of the tundra are captured by A-ka-gua-gan-kak, the giant. They escape and destroy the giant.

ARCTIC LANDS; FOLKTALES—NATIVE AMERICAN—YUPIK; GIANTS.

SLOTE, ALFRED

1335 *Finding Buck McHenry*. HarperCollins, 1991 (0-06-021652-2); LB (0-06-021653-0); pap. (0-06-440469-2). USE LEVEL: M
*African American*
Jason, 11, thinks that he has found a former Negro League baseball player working in his school as a custodian.

SCHOOL; SPORTS—BASEBALL.

SMALL, TERRY

1336 *The Legend of John Henry*. Ill. by the author. Doubleday, 1994 (0-385-31168-0). USE LEVEL: M
*African American*
A rhyming text tells the classic story of John Henry, the "steel-drivin' man."

CHARACTER TRAITS—PERSEVERANCE; CHARACTER TRAITS—PRIDE; FOLKTALES—UNITED STATES; POETRY, RHYME; TRAINS.

SMALLS-HECTOR, IRENE

1337 *Dawn and the Round To-It*. Ill. by Tyrone Geter. Simon & Schuster, 1994 (0-671-87166-8). USE LEVEL: PS/P
*African American*
When five-year-old Dawn wakes up, she is ready to play.

Throughout the day, others in her family seem too busy for her. Dawn finds a way to get their attention.

ACTIVITIES—PLAYING; EMOTIONS—LONELINESS; FAMILY LIFE.

1338 *Irene and the Big, Fine Nickel.* Ill. by Tyrone Geter. Little, Brown, 1991, o.p. USE LEVEL: P/M
*African American*
In Harlem during the 1950s, Irene enjoys the activities in her apartment and neighborhood.

COMMUNITIES, NEIGHBORHOODS; FRIENDSHIP; URBAN LIFE.

1339 *Jonathan and His Mommy.* Ill. by Michael Hays. Little, Brown, 1992 (0-316-79870-3); pap. (0-316-79880-0). USE LEVEL: PS/P
*African American*
Walking around their urban neighborhood, a little boy and his mother use many creative ways of moving, including giant steps, zigzag steps, even bunny steps.

ACTIVITIES—WALKING; COMMUNITIES, NEIGHBORHOODS; FAMILY LIFE—MOTHERS; IMAGINATION; URBAN LIFE.

**SMITH, EDWARD BIKO**
1340 *A Lullaby for Daddy.* Ill. by Susan Anderson. Africa World, 1994 (0-86543-403-4); pap. (0-86543-404-2). USE LEVEL: PS
*African American*
Rosie loves her keyboard, which is like the one Daddy uses at work. One night, Rosie and Daddy write a bedtime song. The next night, Rosie is proud because she remembers the song and sings it for Daddy.

BABIES, TODDLERS; BEDTIME; FAMILY LIFE—FATHERS; LULLABIES; MUSIC.

**SMITH, JOANNE L.**
1341 *Show and Tell.* Ill. by James Buckley. Childrens Pr., 1994, LB (0-516-02026-9). USE LEVEL: P
*African American*
For show and tell, Billy always brings his teddy bear, until one Friday, he brings his dad.

DAYS OF THE WEEK, MONTHS OF THE YEAR; PREDICTABLE TEXT; SCHOOL; TOYS—TEDDY BEARS.

**SMOTHERS, ETHEL FOOTMAN**
1342 *Down in the Piney Woods.* Knopf, 1992 (0-679-80360-2); LB (0-679-90360-7); pap. (0-679-84714-6). USE LEVEL: U
*African American*

In rural Georgia, Annie, ten, resents that her three older half-sisters have moved in with her family. Annie now finds herself being bossed around. That problem seems small when a cross is burned in front of her family's house.

FAMILY LIFE—SIBLINGS; PREJUDICE; RACE RELATIONS; RURAL LIFE.

1343   *Moriah's Pond.* Knopf, 1995 (0-679-84504-6); LB (0-679-94504-0). USE LEVEL: U
*African American*
Annie Rye, ten, and her sisters, Maybaby and Brat, are staying with their great-grandmother Moriah in Georgia in the 1950s. One girl, Betty Jean, seems to want to be a friend, but when Brat is blamed for something Betty Jean did, she does not speak up.

FAMILY LIFE—SIBLINGS; FRIENDSHIP; PREJUDICE; RACE RELATIONS; RURAL LIFE.

### SMUCKER, BARBARA
1344   *Runaway to Freedom: A Story of the Underground Railroad.* Ill. by Charles Lilly. HarperCollins, 1978, pap. (0-06-440106-5). USE LEVEL: U
*African American*
Disguised as boys, Julilly and Liza, who is disabled, escape from Mississippi and follow the Underground Railroad route hoping to reach Canada and freedom.

CHARACTER TRAITS—FREEDOM; HANDICAPS—PHYSICAL; SLAVERY; UNDERGROUND RAILROAD.

### SNEVE, VIRGINIA DRIVING HAWK, SELECTOR
1345   *Dancing Teepees: Poems of American Indian Youth.* Ill. by Stephen Gammell. Holiday, 1989 (0-8234-0724-1); pap. (0-8234-0879-5). USE LEVEL: M
*Native American*
The 19 poems in this book reflect the culture and traditions of diverse native peoples, including Lakota Sioux, Crow, Hopi, and Navajo. Appreciation for the natural world is a theme in many of the poems.

NATURE; POETRY, RHYME.

### SNYDER, DIANNE
1346   *The Boy of the Three-Year Nap.* Ill. by Allen Say. Houghton, 1988 (0-395-44090-4). USE LEVEL: M
*Asian—Japan*
In Japan, a poor widow lives with her lazy son, Taro. When

Taro sees the merchant's wealth, he devises a plan to marry the merchant's daughter. Taro works to succeed, and then continues to work for the merchant.

BEHAVIOR—TRICKERY; CALDECOTT AWARD; CHARACTER TRAITS—LAZINESS; FOLKTALES—ASIA—JAPAN.

**SO, MEILO, RETELLER**

1347    *The Emperor and the Nightingale.* Ill. by the reteller. Macmillan, 1992, o.p. USE LEVEL: M
*Asian—China*
This is a simplified retelling of Andersen's "The Nightingale."

BIRDS—NIGHTINGALES; FOREIGN LANDS—ASIA—CHINA; GIFTS.

**SONNEBORN, RUTH A.**

1348    *Friday Night Is Papa Night.* Ill. by Emily Arnold McCully. Viking, 1970 (0-670-32938-X); Puffin (0-14-050754-X). USE LEVEL: P
*Caribbean American—Puerto Rico*
On Fridays, Pedro and his family wait for Papa to come home from his job. This Friday, it is bedtime and Papa is not home. Pedro wakes up in the middle of the night to welcome his Papa home.

EMOTIONS—LOVE; FAMILY LIFE—FATHERS; POVERTY; URBAN LIFE.

**SOTO, GARY**

1349    *Baseball in April: And Other Stories.* Harcourt, 1990 (0-15-205720-X); pap. (0-15-205721-8). USE LEVEL: U
*Hispanic American*
The 11 stories in this collection describe daily life and experiences of young Hispanics in California. Included is a story of two brothers who try out for Little League and a story about a girl and her Barbie doll.

COMMUNITIES, NEIGHBORHOODS; FAMILY LIFE; FRIENDSHIP; SHORT STORIES.

1350    *Boys at Work.* Ill. by Robert Casilla. Delacorte, 1995 (0-385-32048-5). USE LEVEL: M
*Mexican American*
In Fresno, California, Rudy and Alex have a problem. Rudy accidentally broke Slinky's friend's Discman. Now they are trying to earn money to buy a new one. Their jobs include combing fleas off cats.

FRIENDSHIP; PROBLEM SOLVING.

1351  *Chato's Kitchen*. Ill. by Susan Guevara. Putnam, 1995 (0-399-22658-3). USE LEVEL: M
      *Hispanic*
      In the barrio, Chato the cat meets his new neighbors, a family of mice. Chato and his friend, Novio Boy, invite them for dinner, but the mice bring a guest—Chorizo, a dog.
      ANIMALS—CATS; ANIMALS—MICE; FOOD; FOREIGN LANGUAGES.

1352  *Crazy Weekend*. Scholastic, 1994 (0-590-47814-1); pap. (0-590-47076-0). USE LEVEL: U
      *Hispanic American*
      Hector and his friend Mando visit Hector's Uncle Julio in Fresno for three days. When Uncle Julio takes a photo of an armored car robbery, the boys are interviewed by the newspaper and they become the target of two inept thugs.
      CRIME; FAMILY LIFE—AUNTS, UNCLES; FRIENDSHIP; HUMOR.

1353  *A Fire in My Hands: A Book of Poems*. Ill. by James M. Cardillo. Scholastic, 1990 (0-590-45021-2); pap. (0-590-44579-0). USE LEVEL: U
      *Mexican American*
      There are 23 poems in this collection focusing on life in a Mexican American neighborhood. Each poem is accompanied by a vignette in which Soto provides some background details.
      COMMUNITIES, NEIGHBORHOODS; EMOTIONS; POETRY, RHYME.

1354  *Local News*. Harcourt, 1993 (0-15-248117-6); Scholastic, pap. (0-590-48446-X). USE LEVEL: U
      *Mexican American*
      The 13 stories in this collection feature the everyday activities of families and friends in a Mexican American neighborhood in California. One story, "Blackmail," features the antics of two brothers, another describes Carmen and a kitten, "Push-Up."
      COMMUNITIES, NEIGHBORHOODS; FAMILY LIFE; FRIENDSHIP; SHORT STORIES.

1355  *Neighborhood Odes*. Ill. by David Diaz. Harcourt, 1992 (0-15-256879-4); Scholastic, pap. (0-590-47335-2). USE LEVEL: U
      *Mexican American*
      The 21 poems in this collection describe everyday life in a Mexican American neighborhood. "Ode to La Tortilla," "Ode to the Sprinkler," and "Ode to Pablo's Tennis Shoes" are a few of the poems. Spanish words are incorporated into the poems.
      COMMUNITIES, NEIGHBORHOODS; EMOTIONS; FOREIGN LANGUAGES; POETRY, RHYME.

1356   *The Pool Party*. Ill. by Robert Casilla. Delacorte, 1993 (0-385-30890-6); Dell, pap. (0-440-41010-X). USE LEVEL: M
*Mexican American*
Rudy Herrera has been invited to a pool party at the home of Tiffany Perez, a wealthy schoolmate. His family gives him suggestions about how to behave, but Rudy chooses to be himself.
CHARACTER TRAITS—CONFIDENCE; FAMILY LIFE; FRIENDSHIP; PARTIES.

1357   *The Skirt*. Ill. by Eric Velasquez. Delacorte, 1992 (0-385-30665-2); Dell, pap. (0-440-40924-1). USE LEVEL: M
*Mexican American*
Miata wanted to show off the *folklórico* skirt that she will wear with her dance group. It belonged to her mother when she was a child in Mexico. By accident, Miata has left the skirt on the bus and she needs to get it back.
ACTIVITIES—DANCING; BEHAVIOR—LOSING THINGS; CLOTHING; FAMILY LIFE; FRIENDSHIP.

1358   *Summer on Wheels*. Scholastic, 1995 (0-590-48365-X). USE LEVEL: U
*Mexican American*
Hector and Mando, who were featured in *Crazy Weekend*, are now taking a bike trip to Santa Monica. Their adventures include being in a commercial, recording a rap song, and painting a mural. They also encounter some kooky characters on their trip.
FRIENDSHIP; HUMOR; SPORTS—BICYCLING.

1359   *Taking Sides*. Harcourt, 1991 (0-15-284076-1); pap. (0-15-204077-X). USE LEVEL: U
*Mexican American*
Lincoln Mendoza and his mother have moved to the suburbs and now Lincoln plays basketball for Columbus Junior High School. His new team will be facing his former team from Franklin Junior High, and Lincoln tries to deal with his own feelings.
FRIENDSHIP; PREJUDICE; SCHOOL; SPORTS—BASKETBALL.

**SPAGNOLI, CATHY, ADAPTER**
1360   *Nine-in-One, Grr! Grr! A Folktale from the Hmong People of Laos*. Told by Blia Xiong. Ill. by Nancy Hom. Children's Book Pr., 1989 (0-89239-048-4); pap. (0-89239-110-3). USE LEVEL: M
*Asian—Laos*
Tiger travels to see the great god Shao to find out how many

cubs she will have. Although Shao tells her she will have nine cubs each year, Bird tricks Tiger into thinking it will only be one cub every nine years.

ANIMALS—TIGERS; BEHAVIOR—TRICKERY; BIRDS; FOLKTALES—ASIA—LAOS; POURQUOI TALES.

SPEARE, ELIZABETH GEORGE

1361 *The Sign of the Beaver.* Houghton, 1983 (0-395-33890-5); Dell, pap. (0-440-77900-6). USE LEVEL: M/U
*Native American*
When his father travels to Massachusetts to get the family, Matt, 13, stays in Maine to work on the new cabin. After being stung by bees, Matt is aided by Saknis and Attean, who help him survive and teach him about the resources around him.

NEWBERY AWARD; SURVIVAL; U.S. HISTORY—COLONIAL TIMES.

SPERRY, ARMSTRONG

1362 *Call It Courage.* Ill. by the author. Macmillan, 1940 (0-02-786030-2); pap. (0-689-71391-6). USE LEVEL: U
*Polynesian*
Mafutu has always feared the sea. When he decides to face his fear, he takes his dog Uri and they travel out into the sea. After a storm, they are stranded on an island where Mafutu learns about survival.

CHARACTER TRAITS—BRAVERY; FOREIGN LANDS—POLYNESIA; ISLANDS; NEWBERY AWARD; SEA AND SEASHORE; SURVIVAL.

SPIER, PETER

1363 *People.* Ill. by the author. Doubleday, 1980, LB (0-385-13181-X). USE LEVEL: P/M
*Multicultural*
Information is given about the similarities and differences among people. For example, all people have noses, but they come in different shapes, colors, and sizes.

BEHAVIOR—ACCEPTING DIFFERENCES; CHARACTER TRAITS—APPEARANCE; FOREIGN LANDS; WORLD.

SPINELLI, EILEEN

1364 *If You Want to Find Golden.* Ill. by Stacey Schuett. Whitman, 1993 (0-8075-3585-0). USE LEVEL: P
*Multicultural*
In this urban neighborhood there are many colors—green traffic lights and green vegetables at the open-air market; orange construction cones; and gray pigeons and gray statues.

COMMUNITIES, NEIGHBORHOODS; CONCEPTS—COLOR; URBAN LIFE.

**SPINELLI, JERRY**

1365  *Maniac Magee: A Novel.* Little, Brown, 1990 (0-316-80722-2); Trophy, pap. (0-06-440424-2). USE LEVEL: U
*African American*
Jeffrey Lionel Magee is an orphan who runs to escape his unhappiness. He meets many people, including the Beales, a black family from the East End who befriend him and provide him with love and a home.
ACTIVITIES—RUNNING AWAY; NEWBERY AWARD; ORPHANS; PREJUDICE; RACE RELATIONS.

**SPOHN, DAVID**

1366  *Home Field.* Ill. by the author. Lothrop, 1993 (0-688-11172-6); LB (0-688-11173-4). USE LEVEL: M
*Multicultural*
In this multiracial family, Matt enjoys practicing his baseball skills with his father.
FAMILY LIFE—FATHERS; SPORTS—BASEBALL.

1367  *Nate's Treasure.* Ill. by the author. Lothrop, 1991 (0-688-10092-9). USE LEVEL: M
*Multicultural*
Nate finds the bones of a skunk and he studies them. This was a skunk that had sprayed his dog, Bruno. The illustrations show that Nate is African American and that his father is white.
ANIMALS—SKUNKS; NATURE.

1368  *Starry Night.* Ill. by the author. Lothrop, 1992 (0-688-11170-X); LB (0-688-11171-8). USE LEVEL: M
*Multicultural*
Two boys, who are black, go camping with their father, who is white. They sing songs, tell a ghost story, and appreciate the beauty of the stars on a night in the country.
CAMPS, CAMPING; FAMILY LIFE—FATHERS; NATURE.

1369  *Winter Wood.* Ill. by the author. Lothrop, 1991 (0-688-10093-7); LB (0-688-10094-5). USE LEVEL: M
*Multicultural*
On a winter day, Matt, who is black, goes out with his dad, who is white, to chop wood. While his dad chops, Matt loads the wood onto his sled. During breaks, they watch the birds and talk.
ACTIVITIES—CHOPPING WOOD; FAMILY LIFE; SEASONS—WINTER.

SPURR, ELIZABETH

1370    *Lupe and Me.* Ill. by Enrique O. Sanchez. Harcourt, 1995 (0-15-200522-6). USE LEVEL: M
*Mexican American*
Lupe is 16 when she comes to work as a housekeeper for Sarah, 7, and her family. Sarah and Lupe learn each other's languages and customs, but Lupe disappears when the immigration police begin to investigate her.
CAREERS—HOUSEKEEPERS; FAMILY LIFE; FOREIGN LANGUAGES.

STAMM, CLAUS

1371    *Three Strong Women: A Tall Tale from Japan.* Ill. by Jean Tseng and Mou-sien Tseng. Viking, 1990 (0-670-83323-1); Puffin, pap. (0-14-054530-1). USE LEVEL: M
*Asian—Japan*
Forever-Mountain is a wrestler. He meets Mary-me, her mother, and her grandmother, and each is stronger than he is. They show him how to be strong.
FOLKTALES—ASIA—JAPAN; SPORTS—WRESTLING.

STANEK, MURIEL

1372    *I Speak English for My Mom.* Ill. by Judith Friedman. Whitman, 1989 (0-8075-3659-8). USE LEVEL: P
*Mexican American*
Lupe must help her mother, who does not speak English, cope with life in America. To get a better job, Lupe's mother decides to learn English.
BEHAVIOR—SEEKING BETTER THINGS; FAMILY LIFE; FOREIGN LANGUAGES; SELF-CONCEPT.

STANLEY, DIANE

1373    *Fortune.* Ill. by the author. Morrow, 1990 (0-688-07210-0); LB (0-688-07211-9). USE LEVEL: M
*Middle Eastern—Persia*
A young farmer, Omar, buys a tiger from a strange old woman. The tiger dances and Omar makes his fortune. Now that he is wealthy, Omar breaks his vow to marry Sunny and looks for a princess. Once again, the tiger is his fortune.
ANIMALS—TIGERS; FOREIGN LANDS—MIDDLE EAST—PERSIA; MAGIC.

STANLEY, SANNA

1374    *The Rains Are Coming.* Ill. by the author. Greenwillow, 1993 (0-688-10948-9); LB (0-688-10949-7). USE LEVEL: P
*African—Zaire*
Aimee's father is a missionary and she and her family have been

living in Zaire for four months. Aimee's mother is planning a party, but all of Aimee's friends in the village must finish their work before the rains arrive.

FOREIGN LANDS—AFRICA—ZAIRE; FRIENDSHIP; PARTIES; WEATHER—RAIN.

### STEINER, BARBARA

1375  *Whale Brother.* Ill. by Gretchen Will Mayo. Walker, 1988 (0-8027-6804-0); LB (0-8027-6805-9); pap. (0-8027-7460-1).
USE LEVEL: M
*Native American—Eskimo*
Omu wishes he could do something to make his father proud. He learns to play the harmonica, making the sound of whales and, when a whale dies, he learns to carve a whale, capturing its spirit.

ANIMALS—WHALES; ART; SEA AND SEASHORE; SELF-CONCEPT.

### STEPTOE, JOHN

1376  *Baby Says.* Ill. by the author. Lothrop, 1988 (0-688-07423-5); LB (0-688-07424-3); pap. (0-688-11855-0). USE LEVEL: PS
*African American*
When his little brother keeps distracting him, Big Brother realizes that his little brother needs his attention.

BABIES, TODDLERS; EMOTIONS—LOVE; FAMILY LIFE—SIBLINGS.

1377  *Birthday.* Ill. by the author. Henry Holt, 1972 (0-8050-1849-2). USE LEVEL: P
*African*
Now that his family has left America to live in Africa, Javaka is eager to celebrate his eighth birthday. His party involves the whole community.

BIRTHDAYS; FOREIGN LANDS—AFRICA.

1378  *Daddy Is a Monster . . . Sometimes.* Ill. by the author. HarperCollins, 1980, LB (0-397-31893-6); pap. (0-06-443042-1). USE LEVEL: P
*African American*
Bweela and Javaka love their daddy, but sometimes, when they misbehave, they see him as a monster.

BEHAVIOR—MISBEHAVIOR; EMOTIONS—LOVE; FAMILY LIFE—FATHERS.

1379  *Mufaro's Beautiful Daughters: An African Tale.* Ill. by the author. Lothrop, 1987 (0-688-04045-4); LB (0-688-04046-2); pap. (0-688-12935-8). USE LEVEL: M
*African*

Mufaro has two beautiful daughters, Manyara and Nyasha. Nyasha is kind and considerate. Manyara is vain and bad-tempered. Nyasha is chosen to marry the king.

CALDECOTT AWARD; CHARACTER TRAITS—KINDNESS; CORETTA SCOTT KING AWARD; FOLKTALES—AFRICA; EMOTIONS—ENVY, JEALOUSY; MAGIC.

1380   *Stevie.* Ill. by the author. HarperCollins, 1969 (0-06-025763-6); LB (0-06-025764-4); pap. (0-06-443122-3). USE LEVEL: P
*African American*
Robert resents that Stevie has come to stay with his family. Stevie is little and gets into too many things. When Stevie leaves, Robert misses him.

EMOTIONS—ANGER; FAMILY LIFE; FAMILY LIFE—FOSTER FAMILY.

1381   *The Story of Jumping Mouse: A Native American Legend.* Ill. by the reteller. Lothrop, 1984 (0-688-01902-1); LB (0-688-01903-X); pap. (0-688-08740-X). USE LEVEL: M
*Native American*
A young mouse listens to stories of the beauty and danger in the world. Leaving his safe home, he journeys through the world seeking his own adventures and undergoing many transformations.

ANIMALS; ANIMALS—MICE; CALDECOTT AWARD; FOLKTALES—NATIVE AMERICAN; MAGIC.

**STEVENS, JAN ROMERO**
1382   *Carlos and the Squash Plant/Carlos y la planta de calabaza.* Ill. by Jeanne Arnold. Northland, 1993 (0-87358-559-3). USE LEVEL: P
*Mexican American*
Carlos and his family have a farm in New Mexico. Carlos likes to help grow food, but he does not like to take baths. When he lies about taking his bath, a squash plant begins to grow in his ear.

ACTIVITIES—BATHING; BEHAVIOR—LYING; GARDENS, GARDENING; HUMOR.

**STEVENS, JANET, RETELLER**
1383   *Coyote Steals the Blanket: An Ute Tale.* Ill. by the reteller. Holiday, 1993 (0-8234-0996-1); pap. (0-8234-1129-X). USE LEVEL: M
*Native American—Ute*
Coyote is chased by a rock after he steals a blanket.

ANIMALS—COYOTES; BEHAVIOR—TRICKERY; FOLKTALES—NATIVE AMERICAN—UTE.

STEVENS, PHILIPPA J.

1384   *Bonk! Goes the Ball.* Ill. by Clovis Martin. Childrens Pr., 1990, LB (0-516-02061-7); pap. (0-516-42061-5). USE LEVEL: P

*Asian American*

An Asian American girl demonstrates some simple strategies for soccer.

PREDICTABLE TEXT; SPORTS—SOCCER.

STEWART, DIANNE

1385   *The Dove.* Ill. by Jude Daly. Greenwillow, 1993 (0-688-11264-1); LB (0-688-11265-X). USE LEVEL: P

*African—South Africa*

After their land is flooded, Lindi and her grandmother worry about planting crops and having enough money. A dove comes to their home and they feed it. Lindi then makes a beaded dove, which they find they can sell.

BIRDS—DOVES; FAMILY LIFE—GRANDMOTHERS; FOREIGN LANDS—AFRICA—SOUTH AFRICA; POVERTY.

STEWART, ELISABETH J.

1386   *On the Long Trail Home.* Houghton, 1994 (0-395-68361-0). USE LEVEL: U

*Native American—Cherokee*

Meli and her Cherokee people are being forced from their homes and moved to Oklahoma. Many of her people die, some from deprivation, others from confrontation. Meli has not seen her brother, Tahli, but she knows she must try to go home.

FAMILY LIFE; RELOCATION; U.S. HISTORY.

STOCK, CATHERINE

1387   *Armien's Fishing Trip.* Ill. by the author. Morrow, 1990 (0-688-08395-1); LB (0-688-08396-X). USE LEVEL: P

*African—South Africa*

Armien is visiting his aunt and uncle in Kalk Bay, on the southern tip of Africa. Armien stows away on his uncle's fishing boat. He comes out of his hiding place to help a fisherman who is swept overboard.

BEHAVIOR—BOASTING; CHARACTER TRAITS—BRAVERY; FOREIGN LANDS—AFRICA—SOUTH AFRICA; SPORTS—FISHING.

1388   *Emma's Dragon Hunt.* Ill. by the author. Lothrop, 1984 (0-688-02696-6); LB (0-688-02698-2). USE LEVEL: PS/P

*Asian American—China*

Emma's grandfather, who has just arrived from China, tells her about dragons and some of their powers.
DRAGONS; FAMILY LIFE—GRANDFATHERS; WEATHER.

1389 *Halloween Monster.* Ill. by the author. Macmillan, 1990 (0-02-788404-X). USE LEVEL: P
*African American*
Halloween has made Tommy worried about monsters, ghosts, and witches. He decides to be a monster for Halloween.
BEHAVIOR—WORRYING; EMOTIONS—FEAR; HOLIDAYS—HALLOWEEN.

1390 *Secret Valentine.* Ill. by the author. Macmillan, 1991 (0-02-788372-8). USE LEVEL: P
*African American*
A little girl makes Valentine's cards for everyone in her family, even her cat, Muffety. She decides to make one for the lonely elderly lady who lives next door. On Valentine's Day, she receives a card from a secret friend.
CHARACTER TRAITS—KINDNESS; HOLIDAYS—VALENTINE'S DAY; OLDER ADULTS.

1391 *Where Are You Going, Manyoni?* Ill. by the author. Morrow, 1993 (0-688-10352-9); LB (0-688-10353-7). USE LEVEL: P
*African—Zimbabwe*
In Africa, a girl walks across the veld to go to school, seeing wildlife along the way.
ANIMALS; FOREIGN LANDS—AFRICA—ZIMBABWE; SCHOOL.

**STOLZ, MARY**
1392 *Cezanne Pinto: A Memoir.* Knopf, 1994 (0-679-84917-3). USE LEVEL: U
*African American*
In 1860, Cezanne Pinto escaped from a plantation in Virginia and followed the Underground Railroad to Canada. Now an old man, he looks back on his life, including his time caring for horses in Canada and as a cowboy in the West.
COWBOYS; SLAVERY; UNDERGROUND RAILROAD.

1393 *Coco Grimes.* HarperCollins, 1994 (0-06-024232-9); LB (0-06-024233-7). USE LEVEL: M
*African American*
For his eleventh birthday, Thomas receives a book about the Negro League baseball teams. Thomas and Grandfather travel to Miami and meet Coco Grimes, an elderly man who knew and played ball with many of the early players.

BIRTHDAYS; FAMILY LIFE—GRANDFATHERS; OLDER ADULTS; SPORTS—
BASEBALL.

1394   *Go Fish!* Ill. by Pat Cummings. HarperCollins, 1991 (0-06-
25820-9); LB (0-06-025822-5); pap. (0-06-440466-8). USE
LEVEL: M
*African American*
When Thomas and his grandfather go fishing, Thomas learns
about being patient. Later, Thomas listens to a story about his
African heritage.
FAMILY LIFE—GRANDFATHERS; OLDER ADULTS; SPORTS—FISHING;
STORYTELLING.

1395   *Stealing Home.* Ill. by Pat Cummings. HarperCollins, 1992 (0-
06-021154-7); LB (0-06-021157-1). USE LEVEL: M/U
*African American*
In Florida, Thomas and his grandfather live together and get
along. They enjoy going to baseball games and also fishing.
Things have to change when Great-Aunt Linzy comes to stay.
FAMILY LIFE—GRANDFATHERS; OLDER ADULTS; SPORTS—BASEBALL.

1396   *Storm in the Night.* Ill. by Pat Cummings. HarperCollins, 1988
(0-06-025912-4); LB (0-06-025913-2); pap. (0-06-443256-4).
USE LEVEL: P/M
*African American*
During a storm that has cut off the electricity, a grandfather and
grandson sit together and enjoy the sounds, smells, and feelings
of the rain.
CORETTA SCOTT KING AWARD; EMOTIONS—FEAR; FAMILY LIFE—GRAND-
FATHERS; NIGHT; OLDER ADULTS; WEATHER—STORMS.

1397   *Zekmet, the Stone Carver: A Tale of Ancient Egypt.* Ill. by
Deborah Nourse Lattimore. Harcourt, 1988, o.p. USE LEVEL: M
*African—Egypt*
When the Pharaoh Khafre wants another monument, his vizier
has Zekmet the stone carver plan the project. Zekmet designs
the sphinx, a lion shape with the face of the pharaoh. This is an
original story explaining the origin of this monument.
ANCIENT TIMES; CAREERS—ARTISTS; FOREIGN LANDS—AFRICA—EGYPT;
HISTORY.

**STRAIGHT, SUSAN**
1398   *Bear E. Bear.* Ill. by Marisabina Russo. Hyperion, 1995 (1-
56282-526-7); LB (1-56282-527-5). USE LEVEL: P
*Multicultural*

After her teddy bear falls into the gutter, Gaila waits by the washer and dryer until he is clean and they are together again. While she waits, she thinks of special times she has had with Bear E. Bear.

FAMILY LIFE; LAUNDRY; MARRIAGE, INTERRACIAL; TOYS—TEDDY BEARS.

STRICKLAND, DOROTHY S., EDITOR

1399 *Listen Children: An Anthology of Black Literature.* With a foreword by Coretta Scott King. Ill. by Leo Dillon and Diane Dillon. Bantam, 1982, pap. (0-553-27092-3). USE LEVEL: U
*African American*
This collection features writings that emphasize positive self-esteem and feelings of pride in African American culture, heritage, and life.

POETRY, RHYME; SELF-CONCEPT; SHORT STORIES.

STRICKLAND, DOROTHY S., AND MICHAEL R. STRICKLAND, SELECTORS

1400 *Families: Poems Celebrating the African American Experience.* Ill. by John Ward. Boyds Mills, 1994 (1-56397-288-3). USE LEVEL: M
*African American*
Twenty-three poems celebrate African American families and their experiences. "Aunt Sue's Stories," "Seeing a New Sister," and "Missing Mama" are among the experiences. Poets include Langston Hughes, Lucille Clifton, and Julia Fields.

EMOTIONS; FAMILY LIFE; POETRY, RHYME.

STROUD, VIRGINIA A.

1401 *Doesn't Fall Off His Horse.* Ill. by the author. Dial, 1994 (0-8037-1634-6); LB (0-8037-1635-4). USE LEVEL: M
*Native American—Kiowa*
When Saygee visits her grandfather, she waits for him to tell stories about his childhood with his people, the Kiowa, in Indian Territory. He tells her about how he was given his name, "Doesn't Fall Off His Horse."

ACTIVITIES—REMINISCING; ANIMALS—HORSES; FAMILY LIFE—GRANDFATHERS; NAMES; STORYTELLING.

SULLIVAN, CHARLES, EDITOR

1402 *Children of Promise: African-American Literature and Art for Young People.* Abrams, 1991 (0-8109-3170-2). USE LEVEL: U
*African American*
This collection of literature and art introduces children to interpretations of the African American experience.

ART; LITERATURE; POETRY, RHYME; SELF-CONCEPT.

**SUN, CHYNG FENG**

1403    *Mama Bear.* Ill. by Lolly Robinson. Houghton, 1994 (0-395-63412-1). USE LEVEL: P
*Asian American—China*
Mei-Mei sees a large toy bear that she wants to buy. She and her mother save money for the bear, but by Christmas, there is not enough. Mei-Mei finds that she has something better than the bear—her mother.
EMOTIONS—LOVE; FAMILY LIFE—MOTHERS; HOLIDAYS—CHRISTMAS; TOYS—TEDDY BEARS.

**SURAT, MICHELE MARIA**

1404    *Angel Child, Dragon Child.* Ill. by Vo-Dinh Mai. Raintree, 1983, LB (0-940742-12-8); Scholastic, pap. (0-590-42271-5). USE LEVEL: P
*Asian American—Vietnam*
Ut, a Vietnamese girl, adjusts to life in America even though she misses her mother, who is still in Vietnam. She finds it difficult to be in school and make new friends.
BEHAVIOR—ACCEPTING DIFFERENCES; FAMILY LIFE; FRIENDSHIP; SCHOOL.

**TADJO, VÉRONIQUE, RETELLER**

1405    *Lord of the Dance: An African Retelling.* Ill. by the reteller. HarperCollins, 1989 (0-397-32351-4); LB (0-397-32352-2). USE LEVEL: M
*African—Ivory Coast*
The Mask, the Lord of the Dance, retells a creation story of the Senufo people of the Ivory Coast.
CREATION; FOLKTALES—AFRICA—IVORY COAST; MAGIC.

**TAGORE, RABINDRANATH**

1406    *Paper Boats.* Ill. by Grayce Bochak. Caroline House, 1992 (1-878093-12-6). USE LEVEL: P
*Multicultural*
A young boy sends paper boats down the stream and dreams that someone will find them and know who he is.
BOATS, SHIPS; PAPER; POETRY, RHYME; TOYS.

**TALBERT, MARC**

1407    *A Sunburned Prayer.* Simon & Schuster, 1995 (0-689-80125-4). USE LEVEL: U
*Mexican American*
Eloy wants to make a pilgrimage to Chimayó on Good Friday with the hope of praying for his grandmother, who is dying of

cancer. Disobeying his parents, he walks across the desert and learns about faith and the love of his family.

ANIMALS—DOGS; FAMILY LIFE—GRANDMOTHERS; ILLNESS; RELIGION.

TAN, AMY

1408　*The Chinese Siamese Cat.* Ill. by Gretchen Schields. Macmillan, 1994 (0-02-788835-5). USE LEVEL: M

*Asian—China*

A mother cat tells her kittens the story of their ancestor, Sagwa, a cat who lived in the home of the magistrate. Sagwa's encounter with an ink pot is the reason Siamese cats have such distinctive markings.

ANIMALS—CATS; CHARACTER TRAITS—FOOLISHNESS; FOREIGN LANDS—ASIA—CHINA; POURQUOI TALES.

1409　*Moon Lady.* Ill. by Gretchen Schields. Macmillan, 1992 (0-02-788830-4). USE LEVEL: M

*Asian—China*

When grandmother was a young girl in China, she went to the Moon Festival. She made many foolish wishes, but when she finally saw the Moon Lady, she realized what she really wanted—to be back with her family.

BEHAVIOR—WISHING; FAMILY LIFE—GRANDMOTHERS; FOREIGN LANDS—ASIA—CHINA.

TANAKA, BÉATRICE, RETELLER

1410　*The Chase: A Kutenai Indian Tale.* Ill. by Michel Gay. Crown, 1991, o.p. USE LEVEL: P

*Native American—Kutenai*

When Coyote sees Rabbit running, he and the other animals run too. The animals feel foolish when they find that Rabbit is only hurrying home to his dinner.

ANIMALS; CHARACTER TRAITS—FOOLISHNESS; CUMULATIVE TALES; FOLKTALES—NATIVE AMERICAN—KUTENAI.

TATE, CAROL

1411　*Tale of the Spiteful Spirits: A Kampuchean Folk Tale.* Ill. by the reteller. Bedrick, 1991, LB (0-87226-445-9). USE LEVEL: M

*Asian—Cambodia*

A boy has heard many stories but refuses to share them. The spirits of these stories live in a leather bag. The spirits plan to spoil the boy's wedding day.

FOLKTALES—ASIA—CAMBODIA; STORYTELLING.

**TATE, ELEANORA E.**

1412 *A Blessing in Disguise.* Delacorte, 1995 (0-385-32103-1). USE
LEVEL: U
*African American*
Zambia Brown, 12, thinks her small-town life in South Carolina
with her aunt and uncle is dull. When her father opens a night-
club, Zambee hopes to be part of the excitement. She does not
expect the crime, drugs, and violence that come to her town.
CRIME; DEATH; DRUGS; FAMILY LIFE.

1413 *Front Porch Stories: At the One-Room School.* Ill. by Eric
Velasquez. Bantam, 1992 (0-553-08384-8); Dell, pap. (0-440-
40901-2). USE LEVEL: M
*African American*
Margie, 12, and her cousin Ethel, 7, go with Margie's father to
the one-room schoolhouse and listen to stories. In one story,
the teacher, Daddy's Aunt Daisy, was chased by a shadowy
shape; another tells of a dog that was mistaken for a possum.
HUMOR; SCARY STORIES; SHORT STORIES; STORYTELLING.

1414 *The Secret of Gumbo Grove.* Bantam, pap. (0-553-27226-8). USE
LEVEL: M/U
*African American*
Raisin, 11, lives in a small southern community where blacks are
kept in menial jobs. She begins to work on a project—cleaning
up the cemetery—and she learns about the important contribu-
tions that blacks have made to her community.
COMMUNITIES, NEIGHBORHOODS; PREJUDICE; RACE RELATIONS.

1415 *Thank You, Dr. Martin Luther King, Jr.!* Bantam, pap. (0-553-
15886-4). USE LEVEL: M
*African American*
Mary Elouise Avery is given the opportunity to learn about her
own African American heritage from Imani Afrika and the story-
tellers.
CHARACTER TRAITS—PRIDE; FRIENDSHIP; RACE RELATIONS; SCHOOL;
SELF-CONCEPT.

**TAYLOR, C. J.**

1416 *Bones in the Basket: Native Stories of the Origin of People.* Ill. by
the author. Tundra, 1994 (0-88776-327-8). USE LEVEL: M
*Native American*
There are nine stories of creation from different native peoples

including "From Darkness to Light" from the Mandan, "Big Raven Creates the World" from the Chuckchee, and "Bones in the Basket" from the Modoc.

CREATION; FOLKTALES—NATIVE AMERICAN; SHORT STORIES.

1417 *The Ghost and Lone Warrior: An Arapaho Legend*. Ill. by the author. Tundra, 1991 (0-88776-263-8). USE LEVEL: M
*Native American—Arapaho*
After he hurts his ankle, Lone Warrior is left alone. He is visited by the ghost of his ancestor, who had saved him from being ambushed so he could lead his tribe.

FOLKTALES—NATIVE AMERICAN—ARAPAHO; GHOSTS.

1418 *How Two-Feather Was Saved from Loneliness: An Abenaki Legend*. Ill. by the author. Tundra, 1990 (0-887766-254-9); pap. (0-887766-282-4). USE LEVEL: M
*Native American—Abenaki*
Two-Feather wishes to see another face and the Corn Goddess comes to him. Giving him fire, she shows him how to clear the meadow, then she gives him corn with tassels as soft as her hair.

FOLKTALES—NATIVE AMERICAN—ABENAKI; FOOD.

1419 *How We Saw the World: Nine Native Stories of the Way Things Began*. Ill. by the author. Tundra, 1993 (0-88776-302-2). USE LEVEL: M
*Native American*
From the Bella Coola story "How Eagle Man Created the Islands of the Pacific Coast" to the Algonquin story "The Birth of Niagara Falls," these stories explain natural phenomena and celebrate the beauty of the world.

FOLKTALES—NATIVE AMERICAN; NATURE; POURQUOI TALES; SHORT STORIES.

1420 *Little Water and the Gift of the Animals: A Seneca Legend*. Ill. by the author. Tundra, 1992, LB (0-88776-285-9). USE LEVEL: M
*Native American—Seneca*
Little Water, a hunter, respects the animals and the natural world. When his people are sick, the animals share the cure.

ANIMALS; FOLKTALES—NATIVE AMERICAN—SENECA; ILLNESS; NATURE.

1421 *The Secret of the White Buffalo: An Oglala Legend*. Ill. by the author. Tundra, 1993 (0-88776-321-9). USE LEVEL: M
*Native American—Oglala*
When the people of the village argue, two scouts are sent to look for buffalo. A sacred woman, White Buffalo Woman, tells

Blue Cloud what must be done. She gives them a pipe of peace, which is treasured by the people.

BEHAVIOR—FIGHTING, ARGUING; FOLKTALES—NATIVE AMERICAN—
OGLALA; PROBLEM SOLVING.

**TAYLOR, HARRIET PECK, RETELLER**

1422    *Coyote and the Laughing Butterflies.* Ill. by the reteller.
Macmillan, 1995 (0-02-788846-0). USE LEVEL: M
*Native American—Tewa*
Coyote's wife sends him to the lake for salt crystals. When he gets there, Coyote rests, and the butterflies work together to carry him back to his home. On the third try, the butterflies bring him and some salt back and the animals enjoy a feast.

ANIMALS; ANIMALS—COYOTES; FOLKTALES—NATIVE AMERICAN—TEWA;
INSECTS—BUTTERFLIES, CATERPILLARS; POURQUOI TALES.

1423    *Coyote Places the Stars.* Ill. by the reteller. Macmillan, 1993 (0-02-788845-2). USE LEVEL: M
*Native American—Wasco*
Coyote travels to the moon and, using his arrows, he arranges the stars into the shapes of his animal friends.

ANIMALS—COYOTES; FOLKTALES—NATIVE AMERICAN—WASCO;
POURQUOI TALES; STARS.

**TAYLOR, MILDRED D.**

1424    *The Friendship.* Ill. by Max Ginsburg. Dial, 1987 (0-8037-0417-8); LB (0-8037-0418-6). USE LEVEL: M/U
*African American*
Mr. Tom Bee, an elderly black man, saved a white man's life many years ago. Now the man he rescued, John Wallace, does not want to acknowledge the debt.

CHARACTER TRAITS—MEANNESS; EMOTIONS—FEAR; CORETTA SCOTT
KING AWARD; PREJUDICE; RACE RELATIONS; U.S. HISTORY—DEPRESSION.

1425    *The Friendship/The Gold Cadillac.* Bantam, 1989, pap. (0-553-15765-5). USE LEVEL: M/U
*African American*
Two novels are published together in this paperback.

PREJUDICE; RACE RELATIONS.

1426    *The Gold Cadillac.* Ill. by Michael Hays. Dial, 1987 (0-8037-0342-2); LB (0-8037-0343-0). USE LEVEL: M/U
*African American*
When Wilbert buys a new 1950 gold Cadillac, his daughters are thrilled but his wife is upset. She wanted to save the money for a

better house. On a trip to Mississippi, the family encounters prejudiced behavior that focuses on their expensive car.
EMOTIONS—FEAR; FAMILY LIFE; PREJUDICE; RACE RELATIONS; U.S. HISTORY—THE 1950S.

1427    *Let the Circle Be Unbroken.* Dial, 1981 (0-8037-4748-9); Puffin, pap. (0-14-034892-1). USE LEVEL: U
*African American*
Continuing the story from *Roll of Thunder, Hear My Cry*, the Logan family is uneasy about the upcoming trial of T. J. Avery, a black boy accused of killing a white man. They continue to face prejudice and poverty in the South during the Depression.
CORETTA SCOTT KING AWARD; FAMILY LIFE; PREJUDICE; RACE RELATIONS; U.S. HISTORY—DEPRESSION.

1428    *Mississippi Bridge.* Ill. by Max Ginsburg. Dial, 1990 (0-8037-0426-7); LB (0-8037-0427-5). USE LEVEL: M/U
*African American*
When the bus is full, the black passengers are ordered off to make room for more white passengers. In an ironic twist, this unfair treatment saves the lives of the black passengers. This story is set in Mississippi during the Depression.
DEATH; PREJUDICE; RACE RELATIONS; U.S. HISTORY—DEPRESSION.

1429    *The Road to Memphis.* Dial, 1990 (0-8037-0340-6); Puffin, pap. (0-14-036077-8). USE LEVEL: U
*African American*
In 1941, Cassie Logan is finishing high school in Jackson, Mississippi, and looking to the future. When some white boys taunt some black boys, there is a violent incident. Jeremy Simms, a white boy, may be the only one who knows what happened.
CORETTA SCOTT KING AWARD; FAMILY LIFE; PREJUDICE; RACE RELATIONS; U.S. HISTORY—DEPRESSION.

1430    *Roll of Thunder, Hear My Cry.* Dial, 1976 (0-8037-7473-7); Puffin, pap. (0-14-034893-X). USE LEVEL: U
*African American*
In the rural South during the Depression, the Logan family struggles to keep their land and to demonstrate their dignity and pride. Cassie Logan and her brothers experience the prejudice of their segregated school and community.
CORETTA SCOTT KING AWARD; FAMILY LIFE; NEWBERY AWARD; PREJUDICE; RACE RELATIONS; U.S. HISTORY—DEPRESSION.

1431    *Song of the Trees.* Ill. by Jerry Pinkney. Dial, 1975 (0-8037-5452-3); LB (0-8037-5453-1); Bantam, pap. (0-553-27587-9). USE LEVEL: M/U

*African American*

Cassie Logan loves listening to the sound of the trees on her family's property. During the Depression in Mississippi, there are hardships for the Logan family, one of the few black property owners.

CORETTA SCOTT KING AWARD; PREJUDICE; FAMILY LIFE; RACE RELATIONS; U.S. HISTORY—DEPRESSION.

1432    *The Well: David's Story.* Dial, 1995 (0-8037-1802-0); LB (0-8037-1803-9). USE LEVEL: U

*African American*

When David Logan was a boy, his family's well was the only one with sweet water during a dry spell. David's brother, Hammer, stands up to Charlie Simms, a white boy, and David and Hammer are punished. Later, Charlie and his friends spoil the well.

FAMILY LIFE; PREJUDICE; RACE RELATIONS; SELF-CONCEPT.

**TAYLOR, THEODORE**

1433    *The Cay.* Doubleday, 1969 (0-385-07906-0); pap. (0-380-00142-X). USE LEVEL: U

*Caribbean*

After the boat he is on is torpedoed by a German ship, Phillip finds that he is blind and stranded on a small Caribbean island. He must depend on Timothy, an old black man. Phillip adjusts to his blindness and to his changing attitude toward Timothy.

FOREIGN LANDS—CARIBBEAN ISLANDS; HANDICAPS—BLINDNESS; ISLANDS; PREJUDICE; RACE RELATIONS; WORLD WAR II.

1434    *Timothy of the Cay.* Harcourt, 1993 (0-15-288358-4); Avon, pap. (0-380-72119-8). USE LEVEL: U

*Caribbean*

In this "prequel-sequel," the characters from *The Cay* are featured. Phillip, who was blinded, hopes to regain his sight. Alternate chapters tell of the early life of Timothy, who helped Phillip survive being shipwrecked.

FOREIGN LANDS—CARIBBEAN ISLANDS; HANDICAPS—BLINDNESS; RACE RELATIONS; SURVIVAL.

**TEJIMA**

1435    *Ho-limlim: A Rabbit Tale from Japan.* Ill. by the author.
Putnam, 1990, o.p. USE LEVEL: M
*Asian—Japan*
On a day when spring seems to be almost here, an old rabbit
goes off on an adventure. He thinks he sees a whale, two men
fighting, and a fire, but when he looks closer, it is not as he
thought. He decides to stay near his own home.
ANIMALS—RABBITS; FOLKTALES—ASIA—JAPAN; OLDER ADULTS.

**TEMPLE, FRANCES**

1436    *Grab Hands and Run.* Orchard, 1993 (0-531-05480-2); LB
(0-531-08630-5); Trophy, pap. (0-06-440548-6). USE LEVEL: U
*Central American—El Salvador*
Felipe, 12, loves and admires his father, Jacinto, who speaks out
against the government of El Salvador. When Jacinto disappears, Felipe and his family escape to Canada. Felipe worries
that he should be in El Salvador helping his people.
CHARACTER TRAITS—BRAVERY; FOREIGN LANDS—CENTRAL AMERICA—EL
SALVADOR; REFUGEES.

1437    *Tiger Soup: An Anansi Story from Jamaica.* Ill. by the reteller.
Orchard, 1994 (0-531-06859-5); LB (0-531-08709-3). USE
LEVEL: M
*Caribbean—Jamaica*
Anansi tricks Tiger into letting him eat Tiger's soup, then
Anansi tricks the little monkeys into taking the blame.
ANIMALS—TIGERS; BEHAVIOR—TRICKERY; FOLKTALES—CARIBBEAN
ISLANDS—JAMAICA; FOOD; SPIDERS.

1438    *Tonight, by Sea.* Orchard, 1995 (0-531-06899-4); LB (0-531-
08749-2). USE LEVEL: U
*Caribbean—Haiti*
Belle Fleuve is home for Paulie and her family, yet they plan to
leave to escape the tyranny of the government and the poverty
of their lives. Her parents have left and her uncle's boat-build-
ing activities are illegal and place everyone at risk.
FOREIGN LANDS—CARIBBEAN ISLANDS—HAITI; POVERTY; SEA AND
SEASHORE.

**THOMAS, JANE RESH**

1439    *Lights on the River.* Ill. by Michael Dooling. Hyperion, 1994 (0-
7868-0004-6); LB (0-7868-2003-9). USE LEVEL: M
*Hispanic American*

Teresa watches the babies while her family works in the fields. She thinks of her grandmother in Mexico as she and her family pick crops in America.

FAMILY LIFE; MIGRANT WORKERS.

### THOMAS, JOYCE CAROL

1440  *Brown Honey in Broomwheat Tea: Poems.* Ill. by Floyd Cooper. HarperCollins, 1993 (0-06-021087-7); LB (0-06-021088-5). USE LEVEL: P/M

*African American*

These poems feature the members of a family and use images of nature to show how they are connected.

CORETTA SCOTT KING AWARD; FAMILY LIFE; POETRY, RHYME; SELF-CONCEPT.

### THORNHILL, JAN

1441  *Crow and Fox: And Other Animal Legends.* Ill. by the author. Simon & Schuster, 1993 (0-671-87428-4). USE LEVEL: M

*Multicultural*

The nine stories in this collection are from different cultures, including those of India, China, West Africa, and South America.

ANIMALS; FOLKTALES; SHORT STORIES.

### TILLER, RUTH

1442  *Cinnamon, Mint, & Mothballs: A Visit to Grandmother's House.* Ill. by Aki Sogabe. Harcourt, 1993 (0-15-276617-0). USE LEVEL: P

*Asian American*

Going to Grandmother's means a visit to the farmhouse and barn, feeding the cat and washing hands at the pump, watching the fire and listening to the nighttime sounds. The illustrations depict a family with an Asian heritage.

BEDTIME; FAMILY LIFE—GRANDMOTHERS; RURAL LIFE.

### TIMPANELLI, GIOIA, RETELLER

1443  *Tales from the Roof of the World: Folktales of Tibet.* Ill. by Elizabeth Kelly Lockwood. Viking, 1984, o.p. USE LEVEL: M/U

*Asian—Tibet*

The four stories in this collection introduce readers to the culture and heritage of Tibet. An introduction provides background information about the country and customs.

FOLKTALES—ASIA—TIBET; SHORT STORIES.

TOMPERT, ANN, ADAPTER

1444 *Bamboo Hats and a Rice Cake: A Tale Adapted from Japanese Folklore.* Ill. by Demi. Crown, 1993 (0-517-59272-X); LB (0-517-59273-8). USE LEVEL: M
*Asian—Japan*
An old couple has no rice cakes to celebrate the New Year. The old man goes to the market but cannot sell anything. He only trades for items, ending up with bamboo hats, which he gives to the Jizo statues. They reward him for his gift.
CHARACTER TRAITS—GENEROSITY; FOLKTALES—ASIA—JAPAN; FOREIGN LANGUAGES; HOLIDAYS—NEW YEAR'S.

1445 *Grandfather Tang's Story.* Ill. by Robert Andrew Parker. Crown, 1990 (0-517-57487-X); LB (0-517-57272-9). USE LEVEL: P
*Asian—China*
An old man uses tangrams to tell the story of two foxes that try to outdo each other. The tangram shapes are changed into new animals, each more fierce than the one before.
ANIMALS—FOXES; CONCEPTS—SHAPE; FAMILY LIFE—GRANDFATHERS; FOREIGN LANDS—ASIA—CHINA; TANGRAMS.

1446 *The Silver Whistle.* Ill. by Beth Peck. Macmillan, 1988 (0-02-789160-7). USE LEVEL: P
*Mexican*
Miguel and his family are traveling to town for the Christmas festival. Miguel hopes to sell his clay whistles and buy a silver whistle to place by the manger. Instead, he gives his belongings away to help others.
CHARACTER TRAITS—GENEROSITY; FOREIGN LANDS—MEXICO; GIFTS; HOLIDAYS—CHRISTMAS.

TOPOOCO, EUSEBIO

1447 *Waira's First Journey.* Ill. by the author. Lothrop, 1987 (0-688-12054-7). USE LEVEL: M
*South American—Bolivia*
Waira and her family are going to the market in Topojo. It is a long journey and it is the first time Waira has made the trip. Along the way, Waira and her family see the people and places of her country.
ACTIVITIES—TRAVELING; FAMILY LIFE; FOREIGN LANDS—SOUTH AMERICA—BOLIVIA; MARKETS.

TORRE, BETTY L., RETELLER

1448 *The Luminous Pearl: A Chinese Folktale.* Ill. by Carol Inouye. Orchard, 1990, o.p. USE LEVEL: M
*Asian—China*

Two brothers search for a pearl to win the Dragon King's daughter for a wife. The younger brother, Wa Jing, succeeds in finding the pearl.

CHARACTER TRAITS—HONESTY; CHARACTER TRAITS—KINDNESS; DRAGONS; FOLKTALES—ASIA—CHINA; ROYALTY.

### TORRES, LEYLA

1449 *Saturday Sancocho.* Ill. by the author. Farrar, 1995 (0-374-36418-4). USE LEVEL: P
*South American*
When Maria Lili visits her grandparents on Saturdays, they make chicken sancocho. This week, there is no food and no money, but Mama Ana has a plan. She trades eggs with the vendors in the market to gather the needed ingredients.

ACTIVITIES—COOKING; ACTIVITIES—TRADING; FAMILY LIFE—GRANDPARENTS; FOREIGN LANDS—SOUTH AMERICA; MARKETS.

1450 *Subway Sparrow.* Ill. by the author. Farrar, 1993 (0-374-37285-3). USE LEVEL: P
*Multicultural*
An Asian American girl tries to rescue a sparrow that has flown onto a subway train. The people on the train, who are from diverse backgrounds, help her, and the sparrow is set free.

BIRDS—SPARROWS; CHARACTER TRAITS—KINDNESS; FOREIGN LANGUAGES; TRAINS.

### TREVIÑO, ELIZABETH BORTON DE

1451 *El Güero: A True Adventure Story.* Ill. by Leslie W. Bowman. Farrar, 1989 (0-374-31995-2); pap. (0-374-42028-9). USE LEVEL: U
*Mexican*
El Güero, the Blond One, is the son of a judge. When General Díaz comes to power, the family moves to Baja California. They encounter dangers, including scorpions and bandits. Always, El Güero's father stands up for his beliefs and his family.

ADVENTURE; CHARACTER TRAITS—BRAVERY; FOREIGN LANDS—MEXICO; HISTORY.

1452 *I, Juan de Pareja.* Farrar, 1965 (0-374-33531-1); pap. (0-374-43525-1). USE LEVEL: U
*African heritage*
In Seville, Veláquez is aided by his slave, Juan de Pareja, who develops as an artist in his own right.

ART; NEWBERY AWARD; SLAVERY.

TREZISE, PERCY, AND DICK ROUGHSEY
1453   *Turramulli the Giant Quinkin*. Ill. by the authors. Gareth
Stevens, 1982, o.p. USE LEVEL: M
*Australian—Aborigine*
The Yalanji people decorate their cave walls with story-paint-
ings, some featuring Turramulli the giant, who is dangerous and
evil. Two children, Moonbi and Leealin, are separated from
their parents and cause the death of Turramulli.
FOLKTALES—AUSTRALIA—ABORIGINE; MONSTERS.

TROUGHTON, JOANNA, RETELLER
1454   *How Night Came: A Folk Tale from the Amazon*. Ill. by the
reteller. Bedrick, 1986 (0-87266-093-3). USE LEVEL: M
*South American—Amazon*
The daughter of the Great Snake marries and comes to live on
the earth. She misses the cool darkness of her father's underwa-
ter home. Her husband sends three servants to bring back the
night.
FOLKTALES—SOUTH AMERICA—AMAZON; NIGHT.

1455   *How Rabbit Stole the Fire: A North American Indian Folk Tale*.
Ill. by the reteller. Bedrick, 1986, o.p. USE LEVEL: M
*Native American*
Rabbit, who is full of mischief, goes to the village of the Sky
People. He gets the people to dance and he steals their fire.
ANIMALS—RABBITS; BEHAVIOR—TRICKERY; FIRE; FOLKTALES—NATIVE
AMERICAN.

1456   *How the Birds Changed Their Feathers: A South American
Indian Folk Tale*. Ill. by the reteller. Bedrick, 1976, o.p. USE
LEVEL: M
*South American*
When a boy makes a necklace from some colorful stones, he is
transformed into the Rainbow Snake. The cormorant kills the
snake and claims its skin. All the birds help him carry it, and
their feathers, which were all white, become multicolored.
BIRDS; CONCEPTS—COLOR; FOLKTALES— SOUTH AMERICA; POURQUOI
TALES.

1457   *Make-Believe Tales: A Folk Tale from Burma*. Ill. by the reteller.
Bedrick, 1991, LB (0-87226-451-3). USE LEVEL: M
*Asian—Burma*
A cat, a mouse, a parrot, and a monkey make a bet with a travel-
er that he will not believe their tales. The traveler listens to the

stories and then tells his own story. If the animals believe him, they are his slaves; if not, they lose the bet.

ANIMALS; BEHAVIOR—TRICKERY; FOLKTALES—ASIA—BURMA.

1458    *Tortoise's Dream*. Ill. by the reteller. Bedrick, 1980, o.p. USE LEVEL: M
*African*
Tortoise dreams of a tree filled with all kinds of fruit, but to get the fruit to fall, you must know the name of the tree.

ANIMALS; DREAMS; FOLKTALES—AFRICA; NAMES; REPTILES—TURTLES, TORTOISES; TREES.

1459    *Whale's Canoe: A Folk Tale from Australia*. Ill. by the reteller. Bedrick, 1993, o.p. USE LEVEL: M
*Australian*
The animals want to go to a new land but their canoes are not strong enough. Starfish tricks Whale into falling asleep and the animals use his canoe to travel to the land called Australia. Now Whale must stay in the sea.

ANIMALS; ANIMALS—WHALES; BEHAVIOR—TRICKERY; FOLKTALES—AUSTRALIA; POURQUOI TALES; SEA AND SEASHORE.

1460    *What Made Tiddalik Laugh: An Australian Aborigine Folk Tale*. Ill. by the reteller. Bedrick, 1977 (0-87226-081-X). USE LEVEL: M
*Australian—Aborigine*
Tiddalik the frog has swallowed all the fresh water in the world. The animals try to make Tiddalik laugh, and when Platypus succeeds, the water is returned.

ANIMALS; FOLKTALES—AUSTRALIA—ABORIGINE; FROGS AND TOADS; WATER.

1461    *Who Will Be the Sun? A North American Indian Folk-tale*. Ill. by the reteller. Bedrick, 1985 (0-87226-038-0). USE LEVEL: M
*Native American—Kutenai*
Each animal tries to be the sun. The older Lynx is chosen and his younger brother becomes the moon. Coyote is a trickster.

ANIMALS; FOLKTALES—NATIVE AMERICAN—KUTENAI; SUN.

1462    *The Wizard Punchkin: A Folk Tale from India*. Ill. by the reteller. Bedrick, 1982 (0-87226-162-X). USE LEVEL: M
*Asian—India*
After his brothers are enchanted by the Wizard Punchkin, Chandra finds the way to save his brothers. He steals the wiz-

ard's soul, killing the wizard and releasing all who had been his prisoners.

CHARACTER TRAITS—BRAVERY; FOLKTALES—ASIA—INDIA; MAGIC; WIZARDS.

**TSUTSUI, YORIKO**

1463    *Anna in Charge.* Ill. by Akiko Hayashi. Viking, 1988 (0-670-81672-8); Puffin, pap. (0-14-050733-7). USE LEVEL: P
*Asian—Japan*
When she has to run an errand, Anna's mother leaves Anna at home with Katy, her younger sister, who wanders away. Anna is relieved when she finds Katy.

ACTIVITIES—BABY-SITTING; BEHAVIOR—LOST; EMOTIONS—FEAR; FAMILY LIFE—SIBLINGS; FOREIGN LANDS—ASIA—JAPAN.

1464    *Anna's Secret Friend.* Ill. by Akiko Hayashi. Viking, 1987, o.p.
USE LEVEL: P
*Asian—Japan*
Anna and her family move, and Anna misses her old friends. At her new home, several gifts are left for her. Anna meets the girl who has given her the gifts and they play together.

FAMILY LIFE; FOREIGN LANDS—ASIA—JAPAN; FRIENDSHIP; MOVING.

1465    *Anna's Special Present.* Ill. by Akiko Hayashi. Viking, 1988 (0-670-81671-X); Puffin, pap. (0-14-054219-1). USE LEVEL: P
*Asian—Japan*
When her sister, Katy, is in the hospital, Anna is worried. Anna gives Katy her special doll to show her how much she cares.

FAMILY LIFE—SIBLINGS; FOREIGN LANDS—ASIA—JAPAN; GIFTS; HOSPITALS; ILLNESS; TOYS—DOLLS.

**TURENNE DES PRÉS, FRANÇOIS**

1466    *Children of Yayoute: Folk Tales of Haiti.* Ill. by the author. Universe Publishing, 1993 (0-87663-791-8). USE LEVEL: U
*Caribbean—Haiti*
The 12 stories in this collection include stories of trickery and foolishness. Several stories feature Malice, a Haitian trickster.

BEHAVIOR—TRICKERY; CHARACTER TRAITS—FOOLISHNESS; FOLKTALES—CARIBBEAN ISLANDS—HAITI; SHORT STORIES.

**TURNER, ANN**

1467    *Nettie's Trip South.* Ill. by Ronald Himler. Macmillan, 1987 (0-02-789240-9). USE LEVEL: M
*African American*
In a letter to her friend, Nettie, a young white girl, describes her

journey to Richmond, Virginia, including seeing slaves in her hotel and a slave auction.

ACTIVITIES—TRAVELING; BEHAVIOR—DISBELIEF; FAMILY LIFE; SLAVERY; U.S. HISTORY.

1468    *Through Moon and Stars and Night Skies.* Ill. by James Graham Hale. HarperCollins, 1990 (0-06-026189-7); LB (0-06-026190-0); pap. (0-06-443308-0). USE LEVEL: P
*Asian American*
An Asian boy is adopted by an American family, which welcomes him to his new home.

ADOPTION; EMOTIONS—APPREHENSION; EMOTIONS—FEAR.

**TURNER, GLENNETTE TILLEY**
1469    *Running for Our Lives.* Ill. by Samuel Byrd. Holiday, 1994 (0-8234-1121-4). USE LEVEL: U
*African American*
In the mid 1800s, Luther and his family escape their plantations and travel from Missouri to Canada. Along the Underground Railroad, the family becomes separated, so in addition to the perils of their escape, they must try to find each other.

FOREIGN LANDS—CANADA; SLAVERY; U.S. HISTORY; UNDERGROUND RAILROAD.

**UCHIDA, YOSHIKO**
1470    *The Best Bad Thing.* Macmillan, 1983 (0-689-50290-7); pap. (0-689-71745-8). USE LEVEL: U
*Asian American—Japan*
It is 1935 and Rinko is going to work in the home of Mrs. Hata, a widow with two sons. Rinko thinks this is a "bad thing," but she realizes that she cares about the Hata family and she wants to help them.

CHARACTER TRAITS—HELPFULNESS; FAMILY LIFE; PROBLEM SOLVING.

1471    *The Birthday Visitor.* Ill. by Charles Robinson. Macmillan, 1975, o.p. USE LEVEL: P
*Asian American—Japan*
In California during the 1930s, Emi enjoys the friendship of Mr. and Mrs. Wada, an elderly couple. She is looking forward to her birthday, but not to a visit from Rev. Okura.

BIRTHDAYS; DEATH; FAMILY LIFE; FRIENDSHIP; OLDER ADULTS.

1472    *The Bracelet.* Ill. by Joanna Yardley. Putnam, 1993 (0-399-22503-X). USE LEVEL: M
*Asian American—Japan*

During World War II, Emi and her family are sent to an internment camp for Japanese Americans. Although she loses the bracelet that a friend had given her, she still remembers the feeling of friendship.

FRIENDSHIP; GIFTS; PREJUDICE; RACE RELATIONS; U.S. HISTORY—WORLD WAR II.

1473    *The Happiest Ending.* Macmillan, 1985 (0-689-50326-1). USE LEVEL: U
**Asian American—Japan**
Rinko, 12, interferes in the plans for a Japanese woman to come to California and marry a man she does not know.

BEHAVIOR—GROWING UP; CHARACTER TRAITS—HELPFULNESS; FAMILY LIFE; WEDDINGS.

1474    *In-Between Miya.* Ill. by Susan Bennett. Macmillan, 1967, o.p. USE LEVEL: M
**Asian—Japan**
In Japan, Miya Okamoto, 12, feels that as a middle child she is often overlooked. On her summer vacation, Miya leaves her family's rural village and goes to help relatives in Tokyo. There, Miya begins to appreciate her own home and family.

BEHAVIOR—GROWING UP; FAMILY LIFE; FOREIGN LANDS—ASIA—JAPAN.

1475    *A Jar of Dreams.* Macmillan, 1981 (0-689-50210-9); pap. (0-689-71672-9). USE LEVEL: U
**Asian American—Japan**
Rinko and her family live in California during the Depression. When her Aunt Waka comes to visit from Japan, Rinko learns about herself and her family.

BEHAVIOR—WORRYING; FAMILY LIFE; PREJUDICE; RACE RELATIONS; U.S. HISTORY—DEPRESSION.

1476    *Journey Home.* Ill. by Charles Robinson. Macmillan, 1978 (0-689-50126-9); pap. (0-689-71641-9). USE LEVEL: U
**Asian American—Japan**
Following World War II, Yuki, who is 12, and her family are released from an internment camp. They must adjust to their return to California.

BEHAVIOR—WORRYING; FAMILY LIFE; PREJUDICE; RACE RELATIONS; RELOCATION; U.S. HISTORY—WORLD WAR II.

1477    *Journey to Topaz: A Story of the Japanese-American Evacuation.* Ill. by Donald Carrick. Creative Arts, pap. (0-916870-85-5). USE LEVEL: U
**Asian American—Japan**

After the bombing of Pearl Harbor, Yuki and her family are forced to leave their home in San Francisco and live in a camp in Utah. Each family member adapts differently to the challenges of this experience.

FAMILY LIFE; PREJUDICE; RELOCATION; U.S. HISTORY—WORLD WAR II.

1478    *The Magic Listening Cap: More Folktales from Japan.* Ill. by the reteller. Creative Arts, pap. (0-88739-016-1). USE LEVEL: M/U
        *Asian—Japan*
        The 14 stories in this collection have traditional elements of folktales. There are honest men and fools, unusual creatures, talking animals, and magic.

FOLKTALES—ASIA—JAPAN; HUMOR; SHORT STORIES.

1479    *The Magic Purse.* Ill. by Keiko Narahashi. Macmillan, 1993 (0-689-50559-0). USE LEVEL: M
        *Asian—Japan*
        A poor farmer enters the Black Swamp and encounters a strange young girl. He delivers a letter for her and is rewarded with gold coins and a magic purse.

CHARACTER TRAITS—HONESTY; FOLKTALES—ASIA—JAPAN; MAGIC.

1480    *The Rooster Who Understood Japanese.* Ill. by Charles Robinson. Macmillan, 1976, pap. (0-684-14672-X). USE LEVEL: P
        *Asian American—Japan*
        When their neighbor complains, a family must find a new home for their rooster, Mr. Lincoln.

BIRDS—ROOSTERS; FAMILY LIFE; FRIENDSHIP.

1481    *Sumi and the Goat and the Tokyo Express.* Ill. by Kazue Mizumura. Macmillan, 1969, o.p. USE LEVEL: M
        *Asian—Japan*
        This is an exciting time in Sumi's village. A high-speed train is scheduled to go by and Sumi's 99-year-old friend, Mr. Oda, has a new goat, Miki. The village is surprised when Miki stops the train.

ANIMALS—GOATS; FAMILY LIFE; FOREIGN LANDS—ASIA—JAPAN; OLDER ADULTS; TRAINS.

1482    *Sumi's Prize.* Ill. by Kazue Mizumura. Macmillan, 1964, o.p. USE LEVEL: M
        *Asian—Japan*
        Sumi wants to win a prize and she feels she has a chance in the New Year's Day Kite Contest. Sumi does not win the contest, but she does receive a special prize from the mayor.

CHARACTER TRAITS—AMBITION; FOREIGN LANDS—ASIA—JAPAN; HOLIDAYS—NEW YEAR'S; KITES.

1483 *The Two Foolish Cats: Suggested by a Japanese Folktale.* Ill. by Margot Zemach. Macmillan, 1987, o.p. USE LEVEL: M
*Asian—Japan*
Two cats, Big Daizo and Little Suki, argue over two rice cakes until the monkey teaches them a lesson.
ANIMALS—CATS; BEHAVIOR—FIGHTING, ARGUING; BEHAVIOR—GREED; FOLKTALES—ASIA—JAPAN; FOOD.

1484 *The Wise Old Woman.* Ill. by Martin Springett. Macmillan, 1994 (0-689-50582-5). USE LEVEL: M
*Asian—Japan*
In a village ruled by a cruel young lord, people over age 70 are taken to the mountains to die. A young farmer keeps his elderly mother hidden and when the village is to be attacked by a powerful lord, it is the old woman's wisdom that saves them.
CHARACTER TRAITS—CLEVERNESS; FOLKTALES—ASIA—JAPAN; OLDER ADULTS; PROBLEM SOLVING.

**UDRY, JANICE MAY**
1485 *Mary Jo's Grandmother.* Ill. by Eleanor Mill. Whitman, 1970, o.p. USE LEVEL: P
*African American*
Mary Jo's grandmother lives in her own house in the country. When Grandmother falls, Mary Jo must walk through the snow to get help.
CORETTA SCOTT KING AWARD; FAMILY LIFE—GRANDMOTHERS; ILLNESS; SEASONS—WINTER; WEATHER—SNOW.

1486 *What Mary Jo Shared.* Ill. by Elizabeth Sayles. Scholastic, 1991,©1966, pap. (0-590-43757-7). USE LEVEL: P
*African American*
Mary Jo brings her father for "show and tell." This is a newly illustrated version of the 1966 classic.
CHARACTER TRAITS—SHYNESS; FAMILY LIFE—FATHERS; SCHOOL.

1487 *What Mary Jo Wanted.* Ill. by Eleanor Mill. Whitman, 1968, o.p. USE LEVEL: P
*African American*
Mary Jo wants a dog and her parents decide she is old enough to be responsible. Taking care of her new puppy, Teddy, is hard work for Mary Jo.
ANIMALS—DOGS; FAMILY LIFE; PETS.

**VAN LAAN, NANCY, RETELLER**

1488   *Buffalo Dance: A Blackfoot Legend.* Ill. by Beatriz Vidal. Little,
Brown, 1993 (0-316-89728-0). USE LEVEL: M
*Native American—Blackfoot*
To get food for her people, a Blackfoot woman goes to live with
the buffalo. Her father dies trying to bring her back, but she
calls the Great Spirit and her father is revived. They return to
their people to teach them the dance to honor the buffalo.
ACTIVITIES—DANCING; ANIMALS—BUFFALOES; FOLKTALES—NATIVE
AMERICAN—BLACKFOOT; MAGIC.

1489   *Mama Rocks, Papa Sings.* Ill. by Roberta Smith. Knopf, 1995
(0-679-84016-8); LB (0-679-94016-2). USE LEVEL: P
*Caribbean—Haiti*
Mama and Papa live in Haiti with one baby, but as others in the
village need their help, they take in other children. Always there
is singing, joy, and love.
BABIES, TODDLERS; COUNTING, NUMBERS; EMOTIONS—LOVE; FOREIGN
LANDS—CARIBBEAN ISLANDS—HAITI; POETRY, RHYME.

1490   *Rainbow Crow: A Lenape Tale.* Ill. by Beatriz Vidal. Knopf,
1989, LB (0-394-99577-5); pap. (0-679-81942-8). USE LEVEL:
M
*Native American—Lenape*
Rainbow Crow flies to the Sky Spirit to ask for the snow to
stop. The Sky Spirit does not stop the snow, but gives Crow the
gift of Fire. Crow's rainbow colors are blackened as he carries
Fire back to earth.
BIRDS—CROWS; CONCEPTS—COLOR; FIRE; FOLKTALES—NATIVE
AMERICAN—LENAPE; POURQUOI TALES.

**VAN WOERKOM, DOROTHY, ADAPTER**

1491   *The Rat, the Ox, and the Zodiac: A Chinese Legend.* Ill. by Errol
Le Cain. Crown, 1976, o.p. USE LEVEL: M
*Asian—China*
Rat and Ox both want to be the Beast of the First Year in the
Zodiac. Rat uses his cleverness to be selected.
ANIMALS; ANIMALS—RATS; CHARACTER TRAITS—CLEVERNESS;
FOLKTALES—ASIA—CHINA; ZODIAC.

**VAUGHAN, MARCIA**

1492   *Dorobó the Dangerous.* Ill. by Kazuko Stone. Silver Burdett,
1995 (0-382-24076-6); LB (0-382-24070-7); pap. (0-382-
24453-2). USE LEVEL: M
*Asian—Japan*

In Japan, Crane's fish are stolen by the fox, Doboró the Dangerous. Crane visits Saru the monkey, who tells him how to trick Doboró and keep him from bothering Crane again.

ANIMALS—FOXES; BIRDS—CRANES; FOREIGN LANDS—ASIA—JAPAN.

1493   *Kapoc, the Killer Croc*. Ill. by Eugene Fernandes. Silver Burdett, 1995 (0-382-24075-8); LB (0-382-24069-3); pap. (0-382-24602-0). USE LEVEL: M
*South American—Amazon*
Kapoc brags that she is the fastest creature and she plans to eat Sloth. Instead, they have a contest. Sloth moves through the trees faster than Kapoc swims through the Amazon River, except Sloth has a lot of help.

ANIMALS; BEHAVIOR—TRICKERY; CONTESTS; FOREIGN LANDS—SOUTH AMERICA—AMAZON.

VERTREACE, MARTHA M.
1494   *Kelly in the Mirror*. Ill. by Sandra Speidel. Whitman,1993 (0-8075-4152-4). USE LEVEL: P
*African American*
Kelly feels that she does not fit in with her family, until she realizes that she looks just like her mother did as a little girl.

BEHAVIOR—WORRYING; FAMILY LIFE.

VIDAL, BEATRIZ
1495   *The Legend of El Dorado: A Latin American Tale*. Adapted by Nancy Van Laan. Ill. by the author. Knopf, 1991 (0-679-80136-7). USE LEVEL: M
*Latin American*
This retelling is based on a Chibcha legend. When the serpent of the lake takes the king's wife and daughter, his people create a ceremony covering him with gold dust.

FOLKTALES—LATIN AMERICA; REPTILES—SNAKES; ROYALTY—KINGS.

VOIGT, CYNTHIA
1496   *Come a Stranger*. Macmillan, 1986 (0-689-31289-X); Fawcett, pap. (0-449-70246-4). USE LEVEL: U
*African American*
Mina Smiths attends a dance camp but decides to leave after receiving negative comments and treatment. At home, Tamer Shipp, a young pastor, helps her cope with her changing view of herself and the world.

BEHAVIOR—GROWING UP; EMOTIONS—LOVE; PREJUDICE; RACE RELATIONS; SELF-CONCEPT.

**VUONG, LYNETTE DYER**

1497    *The Brocaded Slipper: And Other Vietnamese Tales.* Ill. by Vo-
Dinh Mai. HarperCollins, 1982, LB (0-397-32508-8); pap. (0-
06-440440-4). USE LEVEL: **M**
*Asian—Vietnam*
Five stories from Vietnam demonstrate how different versions of
a story can appear in many cultures. ("The Brocaded Slipper" is
a Cinderella story.)
CLOTHING—SHOES; EMOTIONS—ENVY, JEALOUSY; FOLKTALES—ASIA—
VIETNAM; SHORT STORIES.

1498    *The Golden Carp: And Other Tales from Vietnam.* Ill. by
Manabu Saito. Lothrop, 1993 (0-688-12514-X). USE LEVEL: **U**
*Asian—Vietnam*
There are six stories in this collection, including "A Friend's
Affection," "The Ogre's Victim," and "Tears of Pearl."
FOLKTALES—ASIA—VIETNAM; MAGIC; SHORT STORIES.

1499    *Sky Legends of Vietnam.* Ill. by Vo-Dinh Mai. HarperCollins,
1993 (0-06-023000-2); LB (0-06-023001-0). USE LEVEL: **U**
*Asian—Vietnam*
Six stories feature elements of the sky—the moon, the sun, and
the stars. Often, a natural phenomenon is explained.
FOLKTALES—ASIA—VIETNAM; POURQUOI TALES; SHORT STORIES; SKY.

**WADE, GINI, RETELLER**

1500    *The Wonderful Bag: An Arabian Tale from The Thousand &*
*One Nights.* Ill. by the reteller. Bedrick/Blackie, 1993 (0-
87226-508-0). USE LEVEL: **M**
*Middle Eastern—Arabia*
When they argue about who owns a damask bag, Ali and
Hamid go before "wise and all-seeing Kadi," who must decide
which man to believe.
BEHAVIOR—FIGHTING, ARGUING; CHARACTER TRAITS—HONESTY;
FOLKTALES—MIDDLE EAST—ARABIA.

**WAGNER, JANE**

1501    *J. T.* Photos by Gordon Parks, Jr. Dell, pap. (0-440-44275-3).
USE LEVEL: **M**
*African American*
J. T. is a loner. His urban neighborhood is run-down and he
does not receive much support at home or at school. When he
befriends a cat, J. T. has something of his own that cares about
him.
ANIMALS—CATS; DEATH; FAMILY LIFE; URBAN LIFE.

**WAHL, JAN**

1502    *Little Eight John.* Ill. by Wil Clay. Dutton, 1992 (0-525-67367-9). USE LEVEL: M
*African American*
Little Eight John was mean and his behavior brought trouble to his family, but he just laughed. He learns his lesson when he is changed into a jam spot on the table.
BEHAVIOR—MISBEHAVIOR; CORETTA SCOTT KING AWARD; FOLKTALES—UNITED STATES; MONSTERS.

1503    *Tailypo!* Ill. by Wil Clay. Henry Holt, 1991 (0-8050-0687-7).
USE LEVEL: M
*African American*
An old man chops off the creature's tail and then eats it. The creature comes looking for its "tailypo."
FOLKTALES—UNITED STATES; MONSTERS; SCARY STORIES.

**WALKER, ALICE**

1504    *To Hell with Dying.* Ill. by Catherine Deeter. Harcourt, 1988 (0-15-289075-0); pap. (0-15-289074-2). USE LEVEL: M
*African American*
When the father says, "These children want Mr. Sweet," Mr. Sweet can be called back from death. It happens every time throughout the young girl's life, but when she is grown, she comes home for Mr. Sweet's final moments.
DEATH; FRIENDSHIP.

**WALL, LINA MAO, RETELLER**

1505    *Judge Rabbit and the Tree Spirit: A Folktale from Cambodia/Bilingual in English and Khmer.* Adapted by Cathy Spagnoli. Ill. by Nancy Hom. Children's Book Pr., 1991, LB (0-89239-071-9). USE LEVEL: M
*Asian—Cambodia*
When the man leaves to fight in the war, the tree spirit takes his shape and his place. When the real husband returns, Judge Rabbit finds a way to outwit the imposter.
ANIMALS—RABBITS; FOLKTALES—ASIA—CAMBODIA; FOREIGN LANGUAGES; MAGIC.

**WALLACE, IAN**

1506    *Chin Chiang and the Dragon's Dance.* Ill. by the author. Macmillan, 1984 (0-689-50299-0) USE LEVEL: P
*Asian American—China*
Chin Chiang is worried about participating in the New Year's dragon dance. At the library, he meets an old woman, Pu Yee, who helps him decide to try.

ACTIVITIES— DANCING; FAMILY LIFE—GRANDFATHERS; HOLIDAYS –
CHINESE NEW YEAR.

**WALSH, JILL PATON**
1507   *Pepi and the Secret Names.* Ill. by Fiona French. Lothrop, 1994
(0-688-13428-9). USE LEVEL: M
*African—Egypt*
Pepi's father is an artist working on the tomb for Prince
Dhutmose. Because Pepi knows the secret name of the lion,
hawk, crocodile, and snake, he is able to get them to come and
be painted and the prince is pleased with the tomb.
ANIMALS; ART; FOREIGN LANDS—AFRICA—EGYPT; HIEROGLYPHICS;
HISTORY; NAMES.

**WALTER, MILDRED PITTS**
1508   *Brother to the Wind.* Ill. by Leo Dillon and Diane Dillon.
Lothrop, 1985, LB (0-688-03812-3). USE LEVEL: P/M
*African*
Emeke herds his family's goats and dreams of flying. Emeke is
helped by Good Snake as he achieves his goal.
ACTIVITIES—FLYING; ANIMALS; FOREIGN LANDS—AFRICA; KITES; MAGIC.

1509   *The Girl on the Outside.* Scholastic, pap. (0-590-46091-9). USE
LEVEL: U
*African American*
In 1957, Eva Collins is one of nine students who will enter
Chatman High School as the first African Americans. Sophia
Stuart and her friends resent the desegregation of their school,
but Sophia can't go along with the mob when they turn on Eva.
PREJUDICE; RACE RELATIONS; SCHOOL; U.S. HISTORY.

1510   *Have a Happy . . .* Ill. by Carole Byard. Lothrop, 1989 (0-688-
06923-1); Avon, pap. (0-380-71314-4). USE LEVEL: M
*African American*
Chris, who is going to be 12, wants to enjoy his birthday, which
is also Christmas Day. It is also during the days of Kwanzaa.
However, his family's economic situation worries him as he
thinks about these celebrations.
BIRTHDAYS; FAMILY LIFE; HOLIDAYS—CHRISTMAS; HOLIDAYS—KWANZAA.

1511   *Justin and the Best Biscuits in the World.* Ill. by Catherine Stock.
Lothrop, 1986 (0-688-06645-3); pap. (0-679-80346-7). USE
LEVEL: M/U
*African American*
Justin spends the summer on his grandfather's ranch and learns

about the history of black cowboys after the Civil War. He also learns about growing up.
BEHAVIOR—GROWING UP; CORETTA SCOTT KING AWARD; COWBOYS; FAMILY LIFE—GRANDFATHERS; SELF-CONCEPT.

1512    *Lillie of Watts: A Birthday Discovery.* Ill. by Leonora E. Prince. Ward Richie Pr., 1969, o.p. USE LEVEL: M
**Native American**
On Lillie's birthday, Lillie is not satisfied with herself. At school, she gets paint on her best sweater. At home, she is frightened by the cat of her mother's employer and she lets the cat run away.
ANIMALS—CATS; BIRTHDAYS; FAMILY LIFE; SELF-CONCEPT; URBAN LIFE.

1513    *Mariah Keeps Cool.* Macmillan, 1990 (0-02-792295-2). USE LEVEL: M
**African American**
Mariah plans to have fun this summer, especially swimming and diving with her friends. They encounter some prejudiced behavior, but Mariah and her friends keep their positive self-image.
FAMILY LIFE; SELF CONCEPT; SPORTS—SWIMMING.

1514    *Mariah Loves Rock.* Troll, pap. (0-8167-1838-5). USE LEVEL: M
**African American**
Mariah, 11, loves rock music, especially Sheik Bashara. She and her friends, called the "Friendly Five," are looking forward to his concert. At home, Mariah is apprehensive about her father's daughter from his first marriage coming to stay.
FAMILY LIFE; FRIENDSHIP; MUSIC.

1515    *My Mama Needs Me.* Ill. by Pat Cummings. Lothrop, 1983 (0-688-01670-7); LB (0-688-01671-5). USE LEVEL: P
**African American**
When Jason's baby sister comes home, Jason feels it is important for him to stay nearby and help, even though there are some activities that would be fun to do.
BABIES, TODDLERS; CORETTA SCOTT KING AWARD; EMOTIONS—LONELINESS; FAMILY LIFE; SELF-CONCEPT.

1516    *Trouble's Child.* Lothrop, 1985 (0-688-04214-7). USE LEVEL: U
**African American**
In rural Louisiana, Martha's grandmother Titay is the midwife and healer. Titay expects Martha to continue her work. Martha dreams of continuing her education, but she worries that her grandmother will not give her her blessing.
BEHAVIOR—SEEKING BETTER THINGS; CORETTA SCOTT KING AWARD; FAMILY LIFE—GRANDMOTHERS; SCHOOL.

1517    *Two and Too Much.* Ill. by Pat Cummings. Macmillan, 1990, pap. (0-02-792290-1). USE LEVEL: P
*African American*
Brandon watches his two-year-old sister, Gina, while their mother gets ready for some guests. Brandon finds that a two-year-old can be a handful.
ACTIVITIES—BABY-SITTING; BABIES, TODDLERS; BEHAVIOR—WORRYING; FAMILY LIFE—SIBLINGS.

1518    *Ty's One-Man Band.* Ill. by Margot Tomes. Macmillan, 1980 (0-02-792300-2); Scholastic, pap. (0-590-40178-5). USE LEVEL: P
*African American*
On a hot day, Ty is bored. At the pond he hears some strange sounds. He meets a peg-legged man, Andro, and finds that the man makes music using spoons, a washboard, a tin pail, and a comb. That night Andro puts on a show for Ty and his friends.
MUSIC; MUSICAL INSTRUMENTS; RURAL LIFE.

**WALTERS, ANNA LEE, RETELLER**
1519    *The Two-Legged Creature: An Otoe Story.* Ill. by Carol Bowles. Northland, 1993 (0-87358-553-4). USE LEVEL: M
*Native American—Otoe*
There was a time when the creatures on the earth lived in harmony. Then Man began to change. He did not listen to the animals and he treated them with cruelty. The animals decided to keep away from Man, with only Dog and Horse staying with him.
ANIMALS; FOLKTALES—NATIVE AMERICAN—OTOE; POURQUOI TALES.

**WANG, ROSALIND C., RETELLER**
1520    *The Fourth Question: A Chinese Tale.* Ill. by Ju-Hong Chen. Holiday, 1991 (0-8234-0855-8). USE LEVEL: M
*Asian—China*
Yee-Lee travels to the Wise Man of Kun-lun Mountain. He has his own question and three for other people, but the Wise Man will answer only three questions, so Yee-Lee does not ask his own question. Still, he is rewarded.
CHARACTER TRAITS—GENEROSITY; CHARACTER TRAITS—KINDNESS; CHARACTER TRAITS—QUESTIONING; FOLKTALES—ASIA—CHINA.

1521    *The Magical Starfruit Tree: A Chinese Folktale.* Ill. by Shao Wei Lieu. Beyond Words Publishing, 1993 (0-941831-89-2). USE LEVEL: M
*Asian—China*

A greedy fruit peddler will not share his fruit with a tired old man. A young boy buys the man a starfruit. The man plants the seed and it magically grows into a tree filled with starfruit, which all enjoy.

BEHAVIOR—GREED; CHARACTER TRAITS—KINDNESS; FOLKTALES—ASIA—CHINA; FOOD.

1522   *The Treasure Chest: A Chinese Tale.* Ill. by Will Hillenbrand. Holiday, 1995 (0-8234-1114-1). USE LEVEL: M
*Asian—China*
Laifu and Pearl are in love and plan to marry. Funtong, an evil ruler, wants Pearl for himself, so he challenges Laifu to three contests. A fish that Laifu had rescued comes to his aid, giving him magical items to defeat Funtong.

CHARACTER TRAITS—KINDNESS; FISH; FOLKTALES—ASIA—CHINA; MAGIC.

WARD, LEILA
1523   *I Am Eyes/Ni Macho.* Ill. by Nonny Hogrogian. Scholastic, pap. (0-590-40990-5). USE LEVEL: P
*African*
When a young girl awakens, she describes what she sees in the countryside of Kenya, including giraffes, elephants, sun and sand, and kites and Kilimanjaro.

ANIMALS; FOREIGN LANDS—AFRICA; NATURE.

WARREN, CATHY
1524   *Fred's First Day.* Ill. by Pat Cummings. Lothrop, 1984, o.p. USE LEVEL: PS
*African American*
Fred is the middle child in his family. He is not quite big enough to do what Sam does and sometimes is too rough to play with Baby Bob. He learns to fit in at the preschool.

FAMILY LIFE—SIBLINGS; FRIENDSHIP; SCHOOL.

WATERS, KATE, AND MADELINE SLOVENZ-LOW
1525   *Lion Dancer: Ernie Wan's Chinese New Year.* Ill. by Martha Cooper. Scholastic, 1990 (0-590-43046-7); pap. (0-590-43047-5). USE LEVEL: P
*Asian American—China*
Ernie Wan, who lives with his family in Chinatown in New York City, is going to celebrate the Chinese New Year by performing his first Lion Dance.

ACTIVITIES—DANCING; HOLIDAYS—CHINESE NEW YEAR; PARADES.

WATKINS, YOKO KAWASHIMA

1526    *My Brother, My Sister, and I.* Macmillan, 1994 (0-02-792526-9). USE LEVEL: U
*Asian—Japan*
In this sequel to *So Far from the Bamboo Grove*, Yoko and her brother and sister are refugees in Japan following World War II. Their mother is dead and their father is missing. They face many difficulties as they try to stay together and survive.
FOREIGN LANDS—ASIA—JAPAN; REFUGEES; SURVIVAL; WORLD WAR II.

1527    *So Far from the Bamboo Grove.* Lothrop, 1986 (0-688-06110-9); Puffin, pap. (0-14-032385-6). USE LEVEL: U
*Asian—Korea/Japan*
In this autobiographical novel, Yoko is a Japanese girl living in northern Korea during World War II. As the war threatens their safety, Yoko, her mother, and her sister flee south and become refugees, eventually reaching Japan.
FOREIGN LANDS—ASIA—KOREA; FOREIGN LANDS—ASIA -JAPAN;
REFUGEES; SURVIVAL; WORLD WAR II.

1528    *Tales from the Bamboo Grove.* Ill. by Jean Tseng and Mou-sien Tseng. Macmillan, 1992 (0-02-792525-0). USE LEVEL: M
*Asian—Japan*
There are six folktales in this collection, including "The Fox Wife," "Yayoi and the Spirit Tree," and "Monkey and Crab."
FOLKTALES—ASIA—JAPAN; SHORT STORIES.

WATSON, PETE

1529    *The Market Lady and the Mango Tree.* Ill. by Mary Watson. Morrow, 1994 (0-688-12970-6); LB (0-688-12971-4). USE LEVEL: M
*African*
The market lady has become so greedy. After she dreams that hippos take all her mangoes, she awakens and changes her ways.
BEHAVIOR—GREED; FOOD; FOREIGN LANDS—AFRICA; MARKETS.

WEIK, MARY HAYS

1530    *The Jazz Man.* Ill. by Ann Grifalconi. Macmillan, 1966 (0-689-71767-9). USE LEVEL: M
*African American*
Zeke lives in Harlem. Because one of his legs is shorter than the other, living on the top floor is difficult for Zeke. Usually, he just stays in the apartment looking out the window and listening to the neighborhood activities.
EMOTIONS—LONELINESS; HANDICAPS; NEWBERY AWARD; POVERTY;
URBAN LIFE.

**WEIR, LaVADA**

1531  *Howdy!* Ill. by William Hoey. Raintree Steck-Vaughn, 1972, o.p. USE LEVEL: P
*African American*
Luke wears his cowboy hat and says "Howdy" to everyone. Pretty soon, everyone is saying "Howdy."
CHARACTER TRAITS—KINDNESS; CLOTHING—HATS; EMOTIONS—HAPPINESS; SELF-CONCEPT.

**WEISMAN, JOAN**

1532  *The Storyteller.* Ill. by David P. Bradley. Rizzoli, 1993 (0-8478-1742-3). USE LEVEL: P
*Native American—Pueblo*
While her father is in the hospital, Rama and her family live in the city. Rama misses her home in Cochiti Pueblo, New Mexico, and hearing the stories of her people. Rama makes friends with Miss Lottie, an elderly neighbor, and they tell stories.
FAMILY LIFE; FRIENDSHIP; OLDER ADULTS; STORYTELLING.

**WEISS, GEORGE DAVID, AND BOB THIEL**

1533  *What a Wonderful World.* Ill. by Ashley Bryan. Macmillan, 1995 (0-689-80087-8). USE LEVEL: P
*Multicultural*
The song that Louis Armstrong made famous is illustrated with brightly colored pictures showing peoples from diverse backgrounds.
SONGS; WORLD.

**WEISS, JACQUELINE SHACHTER, COLLECTOR AND ADAPTER**

1534  *Young Brer Rabbit: And Other Trickster Tales from the Americas.* Ill. by Clinton Arrowood. Stemmer, 1985 (0-88045-037-1); pap. (0-88045-138-1). USE LEVEL: M
*Latin American*
These 15 trickster tales are from Central and South America and the Caribbean. From Colombia comes the story "The Wax Doll," which is a version of "The Tar Baby."
ANIMALS; BEHAVIOR—TRICKERY; FOLKTALES—LATIN AMERICA; SHORT STORIES.

**WEISS, NICKI**

1535  *On a Hot, Hot Day.* Ill. by the author. Putnam, 1992, LB (0-399-22119-0). USE LEVEL: P
*Hispanic American*

Throughout the year in their urban neighborhood, Mama loves her little boy, named Angel.

ACTIVITIES; FAMILY LIFE—MOTHERS; POETRY, RHYME; SEASONS; URBAN LIFE.

**WELLS, RUTH**

1536    *A to Zen: A Book of Japanese Culture.* Ill. by Yoshi. Picture Book, 1992 (0-88708-175-4). USE LEVEL: M
*Asian—Japan*
There are 22 concepts, objects, or activities related to Japanese life and culture featured in this alphabet book. (The Japanese language has no sounds for L, Q, V, and X.) The book is designed to be used from back to front and from right to left.

ABC BOOKS; FOREIGN LANDS—ASIA—JAPAN; FOREIGN LANGUAGES; FORMAT, UNUSUAL.

**WELSCH, ROGER**

1537    *Uncle Smoke Stories: Nehawka Tales of Coyote the Trickster.* Knopf, 1994 (0-679-85450-9); LB (0-679-95450-3). USE LEVEL: M
*Native American*
The author has created a fictional tribe, the Nehawka, which incorporates elements of other peoples (including the Pawnee, Omaha, and Lakota). His storyteller, Uncle Smoke, tells four stories of Coyote.

ANIMALS—COYOTES; BEHAVIOR—TRICKERY; STORYTELLING.

**WHEELER, BERNELDA**

1538    *Where Did You Get Your Moccasins?* Ill. by Herman Bekkering. Peguis Publishers, 1986, pap. (1-895411-50-5). USE LEVEL: P
*Native American*
A young boy describes how his grandmother made his moccasins.

CLOTHING—SHOES; FAMILY LIFE—GRANDMOTHERS; SCHOOL.

**WHEELER, GLORIA**

1539    *Night of the Full Moon.* Ill. by Leslie Bowman. Knopf, 1993 (0-679-84464-3); LB (0-674-94464-8). USE LEVEL: M
*Native American—Potawatomi*
In the 1840s, Libby and her family have a homestead near the Potawatomi people. Libby is a friend of a young girl from the people, Fawn. As more settlers come, Fawn and her family are forced off their land and relocate.

FRIENDSHIP; FRONTIER AND PIONEER LIFE; RELOCATION; U.S. HISTORY.

## WHEELER, M. J.
1540 *Fox Tales.* Ill. by Dana Gustafson. Carolrhoda, 1984, LB (0-87614-255-2). USE LEVEL: M
*Asian—India*
In these three stories, Fox solves a problem between a traveler and a farmer, foolishly plants bones thinking to grow meat, and saves a kind man from a tiger.
ANIMALS—FOXES; FOLKTALES—ASIA—INDIA; SHORT STORIES.

## WHELAN, GLORIA
1541 *Goodbye, Vietnam.* Knopf, 1992 (0-679-82263-1); LB (0-679-92263-6); pap. (0-679-82376-X). USE LEVEL: U
*Asian—Vietnam*
Mai, 13, and her family leave Vietnam to escape from political persecution. Their journey to Hong Kong is filled with danger.
FOREIGN LANDS—ASIA—VIETNAM; REFUGEES.

## WHITE, CAROLYN
1542 *The Tree House Children: An African Tale.* Ill. by Christiane Krömer. Simon & Schuster, 1994 (0-671-79818-9). USE LEVEL: M
*African*
A witch steals two children from their home, planning to eat them. They are rescued by their father, a fisherman. When the witch swallows a fishhook, she dies, and all the children she had eaten are released.
FOLKTALES—AFRICA; MAGIC; WITCHES.

## WHITETHORNE, BAJE
1543 *Sunpainters: Eclipse of the Navajo Sun.* Ill. by the author. Northland, 1994 (0-87358-587-9). USE LEVEL: M
*Native American—Navajo*
During a solar eclipse, grandfather Pipa tells his grandson, Kii Leonard, about the sunpainters who repaint the world, bringing new colors and new life. Kii Leonard learns to value the traditions of his people and to respect the earth.
CONCEPTS—COLOR; FAMILY LIFE—GRANDFATHERS; FOLKTALES—NATIVE AMERICAN—NAVAJO; SUN.

## WHITNEY, ALEX
1544 *Stiff Ears: Animal Folktales of the North American Indian.* Ill. by the author. Walck, 1974, o.p. USE LEVEL: M
*Native American*

Each of the six stories in this collection is from a different Native American people, including the Hopi, the Chippewa, and the Cherokee. Each story is introduced with some background information about the people.

ANIMALS; FOLKTALES—NATIVE AMERICAN; SHORT STORIES.

**WIESNER, WILLIAM**

1545    *Moon Stories.* Ill. by the author. Harper SF, 1973, o.p. USE LEVEL: M

*Multicultural*

In this collection, there are three folktales that feature the moon.

FOLKTALES; MOON.

**WILKINSON, BRENDA**

1546    *Definitely Cool.* Scholastic, 1993 (0-590-46186-9). USE LEVEL: U

*African American*

It is the first day of junior high and Roxanne Williams is worried and excited. She is eager to make friends and fit in. At school, Roxanne has to decide whether to go along with the crowd or to make the right choices for herself.

BEHAVIOR—GROWING UP; FRIENDSHIP; SCHOOL.

1547    *Not Separate, Not Equal.* HarperCollins, 1987, LB (0-06-026482-9). USE LEVEL: U

*African American*

Malene Freeman, 17, is one of six students to integrate the white high school in 1965. As a result, she faces harassment, cruelty, and violence. One man, Wiley Parker, sets his dogs on her and then holds all six students captive.

PREJUDICE; RACE RELATIONS; SCHOOL.

**WILLIAMS, JAY**

1548    *Everyone Knows What a Dragon Looks Like.* Ill. by Mercer Mayer. Macmillan, 1976 (0-02-793090-4); pap. (0-02-045600-X). USE LEVEL: M

*Asian—China*

A dragon appears from an unusual source and saves the town from the enemy's attack.

DRAGONS; FOREIGN LANDS—ASIA—CHINA.

**WILLIAMS, KAREN LYNN**

1549    *Galimoto.* Ill. by Catherine Stock. Lothrop, 1990 (0-688-08789-2); LB (0-688-08790-6); pap. (0-688-10991-8). USE LEVEL: P/M

*African*

Kondi makes a toy car, a "galimoto," out of some wire he has collected. This story is set in Malawi, a country in southeast Africa.

FOREIGN LANDS—AFRICA; IMAGINATION; TOYS.

1550 *Tap-Tap*. Ill. by Catherine Stock. Houghton, 1994 (0-395-65617-6). USE LEVEL: M
*Caribbean—Haiti*

Sasifi and her mother walk to the market and sell oranges. Sasifi uses her spending money to buy them a ride home on a painted truck called the "Tap-Tap."

FAMILY LIFE—MOTHERS; FOREIGN LANDS—CARIBBEAN ISLANDS—HAITI; MARKETS; TRANSPORTATION; TRUCKS.

1551 *When Africa Was Home*. Ill. by Floyd Cooper. Orchard, 1991 (0-531-05925-1); LB (0-531-08525-2); pap. (0-531-07043-3). USE LEVEL: P
*African*

Peter, a golden-haired child, grew up in Africa. When his family moves to America, he misses his friends from the village and the traditions he had shared with them.

ACTIVITIES—PLAYING; FAMILY LIFE; FOREIGN LANDS—AFRICA; FRIENDSHIP.

**WILLIAMS, SHERLEY ANNE**
1552 *Working Cotton*. Ill. by Carole Byard. Harcourt, 1992 (0-15-299624-9). USE LEVEL: M
*African American*

A girl describes the work she and her family do in the cotton fields and the harsh life they have as migrant workers.

CALDECOTT AWARD; CORETTA SCOTT KING AWARD; FAMILY LIFE; MIGRANT WORKERS.

**WILLIAMS, SHERON**
1553 *And in the Beginning* . . . Ill. by Robert Roth. Macmillan, 1992 (0-689-31650-X). USE LEVEL: M
*African*

This story tells how Mahtmi, the Blessed One, created the earth and all the creatures, including the many peoples.

CREATION; FOLKTALES—AFRICA.

WILLIAMS, VERA B.

1554   *A Chair for My Mother.* Ill. by the author. Greenwillow, 1982
       (0-688-00914-X); LB (0-688-00915-8); pap. (0-688-04074-
       8). USE LEVEL: P
       *Hispanic American*
       After a fire, Rosa and her mother use the money in their savings
       jar to buy a chair.
       BEHAVIOR—SEEKING BETTER THINGS; CALDECOTT AWARD; EMOTIONS—
       LOVE; FAMILY LIFE—MOTHERS; FURNITURE—CHAIRS; URBAN LIFE.

1555   *Cherries and Cherry Pits.* Ill. by the author. Greenwillow, 1986
       (0-688-05145-6); LB (0-688-05146-4); pap. (0-688-10478-9).
       USE LEVEL: P
       *African American*
       Bidemmi loves to draw and to tell stories about her pictures.
       Each story in this book tells about people who share cherries.
       ART; COMMUNITIES, NEIGHBORHOODS; CREATIVITY; FOOD;
       IMAGINATION; URBAN LIFE.

1556   *"More, More, More" Said the Baby: 3 Love Stories.* Ill. by the
       author. Greenwillow, 1990 (0-688-09173-3); LB (0-688-
       09174-1). USE LEVEL: P
       *Multicultural*
       Three stories featuring babies in loving environments with a
       father, a mother, and a grandmother.
       BABIES, TODDLERS; CALDECOTT AWARD; FAMILY LIFE.

1557   *Music, Music for Everyone.* Ill. by the author. Greenwillow, 1984
       (0-688-02603-6); LB (0-688-02604-4); pap. (0-688-07811-7).
       USE LEVEL: P
       *Hispanic American*
       Now that Rosa has her accordion she has a delightful time mak-
       ing music.
       EMOTIONS—HAPPINESS; FAMILY LIFE; ILLNESS; MUSIC; URBAN LIFE.

1558   *Scooter.* Ill. by the author. Greenwillow, 1993 (0-688-09376-0);
       LB (0-688-09377-9). USE LEVEL: M
       *Hispanic American*
       When Elana Rose Rosen and her mother move to a new neigh-
       borhood, Elana rides her scooter and makes new friends.
       COMMUNITIES, NEIGHBORHOODS; FRIENDSHIP; SELF-CONCEPT; URBAN
       LIFE.

1559    *Something Special for Me.* Ill. by the author. Greenwillow, 1983
        (0-688-01806-8). USE LEVEL: P
        *Hispanic American*
        Rosa needs to find the present that is just right for her, even if it
        is not something that all her friends have.
        BIRTHDAYS; CHARACTER TRAITS—INDIVIDUALITY; FAMILY LIFE; SELF-
        CONCEPT; MUSIC; URBAN LIFE.

        **WILLIS, MEREDITH SUE**
1560    *The Secret Super Powers of Marco.* HarperCollins, 1994 (0-06-
        023558-6); LB (0-06-023559-4). USE LEVEL: M
        *Multicultural*
        Marco lives with his mother and his sister, Ritzi, in a difficult
        urban neighborhood. He believes he has special powers that will
        help him become a friend of the school bully, Tyrone.
        FAMILY LIFE; FRIENDSHIP; SCHOOL; URBAN LIFE.

        **WILSON, BARBARA KER, RETELLER**
1561    *The Turtle and the Island: A Folktale from Papua New Guinea.*
        Ill. by Frané Lessac. HarperCollins, 1990, o.p. USE LEVEL: M
        *New Guinean*
        A lonely turtle creates an island that becomes filled with people,
        animals, and settlements. It has come to be called New Guinea.
        CREATION; FOLKTALES—NEW GUINEA; ISLANDS; REPTILES—TURTLES,
        TORTOISES.

1562    *Wishbones: A Folk Tale from China.* Ill. by Meilo So. Macmillan,
        1993 (0-02-793125-0). USE LEVEL: M
        *Asian—China*
        A chieftan named Wu has a daughter, Yeh Hsien. Her step-
        mother makes Yeh Hsien do all the work. With the help of the
        bones of a magic fish, Yeh Hsien attends the Cave Festival, loses
        her slipper, and is chosen to be the king's bride.
        FISH; FOLKTALES—ASIA—CHINA; MAGIC.

        **WILSON, BETH P.**
1563    *Jenny.* Ill. by Dolores Johnson. Macmillan, 1990 (0-02-
        793120-X). USE LEVEL: P
        *African American*
        In free-verse vignettes, Jenny tells about her life—her school,
        her family, and her friends.
        FAMILY LIFE; FRIENDSHIP; POETRY, RHYME.

WILSON, JOHNNIECE MARSHALL

1564    *Oh, Brother.* Scholastic, 1988, pap. (0-590-41101-6). USE
LEVEL: M
*African American*
When Alex has to share a room with his older brother, Andrew,
he is resentful. Alex also resents that Andrew seems to get away
with so much.
BEHAVIOR –GROWING UP; FAMILY LIFE—SIBLINGS; SIBLING RIVALRY.

1565    *Poor Girl, Rich Girl.* Scholastic, 1992 (0-590-44732-7); pap.
(0-590-44733-5). USE LEVEL: U
*African American*
Miranda takes some summer jobs—baby-sitting, camp counselor, working at Produceland—to earn money for contact lens-
es. She and her friend Teena have ups and downs in their
friendship, too.
CHARACTER TRAITS—APPEARANCE; FRIENDSHIP; SELF-CONCEPT.

1566    *Robin on His Own.* Scholastic, 1990, pap. (0-590-41809-2).
USE LEVEL: M/U
*African American*
After the death of his mother, Robin must deal with his grief
and with his changing family situation.
DEATH; EMOTIONS—LONELINESS; EMOTIONS—SADNESS; FAMILY LIFE;
PETS.

WINTER, JEANETTE

1567    *Follow the Drinking Gourd.* Ill. by the author. Knopf, 1988 (0-
394-89694-7); LB (0-394-99694-1); pap. (0-679-81997-5).
USE LEVEL: M
*African American*
Peg Leg Joe worked on a plantation that used slaves, and he
helped the slaves escape by teaching them a song about follow-
ing the drinking gourd—the stars of the Big Dipper.
SLAVERY; STARS; U.S. HISTORY; UNDERGROUND RAILROAD.

WINTER, SUSAN

1568    *A Baby Just like Me.* Ill. by the author. Dorling Kindersley, 1994
(1-56458-668-5). USE LEVEL: PS/P
*African American*
Martha is waiting eagerly for her new baby sister but she is disappointed at how little the baby can do and how much of
mother's time she takes.
BABIES, TODDLERS; EMOTIONS—ENVY, JEALOUSY.

**WINTHROP, ELIZABETH**

1569 *Journey to the Bright Kingdom*. Ill. by Charles Mikolaycak. Holiday, 1979, o.p. USE LEVEL: M
*Asian—Japan*
A young woman becomes blind and is sad that she has never seen her daughter, Kiyo. When Kiyo befriends some mice, they open their kingdom to Kiyo and her mother, briefly restoring her mother's sight. This story is based on a Japanese folktale.
ANIMALS —MICE; CHARACTER TRAITS—KINDNESS; FOLKTALES—ASIA—JAPAN; HANDICAPS—BLINDNESS.

**WISNIEWSKI, DAVID**

1570 *Rain Player.* Ill. by the author. Houghton, 1991 (0-395-55112-9). USE LEVEL: M
*Central American—Mayan*
In this original Mayan tale, Chac, the god of rain, is displeased with Pik. To earn Chac's forgiveness, Pik challenges him to play a ball game. If Pik wins, he will be forgiven, and his people will receive rain.
BEHAVIOR—FACING CHALLENGES; CHARACTER TRAITS—BRAVERY; FOREIGN LANDS—CENTRAL AMERICA; GAMES; WEATHER—RAIN.

1571 *The Warrior and the Wise Man*. Ill. by the author. Lothrop, 1989 (0-688-07889-3); LB (0-688 07890-7). USE LEVEL: P/M
*Asian—Japan*
In Japan, many years ago, an emperor had twin sons—Tozaemon, a warrior, and Toemon, a wiseman. To find his successor, the emperor challenges his sons. Intricate cut-paper illustrations enhance the text.
BEHAVIOR—FACING CHALLENGES; CHARACTER TRAITS—BRAVERY; CHARACTER TRAITS—CLEVERNESS; FOREIGN LANDS—ASIA—JAPAN; PROBLEM SOLVING.

1572 *The Wave of the Sea-Wolf.* Ill. by the author. Houghton, 1994 (0-395-66478-0). USE LEVEL: M
*Native American*
In this original story, set in the Pacific Northwest, Kchokeen, a Tlingit princess, is rescued from drowning. Later she saves her people from hostile explorers.
CHARACTER TRAITS—BRAVERY; HISTORY—EXPLORERS; WATER.

**WOLFF, FERIDA**

1573 *The Emperor's Garden*. Ill. by Kathy Osborn. Morrow, 1994 (0-688-11651-5); LB (0-688-11652-3). USE LEVEL: M
*Asian—China*

Every year, the Supreme Emperor travels through a small village but he never stops. The villagers decide to create a garden for him and invite him to visit. Creating the garden brings disagreement among the friendly villagers.

BEHAVIOR—FIGHTING, ARGUING; FOREIGN LANDS—ASIA—CHINA; GARDENS, GARDENING.

**WOLKSTEIN, DIANE**

1574    *The Banza: A Haitian Story.* Ill. by Marc Brown. Dial, 1981 (0-8037-0428-3); LB (0-8037-0429-1); pap. (0-8037-0058-X). USE LEVEL: M

*Caribbean—Haiti*

When she is surrounded by tigers, Cabree the goat plays the Banza, a musical instrument like a banjo, and she is able to get the help she needs.

ANIMALS—GOATS; ANIMALS—TIGERS; CHARACTER TRAITS—BRAVERY; FOLKTALES—CARIBBEAN ISLANDS—HAITI; MUSIC.

1575    *The Magic Orange Tree: And Other Haitian Folktales.* Ill. by Elsa Henriquez. Knopf, 1978, o.p. USE LEVEL: M/U

*Caribbean—Haiti*

This collection of 28 stories is carefully researched and includes folktales and songs. An introduction describes the storytelling traditions of Haiti.

FOLKTALES—CARIBBEAN ISLANDS—HAITI; MUSIC; SHORT STORIES; SONGS.

1576    *The Magic Wings: A Tale from China.* Ill. by Robert Andrew Parker. Dutton,1983 (0-525-44062-3); pap. (0-525-44275-8). USE LEVEL: M

*Asian—China*

In China, a poor goose girl wishes she could fly over the hills and see the beauty of the world. She inspires others to try to fly and she is rewarded with wings.

ACTIVITIES—FLYING; CHARACTER TRAITS—PERSEVERANCE; FOLKTALES—ASIA—CHINA; SEASONS—SPRING.

**WONG, JANET S.**

1577    *Good Luck Gold: And Other Poems.* Macmillan, 1994 (0-689-50617-1). USE LEVEL: M

*Asian American*

In this collection, the importance of the family and of their Asian heritage is celebrated. Some poems feature cultural events while others present images of discrimination. Throughout, there is a sense of pride in identity.

CHARACTER TRAITS—PRIDE; EMOTIONS; FAMILY LIFE; POETRY, RHYME; SELF-CONCEPT.

### WOOD, MARION
1578 *Spirits, Heroes and Hunters from North American Indian Mythology.* Ill. by John Sibbick. Bedrick, 1981 (0-87266-903-5). USE LEVEL: M/U
*Native American*
Pourquoi tales and tales featuring familiar characters like Sedna, Raven, Iktomi, Gluscap, and Scar Face are included among these 27 stories.
FOLKTALES—NATIVE AMERICAN; POURQUOI TALES; SHORT STORIES.

### WOOD, NANCY
1579 *Spirit Walker.* Ill. by Frank Howell. Doubleday, 1993 (0-385-30927-9). USE LEVEL: U
*Native American—Taos Pueblo*
The spirituality of the people of the Taos Pueblo infuses these poems. The interrelationship between people and nature is a theme in many of the poems, like "The Lesson of the Striped Wolf" and "Earth Roots."
NATURE; POETRY, RHYME.

### WOODSON, JACQUELINE
1580 *Between Madison and Palmetto.* Delacorte, 1993 (0-385-30906-6); Dell, pap. (0-440-41062-2). USE LEVEL: U
*African American*
Maizon is back in her neighborhood on Madison Street. She is back with her friends Margaret and Bo and with a new friend, Caroline. She is back with her grandmother. And she finally meets her father, who left her when she was a baby.
FAMILY LIFE—FATHERS; FRIENDSHIP; SELF-CONCEPT.

1581 *Last Summer with Maizon.* Delacorte, 1990 (0-385-30045-X); Dell, pap. (0-440-40555-6). USE LEVEL: U
*African American*
Maizon, who is 11, is Margaret's best friend. When Maizon leaves for a private school, Margaret must adjust to that loss, as well as to the death of her father.
DEATH; FRIENDSHIP; SCHOOL.

1582 *Maizon at Blue Hill.* Delacorte, 1992 (0-385-30796-9); Dell, pap. (0-440-40899-7). USE LEVEL: U
*African American*
Maizon receives a scholarship to Blue Hill, a boarding school for girls. She must leave her grandmother and her best friend,

Margaret, and she must adjust to being one of only five black students at her school.

FAMILY LIFE—GRANDMOTHERS; FRIENDSHIP; RACE RELATIONS; SCHOOL.

**WRIGHT, BETTY REN**

1583    *The Day Our TV Broke Down.* Ill. by Barbara Bejna and Shirlee Jensen. Raintree, 1980, LB (0-8172-1365-1). USE LEVEL: P
*African American*
On Saturday, a boy visits his dad. He enjoys watching cartoons, but when the television breaks, the boy and his father find many things to do together.

ACTIVITIES; FAMILY LIFE—FATHERS; TELEVISION.

**WRIGHT, COURTNI C.**

1584    *Journey to Freedom: A Story of the Underground Railroad.* Ill. by Gershom Griffith. Holiday, 1994 (0-8234-1096-X). USE LEVEL: M
*African American*
Led by Harriet Tubman, Joshua and his family escape from their plantation in Kentucky and travel along the Underground Railroad to freedom in Canada.

CHARACTER TRAITS—FREEDOM; SLAVERY; TUBMAN, HARRIET; U.S. HISTORY; UNDERGROUND RAILROAD.

1585    *Jumping the Broom.* Ill. by Gershom Griffith. Holiday, 1994 (0-8234-1042-0). USE LEVEL: M
*African American*
In the slave quarters there are not many moments to celebrate. Lettie describes the anticipation and activity surrounding her sister Tillie's wedding.

QUILTS; SLAVERY; WEDDINGS.

1586    *Wagon Train: A Family Goes West in 1865.* Ill. by Gershom Griffith. Holiday, 1995 (0-8234-1152-4). USE LEVEL: M
*African American*
Ginny and her family are now free. They are leaving the plantation and heading to California. Their journey is difficult as they cope with snakebite, broken wheels, and harsh weather, but they reach California, where they will homestead.

FRONTIER AND PIONEER LIFE; U.S. HISTORY.

**WYETH, SHARON DENNIS**

1587    *Always My Dad.* Ill. by Raúl Colón. Knopf, 1995 (0-679-83447-8); LB (0-679-93447-2). USE LEVEL: P
*African American*
A girl wishes she could see her father more often, but he does

not live with her family. One summer, while she is staying with her grandparents in the country, her father comes to visit and she and her brothers are glad to be with him, if only for a while.
DIVORCE, SEPARATION; EMOTIONS—LOVE; FAMILY LIFE—FATHERS; RURAL LIFE; SUMMER.

1588  *The World of Daughter McGuire.* Delacorte, 1994 (0-385-31174-5). USE LEVEL: U
*Multicultural*
Daughter McGuire, 11, is becoming more aware of the importance of her background. Her mother is African American and her father is of European descent. After her father leaves, Daughter and her mother and brother move in with Mrs. McGuire's parents.
BEHAVIOR—GROWING UP; MARRIAGE, INTERRACIAL; MOVING; PREJUDICE; SCHOOL; SELF-CONCEPT.

YACOWITZ, CARYN, ADAPTER
1589  *The Jade Stone: A Chinese Folktale.* Ill. by Ju-Hong Chen. Holiday, 1992 (0-8234-0919-8). USE LEVEL: M
*Asian—China*
The Great Emperor wants his jade carved into the shape of a dragon. Chan Lo listens to the spirit of the jade and carves three carp fish.
CAREERS—ARTISTS; FOLKTALES—ASIA—CHINA; ROYALTY—EMPERORS.

YAGAWA, SUMIKO, RETELLER
1590  *The Crane Wife.* Translated from the Japanese by Katherine Paterson. Ill. by Suekichi Akaba. Morrow, 1979, pap. (0-688-07048-5). USE LEVEL: M
*Asian—Japan*
When a poor young man rescues a crane, the bird returns to him as a maiden, who becomes his wife. Her weaving brings them wealth, but his curiosity forces her to become a crane again.
ACTIVITIES—WEAVING; BIRDS—CRANES; CHARACTER TRAITS—CURIOSITY; FOLKTALES—ASIA—JAPAN; MAGIC.

YARBOROUGH, CAMILLE
1591  *Cornrows.* Ill. by Carole Byard. Putnam, 1979, pap. (0-698-20709-2). USE LEVEL: M
*African American*
Sister's Great-Grammaw plaits Ma's hair in cornrows. When

Sister asks about the style, Great Grammaw tells stories about the heritage of this hair style.

CHARACTER TRAITS—APPEARANCE; CORETTA SCOTT KING AWARD; HAIR; SELF-CONCEPT.

1592    *The Shimmershine Queens.* Putnam, 1989 (0-399-21465-8); pap. (0-679-80147-2). USE LEVEL: M/U
*African American*
Angie, a fifth grader, adjusts to her father's moving out. With the help of her 90-year-old cousin, Seatta, Angie learns about the importance of pride in her people's past. When she is to participate in a play, Angie must make some difficult choices.

ACTIVITIES—ACTING; DREAMS; SELF-CONCEPT; URBAN LIFE.

1593    *Tamika and the Wisdom Rings.* Random, 1994, LB (0-679-92749-2); pap. (0-679-82749-8). USE LEVEL: M
*African American*
After her father is killed by drug dealers, Tamika must try to accept the loss. She also must adjust to moving to a new apartment, making new friends, and being in a new school.

CRIME; DEATH; EMOTIONS—SADNESS; FAMILY LIFE; URBAN LIFE.

YASHIMA, MITSU, AND TARO YASHIMA
1594    *Momo's Kitten.* Ill. by Taro Yashima. Viking, 1961; Puffin, pap. (0-14-050200-9). USE LEVEL: P
*Asian American—Japan*
Momo brings home a cat that then has five kittens. Momo is sad to have to give the kittens away.

ANIMALS—CATS; EMOTIONS—SADNESS; PETS.

YASHIMA, TARO
1595    *Crow Boy.* Ill. by the author. Viking, 1955 (0-670-24931-9); Puffin, pap. (0-14-050172-X). USE LEVEL: P
*Asian—Japan*
Crow Boy is rejected by his classmates and he feels isolated and alone. When they realize how shy he is and how they have hurt him, his classmates come to accept him.

CALDECOTT AWARD; CHARACTER TRAITS—SHYNESS; EMOTIONS—LONELINESS; FOREIGN LANDS—ASIA—JAPAN; SCHOOL.

1596    *Umbrella.* Ill. by the author. Viking, 1958 (0-670-73858-1); Puffin, pap. (0-14-050240-8). USE LEVEL: P
*Asian American—Japan*

After she gets a new umbrella and red boots, Momo must wait for it to rain.

CALDECOTT AWARD; UMBRELLAS; URBAN LIFE; WEATHER—RAIN.

YEE, PAUL
1597    *Roses Sing on New Snow: A Delicious Tale*. Ill. by Harvey Chan. Macmillan, 1991 (0-02-793622-8). USE LEVEL: P
*Asian American—China*
Maylin cooks in her father's restaurant in Chinatown, but her father does not let anyone know she is the cook. Instead, he gives credit to his two sons. When a governor from China comes to the restaurant, the secret is discovered.

ACTIVITIES—COOKING; FAMILY LIFE.

1598    *Tales from Gold Mountain: Stories of the Chinese in the New World*. Ill. by Simon Ng. Macmillan, 1989 (0-02-793621-X). USE LEVEL: M
*Asian American—China*
The eight stories in this collection are from the folk traditions of Chinese immigrants to North America. Included is a story about experiences on the railroads and one about a family in Chinatown.

IMMIGRATION; PREJUDICE; SHORT STORIES.

YEH, CHUN-CHUN, AND ALLAN BAILLIE
1599    *Bawshou Rescues the Sun: A Han Folktale*. Ill. by Michelle Powell. Scholastic, 1991, o.p. USE LEVEL: M
*Asian—China*
When the King of Devils steals the sun, Liu Chun searches for it. After Liu Chun becomes a star, his son, Bawshou, who is a giant, continues the quest.

CHARACTER TRAITS—BRAVERY; FOLKTALES—ASIA—CHINA; GIANTS; SUN.

YELLOW ROBE, ROSEBUD
1600    *Tonweya and the Eagles: And Other Lakota Tales*. Ill. by Jerry Pinkney. Dial, 1979 (0-8037-8973-4); LB (0-8037 8974-2). USE LEVEL: U
*Native American—Lakota*
Rosebud Yellow Robe heard these tales from her father, Chief Chauncey Yellow Robe, who heard them from his father. Animals are featured in many of the stories and there is one story about Iktomi.

ANIMALS; FOLKTALES—NATIVE AMERICAN—LAKOTA; SHORT STORIES.

YEN, CLARA, RETELLER

1601    *Why Rat Comes First: A Story of the Chinese Zodiac.* Ill. by Hideo
C. Yoshica. Children's Book Pr., 1991, LB (0-89239-072-7).
USE LEVEL: M
*Asian—China*
The Jade King invites the animals to a feast, but only 12 animals
arrive. They become the creatures of the Chinese years in the
zodiac.
ANIMALS; FOREIGN LANDS—ASIA—CHINA; ROYALTY; ZODIAC.

YEOMAN, JOHN

1602    *The Singing Tortoise: And Other Animal Folktales.* Ill. by
Quentin Blake. Morrow, 1994 (0-688-13366-5). USE LEVEL: M
*Multicultural*
Eleven folktales from diverse peoples all feature animals. "The
Coyote and the Ravens" from the Zuni, "How the Turtle Got
His Shell" from New Guinea, and "The Ranee and the Cobra"
from the Hindi are among the stories in this collection.
ANIMALS; FOLKTALES; POURQUOI TALES; SHORT STORIES.

YEP, LAURENCE

1603    *The Boy Who Swallowed Snakes.* Ill. by Jean Tseng and Mou-Sien
Tseng. Scholastic, 1994 (0-590-46168-0). USE LEVEL: M
*Asian—China*
Little Chou finds a basket of silver coins and a "ku" snake.
When Little Chou swallows the snake, more snakes appear. Mr.
Owyang, a greedy man, eats a snake and he is punished.
BEHAVIOR—GREED; CHARACTER TRAITS—HONESTY; FOLKTALES—ASIA—
CHINA; REPTILES—SNAKES.

1604    *The Butterfly Boy.* Ill. by Jeanne M. Lee. Farrar, 1993 (0-374-
31003-3). USE LEVEL: M
*Asian—China*
A boy imagines he is a butterfly. When he is a butterfly, he
dreams he is a boy. His behavior is considered odd, yet he is sat-
isfied with himself.
FOREIGN LANDS—ASIA—CHINA; IMAGINATION; INSECTS—BUTTERFLIES,
CATERPILLARS; SELF-CONCEPT.

1605    *Child of the Owl.* HarperCollins, 1977, LB (0-06-026743-7);
pap. (0-06-440336-X). USE LEVEL: U
*Asian American—China*
When her father becomes ill, Casey goes to stay with her

grandmother, her Paw-Paw, in Chinatown. She learns about the mother she never knew and she develops a link with her Chinese heritage.

CHARACTER TRAITS—PRIDE; COMMUNITIES, NEIGHBORHOODS; FAMILY LIFE—GRANDMOTHERS.

1606　*Dragon's Gate*. HarperCollins, 1993 (0-06-022971-3); LB (0-06-022972-1); pap. (0-06-440498-7). USE LEVEL: U
*Asian American—China*
In the mid-1800s, Otter has dreams of leaving China and going to America. When his dream comes true, he finds that the opportunities he had hoped for are not there. Instead, he works on the transcontinental railroad and is treated like a slave.
NEWBERY AWARD; PREJUDICE; SLAVERY; TRAINS; U.S. HISTORY.

1607　*Dragonwings*. HarperCollins, 1975, LB (0-06-026738-0); pap. (0-06-440085-9). USE LEVEL: U
*Asian American—China*
In the early 1900s, many Chinese settled in San Francisco's Chinatown. Moon Shadow joins his father Windrider and helps him with his dream of building a flying machine, Dragonwings.
ACTIVITIES—FLYING; CHARACTER TRAITS—PERSISTENCE; FAMILY LIFE—FATHERS; NEWBERY AWARD.

1608　*The Ghost Fox*. Ill. by Jean Tseng and Mou-Sien Tseng. Scholastic, 1994 (0-590-47204-6). USE LEVEL: M
*Asian—China*
While his father is away, Little Lee must try to save his mother from the ghost fox that has bewitched her.
ANIMALS—FOXES; FANTASY; FOREIGN LANDS—ASIA—CHINA; GHOSTS.

1609　*Hiroshima*. Scholastic, 1995 (0-590-20832-2). USE LEVEL: U
*Asian—Japan*
On August 6, 1945, an atomic bomb was dropped on Hiroshima. This book provides perspectives of several people involved in the experience, including Sachi, who is 12, and members of the crew of the *Enola Gay*.
FOREIGN LANDS—ASIA—JAPAN; U.S. HISTORY—WORLD WAR II; WAR.

1610　*The Junior Thunder Lord*. Ill. by Robert Van Nutt. BridgeWater, 1994, LB (0-8167-3454-2). USE LEVEL: M
*Asian—China*
Yue is a merchant who always helps others. When he is kind to Bear Face, he is rewarded. Bear Face is a junior thunder lord who had been sent to earth for three years. Bear Face brings rain to Yue's drought-stricken land.

CHARACTER TRAITS—KINDNESS; FOLKTALES—ASIA—CHINA; WEATHER—DROUGHTS; WEATHER—THUNDER.

1611 *The Man Who Tricked a Ghost.* Ill. by Isadore Seltzer. BridgeWater, 1993 (0-8167-3030-X). USE LEVEL: M
*Asian—China*
Walking home in the dark, Sung encounters the ghost of a warrior. Sung tells the ghost that he is a ghost, too. He tricks the ghost into telling him a secret, which Sung uses to become rich.
BEHAVIOR—TRICKERY; FOLKTALES—ASIA—CHINA; GHOSTS; SCARY STORIES.

1612 *The Rainbow People.* Ill. by David Wiesner. HarperCollins, 1989 (0-06-026760-7); LB (0-06-026761-5); pap. (0-06-440441-2). USE LEVEL: M/U
*Asian—China*
The 20 folktales in this collection reflect many aspects of Chinese culture and folklore. Stories are grouped by "Tricksters," "Fools," "Virtues and Vices," "In Chinese America," and "Love."
FOLKTALES—ASIA—CHINA; MAGIC; SHORT STORIES.

1613 *Sea Glass.* HarperCollins, 1979, o.p. USE LEVEL: U
*Asian American—China*
Craig Chin, 13, is not accepted in his new town. He tries to adjust to this new situation while maintaining some connection with his Chinese heritage. Being overweight and not athletically talented does not help him fit in.
BEHAVIOR—ACCEPTING DIFFERENCES; BEHAVIOR—FACING CHALLENGES; CHARACTER TRAITS—APPEARANCE; FRIENDSHIP; SELF-CONCEPT.

1614 *The Serpent's Children.* HarperCollins, 1984, o.p. USE LEVEL: U
*Asian—China*
In China in the nineteenth century, Cassia and her brother Foxfire live in a rural area. While her father is fighting the invaders, Cassia's mother dies. When her father returns, he focuses the village on facing the invading Manchus and the British.
BEHAVIOR—FIGHTING, ARGUING; FAMILY LIFE; FOREIGN LANDS—ASIA—CHINA; WAR.

1615 *The Shell Woman & the King: A Chinese Folktale.* Ill. by Yang Ming-Yi. Dial, 1993 (0-8037-1394-0); LB (0-8037-1395-9). USE LEVEL: M
*Asian—China*

Uncle Wu marries Shell, an unusual woman who lives near the sea and can change herself into a shell. Uncle Wu brags about her and the king decides to take her for his wife. Shell does three tasks for the king and she is reunited with Uncle Wu.

CHARACTER TRAITS—CLEVERNESS; FOLKTALES—ASIA—CHINA; MAGIC; SEA AND SEASHORE.

1616 *The Star Fisher.* Morrow, 1991 (0-688-09365-5); Puffin, pap. (0-14-036003-4). USE LEVEL: U
*Asian American—China*
When her family moves from Ohio to West Virginia, Joan Lee, 15, must adjust to new people and their prejudices. This novel is set in the 1920s and reflects some of the experiences of the author's family.

FAMILY LIFE; MOVING; PREJUDICE.

1617 *Tongues of Jade.* Ill. by David Wiesner. HarperCollins, 1991 (0-06-022470-3); LB (0-06-022471-1). USE LEVEL: M/U
*Asian American—China*
There are 17 folktales from Chinese communities in the United States reflecting the diverse heritage of these people.

FOLKTALES—ASIAN AMERICAN—CHINESE; SHORT STORIES.

1618 *Tree of Dreams: Ten Tales from the Garden of Night.* Ill. by Isadore Seltzer. BridgeWater, 1995 (0-8167-3498-4). USE LEVEL: U
*Multicultural*
Stories from Japan, India, China, Greece, Brazil, and Senegal are included here. In one story, "The Fighting Cricket," a boy becomes a cricket and then returns to his human form. In another story, Uaicá learns secrets from "The Dream Tree."

DREAMS; FOLKTALES; SHORT STORIES.

YERXA, LEO
1619 *Last Leaf First Snowflake to Fall.* Ill. by the author. Orchard, 1993 (0-531-06824-2); LB (0-531-08674-7). USE LEVEL: M
*Native American*
Poetic language and occasional wordless pages describe a forest trip by foot and canoe. A parent and a child celebrate as the seasons change from fall to winter.

FOREST, WOODS; SEASONS—FALL; SEASONS—WINTER.

YOLEN, JANE
1620 *The Emperor and the Kite.* Ill. by Ed Young. Putnam, 1988 (0-399-21499-2); pap. (0-399-22512-9). USE LEVEL: M
*Asian—China*

The emperor's youngest daughter, Djeow Seow, is so tiny that she is often ignored. When her father is imprisoned, Djeow Seow makes a special kite to save him.

CALDECOTT AWARD; CHARACTER TRAITS—SMALLNESS; FAMILY LIFE.— FATHERS; FOREIGN LANDS—ASIA—CHINA; KITES; ROYALTY.

1621    *Encounter.* Ill. by David Shannon. Harcourt, 1992 (0-15-225962-7). USE LEVEL: M
*Native American—Taino*
When Spanish explorers land on their island, the Taino Indians greet them with gifts and food, yet the sailors take some of the people to be slaves and search for gold.

COLUMBUS, CHRISTOPHER; FOREIGN LANDS—CARIBBEAN ISLANDS; HISTORY—EXPLORERS.

1622    *The Girl Who Loved the Wind.* Ill. by Ed Young. HarperCollins, 1972 (0-690-33100-2); LB (0-690-33101-0); pap. (0-06-443088-X). USE LEVEL: M
*Asian*
In a far eastern country, a merchant loves his daughter, Danina, and he keeps her hidden. The wind sings songs about the world to her, and one day she sails off on the wind.

BEHAVIOR—RUNNING AWAY; FAMILY LIFE—FATHERS; FOREIGN LANDS— ASIA; WEATHER—WIND.

1623    *Rainbow Rider.* Ill. by Michael Foreman. HarperCollins, 1974, LB (0-690-00311-0). USE LEVEL: M
*Native American*
Rainbow Rider lives near the desert and he creates the rainbow, which he rides. Wanting a friend, he tries to make one, but he ends up riding the rainbow and finding a friend. This is an original fantasy with Native American mythological roots.

FRIENDSHIP; IMAGINATION; WEATHER—RAINBOWS.

1624    *The Seeing Stick.* Ill. by Remy Charlip and Demetra Maraslis. HarperCollins, 1977 (0-690-00455-9); LB (0-690-00596-2). USE LEVEL: M
*Asian—China*
In this original fantasy, Hwei Ming, the emperor's daughter, is blind. A blind old man shows her how to "see" using her sense of touch and the carvings on his stick.

FOREIGN LANDS—ASIA—CHINA; HANDICAPS—BLINDNESS; OLDER ADULTS; ROYALTY; SENSES—SEEING.

1625    *Sky Dogs.* Ill. by Barry Moser. Harcourt, 1990 (0-15-275480-6). USE LEVEL: M
*Native American—Blackfoot*

An old man describes how his people felt when they first saw horses. He tells of the fear of horses that later turned to love.
ANIMALS—HORSES; EMOTIONS—FEAR; FOLKTALES—NATIVE AMERICAN—BLACKFOOT.

1626    *Sleep Rhymes Around the World.* Boyds Mills, 1994 (1-56397-243-3). USE LEVEL: P
*Multicultural*
Lullabies and rhymes from many cultures including the Abenaki, Yoruba, Ukraine, and Thai are accompanied by illustrations by an artist from the location. The rhymes are presented in the native language with an English translation.
BEDTIME; FOREIGN LANDS; FOREIGN LANGUAGES; LULLABIES; NIGHT; POETRY, RHYME.

1627    *Street Rhymes Around the World.* Boyds Mills, 1992 (1-878093-53-3). USE LEVEL: P
*Multicultural*
Rhymes from Brazil, Japan, Mexico, and Zambia are among those included. The art work is by 17 international artists and the poems are printed in English and in the native language. There are counting rhymes and rhymes that encourage movement.
ACTIVITIES; COUNTING, NUMBERS; FOREIGN LANDS; FOREIGN LANGUAGES; GAMES; POETRY, RHYME.

**YOUNG, ED**
1628    *Little Plum.* Ill. by the author. Putnam, 1994 (0-399-22683-4). USE LEVEL: M
*Asian—China*
Although Little Plum is no bigger than a plum seed, he is able to recover what is robbed from his village.
CHARACTER TRAITS—BRAVERY; CHARACTER TRAITS—SMALLNESS; ELVES AND LITTLE PEOPLE; FOLKTALES—ASIA—CHINA.

1629    *Lon Po Po: A Red-Riding Hood Story from China.* Ill. by the translator. Putnam, 1989 (0-399-21619-7). USE LEVEL: M
*Asian—China*
A mother leaves her three daughters at home while she goes to visit their grandmother. A wolf, who has seen the mother leave, comes to the house disguised as the grandmother, Po Po.
ANIMALS—WOLVES; BEHAVIOR—TRICKERY; CALDECOTT AWARD; CHARACTER TRAITS—BRAVERY; FOLKTALES—ASIA—CHINA.

1630   *Moon Mother: A Native American Creation Tale*. Ill. by the adapter. HarperCollins, 1993 (0-06-021301-9); LB (0-06-021302-7). USE LEVEL: M
*Native American*
A male spirit person makes the animals and people for the earth. A female spirit person comes to the earth, and she joins the man. They leave the earth and she becomes the moon.
CREATION; FOLKTALES—NATIVE AMERICAN; POURQUOI TALES.

1631   *Red Thread*. Ill. by the author. Putnam, 1993 (0-399-21969-2). USE LEVEL: M
*Asian—China*
Wei Gu visits the matchmaker to find out about his destined bride. He learns that a magical red thread is attached to children's feet at birth, linking those who will marry. Although Wei Gu disdains the prophecy, it is fulfilled.
FOLKTALES—ASIA—CHINA; MAGIC.

1632   *Seven Blind Mice*. Ill. by the author. Putnam, 1992 (0-399-22261-8). USE LEVEL: M
*Asian—India*
Each day, one of the seven blind mice goes to their pond to examine the strange Something. On the seventh day, Sunday, White Mouse examines it completely and reveals that it is an elephant.
ANIMALS—MICE; CALDECOTT AWARD; CONCEPTS—COLOR; DAYS OF THE WEEK, MONTHS OF THE YEAR; FABLES; FOLKTALES—ASIA—INDIA.

1633   *Up a Tree*. Ill. by the author. HarperCollins, 1983, LB (0-06-026814-X). USE LEVEL: P
*Asian*
In this wordless book, a cat chases a butterfly and becomes stuck in a tree. When the cat is bothered by a dog, a group of people try to rescue the cat, which will not come down until some food comes.
ANIMALS—CATS; TREES; WORDLESS BOOKS.

**YOUNG, RONDER THOMAS**
1634   *Learning by Heart*. Houghton, 1993 (0-395-65369-X); Puffin, pap. (0-14-03752-0). USE LEVEL: U
*African American*
Isabella Harris has come to help in Rachel's home. As Rachel

grows up, she becomes more aware of the prejudice that is directed toward Isabella, who is black and a Mennonite.

BEHAVIOR—GROWING UP; FAMILY LIFE; PREJUDICE; RACE RELATIONS.

YOUNG, RUTH

1635    *Golden Bear.* Ill. by Rachel Isadora. Viking, 1992, LB (0-670-82577-8); Puffin, pap. (0-14-050959-3). USE LEVEL: PS/P
*African American*
A young child and a golden teddy bear romp, read, and play together. The rhyming text of this book is also written as a song on the endpapers.

ACTIVITIES—PLAYING; POETRY, RHYME; TOYS—TEDDY BEARS.

ZASLAVSKY, CLAUDIA

1636    *Count on Your Fingers African Style.* Ill. by Jerry Pinkney. HarperCollins, 1980 (0-690-03864-X); LB (0-690-03865-8). USE LEVEL: P
*African*
The counting systems of several African peoples (including Masai, Kamba, and Zulu) are presented and compared to the numbers and counting system in America.

CORETTA SCOTT KING AWARD; COUNTING, NUMBERS; FOREIGN LANDS—AFRICA.

ZUBIZARRETA, ROSALMA, HARRIET ROHMER, AND DAVID SCHECTER

1637    *The Woman Who Outshone the Sun: The Legend of Lucia Zenteno.* Ill. by Fernando Olivera. Children's Book Pr., 1991 (0-89239-101-4); pap. (0-89239-126-X). USE LEVEL: M
*Mexican—Zapotec*
Lucia Zenteno is so beautiful that the people of the village revere and fear her. When the people are mean to her, Lucia leaves. The river leaves with her, bringing a drought.

CHARACTER TRAITS—APPEARANCE; CHARACTER TRAITS—KINDNESS; FOLKTALES—MEXICO—ZAPOTEC; FOREIGN LANGUAGES; WEATHER—DROUGHTS.

# SUBJECT ACCESS

⎯⎯►◄⎯⎯

All titles in the Annotated Bibliography are listed here under as many as six subject headings. Parenthetically following the author(s), title, and entry number is the Use Level abbreviation and the Cultural/Regional designation.

## ABC books

Agard, John. *The Calypso Alphabet*, 34 (P) (Caribbean)

Brusca, María Cristina. *When Jaguars Ate the Moon: And Other Stories about Animals and Plants of the Americas*, 178 (M) (Multicultural)

Feelings, Muriel. *Jambo Means Hello: Swahili Alphabet Book*, 413 (P/M) (African)

Fisher, Leonard Everett. *Alphabet Art: Thirteen ABCs from Around the World*, 423 (P/M) (Multicultural)

Greenfield, Eloise. *Aaron and Gayla's Alphabet Book*, 523 (PS/P) (African American)

Hausman, Gerald. *Turtle Island ABC: A Gathering of Native American Symbols*, 628 (M) (Native American)

Hudson, Cheryl Willis. *Afro-Bets ABC Book*, 684 (PS) (African American)

Lessac, Frané. *Caribbean Alphabet*, 865 (P) (Caribbean)

Musgrove, Margaret. *Ashanti to Zulu: African Traditions*, 1077 (M) (African)

Onyefulu, Ifeoma. *A Is for Africa*, 1128 (P/M) (African)

Rankin, Laura. *The Handmade Alphabet*, 1204 (P/M) (Multicultural)

Reed, Lynn Rowe. *Pedro, His Perro, and the Alphabet Sombrero*, 1212 (P) (Hispanic)

Samton, Sheila. *Amazing Aunt Agatha*, 1267 (P) (African American)

Shelby, Anne. *Potluck*, 1311 (P) (Multicultural)

Wells, Ruth. *A to Zen: A Book of Japanese Culture*, 1536 (M) (Asian—Japan)

## Activities

Agell, Charlotte. *Dancing Feet*, 36 (PS/P) (Multicultural)

Chapman, Christina. *Treasure in the Attic*, 242 (P) (African American)

Greenfield, Eloise. *Aaron and Gayla's Alphabet Book*, 523 (PS/P) (African American)

## Activities (cont.)

Gryski, Camilla. *Cat's Cradle, Owl's Eyes: A Book of String Games*, 564 (M/U) (Multicultural)

*Many Stars & More String Games*, 565 (M) (Multicultural)

*Super String Games*, 566 (M) (Multicultural)

Heo, Yumi. *One Afternoon*, 639 (P) (Asian American—Korea)

Hudson, Wade. *I Love My Family*, 691 (P) (African American)

*Jamal's Busy Day*, 693 (P) (African American)

Jonas, Ann. *When You Were a Baby*, 764 (PS) (African American)

Kroll, Virginia. *Jaha and Jamil Went Down the Hill: An African Mother Goose*, 826 (P) (African)

McMillan, Bruce. *Sense Suspense: A Guessing Game for the Five Senses*, 960 (P) (Multicultural)

Merrill, Jean. *The Toothpaste Millionaire*, 1012 (M) (African American)

Miller, Margaret. *Can You Guess?*, 1021 (PS/P) (Multicultural)

Nunes, Susan. *The Last Dragon*, 1106 (P) (Asian American—China)

Olaleye, Isaac. *The Distant Talking Drum: Poems from Nigeria*, 1125 (M) (African—Nigeria)

Pellowski, Anne. *The Family Storytelling Handbook: How to Use Stories, Anecdotes, Rhymes, Handkerchiefs, Paper, and Other Objects to Enrich Your Family Traditions*, 1159 (M/U) (Multicultural)

*Hidden Stories in Plants: Unusual and Easy-to-Tell Stories from Around the World Together with Creative Things to Do While Telling Them*, 1160 (M/U) (Multicultural)

*The Story Vine: A Source Book of Unusual and Easy-to-Tell Stories from Around the World*, 1161 (M/U) (Multicultural)

Pinkney, Brian. *Max Found Two Sticks*, 1174 (P) (African American)

Rupert, Rona. *Straw Sense*, 1257 (P) (African)

Ryan, Pam Muñoz. *One Hundred Is a Family*, 1258 (PS/P) (Multicultural)

Samton, Sheila. *Amazing Aunt Agatha*, 1267 (P) (African American)

Weiss, Nicki. *On a Hot, Hot Day*, 1535 (P) (Hispanic American)

Wright, Betty Ren. *The Day Our TV Broke Down*, 1583 (P) (African American)

Yolen, Jane, editor. *Street Rhymes Around the World*, 1627 (P) (Multicultural)

## Activities—acting

Boyd, Candy Dawson. *Fall Secrets*, 155 (U) (African American)

Greenfield, Eloise. *Grandpa's Face*, 533 (P) (African American)

Hansen, Joyce. *Yellow Bird and Me*, 607 (M/U) (African American)

Hoffman, Mary. *Amazing Grace*, 658 (P) (African American)

Johnson, Dolores. *The Best Bug to Be*, 743 (P) (African American)

Yarborough, Camille. *The Shimmershine Queens*, 1592 (M/U) (African American)

## Activities—baby-sitting

Clifton, Lucille. *My Brother Fine with Me*, 275 (P) (African American)

Cowen-Fletcher, Jane. *It Takes a Village*, 315 (P) (African—Benin)

Johnson, Angela. *Shoes like Miss Alice's*, 739 (P) (African American)

Johnson, Dolores. *What Kind of Baby-Sitter Is This?*, 747 (P) (African American)

Markel, Michelle. *Gracias, Rosa*, 975 (P) (Central American—Guatemala)

Tsutsui, Yoriko. *Anna in Charge*, 1463 (P) (Asian—Japan)

Walter, Mildred Pitts. *Two and Too Much*, 1517 (P) (African American)

## Activities—bathing

Stevens, Jan Romero. *Carlos and the Squash Plant/Carlos y la planta de calabaza*, 1382 (P) (Mexican American)

## Activities—carving

Gershator, Phillis, reteller. *The Iroko-man: A Yoruba Folktale*, 469 (M) (African—Yoruba)

Shigekawa, Marlene. *Blue Jay in the Desert*, 1320 (M) (Asian American—Japan)

## Activities—chopping wood

Spohn, David. *Winter Wood*, 1369 (M) (Multicultural)

## Activities—cleaning

Cummings, Pat. *Clean Your Room, Harvey Moon!*, 323 (PS/P) (African American)

McKissack, Patricia, and Fredrick McKissack. *Messy Bessey*, 956 (P) (African American)

## Activities—cooking

Heath, Amy. *Sofie's Role*, 636 (P) (African American)

Politi, Leo. *Three Stalks of Corn*, 1184 (M) (Mexican American)

Torres, Leyla. *Saturday Sancocho*, 1449 (P) (South American)

Yee, Paul. *Roses Sing on New Snow: A Delicious Tale*, 1597 (P) (Asian American—China)

## Activities—dancing

Ancona, George. *Powwow*, 49 (M) (Native American)

Bryan, Ashley. *The Dancing Granny*, 183 (M) (Caribbean—West Indies)

Cohen, Miriam. *Born to Dance Samba*, 291 (M) (South American—Brazil)

Deetlefs, Rene, reteller. *Tabu and the Dancing Elephants*, 343 (P) (African)

Fitzhugh, Louise. *Nobody's Family Is Going to Change*, 427 (U) (African American)

Goble, Paul. *Star Boy*, 501 (M) (Native American—Blackfoot)

Jonas, Ann. *Color Dance*, 760 (PS/P) (Multicultural)

Lattimore, Deborah Nourse. *Punga: The Goddess of Ugly*, 847 (M) (New Zealand—Maori)

Lee, Jeanne M. *Silent Lotus*, 859 (M) (Asian—Cambodia)

McKissack, Patricia. *Mirandy and Brother Wind*, 950 (P) (African American)

Maiorano, Robert. *A Little Interlude*, 967 (P) (African American)

Medearis, Angela Shelf. *Dancing with the Indians*, 1001 (P) (Multicultural)

Patrick, Denise Lewis. *Red Dancing Shoes*, 1154 (P) (African American)

## Activities—dancing (cont.)

Soto, Gary. *The Skirt*, 1357 (M) (Mexican American)

Van Laan, Nancy, reteller. *Buffalo Dance: A Blackfoot Legend*, 1488 (M) (Native American—Blackfoot)

Wallace, Ian. *Chin Chiang and the Dragon's Dance*, 1506 (P) (Asian American—China)

Waters, Kate, and Madeline Slovenz-Low. *Lion Dancer: Ernie Wan's Chinese New Year*, 1525 (P) (Asian American—China)

## Activities—drawing

Levine, Arthur A., reteller. *The Boy Who Drew Cats: A Japanese Folktale*, 876 (M) (Asian—Japan)

Moss, Marissa. *Regina's Big Mistake*, 1073 (P) (African American)

## Activities—exploring

Albert, Burton. *Where Does the Trail Lead?*, 37 (PS/P) (African American)

Moses, Amy. *I Am an Explorer*, 1071 (P) (African American)

## Activities—flying

Adoff, Arnold. *Flamboyán*, 25 (P) (Caribbean—Puerto Rico)

Baylor, Byrd. *Hawk, I Am Your Brother*, 102 (P/M) (Native American)

Dorros, Arthur. *Abuela*, 377 (P/M) (Hispanic American)

Keats, Ezra Jack. *The Trip*, 787 (P) (Multicultural)

McDermott, Gerald, reteller. *Coyote: A Trickster Tale from the American Southwest*, 936 (M) (Native American)

Ringgold, Faith. *Aunt Harriet's Underground Railroad in the Sky*, 1220 (P/M) (African American)

*Tar Beach*, 1222 (P/M) (African American)

Walter, Mildred Pitts. *Brother to the Wind*, 1508 (P/M) (African)

Wolkstein, Diane. *The Magic Wings: A Tale from China*, 1576 (M) (Asian—China)

Yep, Laurence. *Dragonwings*, 1607 (U) (Asian American—China)

## Activities—games

Lewin, Hugh. *Jafta and the Wedding*, 880 (P) (African—South Africa)

## Activities—getting dressed

Moore, Dessie. *Getting Dressed*, 1044 (PS) (African American)

## Activities—hiking

Say, Allen. *The Lost Lake*, 1285 (M) (Asian American)

## Activities—jumping rope

Colman, Warren. *Double Dutch and the Voodoo Shoes: A Modern African-American Urban Tale*, 303 (M) (African American)

Greenfield, Eloise. *Koya DeLaney and the Good Girl Blues*, 537 (U) (African American)

## Activities—making things

Ancona, George. *The Piñata Maker/El Piñatero*, 48 (M) (Mexican)

## Activities—painting

Bang, Molly, adapter. *Tye May and the Magic Brush*, 86 (M) (Asian—China)

Clément, Claude. *The Painter and the Wild Swans*, 263 (M) (Asian—Japan)

Demi. *Liang and the Magic Paintbrush*, 355 (M) (Asian—China)

dePaola, Tomie, reteller. *The Legend of the Indian Paintbrush*, 361 (M) (Native American)

Leaf, Margaret. *Eyes of the Dragon*, 855 (M) (Asian—China)

## Activities—paperfolding

Kroll, Virginia. *Pink Paper Swans*, 828 (P) (Multicultural)

Laurin, Anne. *Perfect Crane*, 850 (M) (Asian—Japan)

## Activities—photography

Allen, Judy. *Tiger*, 45 (P) (Asian—China)

Pinkney, Andrea Davis. *Hold Fast to Dreams*, 1172 (U) (African American)

## Activities—picnicking

Choi, Sook Nyul. *Halmoni and the Picnic*, 255 (P) (Asian American—Korea)

## Activities—playing

Bang, Molly. *One Fall Day*, 83 (P) (African American)

*Yellow Ball*, 88 (PS/P) (African American)

Begaye, Lisa Shook. *Building a Bridge*, 110 (P) (Native American—Navajo)

Carlstrom, Nancy White. *Wild Wild Sunflower Child Anna*, 226 (PS/P) (African American)

Chan, Jennifer L. *One Small Girl*, 236 (P) (Asian American—China)

Crews, Nina. *One Hot Summer Day*, 321 (PS/P) (African American)

Ets, Marie Hall. *Gilberto and the Wind*, 407 (P) (Mexican)

Flournoy, Valerie. *The Best Time of Day*, 433 (PS) (African American)

Gomi, Taro. *First Comes Harry*, 508 (PS/P) (Asian—Japan)

Greene, Carol. *Please, Wind*, 520 (PS/P) (African American)

Greenfield, Eloise. *Big Friend, Little Friend*, 526 (PS) (African American)

*Honey, I Love: And Other Love Poems*, 535 (P/M) (African American)

Havill, Juanita. *Jamaica Tag-Along*, 630 (P) (African American)

Johnson, Angela. *Do Like Kyla*, 730 (PS/P) (African American)

Jonas, Ann. *Holes and Peeks*, 761 (PS) (African American)

Keats, Ezra Jack. *The Snowy Day*, 786 (PS/P) (African American)

Lankford, Mary D. *Hopscotch Around the World*, 841 (P/M) (Multicultural)

McDonald, Becky Bring. *Larry and the Cookie*, 943 (PS/P) (African American)

Marzollo, Jean. *Pretend You're a Cat*, 984 (PS/P) (Multicultural)

Mattox, Cheryl Warren, collector and adapter. *Shake It to the One That You Love the Best: Play Songs and Lullabies from Black Musical Traditions*, 990 (M/U) (African American)

## Activities—playing (cont.)

Mills, Claudia. *A Visit to Amy-Claire*, 1026 (PS/P) (Asian American)

Narahashi, Keiko. *Is That Josie?*, 1096 (PS/P) (Asian American)

Nikola-Lisa, W. *Bein' With You This Way*, 1103 (P) (Multicultural)

Oxenbury, Helen. *All Fall Down*, 1143 (PS) (Multicultural)
   *Clap Hands*, 1144 (PS) (Multicultural)
   *Say Goodnight*, 1145 (PS) (Multicultural)
   *Tickle, Tickle*, 1146 (PS) (Multicultural)

Petrie, Catherine. *Joshua James Likes Trucks*, 1166 (P) (African American)

Pringle, Laurence. *Octopus Hug*, 1199 (PS/P) (African American)

Reiser, Lynn. *Margaret and Margarita/Margarita y Margaret*, 1215 (P) (Hispanic American)

Smalls-Hector, Irene. *Dawn and the Round To-It*, 1337 (PS/P) (African American)

Williams, Karen Lynn. *When Africa Was Home*, 1551 (P) (African)

Young, Ruth. *Golden Bear*, 1635 (PS/P) (African American)

## Activities—reading

Johnson, Dolores. *Papa's Stories*, 745 (P) (African American)

Mennen, Ingrid, and Niki Daly. *Somewhere in Africa*, 1010 (P) (African)

## Activities—reminiscing

Ada, Alma Flor. *Where the Flame Trees Bloom*, 21 (M) (Caribbean—Cuba)

Belton, Sandra. *From Miss Ida's Porch*, 115 (M) (African American)
   *May'naise Sandwiches and Sunshine Tea*, 116 (M) (African American)

Crews, Donald. *Bigmama's*, 319 (P) (African American)

Fritz, Jean. *China Homecoming*, 451 (U) (Asian - China)

Gray, Libba Moore. *Dear Willie Rudd*, 514 (P) (African American)

Greenfield, Eloise, and Lessie Jones Little. *Childtimes: A Three-Generation Memoir*, 548 (M/U) (African American)

Haskins, Francine. *I Remember "121,"* 617 (M) (African American)

Igus, Toyomi. *When I Was Little*, 711 (P) (African American)

Johnson, Angela. *Tell Me a Story, Mama*, 740 (P) (African American)

Mathis, Sharon Bell. *The Hundred Penny Box*, 985 (M) (African American)

Meyer, Carolyn. *Rio Grande Stories*, 1013 (U) (Multicultural)

Mitchell, Margaret King. *Uncle Jed's Barbershop*, 1028 (P/M) (African American)

Pomerantz, Charlotte. *The Chalk Doll*, 1185 (P) (Caribbean—Jamaica)

Scott, Ann Herbert. *On Mother's Lap*, 1297 (P) (Native American—Eskimo)

Stroud, Virginia A. *Doesn't Fall Off His Horse*, 1401 (M) (Native American—Kiowa)

## Activities—running away

Spinelli, Jerry. *Maniac Magee: A Novel*, 1365 (U) (African American)

## Activities—sewing

Flournoy, Valerie. *The Patchwork Quilt*, 434 (P/M) (African American)

Guback, Georgia. *Luka's Quilt*, 567 (P) (Hawaiian)

Hopkinson, Deborah. *Sweet Clara and the Freedom Quilt*, 666 (P/M) (African American)

McKissack, Patricia. *Nettie Jo's Friends*, 952 (P) (African American)

## Activities—sharing

McMillan, Bruce. *Eating Fractions*, 959 (P) (Multicultural)

## Activities—shopping

Munsch, Robert. *Where is Gah-Ning?*, 1075 (P) (Asian American—China)

## Activities—singing

Medearis, Angela Shelf, adapter. *The Singing Man: A West African Folktale*, 1004 (M) (African)

Peterson, Jeanne Whitehouse. *My Mama Sings*, 1165 (P) (African American)

## Activities—trading

Torres, Leyla. *Saturday Sancocho*, 1449 (P) (South American)

## Activities—traveling

Aardema, Verna, reteller. *Traveling to Tondo: A Tale of the Nkundo of Zaire*, 12 (M) (African—Zaire)

Brenner, Barbara. *Wagon Wheels*, 160 (P) (African American)

Buffett, Jimmy, and Savannah Jane Buffett. *The Jolly Mon*, 194 (P) (Caribbean)

Caines, Jeannette. *Just Us Women*, 213 (P) (African American)

Fritz, Jean. *China Homecoming*, 451 (U) (Asian - China)

Howard, Elizabeth Fitzgerald. *The Train to Lulu's*, 676 (P) (African American)

Isadora, Rachel. *Over the Green Hills*, 717 (P) (African—South Africa)

Kalman, Maira. *Sayonora, Mrs. Kackleman*, 775 (P) (Asian—Japan)

Lee, Jeanne M., reteller. *Toad Is the Uncle of Heaven: A Vietnamese Folk Tale*, 860 (M) (Asian—Vietnam)

Leigh, Nila K. *Learning to Swim in Swaziland: A Child's-Eye View of a South African Country*, 863 (P) (African—Swaziland)

Lewin, Hugh. *Jafta—The Journey*, 882 (P) (African– South Africa)

*Jafta—The Town*, 883 (P) (African—South Africa)

Lewin, Ted. *Amazon Boy*, 886 (P/M) (South American—Brazil)

Liddell, Janice. *Imani and the Flying Africans*, 894 (M) (African American)

Mohr, Nicholasa. *Going Home*, 1034 (M) (Hispanic American—Puerto Rico)

Pinkney, Gloria Jean. *Back Home*, 1175 (P/M) (African American)

Say, Allen. *Grandfather's Journey*, 1283 (M) (Asian American—Japan)

Sis, Peter. *Komodo!*, 1329 (P) (Indonesian)

Topooco, Eusebio. *Waira's First Journey*, 1447 (M) (South American—Bolivia)

Turner, Ann. *Nettie's Trip South*, 1467 (M) (African American)

## Activities—vacationing

Caines, Jeannette. *Just Us Women*, 213 (P) (African American)

Crews, Donald. *Bigmama's*, 319 (P) (African American)

## Activities—walking

Albert, Burton. *Where Does the Trail Lead?*, 37 (PS/P) (African American)

Buckley, Helen E. *Grandfather and I*, 192 (PS/P) (African American)

Crews, Donald. *Shortcut*, 320 (P) (African American)

Jonas, Ann. *The Trek*, 763 (PS/P) (African American)

Smalls-Hector, Irene. *Jonathan and His Mommy*, 1339 (PS/P) (African American)

## Activities—weaving

Blood, Charles L., and Martin A. Link. *A Goat in the Rug*, 143 (P) (Native American—Navajo)

Castañeda, Omar S. *Abuela's Weave*, 231 (M) (Central American—Guatemala)

Czernecki, Stefan, and Timothy Rhodes. *The Hummingbirds' Gift*, 329 (M) (Mexican)

Demi. *The Magic Tapestry: A Chinese Folktale*, 357 (M) (Asian—China)

Heyer, Marilee, reteller. *The Weaving of a Dream: A Chinese Folktale*, 642 (M) (Asian—China)

Lattimore, Deborah Nourse. *The Dragon's Robe*, 845 (M) (Asian—China)

Matsutani, Miyoko. *The Crane Maiden*, 988 (M) (Asian—Japan)

Oughton, Jerrie. *The Magic Weaver of Rugs: A Tale of the Navaho*, 1141 (M) (Native American—Navajo)

San Souci, Robert D., reteller. *The Enchanted Tapestry: A Chinese Folktale*, 1272 (M) (Asian—China)

Yagawa, Sumiko, reteller. *The Crane Wife*, 1590 (M) (Asian—Japan)

## Activities—whistling

Keats, Ezra Jack. *Whistle for Willie*, 788 (PS/P) (African American)

## Activities—working

Heide, Florence Parry, and Judith Heide Gilliland. *The Day of Ahmed's Secret*, 637 (P/M) (African—Egypt)

## Activities—writing

Cooper, Melrose. *Life Riddles*, 309 (U) (African American)

Heide, Florence Parry, and Judith Heide Gilliland. *The Day of Ahmed's Secret*, 637 (P/M) (African—Egypt)

Keats, Ezra Jack. *A Letter to Amy*, 781 (P) (African American)

## Adoption

Caines, Jeannette. *Abby*, 210 (PS) (African American)

McDonald, Joyce. *Mail-Order Kid*, 944 (M) (Asian American—Korea)

Mora, Pat. *Pablo's Tree*, 1056 (P) (Mexican American)

Myers, Walter Dean. *Me, Mop, and the Moondance Kid*, 1084 (M/U) (African American)

*Mop, Moondance, and the Nagasaki Knights*, 1085 (M/U) (African American)

Rosen, Michael. *Bonesy and Isabel*, 1243 (P) (Hispanic American—El Salvador)

Turner, Ann. *Through Moon and Stars and Night Skies*, 1468 (P) (Asian American)

## Adventure

Cohen, Barbara, and Bahija Lovejoy. *Seven Daughters and Seven Sons*, 289 (U) (Middle Eastern—Arabia)

Dubois, Muriel L. *Abenaki Captive*, 383 (U) (Native American—Abenaki)

McGee, Charmayne. *So Sings the Blue Deer*, 946 (U) (Native American— Huichol)

Myers, Walter Dean. *The Righteous Revenge of Artemis Bonner*, 1087 (U) (African American)

O'Dell, Scott. *The Black Pearl*, 1114 (U) (Mexican)

*Island of the Blue Dolphins*, 1118 (U) (Native American)

*The King's Fifth*, 1119 (U) (Mexican)

*Zia*, 1123 (U) (Native American)

Treviño, Elizabeth Borton de. *El Güero: A True Adventure Story*, 1451 (U) (Mexican)

## Amazon River

Lewin, Ted. *Amazon Boy*, 886 (P/M) (South American—Brazil)

## Anatomy

Agell, Charlotte. *Dancing Feet*, 36 (PS/P) (Multicultural)

Nikola-Lisa, W. *Bein' With You This Way*, 1103 (P) (Multicultural)

## Anatomy—noses

Johnston, Tony, adapter. *The Badger and the Magic Fan: A Japanese Folktale*, 757 (M) (Asian—Japan)

McCoy, Karen Kawamoto, reteller. *A Tale of Two Tengu: A Japanese Folktale*, 933 (M) (Asian—Japan)

## Ancient times

Sabuda, Robert. *Tutankhaman's Gift*, 1259 (M) (African—Egypt)

Stolz, Mary. *Zekmet, the Stone Carver: A Tale of Ancient Egypt*, 1397 (M) (African—Egypt)

## Anderson, Marian

Livingston, Myra Cohn. *Keep On Singing: A Ballad of Marian Anderson*, 903 (M) (African American)

## Animals

Aardema, Verna, reteller. *Rabbit Makes a Monkey of Lion: A Swahili Tale*, 10 (M) (African—Swahili)

*Traveling to Tondo: A Tale of the Nkundo of Zaire*, 12 (M) (African—Zaire)

*The Vingananee and the Tree Toad: A Liberian Tale*, 13 (M) (African—Liberia)

*What's So Funny, Ketu? A Nuer Tale*, 14 (M) (African—Nuer)

*Who's in Rabbit's House? A Masai Tale*, 15 (M) (African—Masai)

Arneach, Lloyd, reteller. *The Animals' Ballgame: A Cherokee Story from the Eastern Band*, 68 (M) (Native American—Cherokee)

Bandes, Hanna. *Sleepy River*, 78 (M) (Native American)

## Animals (cont.)

Bang, Betsy, translator and adapter. *The Old Woman and the Red Pumpkin: A Bengali Folk Tale*, 80 (M) (Asian—India)

Belting, Natalia. *Moon Was Tired of Walking on Air*, 111 (U) (South American)

Bernhard, Emery, reteller. *How Snowshoe Hare Rescued the Sun: A Tale from the Arctic*, 121 (M) (Native American—Yuit Eskimo)

Berry, James. *Spiderman Anancy*, 125 (M) (Caribbean)

Bierhorst, John, reteller. *Doctor Coyote: A Native American Aesop's Fables*, 130 (M) (Mexican—Aztec)

Brown, Marcia, reteller. *Once a Mouse: A Fable Cut in Wood*, 166 (P/M) (Asian—India)

Bruchac, Joseph, reteller. *The Great Ball Game: A Muskogee Story*, 173 (M) (Native American—Muskogee)

Brusca, María Cristina. *When Jaguars Ate the Moon: And Other Stories about Animals and Plants of the Americas*, 178 (M) (Multicultural)

Bryan, Ashley. *Beat the Story-Drum, Pum-Pum*, 181 (M) (African)

   *Lion and the Ostrich Chicks: And Other African Folk Tales*, 185 (M) (African)

   *The Ox of the Wonderful Horns and Other African Folktales*, 186 (M) (African)

Bush, Timothy. *Three at Sea*, 208 (P) (Multicultural)

Cassedy, Sylvia, and Kunihiro Suetake, translators. *Red Dragonfly on My Shoulder: Haiku*, 230 (M) (Asian—Japan)

Chocolate, Deborah M. Newton. *Imani in the Belly*, 248 (M) (African)

Courlander, Harold, and George Herzog. *The Cow-Tail Switch: And Other West African Stories*, 313 (M/U) (African)

Dee, Ruby, reteller. *Two Ways to Count to Ten: A Liberian Folktale*, 342 (M) (African—Liberia)

Demi. *A Chinese Zoo: Fables and Proverbs*, 351 (M) (Asian—China)

   *In the Eyes of the Cat: Japanese Poetry for All Seasons*, 354 (M) (Asian—Japan)

DeSauza, James, reteller, and Harriet Rohmer, adapter. *Brother Anansi and the Cattle Ranch: El Hermano Anansi y el Rancho de Ganado*, 364 (M) (Central American—Nicaragua)

deWit, Dorothy, editor. *The Talking Stone: An Anthology of Native American Tales and Legends*, 367 (U) (Native American)

Duff, Maggie, reteller. *Rum Pum Pum: A Folk Tale from India*, 384 (M) (Asian—India)

Ehlert, Lois. *Moon Rope: A Peruvian Folktale/Un lazo a la luna: Una leyenda peruana*, 395 (M) (South American—Peru)

Fleming, Denise. *In the Small, Small Pond*, 430 (PS) (Asian heritage)

   *In the Tall, Tall Grass*, 431 (PS/P) (Multicultural)

French, Fiona. *Anancy and Mr. Dry-Bone*, 448 (M) (African)

Gleeson, Brian. *Koi and the Kola Nuts*, 482 (M) (African)

Goble, Paul. *The Great Race of the Birds and Animals*, 492 (M) (Native American)

   *Iktomi and the Boulder: A Plains Indian Story*, 495 (M) (Native American—Plains Indians)

Greene, Ellin. *The Legend of the Cranberry: A Paleo-Indian Tale*, 521 (M) (Native American)

Guthrie, Donna W. *Nobiah's Well: A Modern African Folktale*, 569 (M) (African)

Han, Suzanne Crowder. *The Rabbit's Judgment*, 602 (M) (Asian—Korea)

## Animals (cont.)

Mollel, Tololwa M. *The King and the Tortoise*, 1037 (M) (African—Cameroon)

   *Rhinos for Lunch and Elephants for Supper! A Maasai Tale*, 1041 (M) (African—Masai)

Mora, Francisco X. *Juan Tuza and the Magic Pouch*, 1052 (M) (Mexican)

Morgan, Sally. *The Flying Emu: And Other Australian Stories*, 1058 (U) (Australian—Aborigine)

Nunes, Susan. *Tiddalick the Frog*, 1107 (M) (Australian—Aborigine)

Ochs, Carol Partridge. *When I'm Alone*, 1112 (P) (African American)

Onyefulu, Obi, reteller. *Chinye: A West African Folk Tale*, 1130 (M) (African)

Prusski, Jeffrey. *Bring Back the Deer*, 1200 (P) (Native American)

Rees, Ennis. *Brer Rabbit and His Tricks*, 1213 (M) (African American)

   *More of Brer Rabbit's Tricks*, 1214 (M) (African American)

Rose, Anne, reteller. *Akimba and the Magic Cow: A Folktale from Africa*, 1241 (M) (African)

Rosen, Michael. *How the Animals Got Their Colors: Animal Myths from Around the World*, 1247 (M) (Multicultural)

Roth, Susan L. *Fire Came to the Earth People: A Dahomean Folktale*, 1250 (M) (African)

Rucki, Ani. *Turkey's Gift to the People*, 1255 (M) (Native American—Navajo)

Siberell, Anne. *Whale in the Sky*, 1324 (M) (Native American—Northwest Coast)

Sierra, Judy. *The Elephant's Wrestling Match*, 1325 (M) (African)

Steptoe, John, reteller. *The Story of Jumping Mouse: A Native American Legend*, 1381 (M) (Native American)

Stock, Catherine. *Where Are You Going, Manyoni?*, 1391 (P) (African—Zimbabwe)

Tanaka, Béatrice, reteller. *The Chase: A Kutenai Indian Tale*, 1410 (P) (Native American—Kutenai)

Taylor, C. J. *Little Water and the Gift of the Animals: A Seneca Legend*, 1420 (M) (Native American—Seneca)

Taylor, Harriet Peck, reteller. *Coyote and the Laughing Butterflies*, 1422 (M) (Native American—Tewa)

Thornhill, Jan. *Crow and Fox: And Other Animal Legends*, 1441 (M) (Multicultural)

Troughton, Joanna, reteller. *Make-Believe Tales: A Folk Tale from Burma*, 1457 (M) (Asian—Burma)

   *Tortoise's Dream*, 1458 (M) (African)

   *Whale's Canoe: A Folk Tale from Australia*, 1459 (M) (Australian)

   *What Made Tiddalik Laugh: An Australian Aborigine Folk Tale*, 1460 (M) (Australian—Aborigine)

   *Who Will Be the Sun? A North American Indian Folk-tale*, 1461 (M) (Native American—Kutenai)

Van Woerkom, Dorothy, adapter. *The Rat, the Ox, and the Zodiac: A Chinese Legend*, 1491 (M) (Asian—China)

Vaughan, Marcia. *Kapoc, the Killer Croc*, 1493 (M) (South American—Amazon)

Walsh, Jill Paton. *Pepi and the Secret Names*, 1507 (M) (African—Egypt)

Walter, Mildred Pitts. *Brother to the Wind*, 1508 (P/M) (African)

Walters, Anna Lee, reteller. *The Two-Legged Creature: An Otoe Story*, 1519 (M) (Native American—Otoe)

Ward, Leila. *I Am Eyes/Ni Macho*, 1523 (P) (African)

Weiss, Jacqueline Shachter, collector and adapter. *Young Brer Rabbit: And Other Trickster Tales from the Americas*, 1534 (M) (Latin American)

Whitney, Alex. *Stiff Ears: Animal Folktales of the North American Indian*, 1544 (M) (Native American)

Yellow Robe, Rosebud. *Tonweya and the Eagles: And Other Lakota Tales*, 1600 (U) (Native American—Lakota)

Yen, Clara, reteller. *Why Rat Comes First: A Story of the Chinese Zodiac*, 1601 (M) (Asian—China)

Yeoman, John. *The Singing Tortoise: And Other Animal Folktales*, 1602 (M) (Multicultural)

## Animals—aardvarks

Mwalimu, and Adrienne Kennaway. *Awful Aardvark*, 1078 (M) (African)

## Animals—antelopes

Lacapa, Michael, reteller. *Antelope Woman: An Apache Folktale*, 836 (M) (Native American—Apache)

## Animals—baboons

*The Baboon's Umbrella: An African Folktale*, 71 (M) (African)

## Animals—badgers

Johnston, Tony, adapter. *The Badger and the Magic Fan: A Japanese Folktale*, 757 (M) (Asian—Japan)

## Animals—bats

Mollel, Tololwa M. *A Promise to the Sun: An African Story*, 1040 (M) (African)

## Animals—bears

Bird, E. J. *The Rainmakers*, 139 (U) (Native American—Anasazi)

Hinton, Leanne, translator. *Ishi's Tale of Lizard*, 650 (M) (Native American—Yahi)

Lasky, Kathryn. *Cloud Eyes*, 844 (M) (Native American)

Moroney, Lynn, reteller. *The Boy Who Loved Bears: A Pawnee Tale*, 1060 (M) (Native American—Pawnee)

Shetterly, Susan Hand, reteller. *Muwin and the Magic Hare*, 1318 (M) (Native American—Passamaquoddy)

## Animals—buffaloes

Baker, Olaf. *Where the Buffaloes Begin*, 77 (M) (Native American—Plains Indians)

Esbensen, Barbara Juster, reteller. *The Great Buffalo Race: How the Buffalo Got Its Hump/A Seneca Tale*, 403 (M) (Native American—Seneca)

Goble, Paul. *Buffalo Woman*, 486 (M) (Native American—Plains Indians)

*The Great Race of the Birds and Animals*, 492 (M) (Native American)

*Her Seven Brothers*, 493 (M) (Native American—Cheyenne)

Hamada, Cheryl, reteller. *The Farmer, the Buffalo, and the Tiger: A Folktale from Vietnam*, 575 (M) (Asian—Vietnam)

## Animals—buffaloes (cont.)

Van Laan, Nancy, reteller. *Buffalo Dance: A Blackfoot Legend*, 1488 (M) (Native American—Blackfoot)

## Animals—cats

Aardema, Verna, reteller. *Oh, Kojo! How Could You! An Ashanti Tale*, 7 (M) (African—Ashanti)

Armstrong, Jennifer. *Chin Yu Min and the Ginger Cat*, 64 (P) (Asian—China)

Bahous, Sally. *Sitti and the Cats: A Tale of Friendship*, 74 (M) (Middle Eastern—Palestine)

Boivin, Kelly. *Where Is Mittens?*, 146 (PS/P) (African American)

Bryan, Ashley. *The Adventures of Aku: Or How It Came About That We Shall Always See Okra the Cat Lying on a Velvet Cushion, While Okraman the Dog Sleeps Among the Ashes*, 179 (M) (African)

*The Cat's Purr*, 182 (P) (Caribbean—West Indies)

Bunting, Eve. *Smoky Night*, 200 (P/M) (African American)

Burchardt, Nellie. *Project Cat*, 204 (M) (African American)

Ehlert, Lois. *Feathers for Lunch*, 393 (PS/P) (African American)

Gollub, Matthew. *The Twenty-five Mixtec Cats*, 507 (M) (Mexican)

Hunter, Kristin. *Boss Cat*, 702 (M) (African American)

Keats, Ezra Jack. *Hi, Cat!*, 779 (PS/P) (African American)

*Pet Show!*, 784 (PS/P) (African American)

Lattimore, Deborah Nourse. *The Winged Cat: A Tale of Ancient Egypt*, 849 (M) (African—Egypt)

Levine, Arthur A., reteller. *The Boy Who Drew Cats: A Japanese Folktale*, 876 (M) (Asian—Japan)

Polacco, Patricia. *Mrs. Katz and Tush*, 1180 (M) (African American)

Richard, Françoise. *On Cat Mountain*, 1217 (M) (Asian—Japan)

Soto, Gary. *Chato's Kitchen*, 1351 (M) (Hispanic)

Tan, Amy. *The Chinese Siamese Cat*, 1408 (M) (Asian—China)

Uchida, Yoshiko. *The Two Foolish Cats: Suggested by a Japanese Folktale*, 1483 (M) (Asian—Japan)

Wagner, Jane. *J. T.*, 1501 (M) (African American)

Walter, Mildred Pitts. *Lillie of Watts: A Birthday Discovery*, 1512 (M) (Native American)

Yashima, Mitsu, and Taro Yashima. *Momo's Kitten*, 1594 (P) (Asian American—Japan)

Young, Ed. *Up a Tree*, 1633 (P) (Asian)

## Animals—cows

Jameson, Cynthia, reteller. *One for the Price of Two*, 725 (M) (Asian—Japan)

## Animals—coyotes

Aardema, Verna, reteller. *Borreguita and the Coyote: A Tale from Ayutla, Mexico*, 3 (M) (Mexican)

Baylor, Byrd. *Moon Song*, 103 (M) (Native American)

Begay, Shonto. *Ma'ii and Cousin Horned Toad: A Traditional Navajo Story*, 108 (M) (Native American—Navajo)

Bierhorst, John, reteller. *Doctor Coyote: A Native American Aesop's Fables*, 130 (M) (Mexican—Aztec)

Carey, Valerie Scho, adapter. *Quail Song: A Pueblo Indian Tale*, 221 (P) (Native American—Pueblo)

*The Coyote Rings the Wrong Bell: A Mexican Folktale*, 316 (M) (Mexican)

Goble, Paul. *Iktomi and the Ducks: A Plains Indian Story*, 498 (M) (Native American—Plains Indians)

Hausman, Gerald, reteller. *Coyote Walks on Two Legs: A Book of Navaho Myths and Legends*, 626 (M) (Native American—Navajo)

Johnston, Tony. *The Tale of Rabbit and Coyote*, 759 (M) (Native American—Zapotec)

London, Jonathan, reteller. *Fire Race: A Karuk Coyote Tale about How Fire Came to the People*, 911 (M) (Native American—Karuk)

McDermott, Gerald, reteller. *Coyote: A Trickster Tale from the American Southwest*, 936 (M) (Native American)

Mayo, Gretchen Will, reteller. *Meet Tricky Coyote!*, 996 (M) (Native American)

*That Tricky Coyote!*, 998 (M) (Native American)

Oughton, Jerrie. *How the Stars Fell into the Sky: A Navajo Legend*, 1140 (M) (Native American—Navajo)

Stevens, Janet, reteller. *Coyote Steals the Blanket: An Ute Tale*, 1383 (M) (Native American—Ute)

Taylor, Harriet Peck, reteller. *Coyote and the Laughing Butterflies*, 1422 (M) (Native American—Tewa)

*Coyote Places the Stars*, 1423 (M) (Native American—Wasco)

Welsch, Roger. *Uncle Smoke Stories: Nehawka Tales of Coyote the Trickster*, 1537 (M) (Native American)

## Animals—deer

Hodges, Margaret, reteller. *The Golden Deer*, 655 (M) (Asian—India)

McGee, Charmayne. *So Sings the Blue Deer*, 946 (U) (Native American—Huichol)

## Animals—dogs

Aardema, Verna, reteller. *Oh, Kojo! How Could You! An Ashanti Tale*, 7 (M) (African—Ashanti)

Alexander, Martha. *Bobo's Dream*, 41 (PS/P) (African American)

Armstrong, William H. *Sounder*, 67 (U) (African American)

Bogart, Jo Ellen. *Daniel's Dog*, 145 (P) (African American)

Bryan, Ashley. *The Adventures of Aku: Or How It Came About That We Shall Always See Okra the Cat Lying on a Velvet Cushion, While Okraman the Dog Sleeps Among the Ashes*, 179 (M) (African)

Bushey, Jeanne. *A Sled Dog for Moshi*, 209 (P) (Native American—Inuit)

Gardiner, John Reynolds. *Stone Fox*, 457 (M) (Native American)

Jordan, June. *Kimako's Story*, 768 (P) (African American)

Keats, Ezra Jack. *Whistle for Willie*, 788 (PS/P) (African American)

Keats, Ezra Jack, and Pat Cherr. *My Dog Is Lost!*, 789 (P) (Hispanic American—Puerto Rico)

Mora, Francisco X. *The Legend of the Two Moons*, 1053 (M) (Mexican)

## Animals—dogs (cont.)

O'Dell, Scott. *Black Star, Bright Dawn*, 1115 (U) (Native American—Eskimo)
　*Island of the Blue Dolphins*, 1118 (U) (Native American)
Ormerod, Jan. *Joe Can Count*, 1133 (PS) (African American)
Paulsen, Gary. *Dogsong*, 1157 (U) (Native American—Inuit)
Pomerantz, Charlotte. *The Outside Dog*, 1186 (P) (Caribbean—Puerto Rico)
Rosen, Michael. *Bonesy and Isabel*, 1243 (P) (Hispanic American—El Salvador)
Talbert, Marc. *A Sunburned Prayer*, 1407 (U) (Mexican American)
Udry, Janice May. *What Mary Jo Wanted*, 1487 (P) (African American)

## Animals—dolphins

Kendall, Sarita. *Ransom for a River Dolphin*, 795 (U) (South American—
　Colombia)
Orr, Katherine. *Story of a Dolphin*, 1136 (P) (Caribbean)

## Animals—donkeys

Parkison, Jami. *Pequeña the Burro*, 1150 (M) (Mexican)

## Animals—elephants

Allen, Judy. *Elephant*, 44 (P) (African)
Deetlefs, Rene, reteller. *Tabu and the Dancing Elephants*, 343 (P) (African)
Geraghty, Paul. *The Hunter*, 468 (P) (African)
Havill, Juanita. *Sato and the Elephants*, 632 (M) (Asian—Japan)
Oliviero, Jamie. *Som See and the Magic Elephant*, 1127 (M) (Asian—Thailand)
Sierra, Judy. *The Elephant's Wrestling Match*, 1325 (M) (African)

## Animals—endangered animals

Allen, Judy. *Elephant*, 44 (P) (African)
　*Tiger*, 45 (P) (Asian—China)
Bush, Timothy. *Three at Sea*, 208 (P) (Multicultural)
Havill, Juanita. *Sato and the Elephants*, 632 (M) (Asian—Japan)
Schlein, Miriam. *The Year of the Panda*, 1292 (M) (Asian—China)

## Animals—foxes

Ehlert, Lois. *Mole's Hill: A Woodland Tale*, 394 (M) (Native American—
　Woodland)
McDonald, Joyce. *Mail-Order Kid*, 944 (M) (Asian American—Korea)
McKissack, Patricia. *Flossie and the Fox*, 948 (P) (African American)
Tompert, Ann. *Grandfather Tang's Story*, 1445 (P) (Asian—China)
Vaughan, Marcia. *Dorobó the Dangerous*, 1492 (M) (Asian—Japan)
Wheeler, M. J. *Fox Tales*, 1540 (M) (Asian—India)
Yep, Laurence. *The Ghost Fox*, 1608 (M) (Asian—China)

## Animals—gazelles

Bible, Charles, adapter. *Hamdaani: A Traditional Tale from Zanzibar*, 129 (M)
　(African—Zanzibar)

## Animals—giraffes

Jacobs, Shannon K. *Song of the Giraffe*, 721 (M) (African)

Rosen, Michael, reteller. *How Giraffe Got Such a Long Neck . . . and Why Rhino Is So Grumpy: A Tale from East Africa*, 1246 (M) (African—East Africa)

## Animals—goats

Blood, Charles L., and Martin A. Link. *A Goat in the Rug*, 143 (P) (Native American—Navajo)

Kessler, Cristina. *One Night: A Story from the Desert*, 798 (P) (Middle Eastern—Tuareg)

Uchida, Yoshiko. *Sumi and the Goat and the Tokyo Express*, 1481 (M) (Asian—Japan)

Wolkstein, Diane. *The Banza: A Haitian Story*, 1574 (M) (Caribbean—Haiti)

## Animals—gorillas

Aardema, Verna, reteller. *Princess Gorilla and a New Kind of Water: A Mpongwe Tale*, 9 (M) (African—Mpongwe)

## Animals—hamsters

Kline, Suzy. *Song Lee and the Hamster Hunt*, 815 (M) (Asian American—Korea)

## Animals—horses

Bulla, Clyde Robert, and Michael Syson. *Conquista!*, 195 (M) (Native American)

Coerr, Eleanor. *Chang's Paper Pony*, 282 (P) (Asian American—China)

Cohen, Caron Lee, adapter. *The Mud Pony: A Traditional Skidi Pawnee Tale*, 290 (M) (Native American—Pawnee)

Cohlene, Terri, adapter. *Turquoise Boy: A Navajo Legend*, 297 (M) (Native American—Navajo)

Goble, Paul. *The Gift of the Sacred Dog*, 490 (M) (Native American—Plains Indians)

*The Girl Who Loved Wild Horses*, 491 (M) (Native American)

Greenfield, Eloise. *On My Horse*, 542 (PS/P) (African American)

Hewett, Joan. *Laura Loves Horses*, 641 (M) (Hispanic American)

Hurmence, Belinda. *Dixie in the Big Pasture*, 703 (U) (Native American)

Otsuka, Yuzo. *Suho and the White Horse: A Legend of Mongolia*, 1139 (M) (Asian—Mongolia)

Rodanas, Kristina, adapter. *Dance of the Sacred Circle: A Native American Tale*, 1231 (M) (Native American—Blackfoot)

Shefelman, Janice. *A Mare for Young Wolf*, 1310 (P) (Native American)

Stroud, Virginia A. *Doesn't Fall Off His Horse*, 1401 (M) (Native American—Kiowa)

Yolen, Jane. *Sky Dogs*, 1625 (M) (Native American—Blackfoot)

## Animals—hyenas

McKissack, Patricia. *Monkey-Monkey's Trick*, 951 (P) (African)

## Animals—jackals

Aardema, Verna, reteller. *Jackal's Flying Lesson: A Khoikhoi Tale*, 5 (M) (African—Khoikhoi)

Brown, Marcia. *The Blue Jackal*, 165 (M) (Asian—India)

Gleeson, Brian. *The Tiger and the Brahmin*, 483 (M) (Asian—India)

## Animals—leopards

Knutson, Barbara, reteller. *Sungura and Leopard: A Swahili Trickster Tale*, 820 (M) (African—Swahili)

## Animals—lions

Day, Nancy Raines. *The Lion's Whiskers: An Ethiopian Folktale*, 338 (M) (African—Ethiopia)

Fields, Julia. *The Green Lion of Zion Street*, 420 (M) (African American)

MacDonald, Suse. *Nanta's Lion: A Search-and-Find Adventure*, 945 (P) (African—Masai)

Schroeder, Alan. *The Stone Lion*, 1295 (M) (Asian—Tibet)

## Animals—llamas

Alexander, Ellen. *Llama and the Great Flood: A Folktale from Peru*, 39 (M) (South American—Peru)

Palacios, Argentina, adapter. *The Llama's Secret: A Peruvian Legend*, 1149 (M) (South American—Peru)

## Animals—mice

DeArmond, Dale, adapter. *The Seal Oil Lamp: Adapted from an Eskimo Folktale*, 340 (M) (Native American—Eskimo)

Kimmel, Eric A., reteller. *The Greatest of All: A Japanese Folktale*, 805 (M) (Asian—Japan)

Soto, Gary. *Chato's Kitchen*, 1351 (M) (Hispanic)

Steptoe, John, reteller. *The Story of Jumping Mouse: A Native American Legend*, 1381 (M) (Native American)

Winthrop, Elizabeth. *Journey to the Bright Kingdom*, 1569 (M) (Asian—Japan)

Young, Ed. *Seven Blind Mice*, 1632 (M) (Asian—India)

## Animals—moles

Ehlert, Lois. *Mole's Hill: A Woodland Tale*, 394 (M) (Native American—Woodland)

Kwon, Holly H., reteller. *The Moles and the Mireuk: A Korean Folktale*, 834 (M) (Asian—Korea)

## Animals—mongooses

Mwalimu, and Adrienne Kennaway. *Awful Aardvark*, 1078 (M) (African)

## Animals—monkeys

Franklin, Kristine L. *When the Monkeys Came Back*, 443 (P) (Central American—Costa Rica)

Galdone, Paul. *The Monkey and the Crocodile: A Jataka Tale from India*, 454 (M) (Asian—India)

*The Turtle and the Monkey: A Philippine Tale*, 455 (M) (Philippine)

Guy, Rosa, translator and adapter. *Mother Crocodile*, 571 (M) (African)

McKissack, Patricia. *Monkey-Monkey's Trick*, 951 (P) (African)

## Animals—opossums

Mike, Jan M., adapter. *Opossum and the Great Firemaker: A Mexican Legend*, 1016 (M) (Mexican)

## Animals—oxen

Hong, Lily Toy, reteller. *How the Ox Star Fell from Heaven*, 660 (M) (Asian—China)

## Animals—pandas

Schlein, Miriam. *The Year of the Panda*, 1292 (M) (Asian—China)

## Animals—pigs

Johnson, Angela. *Julius*, 734 (P) (African American)

Pitre, Felix, reteller. *Juan Bobo and the Pig: A Puerto Rican Folktale*, 1177 (M) (Caribbean—Puerto Rico)

## Animals—quails

Carey, Valerie Scho, adapter. *Quail Song: A Pueblo Indian Tale*, 221 (P) (Native American—Pueblo)

## Animals—rabbits

Aardema, Verna, reteller. *Rabbit Makes a Monkey of Lion: A Swahili Tale*, 10 (M) (African—Swahili)

*Who's in Rabbit's House? A Masai Tale*, 15 (M) (African—Masai)

Bernhard, Emery, reteller. *How Snowshoe Hare Rescued the Sun: A Tale from the Arctic*, 121 (M) (Native American—Yuit Eskimo)

Bryan, Ashley. *Sh-ko and His Eight Wicked Brothers*, 187 (M) (Asian—Japan)

*The Coyote Rings the Wrong Bell: A Mexican Folktale*, 316 (M) (Mexican)

Grossman, Virginia. *Ten Little Rabbits*, 563 (P) (Native American)

Hamada, Cheryl, reteller. *The White Hare of Inaba: A Japanese Folktale*, 578 (M) (Asian—Japan)

Han, Suzanne Crowder. *The Rabbit's Escape*, 601 (M) (Asian—Korea)

Harris, Joel Chandler. *Jump Again! More Adventures of Brer Rabbit*, 614 (M/U) (African American)

*Jump on Over! The Adventures of Brer Rabbit and His Family*, 615 (M/U) (African American)

Harris, Joel Chandler, and Malcolm Jones. *Jump! The Adventures of Brer Rabbit*, 616 (M/U) (African American)

Johnston, Tony. *The Tale of Rabbit and Coyote*, 759 (M) (Native American—Zapotec)

Knutson, Barbara, reteller. *Sungura and Leopard: A Swahili Trickster Tale*, 820 (M) (African—Swahili)

## Animals—sheep

Aardema, Verna, reteller. *Borreguita and the Coyote: A Tale from Ayutla, Mexico*, 3 (M) (Mexican)

Bryan, Ashley. *The Story of Lightning & Thunder*, 189 (M) (African)

Franklin, Kristine L. *The Shepherd Boy*, 442 (P) (Native American—Navajo)

Hale, Sarah Josepha. *Mary Had a Little Lamb*, 573 (PS/P) (African American)

## Animals—skunks

Spohn, David. *Nate's Treasure*, 1367 (M) (Multicultural)

## Animals—tigers

Allen, Judy. *Tiger*, 45 (P) (Asian—China)

Gleeson, Brian. *The Tiger and the Brahmin*, 483 (M) (Asian—India)

Godden, Rumer. *The Valiant Chatti-Maker*, 503 (M) (Asian—India)

Hamada, Cheryl, reteller. *The Farmer, the Buffalo, and the Tiger: A Folktale from Vietnam*, 575 (M) (Asian—Vietnam)

Mora, Francisco X. *The Tiger and the Rabbit: A Puerto Rican Folktale*, 1054 (M) (Caribbean—Puerto Rico)

Spagnoli, Cathy, adapter. *Nine-in-One, Grr! Grr! A Folktale from the Hmong People of Laos*, 1360 (M) (Asian—Laos)

Stanley, Diane. *Fortune*, 1373 (M) (Middle Eastern—Persia)

Temple, Frances, reteller. *Tiger Soup: An Anansi Story from Jamaica*, 1437 (M) (Caribbean—Jamaica)

Wolkstein, Diane. *The Banza: A Haitian Story*, 1574 (M) (Caribbean—Haiti)

## Animals—whales

George, Jean Craighead. *Water Sky*, 467 (U) (Native American—Inuit)

Rockwell, Anne. *Tuhurahura and the Whale*, 1230 (M) (New Zealand—Maori)

Roy, Ronald. *A Thousand Pails of Water*, 1253 (P) (Asian)

Siberell, Anne. *Whale in the Sky*, 1324 (M) (Native American—Northwest Coast)

Steiner, Barbara. *Whale Brother*, 1375 (M) (Native American—Eskimo)

Troughton, Joanna, reteller. *Whale's Canoe: A Folk Tale from Australia*, 1459 (M) (Australian)

## Animals—wolves

George, Jean Craighead. *Julie*, 463 (U) (Native American—Inuit)

*Julie of the Wolves*, 464 (U) (Native American—Inuit)

Goble, Paul. *Dream Wolf*, 489 (M) (Native American—Plains Indians)

Goble, Paul, and Dorothy Goble. *The Friendly Wolf*, 502 (M) (Native American—Plains Indians)

Powell, Mary, editor. *Wolf Tales: Native American Children's Stories*, 1195 (M) (Native American)

Roth, Susan L. *Kanahéna: A Cherokee Story*, 1251 (M) (Native American—Cherokee)

Young, Ed, translator. *Lon Po Po: A Red-Riding Hood Story from China*, 1629 (M) (Asian—China)

## Animals—worms

Lemieux, Margo. *Full Worm Moon*, 864 (M) (Native American—Algonquian)

## Arctic lands

Andrews, Jan. *Very Last First Time*, 56 (P/M) (Native American—Inuit)

Bernhard, Emery, reteller. *How Snowshoe Hare Rescued the Sun: A Tale from the Arctic*, 121 (M) (Native American—Yuit Eskimo)

Bushey, Jeanne. *A Sled Dog for Moshi*, 209 (P) (Native American—Inuit)

Cohlene, Terri, adapter. *Ka-ha-si and the Loon: An Eskimo Legend*, 294 (M) (Native American—Eskimo)

Davis, Deborah. *The Secret of the Seal*, 334 (M) (Native American—Inuit)

DeArmond, Dale, adapter. *The Seal Oil Lamp: Adapted from an Eskimo Folktale*, 340 (M) (Native American—Eskimo)

George, Jean Craighead. *Julie*, 463 (U) (Native American—Inuit)

*Julie of the Wolves*, 464 (U) (Native American—Inuit)

*Water Sky*, 467 (U) (Native American—Inuit)

Houston, James. *Frozen Fire: A Tale of Courage*, 670 (M) (Native American—Inuit)

Hoyt-Goldsmith, Diane. *Arctic Hunter*, 677 (M) (Native American—Inupiat)

Joosse, Barbara. *Mama, Do You Love Me?*, 767 (PS/P) (Native American—Inuit)

Kendall, Russ. *Eskimo Boy: Life in an Inupiaq Eskimo Village*, 794 (M) (Native American—Inupiaq)

Kroll, Virginia. *The Seasons and Someone*, 829 (M) (Native American—Eskimo)

Luenn, Nancy. *Nessa's Fish*, 921 (P) (Native American—Inuit)

*Nessa's Story*, 922 (P) (Native American—Inuit)

O'Dell, Scott. *Black Star, Bright Dawn*, 1115 (U) (Native American—Eskimo)

Paulsen, Gary. *Dogsong*, 1157 (U) (Native American—Inuit)

Philip, Neil, editor. *Songs Are Thoughts: Poems of the Inuit*, 1170 (M) (Native American—Inuit)

San Souci, Robert D., adapter. *Song of Sedna*, 1278 (M) (Native American—Inuit)

Sis, Peter. *A Small, Tall Tale from the Far, Far North*, 1330 (M) (Native American—Inuit)

Sloat, Teri, reteller. *The Hungry Giant of the Tundra*, 1334 (M) (Native American—Yupik)

## Art

Ancona, George. *The Piñata Maker/El Piñatero*, 48 (M) (Mexican)

Bang, Molly, adapter. *Tye May and the Magic Brush*, 86 (M) (Asian—China)

Baylor, Byrd. *Before You Came This Way*, 100 (P/M) (Native American)

*When Clay Sings*, 105 (P/M) (Native American)

Chapman, Christina. *Treasure in the Attic*, 242 (P) (African American)

Coerr, Eleanor. *Mieko and the Fifth Treasure*, 283 (M) (Asian—Japan)

Demi. *Liang and the Magic Paintbrush*, 355 (M) (Asian—China)

Everett, Gwen. *Li'l Sis and Uncle Willie: A Story Based on the Life and Paintings of William H. Johnson*, 410 (M) (African American)

Hammond, Anna, and Joe Matunis. *This Home We Have Made/Esta Casa Que Hemos Hecho*, 598 (M) (Multicultural)

Hoyt-Goldsmith, Diane. *Totem Pole*, 682 (M) (Native American—Tsimshian)

Johnson, Ryerson. *Kenji and the Magic Geese*, 756 (M) (Asian—Japan)

Lawrence, Jacob. *The Great Migration: An American Story*, 852 (M/U) (African American)

Leaf, Margaret. *Eyes of the Dragon*, 855 (M) (Asian—China)

Lessac, Frané. *Caribbean Canvas*, 866 (M/U) (Caribbean)

Levine, Arthur A., reteller. *The Boy Who Drew Cats: A Japanese Folktale*, 876 (M) (Asian—Japan)

Markun, Patricia Maloney. *The Little Painter of Sabana Grande*, 976 (M) (Central American—Panama)

Say, Allen. *The Ink-Keeper's Apprentice*, 1284 (U) (Asian—Japan)

Shange, Ntozake. *I Live in Music*, 1306 (M) (African American)

Steiner, Barbara. *Whale Brother*, 1375 (M) (Native American—Eskimo)

Sullivan, Charles, editor. *Children of Promise: African-American Literature and Art for Young People*, 1402 (U) (African American)

Treviño, Elizabeth Borton de. *I, Juan de Pareja*, 1452 (U) (African heritage)

Walsh, Jill Paton. *Pepi and the Secret Names*, 1507 (M) (African—Egypt)

Williams, Vera B. *Cherries and Cherry Pits*, 1555 (P) (African American)

## Astronomy

Mayo, Gretchen Will, reteller. *Star Tales: North American Indian Stories about the Stars*, 997 (M/U) (Native American)

Monroe, Jean Guard, and Ray A. Williamson. *They Dance in the Sky: Native American Star Myths*, 1043 (M/U) (Native American)

## Automobiles

Caines, Jeannette. *Just Us Women*, 213 (P) (African American)

Patrick, Denise Lewis. *The Car Washing Street*, 1153 (P) (African American)

## Babies, toddlers

Bogart, Jo Ellen. *Daniel's Dog*, 145 (P) (African American)

Clifton, Lucille. *Everett Anderson's Nine Month Long*, 271 (P) (African American)

Cooke, Trish. *So Much*, 307 (P) (African American)
*When I Grow Bigger*, 308 (PS/P) (African American)

Cowen-Fletcher, Jane. *It Takes a Village*, 315 (P) (African—Benin)

Greenfield, Eloise. *She Come Bringin Me That Little Baby Girl*, 543 (P) (African American)

Hayes, Sarah. *Eat Up, Gemma*, 633 (PS) (African American)
*Happy Christmas, Gemma*, 634 (PS) (African American)

Hudson, Cheryl Willis. *Animal Sounds for Baby*, 686 (PS) (African American)
*Good Morning, Baby*, 687 (PS) (African American)
*Good Night, Baby*, 688 (PS) (African American)
*Let's Count Baby*, 689 (PS) (African American)

Javernick, Ellen. *Where's Brooke?*, 726 (PS/P) (Asian American)

## Babies, toddlers (cont.)

Jonas, Ann. *When You Were a Baby*, 764 (PS) (African American)

Keats, Ezra Jack. *Peter's Chair*, 785 (PS/P) (African American)

Mennen, Ingrid. *One Round Moon and a Star for Me*, 1009 (P) (African)

Narahashi, Keiko. *Is That Josie?*, 1096 (PS/P) (Asian American)

Osofsky, Audrey. *Dreamcatcher*, 1138 (M) (Native American—Ojibway)

Oxenbury, Helen. *All Fall Down*, 1143 (PS) (Multicultural)

   *Clap Hands*, 1144 (PS) (Multicultural)

   *Say Goodnight*, 1145 (PS) (Multicultural)

   *Tickle, Tickle*, 1146 (PS) (Multicultural)

Smith, Edward Biko. *A Lullaby for Daddy*, 1340 (PS) (African American)

Steptoe, John. *Baby Says*, 1376 (PS) (African American)

Van Laan, Nancy. *Mama Rocks, Papa Sings*, 1489 (P) (Caribbean—Haiti)

Walter, Mildred Pitts. *My Mama Needs Me*, 1515 (P) (African American)

   *Two and Too Much*, 1517 (P) (African American)

Williams, Vera B. *"More, More, More" Said the Baby: 3 Love Stories*, 1556 (P) (Multicultural)

Winter, Susan. *A Baby Just like Me*, 1568 (PS/P) (African American)


## Bedtime

Bandes, Hanna. *Sleepy River*, 78 (M) (Native American)

Bang, Molly. *One Fall Day*, 83 (P) (African American)

   *Ten, Nine, Eight*, 85 (PS/P) (African American)

Bozylinsky, Hannah Heritage. *Lala Salama: An African Lullaby in Swahili and English*, 156 (P) (African)

Carlstrom, Nancy White. *Northern Lullaby*, 225 (P) (Native American—Eskimo)

Dragonwagon, Crescent. *Half a Moon and One Whole Star*, 380 (P) (African American)

Greenfield, Eloise. *First Pink Light*, 530, 531 (P) (African American)

Highwater, Jamake. *Moonsong Lullaby*, 644 (P/M) (Native American)

Hudson, Cheryl Willis. *Good Night, Baby*, 688 (PS) (African American)

Johnson, Angela. *Joshua's Night Whispers*, 733 (PS) (African American)

Jonas, Ann. *The Quilt*, 762 (PS/P) (African American)

Melmed, Laura Krauss. *The First Song Ever Sung*, 1007 (P) (Asian—Japan)

Moore, Dessie. *Good Night*, 1046 (PS) (African American)

Owen, Roy. *My Night Forest*, 1142 (PS/P) (Hispanic American)

Oxenbury, Helen. *Say Goodnight*, 1145 (PS) (Multicultural)

Smith, Edward Biko. *A Lullaby for Daddy*, 1340 (PS) (African American)

Tiller, Ruth. *Cinnamon, Mint, & Mothballs: A Visit to Grandmother's House*, 1442 (P) (Asian American)

Yolen, Jane, editor. *Sleep Rhymes Around the World*, 1626 (P) (Multicultural)


## Beggars

Diller, Harriett. *The Waiting Day*, 368 (M) (Asian—China)

## Behavior—accepting differences

Chin-Lee, Cynthia. *Almond Cookies and Dragon Well Tea*, 247 (P) (Asian American—China)

Friedman, Ina R. *How My Parents Learned to Eat*, 450 (P) (Multicultural)

Hamanaka, Sheila. *All the Colors of the Earth*, 579 (PS/P) (Multicultural)

Mohr, Nicholasa. *Going Home*, 1034 (M) (Hispanic American—Puerto Rico)

Perkins, Mitali. *The Sunita Experiment*, 1163 (U) (Asian American—India)

Pettit, Jayne. *My Name Is San Ho*, 1167 (U) (Asian American—Vietnam)

Say, Allen. *The Bicycle Man*, 1282 (M) (Asian—Japan)

Spier, Peter. *People*, 1363 (P/M) (Multicultural)

Surat, Michele Maria. *Angel Child, Dragon Child*, 1404 (P) (Asian American—Vietnam)

Yep, Laurence. *Sea Glass*, 1613 (U) (Asian American—China)

## Behavior—boasting

Grifalconi, Ann. *Osa's Pride*, 557 (P) (African)

Jameson, Cynthia, reteller. *One for the Price of Two*, 725 (M) (Asian—Japan)

Knutson, Barbara, reteller. *Why the Crab Has No Head: An African Tale*, 821 (M) (African—Zaire)

Miller, Moira. *The Moon Dragon*, 1024 (M) (Asian—China)

Stock, Catherine. *Armien's Fishing Trip*, 1387 (P) (African—South Africa)

## Behavior—bullying

Baillie, Allan. *Rebel*, 75 (P) (Asian—Burma)

Keats, Ezra Jack. *Goggles*, 778 (P) (African American)

## Behavior—collecting things

DeGross, Monalisa. *Donavan's Word Jar*, 345 (M) (African American)

Dobkin, Bonnie. *Collecting*, 372 (PS/P) (Asian American)

## Behavior—disbelief

Turner, Ann. *Nettie's Trip South*, 1467 (M) (African American)

## Behavior—dissatisfaction

Demi. *The Stone Cutter*, 358 (M) (Asian—China)

McDermott, Gerald, adapter. *The Stonecutter: A Japanese Folktale*, 939 (M) (Asian—Japan)

## Behavior—facing challenges

Bang, Molly. *The Paper Crane*, 84 (P) (Asian)

Boyd, Candy Dawson. *Breadsticks and Blessing Places*, 152 (U) (African American)

Goble, Paul. *Buffalo Woman*, 486 (M) (Native American—Plains Indians)

*The Gift of the Sacred Dog*, 490 (M) (Native American—Plains Indians)

McDermott, Gerald, adapter. *Arrow to the Sun: A Pueblo Indian Tale*, 935 (P/M) (Native American—Pueblo)

## Behavior—facing challenges (cont.)

Paterson, Katherine. *Park's Quest*, 1151 (U) (Asian American—Vietnam)

Wisniewski, David. *Rain Player*, 1570 (M) (Central American—Mayan)

*The Warrior and the Wise Man*, 1571 (P/M) (Asian—Japan)

Yep, Laurence. *Sea Glass*, 1613 (U) (Asian American—China)

## Behavior—fighting, arguing

Baillie, Allan. *Rebel*, 75 (P) (Asian—Burma)

Barnes, Joyce Annette. *The Baby Grand, the Moon in July, & Me*, 95 (U) (African American)

Bruchac, Joseph, reteller. *The First Strawberries: A Cherokee Story*, 169 (M) (Native American—Cherokee)

Dixon, Ann, reteller. *The Sleeping Lady*, 371 (M) (Native American)

Havill, Juanita. *Jamaica and Brianna*, 629 (P) (African American)

Johnson, Dolores. *Your Dad Was Just Like You*, 749 (P) (African American)

Lattimore, Deborah Nourse. *The Flame of Peace: A Tale of the Aztecs*, 846 (M) (Mexican—Aztec)

*Why There Is No Arguing in Heaven: A Mayan Myth*, 848 (M) (Central American—Mayan)

McCoy, Karen Kawamoto, reteller. *A Tale of Two Tengu: A Japanese Folktale*, 933 (M) (Asian—Japan)

Martin, Francesca. *The Honey Hunters: A Traditional African Tale*, 980 (M) (African)

Namioka, Lensey. *The Coming of the Bear*, 1092 (U) (Asian—Japan)

Shor, Pekay, reteller. *When the Corn Is Red*, 1321 (M) (Native American—Tuscaroran)

Taylor, C. J. *The Secret of the White Buffalo: An Oglala Legend*, 1421 (M) (Native American—Oglala)

Uchida, Yoshiko. *The Two Foolish Cats: Suggested by a Japanese Folktale*, 1483 (M) (Asian—Japan)

Wade, Gini, reteller. *The Wonderful Bag: An Arabian Tale from The Thousand & One Nights*, 1500 (M) (Middle Eastern—Arabia)

Wolff, Ferida. *The Emperor's Garden*, 1573 (M) (Asian—China)

Yep, Laurence. *The Serpent's Children*, 1614 (U) (Asian—China)

## Behavior—getting along with others

Begaye, Lisa Shook. *Building a Bridge*, 110 (P) (Native American—Navajo)

Bunting, Eve. *Smoky Night*, 200 (P/M) (African American)

Havill, Juanita. *Jamaica Tag-Along*, 630 (P) (African American)

Jones, Rebecca C. *Matthew and Tilly*, 766 (P) (African American)

Pinkney, Gloria Jean. *Back Home*, 1175 (P/M) (African American)

## Behavior—gossip

Compton, Patricia A., reteller. *The Terrible EEK: A Japanese Tale*, 304 (M) (Asian—Japan)

## Behavior—greed

Aardema, Verna, reteller. *Sebgugugu the Glutton: A Bantu Tale from Rwanda*, 11 (M) (African—Bantu)

Bahous, Sally. *Sitti and the Cats: A Tale of Friendship*, 74 (M) (Middle Eastern—Palestine)

Bang, Molly, adapter. *Tye May and the Magic Brush*, 86 (M) (Asian—China)

Demi. *Liang and the Magic Paintbrush*, 355 (M) (Asian—China)

*The Magic Tapestry: A Chinese Folktale*, 357 (M) (Asian—China)

*Under the Shade of the Mulberry Tree*, 359 (M) (Asian—China)

Easmon, Carol. *Bisi and the Golden Disc*, 388 (M) (African)

Galdone, Paul. *The Turtle and the Monkey: A Philippine Tale*, 455 (M) (Philippine)

Gerson, Mary-Joan, reteller. *Why the Sky Is Far Away: A Nigerian Folktale*, 473 (M) (African—Nigeria)

Goble, Paul. *Adopted by the Eagles: A Plains Indian Story of Friendship and Treachery*, 484 (M) (Native American—Plains Indians)

Han, Oki S., adapter. *Sir Whong and the Golden Pig*, 600 (M) (Asian—Korea)

Ishii, Momoko, reteller. *The Tongue-cut Sparrow*, 718 (M) (Asian—Japan)

Kurtz, Jane. *Fire on the Mountain*, 833 (M) (African—Ethiopia)

McDermott, Gerald, adapter. *The Stonecutter: A Japanese Folktale*, 939 (M) (Asian—Japan)

Mollel, Tololwa M., reteller. *The Flying Tortoise: An Igbo Tale*, 1036 (M) (African—Igbo)

Newton, Pam, reteller. *The Stonecutter: An Indian Folktale*, 1101 (M) (Asian—India)

Picó, Fernando. *The Red Comb*, 1171 (M) (Caribbean—Puerto Rico)

Reasoner, Charles, reteller. *The Magic Amber: A Korean Legend*, 1211 (M) (Asian—Korea)

Rhee, Nami, reteller. *Magic Spring: A Korean Folktale*, 1216 (M) (Asian—Korea)

Richard, Françoise. *On Cat Mountain*, 1217 (M) (Asian—Japan)

Rohmer, Harriet, Octavio Chow, and Morris Vidaure. *The Invisible Hunters/Los Cazadores Invisibles: A Legend from the Miskito Indians of Nicaragua / Una Leyenda de los Indios Miskitos de Nicaragua*, 1239 (M) (Central American—Nicaragua)

San Souci, Robert D., reteller. *The Enchanted Tapestry: A Chinese Folktale*, 1272 (M) (Asian—China)

Sloat, Teri, reteller. *The Eye of the Needle: Based on a Yupik Tale as Told by Betty Huffman*, 1333 (M) (Native American—Yupik)

Uchida, Yoshiko. *The Two Foolish Cats: Suggested by a Japanese Folktale*, 1483 (M) (Asian—Japan)

Wang, Rosalind C., adapter. *The Magical Starfruit Tree: A Chinese Folktale*, 1521 (M) (Asian—China)

Watson, Pete. *The Market Lady and the Mango Tree*, 1529 (M) (African)

Yep, Laurence. *The Boy Who Swallowed Snakes*, 1603 (M) (Asian—China)

## Behavior—growing up

Bolognese, Don. *Little Hawk's New Name*, 147 (P) (Native American)

Bosse, Malcolm. *Deep Dream of the Rain Forest*, 150 (U) (African—Iban)

## Behavior—growing up (cont.)

O'Dell, Scott. *The Black Pearl*, 1114 (U) (Mexican)

Paterson, Katherine. *Park's Quest*, 1151 (U) (Asian American—Vietnam)

Pettit, Jayne. *My Name Is San Ho*, 1167 (U) (Asian American—Vietnam)

Say, Allen. *The Ink-Keeper's Apprentice*, 1284 (U) (Asian—Japan)

Shefelman, Janice. *A Mare for Young Wolf*, 1310 (P) (Native American)

Uchida, Yoshiko. *The Happiest Ending*, 1473 (U) (Asian American—Japan)
*In-Between Miya*, 1474 (M) (Asian—Japan)

Voigt, Cynthia. *Come a Stranger*, 1496 (U) (African American)

Walter, Mildred Pitts. *Justin and the Best Biscuits in the World*, 1511 (M/U) (African American)

Wilkinson, Brenda. *Definitely Cool*, 1546 (U) (African American)

Wilson, Johnniece Marshall. *Oh, Brother*, 1564 (M) (African American)

Wyeth, Sharon Dennis. *The World of Daughter McGuire*, 1588 (U) (Multicultural)

Young, Ronder Thomas. *Learning by Heart*, 1634 (U) (African American)

## Behavior—hiding

Milios, Rita. *Sneaky Pete*, 1020 (PS/P) (African American)

## Behavior—imitation

Johnson, Angela. *Do Like Kyla*, 730 (PS/P) (African American)

Marzollo, Jean. *Pretend You're a Cat*, 984 (PS/P) (Multicultural)

## Behavior—kindness

Climo, Shirley. *The Egyptian Cinderella*, 278 (M) (African—Egypt)

## Behavior—losing things

Appiah, Sonia. *Amoko and Efua Bear*, 61 (P) (African—Ghana)

Havill, Juanita. *Jamaica's Find*, 631 (P) (African American)

Poydar, Nancy. *Busy Bea*, 1196 (P) (African American)

Soto, Gary. *The Skirt*, 1357 (M) (Mexican American)

## Behavior—lost

Goble, Paul. *Dream Wolf*, 489 (M) (Native American—Plains Indians)
*The Girl Who Loved Wild Horses*, 491 (M) (Native American)

Goble, Paul, and Dorothy Goble. *The Friendly Wolf*, 502 (M) (Native American—Plains Indians)

Keats, Ezra Jack, and Pat Cherr. *My Dog Is Lost!*, 789 (P) (Hispanic American—Puerto Rico)

Tsutsui, Yoriko. *Anna in Charge*, 1463 (P) (Asian—Japan)

## Behavior—lying

Bunting, Eve. *A Day's Work*, 196 (P) (Mexican American)

Cameron, Ann. *Julian's Glorious Summer*, 217 (M) (African American)

Stevens, Jan Romero. *Carlos and the Squash Plant/Carlos y la planta de calabaza*, 1382 (P) (Mexican American)

## Behavior—messy

Cummings, Pat. *Clean Your Room, Harvey Moon!*, 323 (PS/P) (African American)

McKissack, Patricia, and Fredrick McKissack. *Messy Bessey*, 956 (P) (African American)

*Messy Bessey's Closet*, 957 (P) (African American)

Ochs, Carol Partridge. *When I'm Alone*, 1112 (P) (African American)

## Behavior—misbehavior

Cohlene, Terri, adapter. *Clamshell Boy: A Makah Legend*, 292 (M) (Native American—Makah)

Flack, Marjorie. *The Story about Ping*, 428 (P) (Asian—China)

Munsch, Robert. *Where is Gah-Ning?*, 1075 (P) (Asian American—China)

Steptoe, John. *Daddy Is a Monster . . . Sometimes*, 1378 (P) (African American)

Wahl, Jan. *Little Eight John*, 1502 (M) (African American)

## Behavior—mistakes

Martin, Rafe. *Foolish Rabbit's Big Mistake*, 982 (M) (Asian—India)

## Behavior—needing someone

Keats, Ezra Jack. *Louie's Search*, 783 (P) (Multicultural)

Say, Allen. *The Lost Lake*, 1285 (M) (Asian American)

## Behavior—running away

Adoff, Arnold. *Where Wild Willie?*, 33 (P) (African American)

Clifton, Lucille. *My Brother Fine with Me*, 275 (P) (African American)

Fox, Paula. *How Many Miles to Babylon? A Novel*, 438 (M) (African American)

Hamilton, Virginia. *The Planet of Junior Brown*, 594 (U) (African American)

Yolen, Jane. *The Girl Who Loved the Wind*, 1622 (M) (Asian)

## Behavior—secrets

Aardema, Verna, reteller. *What's So Funny, Ketu? A Nuer Tale*, 14 (M) (African—Nuer)

Cohen, Barbara. *213 Valentines*, 288 (M) (African American)

Heide, Florence Parry, and Judith Heide Gilliland. *The Day of Ahmed's Secret*, 637 (P/M) (African—Egypt)

## Behavior—seeking better things

Altman, Linda Jacobs. *Amelia's Road*, 46 (M) (Hispanic American)

Castañeda, Omar S. *Among the Volcanoes*, 232 (U) (Central American—Guatemala)

Hamilton, Virginia. *M. C. Higgins the Great*, 590 (U) (African American)

Johnson, Angela. *The Leaving Morning*, 735 (P) (African American)

Johnson, Dolores. *Papa's Stories*, 745 (P) (African American)

Morris, Winifred. *The Future of Yen-Tzu*, 1067 (M) (Asian—China)

Siberell, Anne. *A Journey to Paradise*, 1323 (M) (Asian—India)

Stanek, Muriel. *I Speak English for My Mom*, 1372 (P) (Mexican American)
Walter, Mildred Pitts. *Trouble's Child*, 1516 (U) (African American)
Williams, Vera B. *A Chair for My Mother*, 1554 (P) (Hispanic American)

## Behavior—sharing

DeGross, Monalisa. *Donavan's Word Jar*, 345 (M) (African American)
Havill, Juanita. *Jamaica Tag-Along*, 630 (P) (African American)
Johnson, Angela. *Do Like Kyla*, 730 (PS/P) (African American)
Johnston, Tony. *The Old Lady and the Birds*, 758 (P) (Mexican)
Jordan, June. *New Life: New Room*, 769 (M) (African American)
Keats, Ezra Jack. *Peter's Chair*, 785 (PS/P) (African American)
McKissack, Patricia, and Fredrick McKissack. *Messy Bessey's Closet*, 957 (P) (African American)

## Behavior—shyness

Kline, Suzy. *Song Lee in Room 2B*, 816 (M) (Asian American—Korea)

## Behavior—solitude

Blue, Rose. *A Quiet Place*, 144 (M) (African American)
Greenfield, Eloise. *Daydreamers*, 529 (M/U) (African American)

## Behavior—stealing

Ada, Alma Flor. *The Gold Coin*, 18 (M) (Central American)
Han, Oki S., adapter. *Sir Whong and the Golden Pig*, 600 (M) (Asian—Korea)

## Behavior—trickery

Aardema, Verna, reteller. *Anansi Finds a Fool: An Ashanti Tale*, 1 (M) (African—Ashanti)
    *Bimwili & the Zimwi: A Tale from Zanzibar*, 2 (M) (African—Zanzibar)
    *Borreguita and the Coyote: A Tale from Ayutla, Mexico*, 3 (M) (Mexican)
    *Jackal's Flying Lesson: A Khoikhoi Tale*, 5 (M) (African—Khoikhoi)
    *Oh, Kojo! How Could You! An Ashanti Tale*, 7 (M) (African—Ashanti)
    *Rabbit Makes a Monkey of Lion: A Swahili Tale*, 10 (M) (African—Swahili)
    *Who's in Rabbit's House? A Masai Tale*, 15 (M) (African—Masai)
Alexander, Lloyd. *The Fortune-Tellers*, 40 (P/M) (African—Cameroon)
Anderson, Bernice G., collector. *Trickster Tales from Prairie Lodgefires*, 51 (M) (Native American)
Appiah, Peggy. *Ananse the Spider: Tales from an Ashanti Village*, 60 (M) (African—Ashanti)
Bang, Betsy, translator and adapter. *The Old Woman and the Red Pumpkin: A Bengali Folk Tale*, 80 (M) (Asian—India)
Bang, Molly, adapter. *Wiley and the Hairy Man: Adapted from an American Folktale*, 87 (P) (African American)
Begay, Shonto. *Ma'ii and Cousin Horned Toad: A Traditional Navajo Story*, 108 (M) (Native American—Navajo)
Bernhard, Emery, reteller. *Spotted Eagle & Black Crow: A Lakota Legend*, 122 (M) (Native American—Lakota)

## Behavior—trickery (cont.)

Han, Suzanne Crowder. *The Rabbit's Judgment*, 602 (M) (Asian—Korea)

Harris, Joel Chandler. *Jump Again! More Adventures of Brer Rabbit*, 614 (M/U) (African American)

*Jump on Over! The Adventures of Brer Rabbit and His Family*, 615 (M/U) (African American)

Harris, Joel Chandler, and Malcolm Jones. *Jump! The Adventures of Brer Rabbit*, 616 (M/U) (African American)

Hausman, Gerald, reteller. *Coyote Walks on Two Legs: A Book of Navaho Myths and Legends*, 626 (M) (Native American—Navajo)

*How Anansi Obtained the Sky God's Stories: An African Folktale from the Ashanti Tribe*, 671 (M) (African—Ashanti)

Hull, Robert, reteller. *Caribbean Stories*, 699 (M) (Caribbean)

Johnston, Tony, adapter. *The Badger and the Magic Fan: A Japanese Folktale*, 757 (M) (Asian—Japan)

*The Tale of Rabbit and Coyote*, 759 (M) (Native American—Zapotec)

Kimmel, Eric A., reteller. *Anansi and the Moss-Covered Rock*, 802 (M) (African)

*Anansi and the Talking Melon*, 803 (M) (African)

*Anansi Goes Fishing*, 804 (M) (African)

Knutson, Barbara, reteller. *Sungura and Leopard: A Swahili Trickster Tale*, 820 (M) (African—Swahili)

Lester, Julius, reteller. *Further Tales of Uncle Remus: The Misadventures of Brer Rabbit, Brer Fox, Brer Wolf, the Doodang, and All the Other Creatures*, 868 (M/U) (African American)

*The Last Tales of Uncle Remus*, 872 (M) (African American)

*More Tales of Uncle Remus: Further Adventures of Brer Rabbit, His Friends, Enemies, and Others*, 874 (M/U) (African American)

*The Tales of Uncle Remus: The Adventures of Brer Rabbit*, 875 (M/U) (African American)

Lyons, Mary E., reteller. *The Butter Tree: Tales of Bruh Rabbit*, 929 (M) (African American)

McDermott, Gerald, reteller. *Coyote: A Trickster Tale from the American Southwest*, 936 (M) (Native American)

*Raven: A Trickster Tale from the Pacific Northwest*, 938 (M) (Native American)

*Zomo the Rabbit: A Trickster Tale from West Africa*, 941 (M) (African)

McKissack, Patricia. *Flossie and the Fox*, 948 (P) (African American)

*Monkey-Monkey's Trick*, 951 (P) (African)

Makhanlall, David. *Brer Anansi and the Boat Race: A Caribbean Folk Tale*, 969 (M) (Caribbean)

Martin, Fran, reteller. *Raven-Who-Sets-Things-Right: Indian Tales of the Northwest Coast*, 979 (M) (Native American—Northwest Coast)

Mayo, Gretchen Will, reteller. *Big Trouble for Tricky Rabbit!*, 994 (M) (Native American)

*Here Comes Tricky Rabbit!*, 995 (M) (Native American)

*Meet Tricky Coyote!*, 996 (M) (Native American)

*That Tricky Coyote!*, 998 (M) (Native American)

Mike, Jan M., adapter. *Opossum and the Great Firemaker: A Mexican Legend*, 1016 (M) (Mexican)

Mollel, Tololwa M. *The King and the Tortoise*, 1037 (M) (African—Cameroon)

## Behavior—trickery (cont.)

Mora, Francisco X. *The Tiger and the Rabbit: A Puerto Rican Folktale*, 1054 (M) (Caribbean—Puerto Rico)

Morgan, Pierr, reteller. *Supper for Crow: A Northwest Coast Indian Tale*, 1057 (M) (Native American—Northwest Coast)

Rees, Ennis. *Brer Rabbit and His Tricks*, 1213 (M) (African American)
  *More of Brer Rabbit's Tricks*, 1214 (M) (African American)

Robinson, Gail, reteller. *Raven the Trickster: Legends of the North American Indians*, 1228 (U) (Native American—Pacific Northwest)

Roth, Susan L. *Kanahéna: A Cherokee Story*, 1251 (M) (Native American—Cherokee)

Sanfield, Steve. *The Adventures of High John the Conqueror*, 1269 (M/U) (African American)

Sherlock, Philip, reteller. *Anansi, the Spider Man: Jamaican Folk Tales*, 1315 (M) (Caribbean—Jamaica)
  *West Indian Folk-Tales*, 1316 (M/U) (Caribbean—West Indies)

Shetterly, Susan Hand, reteller. *Raven's Light: A Myth from the People of the Northwest Coast*, 1319 (M) (Native American)

Snyder, Dianne. *The Boy of the Three-Year Nap*, 1346 (M) (Asian—Japan)

Spagnoli, Cathy, adapter. *Nine-in-One, Grr! Grr! A Folktale from the Hmong People of Laos*, 1360 (M) (Asian—Laos)

Stevens, Janet, reteller. *Coyote Steals the Blanket: An Ute Tale*, 1383 (M) (Native American—Ute)

Temple, Frances, reteller. *Tiger Soup: An Anansi Story from Jamaica*, 1437 (M) (Caribbean—Jamaica)

Troughton, Joanna, reteller. *How Rabbit Stole the Fire: A North American Indian Folk Tale*, 1455 (M) (Native American)
  *Make-Believe Tales: A Folk Tale from Burma*, 1457 (M) (Asian—Burma)
  *Whale's Canoe: A Folk Tale from Australia*, 1459 (M) (Australian)

Turenne des Prés, François. *Children of Yayoute: Folk Tales of Haiti*, 1466 (U) (Caribbean—Haiti)

Vaughan, Marcia. *Kapoc, the Killer Croc*, 1493 (M) (South American—Amazon)

Weiss, Jacqueline Shachter, collector and adapter. *Young Brer Rabbit: And Other Trickster Tales from the Americas*, 1534 (M) (Latin American)

Welsch, Roger. *Uncle Smoke Stories: Nehawka Tales of Coyote the Trickster*, 1537 (M) (Native American)

Yep, Laurence. *The Man Who Tricked a Ghost*, 1611 (M) (Asian—China)

Young, Ed, translator. *Lon Po Po: A Red-Riding Hood Story from China*, 1629 (M) (Asian—China)

## Behavior—wishing

Anderson, Joy. *Juma and the Magic Jinn*, 53 (M) (African)

Brenner, Barbara. *Rosa and Marco and the Three Wishes*, 159 (P) (Hispanic)

Bruchac, Joseph, reteller. *Gluskabe and the Four Wishes*, 172 (M) (Native American—Abenaki)

Caines, Jeannette. *Window Wishing*, 214 (P) (African American)

Demi. *The Stone Cutter*, 358 (M) (Asian—China)

Mollel, Tololwa M. *Big Boy*, 1035 (P) (African)

Newton, Pam, reteller. *The Stonecutter: An Indian Folktale*, 1101 (M) (Asian—India)

Tan, Amy. *Moon Lady*, 1409 (M) (Asian—China)

## Behavior—worrying

Belton, Sandra. *May'naise Sandwiches and Sunshine Tea*, 116 (M) (African American)

Brooks, Bruce. *Everywhere*, 162 (M/U) (African American)

Carlstrom, Nancy White. *Barney Is Best*, 224 (PS/P) (Hispanic American)

Clifton, Lucille. *Amifika*, 265 (P) (African American)

Eisenberg, Phyllis Rose. *You're My Nikki*, 396 (P) (African American)

Greenfield, Eloise. *Talk about a Family*, 545 (M) (African American)

James, Betsy. *The Mud Family*, 724 (M) (Native American—Anasazi)

Stock, Catherine. *Halloween Monster*, 1389 (P) (African American)

Uchida, Yoshiko. *A Jar of Dreams*, 1475 (U) (Asian American—Japan)

   *Journey Home*, 1476 (U) (Asian American—Japan)

Vertreace, Martha M. *Kelly in the Mirror*, 1494 (P) (African American)

Walter, Mildred Pitts. *Two and Too Much*, 1517 (P) (African American)

## Bible

Langstaff, John, editor. *Climbing Jacob's Ladder: Heroes of the Bible in African-American Spirituals*, 839 (P/M) (African American)

## Biography

Altman, Susan, and Susan Lechner. *Followers of the North Star: Rhymes about African American Heroes, Heroines, and Historical Times*, 47 (M/U) (African American)

Cumpián, Carlos. *Latino Rainbow: Poems about Latino Americans*, 325 (M/U) (Hispanic American)

Greenfield, Eloise, and Lessie Jones Little. *Childtimes: A Three-Generation Memoir*, 548 (M/U) (African American)

Izuki, Steven. *Believers in America: Poems about Americans of Asian and Pacific Islander Descent*, 719 (M/U) (Asian American)

Ringgold, Faith. *Dinner at Aunt Connie's House*, 1221 (P/M) (African American)

## Birds

Aardema, Verna, reteller. *Jackal's Flying Lesson: A Khoikhoi Tale*, 5 (M) (African—Khoikhoi)

Arneach, Lloyd, reteller. *The Animals' Ballgame: A Cherokee Story from the Eastern Band*, 68 (M) (Native American—Cherokee)

Bang, Betsy, adapter. *Tuntuni the Tailor Bird: From a Bengali Folktale*, 81 (P) (Asian—India)

Browne, Vee, reteller. *Monster Birds: A Navajo Folktale*, 167 (M) (Native American—Navajo)

Bruchac, Joseph, reteller. *The Great Ball Game: A Muskogee Story*, 173 (M) (Native American—Muskogee)

Ehlert, Lois. *Feathers for Lunch*, 393 (PS/P) (African American)

Keller, Holly. *Grandfather's Dream*, 791 (P) (Asian—Vietnam)

Laurin, Anne. *Perfect Crane*, 850 (M) (Asian—Japan)

Matsutani, Miyoko. *The Crane Maiden*, 988 (M) (Asian—Japan)

Vaughan, Marcia. *Dorobó the Dangerous*, 1492 (M) (Asian—Japan)

Yagawa, Sumiko, reteller. *The Crane Wife*, 1590 (M) (Asian—Japan)

## Birds—crows

Coleman, Evelyn. *The Foot Warmer and the Crow*, 298 (M) (African American)

Goble, Paul, reteller. *Crow Chief: A Plains Indian Story*, 487 (M) (Native American—Plains Indians)

McDermott, Gerald, reteller. *Coyote: A Trickster Tale from the American Southwest*, 936 (M) (Native American)

Morgan, Pierr, reteller. *Supper for Crow: A Northwest Coast Indian Tale*, 1057 (M) (Native American—Northwest Coast)

Rosen, Michael, reteller. *Crow and Hawk: A Traditional Pueblo Indian Story*, 1244 (M) (Native American—Pueblo)

Van Laan, Nancy, reteller. *Rainbow Crow: A Lenape Tale*, 1490 (M) (Native American—Lenape)

## Birds—doves

Stewart, Dianne. *The Dove*, 1385 (P) (African—South Africa)

## Birds—ducks

Berends, Polly Berrien. *The Case of the Elevator Duck*, 118 (M) (African American)

Flack, Marjorie. *The Story about Ping*, 428 (P) (Asian—China)

Garland, Sherry. *Why Ducks Sleep on One Leg*, 459 (M) (Asian—Vietnam)

Paterson, Katherine. *The Tale of the Mandarin Ducks*, 1152 (M) (Asian—Japan)

## Birds—eagles

Allen, Judy. *Eagle*, 43 (P) (Philippine)

Bernhard, Emery, reteller. *Spotted Eagle & Black Crow: A Lakota Legend*, 122 (M) (Native American—Lakota)

Goble, Paul. *Adopted by the Eagles: A Plains Indian Story of Friendship and Treachery*, 484 (M) (Native American—Plains Indians)

Lester, Julius, reteller. *The Man Who Knew Too Much: A Moral Tale from the Baila of Zambia*, 873 (M) (African—Zambia)

## Birds—flamingos

Keller, Holly. *Island Baby*, 792 (P) (Caribbean)

## Birds—geese

Johnson, Ryerson. *Kenji and the Magic Geese*, 756 (M) (Asian—Japan)

## Birds—guinea fowl

Knutson, Barbara, reteller. *How the Guinea Fowl Got Her Spots: A Swahili Tale of Friendship*, 819 (M) (African—Swahili)

## Birds—hawks

Baylor, Byrd. *Hawk, I Am Your Brother*, 102 (P/M) (Native American)

Rosen, Michael, reteller. *Crow and Hawk: A Traditional Pueblo Indian Story*, 1244 (M) (Native American—Pueblo)

## Birds—hummingbirds

Czernecki, Stefan, and Timothy Rhodes. *The Hummingbirds' Gift*, 329 (M) (Mexican)

Palacios, Argentina, adapter. *The Hummingbird King: A Guatemalan Legend*, 1148 (M) (Central American—Guatemala—Mayan)

## Birds—larks

Czernecki, Stefan, and Timothy Rhodes. *The Singing Snake*, 330 (M) (Australian—Aborigine)

## Birds—nightingales

Andersen, Hans Christian. *The Nightingale*, 50 (M) (Asian—China)

Bedard, Michael, reteller. *The Nightingale*, 107 (M) (Asian—China)

So, Meilo, reteller. *The Emperor and the Nightingale*, 1347 (M) (Asian—China)

## Birds—owls

Edmiston, Jim. *Little Eagle Lots of Owls*, 391 (M) (Native American)

Gates, Frieda. *Owl Eyes*, 461 (M) (Native American—Kanienkehaka [Mohawk])

## Birds—parrots

Hamsa, Bobbie. *Polly Wants a Cracker*, 599 (P) (African American)

Mora, Francisco X. *The Legend of the Two Moons*, 1053 (M) (Mexican)

## Birds—quetzals

Palacios, Argentina, adapter. *The Hummingbird King: A Guatemalan Legend*, 1148 (M) (Central American—Guatemala—Mayan)

## Birds—ravens

Dixon, Ann, reteller. *How Raven Brought Light to People*, 370 (M) (Native American—Tlingit)

McDermott, Gerald, reteller. *Raven: A Trickster Tale from the Pacific Northwest*, 938 (M) (Native American)

Martin, Fran, reteller. *Raven-Who-Sets-Things-Right: Indian Tales of the Northwest Coast*, 979 (M) (Native American—Northwest Coast)

Morgan, Pierr, reteller. *Supper for Crow: A Northwest Coast Indian Tale*, 1057 (M) (Native American—Northwest Coast)

Robinson, Gail, reteller. *Raven the Trickster: Legends of the North American Indians*, 1228 (U) (Native American—Pacific Northwest)

Shetterly, Susan Hand, reteller. *Raven's Light: A Myth from the People of the Northwest Coast*, 1319 (M) (Native American)

## Birds—robins

Johnson, Angela. *Mama Bird, Baby Birds*, 736 (PS) (African American)

## Birds—roosters

Ada, Alma Flor, reteller. *The Rooster Who Went to His Uncle's Wedding: A Latin American Folktale*, 20 (M) (Latin American)

González, Lucía M., reteller. *The Bossy Gallito/El Gallo de Bodas: A Traditional Cuban Folktale*, 509 (M) (Caribbean—Cuba)

Uchida, Yoshiko. *The Rooster Who Understood Japanese*, 1480 (P) (Asian American—Japan)

## Birds—sparrows

Fregosi, Claudia. *The Pumpkin Sparrow: Adapted from a Korean Folktale*, 447 (M) (Asian—Korea)

Ishii, Momoko, reteller. *The Tongue-cut Sparrow*, 718 (M) (Asian—Japan)

Jaffe, Nina, reteller. *Older Brother, Younger Brother: A Korean Folktale*, 722 (M) (Asian—Korea)

Newton, Patricia Montgomery, adapter. *The Five Sparrows: A Japanese Folktale*, 1102 (M) (Asian—Japan)

Torres, Leyla. *Subway Sparrow*, 1450 (P) (Multicultural)

## Birds—storks

Hort, Lenny, reteller. *The Tale of the Caliph Stork*, 668 (M) (Middle Eastern—Iraq)

## Birds—swallows

Politi, Leo. *Song of the Swallows*, 1183 (M) (Mexican American)

## Birds—swans

Clément, Claude. *The Painter and the Wild Swans*, 263 (M) (Asian—Japan)

## Birds—turkeys

Rucki, Ani. *Turkey's Gift to the People*, 1255 (M) (Native American—Navajo)

## Birds—wood-hoopoes

Kroll, Virginia. *Wood-hoopoe Willie*, 830 (P) (African American)

## Birth

Fox, Mem. *Sophie*, 437 (P) (African American)

## Birthdays

Ancona, George. *The Piñata Maker/El Piñatero*, 48 (M) (Mexican)

Bunting, Eve. *Flower Garden*, 197 (PS/P) (African American)

Cameron, Ann. *Julian, Dream Doctor*, 215 (M) (African American)

Clifton, Lucille. *Don't You Remember?*, 267 (P) (African American)

Cooke, Trish. *So Much*, 307 (P) (African American)

Cummings, Pat. *Carousel*, 322 (P) (African American)

Frankel, Julie E. *Oh No, Otis*, 440 (PS/P) (African American)

Gordon, Ginger. *My Two Worlds*, 510 (P) (Hispanic American)

Keats, Ezra Jack. *A Letter to Amy*, 781 (P) (African American)

## Birthdays (cont.)

Ketteman, Helen. *Not Yet, Yvette*, 799 (PS/P) (African American)

Lexau, Joan M. *Striped Ice Cream*, 892 (M) (African American)

Little, Lessie Jones, and Eloise Greenfield. *I Can Do It by Myself*, 901 (PS/P) (African American)

Mora, Pat. *A Birthday Basket for Tía*, 1055 (P) (Mexican American)

  *Pablo's Tree*, 1056 (P) (Mexican American)

Myers, Laurie. *Garage Sale Fever*, 1080 (M) (African American)

Parkison, Jami. *Pequeña the Burro*, 1150 (M) (Mexican)

Porter, Connie. *Happy Birthday, Addy: A Springtime Story*, 1193 (M) (African American)

Steptoe, John. *Birthday*, 1377 (P) (African)

Stolz, Mary. *Coco Grimes*, 1393 (M) (African American)

Uchida, Yoshiko. *The Birthday Visitor*, 1471 (P) (Asian American—Japan)

Walter, Mildred Pitts. *Have a Happy . . .* , 1510 (M) (African American)

  *Lillie of Watts: A Birthday Discovery*, 1512 (M) (Native American)

Williams, Vera B. *Something Special for Me*, 1559 (P) (Hispanic American)

## Boats, ships

Demi. *The Magic Boat*, 356 (M) (Asian—China)

Flack, Marjorie. *The Story about Ping*, 428 (P) (Asian—China)

Graham, Lorenz. *Song of the Boat*, 513 (M) (African—West Africa)

Levinson, Riki. *Our Home Is the Sea*, 877 (P) (Asian—Hong Kong)

Tagore, Rabindranath. *Paper Boats*, 1406 (P) (Multicultural)

## Bridges, Ruby

Coles, Robert. *The Story of Ruby Bridges*, 299 (M) (African American)

## Caldecott Award

Aardema, Verna, reteller. *Why Mosquitoes Buzz in People's Ears: A West African Tale*, 16 (M) (African—West Africa)

Andersen, Hans Christian. *The Nightingale*, 50 (M) (Asian—China)

Baker, Olaf. *Where the Buffaloes Begin*, 77 (M) (Native American —Plains Indians)

Bang, Molly. *The Grey Lady and the Strawberry Snatcher*, 82 (P) (African American)

  *Ten, Nine, Eight*, 85 (PS/P) (African American)

Baylor, Byrd. *The Desert Is Theirs*, 101 (M) (Native American—Papago)

  *Hawk, I Am Your Brother*, 102 (P/M) (Native American)

  *When Clay Sings*, 105 (P/M) (Native American)

Belting, Natalia. *The Sun Is a Golden Earring*, 113 (M) (Multicultural)

Brown, Marcia, reteller. *Once a Mouse: A Fable Cut in Wood*, 166 (P/M) (Asian—India)

Bunting, Eve. *Smoky Night*, 200 (P/M) (African American)

Cendrars, Blaise, and Marcia Brown, translator. *Shadow*, 235 (P) (African)

Clark, Ann Nolan. *In My Mother's House*, 259 (P) (Native American)

Dayrell, Elphinstone. *Why the Sun and the Moon Live in the Sky: An African Folktale*, 339 (M) (African)

Ets, Marie Hall, and Aurora Labastida. *Nine Days to Christmas*, 408 (P) (Mexican)

Feelings, Muriel. *Jambo Means Hello: Swahili Alphabet Book*, 413 (P/M) (African)

   *Moja Means One: Swahili Counting Book*, 414 (P/M) (African)

Fleming, Denise. *In the Small, Small Pond*, 430 (PS) (Asian heritage)

Goble, Paul. *The Girl Who Loved Wild Horses*, 491 (M) (Native American)

Grifalconi, Ann. *The Village of Round and Square Houses*, 558 (M) (African)

Haley, Gail E., reteller. *A Story, a Story*, 574 (M) (African)

Handforth, Thomas. *Mei Li*, 603 (P) (Asian—China)

Hodges, Margaret. *The Wave*, 657 (M) (Asian—Japan)

Isadora, Rachel. *Ben's Trumpet*, 716 (P) (African American)

Keats, Ezra Jack. *Goggles*, 778 (P) (African American)

   *The Snowy Day*, 786 (PS/P) (African American)

Lester, Julius. *John Henry*, 870 (M) (African American)

McDermott, Gerald, adapter. *Anansi the Spider: A Tale from the Ashanti*, 934 (P) (African—Ashanti)

   *Arrow to the Sun: A Pueblo Indian Tale*, 935 (P/M) (Native American—Pueblo)

   *Raven: A Trickster Tale from the Pacific Northwest*, 938 (M) (Native American)

McKissack, Patricia. *Mirandy and Brother Wind*, 950 (P) (African American)

Mosel, Arlene, reteller. *The Funny Little Woman*, 1069 (M) (Asian—Japan)

Musgrove, Margaret. *Ashanti to Zulu: African Traditions*, 1077 (M) (African)

Politi, Leo. *Juanita*, 1182 (M) (Mexican American)

   *Song of the Swallows*, 1183 (M) (Mexican American)

Raschka, Chris. *Yo! Yes?*, 1209 (P/M) (Multicultural)

Ringgold, Faith. *Tar Beach*, 1222 (P/M) (African American)

San Souci, Robert D., reteller. *The Talking Eggs: A Folktale from the American South*, 1281 (M) (African American)

Say, Allen. *Grandfather's Journey*, 1283 (M) (Asian American—Japan)

Sleator, William. *The Angry Moon*, 1331 (M) (Native American –Tlingit)

Snyder, Dianne. *The Boy of the Three-Year Nap*, 1346 (M) (Asian—Japan)

Steptoe, John. *Mufaro's Beautiful Daughters: An African Tale*, 1379 (M) (African)

   *The Story of Jumping Mouse: A Native American Legend*, 1381 (M) (Native American)

Williams, Sherley Anne. *Working Cotton*, 1552 (M) (African American)

Williams, Vera B. *A Chair for My Mother*, 1554 (P) (Hispanic American)

   *"More, More, More" Said the Baby: 3 Love Stories*, 1556 (P) (Multicultural)

Yashima, Taro. *Crow Boy*, 1595 (P) (Asian—Japan)

   *Umbrella*, 1596 (P) (Asian American—Japan)

Yolen, Jane. *The Emperor and the Kite*, 1620 (M) (Asian—China)

Young, Ed, translator. *Lon Po Po: A Red-Riding Hood Story from China*, 1629 (M) (Asian—China)

   *Seven Blind Mice*, 1632 (M) (Asian—India)

## Calendar

Fisher, Leonard Everett. *Calendar Art: Thirteen Days, Weeks, Months, and Years from Around the World*, 424 (M) (Multicultural)

## Camps, camping

Hill, Kirkpatrick. *Winter Camp*, 648 (U) (Native American—Athabascan)

Say, Allen. *The Lost Lake*, 1285 (M) (Asian American)

Spohn, David. *Starry Night*, 1368 (M) (Multicultural)

## Careers

Barber, Barbara E. *Saturday at The New You*, 94 (P) (African American)

Greenberg, Melanie Hope. *Aunt Lilly's Laundromat*, 516 (P) (Caribbean—Haiti)

Hudson, Wade. *I'm Gonna Be!*, 692 (P) (African American)

Merrill, Jean. *The Toothpaste Millionaire*, 1012 (M) (African American)

Miller, Margaret. *Whose Hat?*, 1022 (PS/P) (Multicultural)

Moss, Marissa. *Mel's Diner*, 1072 (P) (African American)

## Careers—artists

Demi. *The Artist and the Architect*, 350 (M) (Asian—China)

Everett, Gwen. *Li'l Sis and Uncle Willie: A Story Based on the Life and Paintings of William H. Johnson*, 410 (M) (African American)

Havill, Juanita. *Sato and the Elephants*, 632 (M) (Asian—Japan)

Leaf, Margaret. *Eyes of the Dragon*, 855 (M) (Asian—China)

Littlechild, George. *This Land Is My Land*, 902 (M) (Native American)

Moss, Marissa. *Regina's Big Mistake*, 1073 (P) (African American)

Rosen, Michael. *Elijah's Angel: A Story for Chanukah and Christmas*, 1245 (M) (Multicultural)

Say, Allen. *The Ink-Keeper's Apprentice*, 1284 (U) (Asian—Japan)

Stolz, Mary. *Zekmet, the Stone Carver: A Tale of Ancient Egypt*, 1397 (M) (African—Egypt)

Yacowitz, Caryn, adapter. *The Jade Stone: A Chinese Folktale*, 1589 (M) (Asian—China)

## Careers—astronauts

Barnes, Joyce Annette. *The Baby Grand, the Moon in July, & Me*, 95 (U) (African American)

## Careers—bakers

Heath, Amy. *Sofie's Role*, 636 (P) (African American)

## Careers—barbers

Battle-Lavert, Gwendolyn. *The Barber's Cutting Edge*, 98 (P) (African American)

Mitchell, Margaret King. *Uncle Jed's Barbershop*, 1028 (P/M) (African American)

## Careers—carpenters
Baker, Keith. *The Magic Fan*, 76 (M) (Asian—Japan)

## Careers—factory work
Ackerman, Karen. *By the Dawn's Early Light*, 17 (P) (African American)

## Careers—fishermen
Orr, Katherine. *My Grandpa and the Sea*, 1135 (M) (Caribbean)

## Careers—fortune tellers
Alexander, Lloyd. *The Fortune-Tellers*, 40 (P/M) (African—Cameroon)

## Careers—housekeepers
Spurr, Elizabeth. *Lupe and Me*, 1370 (M) (Mexican American)

## Careers—judges
Edmonds, I. G. *Ooka the Wise: Tales of Old Japan*, 392 (U) (Asian—Japan)

## Careers—miners
Isadora, Rachel. *At the Crossroads*, 715 (P) (African—South Africa)

## Careers—musicians
Isadora, Rachel. *Ben's Trumpet*, 716 (P) (African American)
Raschka, Chris. *Charlie Parker Played Be Bop*, 1208 (P) (African American)

## Careers—shepherds
Franklin, Kristine L. *The Shepherd Boy*, 442 (P) (Native American—Navajo)
Kurtz, Jane. *Fire on the Mountain*, 833 (M) (African—Ethiopia)

## Careers—storekeepers
Schotter, Roni. *A Fruit and Vegetable Man*, 1293 (P) (Asian American)
Shelby, Anne. *We Keep a Store*, 1312 (P) (African American)

## Celebrations
Ancona, George. *Powwow*, 49 (M) (Native American)
Bonnici, Peter. *The Festival*, 148 (P) (Asian—India)
Burden-Patmon, Denise. *Imani's Gift at Kwanzaa*, 205 (P) (African American)
Dorros, Arthur. *Tonight Is Carnaval*, 379 (P/M) (South American—Peru)
George, Jean Craighead. *The First Thanksgiving*, 462 (P) (Native American)
Gollub, Matthew. *The Moon Was at a Fiesta*, 506 (P) (Mexican)
Jacobs, Shannon K. *Song of the Giraffe*, 721 (M) (African)
Kessel, Joyce K. *Squanto and the First Thanksgiving*, 797 (P) (Native American—Patuxet)
Pennington, Daniel. *Itse Selu: Cherokee Harvest Festival*, 1162 (M) (Native American—Cherokee)
Saint James, Synthia. *The Gifts of Kwanzaa*, 1264 (P) (African American)

## Celebrations (cont.)
Shelby, Anne. *Potluck*, 1311 (P) (Multicultural)

## Character traits—ambition
Clark, Ann Nolan. *Secret of the Andes*, 261 (U) (South American—Peru)

Uchida, Yoshiko. *Sumi's Prize*, 1482 (M) (Asian—Japan)

## Character traits—appearance
Brown, Marcia. *The Blue Jackal*, 165 (M) (Asian—India)

Cisneros, Sandra. *Hairs/Pelitos*, 258 (P) (Hispanic American)

Cohlene, Terri, adapter. *Little Firefly: An Algonquian Legend*, 295 (M) (Native American—Algonquian)

Cote, Nancy. *Palm Trees*, 311 (P) (African American)

DeVeaux, Alexis. *An Enchanted Hair Tale*, 366 (M) (African American)

Ginsburg, Mirra, adapter. *The Chinese Mirror: Adapted from a Korean Folktale*, 476 (M) (Asian—Korea)

Hamanaka, Sheila. *All the Colors of the Earth*, 579 (PS/P) (Multicultural)

Kimmel, Eric A., adapter. *The Witch's Face: A Mexican Tale*, 808 (M) (Mexican)

McDermott, Gerald, adapter. *The Magic Tree: A Tale from the Congo*, 937 (M) (African—Zaire)

Maddern, Eric, reteller. *The Fire Children: A West African Creation Tale*, 961 (M) (African)

Mandelbaum, Pili. *You Be Me, I'll Be You*, 970 (P) (Multicultural)

Martin, Rafe. *The Rough-Face Girl*, 983 (M) (Native American—Algonquian)

Mollel, Tololwa M., reteller. *The Princess Who Lost Her Hair: An Akamba Legend*, 1039 (M) (African—Akamba)

San Souci, Robert D., adapter. *The Legend of Scarface: A Blackfeet Indian Tale*, 1274 (M) (Native American—Blackfoot)

*Sootface: An Ojibwa Cinderella Story*, 1279 (M) (Native American—Ojibway)

Schroeder, Alan. *Lily and the Wooden Bowl*, 1294 (M) (Asian—Japan)

Spier, Peter. *People*, 1363 (P/M) (Multicultural)

Wilson, Johnniece Marshall. *Poor Girl, Rich Girl*, 1565 (U) (African American)

Yarborough, Camille. *Cornrows*, 1591 (M) (African American)

Yep, Laurence. *Sea Glass*, 1613 (U) (Asian American—China)

Zubizarreta, Rosalma, Harriet Rohmer, and David Schecter. *The Woman Who Outshone the Sun: The Legend of Lucia Zenteno*, 1637 (M) (Mexican—Zapotec)

## Character traits—bravery
Andrews, Jan. *Very Last First Time*, 56 (P/M) (Native American—Inuit)

Armstrong, Jennifer. *Steal Away*, 65 (U) (African American)

Bang, Betsy, adapter. *Cucumber Stem: From a Bengali Folktale*, 79 (P) (Asian—India)

Bernhard, Emery, reteller. *The Girl Who Wanted to Hunt: A Siberian Tale*, 120 (M) (Asian—Siberia)

*Spotted Eagle & Black Crow: A Lakota Legend*, 122 (M) (Native American—Lakota)

Bierhorst, John. *The Fire Plume: Legends of the American Indians*, 131 (M) (Native American)

Brenner, Barbara. *Little One Inch*, 158 (M) (Asian—Japan)

Brill, Marlene Targ. *Allen Jay and the Underground Railroad*, 161 (M) (African American)

Bruchac, Joseph. *A Boy Called Slow: The True Story of Sitting Bull*, 168 (M) (Native American—Lakota Sioux)

Burchard, Peter. *Bimby*, 202 (M/U) (African American)

*Chinwe*, 203 (M/U) (African American)

Chin, Charlie, reteller. *China's Bravest Girl: The Legend of Hua Mu Lan*, 245 (M) (Asian—China)

Chocolate, Deborah M. Newton. *Imani in the Belly*, 248 (M) (African)

Choi, Sook Nyul. *Echoes of the White Giraffe*, 253 (U) (Asian—Korea)

*Year of Impossible Goodbyes*, 256 (U) (Asian—Korea)

Coerr, Eleanor. *Sadako*, 284 (M/U) (Asian—Japan)

*Sadako and the Thousand Paper Cranes*, 285 (M/U) (Asian - Japan)

Cohlene, Terri, adapter. *Clamshell Boy: A Makah Legend*, 292 (M) (Native American—Makah)

*Ka-ha-si and the Loon: An Eskimo Legend*, 294 (M) (Native American—Eskimo)

Collier, James Lincoln, and Christopher Collier. *Jump Ship to Freedom*, 300 (U) (African American)

*War Comes to Willy Freeman*, 301 (U) (African American)

DeJong, Meindert. *The House of Sixty Fathers*, 346 (M) (Asian—China)

Demi. *The Magic Tapestry: A Chinese Folktale*, 357 (M) (Asian—China)

Duff, Maggie, reteller. *Rum Pum Pum: A Folk Tale from India*, 384 (M) (Asian—India)

Fox, Paula. *The Slave Dancer: A Novel*, 439 (U) (African American)

French, Fiona. *Little Inchkin*, 449 (M) (Asian—Japan)

Goble, Paul. *Buffalo Woman*, 486 (M) (Native American—Plains Indians)

*The Gift of the Sacred Dog*, 490 (M) (Native American—Plains Indians)

Greenfield, Eloise. *Night on Neighborhood Street*, 541 (M) (African American)

Hearn, Lafcadio. *The Voice of the Great Bell*, 635 (M) (Asian—China)

Hest, Amy. *Ruby's Storm*, 640 (P) (Hispanic American)

Heyer, Marilee, reteller. *The Weaving of a Dream: A Chinese Folktale*, 642 (M) (Asian—China)

Highwater, Jamake. *Anpao: An American Indian Odyssey*, 643 (U) (Native American)

Hooks, William H. *The Ballad of Belle Dorcas*, 663 (M) (African American)

*Peach Boy*, 665 (P) (Asian—Japan)

Hughes, Monica, reteller. *Little Fingerling*, 697 (M) (Asian—Japan)

Kesey, Ken. *The Sea Lion: A Story of the Sea Cliff People*, 796 (M) (Native American—Northwest Coast)

Kudlinski, Kathleen V. *Night Bird: A Story of the Seminole Indians*, 832 (M) (Native American—Seminole)

Lattimore, Deborah Nourse. *The Flame of Peace: A Tale of the Aztecs*, 846 (M) (Mexican—Aztec)

## Character traits—bravery (cont.)

Little, Lessie Jones, and Eloise Greenfield. *I Can Do It by Myself*, 901 (PS/P) (African American)

Luenn, Nancy. *Nessa's Fish*, 921 (P) (Native American—Inuit)

Lyons, Mary E. *Letters from a Slave Girl: The Story of Harriet Jacobs*, 930 (U) (African American)

McDermott, Gerald, adapter. *Arrow to the Sun: A Pueblo Indian Tale*, 935 (P/M) (Native American—Pueblo)

Mann, Kenny. *"I Am Not Afraid!": Based on a Masai Tale*, 972 (P) (African—Masai)

Martin, Bill, Jr., and John Archambault. *Knots on a Counting Rope*, 978 (P/M) (Native American)

Mayer, Mercer. *Liza Lou and the Yeller Belly Swamp*, 993 (P) (African American)

Morimoto, Junko. *The Inch Boy*, 1059 (M) (Asian—Japan)

Namioka, Lensey. *The Coming of the Bear*, 1092 (U) (Asian—Japan)

  *Island of Ogres*, 1093 (U) (Asian—Japan)

Nunes, Susan. *To Find the Way*, 1108 (M) (Tahitian)

O'Connor, Jane. *Molly the Brave and Me*, 1113 (P) (African American)

O'Dell, Scott. *Black Star, Bright Dawn*, 1115 (U) (Native American—Eskimo)

  *Child of Fire*, 1117 (U) (Mexican American)

O'Dell, Scott, and Elizabeth Hall. *Thunder Rolling in the Mountains*, 1124 (U) (Native American—Nez Perce)

Oliviero, Jamie. *The Fish Skin*, 1126 (M) (Native American)

Polacco, Patricia. *Pink and Say*, 1181 (M) (African American)

Porter, Connie. *Meet Addy: An American Girl*, 1194 (M) (African American)

Ram, Govinder. *Rama and Sita: An Indian Folk Tale*, 1203 (M) (Asian—India)

Rappaport, Doreen, reteller. *The Journey of Meng: A Chinese Legend*, 1205 (M) (Asian—China)

  *The Long-Haired Girl: A Chinese Legend*, 1206 (M) (Asian—China)

Rodanas, Kristina, adapter. *Dance of the Sacred Circle: A Native American Tale*, 1231 (M) (Native American—Blackfoot)

Sakurai, Gail. *Peach Boy: A Japanese Legend*, 1266 (M) (Asian—Japan)

San Souci, Robert D. *The Boy and the Ghost*, 1270 (P) (African American)

  *The Enchanted Tapestry: A Chinese Folktale*, 1272 (M) (Asian—China)

  *The Legend of Scarface: A Blackfeet Indian Tale*, 1274 (M) (Native American—Blackfoot)

  *The Samurai's Daughter: A Japanese Legend*, 1275 (M) (Asian—Japan)

  *Sukey and the Mermaid*, 1280 (M) (African American)

Schecter, Ellen, reteller. *Sim Chung and the River Dragon: A Folktale from Korea*, 1289 (P) (Asian—Korea)

  *The Warrior Maiden: A Hopi Legend*, 1290 (P) (Native American—Hopi)

Shetterly, Susan Hand, reteller. *The Dwarf-Wizard of Uxmal*, 1317 (M) (Central American—Mayan)

Shute, Linda, reteller. *Momotaro the Peach Boy: A Traditional Japanese Tale*, 1322 (M) (Asian—Japan)

Sperry, Armstrong. *Call It Courage*, 1362 (U) (Polynesian)

Stock, Catherine. *Armien's Fishing Trip*, 1387 (P) (African—South Africa)

Temple, Frances. *Grab Hands and Run*, 1436 (U) (Central American—El Salvador)

Treviño, Elizabeth Borton de. *El Güero: A True Adventure Story*, 1451 (U) (Mexican)

Troughton, Joanna, reteller. *The Wizard Punchkin: A Folk Tale from India*, 1462 (M) (Asian—India)

Wisniewski, David. *Rain Player*, 1570 (M) (Central American—Mayan)

*The Warrior and the Wise Man*, 1571 (P/M) (Asian—Japan)

*The Wave of the Sea-Wolf*, 1572 (M) (Native American)

Wolkstein, Diane. *The Banza: A Haitian Story*, 1574 (M) (Caribbean—Haiti)

Yeh, Chun-Chun, and Allan Baillie. *Bawshou Rescues the Sun: A Han Folktale*, 1599 (M) (Asian—China)

Young, Ed. *Little Plum*, 1628 (M) (Asian—China)

*Lon Po Po: A Red-Riding Hood Story from China*, 1629 (M) (Asian—China)

## Character traits—cleanliness

Cummings, Pat. *Clean Your Room, Harvey Moon!*, 323 (PS/P) (African American)

McKissack, Patricia, and Fredrick McKissack. *Messy Bessey*, 956 (P) (African American)

*Messy Bessey's Closet*, 957 (P) (African American)

## Character traits—cleverness

Aardema, Verna, reteller. *Princess Gorilla and a New Kind of Water: A Mpongwe Tale*, 9 (M) (African—Mpongwe)

Bang, Betsy, translator and adapter. *The Old Woman and the Red Pumpkin: A Bengali Folk Tale*, 80 (M) (Asian—India)

*Tuntuni the Tailor Bird: From a Bengali Folktale*, 81 (P) (Asian—India)

Bang, Molly, adapter. *Wiley and the Hairy Man: Adapted from an American Folktale*, 87 (P) (African American)

Berry, James. *Spiderman Anancy*, 125 (M) (Caribbean)

Bishop, Claire Huchet. *The Five Chinese Brothers*, 141 (M) (Asian—China)

Dee, Ruby, reteller. *Two Ways to Count to Ten: A Liberian Folktale*, 342 (M) (African—Liberia)

Demi. *The Artist and the Architect*, 350 (M) (Asian—China)

*Under the Shade of the Mulberry Tree*, 359 (M) (Asian—China)

Fourie, Corlia. *Ganekwane and the Green Dragon: Four Stories from Africa*, 436 (M) (African)

Galdone, Paul. *The Monkey and the Crocodile: A Jataka Tale from India*, 454 (M) (Asian—India)

*The Turtle and the Monkey: A Philippine Tale*, 455 (M) (Philippine)

Han, Oki S., adapter. *Sir Whong and the Golden Pig*, 600 (M) (Asian—Korea)

Han, Suzanne Crowder. *The Rabbit's Escape*, 601 (M) (Asian—Korea)

Hort, Lenny, reteller. *The Tale of the Caliph Stork*, 668 (M) (Middle Eastern—Iraq)

Lyons, Mary E., reteller. *The Butter Tree: Tales of Bruh Rabbit*, 929 (M) (African American)

McDermott, Gerald, reteller. *Zomo the Rabbit: A Trickster Tale from West Africa*, 941 (M) (African)

McKissack, Patricia. *Flossie and the Fox*, 948 (P) (African American)

*Mirandy and Brother Wind*, 950 (P) (African American)

## Character traits—cleverness

*Monkey-Monkey's Trick*, 951 (P) (African)

Mahy, Margaret. *The Seven Chinese Brothers*, 965 (M) (Asian—China)

Mayer, Mercer. *Liza Lou and the Yeller Belly Swamp*, 993 (P) (African American)

Mollel, Tololwa M. *The King and the Tortoise*, 1037 (M) (African—Cameroon)

Pattison, Darcy. *The River Dragon*, 1155 (M) (Asian—China)

Picó, Fernando. *The Red Comb*, 1171 (M) (Caribbean—Puerto Rico)

Singh, Jacquelin. *Fat Gopal*, 1328 (M) (Asian—India)

Uchida, Yoshiko, reteller. *The Wise Old Woman*, 1484 (M) (Asian—Japan)

Van Woerkom, Dorothy, adapter. *The Rat, the Ox, and the Zodiac: A Chinese Legend*, 1491 (M) (Asian—China)

Wisniewski, David. *The Warrior and the Wise Man*, 1571 (P/M) (Asian—Japan)

Yep, Laurence, reteller. *The Shell Woman & the King: A Chinese Folktale*, 1615 (M) (Asian—China)

## Character traits—conceit

Bible, Charles, adapter. *Hamdaani: A Traditional Tale from Zanzibar*, 129 (M) (African—Zanzibar)

## Character traits—confidence

Barrett, Joyce Durham. *Willie's Not the Hugging Kind*, 96 (P) (African American)

Soto, Gary. *The Pool Party*, 1356 (M) (Mexican American)

## Character traits—courage

Baillie, Allan. *Rebel*, 75 (P) (Asian—Burma)

## Character traits—curiosity

Ginsburg, Mirra, adapter. *The Chinese Mirror: Adapted from a Korean Folktale*, 476 (M) (Asian—Korea)

MacDonald, Suse. *Nanta's Lion: A Search-and-Find Adventure*, 945 (P) (African—Masai)

Matsutani, Miyoko. *The Crane Maiden*, 988 (M) (Asian—Japan)

Mollel, Tololwa M. *The Orphan Boy: A Masai Story*, 1038 (M) (African—Masai)

Yagawa, Sumiko, reteller. *The Crane Wife*, 1590 (M) (Asian—Japan)

## Character traits—foolishness

Aardema, Verna, reteller. *Anansi Finds a Fool: An Ashanti Tale*, 1 (M) (African—Ashanti)

*The Baboon's Umbrella: An African Folktale*, 71 (M) (African)

Brenner, Barbara. *Rosa and Marco and the Three Wishes*, 159 (P) (Hispanic)

Compton, Patricia A., reteller. *The Terrible EEK: A Japanese Tale*, 304 (M) (Asian—Japan)

Ginsburg, Mirra, adapter. *The Chinese Mirror: Adapted from a Korean Folktale*, 476 (M) (Asian—Korea)

Goble, Paul. *Iktomi and the Berries: A Plains Indian Story*, 494 (M) (Native American—Plains Indians)

*Iktomi and the Buffalo Skull: A Plains Indian Story*, 496 (M) (Native American—Plains Indians)

*Iktomi and the Buzzard: A Plains Indian Story*, 497 (M) (Native American—Plains Indians)

Jameson, Cynthia, reteller. *One for the Price of Two*, 725 (M) (Asian—Japan)

Kimmel, Eric A., reteller. *Anansi and the Talking Melon*, 803 (M) (African)

Lobel, Arnold. *Ming Lo Moves the Mountain*, 907 (P) (Asian)

Martin, Rafe. *Foolish Rabbit's Big Mistake*, 982 (M) (Asian—India)

Mora, Francisco X. *The Tiger and the Rabbit: A Puerto Rican Folktale*, 1054 (M) (Caribbean—Puerto Rico)

Morris, Winifred. *The Magic Leaf*, 1068 (M) (Asian—China)

Pitre, Felix, reteller. *Juan Bobo and the Pig: A Puerto Rican Folktale*, 1177 (M) (Caribbean—Puerto Rico)

Rohmer, Harriet, adapter. *Uncle Nacho's Hat: El Sombrero del Tio Nacho*, 1237 (M) (Central American—Nicaragua)

Tan, Amy. *The Chinese Siamese Cat*, 1408 (M) (Asian—China)

Tanaka, Béatrice, reteller. *The Chase: A Kutenai Indian Tale*, 1410 (P) (Native American—Kutenai)

Turenne des Prés, François. *Children of Yayoute: Folk Tales of Haiti*, 1466 (U) (Caribbean—Haiti)

## Character traits—freedom

Baylor, Byrd. *Hawk, I Am Your Brother*, 102 (P/M) (Native American)

Bunting, Eve. *How Many Days to America? A Thanksgiving Story*, 199 (M) (Caribbean)

Coleman, Evelyn. *The Foot Warmer and the Crow*, 298 (M) (African American)

Collier, James Lincoln, and Christopher Collier. *Jump Ship to Freedom*, 300 (U) (African American)

*War Comes to Willy Freeman*, 301 (U) (African American)

*Who Is Carrie?*, 302 (U) (African American)

Dupré, Rick, reteller. *Agassu: Legend of the Leopard King*, 386 (M) (African)

Forrester, Sandra. *Sound the Jubilee*, 435 (U) (African American)

Fox, Paula. *The Slave Dancer: A Novel*, 439 (U) (African American)

Hoobler, Dorothy, and Thomas Hoobler. *Next Stop, Freedom: The Story of a Slave Girl*, 662 (M) (African American)

Lyons, Mary E. *Letters from a Slave Girl: The Story of Harriet Jacobs*, 930 (U) (African American)

Mike, Jan M., reteller. *Gift of the Nile: An Ancient Egyptian Legend*, 1015 (M) (African—Egypt)

Porter, Connie. *Addy's Surprise: A Christmas Story*, 1191 (M) (African American)

*Changes for Addy: A Winter Story*, 1192 (M) (African American)

*Meet Addy: An American Girl*, 1194 (M) (African American)

Ruby, Lois. *Steal Away Home*, 1254 (U) (African American)

Smucker, Barbara. *Runaway to Freedom: A Story of the Underground Railroad*, 1344 (U) (African American)

Samuels, Vyanne. *Carry Go Bring Come*, 1268 (P) (Caribbean—Jamaica)

Schotter, Roni. *A Fruit and Vegetable Man*, 1293 (P) (Asian American)

Uchida, Yoshiko. *The Best Bad Thing*, 1470 (U) (Asian American—Japan)

*The Happiest Ending*, 1473 (U) (Asian American—Japan)

## Character traits—honesty

Aardema, Verna, reteller. *Pedro and the Padre: A Tale from Jalisco, Mexico*, 8 (M) (Mexican)

Bunting, Eve. *A Day's Work*, 196 (P) (Mexican American)

Demi. *The Empty Pot*, 353 (M) (Asian—China)

Havill, Juanita. *Jamaica's Find*, 631 (P) (African American)

Lattimore, Deborah Nourse. *The Winged Cat: A Tale of Ancient Egypt*, 849 (M) (African—Egypt)

Peters, Julie Anne. *The Stinky Sneakers Contest*, 1164 (M) (African American)

Torre, Betty L., reteller. *The Luminous Pearl: A Chinese Folktale*, 1448 (M) (Asian—China)

Uchida, Yoshiko, reteller. *The Magic Purse*, 1479 (M) (Asian—Japan)

Wade, Gini, reteller. *The Wonderful Bag: An Arabian Tale from The Thousand & One Nights*, 1500 (M) (Middle Eastern—Arabia)

Yep, Laurence. *The Boy Who Swallowed Snakes*, 1603 (M) (Asian—China)

## Character traits—individuality

Guy, Rosa. *Billy the Great*, 570 (P) (African American)

Merrill, Jean, adapter. *The Girl Who Loved Caterpillars: A Twelfth Century Tale from Japan*, 1011 (M) (Asian—Japan)

Williams, Vera B. *Something Special for Me*, 1559 (P) (Hispanic American)

## Character traits—kindness

Bahous, Sally. *Sitti and the Cats: A Tale of Friendship*, 74 (M) (Middle Eastern—Palestine)

Bang, Molly. *The Paper Crane*, 84 (P) (Asian)

Bryan, Ashley. *Sh-ko and His Eight Wicked Brothers*, 187 (M) (Asian—Japan)

Clark, Ann Nolan, reteller. *In the Land of Small Dragon*, 260 (M) (Asian—Vietnam)

Climo, Shirley. *The Korean Cinderella*, 279 (M) (Asian—Korea)

Cohlene, Terri, adapter. *Little Firefly: An Algonquian Legend*, 295 (M) (Native American—Algonquian)

DeArmond, Dale, adapter. *The Seal Oil Lamp: Adapted from an Eskimo Folktale*, 340 (M) (Native American—Eskimo)

Fregosi, Claudia. *The Pumpkin Sparrow: Adapted from a Korean Folktale*, 447 (M) (Asian—Korea)

Gleeson, Brian. *The Tiger and the Brahmin*, 483 (M) (Asian—India)

Guthrie, Donna W. *Nobiah's Well: A Modern African Folktale*, 569 (M) (African)

Hamada, Cheryl, reteller. *The Fourth Question: A Chinese Folktale*, 576 (M) (Asian—China)

*Kao and the Golden Fish: A Folktale from Thailand*, 577 (M) (Asian—Thailand)

*The White Hare of Inaba: A Japanese Folktale*, 578 (M) (Asian—Japan)

Han, Suzanne Crowder. *The Rabbit's Judgment*, 602 (M) (Asian—Korea)

Yep, Laurence. *The Junior Thunder Lord*, 1610 (M) (Asian—China)

Zubizarreta, Rosalma, Harriet Rohmer, and David Schecter. *The Woman Who Outshone the Sun: The Legend of Lucia Zenteno*, 1637 (M) (Mexican—Zapotec)

## Character traits—laziness

Aardema, Verna, reteller. *Oh, Kojo! How Could You! An Ashanti Tale*, 7 (M) (African—Ashanti)

*Pedro and the Padre: A Tale from Jalisco, Mexico*, 8 (M) (Mexican)

Hamanaka, Sheila. *Screen of Frogs: An Old Tale*, 580 (M) (Asian—Japan)

Kimmel, Eric A., reteller. *Anansi and the Moss-Covered Rock*, 802 (M) (African)

*Anansi Goes Fishing*, 804 (M) (African)

Snyder, Dianne. *The Boy of the Three-Year Nap*, 1346 (M) (Asian—Japan)

## Character traits—luck

Clifton, Lucille. *The Lucky Stone*, 274 (M) (African American)

Godden, Rumer. *The Valiant Chatti-Maker*, 503 (M) (Asian—India)

## Character traits—meanness

Say, Allen, reteller. *Once Under the Cherry Blossom Tree: An Old Japanese Tale*, 1286 (M) (Asian—Japan)

Taylor, Mildred D. *The Friendship*, 1424 (M/U) (African American)

## Character traits—ostracism

George, Jean Craighead. *The Talking Earth*, 466 (U) (Native American—Seminole)

## Character traits—patience

Day, Nancy Raines. *The Lion's Whiskers: An Ethiopian Folktale*, 338 (M) (African—Ethiopia)

Ketteman, Helen. *Not Yet, Yvette*, 799 (PS/P) (African American)

## Character traits—perseverance

Cohen, Barbara, and Bahija Lovejoy. *Seven Daughters and Seven Sons*, 289 (U) (Middle Eastern—Arabia)

Coles, Robert. *The Story of Ruby Bridges*, 299 (M) (African American)

Grifalconi, Ann. *The Bravest Flute: A Story of Courage in the Mayan Tradition*, 552 (M) (Central American—Mayan)

Jensen, Patsy. *John Henry and His Mighty Hammer*, 729 (P) (African American)

Keats, Ezra Jack. *John Henry: An American Legend*, 780 (M) (African American)

Lester, Julius. *John Henry*, 870 (M) (African American)

Markun, Patricia Maloney. *The Little Painter of Sabana Grande*, 976 (M) (Central American—Panama)

Robinet, Harriette Gillem. *Ride the Red Cycle*, 1226 (M) (African American)

Small, Terry. *The Legend of John Henry*, 1336 (M) (African American)

Wolkstein, Diane. *The Magic Wings: A Tale from China*, 1576 (M) (Asian—China)

## Character traits—persistence

Hoffman, Mary. *Amazing Grace*, 658 (P) (African American)

Yep, Laurence. *Dragonwings*, 1607 (U) (Asian American—China)

## Character traits—pride

Ada, Alma Flor. *My Name Is María Isabel*, 19 (M) (Hispanic American—Puerto Rico)

Armstrong, Jennifer. *Chin Yu Min and the Ginger Cat*, 64 (P) (Asian—China)

Battle-Lavert, Gwendolyn. *The Barber's Cutting Edge*, 98 (P) (African American)

Brown, Marcia, reteller. *Once a Mouse: A Fable Cut in Wood*, 166 (P/M) (Asian—India)

Cameron, Ann. *The Most Beautiful Place in the World*, 219 (M) (Central American—Guatemala)

Clifton, Lucille. *All Us Come Cross the Water*, 264 (P) (African American)

Ginsburg, Mirra, reteller. *The Proud Maiden, Tungak, and the Sun: A Russian Eskimo Tale*, 477 (M) (Native People—Russian Eskimo)

Giovanni, Nikki. *Ego-Tripping: And Other Poems for Young People*, 478 (U) (African American)

Grifalconi, Ann. *Osa's Pride*, 557 (P) (African)

Heide, Florence Parry, and Judith Heide Gilliland. *The Day of Ahmed's Secret*, 637 (P/M) (African—Egypt)

Hoffman, Mary. *Amazing Grace*, 658 (P) (African American)
    *Boundless Grace*, 659 (P) (African American)

Jacobs, Shannon K. *The Boy Who Loved Morning*, 720 (M) (Native American)

Jensen, Patsy. *John Henry and His Mighty Hammer*, 729 (P) (African American)

Johnson, Dolores. *The Best Bug to Be*, 743 (P) (African American)

Keats, Ezra Jack. *John Henry: An American Legend*, 780 (M) (African American)

Kimmel, Eric A., reteller. *The Greatest of All: A Japanese Folktale*, 805 (M) (Asian—Japan)

Kwon, Holly H., reteller. *The Moles and the Mireuk: A Korean Folktale*, 834 (M) (Asian—Korea)

Lacapa, Kathleen, and Michael Lacapa. *Less Than Half, More Than Whole*, 835 (M) (Multicultural)

Lester, Julius. *John Henry*, 870 (M) (African American)

Medearis, Angela Shelf. *Our People*, 1002 (P) (African American)

Mendez, Phil. *The Black Snowman*, 1008 (P/M) (African American)

Myers, Walter Dean. *Brown Angels: An Album of Pictures and Verse*, 1081 (M) (African American)

Robinet, Harriette Gillem. *Ride the Red Cycle*, 1226 (M) (African American)

Sierra, Judy. *The Elephant's Wrestling Match*, 1325 (M) (African)

Small, Terry. *The Legend of John Henry*, 1336 (M) (African American)

Tate, Eleanora E. *Thank You, Dr. Martin Luther King, Jr.!*, 1415 (M) (African American)

Wong, Janet S. *Good Luck Gold: And Other Poems*, 1577 (M) (Asian American)

Yep, Laurence. *Child of the Owl*, 1605 (U) (Asian American—China)

## Character traits—questioning

Aardema, Verna, reteller. *Sebgugugu the Glutton: A Bantu Tale from Rwanda*, 11 (M) (African—Bantu)

Bess, Clayton. *The Truth about the Moon*, 127 (M) (African)

Hamada, Cheryl, reteller. *The Fourth Question: A Chinese Folktale*, 576 (M) (Asian—China)

Ketteman, Helen. *Not Yet, Yvette*, 799 (PS/P) (African American)

Lyon, George Ella. *Who Came Down That Road?*, 928 (P/M) (Native American)

Wang, Rosalind C., reteller. *The Fourth Question: A Chinese Tale*, 1520 (M) (Asian—China)

## Character traits—selfishness

Lattimore, Deborah Nourse. *The Dragon's Robe*, 845 (M) (Asian—China)

## Character traits—shyness

Keats, Ezra Jack. *Louie*, 782 (P) (Multicultural)

Udry, Janice May. *What Mary Jo Shared*, 1486 (P) (African American)

Yashima, Taro. *Crow Boy*, 1595 (P) (Asian—Japan)

## Character traits—smallness

Bang, Betsy, adapter. *Cucumber Stem: From a Bengali Folktale*, 79 (P) (Asian—India)

Brenner, Barbara. *Little One Inch*, 158 (M) (Asian—Japan)

French, Fiona. *Little Inchkin*, 449 (M) (Asian—Japan)

Hamilton, Virginia. *The All Jahdu Storybook*, 581 (M) (African American)
*Jahdu*, 589 (M) (African American)
*The Time-Ago Tales of Jahdu*, 595 (M) (African American)

Hughes, Monica, reteller. *Little Fingerling*, 697 (M) (Asian—Japan)

Morimoto, Junko. *The Inch Boy*, 1059 (M) (Asian—Japan)

Shetterly, Susan Hand, reteller. *The Dwarf-Wizard of Uxmal*, 1317 (M) (Central American—Mayan)

Shute, Linda, reteller. *Momotaro the Peach Boy: A Traditional Japanese Tale*, 1322 (M) (Asian—Japan)

Yolen, Jane. *The Emperor and the Kite*, 1620 (M) (Asian—China)

Young, Ed. *Little Plum*, 1628 (M) (Asian—China)

## Character traits—stubbornness

Leaf, Margaret. *Eyes of the Dragon*, 855 (M) (Asian—China)

## Character traits—vanity

Sierra, Judy. *The Elephant's Wrestling Match*, 1325 (M) (African)

## Character traits—willfulness

Alexander, Sue. *Nadia the Willful*, 42 (P) (Middle Eastern—Arabia)

Ho, Minfong, and Saphan Ros. *The Two Brothers*, 653 (M) (Asian—Cambodia)

## Character traits—wisdom

Edmonds, I. G. *Ooka the Wise: Tales of Old Japan*, 392 (U) (Asian—Japan)

## Charms

Clifton, Lucille. *The Lucky Stone*, 274 (M) (African American)

## Civil rights

Altman, Susan, and Susan Lechner. *Followers of the North Star: Rhymes about African American Heroes, Heroines, and Historical Times*, 47 (M/U) (African American)

Coles, Robert. *The Story of Ruby Bridges*, 299 (M) (African American)

Davis, Ossie. *Just Like Martin*, 335 (U) (African American)

Moore, Yvette. *Freedom Songs*, 1051 (U) (African American)

## Clothing

French, Fiona. *Anancy and Mr. Dry-Bone*, 448 (M) (African)

Lattimore, Deborah Nourse. *The Dragon's Robe*, 845 (M) (Asian—China)

Lloyd, Errol. *Nini at Carnival*, 906 (P) (Mexican)

McKissack, Patricia. *Nettie Jo's Friends*, 952 (P) (African American)

Moore, Dessie. *Getting Dressed*, 1044 (PS) (African American)

Soto, Gary. *The Skirt*, 1357 (M) (Mexican American)

## Clothing—boots

Havill, Juanita. *Jamaica and Brianna*, 629 (P) (African American)

## Clothing—buttons

Freeman, Don. *Corduroy*, 445 (PS/P) (African American)

## Clothing—hats

Howard, Elizabeth Fitzgerald. *Aunt Flossie's Hats (and Crab Cakes Later)*, 672 (P) (African American)

Miller, Margaret. *Whose Hat?*, 1022 (PS/P) (Multicultural)

Morris, Ann. *Hats, Hats, Hats*, 1062 (PS/P) (Multicultural)

Polacco, Patricia. *Chicken Sunday*, 1179 (M) (African American)

Reed, Lynn Rowe. *Pedro, His Perro, and the Alphabet Sombrero*, 1212 (P) (Hispanic)

Rohmer, Harriet, adapter. *Uncle Nacho's Hat: El Sombrero del Tio Nacho*, 1237 (M) (Central American—Nicaragua)

Weir, LaVada. *Howdy!*, 1531 (P) (African American)

## Clothing—pants

Medearis, Angela Shelf. *Poppa's New Pants*, 1003 (P) (African American)

## Clothing—pockets

Freeman, Don. *A Pocket for Corduroy*, 446 (PS/P) (African American)

## Clothing—shoes

Burton, Marilee Robin. *My Best Shoes*, 207 (PS/P) (Multicultural)

Colman, Warren. *Double Dutch and the Voodoo Shoes: A Modern African-American Urban Tale*, 303 (M) (African American)

Daly, Niki. *Not So Fast Songololo*, 332 (P) (African—South Africa)

Hurwitz, Johanna. *New Shoes for Silvia*, 707 (P) (Latin American)

Johnson, Angela. *Shoes like Miss Alice's*, 739 (P) (African American)

Lum, Darrell, reteller. *The Golden Slipper: A Vietnamese Legend*, 923 (M) (Asian—Vietnam)

Miller, Margaret. *Whose Shoe?*, 1023 (PS/P) (Multicultural)

Patrick, Denise Lewis. *Red Dancing Shoes*, 1154 (P) (African American)

Peters, Julie Anne. *The Stinky Sneakers Contest*, 1164 (M) (African American)

Vuong, Lynette Dyer. *The Brocaded Slipper: And Other Vietnamese Tales*, 1497 (M) (Asian—Vietnam)

Wheeler, Bernelda. *Where Did You Get Your Moccasins?*, 1538 (P) (Native American)

## Columbus, Christopher

Yolen, Jane. *Encounter*, 1621 (M) (Native American—Taino)

## Communities, neighborhoods

Angelou, Maya. *My Painted House, My Friendly Chicken, and Me*, 57 (M) (African—South Africa)

Begaye, Lisa Shook. *Building a Bridge*, 110 (P) (Native American—Navajo)

Bunting, Eve. *Smoky Night*, 200 (P/M) (African American)

Clifton, Lucille. *The Boy Who Didn't Believe in Spring*, 266 (P) (African American)

Cowen-Fletcher, Jane. *It Takes a Village*, 315 (P) (African—Benin)

Crews, Nina. *One Hot Summer Day*, 321 (PS/P) (African American)

Davis, Deborah. *The Secret of the Seal*, 334 (M) (Native American—Inuit)

DiSalvo-Ryan, Dyanne. *City Green*, 369 (P) (African American)

Franklin, Kristine L. *The Old, Old Man and the Very Little Boy*, 441 (P) (African)

Giovanni, Nikki. *Spin a Soft Black Song: Poems for Children*, 480 (M/U) (African American)

Gray, Nigel. *A Country Far Away*, 515 (P) (African)

Greenfield, Eloise. *Nathaniel Talking*, 540 (P/M) (African American)

*Night on Neighborhood Street*, 541 (M) (African American)

Grimes, Nikki. *Meet Danitra Brown*, 560 (P/M) (African American)

Gunning, Monica. *Not a Copper Penny in Me House: Poems from the Caribbean*, 568 (M) (Caribbean)

Hansen, Joyce. *The Gift-Giver*, 605 (M/U) (African American)

*Yellow Bird and Me*, 607 (M/U) (African American)

Heo, Yumi. *One Afternoon*, 639 (P) (Asian American—Korea)

Hirschfelder, Arlene B., and Beverly R. Singer, selectors. *Rising Voices: Writings of Young Native Americans*, 651 (U) (Native American)

Isadora, Rachel. *Over the Green Hills*, 717 (P) (African—South Africa)

Johnson, Angela. *The Leaving Morning*, 735 (P) (African American)

## Communities, neighborhoods (cont.)

Jones, Rebecca C. *Matthew and Tilly*, 766 (P) (African American)

Jordan, June. *Kimako's Story*, 768 (P) (African American)

Kroll, Virginia. *Africa Brothers and Sisters*, 825 (P) (African American)

*Masai and I*, 827 (P) (African—Masai)

Lewin, Hugh. *Jafta*, 879 (P) (African—South Africa)

*Jafta and the Wedding*, 880 (P) (African—South Africa)

*Jafta: The Homecoming*, 881 (P) (African—South Africa)

*Jafta—The Journey*, 882 (P) (African—South Africa)

*Jafta—The Town*, 883 (P) (African—South Africa)

*Jafta's Father*, 884 (P) (African—South Africa)

*Jafta's Mother*, 885 (P) (African—South Africa)

Martel, Cruz. *Yagua Days*, 977 (M) (Hispanic American—Puerto Rico)

Mead, Alice. *Crossing the Starlight Bridge*, 1000 (M) (Native American—Penobscot)

Miles, Betty. *Sink or Swim*, 1017 (M) (African American)

Mitchell, Rita Phillips. *Hue Boy*, 1029 (P/M) (Caribbean)

Moore, Emily. *Whose Side Are You On?*, 1050 (M) (African American)

Nikola-Lisa, W. *Bein' With You This Way*, 1103 (P) (Multicultural)

Nunes, Susan. *The Last Dragon*, 1106 (P) (Asian American—China)

Nye, Naomi Shihab. *Sitti's Secrets*, 1109 (P) (Middle Eastern American—Arab)

Patrick, Denise Lewis. *The Car Washing Street*, 1153 (P) (African American)

Quattlebaum, Mary. *Jackson Jones and the Puddle of Thorns*, 1202 (M) (African American)

Smalls-Hector, Irene. *Irene and the Big, Fine Nickel*, 1338 (P/M) (African American)

*Jonathan and His Mommy*, 1339 (PS/P) (African American)

Soto, Gary. *Baseball in April: And Other Stories*, 1349 (U) (Hispanic American)

*A Fire in My Hands: A Book of Poems*, 1353 (U) (Mexican American)

*Local News*, 1354 (U) (Mexican American)

*Neighborhood Odes*, 1355 (U) (Mexican American)

Spinelli, Eileen. *If You Want to Find Golden*, 1364 (P) (Multicultural)

Tate, Eleanora E. *The Secret of Gumbo Grove*, 1414 (M/U) (African American)

Williams, Vera B. *Cherries and Cherry Pits*, 1555 (P) (African American)

*Scooter*, 1558 (M) (Hispanic American)

Yep, Laurence. *Child of the Owl*, 1605 (U) (Asian American—China)


## Concepts

Eastman, Patricia. *Sometimes Things Change*, 389 (P) (Multicultural)

Fisher, Leonard Everett. *Calendar Art: Thirteen Days, Weeks, Months, and Years from Around the World*, 424 (M) (Multicultural)

*Symbol Art: Thirteen Squares, Circles, and Triangles from Around the World*, 426 (M) (Multicultural)

Hausman, Gerald. *Turtle Island ABC: A Gathering of Native American Symbols*, 628 (M) (Native American)

Hudson, Cheryl Willis. *Afro-Bets 123 Book*, 685 (PS) (African American)

## Concepts—color

Caines, Jeannette. *I Need a Lunch Box*, 212 (PS/P) (African American)

Ellis, Veronica Freeman. *Land of the Four Winds: Kpa Nieh Kpau*, 397 (M) (African—Liberia)

Jenkins, Jessica. *Thinking about Colors*, 728 (P) (Multicultural)

Jonas, Ann. *Color Dance*, 760 (PS/P) (Multicultural)

Rosen, Michael. *How the Animals Got Their Colors: Animal Myths from Around the World*, 1247 (M) (Multicultural)

Spinelli, Eileen. *If You Want to Find Golden*, 1364 (P) (Multicultural)

Troughton, Joanna, reteller. *How the Birds Changed Their Feathers: A South American Indian Folk Tale*, 1456 (M) (South American)

Van Laan, Nancy, reteller. *Rainbow Crow: A Lenape Tale*, 1490 (M) (Native American—Lenape)

Whitethorne, Baje. *Sunpainters: Eclipse of the Navajo Sun*, 1543 (M) (Native American—Navajo)

Young, Ed. *Seven Blind Mice*, 1632 (M) (Asian—India)

## Concepts—opposites

Lillie, Patricia. *When This Box Is Full*, 896 (P) (African American)

Moses, Amy. *I Am an Explorer*, 1071 (P) (African American)

## Concepts—shape

Tompert, Ann. *Grandfather Tang's Story*, 1445 (P) (Asian—China)

## Concepts—size

Brown, Marcia, reteller. *Once a Mouse: A Fable Cut in Wood*, 166 (P/M) (Asian—India)

Mitchell, Rita Phillips. *Hue Boy*, 1029 (P/M) (Caribbean)

Mollel, Tololwa M. *Big Boy*, 1035 (P) (African)

## Conservation

Schlein, Miriam. *The Year of the Panda*, 1292 (M) (Asian—China)

## Contests

Aardema, Verna, reteller. *Princess Gorilla and a New Kind of Water: A Mpongwe Tale*, 9 (M) (African—Mpongwe)

Arneach, Lloyd, reteller. *The Animals' Ballgame: A Cherokee Story from the Eastern Band*, 68 (M) (Native American—Cherokee)

Bruchac, Joseph, reteller. *The Great Ball Game: A Muskogee Story*, 173 (M) (Native American—Muskogee)

Dee, Ruby, reteller. *Two Ways to Count to Ten: A Liberian Folktale*, 342 (M) (African—Liberia)

Demi. *The Empty Pot*, 353 (M) (Asian—China)

French, Fiona. *Anancy and Mr. Dry-Bone*, 448 (M) (African)

Peters, Julie Anne. *The Stinky Sneakers Contest*, 1164 (M) (African American)

Pfeffer, Susan Beth. *The Riddle Streak*, 1168 (M) (African American)

Vaughan, Marcia. *Kapoc, the Killer Croc*, 1493 (M) (South American—Amazon)

## Coretta Scott King Award

Adoff, Arnold. *All the Colors of the Race: Poems*, 23 (U) (Multicultural)

Anderson/Sankofa, David A., reteller. *The Origin of Life on Earth: An African Creation Myth*, 54 (M) (African—Yoruba)

Boyd, Candy Dawson. *Circle of Gold*, 154 (U) (African American)

Bryan, Ashley. *All Night, All Day: A Child's First Book of African-American Spirituals*, 180 (P/M) (African American)

  *Beat the Story-Drum, Pum-Pum*, 181 (M) (African)

  *I'm Going to Sing: Black American Spirituals, Vol. 2*, 184 (M) (African American)

  *Lion and the Ostrich Chicks: And Other African Folk Tales*, 185 (M) (African)

Caines, Jeannette. *Just Us Women*, 213 (P) (African American)

Clifton, Lucille. *Don't You Remember?*, 267 (P) (African American)

  *Everett Anderson's Friend*, 269 (P) (African American)

  *Everett Anderson's Goodbye*, 270 (M/U) (African American)

Cummings, Pat. *C.L.O.U.D.S.*, 324 (P) (African American)

DeVeaux, Alexis. *An Enchanted Hair Tale*, 366 (M) (African American)

Dragonwagon, Crescent. *Half a Moon and One Whole Star*, 380 (P) (African American)

Feelings, Tom, selector. *Soul Looks Back In Wonder*, 415 (M/U) (African American)

Fenner, Carol. *The Skates of Uncle Richard*, 417 (M) (African American)

Flournoy, Valerie. *The Patchwork Quilt*, 434 (P/M) (African American)

Greenfield, Eloise. *Africa Dream*, 525 (P) (African American)

  *Daydreamers*, 529 (M/U) (African American)

  *Grandmama's Joy*, 532 (P) (African American)

  *Nathaniel Talking*, 540 (P/M) (African American)

  *Night on Neighborhood Street*, 541 (M) (African American)

  *Under the Sunday Tree: Poems*, 546 (M) (Caribbean)

Greenfield, Eloise, and Lessie Jones Little. *Childtimes: A Three-Generation Memoir*, 548 (M/U) (African American)

Grimes, Nikki. *Meet Danitra Brown*, 560 (P/M) (African American)

  *Something on My Mind*, 561 (M/U) (African American)

Guy, Rosa, translator and adapter. *Mother Crocodile*, 571 (M) (African)

Hamilton, Virginia. *The Bells of Christmas*, 582 (M) (African American)

  *The Magical Adventures of Pretty Pearl*, 591 (U) (African heritage)

  *The People Could Fly: American Black Folktales*, 593 (M/U) (African American)

Hansen, Joyce. *The Captive*, 604 (U) (African)

  *Which Way Freedom?*, 606 (U) (African American)

Johnson, Angela. *Toning the Sweep*, 741 (U) (African American)

  *When I Am Old with You*, 742 (P) (African American)

Johnson, James Weldon. *The Creation*, 751 (P/M) (African American)

Langstaff, John, editor. *What a Morning! The Christmas Story in Black Spirituals*, 840 (P/M) (African American)

Lester, Julius, reteller. *The Tales of Uncle Remus: The Adventures of Brer Rabbit*, 875 (M/U) (African American)

McKissack, Patricia. *The Dark Thirty: Southern Tales of the Supernatural*, 947 (M/U) (African American)

*Mirandy and Brother Wind*, 950 (P) (African American)

McKissack, Patricia, and Fredrick McKissack. *Christmas in the Big House, Christmas in the Quarters*, 954 (M) (African American)

Medearis, Angela Shelf, adapter. *The Singing Man: A West African Folktale*, 1004 (M) (African)

Mitchell, Margaret King. *Uncle Jed's Barbershop*, 1028 (P/M) (African American)

Myers, Walter Dean. *Fast Sam, Cool Clyde, and Stuff*, 1083 (U) (African American)

*The Young Landlords*, 1089 (U) (African American)

Price, Leontyne, reteller. *Aïda*, 1198 (U) (African)

Ringgold, Faith. *Tar Beach*, 1222 (P/M) (African American)

Rohmer, Harriet, Octavio Chow, and Morris Vidaure. *The Invisible Hunters/Los Cazadores Invisibles: A Legend from the Miskito Indians of Nicaragua/Una Leyenda de los Indios Miskitos de Nicaragua*, 1239 (M) (Central American—Nicaragua)

San Souci, Robert D. *Sukey and the Mermaid*, 1280 (M) (African American)

*The Talking Eggs: A Folktale from the American South*, 1281 (M) (African American)

Steptoe, John. *Mufaro's Beautiful Daughters: An African Tale*, 1379 (M) (African)

Stolz, Mary. *Storm in the Night*, 1396 (P/M) (African American)

Taylor, Mildred D. *The Friendship*, 1424 (M/U) (African American)

*Let the Circle Be Unbroken*, 1427 (U) (African American)

*The Road to Memphis*, 1429 (U) (African American)

*Roll of Thunder, Hear My Cry*, 1430 (U) (African American)

*Song of the Trees*, 1431 (M/U) (African American)

Thomas, Joyce Carol. *Brown Honey in Broomwheat Tea: Poems*, 1440 (P/M) (African American)

Udry, Janice May. *Mary Jo's Grandmother*, 1485 (P) (African American)

Wahl, Jan. *Little Eight John*, 1502 (M) (African American)

Walter, Mildred Pitts. *Justin and the Best Biscuits in the World*, 1511 (M/U) (African American)

*My Mama Needs Me*, 1515 (P) (African American)

*Trouble's Child*, 1516 (U) (African American)

Williams, Sherley Anne. *Working Cotton*, 1552 (M) (African American)

Yarborough, Camille. *Cornrows*, 1591 (M) (African American)

Zaslavsky, Claudia. *Count on Your Fingers African Style*, 1636 (P) (African)

## Counting, numbers

Bang, Molly. *Ten, Nine, Eight*, 85 (PS/P) (African American)

Dee, Ruby, reteller. *Two Ways to Count to Ten: A Liberian Folktale*, 342 (M) (African—Liberia)

Falwell, Cathryn. *Feast for 10*, 412 (P) (African American)

Feelings, Muriel. *Moja Means One: Swahili Counting Book*, 414 (P/M) (African)

Fisher, Leonard Everett. *Number Art: Thirteen 1 2 3s from Around the World*, 425 (P/M) (Multicultural)

Garne, S. T. *One White Sail*, 460 (P) (Caribbean)

## Counting, numbers (cont.)

Greenfield, Eloise. *Aaron and Gayla's Counting Book*, 524 (PS/P) (African American)

Grossman, Virginia. *Ten Little Rabbits*, 563 (P) (Native American)

Hamsa, Bobbie. *Polly Wants a Cracker*, 599 (P) (African American)

Haskins, Jim. *Count Your Way Through Africa*, 619 (P) (African)

*Count Your Way Through China*, 620 (P) (Asian—China)

*Count Your Way Through India*, 621 (P) (Asian—India)

*Count Your Way Through Japan*, 622 (P) (Asian—Japan)

*Count Your Way Through Korea*, 623 (P) (Asian—Korea)

*Count Your Way Through Mexico*, 624 (P) (Mexican)

*Count Your Way Through the Arab World*, 625 (P) (Middle Eastern—Arabia)

Hudson, Cheryl Willis. *Afro-Bets 123 Book*, 685 (PS) (African American)

*Let's Count Baby*, 689 (PS) (African American)

Linden, Ann Marie. *One Smiling Grandma: A Caribbean Counting Book*, 898 (PS/P) (Caribbean)

McKissack, Patricia, and Fredrick McKissack. *Bugs!*, 953 (P) (African American)

McMillan, Bruce. *Eating Fractions*, 959 (P) (Multicultural)

Milstein, Linda. *Coconut Mon*, 1027 (P) (Caribbean)

Ochs, Carol Partridge. *When I'm Alone*, 1112 (P) (African American)

Onyefulu, Ifeoma. *Emeka's Gift: An African Counting Story*, 1129 (P) (African)

Ormerod, Jan. *Joe Can Count*, 1133 (PS) (African American)

Ryan, Pam Muñoz. *One Hundred Is a Family*, 1258 (PS/P) (Multicultural)

Van Laan, Nancy. *Mama Rocks, Papa Sings*, 1489 (P) (Caribbean—Haiti)

Yolen, Jane, editor. *Street Rhymes Around the World*, 1627 (P) (Multicultural)

Zaslavsky, Claudia. *Count on Your Fingers African Style*, 1636 (P) (African)

## Cowboys

Stolz, Mary. *Cezanne Pinto: A Memoir*, 1392 (U) (African American)

Walter, Mildred Pitts. *Justin and the Best Biscuits in the World*, 1511 (M/U) (African American)

## Creation

Anderson/Sankofa, David A., reteller. *The Origin of Life on Earth: An African Creation Myth*, 54 (M) (African—Yoruba)

Bierhorst, John, reteller. *The Woman Who Fell from the Sky: The Iroquois Story of Creation*, 137 (M) (Native American—Iroquois)

Bruchac, Joseph, and Michael J. Caduto, retellers. *Native American Stories*, 174 (M/U) (Native American)

Curry, Jane Louise, reteller. *Back in the Beforetime: Tales of the California Indians*, 326 (M/U) (Native American)

Gates, Frieda. *Owl Eyes*, 461 (M) (Native American—Kanienkehaka [Mohawk])

Greger, Shana, reteller. *The Fifth and Final Sun: An Ancient Aztec Myth of the Sun's Origin*, 550 (M) (Mexican—Aztec)

Hamilton, Virginia, reteller. *In the Beginning: Creation Stories from Around the World*, 588 (M) (Multicultural)

Hull, Robert, reteller. *Native North American Stories*, 701 (M) (Native American)

Johnson, James Weldon. *The Creation*, 751 (P/M) (African American)

*The Creation: A Poem*, 752 (P/M) (African American)

Knutson, Barbara, reteller. *Why the Crab Has No Head: An African Tale*, 821 (M) (African—Zaire)

Lattimore, Deborah Nourse. *Why There Is No Arguing in Heaven: A Mayan Myth*, 848 (M) (Central American—Mayan)

Lewis, Richard. *All of You Was Singing*, 888 (M) (Mexican—Aztec)

*In the Night, Still Dark*, 890 (M) (Hawaiian)

Maddern, Eric, reteller. *The Fire Children: A West African Creation Tale*, 961 (M) (African)

Manitonquat (Medicine Story). *The Children of the Morning Light: Wampanoag Tales,* 971 (U) (Native American—Wampanoag)

Morgan, Sally. *The Flying Emu: And Other Australian Stories*, 1058 (U) (Australian—Aborigine)

Rohmer, Harriet, and Mary Anchondo, adapters. *How We Came to the Fifth World/Como vinimos al quinto mundo: A Creation Story from Ancient Mexico*, 1238 (M) (Mexican—Aztec)

Shepherd, Sandy. *Myths and Legends from Around the World*, 1314 (M) (Multicultural)

Tadjo, Véronique, reteller. *Lord of the Dance: An African Retelling*, 1405 (M) (African—Ivory Coast)

Taylor, C. J. *Bones in the Basket: Native Stories of the Origin of People*, 1416 (M) (Native American)

Williams, Sheron. *And in the Beginning . . .* , 1553 (M) (African)

Wilson, Barbara Ker, reteller. *The Turtle and the Island: A Folktale from Papua New Guinea*, 1561 (M) (New Guinean)

Young, Ed, adapter. *Moon Mother: A Native American Creation Tale*, 1630 (M) (Native American)

## Creativity

Williams, Vera B. *Cherries and Cherry Pits*, 1555 (P) (African American)

## Crime

Ada, Alma Flor. *The Gold Coin*, 18 (M) (Central American)

Rodriguez, Anita. *Aunt Martha and the Golden Coin*, 1235 (P) (African American)

Soto, Gary. *Crazy Weekend*, 1352 (U) (Hispanic American)

Tate, Eleanora E. *A Blessing in Disguise*, 1412 (U) (African American)

Yarborough, Camille. *Tamika and the Wisdom Rings*, 1593 (M) (African American)

## Cruelty

Berry, James. *Ajeemah and His Son*, 124 (U) (African)

Fox, Paula. *The Slave Dancer: A Novel*, 439 (U) (African American)

Marie, D. *Tears for Ashan*, 974 (M) (African)

O'Dell, Scott. *My Name Is Not Angelica*, 1120 (U) (Caribbean)

O'Dell, Scott, and Elizabeth Hall. *Thunder Rolling in the Mountains*, 1124 (U) (Native American—Nez Perce)

## Crustacea

Knutson, Barbara, reteller. *Why the Crab Has No Head: An African Tale*, 821 (M) (African—Zaire)

Pitre, Felix, reteller. *Paco and the Witch: A Puerto Rican Folktale*, 1178 (M) (Caribbean—Puerto Rico)

## Cumulative tales

Aardema, Verna, reteller. *Bringing the Rain to Kapiti Plain: A Nandi Tale*, 4 (P/M) (African—Nandi)

   *Traveling to Tondo: A Tale of the Nkundo of Zaire*, 12 (M) (African—Zaire)

   *Who's in Rabbit's House? A Masai Tale*, 15 (M) (African—Masai)

   *Why Mosquitoes Buzz in People's Ears: A West African Tale*, 16 (M) (African—West Africa)

Ada, Alma Flor, reteller. *The Rooster Who Went to His Uncle's Wedding: A Latin American Folktale*, 20 (M) (Latin American)

Chocolate, Deborah M. Newton, reteller. *Talk, Talk: An Ashanti Legend*, 252 (M) (African)

Duff, Maggie, reteller. *Rum Pum Pum: A Folk Tale from India*, 384 (M) (Asian—India)

González, Lucía M., reteller. *The Bossy Gallito/El Gallo de Bodas: A Traditional Cuban Folktale*, 509 (M) (Caribbean—Cuba)

Lee, Jeanne M., reteller. *Toad Is the Uncle of Heaven: A Vietnamese Folk Tale*, 860 (M) (Asian—Vietnam)

Lichtveld, Noni. *I Lost My Arrow in a Kankan Tree*, 893 (M) (South American—Surinam)

Martin, Rafe. *Foolish Rabbit's Big Mistake*, 982 (M) (Asian—India)

Mollel, Tololwa M. *Rhinos for Lunch and Elephants for Supper! A Maasai Tale*, 1041 (M) (African—Masai)

Tanaka, Béatrice, reteller. *The Chase: A Kutenai Indian Tale*, 1410 (P) (Native American—Kutenai)

## Customs

Bunting, Eve. *The Happy Funeral*, 198 (P) (Asian American—China)

Goble, Paul. *Beyond the Ridge*, 485 (M) (Native American—Plains Indians)

Grifalconi, Ann. *Flyaway Girl*, 554 (M) (African)

Miles, Miska. *Annie and the Old One*, 1018 (M) (Native American—Navajo)

Musgrove, Margaret. *Ashanti to Zulu: African Traditions*, 1077 (M) (African)

Nye, Naomi Shihab. *Sitti's Secrets*, 1109 (P) (Middle Eastern American—Arab)

Onyefulu, Ifeoma. *A Is for Africa*, 1128 (P/M) (African)

## Days of the week, months of the year

Bruchac, Joseph, and Jonathan London. *Thirteen Moons on Turtle's Back: A Native American Year of Moons*, 175 (M) (Native American)

Caines, Jeannette. *I Need a Lunch Box*, 212 (PS/P) (African American)

Clifton, Lucille. *Everett Anderson's Year*, 273 (P) (African American)

   *Some of the Days of Everett Anderson*, 277 (P) (African American)

Fisher, Leonard Everett. *Calendar Art: Thirteen Days, Weeks, Months, and Years from Around the World*, 424 (M) (Multicultural)

Lillie, Patricia. *When This Box Is Full*, 896 (P) (African American)

Maher, Ramona. *Alice Yazzie's Year: Poems*, 964 (M) (Native American—Navajo)

Smith, Joanne L. *Show and Tell*, 1341 (P) (African American)

Young, Ed. *Seven Blind Mice*, 1632 (M) (Asian—India)

## Death

Alexander, Sue. *Nadia the Willful*, 42 (P) (Middle Eastern—Arabia)

Anderson, Janet S. *The Key into Winter*, 52 (M) (African American)

Berry, James. *Ajeemah and His Son*, 124 (U) (African)

Bess, Clayton. *Story for a Black Night*, 126 (U) (African)

Boyd, Candy Dawson. *Breadsticks and Blessing Places*, 152 (U) (African American)

Brooks, Bruce. *Everywhere*, 162 (M/U) (African American)

Bruchac, Joseph. *Fox Song*, 171 (P) (Native American)

Bunting, Eve. *The Happy Funeral*, 198 (P) (Asian American—China)

Choi, Sook Nyul. *Gathering of Pearls*, 254 (U) (Asian—Korea)

Clifton, Lucille. *Everett Anderson's Goodbye*, 270 (M/U) (African American)

Coerr, Eleanor. *Sadako*, 284 (M/U) (Asian—Japan)

   *Sadako and the Thousand Paper Cranes*, 285 (M/U) (Asian - Japan)

Cohen, Barbara. *Thank You, Jackie Robinson*, 287 (M) (African American)

Coutant, Helen. *First Snow*, 314 (P) (Asian American—Vietnam)

Davis, Ossie. *Just Like Martin*, 335 (U) (African American)

Eckewa, T. Obinkaram. *The Ancestor Tree*, 390 (M) (African)

Eskridge, Ann E. *The Sanctuary*, 406 (U) (African American)

Fox, Mem. *Sophie*, 437 (P) (African American)

Gardiner, John Reynolds. *Stone Fox*, 457 (M) (Native American)

Goble, Paul. *Beyond the Ridge*, 485 (M) (Native American—Plains Indians)

Greenfield, Eloise. *Sister*, 544 (M) (African American)

Grifalconi, Ann. *Not Home: A Novel*, 556 (U) (African American)

Hamilton, Virginia. *Cousins*, 583 (M) (African American)

Hearn, Lafcadio. *The Voice of the Great Bell*, 635 (M) (Asian—China)

Ho, Minfong. *The Clay Marble*, 652 (U) (Asian—Cambodia)

Krull, Kathleen. *Maria Molina and the Days of the Dead*, 831 (M) (Mexican)

Lacapa, Michael, reteller. *The Flute Player: An Apache Folktale*, 837 (M) (Native American—Apache)

Lehne, Judith Logan. *When the Ragman Sings*, 862 (U) (African American)

Lester, Julius, reteller. *The Man Who Knew Too Much: A Moral Tale from the Baila of Zambia*, 873 (M) (African—Zambia)

Locker, Thomas. *The Land of Gray Wolf*, 908 (P) (Native American)

McDermott, Gerald, reteller. *The Voyage of Osiris: A Myth of Ancient Egypt*, 940 (M) (African—Egypt)

Miles, Miska. *Annie and the Old One*, 1018 (M) (Native American—Navajo)

Miller, Montzalee. *My Grandmother's Cookie Jar*, 1025 (P) (Native American)

Mobley, Jane. *The Star Husband*, 1030 (M) (Native American)

## Death (cont.)

Myers, Christopher A., and Lynne Born Myers. *Forest of the Clouded Leopard*, 1079 (U) (African—Iban)

Nodar, Carmen Santiago. *Abuelita's Paradise*, 1104 (P) (Caribbean—Puerto Rico)

O'Dell, Scott. *Child of Fire*, 1117 (U) (Mexican American)

Oliviero, Jamie. *Som See and the Magic Elephant*, 1127 (M) (Asian—Thailand)

Otsuka, Yuzo. *Suho and the White Horse: A Legend of Mongolia*, 1139 (M) (Asian—Mongolia)

Polacco, Patricia. *Pink and Say*, 1181 (M) (African American)

Porter, Connie. *Addy Saves the Day: A Summer Story*, 1190 (M) (African American)

Prather, Ray. *Fish and Bones*, 1197 (U) (African American)

Price, Leontyne, reteller. *Aïda*, 1198 (U) (African)

Rappaport, Doreen, reteller. *The Journey of Meng: A Chinese Legend*, 1205 (M) (Asian—China)

*The New King: A Madagascan Legend*, 1207 (M) (African—Madagascar)

Rosen, Michael. *Bonesy and Isabel*, 1243 (P) (Hispanic American—El Salvador)

Tate, Eleanora E. *A Blessing in Disguise*, 1412 (U) (African American)

Taylor, Mildred D. *Mississippi Bridge*, 1428 (M/U) (African American)

Uchida, Yoshiko. *The Birthday Visitor*, 1471 (P) (Asian American—Japan)

Wagner, Jane. *J. T.*, 1501 (M) (African American)

Walker, Alice. *To Hell with Dying*, 1504 (M) (African American)

Wilson, Johnniece Marshall. *Robin on His Own*, 1566 (M/U) (African American)

Woodson, Jacqueline. *Last Summer with Maizon*, 1581 (U) (African American)

Yarborough, Camille. *Tamika and the Wisdom Rings*, 1593 (M) (African American)

## Desert

Baylor, Byrd. *The Desert Is Theirs*, 101 (M) (Native American—Papago)

*When Clay Sings*, 105 (P/M) (Native American)

Bird, E. J. *The Rainmakers*, 139 (U) (Native American—Anasazi)

Cohlene, Terri, adapter. *Turquoise Boy: A Navajo Legend*, 297 (M) (Native American—Navajo)

Finley, Mary Pierce. *Soaring Eagle*, 422 (U) (Multicultural)

Franklin, Kristine L. *The Shepherd Boy*, 442 (P) (Native American—Navajo)

Hoyt-Goldsmith, Diane. *Pueblo Storyteller*, 681 (M) (Native American—Cochiti Pueblo)

James, Betsy. *The Mud Family*, 724 (M) (Native American—Anasazi)

Johnson, Angela. *Toning the Sweep*, 741 (U) (African American)

Kessler, Cristina. *One Night: A Story from the Desert*, 798 (P) (Middle Eastern—Tuareg)

Kimmel, Eric A., reteller. *The Three Princes: A Tale from the Middle East*, 807 (M) (Middle Eastern—Arabia)

Maher, Ramona. *Alice Yazzie's Year: Poems*, 964 (M) (Native American—Navajo)

Mora, Francisco X. *Juan Tuza and the Magic Pouch*, 1052 (M) (Mexican)

Paulsen, Gary. *Canyons*, 1156 (U) (Native American—Apache)

## Divorce, separation

Best, Cari. *Taxi! Taxi!*, 128 (P) (Hispanic American)

Caines, Jeannette. *Daddy*, 211 (P) (African American)

Greenfield, Eloise. *Talk about a Family*, 545 (M) (African American)

Mead, Alice. *Crossing the Starlight Bridge*, 1000 (M) (Native American—Penobscot)

Moore, Emily. *Something to Count On*, 1049 (M) (African American)

Wyeth, Sharon Dennis. *Always My Dad*, 1587 (P) (African American)

## Dragons

Hillman, Elizabeth. *Min-Yo and the Moon Dragon*, 649 (M) (Asian—China)

Lattimore, Deborah Nourse. *The Dragon's Robe*, 845 (M) (Asian—China)

Lawson, Julie, reteller. *The Dragon's Pearl*, 854 (M) (Asian—China)

Leaf, Margaret. *Eyes of the Dragon*, 855 (M) (Asian—China)

Lifton, Betty Jean. *Joji and the Dragon*, 895 (P) (Asian—Japan)

Nunes, Susan. *The Last Dragon*, 1106 (P) (Asian American—China)

Pattison, Darcy. *The River Dragon*, 1155 (M) (Asian—China)

Schecter, Ellen, reteller. *Sim Chung and the River Dragon: A Folktale from Korea*, 1289 (P) (Asian—Korea)

Stock, Catherine. *Emma's Dragon Hunt*, 1388 (PS/P) (Asian American—China)

Torre, Betty L., reteller. *The Luminous Pearl: A Chinese Folktale*, 1448 (M) (Asian—China)

Williams, Jay. *Everyone Knows What a Dragon Looks Like*, 1548 (M) (Asian—China)

## Dreams

Adoff, Arnold. *Flamboyán*, 25 (P) (Caribbean—Puerto Rico)

Alexander, Martha. *Bobo's Dream*, 41 (PS/P) (African American)

Bosse, Malcolm. *Deep Dream of the Rain Forest*, 150 (U) (African—Iban)

Cameron, Ann. *Julian, Dream Doctor*, 215 (M) (African American)

Casler, Leigh. *The Boy Who Dreamed of an Acorn*, 229 (M) (Native American)

Cummings, Pat. *Carousel*, 322 (P) (African American)

Dragonwagon, Crescent. *Half a Moon and One Whole Star*, 380 (P) (African American)

Greenfield, Eloise. *Africa Dream*, 525 (P) (African American)

*Daydreamers*, 529 (M/U) (African American)

Hughes, Langston. *The Dream Keeper: And Other Poems*, 695 (M/U) (African American)

*The Dream Keeper: And Other Poems*, 696 (M/U) (African American)

Isadora, Rachel. *Ben's Trumpet*, 716 (P) (African American)

Jacobs, Shannon K. *Song of the Giraffe*, 721 (M) (African)

Jonas, Ann. *The Quilt*, 762 (PS/P) (African American)

Keats, Ezra Jack. *Dreams*, 777 (PS/P) (Hispanic American)

## Dreams (cont.)

Moss, Thylias. *I Want to Be*, 1074 (P/M) (African American)

Osofsky, Audrey. *Dreamcatcher*, 1138 (M) (Native American—Ojibway)

Rodriguez, Anita. *Jamal and the Angel*, 1236 (P) (African American)

Say, Allen. *A River Dream*, 1287 (P) (Asian American)

Troughton, Joanna, reteller. *Tortoise's Dream*, 1458 (M) (African)

Yarborough, Camille. *The Shimmershine Queens*, 1592 (M/U) (African American)

Yep, Laurence. *Tree of Dreams: Ten Tales from the Garden of Night*, 1618 (U) (Multicultural)

## Drugs

Tate, Eleanora E. *A Blessing in Disguise*, 1412 (U) (African American)

## Ecology

Allen, Judy. *Elephant*, 44 (P) (African)

Baylor, Byrd. *The Desert Is Theirs*, 101 (M) (Native American—Papago)

Cherry, Lynne. *The Great Kapok Tree: A Tale of the Amazon Rain Forest*, 243 (M) (South American)

Franklin, Kristine L. *When the Monkeys Came Back*, 443 (P) (Central American—Costa Rica)

George, Jean Craighead. *Julie*, 463 (U) (Native American—Inuit)

Geraghty, Paul. *The Hunter*, 468 (P) (African)

Glaser, Linda. *Tanya's Big Green Dream*, 481 (M) (Multicultural)

Hamilton, Virginia. *M. C. Higgins the Great*, 590 (U) (African American)

Jones, Hettie, selector. *The Trees Stand Shining: Poetry of the North American Indians*, 765 (M) (Native American)

Keller, Holly. *Grandfather's Dream*, 791 (P) (Asian—Vietnam)
*Island Baby*, 792 (P) (Caribbean)

Kendall, Sarita. *Ransom for a River Dolphin*, 795 (U) (South American—Colombia)

Lewin, Ted. *Amazon Boy*, 886 (P/M) (South American—Brazil)

Longfellow, Henry Wadsworth. *Hiawatha*, 913 (M) (Native American)
*Hiawatha's Childhood*, 914 (M) (Native American)

McGee, Charmayne. *So Sings the Blue Deer*, 946 (U) (Native American—Huichol)

Rose, Deborah Lee, adapter. *The People Who Hugged the Trees: An Environmental Folktale*, 1242 (M) (Asian—India)

Seattle, Chief. *Brother Eagle, Sister Sky: A Message from Chief Seattle*, 1299 (M) (Native American)

## Eggs

San Souci, Robert D., reteller. *The Talking Eggs: A Folktale from the American South*, 1281 (M) (African American)

## Elections

Hurwitz, Johanna. *Class President*, 706 (M) (Hispanic American—Puerto Rico)

## Elves and little people

Bang, Betsy, adapter. *Cucumber Stem: From a Bengali Folktale*, 79 (P) (Asian—India)

Brenner, Barbara. *Little One Inch*, 158 (M) (Asian—Japan)

French, Fiona. *Little Inchkin*, 449 (M) (Asian—Japan)

Hamilton, Virginia. *The All Jahdu Storybook*, 581 (M) (African American)

*Jahdu*, 589 (M) (African American)

*The Time-Ago Tales of Jahdu*, 595 (M) (African American)

Hughes, Monica, reteller. *Little Fingerling*, 697 (M) (Asian—Japan)

Morimoto, Junko. *The Inch Boy*, 1059 (M) (Asian—Japan)

Shetterly, Susan Hand, reteller. *The Dwarf-Wizard of Uxmal*, 1317 (M) (Central American—Mayan)

Shute, Linda, reteller. *Momotaro the Peach Boy: A Traditional Japanese Tale*, 1322 (M) (Asian—Japan)

Young, Ed. *Little Plum*, 1628 (M) (Asian—China)

## Emotions

Adoff, Arnold. *All the Colors of the Race: Poems*, 23 (U) (Multicultural)

*I Am the Darker Brother: An Anthology of Modern Poems by Negro Americans*, 27 (M/U) (African American)

*My Black Me: A Beginning Book of Black Poetry*, 30, 31 (M/U) (African American)

*OUTside INside Poems*, 32 (M) (African American)

Curtis, Gavin. *Grandma's Baseball*, 328 (P) (African American)

Eskridge, Ann E. *The Sanctuary*, 406 (U) (African American)

Giovanni, Nikki. *Ego-Tripping: And Other Poems for Young People*, 478 (U) (African American)

*Spin a Soft Black Song: Poems for Children*, 480 (M/U) (African American)

Greenfield, Eloise. *Daydreamers*, 529 (M/U) (African American)

Grimes, Nikki. *From a Child's Heart: Poems*, 559 (P) (African American)

*Something on My Mind*, 561 (M/U) (African American)

Hughes, Langston. *The Dream Keeper: And Other Poems*, 695 (M/U) (African American)

*The Dream Keeper: And Other Poems*, 696 (M/U) (African American)

Jenkins, Jessica. *Thinking about Colors*, 728 (P) (Multicultural)

Lacapa, Kathleen, and Michael Lacapa. *Less Than Half, More Than Whole*, 835 (M) (Multicultural)

Lewin, Hugh. *Jafta*, 879 (P) (African—South Africa)

*Jafta—The Town*, 883 (P) (African—South Africa)

Livingston, Myra Cohn. *Let Freedom Ring: A Ballad of Martin Luther King, Jr.*, 904 (M) (African American)

Medearis, Angela Shelf. *Skin Deep: And Other Teenage Reflections*, 1005 (U) (African American)

Moss, Marissa. *Regina's Big Mistake*, 1073 (P) (African American)

Navasky, Bruno, selector and translator. *Festival in My Heart: Poems by Japanese Children*, 1097 (U) (Asian—Japan)

## Emotions (cont.)

Soto, Gary. *A Fire in My Hands: A Book of Poems*, 1353 (U) (Mexican American)

   *Neighborhood Odes*, 1355 (U) (Mexican American)

Strickland, Dorothy S., and Michael R. Strickland, selectors. *Families: Poems Celebrating the African American Experience*, 1400 (M) (African American)

Wong, Janet S. *Good Luck Gold: And Other Poems*, 1577 (M) (Asian American)

## Emotions—anger

Bunting, Eve. *Summer Wheels*, 201 (M) (African American)

Clymer, Eleanor. *Luke Was There*, 281 (M) (African American)

Gordon, Sheila. *Waiting for the Rain: A Novel of South Africa*, 512 (U) (African—South Africa)

Greenfield, Eloise. *Koya DeLaney and the Good Girl Blues*, 537 (U) (African American)

   *Talk about a Family*, 545 (M) (African American)

Steptoe, John. *Stevie*, 1380 (P) (African American)

## Emotions—apprehension

Carlstrom, Nancy White. *Barney Is Best*, 224 (PS/P) (Hispanic American)

Clifton, Lucille. *Amifika*, 265 (P) (African American)

Johnson, Angela. *The Leaving Morning*, 735 (P) (African American)

Johnson, Dolores. *What Will Mommy Do When I'm at School?*, 748 (PS/P) (African American)

Pinkney, Gloria Jean. *Back Home*, 1175 (P/M) (African American)

Richardson, Jean. *The Courage Seed*, 1218 (M) (Native American)

Sacks, Margaret. *Thembu*, 1260 (M) (African—South Africa)

Turner, Ann. *Through Moon and Stars and Night Skies*, 1468 (P) (Asian American)

## Emotions—embarrassment

Cote, Nancy. *Palm Trees*, 311 (P) (African American)

Namioka, Lensey. *Yang the Third and Her Impossible Family*, 1094 (M) (Asian American—China)

## Emotions—envy, jealousy

Bernhard, Emery, reteller. *Spotted Eagle & Black Crow: A Lakota Legend*, 122 (M) (Native American—Lakota)

Caines, Jeannette. *I Need a Lunch Box*, 212 (PS/P) (African American)

Clark, Ann Nolan, reteller. *In the Land of Small Dragon*, 260 (M) (Asian—Vietnam)

Climo, Shirley. *The Egyptian Cinderella*, 278 (M) (African—Egypt)

   *The Korean Cinderella*, 279 (M) (Asian—Korea)

Cohen, Miriam. *Born to Dance Samba*, 291 (M) (South American—Brazil)

Demi. *The Artist and the Architect*, 350 (M) (Asian—China)

Greenfield, Eloise. *She Come Bringin Me That Little Baby Girl*, 543 (P) (African American)

Hamilton, Virginia. *Cousins*, 583 (M) (African American)

Havill, Juanita. *Jamaica and Brianna*, 629 (P) (African American)

Louie, Ai-Ling, reteller. *Yeh-Shen: A Cinderella Story from China*, 918 (M) (Asian—China)

Lum, Darrell, reteller. *The Golden Slipper: A Vietnamese Legend*, 923 (M) (Asian—Vietnam)

Mills, Claudia. *A Visit to Amy-Claire*, 1026 (PS/P) (Asian American)

Newton, Pam, reteller. *The Stonecutter: An Indian Folktale*, 1101 (M) (Asian—India)

Steptoe, John. *Mufaro's Beautiful Daughters: An African Tale*, 1379 (M) (African)

Vuong, Lynette Dyer. *The Brocaded Slipper: And Other Vietnamese Tales*, 1497 (M) (Asian—Vietnam)

Winter, Susan. *A Baby Just like Me*, 1568 (PS/P) (African American)


## Emotions—fear

Brill, Marlene Targ. *Allen Jay and the Underground Railroad*, 161 (M) (African American)

Bulla, Clyde Robert, and Michael Syson. *Conquista!*, 195 (M) (Native American)

Cameron, Ann. *Julian's Glorious Summer*, 217 (M) (African American)

Clymer, Eleanor. *Luke Was There*, 281 (M) (African American)

Coleman, Evelyn. *The Foot Warmer and the Crow*, 298 (M) (African American)

Compton, Patricia A., reteller. *The Terrible EEK: A Japanese Tale*, 304 (M) (Asian—Japan)

Crews, Donald. *Shortcut*, 320 (P) (African American)

Dalgliesh, Alice. *The Courage of Sarah Noble*, 331 (M) (Native American)

Greenfield, Eloise. *Grandpa's Face*, 533 (P) (African American)

Grifalconi, Ann. *Darkness and the Butterfly*, 553 (P) (African)

Jonas, Ann. *Holes and Peeks*, 761 (PS) (African American)

Little, Lessie Jones, and Eloise Greenfield. *I Can Do It by Myself*, 901 (PS/P) (African American)

Mann, Kenny. *"I Am Not Afraid!": Based on a Masai Tale*, 972 (P) (African—Masai)

Milich, Melissa. *Can't Scare Me!*, 1019 (M) (African American)

Mollel, Tololwa M. *Rhinos for Lunch and Elephants for Supper! A Maasai Tale*, 1041 (M) (African—Masai)

Stock, Catherine. *Halloween Monster*, 1389 (P) (African American)

Stolz, Mary. *Storm in the Night*, 1396 (P/M) (African American)

Taylor, Mildred D. *The Friendship*, 1424 (M/U) (African American)
   *The Gold Cadillac*, 1426 (M/U) (African American)

Tsutsui, Yoriko. *Anna in Charge*, 1463 (P) (Asian—Japan)

Turner, Ann. *Through Moon and Stars and Night Skies*, 1468 (P) (Asian American)

Yolen, Jane. *Sky Dogs*, 1625 (M) (Native American—Blackfoot)


## Emotions—happiness

Moss, Thylias. *I Want to Be*, 1074 (P/M) (African American)

Raschka, Chris. *Yo! Yes?*, 1209 (P/M) (Multicultural)

Scott, Ann Herbert. *Hi*, 1296 (P) (Hispanic American)

## Emotions—happiness (cont.)

Weir, LaVada. *Howdy!*, 1531 (P) (African American)

Williams, Vera B. *Music, Music for Everyone*, 1557 (P) (Hispanic American)

## Emotions—homesickness

Say, Allen. *Grandfather's Journey*, 1283 (M) (Asian American—Japan)

## Emotions—loneliness

Keats, Ezra Jack. *Louie*, 782 (P) (Multicultural)

  *The Trip*, 787 (P) (Multicultural)

Kidd, Diana. *Onion Tears*, 801 (M) (Asian—Vietnam)

Scott, Ann Herbert. *Sam*, 1298 (P) (African American)

Smalls-Hector, Irene. *Dawn and the Round To-It*, 1337 (PS/P) (African American)

Walter, Mildred Pitts. *My Mama Needs Me*, 1515 (P) (African American)

Weik, Mary Hays. *The Jazz Man*, 1530 (M) (African American)

Wilson, Johnniece Marshall. *Robin on His Own*, 1566 (M/U) (African American)

Yashima, Taro. *Crow Boy*, 1595 (P) (Asian—Japan)

## Emotions—love

Alexander, Sue. *Nadia the Willful*, 42 (P) (Middle Eastern—Arabia)

Barrett, Joyce Durham. *Willie's Not the Hugging Kind*, 96 (P) (African American)

Birdseye, Tom, adapter. *A Song of Stars: An Asian Legend*, 140 (M) (Asian—China)

Brooks, Bruce. *Everywhere*, 162 (M/U) (African American)

Buckley, Helen E. *Grandmother and I*, 193 (PS/P) (African American)

Caines, Jeannette. *Abby*, 210 (PS) (African American)

  *Daddy*, 211 (P) (African American)

Clark, Ann Nolan. *In My Mother's House*, 259 (P) (Native American)

Clifton, Lucille. *Everett Anderson's Goodbye*, 270 (M/U) (African American)

  *My Brother Fine with Me*, 275 (P) (African American)

Cohen, Barbara, and Bahija Lovejoy. *Seven Daughters and Seven Sons*, 289 (U) (Middle Eastern—Arabia)

Eisenberg, Phyllis Rose. *You're My Nikki*, 396 (P) (African American)

Freeman, Don. *Corduroy*, 445 (PS/P) (African American)

  *A Pocket for Corduroy*, 446 (PS/P) (African American)

Goble, Paul. *Love Flute*, 500 (M) (Native American—Plains Indians)

Greenfield, Eloise. *First Pink Light*, 530, 531 (P) (African American)

  *Grandmama's Joy*, 532 (P) (African American)

  *Honey, I Love*, 534 (PS/P) (African American)

  *Honey, I Love: And Other Love Poems*, 535 (P/M) (African American)

Grifalconi, Ann. *Kinda Blue*, 555 (P) (African American)

Hamanaka, Sheila. *All the Colors of the Earth*, 579 (PS/P) (Multicultural)

Hort, Lenny. *How Many Stars in the Sky?*, 667 (P) (African American)

Hudson, Wade. *I Love My Family*, 691 (P) (African American)

Johnson, Angela. *Mama Bird, Baby Birds*, 736 (PS) (African American)
  *One of Three*, 737 (P) (African American)

Johnson, Dolores. *Your Dad Was Just Like You*, 749 (P) (African American)

Joosse, Barbara. *Mama, Do You Love Me?*, 767 (PS/P) (Native American—Inuit)

Lacapa, Michael, reteller. *The Flute Player: An Apache Folktale*, 837 (M) (Native American—Apache)

Lauture, Denizé. *Father and Son*, 851 (P) (African American)

Lewin, Hugh. *Jafta—The Journey*, 882 (P) (African—South Africa)
  *Jafta's Father*, 884 (P) (African—South Africa)

Loh, Morag Jeanette. *Tucking Mommy In*, 909 (P) (Multicultural)

Mayer, Marianna. *The Golden Swan: An East Indian Tale of Love from the Mahabharata*, 992 (M) (Asian—India)

Meeker, Clare Hodgson, adapter. *A Tale of Two Rice Birds: A Folktale from Thailand*, 1006 (M) (Asian—Thailand)

Mitchell, Rita Phillips. *Hue Boy*, 1029 (P/M) (Caribbean)

Morris, Ann. *Loving*, 1064 (PS/P) (Multicultural)

O'Brien, Anne Sibley, adapter. *The Princess and the Beggar: A Korean Folktale*, 1111 (M) (Asian—Korea)

Peterson, Jeanne Whitehouse. *My Mama Sings*, 1165 (P) (African American)

Scott, Ann Herbert. *On Mother's Lap*, 1297 (P) (Native American—Eskimo)

Sonneborn, Ruth A. *Friday Night Is Papa Night*, 1348 (P) (Caribbean - Puerto Rico)

Steptoe, John. *Baby Says*, 1376 (PS) (African American)
  *Daddy Is a Monster . . . Sometimes*, 1378 (P) (African American)

Sun, Chyng Feng. *Mama Bear*, 1403 (P) (Asian American—China)

Van Laan, Nancy. *Mama Rocks, Papa Sings*, 1489 (P) (Caribbean—Haiti)

Voigt, Cynthia. *Come a Stranger*, 1496 (U) (African American)

Williams, Vera B. *A Chair for My Mother*, 1554 (P) (Hispanic American)

Wyeth, Sharon Dennis. *Always My Dad*, 1587 (P) (African American)


## Emotions—sadness

Alexander, Sue. *Nadia the Willful*, 42 (P) (Middle Eastern—Arabia)

Clifton, Lucille. *Everett Anderson's Goodbye*, 270 (M/U) (African American)

Coerr, Eleanor. *Sadako*, 284 (M/U) (Asian—Japan)
  *Sadako and the Thousand Paper Cranes*, 285 (M/U) (Asian - Japan)

Gray, Libba Moore. *Dear Willie Rudd*, 514 (P) (African American)

Grifalconi, Ann. *Kinda Blue*, 555 (P) (African American)
  *Osa's Pride*, 557 (P) (African)

Kidd, Diana. *Onion Tears*, 801 (M) (Asian—Vietnam)

Lewin, Hugh. *Jafta's Father*, 884 (P) (African—South Africa)

Marie, D. *Tears for Ashan*, 974 (M) (African)

Nodar, Carmen Santiago. *Abuelita's Paradise*, 1104 (P) (Caribbean—Puerto Rico)

Richardson, Jean. *The Courage Seed*, 1218 (M) (Native American)

## Family life (cont.)

*Evan's Corner*, 647 (P/M) (African American)

Hill, Kirkpatrick. *Winter Camp*, 648 (U) (Native American—Athabascan)

Hirschfelder, Arlene B., and Beverly R. Singer, selectors. *Rising Voices: Writings of Young Native Americans*, 651 (U) (Native American)

Hoffman, Mary. *Boundless Grace*, 659 (P) (African American)

Hong, Lily Toy, reteller. *Two of Everything: A Chinese Folktale*, 661 (M) (Asian—China)

Howard, Elizabeth Fitzgerald. *Chita's Christmas Tree*, 673 (P) (African American)

Hoyt-Goldsmith, Diane. *Arctic Hunter*, 677 (M) (Native American—Inupiat)

*Celebrating Kwanzaa*, 678 (M) (African American)

*Cherokee Summer*, 679 (M) (Native American—Cherokee)

*Hoang Anh: A Vietnamese American Boy*, 680 (M) (Asian American—Vietnam)

*Pueblo Storyteller*, 681 (M) (Native American—Cochiti Pueblo)

*Totem Pole*, 682 (M) (Native American—Tsimshian)

Hru, Dakari. *Joshua's Masai Mask*, 683 (M) (African American)

Hudson, Wade. *I Love My Family*, 691 (P) (African American)

*Jamal's Busy Day*, 693 (P) (African American)

Hunter, Kristin. *Boss Cat*, 702 (M) (African American)

Hurmence, Belinda. *A Girl Called Boy*, 704 (U) (African American)

*Tough Tiffany*, 705 (M/U) (African American)

Hurwitz, Johanna. *New Shoes for Silvia*, 707 (P) (Latin American)

Hyppolite, Joanne. *Seth and Samona*, 710 (U) (Caribbean American—Haiti)

Isadora, Rachel. *Over the Green Hills*, 717 (P) (African—South Africa)

Johnson, Angela. *Joshua by the Sea*, 732 (PS) (African American)

*Julius*, 734 (P) (African American)

*The Leaving Morning*, 735 (P) (African American)

Johnson, Dolores. *Papa's Stories*, 745 (P) (African American)

*Seminole Diary*, 746 (M) (African American)

Jordan, June. *Kimako's Story*, 768 (P) (African American)

*New Life: New Room*, 769 (M) (African American)

Joseph, Lynn. *An Island Christmas*, 771 (P) (Caribbean)

Keats, Ezra Jack. *Louie's Search*, 783 (P) (Multicultural)

*Peter's Chair*, 785 (PS/P) (African American)

Keegan, Marcia. *Pueblo Boy: Growing Up in Two Worlds*, 790 (M) (Native American—Pueblo)

Kendall, Russ. *Eskimo Boy: Life in an Inupiaq Eskimo Village*, 794 (M) (Native American—Inupiaq)

Kessler, Cristina. *One Night: A Story from the Desert*, 798 (P) (Middle Eastern—Tuareg)

Ketteman, Helen. *Not Yet, Yvette*, 799 (PS/P) (African American)

Kroll, Virginia. *Masai and I*, 827 (P) (African—Masai)

Krull, Kathleen. *Maria Molina and the Days of the Dead*, 831 (M) (Mexican)

Lacapa, Kathleen, and Michael Lacapa. *Less Than Half, More Than Whole*, 835 (M) (Multicultural)

Lee, Huy Voun. *At the Beach*, 856 (P) (Asian—China)

## Family life (cont.)

Lee, Marie G. *If It Hadn't Been for Yoon Jun*, 861 (U) (Asian American—Korea)

Lemieux, Margo. *Full Worm Moon*, 864 (M) (Native American—Algonquian)

Levinson, Riki. *Our Home Is the Sea*, 877 (P) (Asian—Hong Kong)

Levitin, Sonia. *The Golem and the Dragon Girl*, 878 (U) (Multicultural)

Lewin, Hugh. *Jafta*, 879 (P) (African—South Africa)

  *Jafta—The Town*, 883 (P) (African—South Africa)

Lexau, Joan M. *Striped Ice Cream*, 892 (M) (African American)

Linden, Ann Marie. *Emerald Blue*, 897 (P) (Caribbean)

Lomas Garza, Carmen. *Family Pictures/Cuadros de Familia*, 910 (P/M) (Hispanic American)

Lotz, Karen E. *Can't Sit Still*, 917 (P) (African American)

Lovelace, Maud Hart. *The Trees Kneel at Christmas*, 919 (M) (Middle Eastern American—Lebanon)

Luenn, Nancy. *Nessa's Story*, 922 (P) (Native American—Inuit)

Lyon, George Ella. *Dreamplace*, 925 (P) (Native American—Pueblo)

  *Who Came Down That Road?*, 928 (P/M) (Native American)

McDonald, Becky Bring. *Katie Couldn't*, 942 (PS/P) (Asian American)

McDonald, Joyce. *Mail-Order Kid*, 944 (M) (Asian American—Korea)

McKissack, Patricia. *Nettie Jo's Friends*, 952 (P) (African American)

Mahy, Margaret. *The Seven Chinese Brothers*, 965 (M) (Asian—China)

Maiorano, Robert. *Francisco*, 966 (P) (West Indian)

Martel, Cruz. *Yagua Days*, 977 (M) (Hispanic American—Puerto Rico)

Mead, Alice. *Crossing the Starlight Bridge*, 1000 (M) (Native American—Penobscot)

Medearis, Angela Shelf. *Poppa's New Pants*, 1003 (P) (African American)

Meyer, Carolyn. *Rio Grande Stories*, 1013 (U) (Multicultural)

  *White Lilacs*, 1014 (U) (African American)

Mills, Claudia. *A Visit to Amy-Claire*, 1026 (PS/P) (Asian American)

Mohr, Nicholasa. *Felita*, 1033 (M) (Hispanic American—Puerto Rico)

  *Going Home*, 1034 (M) (Hispanic American—Puerto Rico)

Mollel, Tololwa M. *Big Boy*, 1035 (P) (African)

Moore, Emily. *Just My Luck*, 1048 (M) (African American)

  *Something to Count On*, 1049 (M) (African American)

Morris, Ann. *Houses and Homes*, 1063 (PS/P) (Multicultural)

  *Loving*, 1064 (PS/P) (Multicultural)

Moss, Marissa. *Mel's Diner*, 1072 (P) (African American)

Munsch, Robert. *Where is Gah-Ning?*, 1075 (P) (Asian American—China)

Myers, Walter Dean. *Darnell Rock Reporting*, 1082 (U) (African American)

  *Me, Mop, and the Moondance Kid*, 1084 (M/U) (African American)

  *Mop, Moondance, and the Nagasaki Knights*, 1085 (M/U) (African American)

Naidoo, Beverley. *Journey to Jo'burg: A South African Story*, 1091 (U) (African—South Africa)

Namioka, Lensey. *Yang the Third and Her Impossible Family*, 1094 (M) (Asian American—China)

  *Yang the Youngest and His Terrible Ear*, 1095 (M) (Asian American—China)

Neasi, Barbara J. *Listen to Me*, 1098 (PS/P) (African American)

Neville, Emily Cheney. *The China Year: A Novel*, 1100 (U) (Asian—China)

Onyefulu, Ifeoma. *Emeka's Gift: An African Counting Story*, 1129 (P) (African)

Oodgeroo. *Dreamtime: Aboriginal Stories*, 1131 (M) (Australian—Aborigine)

Osofsky, Audrey. *Dreamcatcher*, 1138 (M) (Native American—Ojibway)

Palacios, Argentina. *A Christmas Surprise for Chabelita*, 1147 (M) (Central American—Panama)

Paterson, Katherine. *Park's Quest*, 1151 (U) (Asian American—Vietnam)

Pettit, Jayne. *My Name Is San Ho*, 1167 (U) (Asian American—Vietnam)

Pinkney, Andrea Davis. *Hold Fast to Dreams*, 1172 (U) (African American)

*Seven Candles for Kwanzaa*, 1173 (P/M) (African American)

Pinkney, Gloria Jean. *Back Home*, 1175 (P/M) (African American)

Politi, Leo. *Juanita*, 1182 (M) (Mexican American)

*Three Stalks of Corn*, 1184 (M) (Mexican American)

Porte, Barbara Ann. *"Leave That Cricket Be, Alan Lee,"* 1188 (P) (Asian American—China)

Porter, Connie. *Addy Saves the Day: A Summer Story*, 1190 (M) (African American)

*Addy's Surprise: A Christmas Story*, 1191 (M) (African American)

*Changes for Addy: A Winter Story*, 1192 (M) (African American)

*Meet Addy: An American Girl*, 1194 (M) (African American)

Poydar, Nancy. *Busy Bea*, 1196 (P) (African American)

Prusski, Jeffrey. *Bring Back the Deer*, 1200 (P) (Native American)

Quattlebaum, Mary. *Jackson Jones and the Puddle of Thorns*, 1202 (M) (African American)

Rattigan, Jama Kim. *Dumpling Soup*, 1210 (P) (Hawaiian)

Ringgold, Faith. *Aunt Harriet's Underground Railroad in the Sky*, 1220 (P/M) (African American)

*Dinner at Aunt Connie's House*, 1221 (P/M) (African American)

*Tar Beach*, 1222 (P/M) (African American)

Ryan, Pam Muñoz. *One Hundred Is a Family*, 1258 (PS/P) (Multicultural)

Saint James, Synthia. *The Gifts of Kwanzaa*, 1264 (P) (African American)

Samuels, Vyanne. *Carry Go Bring Come*, 1268 (P) (Caribbean—Jamaica)

Say, Allen. *The Lost Lake*, 1285 (M) (Asian American)

*Tree of Cranes*, 1288 (P/M) (Asian American—Japan)

Schermbrucker, Reviva. *Charlie's House*, 1291 (P/M) (African—South Africa)

Scott, Ann Herbert. *Sam*, 1298 (P) (African American)

Sebestyen, Ouida. *Words by Heart*, 1300 (U) (African American)

Seed, Jenny. *Ntombi's Song*, 1301 (PS/P) (African—South Africa)

Seltzer, Isadore. *The House I Live In: At Home in America*, 1303 (P) (Multicultural)

Sewell, Marcia. *People of the Breaking Day*, 1305 (M) (Native American—Wampanoag)

Shelby, Anne. *We Keep a Store*, 1312 (P) (African American)

Smalls-Hector, Irene. *Dawn and the Round To-It*, 1337 (PS/P) (African American)

Soto, Gary. *Baseball in April: And Other Stories*, 1349 (U) (Hispanic American)

Weisman, Joan. *The Storyteller*, 1532 (P) (Native American—Pueblo)

Williams, Karen Lynn. *When Africa Was Home*, 1551 (P) (African)

Williams, Sherley Anne. *Working Cotton*, 1552 (M) (African American)

Williams, Vera B. *"More, More, More" Said the Baby: 3 Love Stories*, 1556 (P) (Multicultural)

    *Music, Music for Everyone*, 1557 (P) (Hispanic American)

    *Something Special for Me*, 1559 (P) (Hispanic American)

Willis, Meredith Sue. *The Secret Super Powers of Marco*, 1560 (M) (Multicultural)

Wilson, Beth P. *Jenny*, 1563 (P) (African American)

Wilson, Johnniece Marshall. *Robin on His Own*, 1566 (M/U) (African American)

Wong, Janet S. *Good Luck Gold: And Other Poems*, 1577 (M) (Asian American)

Yarborough, Camille. *Tamika and the Wisdom Rings*, 1593 (M) (African American)

Yee, Paul. *Roses Sing on New Snow: A Delicious Tale*, 1597 (P) (Asian American—China)

Yep, Laurence. *The Serpent's Children*, 1614 (U) (Asian—China)

    *The Star Fisher*, 1616 (U) (Asian American—China)

Young, Ronder Thomas. *Learning by Heart*, 1634 (U) (African American)

## Family life—aunts, uncles

Caines, Jeannette. *Just Us Women*, 213 (P) (African American)

Everett, Gwen. *Li'l Sis and Uncle Willie: A Story Based on the Life and Paintings of William H. Johnson*, 410 (M) (African American)

Grifalconi, Ann. *Kinda Blue*, 555 (P) (African American)

Howard, Elizabeth Fitzgerald. *Aunt Flossie's Hats (and Crab Cakes Later)*, 672 (P) (African American)

    *Mac & Marie & the Train Toss Surprise*, 674 (P) (African American)

Johnson, Angela. *The Girl Who Wore Snakes*, 731 (P) (African American)

Mathis, Sharon Bell. *The Hundred Penny Box*, 985 (M) (African American)

Mitchell, Margaret King. *Uncle Jed's Barbershop*, 1028 (P/M) (African American)

Mora, Pat. *A Birthday Basket for Tia*, 1055 (P) (Mexican American)

Nunes, Susan. *The Last Dragon*, 1106 (P) (Asian American—China)

O'Dell, Scott. *Zia*, 1123 (U) (Native American)

Oliviero, Jamie. *Som See and the Magic Elephant*, 1127 (M) (Asian—Thailand)

Pinkney, Gloria Jean. *The Sunday Outing*, 1176 (P/M) (African American)

Say, Allen. *A River Dream*, 1287 (P) (Asian American)

Soto, Gary. *Crazy Weekend*, 1352 (U) (Hispanic American)

## Family life—cousins

Hamilton, Virginia. *Cousins*, 583 (M) (African American)

## Family life—fathers

Bang, Molly. *Ten, Nine, Eight*, 85 (PS/P) (African American)

Best, Cari. *Taxi! Taxi!*, 128 (P) (Hispanic American)

## Family life—fathers (cont.)

Caines, Jeannette. *Daddy*, 211 (P) (African American)

Cameron, Ann. *Julian, Dream Doctor*, 215 (M) (African American)

Cazet, Denys. *Born in the Gravy*, 233 (P) (Mexican American)

Chang, Margaret, and Raymond Chang. *In the Eye of War*, 240 (U) (Asian—China)

Clifton, Lucille. *Amifika*, 265 (P) (African American)

Greenfield, Eloise. *Daddy and I*, 527 (PS) (African American)

First Pink Light, 530, 531 (P) (African American)

Hort, Lenny. *How Many Stars in the Sky?*, 667 (P) (African American)

Howard, Elizabeth Fitzgerald. *Papa Tells Chita a Story*, 675 (P) (African American)

Isadora, Rachel. *At the Crossroads*, 715 (P) (African—South Africa)

Johnson, Angela. *Joshua's Night Whispers*, 733 (PS) (African American)

Johnson, Dolores. *Your Dad Was Just Like You*, 749 (P) (African American)

Kroll, Virginia. *Africa Brothers and Sisters*, 825 (P) (African American)

Lauture, Denizé. *Father and Son*, 851 (P) (African American)

Lewin, Hugh. *Jafta: The Homecoming*, 881 (P) (African—South Africa)

Jafta—The Journey, 882 (P) (African—South Africa)

Jafta's Father, 884 (P) (African—South Africa)

Mandelbaum, Pili. *You Be Me, I'll Be You*, 970 (P) (Multicultural)

Medearis, Angela Shelf. *Our People*, 1002 (P) (African American)

Mitchell, Rita Phillips. *Hue Boy*, 1029 (P/M) (Caribbean)

Myers, Christopher A., and Lynne Born Myers. *Forest of the Clouded Leopard*, 1079 (U) (African—Iban)

Patrick, Denise Lewis. *The Car Washing Street*, 1153 (P) (African American)

Pringle, Laurence. *Octopus Hug*, 1199 (PS/P) (African American)

Roy, Ronald. *A Thousand Pails of Water*, 1253 (P) (Asian)

Sacks, Margaret. *Themba*, 1260 (M) (African—South Africa)

Smith, Edward Biko. *A Lullaby for Daddy*, 1340 (PS) (African American)

Sonneborn, Ruth A. *Friday Night Is Papa Night*, 1348 (P) (Caribbean—Puerto Rico)

Spohn, David. *Home Field*, 1366 (M) (Multicultural)

Starry Night, 1368 (M) (Multicultural)

Steptoe, John. *Daddy Is a Monster . . . Sometimes*, 1378 (P) (African American)

Udry, Janice May. *What Mary Jo Shared*, 1486 (P) (African American)

Woodson, Jacqueline. *Between Madison and Palmetto*, 1580 (U) (African American)

Wright, Betty Ren. *The Day Our TV Broke Down*, 1583 (P) (African American)

Wyeth, Sharon Dennis. *Always My Dad*, 1587 (P) (African American)

Yep, Laurence. *Dragonwings*, 1607 (U) (Asian American—China)

Yolen, Jane. *The Emperor and the Kite*, 1620 (M) (Asian—China)

The Girl Who Loved the Wind, 1622 (M) (Asian)

## Family life—foster family

Blue, Rose. *A Quiet Place*, 144 (M) (African American)

Grifalconi, Ann. *Not Home: A Novel*, 556 (U) (African American)

Steptoe, John. *Stevie*, 1380 (P) (African American)

## Family life—grandfathers

Brooks, Bruce. *Everywhere*, 162 (M/U) (African American)

Buckley, Helen E. *Grandfather and I*, 192 (PS/P) (African American)

Bunting, Eve. *A Day's Work*, 196 (P) (Mexican American)

Coerr, Eleanor. *Chang's Paper Pony*, 282 (P) (Asian American—China)

Engel, Diana. *Fishing*, 401 (P) (African American)

Gardiner, John Reynolds. *Stone Fox*, 457 (M) (Native American)

Greenfield, Eloise. *Grandpa's Face*, 533 (P) (African American)

Igus, Toyomi. *When I Was Little*, 711 (P) (African American)

Jacobs, Shannon K. *The Boy Who Loved Morning*, 720 (M) (Native American)

Johnson, Angela. *When I Am Old with You*, 742 (P) (African American)

Johnson, Dolores. *Your Dad Was Just Like You*, 749 (P) (African American)

Keller, Holly. *Grandfather's Dream*, 791 (P) (Asian—Vietnam)

Kroll, Virginia. *Wood-hoopoe Willie*, 830 (P) (African American)

Martin, Bill, Jr., and John Archambault. *Knots on a Counting Rope*, 978 (P/M) (Native American)

Mora, Pat. *Pablo's Tree*, 1056 (P) (Mexican American)

Orr, Katherine. *My Grandpa and the Sea*, 1135 (M) (Caribbean)

Pomerantz, Charlotte. *The Outside Dog*, 1186 (P) (Caribbean—Puerto Rico)

Rochelle, Belinda. *When Jo Louis Won the Title*, 1229 (P/M) (African American)

Say, Allen. *Grandfather's Journey*, 1283 (M) (Asian American—Japan)

Shigekawa, Marlene. *Blue Jay in the Desert*, 1320 (M) (Asian American—Japan)

Stock, Catherine. *Emma's Dragon Hunt*, 1388 (PS/P) (Asian American—China)

Stolz, Mary. *Coco Grimes*, 1393 (M) (African American)

  *Go Fish!*, 1394 (M) (African American)

  *Stealing Home*, 1395 (M/U) (African American)

  *Storm in the Night*, 1396 (P/M) (African American)

Stroud, Virginia A. *Doesn't Fall Off His Horse*, 1401 (M) (Native American—Kiowa)

Tompert, Ann. *Grandfather Tang's Story*, 1445 (P) (Asian—China)

Wallace, Ian. *Chin Chiang and the Dragon's Dance*, 1506 (P) (Asian American—China)

Walter, Mildred Pitts. *Justin and the Best Biscuits in the World*, 1511 (M/U) (African American)

Whitethorne, Baje. *Sunpainters: Eclipse of the Navajo Sun*, 1543 (M) (Native American—Navajo)

## Family life—grandmothers

Ackerman, Karen. *By the Dawn's Early Light*, 17 (P) (African American)

Anderson, Janet S. *The Key into Winter*, 52 (M) (African American)

## Family life—grandmothers (cont.)

Belton, Sandra. *May'naise Sandwiches and Sunshine Tea*, 116 (M) (African American)

Bruchac, Joseph. *Fox Song*, 171 (P) (Native American)

Bryan, Ashley. *Turtle Knows Your Name*, 190 (M) (Caribbean—West Indies)

Buckley, Helen E. *Grandmother and I*, 193 (PS/P) (African American)

Caines, Jeannette. *Window Wishing*, 214 (P) (African American)

Cameron, Ann. *The Most Beautiful Place in the World*, 219 (M) (Central American—Guatemala)

Castañeda, Omar S. *Abuela's Weave*, 231 (M) (Central American—Guatemala)

Choi, Sook Nyul. *Halmoni and the Picnic*, 255 (P) (Asian American—Korea)

Coutant, Helen. *First Snow*, 314 (P) (Asian American—Vietnam)

Curtis, Gavin. *Grandma's Baseball*, 328 (P) (African American)

Daly, Niki. *Not So Fast Songololo*, 332 (P) (African—South Africa)

DeGross, Monalisa. *Donavan's Word Jar*, 345 (M) (African American)

Dorros, Arthur. *Abuela*, 377 (P/M) (Hispanic American)

Dupré, Rick. *The Wishing Chair*, 387 (P) (African American)

Flournoy, Valerie. *The Patchwork Quilt*, 434 (P/M) (African American)

Garland, Sherry. *The Lotus Seed*, 458 (P) (Asian American—Vietnam)

Greenfield, Eloise. *Grandmama's Joy*, 532 (P) (African American)
  *William and the Good Old Days*, 547 (P) (African American)

Guback, Georgia. *Luka's Quilt*, 567 (P) (Hawaiian)

Hamilton, Virginia. *Cousins*, 583 (M) (African American)

Johnson, Angela. *Toning the Sweep*, 741 (U) (African American)

Luenn, Nancy. *Nessa's Fish*, 921 (P) (Native American—Inuit)

Miles, Miska. *Annie and the Old One*, 1018 (M) (Native American –Navajo)

Miller, Montzalee. *My Grandmother's Cookie Jar*, 1025 (P) (Native American)

Nodar, Carmen Santiago. *Abuelita's Paradise*, 1104 (P) (Caribbean—Puerto Rico)

Nye, Naomi Shihab. *Sitti's Secrets*, 1109 (P) (Middle Eastern American—Arab)

Patrick, Denise Lewis. *Red Dancing Shoes*, 1154 (P) (African American)

Polacco, Patricia. *Chicken Sunday*, 1179 (M) (African American)

Sakai, Kimiko. *Sachiko Means Happiness*, 1265 (P) (Asian American—Japan)

Sloat, Teri, reteller. *The Eye of the Needle: Based on a Yupik Tale as Told by Betty Huffman*, 1333 (M) (Native American—Yupik)

Stewart, Dianne. *The Dove*, 1385 (P) (African—South Africa)

Talbert, Marc. *A Sunburned Prayer*, 1407 (U) (Mexican American)

Tan, Amy. *Moon Lady*, 1409 (M) (Asian—China)

Tiller, Ruth. *Cinnamon, Mint, & Mothballs: A Visit to Grandmother's House*, 1442 (P) (Asian American)

Udry, Janice May. *Mary Jo's Grandmother*, 1485 (P) (African American)

Walter, Mildred Pitts. *Trouble's Child*, 1516 (U) (African American)

Wheeler, Bernelda. *Where Did You Get Your Moccasins?*, 1538 (P) (Native American)

Woodson, Jacqueline. *Maizon at Blue Hill*, 1582 (U) (African American)

Yep, Laurence. *Child of the Owl*, 1605 (U) (Asian American—China)

## Family life—grandparents

Brusca, María Cristina. *On the Pampas*, 177 (P) (South American—Argentina)

Gordon, Ginger. *My Two Worlds*, 510 (P) (Hispanic American)

Hest, Amy. *Ruby's Storm*, 640 (P) (Hispanic American)

Johnson, Herschel. *A Visit to the Country*, 750 (P) (African American)

Liddell, Janice. *Imani and the Flying Africans*, 894 (M) (African American)

Oppenheim, Shulamith Levey. *Fireflies for Nathan*, 1132 (P) (African American)

Perkins, Mitali. *The Sunita Experiment*, 1163 (U) (Asian American—India)

Torres, Leyla. *Saturday Sancocho*, 1449 (P) (South American)

## Family life—great-grandparents

Clifton, Lucille. *The Lucky Stone*, 274 (M) (African American)

## Family life—mothers

Ackerman, Karen. *By the Dawn's Early Light*, 17 (P) (African American)

Barber, Barbara E. *Saturday at The New You*, 94 (P) (African American)

Chapman, Christina. *Treasure in the Attic*, 242 (P) (African American)

Clark, Ann Nolan. *In My Mother's House*, 259 (P) (Native American)

Eisenberg, Phyllis Rose. *You're My Nikki*, 396 (P) (African American)

Gilcrist, Jan Spivey. *Indigo and Moonlight Gold*, 474 (P) (African American)

Johnson, Angela. *Mama Bird, Baby Birds*, 736 (PS) (African American)

   *Tell Me a Story, Mama*, 740 (P) (African American)

Johnson, Dolores. *What Will Mommy Do When I'm at School?*, 748 (PS/P) (African American)

Joosse, Barbara. *Mama, Do You Love Me?*, 767 (PS/P) (Native American—Inuit)

Joseph, Lynn. *Jasmine's Parlour Day*, 772 (P) (Caribbean—Trinidad)

Lehne, Judith Logan. *When the Ragman Sings*, 862 (U) (African American)

Lewin, Hugh. *Jafta's Mother*, 885 (P) (African—South Africa)

Loh, Morag Jeanette. *Tucking Mommy In*, 909 (P) (Multicultural)

Peterson, Jeanne Whitehouse. *My Mama Sings*, 1165 (P) (African American)

Pomerantz, Charlotte. *The Chalk Doll*, 1185 (P) (Caribbean—Jamaica)

Scott, Ann Herbert. *On Mother's Lap*, 1297 (P) (Native American—Eskimo)

Smalls-Hector, Irene. *Jonathan and His Mommy*, 1339 (PS/P) (African American)

Sun, Chyng Feng. *Mama Bear*, 1403 (P) (Asian American—China)

Weiss, Nicki. *On a Hot, Hot Day*, 1535 (P) (Hispanic American)

Williams, Karen Lynn. *Tap-Tap*, 1550 (M) (Caribbean—Haiti)

Williams, Vera B. *A Chair for My Mother*, 1554 (P) (Hispanic American)

## Family life—siblings

Adoff, Arnold. *Hard to Be Six*, 26 (P) (Multicultural)

Banks, Jacqueline Turner. *Egg-Drop Blues*, 90 (U) (African American)

Bishop, Claire Huchet. *The Five Chinese Brothers*, 141 (M) (Asian—China)

Blackman, Malorie. *Girl Wonder and the Terrific Twins*, 142 (M) (African American)

Brenner, Barbara. *Rosa and Marco and the Three Wishes*, 159 (P) (Hispanic)

## Family life—siblings (cont.)

Caines, Jeannette. *Abby*, 210 (PS) (African American)

Clifton, Lucille. *My Brother Fine with Me*, 275 (P) (African American)

Cohlene, Terri, adapter. *Little Firefly: An Algonquian Legend*, 295 (M) (Native American—Algonquian)

Cooper, Susan. *Jethro and the Jumbie*, 310 (M) (Caribbean)

Cowen-Fletcher, Jane. *It Takes a Village*, 315 (P) (African—Benin)

Dorris, Michael. *Morning Girl*, 376 (U) (Native American—Taino)

Duncan, Alice Faye. *Willie Jerome*, 385 (P) (African American)

Greenfield, Eloise. *She Come Bringin Me That Little Baby Girl*, 543 (P) (African American)

   *Sister*, 544 (M) (African American)

Grifalconi, Ann. *Not Home: A Novel*, 556 (U) (African American)

Havill, Juanita. *Jamaica Tag-Along*, 630 (P) (African American)

Hayes, Sarah. *Eat Up, Gemma*, 633 (PS) (African American)

   *Happy Christmas, Gemma*, 634 (PS) (African American)

Ho, Minfong, and Saphan Ros. *The Two Brothers*, 653 (M) (Asian—Cambodia)

Howard, Elizabeth Fitzgerald. *The Train to Lulu's*, 676 (P) (African American)

Jaffe, Nina, reteller. *Older Brother, Younger Brother: A Korean Folktale*, 722 (M) (Asian—Korea)

Johnson, Angela. *Do Like Kyla*, 730 (PS/P) (African American)

   *One of Three*, 737 (P) (African American)

Kalman, Maira. *Sayonora, Mrs. Kackleman*, 775 (P) (Asian—Japan)

Kurtz, Jane. *Fire on the Mountain*, 833 (M) (African—Ethiopia)

Martin, Rafe. *The Rough-Face Girl*, 983 (M) (Native American—Algonquian)

Myers, Walter Dean. *Scorpions*, 1088 (U) (African American)

Pfeffer, Susan Beth. *The Riddle Streak*, 1168 (M) (African American)

San Souci, Robert D., reteller. *Sootface: An Ojibwa Cinderella Story*, 1279 (M) (Native American—Ojibway)

Schroeder, Alan. *The Stone Lion*, 1295 (M) (Asian—Tibet)

Smothers, Ethel Footman. *Down in the Piney Woods*, 1342 (U) (African American)

   *Moriah's Pond*, 1343 (U) (African American)

Steptoe, John. *Baby Says*, 1376 (PS) (African American)

Tsutsui, Yoriko. *Anna in Charge*, 1463 (P) (Asian—Japan)

   *Anna's Special Present*, 1465 (P) (Asian—Japan)

Walter, Mildred Pitts. *Two and Too Much*, 1517 (P) (African American)

Warren, Cathy. *Fred's First Day*, 1524 (PS) (African American)

Wilson, Johnniece Marshall. *Oh, Brother*, 1564 (M) (African American)

## Family life—step families

Day, Nancy Raines. *The Lion's Whiskers: An Ethiopian Folktale*, 338 (M) (African—Ethiopia)

## Fans

Singer, Marilyn. *The Painted Fan*, 1327 (M) (Asian—China)

## Fantasy

Anderson, Janet S. *The Key into Winter*, 52 (M) (African American)

Chew, Ruth. *Royal Magic*, 244 (M) (African American)

Cummings, Pat. *C.L.O.U.D.S.*, 324 (P) (African American)

Goldberg, Whoopi. *Alice*, 504 (M) (African American)

Hamilton, Virginia. *The Magical Adventures of Pretty Pearl*, 591 (U) (African heritage)

Hurmence, Belinda. *A Girl Called Boy*, 704 (U) (African American)

Paulsen, Gary. *Canyons*, 1156 (U) (Native American—Apache)

Richemont, Enid. *The Magic Skateboard*, 1219 (M) (African heritage)

Singer, Marilyn. *The Painted Fan*, 1327 (M) (Asian—China)

Yep, Laurence. *The Ghost Fox*, 1608 (M) (Asian—China)

## Farms

Hamilton, Virginia. *Drylongso*, 585 (M) (African American)

## Format, unusual—board books

Hudson, Cheryl Willis. *Animal Sounds for Baby*, 686 (PS) (African American)

## Festivals

Cohen, Miriam. *Born to Dance Samba*, 291 (M) (South American—Brazil)

Delacre, Lulu. *Vejigante Masquerader*, 349 (M) (Caribbean—Puerto Rico)

Dorros, Arthur. *Tonight Is Carnaval*, 379 (P/M) (South American—Peru)

Gollub, Matthew. *The Moon Was at a Fiesta*, 506 (P) (Mexican)

Lloyd, Errol. *Nini at Carnival*, 906 (P) (Mexican)

Pennington, Daniel. *Itse Selu: Cherokee Harvest Festival*, 1162 (M) (Native American—Cherokee)

## Fields, meadows

Carlstrom, Nancy White. *Wild Wild Sunflower Child Anna*, 226 (PS/P) (African American)

## Fire

Crespo, George, reteller. *How Iwariwa the Cayman Learned to Share: A Yanomami Myth*, 317 (M) (South American—Yanomamo Indians)

London, Jonathan, reteller. *Fire Race: A Karuk Coyote Tale about How Fire Came to the People*, 911 (M) (Native American—Karuk)

Maddern, Eric. *Rainbow Bird: An Aboriginal Folktale from Northern Australia*, 962 (M) (Australian—Aborigine)

Roth, Susan L. *Fire Came to the Earth People: A Dahomean Folktale*, 1250 (M) (African)

Troughton, Joanna, reteller. *How Rabbit Stole the Fire: A North American Indian Folk Tale*, 1455 (M) (Native American)

Van Laan, Nancy, reteller. *Rainbow Crow: A Lenape Tale*, 1490 (M) (Native American—Lenape)

## Fireworks

Flora, James. *The Fabulous Firework Family*, 432 (M) (Mexican)

## Fish

Hamada, Cheryl, reteller. *Kao and the Golden Fish: A Folktale from Thailand*, 577 (M) (Asian—Thailand)

Louie, Ai-Ling, reteller. *Yeh-Shen: A Cinderella Story from China*, 918 (M) (Asian—China)

Wang, Rosalind C., reteller. *The Treasure Chest: A Chinese Tale*, 1522 (M) (Asian—China)

Wilson, Barbara Ker. *Wishbones: A Folk Tale from China*, 1562 (M) (Asian—China)

## Fish—sharks

George, Jean Craighead. *Shark Beneath the Reef*, 465 (U) (Mexican)

## Flowers

Bunting, Eve. *Flower Garden*, 197 (PS/P) (African American)

dePaola, Tomie, reteller. *The Legend of the Bluebonnet: An Old Tale of Texas*, 360 (M) (Native American)

*The Legend of the Indian Paintbrush*, 361 (M) (Native American)

*The Legend of the Poinsettia*, 363 (M) (Mexican)

Esbensen, Barbara Juster, reteller. *The Star Maiden: An Ojibway Tale*, 405 (M) (Native American—Ojibway)

Garland, Sherry. *The Lotus Seed*, 458 (P) (Asian American—Vietnam)

## Folktales

Baumgartner, Barbara. *Crocodile! Crocodile! Stories Told Around the World*, 99 (M) (Multicultural)

Belting, Natalia. *The Sun Is a Golden Earring*, 113 (M) (Multicultural)

Brusca, María Cristina. *When Jaguars Ate the Moon: And Other Stories about Animals and Plants of the Americas*, 178 (M) (Multicultural)

Climo, Shirley. *Someone Saw a Spider: Spider Facts and Folktales*, 280 (M) (Multicultural)

DeSpain, Pleasant. *Thirty-Three Multicultural Tales to Tell*, 365 (U) (Multicultural)

Hamilton, Virginia, reteller. *The Dark Way: Stories from the Spirit World*, 584 (U) (Multicultural)

*In the Beginning: Creation Stories from Around the World*, 588 (M) (Multicultural)

Hodges, Margaret, reteller. *Hauntings: Ghosts and Ghouls from Around the World*, 656 (M) (Multicultural)

Ingpen, Robert, and Barbara Hayes. *Folk Tales and Fables of the Americas and the Pacific*, 713 (U) (Multicultural)

Kherdian, David, reteller. *Feathers and Tails: Animal Fables from Around the World*, 800 (M) (Multicultural)

Mayo, Margaret, reteller. *Magical Tales from Many Lands*, 999 (M) (Multicultural)

Osborne, Mary Pope, reteller. *Mermaid Tales from Around the World*, 1137 (M) (Multicultural)

Pellowski, Anne. *Hidden Stories in Plants: Unusual and Easy-to-Tell Stories from Around the World Together with Creative Things to Do While Telling Them*, 1160 (M/U) (Multicultural)

Riordan, James. *The Woman in the Moon: And Other Tales of Forgotten Heroines*, 1223 (M/U) (Multicultural)

Rosen, Michael. *How the Animals Got Their Colors: Animal Myths from Around the World*, 1247 (M) (Multicultural)

*South and North, East and West: The Oxfam Book of Children's Stories*, 1248 (M) (Multicultural)

San Souci, Robert D., reteller. *Short and Shivery: Thirty Chilling Tales*, 1276 (M/U) (Multicultural)

Shannon, George, reteller. *More Stories to Solve: Fifteen Folktales from Around the World*, 1307 (M) (Multicultural)

*Still More Stories to Solve: Fourteen Folktales from Around the World*, 1308 (M) (Multicultural)

*Stories to Solve: Folktales from Around the World*, 1309 (M) (Multicultural)

Shepherd, Sandy. *Myths and Legends from Around the World*, 1314 (M) (Multicultural)

Thornhill, Jan. *Crow and Fox: And Other Animal Legends*, 1441 (M) (Multicultural)

Wiesner, William. *Moon Stories*, 1545 (M) (Multicultural)

Yeoman, John. *The Singing Tortoise: And Other Animal Folktales*, 1602 (M) (Multicultural)

Yep, Laurence. *Tree of Dreams: Ten Tales from the Garden of Night*, 1618 (U) (Multicultural)

## Folktales—Africa

*The Baboon's Umbrella: An African Folktale*, 71 (M) (African)

Berger, Terry. *Black Fairy Tales*, 119 (M) (African)

Bowden, Joan Chase. *Why the Tides Ebb and Flow*, 151 (M) (African)

Bryan, Ashley. *The Adventures of Aku: Or How It Came About That We Shall Always See Okra the Cat Lying on a Velvet Cushion, While Okraman the Dog Sleeps Among the Ashes*, 179 (M) (African)

*Beat the Story-Drum, Pum-Pum*, 181 (M) (African)

*Lion and the Ostrich Chicks: And Other African Folk Tales*, 185 (M) (African)

*The Ox of the Wonderful Horns and Other African Folktales*, 186 (M) (African)

*The Story of Lightning & Thunder*, 189 (M) (African)

Chocolate, Deborah M. Newton. *Imani in the Belly*, 248 (M) (African)

*Talk, Talk: An Ashanti Legend*, 252 (M) (African)

Courlander, Harold, compiler. *The Crest and the Hide: And Other African Stories of Chiefs, Bards, Hunters, Sorcerers, and Common People*, 312 (M/U) (African)

Courlander, Harold, and George Herzog. *The Cow-Tail Switch: And Other West African Stories*, 313 (M/U) (African)

Dayrell, Elphinstone. *Why the Sun and the Moon Live in the Sky: An African Folktale*, 339 (M) (African)

Dee, Ruby, reteller. *Tower to Heaven*, 341 (M) (African)

Dupré, Rick, reteller. *Agassu: Legend of the Leopard King*, 386 (M) (African)

Fairman, Tony, reteller. *Bury My Bones, But Keep My Words: African Tales for Retelling*, 411 (U) (African)

## Folktales—Africa (cont.)

French, Fiona. *Anancy and Mr. Dry-Bone*, 448 (M) (African)

Gleeson, Brian. *Koi and the Kola Nuts*, 482 (M) (African)

Grifalconi, Ann. *The Village of Round and Square Houses*, 558 (M) (African)

Guy, Rosa, translator and adapter. *Mother Crocodile*, 571 (M) (African)

Haley, Gail E., reteller. *A Story, a Story*, 574 (M) (African)

Hull, Robert, reteller. *African Stories*, 698 (M) (African)

Ingpen, Robert, and Barbara Hayes. *Folk Tales and Fables of the Middle East and Africa*, 714 (U) (Multicultural)

Kimmel, Eric A., reteller. *Anansi and the Moss-Covered Rock*, 802 (M) (African)

　*Anansi and the Talking Melon*, 803 (M) (African)

　*Anansi Goes Fishing*, 804 (M) (African)

Lester, Julius. *How Many Spots Does a Leopard Have? and Other Tales*, 869 (M) (African)

McDermott, Gerald, adapter. *Anansi the Spider: A Tale from the Ashanti*, 934 (P) (African—Ashanti)

　*Zomo the Rabbit: A Trickster Tale from West Africa*, 941 (M) (African)

McKissack, Patricia. *Monkey-Monkey's Trick*, 951 (P) (African)

Maddern, Eric, reteller. *The Fire Children: A West African Creation Tale*, 961 (M) (African)

Martin, Francesca. *The Honey Hunters: A Traditional African Tale*, 980 (M) (African)

Medearis, Angela Shelf, adapter. *The Singing Man: A West African Folktale*, 1004 (M) (African)

Mogensen, Jan. *Kakalambalala*, 1032 (M) (African)

Mollel, Tololwa M. *A Promise to the Sun: An African Story*, 1040 (M) (African)

Mwalimu, and Adrienne Kennaway. *Awful Aardvark*, 1078 (M) (African)

Onyefulu, Obi, reteller. *Chinye: A West African Folk Tale*, 1130 (M) (African)

Rose, Anne, reteller. *Akimba and the Magic Cow: A Folktale from Africa*, 1241 (M) (African)

Roth, Susan L. *Fire Came to the Earth People: A Dahomean Folktale*, 1250 (M) (African)

Sierra, Judy. *The Elephant's Wrestling Match*, 1325 (M) (African)

Steptoe, John. *Mufaro's Beautiful Daughters: An African Tale*, 1379 (M) (African)

Troughton, Joanna, reteller. *Tortoise's Dream*, 1458 (M) (African)

White, Carolyn. *The Tree House Children: An African Tale*, 1542 (M) (African)

Williams, Sheron. *And in the Beginning . . .* , 1553 (M) (African)

## Folktales—Africa—Akamba

Mollel, Tololwa M., reteller. *The Princess Who Lost Her Hair: An Akamba Legend*, 1039 (M) (African –Akamba)

## Folktales—Africa—Akan

Chocolate, Deborah M. Newton, reteller. *Spider and the Sky God: An Akan Legend*, 251 (M) (African—Akan)

## Folktales—Africa—Ashanti

Aardema, Verna, reteller. *Anansi Finds a Fool: An Ashanti Tale*, 1 (M) (African—Ashanti)

*Oh, Kojo! How Could You! An Ashanti Tale*, 7 (M) (African—Ashanti)

Appiah, Peggy. *Ananse the Spider: Tales from an Ashanti Village*, 60 (M) (African—Ashanti)

*How Anansi Obtained the Sky God's Stories: An African Folktale from the Ashanti Tribe*, 671 (M) (African—Ashanti)

## Folktales—Africa—Bantu

Aardema, Verna, reteller. *Sebgugugu the Glutton: A Bantu Tale from Rwanda*, 11 (M) (African—Bantu)

Lottridge, Celia Barker, reteller. *The Name of the Tree: A Bantu Folktale*, 916 (M) (African—Bantu)

## Folktales—Africa—Cameroon

Mollel, Tololwa M. *The King and the Tortoise*, 1037 (M) (African—Cameroon)

## Folktales—Africa—East Africa

Rosen, Michael, reteller. *How Giraffe Got Such a Long Neck . . . and Why Rhino Is So Grumpy: A Tale from East Africa*, 1246 (M) (African—East Africa)

## Folktales—Africa—Egypt

Climo, Shirley. *The Egyptian Cinderella*, 278 (M) (African—Egypt)

Lattimore, Deborah Nourse. *The Winged Cat: A Tale of Ancient Egypt*, 849 (M) (African—Egypt)

McDermott, Gerald, reteller. *The Voyage of Osiris: A Myth of Ancient Egypt*, 940 (M) (African—Egypt)

Manniche, Lise, translator. *The Prince Who Knew His Fate: An Ancient Egyptian Tale*, 973 (M) (African—Egypt)

Mike, Jan M., reteller. *Gift of the Nile: An Ancient Egyptian Legend*, 1015 (M) (African—Egypt)

## Folktales—Africa—Ethiopia

Day, Nancy Raines. *The Lion's Whiskers: An Ethiopian Folktale*, 338 (M) (African—Ethiopia)

Kurtz, Jane. *Fire on the Mountain*, 833 (M) (African—Ethiopia)

## Folktales—Africa—Igbo

Mollel, Tololwa M., reteller. *The Flying Tortoise: An Igbo Tale*, 1036 (M) (African—Igbo)

## Folktales—Africa—Ivory Coast

Roddy, Patricia. *Api and the Boy Stranger: A Village Creation Tale*, 1234 (M) (African—Ivory Coast)

Tadjo, Véronique, reteller. *Lord of the Dance: An African Retelling*, 1405 (M) (African—Ivory Coast)

## Folktales—Africa—Khoikhoi

Aardema, Verna, reteller. *Jackal's Flying Lesson: A Khoikhoi Tale*, 5 (M) (African—Khoikhoi)

## Folktales—Africa—Liberia

Aardema, Verna, reteller. *The Vingananee and the Tree Toad: A Liberian Tale*, 13 (M) (African—Liberia)

Dee, Ruby, reteller. *Two Ways to Count to Ten: A Liberian Folktale*, 342 (M) (African—Liberia)

Ellis, Veronica Freeman. *Land of the Four Winds: Kpa Nieh Kpau*, 397 (M) (African—Liberia)

## Folktales—Africa—Madagascar

Rappaport, Doreen. *The New King: A Madagascan Legend*, 1207 (M) (African—Madagascar)

## Folktales—Africa—Masai

Aardema, Verna, reteller. *Who's in Rabbit's House? A Masai Tale*, 15 (M) (African—Masai)

Mann, Kenny. *"I Am Not Afraid!": Based on a Masai Tale*, 972 (P) (African—Masai)

Mollel, Tololwa M. *The Orphan Boy: A Masai Story*, 1038 (M) (African—Masai)
   *Rhinos for Lunch and Elephants for Supper! A Maasai Tale*, 1041 (M) (African—Masai)

## Folktales—Africa—Mpongwe

Aardema, Verna, reteller. *Princess Gorilla and a New Kind of Water: A Mpongwe Tale*, 9 (M) (African—Mpongwe)

## Folktales—Africa—Nandi

Aardema, Verna, reteller. *Bringing the Rain to Kapiti Plain: A Nandi Tale*, 4 (P/M) (African—Nandi)

## Folktales—Africa—Nigeria

Daly, Niki, reteller. *Why the Sun and the Moon Live in the Sky*, 333 (M) (African—Nigeria)

Gerson, Mary-Joan, reteller. *Why the Sky Is Far Away: A Nigerian Folktale*, 473 (M) (African—Nigeria)

## Folktales—Africa—Nuer

Aardema, Verna, reteller. *What's So Funny, Ketu? A Nuer Tale*, 14 (M) (African—Nuer)

## Folktales—Africa—Swahili

Aardema, Verna, reteller. *Rabbit Makes a Monkey of Lion: A Swahili Tale*, 10 (M) (African—Swahili)

Knutson, Barbara, reteller. *How the Guinea Fowl Got Her Spots: A Swahili Tale of Friendship*, 819 (M) (African—Swahili)
   *Sungura and Leopard: A Swahili Trickster Tale*, 820 (M) (African—Swahili)

## Folktales—Africa—Uganda

Serwadda, W. Moses. *Songs and Stories from Uganda*, 1304 (M) (African—Uganda)

## Folktales—Africa—West Africa

Aardema, Verna, reteller. *Why Mosquitoes Buzz in People's Ears: A West African Tale*, 16 (M) (African—West Africa)

Arkhurst, Joyce Cooper, reteller. *The Adventures of Spider: West African Folk Tales*, 62 (M) (African—West Africa)

*More Adventures of Spider: West African Folk Tales*, 63 (M) (African—West Africa)

## Folktales—Africa—Yoruba

Anderson/Sankofa, David A., reteller. *The Origin of Life on Earth: An African Creation Myth*, 54 (M) (African—Yoruba)

Gershator, Phillis, reteller. *The Iroko-man: A Yoruba Folktale*, 469 (M) (African—Yoruba)

## Folktales—Africa—Zaire

Aardema, Verna, reteller. *Traveling to Tondo: A Tale of the Nkundo of Zaire*, 12 (M) (African—Zaire)

Knutson, Barbara, reteller. *Why the Crab Has No Head: An African Tale*, 821 (M) (African—Zaire)

McDermott, Gerald, adapter. *The Magic Tree: A Tale from the Congo*, 937 (M) (African—Zaire)

## Folktales—Africa—Zambia

Lester, Julius, reteller. *The Man Who Knew Too Much: A Moral Tale from the Baila of Zambia*, 873 (M) (African—Zambia)

## Folktales—Africa—Zanzibar

Aardema, Verna, reteller. *Bimwili & the Zimwi: A Tale from Zanzibar*, 2 (M) (African—Zanzibar)

Bible, Charles, adapter. *Hamdaani: A Traditional Tale from Zanzibar*, 129 (M) (African—Zanzibar)

## Folktales—Asia

Davison, Katherine. *Moon Magic: Stories from Asia*, 336 (M) (Asian)

Ingpen, Robert, and Barbara Hayes. *Folk Tales and Fables of Asia and Australia*, 712 (U) (Multicultural)

Livo, Norma J., and Dia Cha. *Folk Stories of the Hmong: Peoples of Laos, Thailand, and Vietnam*, 905 (U) (Asian)

Long, Hua. *The Moon Maiden: And Other Asian Folktales*, 912 (M) (Asian)

## Folktales—Asia—Burma

Troughton, Joanna, reteller. *Make-Believe Tales: A Folk Tale from Burma*, 1457 (M) (Asian—Burma)

## Folktales—Asia—Cambodia

Ho, Minfong, and Saphan Ros. *The Two Brothers*, 653 (M) (Asian—Cambodia)

## Folktales—Asia—Cambodia (cont.)

Tate, Carol. *Tale of the Spiteful Spirits: A Kampuchean Folk Tale*, 1411 (M) (Asian—Cambodia)

Wall, Lina Mao, reteller. *Judge Rabbit and the Tree Spirit: A Folktale from Cambodia/Bilingual in English and Khmer*, 1505 (M) (Asian—Cambodia)

## Folktales—Asia—China

Birdseye, Tom, adapter. *A Song of Stars: An Asian Legend*, 140 (M) (Asian—China)

Bishop, Claire Huchet. *The Five Chinese Brothers*, 141 (M) (Asian—China)

Chang, Cindy, reteller. *The Seventh Sister: A Chinese Legend*, 237 (M) (Asian—China)

Chang, Margaret, and Raymond Chang, retellers. *The Cricket Warrior: A Chinese Tale*, 239 (M) (Asian—China)

Chin, Charlie, reteller. *China's Bravest Girl: The Legend of Hua Mu Lan*, 245 (M) (Asian—China)

Demi. *The Artist and the Architect*, 350 (M) (Asian—China)

　*A Chinese Zoo: Fables and Proverbs*, 351 (M) (Asian—China)

　*The Empty Pot*, 353 (M) (Asian—China)

　*The Magic Boat*, 356 (M) (Asian—China)

　*The Magic Tapestry: A Chinese Folktale*, 357 (M) (Asian—China)

　*The Stone Cutter*, 358 (M) (Asian—China)

　*Under the Shade of the Mulberry Tree*, 359 (M) (Asian—China)

Flack, Marjorie. *The Story about Ping*, 428 (P) (Asian—China)

Hamada, Cheryl, reteller. *The Fourth Question: A Chinese Folktale*, 576 (M) (Asian—China)

Hearn, Lafcadio. *The Voice of the Great Bell*, 635 (M) (Asian—China)

Heyer, Marilee, reteller. *The Weaving of a Dream: A Chinese Folktale*, 642 (M) (Asian—China)

Hillman, Elizabeth. *Min-Yo and the Moon Dragon*, 649 (M) (Asian—China)

Hong, Lily Toy, reteller. *How the Ox Star Fell from Heaven*, 660 (M) (Asian—China)

　*Two of Everything: A Chinese Folktale*, 661 (M) (Asian—China)

Kendall, Carol, and Yao-wen Li, retellers. *Sweet and Sour: Tales from China*, 793 (M) (Asian—China)

Lattimore, Deborah Nourse. *The Dragon's Robe*, 845 (M) (Asian—China)

Lawson, Julie, reteller. *The Dragon's Pearl*, 854 (M) (Asian—China)

Lee, Jeanne M., reteller. *Legend of the Milky Way*, 858 (M) (Asian—China)

Louie, Ai-Ling, reteller. *Yeh-Shen: A Cinderella Story from China*, 918 (M) (Asian—China)

Mahy, Margaret. *The Seven Chinese Brothers*, 965 (M) (Asian—China)

Miller, Moira. *The Moon Dragon*, 1024 (M) (Asian—China)

Morris, Winifred. *The Future of Yen-Tzu*, 1067 (M) (Asian—China)

　*The Magic Leaf*, 1068 (M) (Asian—China)

Mosel, Arlene, reteller. *Tikki Tikki Tembo*, 1070 (M) (Asian—China)

Rappaport, Doreen, reteller. *The Journey of Meng: A Chinese Legend*, 1205 (M) (Asian—China)

　*The Long-Haired Girl: A Chinese Legend*, 1206 (M) (Asian—China)

## Folktales—Asia—India

## Folktales— Asia—India (cont.)

## Folktales—Asia—Japan

Newton, Patricia Montgomery, adapter. *The Five Sparrows: A Japanese Folktale*, 1102 (M) (Asian—Japan)

Paterson, Katherine. *The Tale of the Mandarin Ducks*, 1152 (M) (Asian—Japan)

Quale, Eric. *The Shining Princess: And Other Japanese Legends*, 1201 (M/U) (Asian—Japan)

Richard, Françoise. *On Cat Mountain*, 1217 (M) (Asian—Japan)

Sakurai, Gail. *Peach Boy: A Japanese Legend*, 1266 (M) (Asian—Japan)

San Souci, Robert D., reteller. *The Samurai's Daughter: A Japanese Legend*, 1275 (M) (Asian—Japan)

*The Snow Wife*, 1277 (M) (Asian—Japan)

Say, Allen, reteller. *Once Under the Cherry Blossom Tree: An Old Japanese Tale*, 1286 (M) (Asian—Japan)

Schroeder, Alan. *Lily and the Wooden Bowl*, 1294 (M) (Asian—Japan)

Shute, Linda, reteller. *Momotaro the Peach Boy: A Traditional Japanese Tale*, 1322 (M) (Asian—Japan)

Snyder, Dianne. *The Boy of the Three-Year Nap*, 1346 (M) (Asian—Japan)

Stamm, Claus. *Three Strong Women: A Tall Tale from Japan*, 1371 (M) (Asian—Japan)

Tejima. *Ho-limlim: A Rabbit Tale from Japan*, 1435 (M) (Asian—Japan)

Tompert, Ann, adapter. *Bamboo Hats and a Rice Cake: A Tale Adapted from Japanese Folklore*, 1444 (M) (Asian—Japan)

Uchida, Yoshiko, reteller. *The Magic Listening Cap: More Folktales from Japan*, 1478 (M/U) (Asian—Japan)

*The Magic Purse*, 1479 (M) (Asian—Japan)

*The Two Foolish Cats: Suggested by a Japanese Folktale*, 1483 (M) (Asian—Japan)

*The Wise Old Woman*, 1484 (M) (Asian—Japan)

Watkins, Yoko Kawashima. *Tales from the Bamboo Grove*, 1528 (M) (Asian—Japan)

Winthrop, Elizabeth. *Journey to the Bright Kingdom*, 1569 (M) (Asian—Japan)

Yagawa, Sumiko, reteller. *The Crane Wife*, 1590 (M) (Asian—Japan)

## Folktales—Asia—Korea

Climo, Shirley. *The Korean Cinderella*, 279 (M) (Asian—Korea)

Fregosi, Claudia. *The Pumpkin Sparrow: Adapted from a Korean Folktale*, 447 (M) (Asian—Korea)

Ginsburg, Mirra, adapter. *The Chinese Mirror: Adapted from a Korean Folktale*, 476 (M) (Asian—Korea)

Han, Oki S., adapter. *Sir Whong and the Golden Pig*, 600 (M) (Asian—Korea)

Han, Suzanne Crowder. *The Rabbit's Escape*, 601 (M) (Asian—Korea)

*The Rabbit's Judgment*, 602 (M) (Asian—Korea)

Jaffe, Nina, reteller. *Older Brother, Younger Brother: A Korean Folktale*, 722 (M) (Asian—Korea)

Kwon, Holly H., reteller. *The Moles and the Mireuk: A Korean Folktale*, 834 (M) (Asian—Korea)

O'Brien, Anne Sibley, adapter. *The Princess and the Beggar: A Korean Folktale*, 1111 (M) (Asian—Korea)

## Folktales—Asia—Korea (cont.)

Reasoner, Charles, reteller. *The Magic Amber: A Korean Legend*, 1211 (M) (Asian—Korea)

Rhee, Nami, reteller. *Magic Spring: A Korean Folktale*, 1216 (M) (Asian—Korea)

Schecter, Ellen, reteller. *Sim Chung and the River Dragon: A Folktale from Korea*, 1289 (P) (Asian—Korea)

## Folktales—Asia—Laos

Spagnoli, Cathy, adapter. *Nine-in-One, Grr! Grr! A Folktale from the Hmong People of Laos*, 1360 (M) (Asian—Laos)

## Folktales—Asia—Mongolia

Otsuka, Yuzo. *Suho and the White Horse: A Legend of Mongolia*, 1139 (M) (Asian—Mongolia)

## Folktales—Asia—Pakistan

Shepard, Aaron, reteller. *The Gifts of Wali Dad: A Tale of India and Pakistan*, 1313 (M) (Asian—India/Pakistan)

## Folktales—Asia—Siberia

Bernhard, Emery, reteller. *The Girl Who Wanted to Hunt: A Siberian Tale*, 120 (M) (Asian—Siberia)

## Folktales—Asia—Thailand

Hamada, Cheryl, reteller. *Kao and the Golden Fish: A Folktale from Thailand*, 577 (M) (Asian—Thailand)

Meeker, Clare Hodgson, adapter. *A Tale of Two Rice Birds: A Folktale from Thailand*, 1006 (M) (Asian—Thailand)

## Folktales—Asia—Tibet

Schroeder, Alan. *The Stone Lion*, 1295 (M) (Asian—Tibet)

Timpanelli, Gioia, reteller. *Tales from the Roof of the World: Folktales of Tibet*, 1443 (M/U) (Asian—Tibet)

## Folktales—Asia—Vietnam

Clark, Ann Nolan, reteller. *In the Land of Small Dragon*, 260 (M) (Asian—Vietnam)

Garland, Sherry. *Why Ducks Sleep on One Leg*, 459 (M) (Asian—Vietnam)

Hamada, Cheryl, reteller. *The Farmer, the Buffalo, and the Tiger: A Folktale from Vietnam*, 575 (M) (Asian—Vietnam)

Lee, Jeanne M., reteller. *Toad Is the Uncle of Heaven: A Vietnamese Folk Tale*, 860 (M) (Asian—Vietnam)

Lum, Darrell, reteller. *The Golden Slipper: A Vietnamese Legend*, 923 (M) (Asian—Vietnam)

Vuong, Lynette Dyer. *The Brocaded Slipper: And Other Vietnamese Tales*, 1497 (M) (Asian—Vietnam)

*The Golden Carp: And Other Tales from Vietnam*, 1498 (U) (Asian—Vietnam)

*Sky Legends of Vietnam*, 1499 (U) (Asian—Vietnam)

## Folktales—Asian American—Chinese

Yep, Laurence. *Tongues of Jade*, 1617 (M/U) (Asian American—China)

## Folktales—Australia

Ingpen, Robert, and Barbara Hayes. *Folk Tales and Fables of Asia and Australia*, 712 (U) (Multicultural)

Troughton, Joanna, reteller. *Whale's Canoe: A Folk Tale from Australia*, 1459 (M) (Australian)

## Folktales—Australia—Aborigine

Czernecki, Stefan, and Timothy Rhodes. *The Singing Snake*, 330 (M) (Australian—Aborigine)

Maddern, Eric. *Rainbow Bird: An Aboriginal Folktale from Northern Australia*, 962 (M) (Australian—Aborigine)

Morgan, Sally. *The Flying Emu: And Other Australian Stories*, 1058 (U) (Australian—Aborigine)

Nunes, Susan. *Tiddalick the Frog*, 1107 (M) (Australian—Aborigine)

Oodgeroo. *Dreamtime: Aboriginal Stories*, 1131 (M) (Australian—Aborigine)

Trezise, Percy, and Dick Roughsey. *Turramulli the Giant Quinkin*, 1453 (M) (Australian—Aborigine)

Troughton, Joanna, reteller. *What Made Tiddalik Laugh: An Australian Aborigine Folk Tale*, 1460 (M) (Australian—Aborigine)

## Folktales—Caribbean Islands

Berry, James. *Spiderman Anancy*, 125 (M) (Caribbean)

Bryan, Ashley. *The Cat's Purr*, 182 (P) (Caribbean—West Indies)

Hull, Robert, reteller. *Caribbean Stories*, 699 (M) (Caribbean)

Joseph, Lynn. *The Mermaid's Twin Sister: More Stories from Trinidad*, 773 (M) (Caribbean)

　*A Wave in Her Pocket: Stories from Trinidad*, 774 (M/U) (Caribbean)

Lyons, Mary E., selector. *Raw Head, Bloody Bones: African-American Tales of the Supernatural*, 931 (U) (African American)

Makhanlall, David. *Brer Anansi and the Boat Race: A Caribbean Folk Tale*, 969 (M) (Caribbean)

## Folktales—Caribbean Islands—Cuba

González, Lucía M., reteller. *The Bossy Gallito/El Gallo de Bodas: A Traditional Cuban Folktale*, 509 (M) (Caribbean—Cuba)

## Folktales—Caribbean Islands—Haiti

Turenne des Prés, François. *Children of Yayoute: Folk Tales of Haiti*, 1466 (U) (Caribbean—Haiti)

Wolkstein, Diane. *The Banza: A Haitian Story*, 1574 (M) (Caribbean—Haiti)

　*The Magic Orange Tree: And Other Haitian Folktales*, 1575 (M/U) (Caribbean—Haiti)

## Folktales—Caribbean Islands—Jamaica

Sherlock, Philip, reteller. *Anansi, the Spider Man: Jamaican Folk Tales*, 1315 (M) (Caribbean—Jamaica)

Temple, Frances, reteller. *Tiger Soup: An Anansi Story from Jamaica*, 1437 (M) (Caribbean—Jamaica)

## Folktales—Caribbean Islands—Puerto Rico

Mora, Francisco X. *The Tiger and the Rabbit: A Puerto Rican Folktale*, 1054 (M) (Caribbean—Puerto Rico)

Pitre, Felix, reteller. *Juan Bobo and the Pig: A Puerto Rican Folktale*, 1177 (M) (Caribbean—Puerto Rico)

*Paco and the Witch: A Puerto Rican Folktale*, 1178 (M) (Caribbean—Puerto Rico)

## Folktales—Caribbean Islands—West Indies

Bryan, Ashley. *The Cat's Purr*, 182 (P) (Caribbean—West Indies)

*The Dancing Granny*, 183 (M) (Caribbean—West Indies)

*Turtle Knows Your Name*, 190 (M) (Caribbean—West Indies)

Gershator, Phillis, reteller. *Tukama Tootles the Flute: A Tale from the Antilles*, 471 (M) (Caribbean—West Indies)

Hausman, Gerald. *Duppy Talk: West Indian Tales of Mystery and Magic*, 627 (U) (Caribbean—West Indies)

Sherlock, Philip, reteller. *West Indian Folk-Tales*, 1316 (M/U) (Caribbean—West Indies)

## Folktales—Central America—Guatemala—Mayan

Palacios, Argentina, adapter. *The Hummingbird King: A Guatemalan Legend*, 1148 (M) (Central American—Guatemala—Mayan)

## Folktales—Central America—Mayan

Bierhorst, John, editor. *The Monkey's Haircut: And Other Stories Told by the Maya*, 133 (M/U) (Central American—Mayan)

Lattimore, Deborah Nourse. *Why There Is No Arguing in Heaven: A Mayan Myth*, 848 (M) (Central American—Mayan)

Shetterly, Susan Hand, reteller. *The Dwarf-Wizard of Uxmal*, 1317 (M) (Central American—Mayan)

## Folktales—Central America—Nicaragua

DeSauza, James, reteller, and Harriet Rohmer, adapter. *Brother Anansi and the Cattle Ranch: El Hermano Anansi y el Rancho de Ganado*, 364 (M) (Central American—Nicaragua)

Rohmer, Harriet, adapter. *Uncle Nacho's Hat: El Sombrero del Tio Nacho*, 1237 (M) (Central American—Nicaragua)

Rohmer, Harriet, Octavio Chow, and Morris Vidaure. *The Invisible Hunters/Los Cazadores Invisibles: A Legend from the Miskito Indians of Nicaragua/Una Leyenda de los Indios Miskitos de Nicaragua*, 1239 (M) (Central American—Nicaragua)

## Folktales—Latin America

Ada, Alma Flor, reteller. *The Rooster Who Went to His Uncle's Wedding: A Latin American Folktale*, 20 (M) (Latin American)

Vidal, Beatriz. *The Legend of El Dorado: A Latin American Tale*, 1495 (M) (Latin American)

Weiss, Jacqueline Shachter, collector and adapter. *Young Brer Rabbit: And Other Trickster Tales from the Americas*, 1534 (M) (Latin American)

## Folktales—Mexico

Aardema, Verna, reteller. *Borreguita and the Coyote: A Tale from Ayutla, Mexico*, 3 (M) (Mexican)

*Pedro and the Padre: A Tale from Jalisco, Mexico*, 8 (M) (Mexican)

Brenner, Anita. *The Boy Who Could Do Anything: And Other Mexican Folk Tales*, 157 (M/U) (Mexican)

*The Coyote Rings the Wrong Bell: A Mexican Folktale*, 316 (M) (Mexican)

dePaola, Tomie, reteller. *The Legend of the Poinsettia*, 363 (M) (Mexican)

Kimmel, Eric A., adapter. *The Witch's Face: A Mexican Tale*, 808 (M) (Mexican)

Mike, Jan M., adapter. *Opossum and the Great Firemaker: A Mexican Legend*, 1016 (M) (Mexican)

Mora, Francisco X. *The Legend of the Two Moons*, 1053 (M) (Mexican)

## Folktales—Mexico—Aztec

Bierhorst, John, reteller. *Doctor Coyote: A Native American Aesop's Fables*, 130 (M) (Mexican—Aztec)

Greger, Shana, reteller. *The Fifth and Final Sun: An Ancient Aztec Myth of the Sun's Origin*, 550 (M) (Mexican—Aztec)

Lattimore, Deborah Nourse. *The Flame of Peace: A Tale of the Aztecs*, 846 (M) (Mexican—Aztec)

Lewis, Richard. *All of You Was Singing*, 888 (M) (Mexican—Aztec)

Ober, Hal, reteller. *How Music Came to the World: An Ancient Mexican Myth*, 1110 (M) (Mexican—Aztec)

Rohmer, Harriet, and Mary Anchondo, adapters. *How We Came to the Fifth World/Como vinimos al quinto mundo: A Creation Story from Ancient Mexico*, 1238 (M) (Mexican—Aztec)

## Folktales—Mexico—Zapotec

Zubizarreta, Rosalma, Harriet Rohmer, and David Schecter. *The Woman Who Outshone the Sun: The Legend of Lucia Zenteno*, 1637 (M) (Mexican—Zapotec)

## Folktales—Middle East

Ingpen, Robert, and Barbara Hayes. *Folk Tales and Fables of the Middle East and Africa*, 714 (U) (Multicultural)

## Folktales—Middle East—Arabia

Carrick, Carol. *Aladdin and the Wonderful Lamp*, 227 (M) (Middle Eastern—Arabia)

Kimmel, Eric A., reteller. *The Tale of Aladdin and the Wonderful Lamp: A Story from the Arabian Nights*, 806 (M) (Middle Eastern—Arabia)

Greene, Ellin. *The Legend of the Cranberry: A Paleo-Indian Tale*, 521 (M) (Native American)

Highwater, Jamake. *Anpao: An American Indian Odyssey*, 643 (U) (Native American)

Hull, Robert, reteller. *Native North American Stories*, 701 (M) (Native American)

McDermott, Gerald, reteller. *Coyote: A Trickster Tale from the American Southwest*, 936 (M) (Native American)

  *Raven: A Trickster Tale from the Pacific Northwest*, 938 (M) (Native American)

Mayo, Gretchen Will, reteller. *Big Trouble for Tricky Rabbit!*, 994 (M) (Native American)

  *Here Comes Tricky Rabbit!*, 995 (M) (Native American)

  *Meet Tricky Coyote!*, 996 (M) (Native American)

  *Star Tales: North American Indian Stories about the Stars*, 997 (M/U) (Native American)

  *That Tricky Coyote!*, 998 (M) (Native American)

Mobley, Jane. *The Star Husband*, 1030 (M) (Native American)

Monroe, Jean Guard, and Ray A. Williamson. *They Dance in the Sky: Native American Star Myths*, 1043 (M/U) (Native American)

Norman, Howard. *How Glooskap Outwits the Ice Giants: And Other Tales of the Maritime Indians*, 1105 (M) (Native American)

Oliviero, Jamie. *The Fish Skin*, 1126 (M) (Native American)

Powell, Mary, editor. *Wolf Tales: Native American Children's Stories*, 1195 (M) (Native American)

Robinson, Gail, reteller. *Raven the Trickster: Legends of the North American Indians*, 1228 (U) (Native American—Pacific Northwest)

Shetterly, Susan Hand, reteller. *Raven's Light: A Myth from the People of the Northwest Coast*, 1319 (M) (Native American)

Steptoe, John, reteller. *The Story of Jumping Mouse: A Native American Legend*, 1381 (M) (Native American)

Taylor, C. J. *Bones in the Basket: Native Stories of the Origin of People*, 1416 (M) (Native American)

  *How We Saw the World: Nine Native Stories of the Way Things Began*, 1419 (M) (Native American)

Troughton, Joanna, reteller. *How Rabbit Stole the Fire: A North American Indian Folk Tale*, 1455 (M) (Native American)

Whitney, Alex. *Stiff Ears: Animal Folktales of the North American Indian*, 1544 (M) (Native American)

Wood, Marion. *Spirits, Heroes and Hunters from North American Indian Mythology*, 1578 (M/U) (Native American)

Young, Ed, adapter. *Moon Mother: A Native American Creation Tale*, 1630 (M) (Native American)

## Folktales—Native American—Abenaki

Bruchac, Joseph, reteller. *Gluskabe and the Four Wishes*, 172 (M) (Native American—Abenaki)

Taylor, C. J. *How Two-Feather Was Saved from Loneliness: An Abenaki Legend*, 1418 (M) (Native American—Abenaki)

## Folktales—Native American—Algonquian

Cohlene, Terri, adapter. *Little Firefly: An Algonquian Legend*, 295 (M) (Native American—Algonquian)

Martin, Rafe. *The Rough-Face Girl*, 983 (M) (Native American—Algonquian)

## Folktales—Native American—Apache

Lacapa, Michael, reteller. *Antelope Woman: An Apache Folktale*, 836 (M) (Native American—Apache)

*The Flute Player: An Apache Folktale*, 837 (M) (Native American—Apache)

## Folktales—Native American—Arapaho

Taylor, C. J. *The Ghost and Lone Warrior: An Arapaho Legend*, 1417 (M) (Native American—Arapaho)

## Folktales—Native American—Blackfoot

Goble, Paul. *The Lost Children: The Boys Who Were Neglected*, 499 (M) (Native American—Blackfoot)

*Star Boy*, 501 (M) (Native American—Blackfoot)

Rodanas, Kristina, adapter. *Dance of the Sacred Circle: A Native American Tale*, 1231 (M) (Native American—Blackfoot)

San Souci, Robert D., adapter. *The Legend of Scarface: A Blackfeet Indian Tale*, 1274 (M) (Native American—Blackfoot)

Van Laan, Nancy, reteller. *Buffalo Dance: A Blackfoot Legend*, 1488 (M) (Native American—Blackfoot)

Yolen, Jane. *Sky Dogs*, 1625 (M) (Native American—Blackfoot)

## Folktales—Native American—Cherokee

Arneach, Lloyd, reteller. *The Animals' Ballgame: A Cherokee Story from the Eastern Band*, 68 (M) (Native American—Cherokee)

Bruchac, Joseph, reteller. *The First Strawberries: A Cherokee Story*, 169 (M) (Native American—Cherokee)

Cohlene, Terri, adapter. *Dancing Drum: A Cherokee Legend*, 293 (M) (Native American—Cherokee)

Hoyt-Goldsmith, Diane. *Cherokee Summer*, 679 (M) (Native American—Cherokee)

Ross, Gayle, reteller. *How Turtle's Back Was Cracked: A Traditional Cherokee Tale*, 1249 (M) (Native American—Cherokee)

Roth, Susan L. *Kanahéna: A Cherokee Story*, 1251 (M) (Native American—Cherokee)

*The Story of Light*, 1252 (M) (Native American—Cherokee)

## Folktales—Native American—Cheyenne

Cohlene, Terri, adapter. *Quillworker: A Cheyenne Legend*, 296 (M) (Native American—Cheyenne)

Goble, Paul. *Her Seven Brothers*, 493 (M) (Native American—Cheyenne)

## Folktales—Native American—Chinook

Martin, Rafe. *The Boy Who Lived with the Seals*, 981 (M) (Native American—Chinook)

## Folktales—Native American—Chippewa

Greene, Jacqueline Dembar, reteller. *Manabozho's Gifts: Three Chippewa Tales*, 522 (M) (Native American—Chippewa)

## Folktales—Native American—Choctaw

Harrell, Beatrice Orcutt. *How Thunder and Lightning Came to Be: A Choctaw Legend*, 608 (M) (Native American—Choctaw)

## Folktales—Native American—Cochiti Pueblo

Hoyt-Goldsmith, Diane. *Pueblo Storyteller*, 681 (M) (Native American—Cochiti Pueblo)

## Folktales—Native American—Eskimo

Cohlene, Terri, adapter. *Ka-ha-si and the Loon: An Eskimo Legend*, 294 (M) (Native American—Eskimo)

DeArmond, Dale, adapter. *The Seal Oil Lamp: Adapted from an Eskimo Folktale*, 340 (M) (Native American—Eskimo)

Kroll, Virginia. *The Seasons and Someone*, 829 (M) (Native American—Eskimo)

## Folktales—Native American—Hopi

Schecter, Ellen. *The Warrior Maiden: A Hopi Legend*, 1290 (P) (Native American—Hopi)

## Folktales—Native American—Huichol

Bernhard, Emery, reteller. *The Tree That Rains: The Flood Myth of the Huichol Indians of Mexico*, 123 (M) (Native American—Huichol)

## Folktales—Native American—Inuit

Cleaver, Elizabeth. *The Enchanted Caribou*, 262 (M) (Native American—Inuit)

Munsch, Robert, and Michael Kusugak. *A Promise Is a Promise*, 1076 (P) (Native American—Inuit)

San Souci, Robert D., adapter. *Song of Sedna*, 1278 (M) (Native American—Inuit)

## Folktales—Native American—Iroquois

Bierhorst, John, editor. *The Naked Bear: Folktales of the Iroquois*, 134 (M/U) (Native American—Iroquois)

*The Woman Who Fell from the Sky: The Iroquois Story of Creation*, 137 (M) (Native American—Iroquois)

## Folktales—Native American—Kanienkehaka (Mohawk)

Gates, Frieda. *Owl Eyes*, 461 (M) (Native American—Kanienkehaka [Mohawk])

## Folktales—Native American—Karuk

London, Jonathan, reteller. *Fire Race: A Karuk Coyote Tale about How Fire Came to the People*, 911 (M) (Native American—Karuk)

## Folktales—Native American—Kutenai

Tanaka, Béatrice, reteller. *The Chase: A Kutenai Indian Tale*, 1410 (P) (Native American—Kutenai)

Troughton, Joanna, reteller. *Who Will Be the Sun? A North American Indian Folk-tale*, 1461 (M) (Native American—Kutenai)

## Folktales—Native American—Lakota

Bernhard, Emery, reteller. *Spotted Eagle & Black Crow: A Lakota Legend*, 122 (M) (Native American—Lakota)

Yellow Robe, Rosebud. *Tonweya and the Eagles: And Other Lakota Tales*, 1600 (U) (Native American—Lakota)

## Folktales—Native American—Lenape

Van Laan, Nancy, reteller. *Rainbow Crow: A Lenape Tale*, 1490 (M) (Native American—Lenape)

## Folktales—Native American—Makah

Cohlene, Terri, adapter. *Clamshell Boy: A Makah Legend*, 292 (M) (Native American—Makah)

## Folktales—Native American—Muskogee

Bruchac, Joseph, reteller. *The Great Ball Game: A Muskogee Story*, 173 (M) (Native American—Muskogee)

## Folktales—Native American—Navajo

Begay, Shonto. *Ma'ii and Cousin Horned Toad: A Traditional Navajo Story*, 108 (M) (Native American—Navajo)

Browne, Vee, reteller. *Monster Birds: A Navajo Folktale*, 167 (M) (Native American—Navajo)

Cohlene, Terri, adapter. *Turquoise Boy: A Navajo Legend*, 297 (M) (Native American—Navajo)

Hausman, Gerald, reteller. *Coyote Walks on Two Legs: A Book of Navaho Myths and Legends*, 626 (M) (Native American—Navajo)

Oughton, Jerrie. *How the Stars Fell into the Sky: A Navajo Legend*, 1140 (M) (Native American—Navajo)

*The Magic Weaver of Rugs: A Tale of the Navaho*, 1141 (M) (Native American—Navajo)

Rucki, Ani. *Turkey's Gift to the People*, 1255 (M) (Native American—Navajo)

Whitethorne, Baje. *Sunpainters: Eclipse of the Navajo Sun*, 1543 (M) (Native American—Navajo)

## Folktales—Native American—Northwest Coast

Harris, Christie. *Mouse Woman and the Mischief-Makers*, 609 (U) (Native American—Northwest Coast)

*Mouse Woman and the Muddleheads*, 610 (U) (Native American—Northwest Coast)

*Mouse Woman and the Vanished Princesses*, 611 (U) (Native American—Northwest Coast)

*Once More Upon a Totem*, 612 (U) (Native American—Northwest Coast)

*Once Upon a Totem*, 613 (U) (Native American—Northwest Coast)

Martin, Fran, reteller. *Raven-Who-Sets-Things-Right: Indian Tales of the Northwest Coast*, 979 (M) (Native American—Northwest Coast)

Morgan, Pierr, reteller. *Supper for Crow: A Northwest Coast Indian Tale*, 1057 (M) (Native American—Northwest Coast)

Siberell, Anne. *Whale in the Sky*, 1324 (M) (Native American—Northwest Coast)

## Folktales—Native American—Oglala

Taylor, C. J. *The Secret of the White Buffalo: An Oglala Legend*, 1421 (M) (Native American—Oglala)

## Folktales—Native American—Ojibway

Esbensen, Barbara Juster, reteller. *Ladder to the Sky: How the Gift of Healing Came to the Ojibway Nation*, 404 (M) (Native American—Ojibway)

*The Star Maiden: An Ojibway Tale*, 405 (M) (Native American—Ojibway)

Larry, Charles, reteller. *Peboan and Seegwun*, 843 (M) (Native American—Ojibway)

Osofsky, Audrey. *Dreamcatcher*, 1138 (M) (Native American—Ojibway)

San Souci, Robert D., reteller. *Sootface: An Ojibwa Cinderella Story*, 1279 (M) (Native American—Ojibway)

## Folktales—Native American—Otoe

Walters, Anna Lee, reteller. *The Two-Legged Creature: An Otoe Story*, 1519 (M) (Native American—Otoe)

## Folktales—Native American—Passamaquoddy

Shetterly, Susan Hand, reteller. *Muwin and the Magic Hare*, 1318 (M) (Native American—Passamaquoddy)

## Folktales—Native American—Pawnee

Cohen, Caron Lee, adapter. *The Mud Pony: A Traditional Skidi Pawnee Tale*, 290 (M) (Native American—Pawnee)

Moroney, Lynn, reteller. *The Boy Who Loved Bears: A Pawnee Tale*, 1060 (M) (Native American—Pawnee)

## Folktales—Native American—Plains Indians

Baker, Olaf. *Where the Buffaloes Begin*, 77 (M) (Native American—Plains Indians)

Goble, Paul. *Adopted by the Eagles: A Plains Indian Story of Friendship and Treachery*, 484 (M) (Native American—Plains Indians)

*Beyond the Ridge*, 485 (M) (Native American—Plains Indians)

*Buffalo Woman*, 486 (M) (Native American—Plains Indians)

*Crow Chief: A Plains Indian Story*, 487 (M) (Native American—Plains Indians)

## Folktales—Native American—Plains Indians (cont.)

## Folktales—Native American—Pueblo

## Folktales—Native American—Seneca

## Folktales—Native American—Skagit

## Folktales—Native American—Tewa

## Folktales—Native American—Tlingit

## Folktales—Native American—Tsimshian

## Folktales—Native American—Tuscaroran

Shor, Pekay, reteller. *When the Corn Is Red*, 1321 (M) (Native American—Tuscaroran)

## Folktales—Native American—Ute

Stevens, Janet, reteller. *Coyote Steals the Blanket: An Ute Tale*, 1383 (M) (Native American—Ute)

## Folktales—Native American—Wampanoag

Fritz, Jean. *The Good Giants and the Bad Pukwudgies*, 452 (M) (Native American—Wampanoag)

Manitonquat (Medicine Story). *The Children of the Morning Light: Wampanoag Tales*, 971 (U) (Native American—Wampanoag)

## Folktales—Native American—Wasco

Taylor, Harriet Peck, reteller. *Coyote Places the Stars*, 1423 (M) (Native American—Wasco)

## Folktales—Native American—Woodland

Ehlert, Lois. *Mole's Hill: A Woodland Tale*, 394 (M) (Native American—Woodland)

## Folktales—Native American—Yahi

Hinton, Leanne, translator. *Ishi's Tale of Lizard*, 650 (M) (Native American—Yahi)

## Folktales—Native American—Yuit Eskimo

Bernhard, Emery, reteller. *How Snowshoe Hare Rescued the Sun: A Tale from the Arctic*, 121 (M) (Native American—Yuit Eskimo)

## Folktales—Native American—Yupik

Sloat, Teri, reteller. *The Eye of the Needle: Based on a Yupik Tale as Told by Betty Huffman*, 1333 (M) (Native American—Yupik)

*The Hungry Giant of the Tundra*, 1334 (M) (Native American—Yupik)

## Folktales—Native American—Zapotec

Johnston, Tony. *The Tale of Rabbit and Coyote*, 759 (M) (Native American—Zapotec)

## Folktales—Native American—Zuni

Rodanas, Kristina, reteller. *Dragonfly's Tale*, 1232 (M) (Native American—Zuni)

## Folktales—Native People—Russian Eskimo

Ginsburg, Mirra, reteller. *The Proud Maiden, Tungak, and the Sun: A Russian Eskimo Tale*, 477 (M) (Native People—Russian Eskimo)

## Folktales—South America—Yanomamo

Crespo, George, reteller. *How Iwariwa the Cayman Learned to Share: A Yanomami Myth*, 317 (M) (South American—Yanomamo Indians)

## Folktales—Taino

Crespo, George, reteller. *How the Sea Began: A Taino Myth*, 318 (M) (Native American—Taino)

## Folktales—United States

Bang, Molly, adapter. *Wiley and the Hairy Man: Adapted from an American Folktale*, 87 (P) (African American)

Hamilton, Virginia, reteller. *Her Stories: African American Folktales, Fairy Tales, and True Tales*, 586 (U) (African American)

*The People Could Fly: American Black Folktales*, 593 (M/U) (African American)

Harris, Joel Chandler. *Jump Again! More Adventures of Brer Rabbit*, 614 (M/U) (African American)

*Jump on Over! The Adventures of Brer Rabbit and His Family*, 615 (M/U) (African American)

Harris, Joel Chandler, and Malcolm Jones. *Jump! The Adventures of Brer Rabbit*, 616 (M/U) (African American)

Haskins, James. *The Headless Haunt: And Other African-American Ghost Stories*, 618 (U) (African American)

Jensen, Patsy. *John Henry and His Mighty Hammer*, 729 (P) (African American)

Keats, Ezra Jack. *John Henry: An American Legend*, 780 (M) (African American)

Lester, Julius, reteller. *Further Tales of Uncle Remus: The Misadventures of Brer Rabbit, Brer Fox, Brer Wolf, the Doodang, and All the Other Creatures*, 868 (M/U) (African American)

*John Henry*, 870 (M) (African American)

*The Knee-High Man: And Other Tales*, 871 (M) (African American)

*The Last Tales of Uncle Remus*, 872 (M) (African American)

*More Tales of Uncle Remus: Further Adventures of Brer Rabbit, His Friends, Enemies, and Others*, 874 (M/U) (African American)

*The Tales of Uncle Remus: The Adventures of Brer Rabbit*, 875 (M/U) (African American)

Lyons, Mary E., reteller. *The Butter Tree: Tales of Bruh Rabbit*, 929 (M) (African American)

*Raw Head, Bloody Bones: African-American Tales of the Supernatural*, 931 (U) (African American)

McKissack, Patricia. *The Dark Thirty: Southern Tales of the Supernatural*, 947 (M/U) (African American)

Rees, Ennis. *Brer Rabbit and His Tricks*, 1213 (M) (African American)

*More of Brer Rabbit's Tricks*, 1214 (M) (African American)

Sanfield, Steve. *The Adventures of High John the Conqueror*, 1269 (M/U) (African American)

San Souci, Robert D., collector and adapter. *Cut from the Same Cloth: American Women of Myth, Legend, and Tall Tale*, 1271 (U) (Multicultural)

*Larger Than Life: The Adventures of American Legendary Heroes*, 1273 (M) (Multicultural)

*Sukey and the Mermaid*, 1280 (M) (African American)

## Folktales—United States (cont.)

*The Talking Eggs: A Folktale from the American South*, 1281 (M) (African American)

Small, Terry. *The Legend of John Henry*, 1336 (M) (African American)

Wahl, Jan. *Little Eight John*, 1502 (M) (African American)

*Tailypo!*, 1503 (M) (African American)

## Food

Andrews, Jan. *Very Last First Time*, 56 (P/M) (Native American—Inuit)

Baer, Edith. *This Is the Way We Eat Our Lunch: A Book about Children Around the World*, 72 (P) (Multicultural)

Bang, Molly. *The Grey Lady and the Strawberry Snatcher*, 82 (P) (African American)

Bruchac, Joseph, reteller. *The First Strawberries: A Cherokee Story*, 169 (M) (Native American—Cherokee)

Falwell, Cathryn. *Feast for 10*, 412 (P) (African American)

Friedman, Ina R. *How My Parents Learned to Eat*, 450 (P) (Multicultural)

Greene, Ellin. *The Legend of the Cranberry: A Paleo-Indian Tale*, 521 (M) (Native American)

Hayes, Sarah. *Eat Up, Gemma*, 633 (PS) (African American)

Lasky, Kathryn. *Cloud Eyes*, 844 (M) (Native American)

Lexau, Joan M. *Striped Ice Cream*, 892 (M) (African American)

Lyon, George Ella. *The Outside Inn*, 926 (P) (Multicultural)

McDonald, Becky Bring. *Larry and the Cookie*, 943 (PS/P) (African American)

Milstein, Linda. *Coconut Mon*, 1027 (P) (Caribbean)

Morris, Ann. *Bread, Bread, Bread*, 1061 (PS/P) (Multicultural)

Mosel, Arlene, reteller. *The Funny Little Woman*, 1069 (M) (Asian   Japan)

Paulsen, Gary. *The Tortilla Factory*, 1158 (P) (Mexican)

Polacco, Patricia. *Chicken Sunday*, 1179 (M) (African American)

Politi, Leo. *Three Stalks of Corn*, 1184 (M) (Mexican American)

Rattigan, Jama Kim. *Dumpling Soup*, 1210 (P) (Hawaiian)

Rodanas, Kristina, reteller. *Dragonfly's Tale*, 1232 (M) (Native American—Zuni)

Schotter, Roni. *A Fruit and Vegetable Man*, 1293 (P) (Asian American)

Shelby, Anne. *Potluck*, 1311 (P) (Multicultural)

Shor, Pekay, reteller. *When the Corn Is Red*, 1321 (M) (Native American—Tuscaroran)

Soto, Gary. *Chato's Kitchen*, 1351 (M) (Hispanic)

Taylor, C. J. *How Two-Feather Was Saved from Loneliness: An Abenaki Legend*, 1418 (M) (Native American—Abenaki)

Temple, Frances, reteller. *Tiger Soup: An Anansi Story from Jamaica*, 1437 (M) (Caribbean—Jamaica)

Uchida, Yoshiko. *The Two Foolish Cats: Suggested by a Japanese Folktale*, 1483 (M) (Asian—Japan)

Wang, Rosalind C., adapter. *The Magical Starfruit Tree: A Chinese Folktale*, 1521 (M) (Asian—China)

Watson, Pete. *The Market Lady and the Mango Tree*, 1529 (M) (African)

Williams, Vera B. *Cherries and Cherry Pits*, 1555 (P) (African American)

## Foreign lands

Anno, Mitsumasa, and Raymond Briggs. *All in a Day*, 58 (M) (Multicultural)

Baer, Edith. *This Is the Way We Eat Our Lunch: A Book about Children Around the World*, 72 (P) (Multicultural)

*This Is the Way We Go to School: A Book about Children Around the World*, 73 (P) (Multicultural)

Fisher, Leonard Everett. *Alphabet Art: Thirteen ABCs from Around the World*, 423 (P/M) (Multicultural)

*Number Art: Thirteen 1 2 3s from Around the World*, 425 (P/M) (Multicultural)

*Symbol Art: Thirteen Squares, Circles, and Triangles from Around the World*, 426 (M) (Multicultural)

Knight, Margy Burns. *Talking Walls*, 817 (M) (Multicultural)

Lankford, Mary D. *Hopscotch Around the World*, 841 (P/M) (Multicultural)

Morris, Ann. *Bread, Bread, Bread*, 1061 (PS/P) (Multicultural)

*Hats, Hats, Hats*, 1062 (PS/P) (Multicultural)

*Houses and Homes*, 1063 (PS/P) (Multicultural)

*Loving*, 1064 (PS/P) (Multicultural)

*On the Go*, 1065 (PS/P) (Multicultural)

*Tools*, 1066 (PS/P) (Multicultural)

Roy, Ronald. *A Thousand Pails of Water*, 1253 (P) (Asian)

Seltzer, Isadore. *The House I Live In: At Home in America*, 1303 (P) (Multicultural)

Singer, Marilyn. *Nine O'Clock Lullaby*, 1326 (P) (Multicultural)

Spier, Peter. *People*, 1363 (P/M) (Multicultural)

Yolen, Jane, editor. *Sleep Rhymes Around the World*, 1626 (P) (Multicultural)

*Street Rhymes Around the World*, 1627 (P) (Multicultural)

## Foreign lands—Africa

Aardema, Verna. *Ji-Nongo-Nongo Means Riddles*, 6 (P/M) (African)

Adoff, Arnold. *Ma nDa La*, 29 (P) (African)

Allen, Judy. *Elephant*, 44 (P) (African)

Anderson, Joy. *Juma and the Magic Jinn*, 53 (M) (African)

Anderson/Sankofa, David A. *The Rebellion of Humans: An African Spiritual Journey*, 55 (M) (African)

Berry, James. *Ajeemah and His Son*, 124 (U) (African)

Bess, Clayton. *Story for a Black Night*, 126 (U) (African)

*The Truth about the Moon*, 127 (M) (African)

Bosse, Malcolm. *Deep Dream of the Rain Forest*, 150 (U) (African—Iban)

Bozylinsky, Hannah Heritage. *Lala Salama: An African Lullaby in Swahili and English*, 156 (P) (African)

Cendrars, Blaise, and Marcia Brown, translator. *Shadow*, 235 (P) (African)

Deetlefs, Rene, reteller. *Tabu and the Dancing Elephants*, 343 (P) (African)

Easmon, Carol. *Bisi and the Golden Disc*, 388 (M) (African)

Eckewa, T. Obinkaram. *The Ancestor Tree*, 390 (M) (African)

Equiano, Olaudah, and Ann Cameron, adapter. *The Kidnapped Prince: The Life of Olaudah Equiano*, 402 (U) (African)

## Foreign lands—Africa (cont.)

Feelings, Muriel. *Jambo Means Hello: Swahili Alphabet Book*, 413 (P/M)
  (African)

  *Moja Means One: Swahili Counting Book*, 414 (P/M) (African)

Fourie, Corlia. *Ganekwane and the Green Dragon: Four Stories from Africa*, 436
  (M) (African)

Franklin, Kristine L. *The Old, Old Man and the Very Little Boy*, 441 (P) (African)

Geraghty, Paul. *The Hunter*, 468 (P) (African)

Graham, Lorenz. *Song of the Boat*, 513 (M) (African—West Africa)

Gray, Nigel. *A Country Far Away*, 515 (P) (African)

Greenfield, Eloise. *Africa Dream*, 525 (P) (African American)

Grifalconi, Ann. *Darkness and the Butterfly*, 553 (P) (African)

  *Flyaway Girl*, 554 (M) (African)

  *Osa's Pride*, 557 (P) (African)

Guthrie, Donna W. *Nobiah's Well: A Modern African Folktale*, 569 (M) (African)

Hamilton, Virginia. *The All Jahdu Storybook*, 581 (M) (African American)

  *Jahdu*, 589 (M) (African American)

  *The Time-Ago Tales of Jahdu*, 595 (M) (African American)

Hansen, Joyce. *The Captive*, 604 (U) (African)

Haskins, Jim. *Count Your Way Through Africa*, 619 (P) (African)

Hoffman, Mary. *Boundless Grace*, 659 (P) (African American)

Jacobs, Shannon K. *Song of the Giraffe*, 721 (M) (African)

Kroll, Virginia. *Africa Brothers and Sisters*, 825 (P) (African American)

  *Jaha and Jamil Went Down the Hill: An African Mother Goose*, 826 (P)
  (African)

Langer, Nola. *Rafiki*, 838 (P) (African)

Marie, D. *Tears for Ashan*, 974 (M) (African)

Mennen, Ingrid. *One Round Moon and a Star for Me*, 1009 (P) (African)

Mennen, Ingrid, and Niki Daly. *Somewhere in Africa*, 1010 (P) (African)

Mollel, Tololwa M. *Big Boy*, 1035 (P) (African)

Musgrove, Margaret. *Ashanti to Zulu: African Traditions*, 1077 (M) (African)

Onyefulu, Ifeoma. *A Is for Africa*, 1128 (P/M) (African)

  *Emeka's Gift: An African Counting Story*, 1129 (P) (African)

Price, Leontyne, reteller. *Aïda*, 1198 (U) (African)

Robinson, Adjai. *Three African Tales*, 1227 (M) (African)

Rupert, Rona. *Straw Sense*, 1257 (P) (African)

Steptoe, John. *Birthday*, 1377 (P) (African)

Walter, Mildred Pitts. *Brother to the Wind*, 1508 (P/M) (African)

Ward, Leila. *I Am Eyes/Ni Macho*, 1523 (P) (African)

Watson, Pete. *The Market Lady and the Mango Tree*, 1529 (M) (African)

Williams, Karen Lynn. *Galimoto*, 1549 (P/M) (African)

  *When Africa Was Home*, 1551 (P) (African)

Zaslavsky, Claudia. *Count on Your Fingers African Style*, 1636 (P) (African)

## Foreign lands—Africa—Benin

Cowen-Fletcher, Jane. *It Takes a Village*, 315 (P) (African—Benin)

## Foreign lands—Africa—Cameroon

Alexander, Lloyd. *The Fortune-Tellers*, 40 (P/M) (African—Cameroon)

## Foreign lands—Africa—Egypt

Heide, Florence Parry, and Judith Heide Gilliland. *The Day of Ahmed's Secret*, 637 (P/M) (African—Egypt)

Sabuda, Robert. *Tutankhaman's Gift*, 1259 (M) (African—Egypt)

Stolz, Mary. *Zekmet, the Stone Carver: A Tale of Ancient Egypt*, 1397 (M) (African—Egypt)

Walsh, Jill Paton. *Pepi and the Secret Names*, 1507 (M) (African—Egypt)

## Foreign lands—Africa—Ghana

Appiah, Sonia. *Amoko and Efua Bear*, 61 (P) (African—Ghana)

## Foreign lands—Africa—Iban

Myers, Christopher A., and Lynne Born Myers. *Forest of the Clouded Leopard*, 1079 (U) (African—Iban)

## Foreign lands—Africa—Masai

Hru, Dakari. *Joshua's Masai Mask*, 683 (M) (African American)

Kroll, Virginia. *Masai and I*, 827 (P) (African—Masai)

MacDonald, Suse. *Nanta's Lion: A Search-and-Find Adventure*, 945 (P) (African—Masai)

## Foreign lands—Africa—Namibia

Beake, Lesley. *Song of Be*, 106 (U) (African—Namibia)

Haarhoff, Dorian. *Desert December*, 572 (P) (African—Namibia)

## Foreign lands—Africa—Nigeria

Olaleye, Isaac. *The Distant Talking Drum: Poems from Nigeria*, 1125 (M) (African—Nigeria)

## Foreign lands—Africa—South Africa

Angelou, Maya. *My Painted House, My Friendly Chicken, and Me*, 57 (M) (African—South Africa)

Case, Dianne. *92 Queens Road*, 228 (U) (African—South Africa)

Daly, Niki. *Not So Fast Songololo*, 332 (P) (African—South Africa)

Gordon, Sheila. *The Middle of Somewhere: A Story of South Africa*, 511 (U) (African—South Africa)

   *Waiting for the Rain: A Novel of South Africa*, 512 (U) (African—South Africa)

Isadora, Rachel. *At the Crossroads*, 715 (P) (African—South Africa)

   *Over the Green Hills*, 717 (P) (African—South Africa)

Lewin, Hugh. *Jafta*, 879 (P) (African—South Africa)

Foreign lands—Africa—South Africa (cont.)
*Jafta and the Wedding*, 880 (P) (African—South Africa)
*Jafta: The Homecoming*, 881 (P) (African—South Africa)
*Jafta—The Journey*, 882 (P) (African—South Africa)
*Jafta—The Town*, 883 (P) (African—South Africa)
*Jafta's Father*, 884 (P) (African—South Africa)
*Jafta's Mother*, 885 (P) (African—South Africa)
Maartens, Maretha. *Paper Bird: A Novel of South Africa*, 932 (U) (African—South Africa)
Naidoo, Beverley. *Chain of Fire*, 1090 (U) (African—South Africa)
*Journey to Jo'burg: A South African Story*, 1091 (U) (African—South Africa)
Sacks, Margaret. *Themba*, 1260 (M) (African—South Africa)
Schermbrucker, Reviva. *Charlie's House*, 1291 (P/M) (African—South Africa)
Seed, Jenny. *Ntombi's Song*, 1301 (PS/P) (African—South Africa)
Seeger, Pete. *Abiyoyo: Based on a South African Lullaby and Folk Song*, 1302 (M) (African—South Africa)
Stewart, Dianne. *The Dove*, 1385 (P) (African—South Africa)
Stock, Catherine. *Armien's Fishing Trip*, 1387 (P) (African—South Africa)

Foreign lands—Africa—Swaziland
Leigh, Nila K. *Learning to Swim in Swaziland: A Child's-Eye View of a South African Country*, 863 (P) (African—Swaziland)

Foreign lands—Africa—Yoruba
Rupert, Janet E. *The African Mask*, 1256 (U) (African—Yoruba)

Foreign lands—Africa—Zaire
Stanley, Sanna. *The Rains Are Coming*, 1374 (P) (African—Zaire)

Foreign lands—Africa—Zimbabwe
Stock, Catherine. *Where Are You Going, Manyoni?*, 1391 (P) (African—Zimbabwe)

Foreign lands—Asia
Bang, Molly. *The Paper Crane*, 84 (P) (Asian)
Yolen, Jane. *The Girl Who Loved the Wind*, 1622 (M) (Asian)

Foreign lands—Asia—Burma
Baillie, Allan. *Rebel*, 75 (P) (Asian—Burma)

Foreign lands—Asia—Cambodia
Ho, Minfong. *The Clay Marble*, 652 (U) (Asian—Cambodia)
Lee, Jeanne M. *Silent Lotus*, 859 (M) (Asian—Cambodia)

Foreign lands—Asia—China
Allen, Judy. *Tiger*, 45 (P) (Asian—China)

Andersen, Hans Christian. *The Nightingale*, 50 (M) (Asian—China)

Armstrong, Jennifer. *Chin Yu Min and the Ginger Cat*, 64 (P) (Asian—China)
  *Wan Hu Is in the Stars*, 66 (M) (Asian—China)

Bang, Molly, adapter. *Tye May and the Magic Brush*, 86 (M) (Asian—China)

Bedard, Michael, reteller. *The Nightingale*, 107 (M) (Asian—China)

Chang, Margaret, and Raymond Chang. *In the Eye of War*, 240 (U) (Asian—China)

DeJong, Meindert. *The House of Sixty Fathers*, 346 (M) (Asian—China)

Demi. *Dragon Kites and Dragonflies: A Collection of Chinese Nursery Rhymes*, 352 (P/M) (Asian—China)
  *Liang and the Magic Paintbrush*, 355 (M) (Asian—China)

Diller, Harriett. *The Waiting Day*, 368 (M) (Asian—China)

Fritz, Jean. *China Homecoming*, 451 (U) (Asian - China)
  *Homesick: My Own Story*, 453 (U) (Asian—China)

Handforth, Thomas. *Mei Li*, 603 (P) (Asian—China)

Haskins, Jim. *Count Your Way Through China*, 620 (P) (Asian—China)

Leaf, Margaret. *Eyes of the Dragon*, 855 (M) (Asian—China)

Lewis, Elizabeth Foreman. *Young Fu of the Upper Yangtze*, 887 (U) (Asian—China)

Neville, Emily Cheney. *The China Year: A Novel*, 1100 (U) (Asian—China)

Pattison, Darcy. *The River Dragon*, 1155 (M) (Asian—China)

Schlein, Miriam. *The Year of the Panda*, 1292 (M) (Asian—China)

Singer, Marilyn. *The Painted Fan*, 1327 (M) (Asian—China)

So, Meilo, reteller. *The Emperor and the Nightingale*, 1347 (M) (Asian—China)

Tan, Amy. *The Chinese Siamese Cat*, 1408 (M) (Asian—China)
  *Moon Lady*, 1409 (M) (Asian—China)

Tompert, Ann. *Grandfather Tang's Story*, 1445 (P) (Asian—China)

Williams, Jay. *Everyone Knows What a Dragon Looks Like*, 1548 (M) (Asian—China)

Wolff, Ferida. *The Emperor's Garden*, 1573 (M) (Asian—China)

Yen, Clara, reteller. *Why Rat Comes First: A Story of the Chinese Zodiac*, 1601 (M) (Asian—China)

Yep, Laurence. *The Butterfly Boy*, 1604 (M) (Asian—China)
  *The Ghost Fox*, 1608 (M) (Asian—China)
  *The Serpent's Children*, 1614 (U) (Asian—China)

Yolen, Jane. *The Emperor and the Kite*, 1620 (M) (Asian—China)
  *The Seeing Stick*, 1624 (M) (Asian—China)

## Foreign lands—Asia—Hong Kong
Levinson, Riki. *Our Home Is the Sea*, 877 (P) (Asian—Hong Kong)

## Foreign lands—Asia—India
Bonnici, Peter. *The Festival*, 148 (P) (Asian—India)
  *The First Rains*, 149 (P) (Asian—India)

Haskins, Jim. *Count Your Way Through India*, 621 (P) (Asian—India)

Kamal, Aleph. *The Bird Who Was an Elephant*, 776 (M) (Asian—India)

Yashima, Taro. *Crow Boy*, 1595 (P) (Asian—Japan)

Yep, Laurence. *Hiroshima*, 1609 (U) (Asian—Japan)

## Foreign lands—Asia—Korea

Choi, Sook Nyul. *Echoes of the White Giraffe*, 253 (U) (Asian—Korea)

 *Gathering of Pearls*, 254 (U) (Asian—Korea)

 *Year of Impossible Goodbyes*, 256 (U) (Asian—Korea)

Haskins, Jim. *Count Your Way Through Korea*, 623 (P) (Asian—Korea)

Watkins, Yoko Kawashima. *So Far from the Bamboo Grove*, 1527 (U) (Asian—Korea/Japan)

## Foreign lands—Asia—Thailand

Oliviero, Jamie. *Som See and the Magic Elephant*, 1127 (M) (Asian—Thailand)

## Foreign lands—Asia—Vietnam

Garland, Sherry. *The Lotus Seed*, 458 (P) (Asian American—Vietnam)

Keller, Holly. *Grandfather's Dream*, 791 (P) (Asian—Vietnam)

Kidd, Diana. *Onion Tears*, 801 (M) (Asian—Vietnam)

Lee, Jeanne M. *Ba-Nam*, 857 (P) (Asian—Vietnam)

Whelan, Gloria. *Goodbye, Vietnam*, 1541 (U) (Asian—Vietnam)

## Foreign lands—Australia

Kidd, Diana. *Onion Tears*, 801 (M) (Asian—Vietnam)

## Foreign lands—Australia—Aborigine

Adams, Jeanie. *Going for Oysters*, 22 (P) (Australian—Aborigine)

## Foreign lands—Canada

Andrews, Jan. *Very Last First Time*, 56 (P/M) (Native American—Inuit)

Dubois, Muriel L. *Abenaki Captive*, 383 (U) (Native American—Abenaki)

Houston, James. *The Falcon Bow: An Arctic Legend*, 669 (U) (Native American—Inuit)

 *Frozen Fire: A Tale of Courage*, 670 (M) (Native American—Inuit)

Munsch, Robert, and Michael Kusugak. *A Promise Is a Promise*, 1076 (P) (Native American—Inuit)

Turner, Glennette Tilley. *Running for Our Lives*, 1469 (U) (African American)

## Foreign lands—Caribbean Islands

Agard, John. *The Calypso Alphabet*, 34 (P) (Caribbean)

Agard, John, and Grace Nichols, eds. *A Caribbean Dozen: Poems from Caribbean Poets*, 35 (M/U) (Caribbean)

Berry, James. *Ajeemah and His Son*, 124 (U) (African)

Binch, Caroline. *Gregory Cool*, 138 (M) (Caribbean)

Buffett, Jimmy, and Savannah Jane Buffett. *The Jolly Mon*, 194 (P) (Caribbean)

Bunting, Eve. *How Many Days to America? A Thanksgiving Story*, 199 (M) (Caribbean)

## Foreign lands—Caribbean Islands—Puerto Rico

Adoff, Arnold. *Flamboyán*, 25 (P) (Caribbean—Puerto Rico)

Delacre, Lulu. *Vejigante Masquerader*, 349 (M) (Caribbean—Puerto Rico)

Martel, Cruz. *Yagua Days*, 977 (M) (Hispanic American—Puerto Rico)

Mohr, Nicholasa. *Going Home*, 1034 (M) (Hispanic American—Puerto Rico)

Nodar, Carmen Santiago. *Abuelita's Paradise*, 1104 (P) (Caribbean—Puerto Rico)

Picó, Fernando. *The Red Comb*, 1171 (M) (Caribbean—Puerto Rico)

Pomerantz, Charlotte. *The Outside Dog*, 1186 (P) (Caribbean—Puerto Rico)

## Foreign lands—Caribbean Islands—Trinidad

Joseph, Lynn. *Jasmine's Parlour Day*, 772 (P) (Caribbean—Trinidad)

## Foreign lands—Central America

Ada, Alma Flor. *The Gold Coin*, 18 (M) (Central American)

Grifalconi, Ann. *The Bravest Flute: A Story of Courage in the Mayan Tradition*, 552 (M) (Central American—Mayan)

O'Dell, Scott. *The Captive*, 1116 (U) (Central American—Mayan)

Wisniewski, David. *Rain Player*, 1570 (M) (Central American—Mayan)

## Foreign lands—Central America—Costa Rica

Franklin, Kristine L. *When the Monkeys Came Back*, 443 (P) (Central American—Costa Rica)

## Foreign lands—Central America—El Salvador

Temple, Frances. *Grab Hands and Run*, 1436 (U) (Central American—El Salvador)

## Foreign lands—Central America—Guatemala

Cameron, Ann. *The Most Beautiful Place in the World*, 219 (M) (Central American—Guatemala)

Castañeda, Omar S. *Abuela's Weave*, 231 (M) (Central American—Guatemala)

*Among the Volcanoes*, 232 (U) (Central American—Guatemala)

Markel, Michelle. *Gracias, Rosa*, 975 (P) (Central American—Guatemala)

## Foreign lands—Central America—Panama

Markun, Patricia Maloney. *The Little Painter of Sabana Grande*, 976 (M) (Central American—Panama)

Palacios, Argentina. *A Christmas Surprise for Chabelita*, 1147 (M) (Central American—Panama)

## Foreign lands—Dominican Republic

Gordon, Ginger. *My Two Worlds*, 510 (P) (Hispanic American)

Maiorano, Robert. *Francisco*, 966 (P) (West Indian)

## Foreign lands—England

Richemont, Enid. *The Magic Skateboard*, 1219 (M) (African heritage)

## Foreign lands—Indonesia

Sis, Peter. *Komodo!*, 1329 (P) (Indonesian)

## Foreign lands—Latin America

Carlson, Lori M., and Cynthia L. Ventura, editors. *Where Angels Glide at Dawn: New Stories from Latin America*, 222 (U) (Latin American)

Delacre, Lulu, selector. *Arroz Con Leche: Popular Songs and Rhymes from Latin America*, 347 (P/M) (Latin American)

Griego, Margot C., et al., selectors. *Tortillitas Para Mamá: And Other Nursery Rhymes*, 551 (P) (Latin American)

Hurwitz, Johanna. *New Shoes for Silvia*, 707 (P) (Latin American)

Orozco, José-Luis, selector, arranger, and translator. *De Colores: And Other Latin-American Folk Songs for Children*, 1134 (M/U) (Latin American)

## Foreign lands—Mexico

Ancona, George. *The Piñata Maker/El Piñatero*, 48 (M) (Mexican)

Czernecki, Stefan, and Timothy Rhodes. *The Hummingbirds' Gift*, 329 (M) (Mexican)

DeGerez, Toni, adapter. *My Song Is a Piece of Jade: Songs of Ancient Mexico in English and Spanish*, 344 (M) (Mexican)

Ets, Marie Hall. *Gilberto and the Wind*, 407 (P) (Mexican)

Ets, Marie Hall, and Aurora Labastida. *Nine Days to Christmas*, 408 (P) (Mexican)

Flora, James. *The Fabulous Firework Family*, 432 (M) (Mexican)

George, Jean Craighead. *Shark Beneath the Reef*, 465 (U) (Mexican)

Gollub, Matthew. *The Moon Was at a Fiesta*, 506 (P) (Mexican)

  *The Twenty-five Mixtec Cats*, 507 (M) (Mexican)

Grossman, Patricia. *Saturday Market*, 562 (P) (Mexican)

Haskins, Jim. *Count Your Way Through Mexico*, 624 (P) (Mexican)

Johnston, Tony. *The Old Lady and the Birds*, 758 (P) (Mexican)

Krull, Kathleen. *Maria Molina and the Days of the Dead*, 831 (M) (Mexican)

Lewis, Thomas P. *Hill of Fire*, 891 (P) (Mexican)

Lloyd, Errol. *Nini at Carnival*, 906 (P) (Mexican)

McGee, Charmayne. *So Sings the Blue Deer*, 946 (U) (Native American—Huichol)

Mora, Francisco X. *Juan Tuza and the Magic Pouch*, 1052 (M) (Mexican)

O'Dell, Scott. *The Black Pearl*, 1114 (U) (Mexican)

  *Child of Fire*, 1117 (U) (Mexican American)

  *The King's Fifth*, 1119 (U) (Mexican)

Parkison, Jami. *Pequeña the Burro*, 1150 (M) (Mexican)

Paulsen, Gary. *The Tortilla Factory*, 1158 (P) (Mexican)

Tompert, Ann. *The Silver Whistle*, 1446 (P) (Mexican)

Treviño, Elizabeth Borton de. *El Güero: A True Adventure Story*, 1451 (U) (Mexican)

## Foreign lands—Middle East—Arabia

Alexander, Sue. *Nadia the Willful*, 42 (P) (Middle Eastern—Arabia)

Cohen, Barbara, and Bahija Lovejoy. *Seven Daughters and Seven Sons*, 289 (U) (Middle Eastern—Arabia)

Haskins, Jim. *Count Your Way Through the Arab World*, 625 (P) (Middle Eastern—Arabia)

## Foreign lands—Middle East—Lebanon

Heide, Florence Parry, and Judith Heide Gilliland. *Sami and the Time of the Troubles*, 638 (M) (Middle Eastern—Lebanon)

## Foreign lands—Middle East—Palestine

Nye, Naomi Shihab. *Sitti's Secrets*, 1109 (P) (Middle Eastern American—Arab)

## Foreign lands—Middle East—Persia

Stanley, Diane. *Fortune*, 1373 (M) (Middle Eastern—Persia)

## Foreign lands—Middle East—Tuareg

Kessler, Cristina. *One Night: A Story from the Desert*, 798 (P) (Middle Eastern—Tuareg)

## Foreign lands—Philippines

Allen, Judy. *Eagle*, 43 (P) (Philippine)

## Foreign lands—Polynesia

Sperry, Armstrong. *Call It Courage*, 1362 (U) (Polynesian)

## Foreign lands—South America

Alexander, Ellen. *Chaska and the Golden Doll*, 38 (M) (South American)

Cherry, Lynne. *The Great Kapok Tree: A Tale of the Amazon Rain Forest*, 243 (M) (South American)

Torres, Leyla. *Saturday Sancocho*, 1449 (P) (South American)

## Foreign lands—South America—Amazon

Vaughan, Marcia. *Kapoc, the Killer Croc*, 1493 (M) (South American—Amazon)

## Foreign lands—South America—Argentina

Brusca, María Cristina. *On the Pampas*, 177 (P) (South American—Argentina)

## Foreign lands—South America—Bolivia

Topooco, Eusebio. *Waira's First Journey*, 1447 (M) (South American—Bolivia)

## Foreign lands—South America—Brazil

Cohen, Miriam. *Born to Dance Samba*, 291 (M) (South American—Brazil)

Lewin, Ted. *Amazon Boy*, 886 (P/M) (South American—Brazil)

## Foreign lands—South America—Colombia

Kendall, Sarita. *Ransom for a River Dolphin*, 795 (U) (South American—Colombia)

## Foreign lands—South America—Peru

Clark, Ann Nolan. *Secret of the Andes*, 261 (U) (South American—Peru)

Dorros, Arthur. *Tonight Is Carnaval*, 379 (P/M) (South American—Peru)

## Foreign lands—South America—Surinam

Lichtveld, Noni. *I Lost My Arrow in a Kankan Tree*, 893 (M) (South American—Surinam)

## Foreign lands—Tahiti

Nunes, Susan. *To Find the Way*, 1108 (M) (Tahitian)

## Foreign languages

Ancona, George. *The Piñata Maker/El Piñatero*, 48 (M) (Mexican)

Anzaldúa, Gloria. *Friends from the Other Side/Amigos del Otro Lado*, 59 (M) (Mexican American)

Bozylinsky, Hannah Heritage. *Lala Salama: An African Lullaby in Swahili and English*, 156 (P) (African)

Cazet, Denys. *Born in the Gravy*, 233 (P) (Mexican American)

Chin, Charlie, reteller. *China's Bravest Girl: The Legend of Hua Mu Lan*, 245 (M) (Asian—China)

Chocolate, Deborah M. Newton. *Kwanzaa*, 249 (P/M) (African American)

*My First Kwanzaa Book*, 250 (PS/P) (African American)

Cisneros, Sandra. *Hairs/Pelitos*, 258 (P) (Hispanic American)

DeGerez, Toni, adapter. *My Song Is a Piece of Jade: Songs of Ancient Mexico in English and Spanish*, 344 (M) (Mexican)

Delacre, Lulu, selector. *Arroz Con Leche: Popular Songs and Rhymes from Latin America*, 347 (P/M) (Latin American)

*Las Navidades: Popular Christmas Songs from Latin America*, 348 (P/M) (Latin American)

*Vejigante Masquerader*, 349 (M) (Caribbean—Puerto Rico)

DeSauza, James, reteller, and Harriet Rohmer, adapter. *Brother Anansi and the Cattle Ranch: El Hermano Anansi y el Rancho de Ganado*, 364 (M) (Central American—Nicaragua)

Dorros, Arthur. *Abuela*, 377 (P/M) (Hispanic American)

*Radio Man: A Story in English and Spanish/Don Radio: Un Cuento en Inglés y Español*, 378 (P) (Mexican American)

*Tonight Is Carnaval*, 379 (P/M) (South American—Peru)

Ehlert, Lois. *Moon Rope: A Peruvian Folktale/Un lazo a la luna: Una leyenda peruana*, 395 (M) (South American—Peru)

Feelings, Muriel. *Jambo Means Hello: Swahili Alphabet Book*, 413 (P/M) (African)

*Moja Means One: Swahili Counting Book*, 414 (P/M) (African)

Flora, James. *The Fabulous Firework Family*, 432 (M) (Mexican)

Goble, Paul. *Adopted by the Eagles: A Plains Indian Story of Friendship and Treachery*, 484 (M) (Native American—Plains Indians)

González, Lucía M., reteller. *The Bossy Gallito/El Gallo de Bodas: A Traditional Cuban Folktale*, 509 (M) (Caribbean—Cuba)

Griego, Margot C., et al., selectors. *Tortillitas Para Mamá: And Other Nursery Rhymes*, 551 (P) (Latin American)

Grossman, Patricia. *Saturday Market*, 562 (P) (Mexican)

Han, Suzanne Crowder. *The Rabbit's Escape*, 601 (M) (Asian—Korea)

*The Rabbit's Judgment*, 602 (M) (Asian—Korea)

Haskins, Jim. *Count Your Way Through Africa*, 619 (P) (African)

*Count Your Way Through China*, 620 (P) (Asian—China)

*Count Your Way Through India*, 621(P) (Asian—India)

*Count Your Way Through Japan*, 622 (P) (Asian—Japan)

*Count Your Way Through Korea*, 623 (P) (Asian—Korea)

*Count Your Way Through Mexico*, 624 (P) (Mexican)

*Count Your Way Through the Arab World*, 625 (P) (Middle Eastern—Arabia)

Hoyt-Goldsmith, Diane. *Celebrating Kwanzaa*, 678 (M) (African American)

Johnston, Tony. *The Old Lady and the Birds*, 758 (P) (Mexican)

Kalman, Maira. *Sayonora, Mrs. Kackleman*, 775 (P) (Asian—Japan)

Kamal, Aleph. *The Bird Who Was an Elephant*, 776 (M) (Asian—India)

Keats, Ezra Jack, and Pat Cherr. *My Dog Is Lost!*, 789 (P) (Hispanic American—Puerto Rico)

Lee, Huy Voun. *At the Beach*, 856 (P) (Asian—China)

Lomas Garza, Carmen. *Family Pictures/Cuadros de Familia*, 910 (P/M) (Hispanic American)

McMillan, Bruce. *Sense Suspense: A Guessing Game for the Five Senses*, 960 (P) (Multicultural)

Mado, Michio. *The Animals: Selected Poems*, 963 (M/U) (Asian—Japan)

Markel, Michelle. *Gracias, Rosa*, 975 (P) (Central American—Guatemala)

Mora, Francisco X. *Juan Tuza and the Magic Pouch*, 1052 (M) (Mexican)

*The Legend of the Two Moons*, 1053 (M) (Mexican)

Onyefulu, Ifeoma. *Emeka's Gift: An African Counting Story*, 1129 (P) (African)

Orozco, José-Luis, selector, arranger, and translator. *De Colores: And Other Latin-American Folk Songs for Children*, 1134 (M/U) (Latin American)

Pinkney, Andrea Davis. *Seven Candles for Kwanzaa*, 1173 (P/M) (African American)

Politi, Leo. *Juanita*, 1182 (M) (Mexican American)

*Three Stalks of Corn*, 1184 (M) (Mexican American)

Pomerantz, Charlotte. *The Tamarindo Puppy: And Other Poems*, 1187 (M) (Hispanic)

Reed, Lynn Rowe. *Pedro, His Perro, and the Alphabet Sombrero*, 1212 (P) (Hispanic)

Reiser, Lynn. *Margaret and Margarita/Margarita y Margaret*, 1215 (P) (Hispanic American)

Rohmer, Harriet, adapter. *Uncle Nacho's Hat: El Sombrero del Tio Nacho*, 1237 (M) (Central American—Nicaragua)

Rohmer, Harriet, and Mary Anchondo, adapters. *How We Came to the Fifth World/Como vinimos al quinto mundo: A Creation Story from Ancient Mexico*, 1238 (M) (Mexican—Aztec)

Rohmer, Harriet, Octavio Chow, and Morris Vidaure. *The Invisible Hunters/Los Cazadores Invisibles: A Legend from the Miskito Indians of Nicaragua/Una*

## Foreign languages (cont.)

*Leyenda de los Indios Miskitos de Nicaragua*, 1239 (M) (Central American—Nicaragua)

Serwadda, W. Moses. *Songs and Stories from Uganda*, 1304 (M) (African—Uganda)

Soto, Gary. *Chato's Kitchen*, 1351 (M) (Hispanic)

*Neighborhood Odes*, 1355 (U) (Mexican American)

Spurr, Elizabeth. *Lupe and Me*, 1370 (M) (Mexican American)

Stanek, Muriel. *I Speak English for My Mom*, 1372 (P) (Mexican American)

Tompert, Ann, adapter. *Bamboo Hats and a Rice Cake: A Tale Adapted from Japanese Folklore*, 1444 (M) (Asian—Japan)

Torres, Leyla. *Subway Sparrow*, 1450 (P) (Multicultural)

Wall, Lina Mao, reteller. *Judge Rabbit and the Tree Spirit: A Folktale from Cambodia/Bilingual in English and Khmer*, 1505 (M) (Asian—Cambodia)

Wells, Ruth. *A to Zen: A Book of Japanese Culture*, 1536 (M) (Asian—Japan)

Yolen, Jane, editor. *Sleep Rhymes Around the World*, 1626 (P) (Multicultural)

*Street Rhymes Around the World*, 1627 (P) (Multicultural)

Zubizarreta, Rosalma, Harriet Rohmer, and David Schecter. *The Woman Who Outshone the Sun: The Legend of Lucia Zenteno*, 1637 (M) (Mexican—Zapotec)

## Forest, woods

Prusski, Jeffrey. *Bring Back the Deer*, 1200 (P) (Native American)

Yerxa, Leo. *Last Leaf First Snowflake to Fall*, 1619 (M) (Native American)

## Format, unusual

Wells, Ruth. *A to Zen: A Book of Japanese Culture*, 1536 (M) (Asian—Japan)

## Format, unusual—board books

Greenfield, Eloise. *Big Friend, Little Friend*, 526 (PS) (African American)

*Daddy and I*, 527 (PS) (African American)

*I Make Music*, 536 (PS) (African American)

*My Doll, Keshia*, 539 (PS) (African American)

Hudson, Cheryl Willis. *Animal Sounds for Baby*, 686 (PS) (African American)

*Good Morning, Baby*, 687 (PS) (African American)

*Good Night, Baby*, 688 (PS) (African American)

*Let's Count Baby*, 689 (PS) (African American)

Johnson, Angela. *Joshua by the Sea*, 732 (PS) (African American)

*Joshua's Night Whispers*, 733 (PS) (African American)

*Mama Bird, Baby Birds*, 736 (PS) (African American)

*Rain Feet*, 738 (PS) (African American)

Moore, Dessie. *Getting Dressed*, 1044 (PS) (African American)

*Good Morning*, 1045 (PS) (African American)

*Good Night*, 1046 (PS) (African American)

*Let's Pretend*, 1047 (PS) (African American)

Oxenbury, Helen. *All Fall Down*, 1143 (PS) (Multicultural)

*Clap Hands*, 1144 (PS) (Multicultural)

*Say Goodnight*, 1145 (PS) (Multicultural)

*Tickle, Tickle*, 1146 (PS) (Multicultural)

## Fractions

McMillan, Bruce. *Eating Fractions*, 959 (P) (Multicultural)

## Friendship

Anzaldúa, Gloria. *Friends from the Other Side/Amigos del Otro Lado*, 59 (M) (Mexican American)

Armstrong, Jennifer. *Chin Yu Min and the Ginger Cat*, 64 (P) (Asian—China)

Banim, Lisa. *American Dreams*, 89 (M) (Asian American—Japan)

Banks, Jacqueline Turner. *The New One*, 91 (U) (African American)

*Project Wheels*, 92 (U) (African American)

Barrett, Joyce Durham. *Willie's Not the Hugging Kind*, 96 (P) (African American)

Barrett, Mary Brigid. *Sing to the Stars*, 97 (P) (African American)

Begaye, Lisa Shook. *Building a Bridge*, 110 (P) (Native American—Navajo)

Belton, Sandra. *From Miss Ida's Porch*, 115 (M) (African American)

Binch, Caroline. *Gregory Cool*, 138 (M) (Caribbean)

Bird, E. J. *The Rainmakers*, 139 (U) (Native American—Anasazi)

Bosse, Malcolm. *Deep Dream of the Rain Forest*, 150 (U) (African—Iban)

Boyd, Candy Dawson. *Breadsticks and Blessing Places*, 152 (U) (African American)

Brooks, Bruce. *Everywhere*, 162 (M/U) (African American)

*The Moves Make the Man*, 163 (U) (African American)

Bunting, Eve. *Summer Wheels*, 201 (M) (African American)

Burden-Patmon, Denise. *Imani's Gift at Kwanzaa*, 205 (P) (African American)

Bushey, Jeanne. *A Sled Dog for Moshi*, 209 (P) (Native American—Inuit)

Cameron, Ann. *Julian, Dream Doctor*, 215 (M) (African American)

*Julian, Secret Agent*, 216 (M) (African American)

*Julian's Glorious Summer*, 217 (M) (African American)

*More Stories Julian Tells*, 218 (M) (African American)

*The Stories Julian Tells*, 220 (M) (African American)

Chang, Heidi. *Elaine and the Flying Frog*, 238 (M) (Asian American—China)

Chin-Lee, Cynthia. *Almond Cookies and Dragon Well Tea*, 247 (P) (Asian American—China)

Choi, Sook Nyul. *Echoes of the White Giraffe*, 253 (U) (Asian—Korea)

Christopher, Matt. *Shortstop from Tokyo*, 257 (M) (Asian American—Japan)

Clifton, Lucille. *Everett Anderson's Friend*, 269 (P) (African American)

*My Friend Jacob*, 276 (P) (African American)

Clymer, Eleanor. *Luke Was There*, 281 (M) (African American)

Cohen, Barbara. *Thank You, Jackie Robinson*, 287 (M) (African American)

*213 Valentines*, 288 (M) (African American)

Collier, James Lincoln, and Christopher Collier. *Who Is Carrie?*, 302 (U) (African American)

Colman, Warren. *Double Dutch and the Voodoo Shoes: A Modern African-American Urban Tale*, 303 (M) (African American)

## Friendship (cont.)

*Horrible Harry and the Kickball Wedding*, 812 (M) (Asian American—Korea)

*Horrible Harry in Room 2B*, 813 (M) (Asian American—Korea)

*Horrible Harry's Secret*, 814 (M) (Asian American—Korea)

*Song Lee and the Hamster Hunt*, 815 (M) (Asian American—Korea)

*Song Lee in Room 2B*, 816 (M) (Asian American—Korea)

Knutson, Barbara, reteller. *How the Guinea Fowl Got Her Spots: A Swahili Tale of Friendship*, 819 (M) (African—Swahili)

Konigsburg, E. L. *Jennifer, Hecate, Macbeth, William McKinley, and Me, Elizabeth*, 822 (M) (African American)

Kroll, Virginia. *Pink Paper Swans*, 828 (P) (Multicultural)

Lee, Marie G. *If It Hadn't Been for Yoon Jun*, 861 (U) (Asian American—Korea)

Lehne, Judith Logan. *When the Ragman Sings*, 862 (U) (African American)

Lessac, Frané. *My Little Island*, 867 (P) (Caribbean)

Levitin, Sonia. *The Golem and the Dragon Girl*, 878 (U) (Multicultural)

Lloyd, Errol. *Nini at Carnival*, 906 (P) (Mexican)

Lord, Bette Bao. *In the Year of the Boar and Jackie Robinson*, 915 (M) (Asian American—China)

Lyon, George Ella. *Together*, 927 (P) (Multicultural)

Maiorano, Robert. *A Little Interlude*, 967 (P) (African American)

Mathis, Sharon Bell. *Sidewalk Story*, 987 (M) (African American)

Merrill, Jean. *The Toothpaste Millionaire*, 1012 (M) (African American)

Miles, Betty. *Sink or Swim*, 1017 (M) (African American)

Moore, Emily. *Just My Luck*, 1048 (M) (African American)

*Something to Count On*, 1049 (M) (African American)

*Whose Side Are You On?*, 1050 (M) (African American)

Myers, Laurie. *Garage Sale Fever*, 1080 (M) (African American)

Myers, Walter Dean. *Fast Sam, Cool Clyde, and Stuff*, 1083 (U) (African American)

*Me, Mop, and the Moondance Kid*, 1084 (M/U) (African American)

*The Mouse Rap*, 1086 (U) (African American)

*The Young Landlords*, 1089 (U) (African American)

Namioka, Lensey. *Yang the Third and Her Impossible Family*, 1094 (M) (Asian American—China)

*Yang the Youngest and His Terrible Ear*, 1095 (M) (Asian American—China)

Nelson, Vaunda Micheaux. *Mayfield Crossing*, 1099 (U) (African American)

O'Connor, Jane. *Molly the Brave and Me*, 1113 (P) (African American)

Perkins, Mitali. *The Sunita Experiment*, 1163 (U) (Asian American—India)

Peters, Julie Anne. *The Stinky Sneakers Contest*, 1164 (M) (African American)

Pinkney, Gloria Jean. *Back Home*, 1175 (P/M) (African American)

Polacco, Patricia. *Chicken Sunday*, 1179 (M) (African American)

*Mrs. Katz and Tush*, 1180 (M) (African American)

*Pink and Say*, 1181 (M) (African American)

Porter, Connie. *Addy Learns a Lesson: A School Story*, 1189 (M) (African American)

*Addy Saves the Day: A Summer Story*, 1190 (M) (African American)

*Happy Birthday, Addy: A Springtime Story*, 1193 (M) (African American)

## Friendship (cont.)

Quattlebaum, Mary. *Jackson Jones and the Puddle of Thorns*, 1202 (M) (African American)

Raschka, Chris. *Yo! Yes?*, 1209 (P/M) (Multicultural)

Reiser, Lynn. *Margaret and Margarita/Margarita y Margaret*, 1215 (P) (Hispanic American)

Rosen, Michael. *Elijah's Angel: A Story for Chanukah and Christmas*, 1245 (M) (Multicultural)

Rupert, Rona. *Straw Sense*, 1257 (P) (African)

Scott, Ann Herbert. *Hi*, 1296 (P) (Hispanic American)

Smalls-Hector, Irene. *Irene and the Big, Fine Nickel*, 1338 (P/M) (African American)

Smothers, Ethel Footman. *Moriah's Pond*, 1343 (U) (African American)

Soto, Gary. *Baseball in April: And Other Stories*, 1349 (U) (Hispanic American)

  *Boys at Work*, 1350 (M) (Mexican American)

  *Crazy Weekend*, 1352 (U) (Hispanic American)

  *Local News*, 1354 (U) (Mexican American)

  *The Pool Party*, 1356 (M) (Mexican American)

  *The Skirt*, 1357 (M) (Mexican American)

  *Summer on Wheels*, 1358 (U) (Mexican American)

  *Taking Sides*, 1359 (U) (Mexican American)

Stanley, Sanna. *The Rains Are Coming*, 1374 (P) (African—Zaire)

Surat, Michele Maria. *Angel Child, Dragon Child*, 1404 (P) (Asian American—Vietnam)

Tate, Eleanora E. *Thank You, Dr. Martin Luther King, Jr.!*, 1415 (M) (African American)

Tsutsui, Yoriko. *Anna's Secret Friend*, 1464 (P) (Asian—Japan)

Uchida, Yoshiko. *The Birthday Visitor*, 1471 (P) (Asian American—Japan)

  *The Bracelet*, 1472 (M) (Asian American—Japan)

  *The Rooster Who Understood Japanese*, 1480 (P) (Asian American—Japan)

Walker, Alice. *To Hell with Dying*, 1504 (M) (African American)

Walter, Mildred Pitts. *Mariah Loves Rock*, 1514 (M) (African American)

Warren, Cathy. *Fred's First Day*, 1524 (PS) (African American)

Weisman, Joan. *The Storyteller*, 1532 (P) (Native American—Pueblo)

Wheeler, Gloria. *Night of the Full Moon*, 1539 (M) (Native American—Potawatomi)

Wilkinson, Brenda. *Definitely Cool*, 1546 (U) (African American)

Williams, Karen Lynn. *When Africa Was Home*, 1551 (P) (African)

Williams, Vera B. *Scooter*, 1558 (M) (Hispanic American)

Willis, Meredith Sue. *The Secret Super Powers of Marco*, 1560 (M) (Multicultural)

Wilson, Beth P. *Jenny*, 1563 (P) (African American)

Wilson, Johnniece Marshall. *Poor Girl, Rich Girl*, 1565 (U) (African American)

Woodson, Jacqueline. *Between Madison and Palmetto*, 1580 (U) (African American)

  *Last Summer with Maizon*, 1581 (U) (African American)

  *Maizon at Blue Hill*, 1582 (U) (African American)

Yep, Laurence. *Sea Glass*, 1613 (U) (Asian American—China)

Yolen, Jane. *Rainbow Rider*, 1623 (M) (Native American)

## Frogs and toads

Aardema, Verna, reteller. *The Vingananee and the Tree Toad: A Liberian Tale*, 13 (M) (African—Liberia)

Begay, Shonto. *Ma'ii and Cousin Horned Toad: A Traditional Navajo Story*, 108 (M) (Native American—Navajo)

Hamanaka, Sheila. *Screen of Frogs: An Old Tale*, 580 (M) (Asian—Japan)

Lee, Jeanne M., reteller. *Toad Is the Uncle of Heaven: A Vietnamese Folk Tale*, 860 (M) (Asian—Vietnam)

Nunes, Susan. *Tiddalick the Frog*, 1107 (M) (Australian—Aborigine)

Troughton, Joanna, reteller. *What Made Tiddalik Laugh: An Australian Aborigine Folk Tale*, 1460 (M) (Australian—Aborigine)

## Frontier and pioneer life

Brenner, Barbara. *Wagon Wheels*, 160 (P) (African American)

Dalgliesh, Alice. *The Courage of Sarah Noble*, 331 (M) (Native American)

Hurmence, Belinda. *Dixie in the Big Pasture*, 703 (U) (Native American)

O'Dell, Scott. *Streams to the River, River to the Sea: A Novel of Sacagawea*, 1122 (U) (Native American)

Wheeler, Gloria. *Night of the Full Moon*, 1539 (M) (Native American—Potawatomi)

Wright, Courtni C. *Wagon Train: A Family Goes West in 1865*, 1586 (M) (African American)

## Furniture—carpets

dePaola, Tomie, reteller. *The Legend of the Persian Carpet*, 362 (M) (Middle Eastern—Iran)

## Furniture—chairs

Keats, Ezra Jack. *Peter's Chair*, 785 (PS/P) (African American)

Williams, Vera B. *A Chair for My Mother*, 1554 (P) (Hispanic American)

## Games

Delacre, Lulu, selector. *Arroz Con Leche: Popular Songs and Rhymes from Latin America*, 347 (P/M) (Latin American)

Gryski, Camilla. *Cat's Cradle, Owl's Eyes: A Book of String Games*, 564 (M/U) (Multicultural)

*Many Stars & More String Games*, 565 (M) (Multicultural)

*Super String Games*, 566 (M) (Multicultural)

Jonas, Ann. *The Trek*, 763 (PS/P) (African American)

Lankford, Mary D. *Hopscotch Around the World*, 841 (P/M) (Multicultural)

Mattox, Cheryl Warren, collector and adapter. *Shake It to the One That You Love the Best: Play Songs and Lullabies from Black Musical Traditions*, 990 (M/U) (African American)

Oxenbury, Helen. *All Fall Down*, 1143 (PS) (Multicultural)

Pringle, Laurence. *Octopus Hug*, 1199 (PS/P) (African American)

## Games (cont.)

Say, Allen. *The Bicycle Man*, 1282 (M) (Asian—Japan)

Wisniewski, David. *Rain Player*, 1570 (M) (Central American—Mayan)

Yolen, Jane, editor. *Street Rhymes Around the World*, 1627 (P) (Multicultural)

## Gangs

Myers, Walter Dean. *Scorpions*, 1088 (U) (African American)

O'Dell, Scott. *Child of Fire*, 1117 (U) (Mexican American)

## Gardens, gardening

Bunting, Eve. *A Day's Work*, 196 (P) (Mexican American)

  *Flower Garden*, 197 (PS/P) (African American)

DiSalvo-Ryan, Dyanne. *City Green*, 369 (P) (African American)

McKissack, Patricia, and Fredrick McKissack. *Messy Bessey's Garden*, 958 (P) (African American)

Quattlebaum, Mary. *Jackson Jones and the Puddle of Thorns*, 1202 (M) (African American)

Stevens, Jan Romero. *Carlos and the Squash Plant/Carlos y la planta de calabaza*, 1382 (P) (Mexican American)

Wolff, Ferida. *The Emperor's Garden*, 1573 (M) (Asian—China)

## Gauchos

Brusca, María Cristina. *On the Pampas*, 177 (P) (South American—Argentina)

## Ghosts

Haskins, James. *The Headless Haunt: And Other African-American Ghost Stories*, 618 (U) (African American)

Hausman, Gerald. *Duppy Talk: West Indian Tales of Mystery and Magic*, 627 (U) (Caribbean—West Indies)

Milich, Melissa. *Can't Scare Me!*, 1019 (M) (African American)

San Souci, Robert D. *The Boy and the Ghost*, 1270 (P) (African American)

  *Short and Shivery: Thirty Chilling Tales*, 1276 (M/U) (Multicultural)

Taylor, C. J. *The Ghost and Lone Warrior: An Arapaho Legend*, 1417 (M) (Native American—Arapaho)

Yep, Laurence. *The Ghost Fox*, 1608 (M) (Asian—China)

  *The Man Who Tricked a Ghost*, 1611 (M) (Asian—China)

## Giants

Cohlene, Terri, adapter. *Clamshell Boy: A Makah Legend*, 292 (M) (Native American—Makah)

Fritz, Jean. *The Good Giants and the Bad Pukwudgies*, 452 (M) (Native American—Wampanoag)

Gershator, Phillis, reteller. *Tukama Tootles the Flute: A Tale from the Antilles*, 471 (M) (Caribbean—West Indies)

Norman, Howard. *How Glooskap Outwits the Ice Giants: And Other Tales of the Maritime Indians*, 1105 (M) (Native American)

Seeger, Pete. *Abiyoyo: Based on a South African Lullaby and Folk Song*, 1302 (M) (African—South Africa)

Sloat, Teri, reteller. *The Hungry Giant of the Tundra*, 1334 (M) (Native American—Yupik)

Yeh, Chun-Chun, and Allan Baillie. *Bawshou Rescues the Sun: A Han Folktale*, 1599 (M) (Asian—China)

## Gifts

Andersen, Hans Christian. *The Nightingale*, 50 (M) (Asian—China)

Banks, Jacqueline Turner. *Project Wheels*, 92 (U) (African American)

Bedard, Michael, reteller. *The Nightingale*, 107 (M) (Asian—China)

Boyd, Candy Dawson. *Circle of Gold*, 154 (U) (African American)

dePaola, Tomie, reteller. *The Legend of the Poinsettia*, 363 (M) (Mexican)

Edmiston, Jim. *Little Eagle Lots of Owls*, 391 (M) (Native American)

Hurwitz, Johanna. *New Shoes for Silvia*, 707 (P) (Latin American)

Lexau, Joan M. *Striped Ice Cream*, 892 (M) (African American)

Little, Lessie Jones, and Eloise Greenfield. *I Can Do It by Myself*, 901 (PS/P) (African American)

Markel, Michelle. *Gracias, Rosa*, 975 (P) (Central American—Guatemala)

Mora, Pat. *A Birthday Basket for Tia*, 1055 (P) (Mexican American)

Myers, Laurie. *Garage Sale Fever*, 1080 (M) (African American)

Patrick, Denise Lewis. *Red Dancing Shoes*, 1154 (P) (African American)

So, Meilo, reteller. *The Emperor and the Nightingale*, 1347 (M) (Asian—China)

Tompert, Ann. *The Silver Whistle*, 1446 (P) (Mexican)

Tsutsui, Yoriko. *Anna's Special Present*, 1465 (P) (Asian—Japan)

Uchida, Yoshiko. *The Bracelet*, 1472 (M) (Asian American—Japan)

## Glasses

Keats, Ezra Jack. *Goggles*, 778 (P) (African American)

## Gypsies

Hooks, William H. *Circle of Fire*, 664 (U) (African American)

## Haiku

Cassedy, Sylvia, and Kunihiro Suetake, translators. *Red Dragonfly on My Shoulder: Haiku*, 230 (M) (Asian—Japan)

Demi. *In the Eyes of the Cat: Japanese Poetry for All Seasons*, 354 (M) (Asian—Japan)

Lewis, Richard, editor. *In a Spring Garden*, 889 (M) (Asian—Japan)

## Hair

Cisneros, Sandra. *Hairs/Pelitos*, 258 (P) (Hispanic American)

Cote, Nancy. *Palm Trees*, 311 (P) (African American)

DeVeaux, Alexis. *An Enchanted Hair Tale*, 366 (M) (African American)

Mollel, Tololwa M., reteller. *The Princess Who Lost Her Hair: An Akamba Legend*, 1039 (M) (African—Akamba)

Yarborough, Camille. *Cornrows*, 1591 (M) (African American)

## Handicaps

Banks, Jacqueline Turner. *Egg-Drop Blues*, 90 (U) (African American)

Clifton, Lucille. *My Friend Jacob*, 276 (P) (African American)

Rankin, Laura. *The Handmade Alphabet*, 1204 (P/M) (Multicultural)

Robinet, Harriette Gillem. *Ride the Red Cycle*, 1226 (M) (African American)

Rupert, Rona. *Straw Sense*, 1257 (P) (African)

Weik, Mary Hays. *The Jazz Man*, 1530 (M) (African American)

## Handicaps—blindness

Barrett, Mary Brigid. *Sing to the Stars*, 97 (P) (African American)

Chanin, Michael. *Grandfather Four Winds and the Rising Moon*, 241 (M) (Native American)

DeArmond, Dale, adapter. *The Seal Oil Lamp: Adapted from an Eskimo Folktale*, 340 (M) (Native American—Eskimo)

Martin, Bill, Jr., and John Archambault. *Knots on a Counting Rope*, 978 (P/M) (Native American)

Porter, Connie. *Happy Birthday, Addy: A Springtime Story*, 1193 (M) (African American)

Schecter, Ellen, reteller. *Sim Chung and the River Dragon: A Folktale from Korea*, 1289 (P) (Asian—Korea)

Taylor, Theodore. *The Cay*, 1433 (U) (Caribbean)

  *Timothy of the Cay*, 1434 (U) (Caribbean)

Winthrop, Elizabeth. *Journey to the Bright Kingdom*, 1569 (M) (Asian—Japan)

Yolen, Jane. *The Seeing Stick*, 1624 (M) (Asian—China)

## Handicaps—deafness

Lee, Jeanne M. *Silent Lotus*, 859 (M) (Asian—Cambodia)

## Handicaps—physical

Banks, Jacqueline Turner. *Project Wheels*, 92 (U) (African American)

Dobkin, Bonnie. *Just a Little Different*, 374 (PS/P) (Multicultural)

Greenfield, Eloise. *Darlene*, 528 (P) (African American)

Greenfield, Eloise, and Alesia Revis. *Alesia*, 549 (M/U) (African American)

Kesey, Ken. *The Sea Lion: A Story of the Sea Cliff People*, 796 (M) (Native American—Northwest Coast)

Lee, Jeanne M. *Silent Lotus*, 859 (M) (Asian—Cambodia)

Smucker, Barbara. *Runaway to Freedom: A Story of the Underground Railroad*, 1344 (U) (African American)

## Hawaii

Guback, Georgia. *Luka's Quilt*, 567 (P) (Hawaiian)

Lewis, Richard. *In the Night, Still Dark*, 890 (M) (Hawaiian)

## Hibernation

Shetterly, Susan Hand, reteller. *Muwin and the Magic Hare*, 1318 (M) (Native American—Passamaquoddy)

## Hieroglyphics

Manniche, Lise, translator. *The Prince Who Knew His Fate: An Ancient Egyptian Tale*, 973 (M) (African—Egypt)

Walsh, Jill Paton. *Pepi and the Secret Names*, 1507 (M) (African—Egypt)

## History

Baylor, Byrd. *When Clay Sings*, 105 (P/M) (Native American)

Berry, James. *Ajeemah and His Son*, 124 (U) (African)

Bulla, Clyde Robert, and Michael Syson. *Conquista!*, 195 (M) (Native American)

Choi, Sook Nyul. *Year of Impossible Goodbyes*, 256 (U) (Asian—Korea)

DeJong, Meindert. *The House of Sixty Fathers*, 346 (M) (Asian—China)

Dubois, Muriel L. *Abenaki Captive*, 383 (U) (Native American—Abenaki)

Fisher, Leonard Everett. *Alphabet Art: Thirteen ABCs from Around the World*, 423 (P/M) (Multicultural)

*Number Art: Thirteen 1 2 3s from Around the World*, 425 (P/M) (Multicultural)

*Symbol Art: Thirteen Squares, Circles, and Triangles from Around the World*, 426 (M) (Multicultural)

Fritz, Jean. *Homesick: My Own Story*, 453 (U) (Asian—China)

Knight, Margy Burns. *Talking Walls*, 817 (M) (Multicultural)

Lewis, Elizabeth Foreman. *Young Fu of the Upper Yangtze*, 887 (U) (Asian—China)

Namioka, Lensey. *The Coming of the Bear*, 1092 (U) (Asian—Japan)

*Island of Ogres*, 1093 (U) (Asian—Japan)

O'Dell, Scott. *The Captive*, 1116 (U) (Central American—Mayan)

*The King's Fifth*, 1119 (U) (Mexican)

*My Name Is Not Angelica*, 1120 (U) (Caribbean)

Rupert, Janet E. *The African Mask*, 1256 (U) (African—Yoruba)

Sabuda, Robert. *Tutankhamen's Gift*, 1259 (M) (African—Egypt)

Stolz, Mary. *Zekmet, the Stone Carver: A Tale of Ancient Egypt*, 1397 (M) (African—Egypt)

Treviño, Elizabeth Borton de. *El Güero: A True Adventure Story*, 1451 (U) (Mexican)

Walsh, Jill Paton. *Pepi and the Secret Names*, 1507 (M) (African—Egypt)

## History—explorers

Dorris, Michael. *Morning Girl*, 376 (U) (Native American—Taino)

O'Dell, Scott. *Streams to the River, River to the Sea: A Novel of Sacagawea*, 1122 (U) (Native American)

Sis, Peter. *A Small, Tall Tale from the Far, Far North*, 1330 (M) (Native American—Inuit)

Wisniewski, David. *The Wave of the Sea-Wolf*, 1572 (M) (Native American)

Yolen, Jane. *Encounter*, 1621 (M) (Native American—Taino)

## Holidays

Krull, Kathleen. *Maria Molina and the Days of the Dead*, 831 (M) (Mexican)

## Holidays (cont.)

Pennington, Daniel. *Itse Selu: Cherokee Harvest Festival*, 1162 (M) (Native American—Cherokee)

## Holidays—Chinese New Year

Chin, Steven A. *Dragon Parade: A Chinese New Year Story*, 246 (M) (Asian American—China)

Goldin, Barbara Diamond. *Red Means Good Fortune: A Story of San Francisco's Chinatown*, 505 (M) (Asian American—China)

Handforth, Thomas. *Mei Li*, 603 (P) (Asian—China)

Wallace, Ian. *Chin Chiang and the Dragon's Dance*, 1506 (P) (Asian American—China)

Waters, Kate, and Madeline Slovenz-Low. *Lion Dancer: Ernie Wan's Chinese New Year*, 1525 (P) (Asian American—China)

## Holidays—Christmas

Clifton, Lucille. *Everett Anderson's Christmas Coming*, 268 (P) (African American)

Delacre, Lulu, selector. *Las Navidades: Popular Christmas Songs from Latin America*, 348 (P/M) (Latin American)

dePaola, Tomie, reteller. *The Legend of the Poinsettia*, 363 (M) (Mexican)

Ets, Marie Hall, and Aurora Labastida. *Nine Days to Christmas*, 408 (P) (Mexican)

Fenner, Carol. *The Skates of Uncle Richard*, 417 (M) (African American)

Gordon, Ginger. *My Two Worlds*, 510 (P) (Hispanic American)

Haarhoff, Dorian. *Desert December*, 572 (P) (African—Namibia)

Hamilton, Virginia. *The Bells of Christmas*, 582 (M) (African American)

Hayes, Sarah. *Happy Christmas, Gemma*, 634 (PS) (African American)

Heath, Amy. *Sofie's Role*, 636 (P) (African American)

Howard, Elizabeth Fitzgerald. *Chita's Christmas Tree*, 673 (P) (African American)

Joseph, Lynn. *An Island Christmas*, 771 (P) (Caribbean)

Kline, Suzy. *Horrible Harry and the Christmas Surprise*, 810 (M) (Asian American—Korea)

Langstaff, John, editor. *What a Morning! The Christmas Story in Black Spirituals*, 840 (P/M) (African American)

Lovelace, Maud Hart. *The Trees Kneel at Christmas*, 919 (M) (Middle Eastern American—Lebanon)

McKissack, Patricia, and Fredrick McKissack. *Christmas in the Big House, Christmas in the Quarters*, 954 (M) (African American)

Mattingly, Christobel. *The Miracle Tree*, 989 (M) (Asian—Japan)

Mendez, Phil. *The Black Snowman*, 1008 (P/M) (African American)

Palacios, Argentina. *A Christmas Surprise for Chabelita*, 1147 (M) (Central American—Panama)

Porter, Connie. *Addy's Surprise: A Christmas Story*, 1191 (M) (African American)

Richemont, Enid. *The Magic Skateboard*, 1219 (M) (African heritage)

Rollins, Charlemae Hill, compiler. *Christmas Gif': An Anthology of Christmas Poems, Songs, and Stories Written by and About Black People*, 1240 (M/U) (African American)

Rosen, Michael. *Elijah's Angel: A Story for Chanukah and Christmas*, 1245 (M) (Multicultural)

Say, Allen. *Tree of Cranes*, 1288 (P/M) (Asian American—Japan)

Sun, Chyng Feng. *Mama Bear*, 1403 (P) (Asian American—China)

Tompert, Ann. *The Silver Whistle*, 1446 (P) (Mexican)

Walter, Mildred Pitts. *Have a Happy . . .* , 1510 (M) (African American)

## Holidays—Easter

Polacco, Patricia. *Chicken Sunday*, 1179 (M) (African American)

## Holidays—Halloween

Elmore, Patricia. *Susannah and the Poison Green Halloween*, 398 (U) (African American)

Hamilton, Virginia. *Willie Bea and the Time the Martians Landed*, 596 (U) (African American)

Keats, Ezra Jack. *The Trip*, 787 (P) (Multicultural)

Stock, Catherine. *Halloween Monster*, 1389 (P) (African American)

## Holidays—Hanukkah

Conway, Diana Cohen. *Northern Lights: A Hanukkah Story*, 305 (P) (Multicultural)

Rosen, Michael. *Elijah's Angel: A Story for Chanukah and Christmas*, 1245 (M) (Multicultural)

## Holidays—Kwanzaa

Burden-Patmon, Denise. *Imani's Gift at Kwanzaa*, 205 (P) (African American)

Chocolate, Deborah M. Newton. *Kwanzaa*, 249 (P/M) (African American)

*My First Kwanzaa Book*, 250 (PS/P) (African American)

Hoyt-Goldsmith, Diane. *Celebrating Kwanzaa*, 678 (M) (African American)

Kroll, Virginia. *Wood-hoopoe Willie*, 830 (P) (African American)

Pinkney, Andrea Davis. *Seven Candles for Kwanzaa*, 1173 (P/M) (African American)

Saint James, Synthia. *The Gifts of Kwanzaa*, 1264 (P) (African American)

Walter, Mildred Pitts. *Have a Happy . . .* , 1510 (M) (African American)

## Holidays—Mother's Day

Boyd, Candy Dawson. *Circle of Gold*, 154 (U) (African American)

## Holidays—New Year's

Grifalconi, Ann. *The Bravest Flute: A Story of Courage in the Mayan Tradition*, 552 (M) (Central American—Mayan)

Rattigan, Jama Kim. *Dumpling Soup*, 1210 (P) (Hawaiian)

Tompert, Ann, adapter. *Bamboo Hats and a Rice Cake: A Tale Adapted from Japanese Folklore*, 1444 (M) (Asian—Japan)

## Holidays—New Year's (cont.)

Uchida, Yoshiko. *Sumi's Prize*, 1482 (M) (Asian—Japan)

## Holidays—Passover

Polacco, Patricia. *Mrs. Katz and Tush*, 1180 (M) (African American)

## Holidays—Thanksgiving

Bunting, Eve. *How Many Days to America? A Thanksgiving Story*, 199 (M) (Caribbean)

George, Jean Craighead. *The First Thanksgiving*, 462 (P) (Native American)

Kessel, Joyce K. *Squanto and the First Thanksgiving*, 797 (P) (Native American—Patuxet)

## Holidays—Valentine's Day

Cohen, Barbara. *213 Valentines*, 288 (M) (African American)

Kline, Suzy. *Horrible Harry and the Kickball Wedding*, 812 (M) (Asian American—Korea)

Stock, Catherine. *Secret Valentine*, 1390 (P) (African American)

## Homelessness

Hammond, Anna, and Joe Matunis. *This Home We Have Made/Esta Casa Que Hemos Hecho*, 598 (M) (Multicultural)

Myers, Walter Dean. *Darnell Rock Reporting*, 1082 (U) (African American)

*Mop, Moondance, and the Nagasaki Knights*, 1085 (M/U) (African American)

## Hope

Coerr, Eleanor. *Sadako*, 284 (M/U) (Asian—Japan)

*Sadako and the Thousand Paper Cranes*, 285 (M/U) (Asian - Japan)

## Hospitals

Carlstrom, Nancy White. *Barney Is Best*, 224 (PS/P) (Hispanic American)

Tsutsui, Yoriko. *Anna's Special Present*, 1465 (P) (Asian—Japan)

## Houses

Clark, Ann Nolan. *In My Mother's House*, 259 (P) (Native American)

Dragonwagon, Crescent. *Home Place*, 381 (P) (African American)

Grifalconi, Ann. *The Village of Round and Square Houses*, 558 (M) (African)

Levinson, Riki. *Our Home Is the Sea*, 877 (P) (Asian—Hong Kong)

Lobel, Arnold. *Ming Lo Moves the Mountain*, 907 (P) (Asian)

Morris, Ann. *Houses and Homes*, 1063 (PS/P) (Multicultural)

San Souci, Robert D. *The Boy and the Ghost*, 1270 (P) (African American)

Schermbrucker, Reviva. *Charlie's House*, 1291 (P/M) (African—South Africa)

Seltzer, Isadore. *The House I Live In: At Home in America*, 1303 (P) (Multicultural)

# Humor

Aardema, Verna, reteller. *Princess Gorilla and a New Kind of Water: A Mpongwe Tale*, 9 (M) (African—Mpongwe)

Alexander, Lloyd. *The Fortune-Tellers*, 40 (P/M) (African—Cameroon)

Bierhorst, John, editor. *Lightning Inside You: And Other Native American Riddles*, 132 (M) (Native American)

Cameron, Ann. *Julian, Dream Doctor*, 215 (M) (African American)

*Julian, Secret Agent*, 216 (M) (African American)

*Julian's Glorious Summer*, 217 (M) (African American)

*More Stories Julian Tells*, 218 (M) (African American)

*The Stories Julian Tells*, 220 (M) (African American)

Cooke, Trish. *Mr. Pam Pam and the Hullabazoo*, 306 (P) (African American)

Gilson, Jamie. *Hello, My Name Is Scrambled Eggs*, 475 (M) (Asian American—Vietnam)

Lobel, Arnold. *Ming Lo Moves the Mountain*, 907 (P) (Asian)

Myers, Walter Dean. *The Righteous Revenge of Artemis Bonner*, 1087 (U) (African American)

Soto, Gary. *Crazy Weekend*, 1352 (U) (Hispanic American)

*Summer on Wheels*, 1358 (U) (Mexican American)

Stevens, Jan Romero. *Carlos and the Squash Plant/Carlos y la planta de calabaza*, 1382 (P) (Mexican American)

Tate, Eleanora E. *Front Porch Stories: At the One-Room School*, 1413 (M) (African American)

Uchida, Yoshiko, reteller. *The Magic Listening Cap: More Folktales from Japan*, 1478 (M/U) (Asian—Japan)


# Illness

Bess, Clayton. *Story for a Black Night*, 126 (U) (African)

Esbensen, Barbara Juster, reteller. *Ladder to the Sky: How the Gift of Healing Came to the Ojibway Nation*, 404 (M) (Native American—Ojibway)

Flournoy, Valerie. *The Patchwork Quilt*, 434 (P/M) (African American)

Greenfield, Eloise. *William and the Good Old Days*, 547 (P) (African American)

Grifalconi, Ann. *Not Home: A Novel*, 556 (U) (African American)

Han, Suzanne Crowder. *The Rabbit's Escape*, 601 (M) (Asian—Korea)

Johnson, Angela. *Toning the Sweep*, 741 (U) (African American)

Kroll, Virginia. *Pink Paper Swans*, 828 (P) (Multicultural)

Say, Allen. *A River Dream*, 1287 (P) (Asian American)

Talbert, Marc. *A Sunburned Prayer*, 1407 (U) (Mexican American)

Taylor, C. J. *Little Water and the Gift of the Animals: A Seneca Legend*, 1420 (M) (Native American—Seneca)

Tsutsui, Yoriko. *Anna's Special Present*, 1465 (P) (Asian—Japan)

Udry, Janice May. *Mary Jo's Grandmother*, 1485 (P) (African American)

Williams, Vera B. *Music, Music for Everyone*, 1557 (P) (Hispanic American)


# Illness—Alzheimer's

Sakai, Kimiko. *Sachiko Means Happiness*, 1265 (P) (Asian American—Japan)

# Imagination

Alexander, Martha. *Bobo's Dream*, 41 (PS/P) (African American)

Baker, Keith. *The Magic Fan*, 76 (M) (Asian—Japan)

Bang, Molly. *The Grey Lady and the Strawberry Snatcher*, 82 (P) (African American)

Cooke, Trish. *Mr. Pam Pam and the Hullabazoo*, 306 (P) (African American)

Dorros, Arthur. *Abuela*, 377 (P/M) (Hispanic American)

Ets, Marie Hall. *Gilberto and the Wind*, 407 (P) (Mexican)

Feelings, Tom. *Tommy Traveler in the World of Black History*, 416 (M/U) (African American)

Fields, Julia. *The Green Lion of Zion Street*, 420 (M) (African American)

Fox, Paula. *How Many Miles to Babylon? A Novel*, 438 (M) (African American)

Gershator, Phillis. *Rata-pata-scata-fata: A Caribbean Story*, 470 (M) (Caribbean)

Gilcrist, Jan Spivey. *Indigo and Moonlight Gold*, 474 (P) (African American)

Greene, Carol. *Hi, Clouds*, 519 (PS/P) (African American)

Greenfield, Eloise. *Honey, I Love: And Other Love Poems*, 535 (P/M) (African American)

  *On My Horse*, 542 (PS/P) (African American)

Hammond, Anna, and Joe Matunis. *This Home We Have Made/Esta Casa Que Hemos Hecho*, 598 (M) (Multicultural)

Johnson, Angela. *Julius*, 734 (P) (African American)

  *When I Am Old with You*, 742 (P) (African American)

Jonas, Ann. *The Trek*, 763 (PS/P) (African American)

Keats, Ezra Jack. *Dreams*, 777 (PS/P) (Hispanic American)

  *The Trip*, 787 (P) (Multicultural)

Luenn, Nancy. *Nessa's Story*, 922 (P) (Native American—Inuit)

Lyon, George Ella. *The Outside Inn*, 926 (P) (Multicultural)

McKissack, Patricia. *A Million Fish . . . More or Less*, 949 (M) (African American)

Marzollo, Jean. *Pretend You're a Cat*, 984 (PS/P) (Multicultural)

Moore, Dessie. *Let's Pretend*, 1047 (PS) (African American)

Moses, Amy. *I Am an Explorer*, 1071 (P) (African American)

Moss, Thylias. *I Want to Be*, 1074 (P/M) (African American)

Narahashi, Keiko. *Is That Josie?*, 1096 (PS/P) (Asian American)

Ochs, Carol Partridge. *When I'm Alone*, 1112 (P) (African American)

Owen, Roy. *My Night Forest*, 1142 (PS/P) (Hispanic American)

Pinkney, Brian. *Max Found Two Sticks*, 1174 (P) (African American)

Ringgold, Faith. *Aunt Harriet's Underground Railroad in the Sky*, 1220 (P/M) (African American)

  *Dinner at Aunt Connie's House*, 1221 (P/M) (African American)

  *Tar Beach*, 1222 (P/M) (African American)

Schermbrucker, Reviva. *Charlie's House*, 1291 (P/M) (African—South Africa)

Smalls-Hector, Irene. *Jonathan and His Mommy*, 1339 (PS/P) (African American)

Williams, Karen Lynn. *Galimoto*, 1549 (P/M) (African)

Williams, Vera B. *Cherries and Cherry Pits*, 1555 (P) (African American)

Yep, Laurence. *The Butterfly Boy*, 1604 (M) (Asian—China)

Yolen, Jane. *Rainbow Rider*, 1623 (M) (Native American)

## Imagination—imaginary friends

Bogart, Jo Ellen. *Daniel's Dog*, 145 (P) (African American)

Greenfield, Eloise. *Me and Neesie*, 538 (P) (African American)

## Immigration

Anzaldúa, Gloria. *Friends from the Other Side/Amigos del Otro Lado*, 59 (M) (Mexican American)

Goldin, Barbara Diamond. *Red Means Good Fortune: A Story of San Francisco's Chinatown*, 505 (M) (Asian American—China)

Lee, Marie G. *If It Hadn't Been for Yoon Jun*, 861 (U) (Asian American—Korea)

Lord, Bette Bao. *In the Year of the Boar and Jackie Robinson*, 915 (M) (Asian American—China)

Yee, Paul. *Tales from Gold Mountain: Stories of the Chinese in the New World*, 1598 (M) (Asian American—China)

## Insects

McKissack, Patricia, and Fredrick McKissack. *Bugs!*, 953 (P) (African American)

Rodanas, Kristina, reteller. *Dragonfly's Tale*, 1232 (M) (Native American—Zuni)

## Insects—ants

Kline, Suzy. *Horrible Harry and the Ant Invasion*, 809 (M) (Asian American—Korea)

## Insects—bees

Johnson, Dolores. *The Best Bug to Be*, 743 (P) (African American)

Lasky, Kathryn. *Cloud Eyes*, 844 (M) (Native American)

## Insects—butterflies, caterpillars

Aardema, Verna, reteller. *Who's in Rabbit's House? A Masai Tale*, 15 (M) (African—Masai)

Grifalconi, Ann. *Darkness and the Butterfly*, 553 (P) (African)

Merrill, Jean, adapter. *The Girl Who Loved Caterpillars: A Twelfth Century Tale from Japan*, 1011 (M) (Asian—Japan)

Mollel, Tololwa M. *Rhinos for Lunch and Elephants for Supper! A Maasai Tale*, 1041 (M) (African—Masai)

Taylor, Harriet Peck, reteller. *Coyote and the Laughing Butterflies*, 1422 (M) (Native American—Tewa)

Yep, Laurence. *The Butterfly Boy*, 1604 (M) (Asian—China)

## Insects—crickets

Chang, Margaret, and Raymond Chang, retellers. *The Cricket Warrior: A Chinese Tale*, 239 (M) (Asian—China)

Porte, Barbara Ann. *"Leave That Cricket Be, Alan Lee,"* 1188 (P) (Asian American—China)

## Insects—fireflies

Oppenheim, Shulamith Levey. *Fireflies for Nathan*, 1132 (P) (African American)

## Insects—mosquitoes

Aardema, Verna, reteller. *Why Mosquitoes Buzz in People's Ears: A West African Tale*, 16 (M) (African—West Africa)

## Islands

Agard, John. *The Calypso Alphabet*, 34 (P) (Caribbean)

Agard, John, and Grace Nichols, eds. *A Caribbean Dozen: Poems from Caribbean Poets*, 35 (M/U) (Caribbean)

Albert, Burton. *Where Does the Trail Lead?*, 37 (PS/P) (African American)

Binch, Caroline. *Gregory Cool*, 138 (M) (Caribbean)

Burgie, Irving. *Caribbean Carnival: Songs of the West Indies*, 206 (M) (Caribbean)

Carlstrom, Nancy White. *Baby-O*, 223 (P) (Caribbean)

Crespo, George, reteller. *How the Sea Began: A Taino Myth*, 318 (M) (Native American—Taino)

George, Jean Craighead. *Shark Beneath the Reef*, 465 (U) (Mexican)

Greenfield, Eloise. *Under the Sunday Tree: Poems*, 546 (M) (Caribbean)

Gunning, Monica. *Not a Copper Penny in Me House: Poems from the Caribbean*, 568 (M) (Caribbean)

Joseph, Lynn. *Coconut Kind of Day: Island Poems*, 770 (M) (Caribbean)

  *Jasmine's Parlour Day*, 772 (P) (Caribbean—Trinidad)

  *A Wave in Her Pocket: Stories from Trinidad*, 774 (M/U) (Caribbean)

Keller, Holly. *Island Baby*, 792 (P) (Caribbean)

Lessac, Frané. *Caribbean Alphabet*, 865 (P) (Caribbean)

  *Caribbean Canvas*, 866 (M/U) (Caribbean)

  *My Little Island*, 867 (P) (Caribbean)

Linden, Ann Marie. *Emerald Blue*, 897 (P) (Caribbean)

  *One Smiling Grandma: A Caribbean Counting Book*, 898 (PS/P) (Caribbean)

O'Dell, Scott. *Island of the Blue Dolphins*, 1118 (U) (Native American)

Orr, Katherine. *Story of a Dolphin*, 1136 (P) (Caribbean)

Rockwell, Anne. *Tuhurahura and the Whale*, 1230 (M) (New Zealand—Maori)

Sperry, Armstrong. *Call It Courage*, 1362 (U) (Polynesian)

Taylor, Theodore. *The Cay*, 1433 (U) (Caribbean)

Wilson, Barbara Ker, reteller. *The Turtle and the Island: A Folktale from Papua New Guinea*, 1561 (M) (New Guinean)

## Jacobs, Harriet A.

Lyons, Mary E. *Letters from a Slave Girl: The Story of Harriet Jacobs*, 930 (U) (African American)

## Jungles

Aardema, Verna, reteller. *Rabbit Makes a Monkey of Lion: A Swahili Tale*, 10 (M) (African—Swahili)

Allen, Judy. *Eagle*, 43 (P) (Philippine)

## King, Dr. Martin Luther, Jr.

Livingston, Myra Cohn. *Let Freedom Ring: A Ballad of Martin Luther King, Jr.*, 904 (M) (African American)

## Kites

Chang, Heidi. *Elaine and the Flying Frog*, 238 (M) (Asian American—China)

Greene, Carol. *Please, Wind*, 520 (PS/P) (African American)

Miller, Moira. *The Moon Dragon*, 1024 (M) (Asian—China)

Uchida, Yoshiko. *Sumi's Prize*, 1482 (M) (Asian -Japan)

Walter, Mildred Pitts. *Brother to the Wind*, 1508 (P/M) (African)

Yolen, Jane. *The Emperor and the Kite*, 1620 (M) (Asian—China)

## Ku Klux Klan

Hooks, William H. *Circle of Fire*, 664 (U) (African American)

Meyer, Carolyn. *White Lilacs*, 1014 (U) (African American)

## Language

Battle-Lavert, Gwendolyn. *The Barber's Cutting Edge*, 98 (P) (African American)

DeGross, Monalisa. *Donavan's Word Jar*, 345 (M) (African American)

Miller, Margaret. *Can You Guess?*, 1021 (PS/P) (Multicultural)

## Laundry

Freeman, Don. *A Pocket for Corduroy*, 446 (PS/P) (African American)

Greenberg, Melanie Hope. *Aunt Lilly's Laundromat*, 516 (P) (Caribbean—Haiti)

Straight, Susan. *Bear E. Bear*, 1398 (P) (Multicultural)

## Letters

Keats, Ezra Jack. *A Letter to Amy*, 781 (P) (African American)

## Libraries

Blue, Rose. *A Quiet Place*, 144 (M) (African American)

Mennen, Ingrid, and Niki Daly. *Somewhere in Africa*, 1010 (P) (African)

## Literature

Sullivan, Charles, editor. *Children of Promise: African-American Literature and Art for Young People*, 1402 (U) (African American)

## Lullabies

Bozylinsky, Hannah Heritage. *Lala Salama: An African Lullaby in Swahili and English*, 156 (P) (African)

Carlstrom, Nancy White. *Northern Lullaby*, 225 (P) (Native American—Eskimo)

Highwater, Jamake. *Moonsong Lullaby*, 644 (P/M) (Native American)

Smith, Edward Biko. *A Lullaby for Daddy*, 1340 (PS) (African American)

Yolen, Jane, editor. *Sleep Rhymes Around the World*, 1626 (P) (Multicultural)

Harris, Christie. *Mouse Woman and the Muddleheads*, 610 (U) (Native American—Northwest Coast)

Hausman, Gerald. *Duppy Talk: West Indian Tales of Mystery and Magic*, 627 (U) (Caribbean—West Indies)

Hong, Lily Toy, reteller. *Two of Everything: A Chinese Folktale*, 661 (M) (Asian—China)

Hooks, William H. *The Ballad of Belle Dorcas*, 663 (M) (African American)

Hort, Lenny, reteller. *The Tale of the Caliph Stork*, 668 (M) (Middle Eastern—Iraq)

Hru, Dakari. *Joshua's Masai Mask*, 683 (M) (African American)

Jaffrey, Madhur. *Seasons of Splendour: Tales, Myths, and Legends of India*, 723 (U) (Asian—India)

Johnson, Ryerson. *Kenji and the Magic Geese*, 756 (M) (Asian—Japan)

Johnston, Tony, adapter. *The Badger and the Magic Fan: A Japanese Folktale*, 757 (M) (Asian—Japan)

Kesey, Ken. *The Sea Lion: A Story of the Sea Cliff People*, 796 (M) (Native American—Northwest Coast)

Kimmel, Eric A., reteller. *The Tale of Aladdin and the Wonderful Lamp: A Story from the Arabian Nights*, 806 (M) (Middle Eastern—Arabia)

*The Three Princes: A Tale from the Middle East*, 807 (M) (Middle Eastern—Arabia)

*The Witch's Face: A Mexican Tale*, 808 (M) (Mexican)

Laurin, Anne. *Perfect Crane*, 850 (M) (Asian—Japan)

Lawson, Julie, reteller. *The Dragon's Pearl*, 854 (M) (Asian—China)

Liddell, Janice. *Imani and the Flying Africans*, 894 (M) (African American)

Livo, Norma J., and Dia Cha. *Folk Stories of the Hmong: Peoples of Laos, Thailand, and Vietnam*, 905 (U) (Asian)

Long, Hua. *The Moon Maiden: And Other Asian Folktales*, 912 (M) (Asian)

Louie, Ai-Ling, reteller. *Yeh-Shen: A Cinderella Story from China*, 918 (M) (Asian—China)

McDermott, Gerald, adapter. *The Magic Tree: A Tale from the Congo*, 937 (M) (African—Zaire)

Manniche, Lise, translator. *The Prince Who Knew His Fate: An Ancient Egyptian Tale*, 973 (M) (African—Egypt)

Matsutani, Miyoko. *The Crane Maiden*, 988 (M) (Asian—Japan)

Mayer, Marianna, reteller. *Aladdin and the Enchanted Lamp*, 991 (M) (Middle Eastern—Arabia)

Mora, Francisco X. *Juan Tuza and the Magic Pouch*, 1052 (M) (Mexican)

Mosel, Arlene, reteller. *The Funny Little Woman*, 1069 (M) (Asian—Japan)

Oliviero, Jamie. *The Fish Skin*, 1126 (M) (Native American)

Onyefulu, Obi, reteller. *Chinye: A West African Folk Tale*, 1130 (M) (African)

Philip, Neil. *The Arabian Nights*, 1169 (U) (Middle Eastern—Arabia)

Reasoner, Charles, reteller. *The Magic Amber: A Korean Legend*, 1211 (M) (Asian—Korea)

Rhee, Nami, reteller. *Magic Spring: A Korean Folktale*, 1216 (M) (Asian—Korea)

Richemont, Enid. *The Magic Skateboard*, 1219 (M) (African heritage)

Rodriguez, Anita. *Aunt Martha and the Golden Coin*, 1235 (P) (African American)

## Magic (cont.)

Rohmer, Harriet, Octavio Chow, and Morris Vidaure. *The Invisible Hunters/Los Cazadores Invisibles: A Legend from the Miskito Indians of Nicaragua/Una Leyenda de los Indios Miskitos de Nicaragua*, 1239 (M) (Central American—Nicaragua)

Rose, Anne, reteller. *Akimba and the Magic Cow: A Folktale from Africa*, 1241 (M) (African)

Rosen, Michael, reteller. *How Giraffe Got Such a Long Neck . . . and Why Rhino Is So Grumpy: A Tale from East Africa*, 1246 (M) (African—East Africa)

Sadler, Catherine Edwards. *Treasure Mountain: Folktales from Southern China*, 1262 (M) (Asian—China)

San Souci, Robert D., reteller. *The Talking Eggs: A Folktale from the American South*, 1281 (M) (African American)

Schroeder, Alan. *Lily and the Wooden Bowl*, 1294 (M) (Asian—Japan)

Seeger, Pete. *Abiyoyo: Based on a South African Lullaby and Folk Song*, 1302 (M) (African—South Africa)

Shetterly, Susan Hand, reteller. *The Dwarf-Wizard of Uxmal*, 1317 (M) (Central American—Mayan)

Siberell, Anne. *A Journey to Paradise*, 1323 (M) (Asian—India)

Sleator, William. *The Angry Moon*, 1331 (M) (Native American—Tlingit)

Stanley, Diane. *Fortune*, 1373 (M) (Middle Eastern—Persia)

Steptoe, John. *Mufaro's Beautiful Daughters: An African Tale*, 1379 (M) (African)

    *The Story of Jumping Mouse: A Native American Legend*, 1381 (M) (Native American)

Tadjo, Véronique, reteller. *Lord of the Dance: An African Retelling*, 1405 (M) (African—Ivory Coast)

Troughton, Joanna, reteller. *The Wizard Punchkin: A Folk Tale from India*, 1462 (M) (Asian—India)

Uchida, Yoshiko, reteller. *The Magic Purse*, 1479 (M) (Asian—Japan)

Van Laan, Nancy, reteller. *Buffalo Dance: A Blackfoot Legend*, 1488 (M) (Native American—Blackfoot)

Vuong, Lynette Dyer. *The Golden Carp: And Other Tales from Vietnam*, 1498 (U) (Asian—Vietnam)

Wall, Lina Mao, reteller. *Judge Rabbit and the Tree Spirit: A Folktale from Cambodia/Bilingual in English and Khmer*, 1505 (M) (Asian—Cambodia)

Walter, Mildred Pitts. *Brother to the Wind*, 1508 (P/M) (African)

Wang, Rosalind C., reteller. *The Treasure Chest: A Chinese Tale*, 1522 (M) (Asian—China)

White, Carolyn. *The Tree House Children: An African Tale*, 1542 (M) (African)

Wilson, Barbara Ker. *Wishbones: A Folk Tale from China*, 1562 (M) (Asian—China)

Yagawa, Sumiko, reteller. *The Crane Wife*, 1590 (M) (Asian—Japan)

Yep, Laurence, reteller. *The Rainbow People*, 1612 (M/U) (Asian—China)

    *The Shell Woman & the King: A Chinese Folktale*, 1615 (M) (Asian—China)

Young, Ed. *Red Thread*, 1631 (M) (Asian—China)

## Markets

Grossman, Patricia. *Saturday Market*, 562 (P) (Mexican)

Joseph, Lynn. *Jasmine's Parlour Day*, 772 (P) (Caribbean—Trinidad)

Topooco, Eusebio. *Waira's First Journey*, 1447 (M) (South American—Bolivia)

Torres, Leyla. *Saturday Sancocho*, 1449 (P) (South American)

Watson, Pete. *The Market Lady and the Mango Tree*, 1529 (M) (African)

Williams, Karen Lynn. *Tap-Tap*, 1550 (M) (Caribbean—Haiti)

## Marriage, interracial

Davol, Marguerite W. *Black, White, Just Right!*, 337 (PS/P) (Multicultural)

Lacapa, Kathleen, and Michael Lacapa. *Less Than Half, More Than Whole*, 835 (M) (Multicultural)

Mandelbaum, Pili. *You Be Me, I'll Be You*, 970 (P) (Multicultural)

Straight, Susan. *Bear E. Bear*, 1398 (P) (Multicultural)

Wyeth, Sharon Dennis. *The World of Daughter McGuire*, 1588 (U) (Multicultural)

## Masks

Delacre, Lulu. *Vejigante Masquerader*, 349 (M) (Caribbean—Puerto Rico)

## Mathematics

McMillan, Bruce. *Eating Fractions*, 959 (P) (Multicultural)

## Merry-go-rounds

Cummings, Pat. *Carousel*, 322 (P) (African American)

## Migrant workers

Altman, Linda Jacobs. *Amelia's Road*, 46 (M) (Hispanic American)

Dorros, Arthur. *Radio Man: A Story in English and Spanish/Don Radio: Un Cuento en Inglés y Español*, 378 (P) (Mexican American)

Thomas, Jane Resh. *Lights on the River*, 1439 (M) (Hispanic American)

Williams, Sherley Anne. *Working Cotton*, 1552 (M) (African American)

## Mining

Coerr, Eleanor. *Chang's Paper Pony*, 282 (P) (Asian American—China)

## Missions

Politi, Leo. *Song of the Swallows*, 1183 (M) (Mexican American)

## Money

Boyd, Candy Dawson. *Circle of Gold*, 154 (U) (African American)

Myers, Laurie. *Garage Sale Fever*, 1080 (M) (African American)

## Monsters

Aardema, Verna, reteller. *Bimwili & the Zimwi: A Tale from Zanzibar*, 2 (M) (African—Zanzibar)

*The Vingananee and the Tree Toad: A Liberian Tale*, 13 (M) (African—Liberia)

## Monsters (cont.)

## Moon

McDermott, Gerald, adapter. *Anansi the Spider: A Tale from the Ashanti*, 934 (P) (African—Ashanti)

Mora, Francisco X. *The Legend of the Two Moons*, 1053 (M) (Mexican)

Sleator, William. *The Angry Moon*, 1331 (M) (Native American—Tlingit)

Wiesner, William. *Moon Stories*, 1545 (M) (Multicultural)

## Morning

Jacobs, Shannon K. *The Boy Who Loved Morning*, 720 (M) (Native American)

Moore, Dessie. *Good Morning*, 1045 (PS) (African American)

## Moving

Chang, Heidi. *Elaine and the Flying Frog*, 238 (M) (Asian American—China)

Engel, Diana. *Fishing*, 401 (P) (African American)

Fenner, Carol. *Yolanda's Genius*, 418 (U) (African American)

Greenfield, Eloise. *Grandmama's Joy*, 532 (P) (African American)

Haskins, Francine. *I Remember "121,"* 617 (M) (African American)

Johnson, Angela. *The Leaving Morning*, 735 (P) (African American)

Keats, Ezra Jack. *The Trip*, 787 (P) (Multicultural)

Levitin, Sonia. *The Golem and the Dragon Girl*, 878 (U) (Multicultural)

Lobel, Arnold. *Ming Lo Moves the Mountain*, 907 (P) (Asian)

Mead, Alice. *Crossing the Starlight Bridge*, 1000 (M) (Native American—Penobscot)

Mohr, Nicholasa. *Felita*, 1033 (M) (Hispanic American—Puerto Rico)

Pettit, Jayne. *My Name Is San Ho*, 1167 (U) (Asian American—Vietnam)

Pinkney, Andrea Davis. *Hold Fast to Dreams*, 1172 (U) (African American)

Richardson, Jean. *The Courage Seed*, 1218 (M) (Native American)

Rochelle, Belinda. *When Jo Louis Won the Title*, 1229 (P/M) (African American)

Tsutsui, Yoriko. *Anna's Secret Friend*, 1464 (P) (Asian—Japan)

Wyeth, Sharon Dennis. *The World of Daughter McGuire*, 1588 (U) (Multicultural)

Yep, Laurence. *The Star Fisher*, 1616 (U) (Asian American—China)

## Museums

Everett, Gwen. *Li'l Sis and Uncle Willie: A Story Based on the Life and Paintings of William H. Johnson*, 410 (M) (African American)

## Music

Barnes, Joyce Annette. *The Baby Grand, the Moon in July, & Me*, 95 (U) (African American)

Barrett, Mary Brigid. *Sing to the Stars*, 97 (P) (African American)

Bryan, Ashley. *All Night, All Day: A Child's First Book of African-American Spirituals*, 180 (P/M) (African American)

*I'm Going to Sing: Black American Spirituals, Vol. 2*, 184 (M) (African American)

*Walk Together Children: Black American Spirituals*, 191 (M) (African American)

Buffett, Jimmy, and Savannah Jane Buffett. *The Jolly Mon*, 194 (P) (Caribbean)

## Music (cont.)

Burgie, Irving. *Caribbean Carnival: Songs of the West Indies*, 206 (M) (Caribbean)

Delacre, Lulu, selector. *Arroz Con Leche: Popular Songs and Rhymes from Latin America*, 347 (P/M) (Latin American)

*Las Navidades: Popular Christmas Songs from Latin America*, 348 (P/M) (Latin American)

Duncan, Alice Faye. *Willie Jerome*, 385 (P) (African American)

Fenner, Carol. *Yolanda's Genius*, 418 (U) (African American)

Fichter, George S. *American Indian Music and Musical Instruments: With Instructions for Making the Instruments*, 419 (M/U) (Native American)

Gershator, Phillis, reteller. *Tukama Tootles the Flute: A Tale from the Antilles*, 471 (M) (Caribbean—West Indies)

Goble, Paul. *Love Flute*, 500 (M) (Native American—Plains Indians)

Greenfield, Eloise. *I Make Music*, 536 (PS) (African American)

Grifalconi, Ann. *The Bravest Flute: A Story of Courage in the Mayan Tradition*, 552 (M) (Central American—Mayan)

Hru, Dakari. *Joshua's Masai Mask*, 683 (M) (African American)

Isadora, Rachel. *Ben's Trumpet*, 716 (P) (African American)

Johnson, James Weldon. *Lift Every Voice and Sing*, 753 (P/M) (African American)

*Lift Ev'ry Voice and Sing*, 754 (M) (African American)

Kroll, Virginia. *Wood-hoopoe Willie*, 830 (P) (African American)

Lacapa, Michael, reteller. *The Flute Player: An Apache Folktale*, 837 (M) (Native American—Apache)

Langstaff, John, editor. *Climbing Jacob's Ladder: Heroes of the Bible in African-American Spirituals*, 839 (P/M) (African American)

*What a Morning! The Christmas Story in Black Spirituals*, 840 (P/M) (African American)

Lewis, Richard. *All of You Was Singing*, 888 (M) (Mexican—Aztec)

Livingston, Myra Cohn. *Keep On Singing: A Ballad of Marian Anderson*, 903 (M) (African American)

Maiorano, Robert. *A Little Interlude*, 967 (P) (African American)

Medearis, Angela Shelf, adapter. *The Singing Man: A West African Folktale*, 1004 (M) (African)

Moore, Yvette. *Freedom Songs*, 1051 (U) (African American)

Namioka, Lensey. *Yang the Youngest and His Terrible Ear*, 1095 (M) (Asian American—China)

Ober, Hal, reteller. *How Music Came to the World: An Ancient Mexican Myth*, 1110 (M) (Mexican—Aztec)

Orozco, José-Luis, selector, arranger, and translator. *De Colores: And Other Latin American Folk Songs for Children*, 1134 (M/U) (Latin American)

Peterson, Jeanne Whitehouse. *My Mama Sings*, 1165 (P) (African American)

Pinkney, Brian. *Max Found Two Sticks*, 1174 (P) (African American)

Politi, Leo. *Juanita*, 1182 (M) (Mexican American)

Price, Leontyne, reteller. *Aïda*, 1198 (U) (African)

Raschka, Chris. *Charlie Parker Played Be Bop*, 1208 (P) (African American)

Rodriguez, Anita. *Jamal and the Angel*, 1236 (P) (African American)

Sage, James. *The Little Band*, 1263 (P) (Multicultural)

Serwadda, W. Moses. *Songs and Stories from Uganda*, 1304 (M) (African – Uganda)

Shange, Ntozake. *I Live in Music*, 1306 (M) (African American)

Smith, Edward Biko. *A Lullaby for Daddy*, 1340 (PS) (African American)

Walter, Mildred Pitts. *Mariah Loves Rock*, 1514 (M) (African American)

*Ty's One-Man Band*, 1518 (P) (African American)

Williams, Vera B. *Music, Music for Everyone*, 1557 (P) (Hispanic American)

*Something Special for Me*, 1559 (P) (Hispanic American)

Wolkstein, Diane. *The Banza: A Haitian Story*, 1574 (M) (Caribbean—Haiti)

*The Magic Orange Tree: And Other Haitian Folktales*, 1575 (M/U) (Caribbean—Haiti)

## Musical instruments

Fichter, George S. *American Indian Music and Musical Instruments: With Instructions for Making the Instruments*, 419 (M/U) (Native American)

Goble, Paul. *Love Flute*, 500 (M) (Native American—Plains Indians)

Pinkney, Brian. *Max Found Two Sticks*, 1174 (P) (African American)

Walter, Mildred Pitts. *Ty's One-Man Band*, 1518 (P) (African American)

## Mystery and detective stories

Berends, Polly Berrien. *The Case of the Elevator Duck*, 118 (M) (African American)

Cameron, Ann. *Julian, Secret Agent*, 216 (M) (African American)

Chew, Ruth. *Royal Magic*, 244 (M) (African American)

Elmore, Patricia. *Susannah and the Blue House Mystery*, 399 (U) (African American)

*Susannah and the Poison Green Halloween*, 398 (U) (African American)

*Susannah and the Purple Mongoose Mystery*, 400 (U) (African American)

Hamilton, Virginia. *The House of Dies Drear*, 587 (M) (African American)

*The Mystery of Drear House: The Conclusion of the Dies Drear Chronicle*, 592 (M) (African American)

Myers, Walter Dean. *The Mouse Rap*, 1086 (U) (African American)

Prather, Ray. *Fish and Bones*, 1197 (U) (African American)

Ruby, Lois. *Steal Away Home*, 1254 (U) (African American)

## Mythical creatures

Shepherd, Sandy. *Myths and Legends from Around the World*, 1314 (M) (Multicultural)

## Mythical creatures—mermaids

Osborne, Mary Pope, reteller. *Mermaid Tales from Around the World*, 1137 (M) (Multicultural)

San Souci, Robert D. *Sukey and the Mermaid*, 1280 (M) (African American)

## Names

Ada, Alma Flor. *My Name Is María Isabel*, 19 (M) (Hispanic American—Puerto Rico)

Bolognese, Don. *Little Hawk's New Name*, 147 (P) (Native American)

Bruchac, Joseph. *A Boy Called Slow: The True Story of Sitting Bull*, 168 (M) (Native American—Lakota Sioux)

Bryan, Ashley. *Turtle Knows Your Name*, 190 (M) (Caribbean—West Indies)

Edmiston, Jim. *Little Eagle Lots of Owls*, 391 (M) (Native American)

Jacobs, Shannon K. *The Boy Who Loved Morning*, 720 (M) (Native American)

Lottridge, Celia Barker, reteller. *The Name of the Tree: A Bantu Folktale*, 916 (M) (African—Bantu)

Mogensen, Jan. *Kakalambalala*, 1032 (M) (African)

Mosel, Arlene, reteller. *Tikki Tikki Tembo*, 1070 (M) (Asian—China)

Pitre, Felix, reteller. *Paco and the Witch: A Puerto Rican Folktale*, 1178 (M) (Caribbean—Puerto Rico)

Rochelle, Belinda. *When Jo Louis Won the Title*, 1229 (P/M) (African American)

Stroud, Virginia A. *Doesn't Fall Off His Horse*, 1401 (M) (Native American—Kiowa)

Troughton, Joanna, reteller. *Tortoise's Dream*, 1458 (M) (African)

Walsh, Jill Paton. *Pepi and the Secret Names*, 1507 (M) (African—Egypt)


## Nature

Allen, Judy. *Elephant*, 44 (P) (African)

Anderson/Sankofa, David A. *The Rebellion of Humans: An African Spiritual Journey*, 55 (M) (African)

Bandes, Hanna. *Sleepy River*, 78 (M) (Native American)

Baylor, Byrd. *The Desert Is Theirs*, 101 (M) (Native American—Papago)

Begay, Shonto. *Navajo: Visions and Voices Across the Mesa*, 109 (U) (Native American—Navajo)

Belting, Natalia. *Moon Was Tired of Walking on Air*, 111 (U) (South American)
  *Our Fathers Had Powerful Songs*, 112 (M) (Native American)
  *Whirlwind Is a Ghost Dancing*, 114 (M) (Native American)

Bierhorst, John, editor. *Lightning Inside You: And Other Native American Riddles*, 132 (M) (Native American)

Bruchac, Joseph. *Fox Song*, 171 (P) (Native American)

Bruchac, Joseph, and Michael J. Caduto, retellers. *Native American Stories*, 174 (M/U) (Native American)

Brusca, María Cristina. *When Jaguars Ate the Moon: And Other Stories about Animals and Plants of the Americas*, 178 (M) (Multicultural)

Carlstrom, Nancy White. *Northern Lullaby*, 225 (P) (Native American—Eskimo)

Cassedy, Sylvia, and Kunihiro Suetake, translators. *Red Dragonfly on My Shoulder: Haiku*, 230 (M) (Asian—Japan)

Chanin, Michael. *Grandfather Four Winds and the Rising Moon*, 241 (M) (Native American)

Cherry, Lynne. *The Great Kapok Tree: A Tale of the Amazon Rain Forest*, 243 (M) (South American)

Davis, Deborah. *The Secret of the Seal*, 334 (M) (Native American—Inuit)

DeGerez, Toni, adapter. *My Song Is a Piece of Jade: Songs of Ancient Mexico in English and Spanish*, 344 (M) (Mexican)

Diller, Harriett. *The Waiting Day*, 368 (M) (Asian—China)

Eastman, Patricia. *Sometimes Things Change*, 389 (P) (Multicultural)

Esbensen, Barbara Juster, reteller. *The Star Maiden: An Ojibway Tale*, 405 (M) (Native American—Ojibway)

Fleming, Denise. *In the Small, Small Pond*, 430 (PS) (Asian heritage)

*In the Tall, Tall Grass*, 431 (PS/P) (Multicultural)

George, Jean Craighead. *The Talking Earth*, 466 (U) (Native American—Seminole)

*Water Sky*, 467 (U) (Native American—Inuit)

Goble, Paul. *Buffalo Woman*, 486 (M) (Native American—Plains Indians)

Jones, Hettie, selector. *The Trees Stand Shining: Poetry of the North American Indians*, 765 (M) (Native American)

Keller, Holly. *Island Baby*, 792 (P) (Caribbean)

Kendall, Sarita. *Ransom for a River Dolphin*, 795 (U) (South American—Colombia)

Lacapa, Michael, reteller. *Antelope Woman: An Apache Folktale*, 836 (M) (Native American—Apache)

Lemieux, Margo. *Full Worm Moon*, 864 (M) (Native American—Algonquian)

Lewis, Richard, editor. *In a Spring Garden*, 889 (M) (Asian—Japan)

Longfellow, Henry Wadsworth. *Hiawatha*, 913 (M) (Native American)

*Hiawatha's Childhood*, 914 (M) (Native American)

Lyon, George Ella. *The Outside Inn*, 926 (P) (Multicultural)

McGee, Charmayne. *So Sings the Blue Deer*, 946 (U) (Native American—Huichol)

Major, Beverly. *Over Back*, 968 (M) (African American)

Pellowski, Anne. *Hidden Stories in Plants: Unusual and Easy-to-Tell Stories from Around the World Together with Creative Things to Do While Telling Them*, 1160 (M/U) (Multicultural)

Seattle, Chief. *Brother Eagle, Sister Sky: A Message from Chief Seattle*, 1299 (M) (Native American)

Sneve, Virginia Driving Hawk, selector. *Dancing Teepees: Poems of American Indian Youth*, 1345 (M) (Native American)

Spohn, David. *Nate's Treasure*, 1367 (M) (Multicultural)

*Starry Night*, 1368 (M) (Multicultural)

Taylor, C. J. *How We Saw the World: Nine Native Stories of the Way Things Began*, 1419 (M) (Native American)

*Little Water and the Gift of the Animals: A Seneca Legend*, 1420 (M) (Native American—Seneca)

Ward, Leila. *I Am Eyes/Ni Macho*, 1523 (P) (African)

Wood, Nancy. *Spirit Walker*, 1579 (U) (Native American—Taos Pueblo)

## Newbery Award

Armstrong, William H. *Sounder*, 67 (U) (African American)

Brooks, Bruce. *The Moves Make the Man*, 163 (U) (African American)

Clark, Ann Nolan. *Secret of the Andes*, 261 (U) (South American—Peru)

## Newbery Award (cont.)

Courlander, Harold, and George Herzog. *The Cow-Tail Switch: And Other West African Stories*, 313 (M/U) (African)

Dalgliesh, Alice. *The Courage of Sarah Noble*, 331 (M) (Native American)

DeJong, Meindert. *The House of Sixty Fathers*, 346 (M) (Asian—China)

Finger, Charles J. *Tales from Silver Lands*, 421 (U) (South American)

Fox, Paula. *The Slave Dancer: A Novel*, 439 (U) (African American)

Fritz, Jean. *Homesick: My Own Story*, 453 (U) (Asian—China)

George, Jean Craighead. *Julie of the Wolves*, 464 (U) (Native American—Inuit)

Greene, Bette. *Philip Hall Likes Me, I Reckon Maybe*, 518 (M) (African American)

Hamilton, Virginia, reteller. *In the Beginning: Creation Stories from Around the World*, 588 (M) (Multicultural)

  *M. C. Higgins the Great*, 590 (U) (African American)

  *The Planet of Junior Brown*, 594 (U) (African American)

Highwater, Jamake. *Anpao: An American Indian Odyssey*, 643 (U) (Native American)

Konigsburg, E. L. *Jennifer, Hecate, Macbeth, William McKinley, and Me, Elizabeth*, 822 (M) (African American)

Lewis, Elizabeth Foreman. *Young Fu of the Upper Yangtze*, 887 (U) (Asian—China)

McKissack, Patricia. *The Dark Thirty: Southern Tales of the Supernatural*, 947 (M/U) (African American)

Mathis, Sharon Bell. *The Hundred Penny Box*, 985 (M) (African American)

Miles, Miska. *Annie and the Old One*, 1018 (M) (Native American—Navajo)

Myers, Walter Dean. *Scorpions*, 1088 (U) (African American)

O'Dell, Scott. *The Black Pearl*, 1114 (U) (Mexican)

  *Island of the Blue Dolphins*, 1118 (U) (Native American)

  *The King's Fifth*, 1119 (U) (Mexican)

  *Sing Down the Moon*, 1121 (U) (Native American)

Paulsen, Gary. *Dogsong*, 1157 (U) (Native American—Inuit)

Speare, Elizabeth George. *The Sign of the Beaver*, 1361 (M/U) (Native American)

Sperry, Armstrong. *Call It Courage*, 1362 (U) (Polynesian)

Spinelli, Jerry. *Maniac Magee: A Novel*, 1365 (U) (African American)

Taylor, Mildred D. *Roll of Thunder, Hear My Cry*, 1430 (U) (African American)

Treviño, Elizabeth Borton de. *I, Juan de Pareja*, 1452 (U) (African heritage)

Weik, Mary Hays. *The Jazz Man*, 1530 (M) (African American)

Yep, Laurence. *Dragon's Gate*, 1606 (U) (Asian American—China)

  *Dragonwings*, 1607 (U) (Asian American— China)

## Night

Ackerman, Karen. *By the Dawn's Early Light*, 17 (P) (African American)

Bandes, Hanna. *Sleepy River*, 78 (M) (Native American)

Bierhorst, John, selector. *On the Road of Stars: Native American Night Poems and Sleep Charms*, 135 (M) (Native American)

Dragonwagon, Crescent. *Half a Moon and One Whole Star*, 380 (P) (African American)

Gerson, Mary-Joan, reteller. *How Night Came from the Sea: A Story from Brazil*, 472 (M) (South American—Brazil)

Greenfield, Eloise. *First Pink Light*, 530, 531 (P) (African American)

*Night on Neighborhood Street*, 541 (M) (African American)

Grifalconi, Ann. *Darkness and the Butterfly*, 553 (P) (African)

Highwater, Jamake. *Moonsong Lullaby*, 644 (P/M) (Native American)

Johnson, Angela. *Joshua's Night Whispers*, 733 (PS) (African American)

Keats, Ezra Jack. *Dreams*, 777 (PS/P) (Hispanic American)

Larrick, Nancy, selector. *The Night of the Whippoorwill: Poems*, 842 (M) (Multicultural)

Lippert, Margaret H., adapter. *The Sea Serpent's Daughter: A Brazilian Legend*, 899 (M) (South American—Brazil)

Mennen, Ingrid. *One Round Moon and a Star for Me*, 1009 (P) (African)

Mwalimu, and Adrienne Kennaway. *Awful Aardvark*, 1078 (M) (African)

Oppenheim, Shulamith Levey. *Fireflies for Nathan*, 1132 (P) (African American)

Stolz, Mary. *Storm in the Night*, 1396 (P/M) (African American)

Troughton, Joanna, reteller. *How Night Came: A Folk Tale from the Amazon*, 1454 (M) (South American—Amazon)

Yolen, Jane, editor. *Sleep Rhymes Around the World*, 1626 (P) (Multicultural)

## Nursery rhymes

Demi. *Dragon Kites and Dragonflies: A Collection of Chinese Nursery Rhymes*, 352 (P/M) (Asian—China)

Griego, Margot C., et al., selectors. *Tortillitas Para Mamá: And Other Nursery Rhymes*, 551 (P) (Latin American)

Hale, Sarah Josepha. *Mary Had a Little Lamb*, 573 (PS/P) (African American)

Kroll, Virginia. *Jaha and Jamil Went Down the Hill: An African Mother Goose*, 826 (P) (African)

## Older adults

Belton, Sandra. *From Miss Ida's Porch*, 115 (M) (African American)

Bunting, Eve. *Summer Wheels*, 201 (M) (African American)

DeGross, Monalisa. *Donavan's Word Jar*, 345 (M) (African American)

Eskridge, Ann E. *The Sanctuary*, 406 (U) (African American)

Franklin, Kristine L. *The Old, Old Man and the Very Little Boy*, 441 (P) (African)

Greenfield, Eloise. *Grandpa's Face*, 533 (P) (African American)

Hong, Lily Toy, reteller. *Two of Everything: A Chinese Folktale*, 661 (M) (Asian—China)

Howard, Elizabeth Fitzgerald. *Aunt Flossie's Hats (and Crab Cakes Later)*, 672 (P) (African American)

Johnson, Angela. *When I Am Old with You*, 742 (P) (African American)

Kroll, Virginia. *Pink Paper Swans*, 828 (P) (Multicultural)

Lee, Jeanne M. *Ba-Nam*, 857 (P) (Asian—Vietnam)

Mathis, Sharon Bell. *The Hundred Penny Box*, 985 (M) (African American)

Medearis, Angela Shelf. *Poppa's New Pants*, 1003 (P) (African American)

Miles, Miska. *Annie and the Old One*, 1018 (M) (Native American—Navajo)

## Older adults (cont.)

Porter, Connie. *Happy Birthday, Addy: A Springtime Story*, 1193 (M) (African American)

Sakai, Kimiko. *Sachiko Means Happiness*, 1265 (P) (Asian American—Japan)

Stock, Catherine. *Secret Valentine*, 1390 (P) (African American)

Stolz, Mary. *Coco Grimes*, 1393 (M) (African American)

  *Go Fish!*, 1394 (M) (African American)

  *Stealing Home*, 1395 (M/U) (African American)

  *Storm in the Night*, 1396 (P/M) (African American)

Tejima. *Ho-limlim: A Rabbit Tale from Japan*, 1435 (M) (Asian—Japan)

Uchida, Yoshiko. *The Birthday Visitor*, 1471 (P) (Asian American—Japan)

  *Sumi and the Goat and the Tokyo Express*, 1481 (M) (Asian—Japan)

  *The Wise Old Woman*, 1484 (M) (Asian—Japan)

Weisman, Joan. *The Storyteller*, 1532 (P) (Native American—Pueblo)

Yolen, Jane. *The Seeing Stick*, 1624 (M) (Asian—China)

## Orphans

Spinelli, Jerry. *Maniac Magee: A Novel*, 1365 (U) (African American)

## Paper

Tagore, Rabindranath. *Paper Boats*, 1406 (P) (Multicultural)

## Parades

Sage, James. *The Little Band*, 1263 (P) (Multicultural)

Waters, Kate, and Madeline Slovenz-Low. *Lion Dancer: Ernie Wan's Chinese New Year*, 1525 (P) (Asian American—China)

## Parties

Keats, Ezra Jack. *A Letter to Amy*, 781 (P) (African American)

Ketteman, Helen. *Not Yet, Yvette*, 799 (PS/P) (African American)

Soto, Gary. *The Pool Party*, 1356 (M) (Mexican American)

Stanley, Sanna. *The Rains Are Coming*, 1374 (P) (African—Zaire)

## Pets

Burchardt, Nellie. *Project Cat*, 204 (M) (African American)

Bushey, Jeanne. *A Sled Dog for Moshi*, 209 (P) (Native American—Inuit)

Cebulash, Mel. *Willie's Wonderful Pet*, 234 (P) (African American)

Hunter, Kristin. *Boss Cat*, 702 (M) (African American)

Johnson, Angela. *The Girl Who Wore Snakes*, 731 (P) (African American)

Jordan, June. *Kimako's Story*, 768 (P) (African American)

Keats, Ezra Jack. *Hi, Cat!*, 779 (PS/P) (African American)

  *Pet Show!*, 784 (PS/P) (African American)

  *Whistle for Willie*, 788 (PS/P) (African American)

Kline, Suzy. *Song Lee and the Hamster Hunt*, 815 (M) (Asian American—Korea)

Namioka, Lensey. *Yang the Third and Her Impossible Family*, 1094 (M) (Asian American—China)

Rosen, Michael. *Bonesy and Isabel,* 1243 (P) (Hispanic American—El Salvador)

Udry, Janice May. *What Mary Jo Wanted,* 1487 (P) (African American)

Wilson, Johnniece Marshall. *Robin on His Own,* 1566 (M/U) (African American)

Yashima, Mitsu, and Taro Yashima. *Momo's Kitten,* 1594 (P) (Asian American—Japan)

## Plants

Brusca, María Cristina. *When Jaguars Ate the Moon: And Other Stories about Animals and Plants of the Americas,* 178 (M) (Multicultural)

Demi. *The Empty Pot,* 353 (M) (Asian—China)

Fregosi, Claudia. *The Pumpkin Sparrow: Adapted from a Korean Folktale,* 447 (M) (Asian—Korea)

Little, Lessie Jones, and Eloise Greenfield. *I Can Do It by Myself,* 901 (PS/P) (African American)

Pellowski, Anne. *Hidden Stories in Plants: Unusual and Easy-to-Tell Stories from Around the World Together with Creative Things to Do While Telling Them,* 1160 (M/U) (Multicultural)

## Poetry, rhyme

Aardema, Verna, reteller. *Bringing the Rain to Kapiti Plain: A Nandi Tale,* 4 (P/M) (African—Nandi)

Adoff, Arnold. *Black Is Brown Is Tan,* 24 (P) (Multicultural)

*Hard to Be Six,* 26 (P) (Multicultural)

*I Am the Darker Brother: An Anthology of Modern Poems by Negro Americans,* 27 (M/U) (African American)

*In for Winter, Out for Spring,* 28 (P/M) (African American)

*My Black Me: A Beginning Book of Black Poetry,* 30, 31 (M/U) (African American)

*OUTside INside Poems,* 32 (M) (African American)

*Where Wild Willie?,* 33 (P) (African American)

Agard, John, and Grace Nichols, eds. *A Caribbean Dozen: Poems from Caribbean Poets,* 35 (M/U) (Caribbean)

Agell, Charlotte. *Dancing Feet,* 36 (PS/P) (Multicultural)

Altman, Susan, and Susan Lechner. *Followers of the North Star: Rhymes about African American Heroes, Heroines, and Historical Times,* 47 (M/U) (African American)

Baer, Edith. *This Is the Way We Eat Our Lunch: A Book about Children Around the World,* 72 (P) (Multicultural)

*This Is the Way We Go to School: A Book about Children Around the World,* 73 (P) (Multicultural)

Bang, Molly. *Ten, Nine, Eight,* 85 (PS/P) (African American)

Baylor, Byrd. *The Desert Is Theirs,* 101 (M) (Native American—Papago)

*The Way to Start a Day,* 104 (M) (Multicultural)

Begay, Shonto. *Navajo: Visions and Voices Across the Mesa,* 109 (U) (Native American—Navajo)

Belting, Natalia. *Our Fathers Had Powerful Songs,* 112 (M) (Native American)

*The Sun Is a Golden Earring,* 113 (M) (Multicultural)

*Whirlwind Is a Ghost Dancing,* 114 (M) (Native American)

Frankel, Julie E. *Oh No, Otis*, 440 (PS/P) (African American)

Garne, S. T. *One White Sail*, 460 (P) (Caribbean)

Giovanni, Nikki. *Ego-Tripping: And Other Poems for Young People*, 478 (U) (African American)

    *Knoxville, Tennessee*, 479 (P) (African American)

    *Spin a Soft Black Song: Poems for Children*, 480 (M/U) (African American)

Greene, Carol. *Hi, Clouds*, 519 (PS/P) (African American)

Greenfield, Eloise. *Daddy and I*, 527 (PS) (African American)

    *Daydreamers*, 529 (M/U) (African American)

    *Honey, I Love*, 534 (PS/P) (African American)

    *Honey, I Love: And Other Love Poems*, 535 (P/M) (African American)

    *I Make Music*, 536 (PS) (African American)

    *My Doll, Keshia*, 539 (PS) (African American)

    *Nathaniel Talking*, 540 (P/M) (African American)

    *Night on Neighborhood Street*, 541 (M) (African American)

    *On My Horse*, 542 (PS/P) (African American)

    *Under the Sunday Tree: Poems*, 546 (M) (Caribbean)

Griego, Margot C., et al., selectors. *Tortillitas Para Mamá: And Other Nursery Rhymes*, 551 (P) (Latin American)

Grimes, Nikki. *From a Child's Heart: Poems*, 559 (P) (African American)

    *Meet Danitra Brown*, 560 (P/M) (African American)

    *Something on My Mind*, 561 (M/U) (African American)

Grossman, Virginia. *Ten Little Rabbits*, 563 (P) (Native American)

Gunning, Monica. *Not a Copper Penny in Me House: Poems from the Caribbean*, 568 (M) (Caribbean)

Hale, Sarah Josepha. *Mary Had a Little Lamb*, 573 (PS/P) (African American)

Hamanaka, Sheila. *All the Colors of the Earth*, 579 (PS/P) (Multicultural)

Hamsa, Bobbie. *Polly Wants a Cracker*, 599 (P) (African American)

Highwater, Jamake. *Moonsong Lullaby*, 644 (P/M) (Native American)

Hirschfelder, Arlene B., and Beverly R. Singer, selectors. *Rising Voices: Writings of Young Native Americans*, 651 (U) (Native American)

Hoberman, Mary Ann, selector. *My Song Is Beautiful: A Celebration of Multicultural Poems and Pictures*, 654 (P/M) (Multicultural)

Hudson, Cheryl Willis. *Animal Sounds for Baby*, 686 (PS) (African American)

    *Good Morning, Baby*, 687 (PS) (African American)

    *Good Night, Baby*, 688 (PS) (African American)

    *Let's Count Baby*, 689 (PS) (African American)

Hudson, Cheryl Willis, and Bernette G. Ford. *Bright Eyes, Brown Skin*, 690 (PS) (African American)

Hudson, Wade, selector. *Pass It On: African-American Poetry for Children*, 694 (P/M) (African American)

Hughes, Langston. *The Dream Keeper: And Other Poems*, 695 (M/U) (African American)

    *The Dream Keeper: And Other Poems*, 696 (M/U) (African American)

Izuki, Steven. *Believers in America: Poems about Americans of Asian and Pacific Islander Descent*, 719 (M/U) (Asian American)

Javernick, Ellen. *Where's Brooke?*, 726 (PS/P) (Asian American)

## Post office

Scott, Ann Herbert. *Hi*, 1296 (P) (Hispanic American)

## Pourquoi tales

Aardema, Verna, reteller. *Oh, Kojo! How Could You! An Ashanti Tale*, 7 (M) (African—Ashanti)

   *Why Mosquitoes Buzz in People's Ears: A West African Tale*, 16 (M) (African—West Africa)

Appiah, Peggy. *Ananse the Spider: Tales from an Ashanti Village*, 60 (M) (African—Ashanti)

Arkhurst, Joyce Cooper, reteller. *The Adventures of Spider: West African Folk Tales*, 62 (M) (African—West Africa)

   *More Adventures of Spider: West African Folk Tales*, 63 (M) (African—West Africa)

Arneach, Lloyd, reteller. *The Animals' Ballgame: A Cherokee Story from the Eastern Band*, 68 (M) (Native American—Cherokee)

Baylor, Byrd. *Moon Song*, 103 (M) (Native American)

Belting, Natalia. *Moon Was Tired of Walking on Air*, 111 (U) (South American)

Bess, Clayton. *The Truth about the Moon*, 127 (M) (African)

Bierhorst, John, reteller. *The Woman Who Fell from the Sky: The Iroquois Story of Creation*, 137 (M) (Native American—Iroquois)

Bowden, Joan Chase. *Why the Tides Ebb and Flow*, 151 (M) (African)

Bruchac, Joseph, reteller. *The First Strawberries: A Cherokee Story*, 169 (M) (Native American—Cherokee)

   *The Great Ball Game: A Muskogee Story*, 173 (M) (Native American—Muskogee)

Bryan, Ashley. *The Adventures of Aku: Or How It Came About That We Shall Always See Okra the Cat Lying on a Velvet Cushion, While Okraman the Dog Sleeps Among the Ashes*, 179 (M) (African)

   *Beat the Story-Drum, Pum-Pum*, 181 (M) (African)

   *The Cat's Purr*, 182 (P) (Caribbean—West Indies)

   *The Story of Lightning & Thunder*, 189 (M) (African)

Chocolate, Deborah M. Newton, reteller. *Spider and the Sky God: An Akan Legend*, 251 (M) (African—Akan)

Cohlene, Terri, adapter. *Quillworker: A Cheyenne Legend*, 296 (M) (Native American—Cheyenne)

Crespo, George, reteller. *How the Sea Began: A Taino Myth*, 318 (M) (Native American—Taino)

Curry, Jane Louise, reteller. *Back in the Beforetime: Tales of the California Indians*, 326 (M/U) (Native American)

Czernecki, Stefan, and Timothy Rhodes. *The Singing Snake*, 330 (M) (Australian—Aborigine)

Daly, Niki, reteller. *Why the Sun and the Moon Live in the Sky*, 333 (M) (African—Nigeria)

Davison, Katherine. *Moon Magic: Stories from Asia*, 336 (M) (Asian)

Dayrell, Elphinstone. *Why the Sun and the Moon Live in the Sky: An African Folktale*, 339 (M) (African)

deWit, Dorothy, editor. *The Talking Stone: An Anthology of Native American Tales and Legends*, 367 (U) (Native American)

## Pourquoi tales (cont.)

*Whale's Canoe: A Folk Tale from Australia*, 1459 (M) (Australian)

Van Laan, Nancy, reteller. *Rainbow Crow: A Lenape Tale*, 1490 (M) (Native American—Lenape)

Vuong, Lynette Dyer. *Sky Legends of Vietnam*, 1499 (U) (Asian—Vietnam)

Walters, Anna Lee, reteller. *The Two-Legged Creature: An Otoe Story*, 1519 (M) (Native American—Otoe)

Wood, Marion. *Spirits, Heroes and Hunters from North American Indian Mythology*, 1578 (M/U) (Native American)

Yeoman, John. *The Singing Tortoise: And Other Animal Folktales*, 1602 (M) (Multicultural)

Young, Ed, adapter. *Moon Mother: A Native American Creation Tale*, 1630 (M) (Native American)

## Poverty

Anzaldúa, Gloria. *Friends from the Other Side/Amigos del Otro Lado*, 59 (M) (Mexican American)

Binch, Caroline. *Gregory Cool*, 138 (M) (Caribbean)

Hurmence, Belinda. *Tough Tiffany*, 705 (M/U) (African American)

Maartens, Maretha. *Paper Bird: A Novel of South Africa*, 932 (U) (African—South Africa)

Maiorano, Robert. *Francisco*, 966 (P) (West Indian)

Markel, Michelle. *Gracias, Rosa*, 975 (P) (Central American—Guatemala)

Mathis, Sharon Bell. *Sidewalk Story*, 987 (M) (African American)

Schermbrucker, Reviva. *Charlie's House*, 1291 (P/M) (African—South Africa)

Sonneborn, Ruth A. *Friday Night Is Papa Night*, 1348 (P) (Caribbean—Puerto Rico)

Stewart, Dianne. *The Dove*, 1385 (P) (African—South Africa)

Temple, Frances. *Tonight, by Sea*, 1438 (U) (Caribbean—Haiti)

Weik, Mary Hays. *The Jazz Man*, 1530 (M) (African American)

## Predictable text

Boivin, Kelly. *Where Is Mittens?*, 146 (PS/P) (African American)

Dobkin, Bonnie. *Collecting*, 372 (PS/P) (Asian American)

   *Everybody Says*, 373 (PS/P) (African American)

   *Just a Little Different*, 374 (PS/P) (Multicultural)

Eastman, Patricia. *Sometimes Things Change*, 389 (P) (Multicultural)

Frankel, Julie E. *Oh No, Otis*, 440 (PS/P) (African American)

Greene, Carol. *Hi, Clouds*, 519 (PS/P) (African American)

   *Please, Wind*, 520 (PS/P) (African American)

Hamsa, Bobbie. *Polly Wants a Cracker*, 599 (P) (African American)

Javernick, Ellen. *Where's Brooke?*, 726 (PS/P) (Asian American)

Johnson, Mildred D. *Wait, Skates!*, 755 (PS/P) (African American)

Lunn, Carolyn. *Bobby's Zoo*, 924 (PS/P) (African American)

McDonald, Becky Bring. *Katie Couldn't*, 942 (PS/P) (Asian American)

   *Larry and the Cookie*, 943 (PS/P) (African American)

McKissack, Patricia, and Fredrick McKissack. *Bugs!*, 953 (P) (African American)

   *Constance Stumbles*, 955 (P) (African American)

## Predictable text (cont.)

*Messy Bessey*, 956 (P) (African American)

*Messy Bessey's Closet*, 957 (P) (African American)

*Messy Bessey's Garden*, 958 (P) (African American)

Milios, Rita. *Sneaky Pete*, 1020 (PS/P) (African American)

Moore, Dessie. *Getting Dressed*, 1044 (PS) (African American)

*Good Morning*, 1045 (PS) (African American)

*Good Night*, 1046 (PS) (African American)

*Let's Pretend*, 1047 (PS) (African American)

Moses, Amy. *I Am an Explorer*, 1071 (P) (African American)

Neasi, Barbara J. *Listen to Me*, 1098 (PS/P) (African American)

Petrie, Catherine. *Joshua James Likes Trucks*, 1166 (P) (African American)

Smith, Joanne L. *Show and Tell*, 1341 (P) (African American)

Stevens, Philippa J. *Bonk! Goes the Ball*, 1384 (P) (Asian American)

## Prejudice

Adoff, Arnold, editor. *My Black Me: A Beginning Book of Black Poetry*, 30, 31 (M/U) (African American)

Armstrong, William H. *Sounder*, 67 (U) (African American)

Banim, Lisa. *American Dreams*, 89 (M) (Asian American—Japan)

Banks, Jacqueline Turner. *The New One*, 91 (U) (African American)

Brooks, Bruce. *The Moves Make the Man*, 163 (U) (African American)

Bunting, Eve. *Smoky Night*, 200 (P/M) (African American)

Case, Dianne. *92 Queens Road*, 228 (U) (African—South Africa)

Coles, Robert. *The Story of Ruby Bridges*, 299 (M) (African American)

Davis, Ossie. *Just Like Martin*, 335 (U) (African American)

Gordon, Sheila. *The Middle of Somewhere: A Story of South Africa*, 511 (U) (African—South Africa)

*Waiting for the Rain: A Novel of South Africa*, 512 (U) (African—South Africa)

Hooks, William H. *Circle of Fire*, 664 (U) (African American)

Hurmence, Belinda. *Dixie in the Big Pasture*, 703 (U) (Native American)

Knight, Margy Burns. *Who Belongs Here? An American Story*, 818 (M) (Asian American—Cambodia)

Krensky, Stephen. *The Iron Dragon Never Sleeps*, 824 (U) (Asian American—China)

Livingston, Myra Cohn. *Keep On Singing: A Ballad of Marian Anderson*, 903 (M) (African American)

Meyer, Carolyn. *White Lilacs*, 1014 (U) (African American)

Mochizuki, Ken. *Baseball Saved Us*, 1031 (M) (Asian American—Japan)

Mohr, Nicholasa. *Felita*, 1033 (M) (Hispanic American—Puerto Rico)

Moore, Yvette. *Freedom Songs*, 1051 (U) (African American)

Naidoo, Beverley. *Chain of Fire*, 1090 (U) (African—South Africa)

*Journey to Jo'burg: A South African Story*, 1091 (U) (African—South Africa)

Nelson, Vaunda Micheaux. *Mayfield Crossing*, 1099 (U) (African American)

Pinkney, Andrea Davis. *Hold Fast to Dreams*, 1172 (U) (African American)

Porter, Connie. *Happy Birthday, Addy: A Springtime Story*, 1193 (M) (African American)

Prather, Ray. *Fish and Bones*, 1197 (U) (African American)

Robinet, Harriette Gillem. *Mississippi Chariot*, 1225 (U) (African American)

Sebestyen, Ouida. *Words by Heart*, 1300 (U) (African American)

Smothers, Ethel Footman. *Down in the Piney Woods*, 1342 (U) (African American)

   *Moriah's Pond*, 1343 (U) (African American)

Soto, Gary. *Taking Sides*, 1359 (U) (Mexican American)

Spinelli, Jerry. *Maniac Magee: A Novel*, 1365 (U) (African American)

Tate, Eleanora E. *The Secret of Gumbo Grove*, 1414 (M/U) (African American)

Taylor, Mildred D. *The Friendship*, 1424 (M/U) (African American)

   *The Friendship/The Gold Cadillac*, 1425 (M/U) (African American)

   *The Gold Cadillac*, 1426 (M/U) (African American)

   *Let the Circle Be Unbroken*, 1427 (U) (African American)

   *Mississippi Bridge*, 1428 (M/U) (African American)

   *The Road to Memphis*, 1429 (U) (African American)

   *Roll of Thunder, Hear My Cry*, 1430 (U) (African American)

   *Song of the Trees*, 1431 (M/U) (African American)

   *The Well: David's Story*, 1432 (U) (African American)

Taylor, Theodore. *The Cay*, 1433 (U) (Caribbean)

Uchida, Yoshiko. *The Bracelet*, 1472 (M) (Asian American—Japan)

   *A Jar of Dreams*, 1475 (U) (Asian American—Japan)

   *Journey Home*, 1476 (U) (Asian American—Japan)

   *Journey to Topaz: A Story of the Japanese-American Evacuation*, 1477 (U) (Asian American—Japan)

Voigt, Cynthia. *Come a Stranger*, 1496 (U) (African American)

Walter, Mildred Pitts. *The Girl on the Outside*, 1509 (U) (African American)

Wilkinson, Brenda. *Not Separate, Not Equal*, 1547 (U) (African American)

Wyeth, Sharon Dennis. *The World of Daughter McGuire*, 1588 (U) (Multicultural)

Yee, Paul. *Tales from Gold Mountain: Stories of the Chinese in the New World*, 1598 (M) (Asian American—China)

Yep, Laurence. *Dragon's Gate*, 1606 (U) (Asian American—China)

   *The Star Fisher*, 1616 (U) (Asian American—China)

Young, Ronder Thomas. *Learning by Heart*, 1634 (U) (African American)

## Problem solving

dePaola, Tomie, reteller. *The Legend of the Persian Carpet*, 362 (M) (Middle Eastern—Iran)

Hillman, Elizabeth. *Min-Yo and the Moon Dragon*, 649 (M) (Asian—China)

Jonas, Ann. *Holes and Peeks*, 761 (PS) (African American)

Keats, Ezra Jack. *Goggles*, 778 (P) (African American)

   *Whistle for Willie*, 788 (PS/P) (African American)

Lasky, Kathryn. *Cloud Eyes*, 844 (M) (Native American)

## Problem solving (cont.)

Lunn, Carolyn. *Bobby's Zoo*, 924 (PS/P) (African American)

Maiorano, Robert. *Francisco*, 966 (P) (West Indian)

Seed, Jenny. *Ntombi's Song*, 1301 (PS/P) (African—South Africa)

Singh, Jacquelin. *Fat Gopal*, 1328 (M) (Asian—India)

Soto, Gary. *Boys at Work*, 1350 (M) (Mexican American)

Taylor, C. J. *The Secret of the White Buffalo: An Oglala Legend*, 1421 (M) (Native American—Oglala)

Uchida, Yoshiko. *The Best Bad Thing*, 1470 (U) (Asian American—Japan)
*The Wise Old Woman*, 1484 (M) (Asian—Japan)

Wisniewski, David. *The Warrior and the Wise Man*, 1571 (P/M) (Asian—Japan)

## Protest

Neville, Emily Cheney. *The China Year: A Novel*, 1100 (U) (Asian—China)

## Proverbs

Demi. *A Chinese Zoo: Fables and Proverbs*, 351 (M) (Asian—China)

## Pueblos

Lyon, George Ella. *Dreamplace*, 925 (P) (Native American—Pueblo)

## Puppets

Baumgartner, Barbara. *Crocodile! Crocodile! Stories Told Around the World*, 99 (M) (Multicultural)

Cleaver, Elizabeth. *The Enchanted Caribou*, 262 (M) (Native American– Inuit)

Keats, Ezra Jack. *Louie*, 782 (P) (Multicultural)

## Quilts

Flournoy, Valerie. *The Patchwork Quilt*, 434 (P/M) (African American)

Guback, Georgia. *Luka's Quilt*, 567 (P) (Hawaiian)

Hopkinson, Deborah. *Sweet Clara and the Freedom Quilt*, 666 (P/M) (African American)

Jonas, Ann. *The Quilt*, 762 (PS/P) (African American)

Wright, Courtni C. *Jumping the Broom*, 1585 (M) (African American)

## Race relations

Adoff, Arnold. *All the Colors of the Race: Poems*, 23 (U) (Multicultural)
*Black Is Brown Is Tan*, 24 (P) (Multicultural)

Armstrong, William H. *Sounder*, 67 (U) (African American)

Banim, Lisa. *American Dreams*, 89 (M) (Asian American—Japan)

Banks, Sara H. *Remember My Name*, 93 (U) (Native American—Cherokee)

Beake, Lesley. *Song of Be*, 106 (U) (African—Namibia)

Brooks, Bruce. *The Moves Make the Man*, 163 (U) (African American)

Case, Dianne. *92 Queens Road*, 228 (U) (African—South Africa)

Coles, Robert. *The Story of Ruby Bridges*, 299 (M) (African American)

Gordon, Sheila. *The Middle of Somewhere: A Story of South Africa*, 511 (U) (African—South Africa)

    *Waiting for the Rain: A Novel of South Africa*, 512 (U) (African—South Africa)

Gray, Libba Moore. *Dear Willie Rudd*, 514 (P) (African American)

Hooks, William H. *Circle of Fire*, 664 (U) (African American)

Hurmence, Belinda. *Dixie in the Big Pasture*, 703 (U) (Native American)

Lehne, Judith Logan. *When the Ragman Sings*, 862 (U) (African American)

Livingston, Myra Cohn. *Keep On Singing: A Ballad of Marian Anderson*, 903 (M) (African American)

Maartens, Maretha. *Paper Bird: A Novel of South Africa*, 932 (U) (African—South Africa)

Meyer, Carolyn. *White Lilacs*, 1014 (U) (African American)

Mitchell, Margaret King. *Uncle Jed's Barbershop*, 1028 (P/M) (African American)

Mochizuki, Ken. *Baseball Saved Us*, 1031 (M) (Asian American—Japan)

Moore, Yvette. *Freedom Songs*, 1051 (U) (African American)

Naidoo, Beverley. *Chain of Fire*, 1090 (U) (African—South Africa)

    *Journey to Jo'burg: A South African Story*, 1091 (U) (African—South Africa)

Nelson, Vaunda Micheaux. *Mayfield Crossing*, 1099 (U) (African American)

Polacco, Patricia. *Pink and Say*, 1181 (M) (African American)

Prather, Ray. *Fish and Bones*, 1197 (U) (African American)

Raschka, Chris. *Yo! Yes?*, 1209 (P/M) (Multicultural)

Robinet, Harriette Gillem. *Mississippi Chariot*, 1225 (U) (African American)

Sebestyen, Ouida. *Words by Heart*, 1300 (U) (African American)

Smothers, Ethel Footman. *Down in the Piney Woods*, 1342 (U) (African American)

    *Moriah's Pond*, 1343 (U) (African American)

Spinelli, Jerry. *Maniac Magee: A Novel*, 1365 (U) (African American)

Tate, Eleanora E. *The Secret of Gumbo Grove*, 1414 (M/U) (African American)

    *Thank You, Dr. Martin Luther King, Jr.!*, 1415 (M) (African American)

Taylor, Mildred D. *The Friendship*, 1424 (M/U) (African American)

    *The Friendship/The Gold Cadillac*, 1425 (M/U) (African American)

    *The Gold Cadillac*, 1426 (M/U) (African American)

    *Let the Circle Be Unbroken*, 1427 (U) (African American)

    *Mississippi Bridge*, 1428 (M/U) (African American)

    *The Road to Memphis*, 1429 (U) (African American)

    *Roll of Thunder, Hear My Cry*, 1430 (U) (African American)

    *Song of the Trees*, 1431 (M/U) (African American)

    *The Well: David's Story*, 1432 (U) (African American)

Taylor, Theodore. *The Cay*, 1433 (U) (Caribbean)

    *Timothy of the Cay*, 1434 (U) (Caribbean)

Uchida, Yoshiko. *The Bracelet*, 1472 (M) (Asian American—Japan)

    *A Jar of Dreams*, 1475 (U) (Asian American—Japan)

    *Journey Home*, 1476 (U) (Asian American—Japan)

Voigt, Cynthia. *Come a Stranger*, 1496 (U) (African American)

## Race relations (cont.)

Walter, Mildred Pitts. *The Girl on the Outside*, 1509 (U) (African American)

Wilkinson, Brenda. *Not Separate, Not Equal*, 1547 (U) (African American)

Woodson, Jacqueline. *Maizon at Blue Hill*, 1582 (U) (African American)

Young, Ronder Thomas. *Learning by Heart*, 1634 (U) (African American)

## Radios

Dorros, Arthur. *Radio Man: A Story in English and Spanish/Don Radio: Un Cuento en Inglés y Español*, 378 (P) (Mexican American)

## Rain forest

Cherry, Lynne. *The Great Kapok Tree: A Tale of the Amazon Rain Forest*, 243 (M) (South American)

## Ranch life

Brusca, María Cristina. *On the Pampas*, 177 (P) (South American—Argentina)

## Refugees

Bunting, Eve. *How Many Days to America? A Thanksgiving Story*, 199 (M) (Caribbean)

Ho, Minfong. *The Clay Marble*, 652 (U) (Asian—Cambodia)

Knight, Margy Burns. *Who Belongs Here? An American Story*, 818 (M) (Asian American—Cambodia)

Temple, Frances. *Grab Hands and Run*, 1436 (U) (Central American—El Salvador)

Watkins, Yoko Kawashima. *My Brother, My Sister, and I*, 1526 (U) (Asian—Japan)

*So Far from the Bamboo Grove*, 1527 (U) (Asian—Korea/Japan)

Whelan, Gloria. *Goodbye, Vietnam*, 1541 (U) (Asian—Vietnam)

## Religion

Anderson/Sankofa, David A., reteller. *The Origin of Life on Earth: An African Creation Myth*, 54 (M) (African—Yoruba)

Bryan, Ashley. *All Night, All Day: A Child's First Book of African-American Spirituals*, 180 (P/M) (African American)

*I'm Going to Sing: Black American Spirituals, Vol. 2*, 184 (M) (African American)

*Walk Together Children: Black American Spirituals*, 191 (M) (African American)

dePaola, Tomie, reteller. *The Legend of the Poinsettia*, 363 (M) (Mexican)

Grimes, Nikki. *From a Child's Heart: Poems*, 559 (P) (African American)

Hamilton, Virginia, reteller. *In the Beginning: Creation Stories from Around the World*, 588 (M) (Multicultural)

Johnson, James Weldon. *The Creation*, 751 (P/M) (African American)

*The Creation: A Poem*, 752 (P/M) (African American)

Langstaff, John, editor. *Climbing Jacob's Ladder: Heroes of the Bible in African-American Spirituals*, 839 (P/M) (African American)

*What a Morning! The Christmas Story in Black Spirituals*, 840 (P/M) (African American)

McDermott, Gerald, reteller. *The Voyage of Osiris: A Myth of Ancient Egypt*, 940 (M) (African—Egypt)

Talbert, Marc. *A Sunburned Prayer*, 1407 (U) (Mexican American)

## Relocation

Banim, Lisa. *American Dreams*, 89 (M) (Asian American—Japan)

Banks, Sara H. *Remember My Name*, 93 (U) (Native American—Cherokee)

Case, Dianne. *92 Queens Road*, 228 (U) (African—South Africa)

Hoyt-Goldsmith, Diane. *Cherokee Summer*, 679 (M) (Native American—Cherokee)

Johnson, Dolores. *Seminole Diary*, 746 (M) (African American)

Kudlinski, Kathleen V. *Night Bird: A Story of the Seminole Indians*, 832 (M) (Native American—Seminole)

Meyer, Carolyn. *White Lilacs*, 1014 (U) (African American)

Naidoo, Beverley. *Chain of Fire*, 1090 (U) (African—South Africa)

O'Dell, Scott. *Sing Down the Moon*, 1121 (U) (Native American)

O'Dell, Scott, and Elizabeth Hall. *Thunder Rolling in the Mountains*, 1124 (U) (Native American—Nez Perce)

Shigekawa, Marlene. *Blue Jay in the Desert*, 1320 (M) (Asian American—Japan)

Stewart, Elisabeth J. *On the Long Trail Home*, 1386 (U) (Native American—Cherokee)

Uchida, Yoshiko. *Journey Home*, 1476 (U) (Asian American—Japan)

*Journey to Topaz: A Story of the Japanese-American Evacuation*, 1477 (U) (Asian American—Japan)

Wheeler, Gloria. *Night of the Full Moon*, 1539 (M) (Native American—Potawatomi)

## Reptiles—alligators, crocodiles

Crespo, George, reteller. *How Iwariwa the Cayman Learned to Share: A Yanomami Myth*, 317 (M) (South American—Yanomamo Indians)

Galdone, Paul. *The Monkey and the Crocodile: A Jataka Tale from India*, 454 (M) (Asian—India)

Guy, Rosa, translator and adapter. *Mother Crocodile*, 571 (M) (African)

Hamada, Cheryl, reteller. *The White Hare of Inaba: A Japanese Folktale*, 578 (M) (Asian—Japan)

Maddern, Eric. *Rainbow Bird: An Aboriginal Folktale from Northern Australia*, 962 (M) (Australian—Aborigine)

## Reptiles—iguanas

Mike, Jan M., adapter. *Opossum and the Great Firemaker: A Mexican Legend*, 1016 (M) (Mexican)

## Reptiles—Komodo dragons

Sis, Peter. *Komodo!*, 1329 (P) (Indonesian)

Lewin, Ted. *Amazon Boy*, 886 (P/M) (South American—Brazil)

## Roads

Lyon, George Ella. *Who Came Down That Road?*, 928 (P/M) (Native American)

## Royalty

Bang, Betsy, adapter. *Tuntuni the Tailor Bird: From a Bengali Folktale*, 81 (P) (Asian—India)

Berger, Terry. *Black Fairy Tales*, 119 (M) (African)

Chew, Ruth. *Royal Magic*, 244 (M) (African American)

Climo, Shirley. *The Egyptian Cinderella*, 278 (M) (African—Egypt)

Kimmel, Eric A., reteller. *The Three Princes: A Tale from the Middle East*, 807 (M) (Middle Eastern—Arabia)

McDermott, Gerald, reteller. *The Voyage of Osiris: A Myth of Ancient Egypt*, 940 (M) (African—Egypt)

Mayer, Marianna. *The Golden Swan: An East Indian Tale of Love from the Mahabharata*, 992 (M) (Asian—India)

Rappaport, Doreen. *The New King: A Madagascan Legend*, 1207 (M) (African—Madagascar)

Rodanas, Kristina, reteller. *The Story of Wali Dâd*, 1233 (M) (Asian—India)

Sabuda, Robert. *Tutankhamen's Gift*, 1259 (M) (African—Egypt)

Shepard, Aaron, reteller. *The Gifts of Wali Dad: A Tale of India and Pakistan*, 1313 (M) (Asian—India/Pakistan)

Singh, Jacquelin. *Fat Gopal*, 1328 (M) (Asian—India)

Torre, Betty L., reteller. *The Luminous Pearl: A Chinese Folktale*, 1448 (M) (Asian—China)

Yen, Clara, reteller. *Why Rat Comes First: A Story of the Chinese Zodiac*, 1601 (M) (Asian—China)

Yolen, Jane. *The Emperor and the Kite*, 1620 (M) (Asian—China)

*The Seeing Stick*, 1624 (M) (Asian—China)

## Royalty—emperors

Morris, Winifred. *The Future of Yen-Tzu*, 1067 (M) (Asian—China)

Yacowitz, Caryn, adapter. *The Jade Stone: A Chinese Folktale*, 1589 (M) (Asian—China)

## Royalty—kings

Buffett, Jimmy, and Savannah Jane Buffett. *The Jolly Mon*, 194 (P) (Caribbean)

Vidal, Beatriz. *The Legend of El Dorado: A Latin American Tale*, 1495 (M) (Latin American)

## Royalty—princes

Manniche, Lise, translator. *The Prince Who Knew His Fate: An Ancient Egyptian Tale*, 973 (M) (African—Egypt)

## Rugs

Blood, Charles L., and Martin A. Link. *A Goat in the Rug*, 143 (P) (Native American—Navajo)

## Rural life

Crews, Donald. *Bigmama's*, 319 (P) (African American)

  *Shortcut*, 320 (P) (African American)

Giovanni, Nikki. *Knoxville, Tennessee*, 479 (P) (African American)

Greene, Bette. *Get On Out of Here, Philip Hall*, 517 (M) (African American)

  *Philip Hall Likes Me, I Reckon Maybe*, 518 (M) (African American)

Grifalconi, Ann. *Kinda Blue*, 555 (P) (African American)

Hamilton, Virginia. *Zeely*, 597 (M) (African American)

Howard, Elizabeth Fitzgerald. *Mac & Marie & the Train Toss Surprise*, 674 (P) (African American)

Hurmence, Belinda. *Tough Tiffany*, 705 (M/U) (African American)

Igus, Toyomi. *When I Was Little*, 711 (P) (African American)

McKissack, Patricia. *Flossie and the Fox*, 948 (P) (African American)

Major, Beverly. *Over Back*, 968 (M) (African American)

Medearis, Angela Shelf. *Poppa's New Pants*, 1003 (P) (African American)

Miles, Betty. *Sink or Swim*, 1017 (M) (African American)

Oppenheim, Shulamith Levey. *Fireflies for Nathan*, 1132 (P) (African American)

Pinkney, Gloria Jean. *Back Home*, 1175 (P/M) (African American)

Prather, Ray. *Fish and Bones*, 1197 (U) (African American)

Shelby, Anne. *We Keep a Store*, 1312 (P) (African American)

Smothers, Ethel Footman. *Down in the Piney Woods*, 1342 (U) (African American)

  *Moriah's Pond*, 1343 (U) (African American)

Tiller, Ruth. *Cinnamon, Mint, & Mothballs: A Visit to Grandmother's House*, 1442 (P) (Asian American)

Walter, Mildred Pitts. *Ty's One-Man Band*, 1518 (P) (African American)

Wyeth, Sharon Dennis. *Always My Dad*, 1587 (P) (African American)

## Sacagawea

O'Dell, Scott. *Streams to the River, River to the Sea: A Novel of Sacagawea*, 1122 (U) (Native American)

## Scarecrows

Lifton, Betty Jean. *Joji and the Dragon*, 895 (P) (Asian—Japan)

## Scary stories

Bierhorst, John, editor. *The Whistling Skeleton: American Indian Tales of the Supernatural*, 136 (M/U) (Native American)

Hamilton, Virginia, reteller. *The Dark Way: Stories from the Spirit World*, 584 (U) (Multicultural)

  *The People Could Fly: American Black Folktales*, 593 (M/U) (African American)

Hodges, Margaret, reteller. *Hauntings: Ghosts and Ghouls from Around the World*, 656 (M) (Multicultural)

Lyons, Mary E., selector. *Raw Head, Bloody Bones: African-American Tales of the Supernatural*, 931 (U) (African American)

McKissack, Patricia. *The Dark Thirty: Southern Tales of the Supernatural*, 947 (M/U) (African American)

Milich, Melissa. *Can't Scare Me!*, 1019 (M) (African American)

San Souci, Robert D. *The Boy and the Ghost*, 1270 (P) (African American)

    *Short and Shivery: Thirty Chilling Tales*, 1276 (M/U) (Multicultural)

Tate, Eleanora E. *Front Porch Stories: At the One-Room School*, 1413 (M) (African American)

Wahl, Jan, reteller. *Tailypo!*, 1503 (M) (African American)

Yep, Laurence. *The Man Who Tricked a Ghost*, 1611 (M) (Asian—China)

## School

Ada, Alma Flor. *My Name Is María Isabel*, 19 (M) (Hispanic American—Puerto Rico)

Alexander, Ellen. *Chaska and the Golden Doll*, 38 (M) (South American)

Ashley, Bernard. *Cleversticks*, 69 (PS/P) (Asian American)

Baer, Edith. *This Is the Way We Go to School: A Book about Children Around the World*, 73 (P) (Multicultural)

Banks, Jacqueline Turner. *Egg-Drop Blues*, 90 (U) (African American)

    *The New One*, 91 (U) (African American)

    *Project Wheels*, 92 (U) (African American)

Begaye, Lisa Shook. *Building a Bridge*, 110 (P) (Native American—Navajo)

Boyd, Candy Dawson. *Breadsticks and Blessing Places*, 152 (U) (African American)

    *Fall Secrets*, 155 (U) (African American)

Brooks, Bruce. *The Moves Make the Man*, 163 (U) (African American)

Cazet, Denys. *Born in the Gravy*, 233 (P) (Mexican American)

Cebulash, Mel. *Willie's Wonderful Pet*, 234 (P) (African American)

Chang, Heidi. *Elaine and the Flying Frog*, 238 (M) (Asian American—China)

Choi, Sook Nyul. *Gathering of Pearls*, 254 (U) (Asian—Korea)

    *Halmoni and the Picnic*, 255 (P) (Asian American—Korea)

Clifton, Lucille. *All Us Come Cross the Water*, 264 (P) (African American)

Cohen, Barbara. *213 Valentines*, 288 (M) (African American)

Coles, Robert. *The Story of Ruby Bridges*, 299 (M) (African American)

Evans, Mari. *JD*, 409 (M) (African American)

Glaser, Linda. *Tanya's Big Green Dream*, 481 (M) (Multicultural)

Greenfield, Eloise. *Me and Neesie*, 538 (P) (African American)

Hale, Sarah Josepha. *Mary Had a Little Lamb*, 573 (PS/P) (African American)

Hoffman, Mary. *Amazing Grace*, 658 (P) (African American)

Hru, Dakari. *Joshua's Masai Mask*, 683 (M) (African American)

Hudson, Cheryl Willis, and Bernette G. Ford. *Bright Eyes, Brown Skin*, 690 (PS) (African American)

Hudson, Wade. *Jamal's Busy Day*, 693 (P) (African American)

Hurmence, Belinda. *Tough Tiffany*, 705 (M/U) (African American)

Hurwitz, Johanna. *Class President*, 706 (M) (Hispanic American—Puerto Rico)

    *School Spirit*, 708 (M) (Hispanic American—Puerto Rico)

## School (cont.)

Johnson, Dolores. *The Best Bug to Be*, 743 (P) (African American)

Kline, Suzy. *Horrible Harry and the Ant Invasion*, 809 (M) (Asian American—Korea)

   *Horrible Harry and the Christmas Surprise*, 810 (M) (Asian American—Korea)

   *Horrible Harry and the Green Slime*, 811 (M) (Asian American—Korea)

   *Horrible Harry and the Kickball Wedding*, 812 (M) (Asian American—Korea)

   *Horrible Harry in Room 2B*, 813 (M) (Asian American—Korea)

   *Horrible Harry's Secret*, 814 (M) (Asian American—Korea)

   *Song Lee and the Hamster Hunt*, 815 (M) (Asian American—Korea)

   *Song Lee in Room 2B*, 816 (M) (Asian American—Korea)

Konigsburg, E. L. *Jennifer, Hecate, Macbeth, William McKinley, and Me, Elizabeth*, 822 (M) (African American)

Lord, Bette Bao. *In the Year of the Boar and Jackie Robinson*, 915 (M) (Asian American—China)

Meyer, Carolyn. *Rio Grande Stories*, 1013 (U) (Multicultural)

Moore, Emily. *Something to Count On*, 1049 (M) (African American)

   *Whose Side Are You On?*, 1050 (M) (African American)

Moss, Marissa. *Regina's Big Mistake*, 1073 (P) (African American)

Myers, Laurie. *Garage Sale Fever*, 1080 (M) (African American)

Myers, Walter Dean. *Darnell Rock Reporting*, 1082 (U) (African American)

Nelson, Vaunda Micheaux. *Mayfield Crossing*, 1099 (U) (African American)

Neville, Emily Cheney. *The China Year: A Novel*, 1100 (U) (Asian—China)

Perkins, Mitali. *The Sunita Experiment*, 1163 (U) (Asian American—India)

Porter, Connie. *Addy Learns a Lesson: A School Story*, 1189 (M) (African American)

Richardson, Jean. *The Courage Seed*, 1218 (M) (Native American)

Slote, Alfred. *Finding Buck McHenry*, 1335 (M) (African American)

Smith, Joanne L. *Show and Tell*, 1341 (P) (African American)

Soto, Gary. *Taking Sides*, 1359 (U) (Mexican American)

Stock, Catherine. *Where Are You Going, Manyoni?*, 1391 (P) (African-Zimbabwe)

Surat, Michele Maria. *Angel Child, Dragon Child*, 1404 (P) (Asian American—Vietnam)

Tate, Eleanora E. *Thank You, Dr. Martin Luther King, Jr.!*, 1415 (M) (African American)

Udry, Janice May. *What Mary Jo Shared*, 1486 (P) (African American)

Walter, Mildred Pitts. *The Girl on the Outside*, 1509 (U) (African American)

   *Trouble's Child*, 1516 (U) (African American)

Warren, Cathy. *Fred's First Day*, 1524 (PS) (African American)

Wheeler, Bernelda. *Where Did You Get Your Moccasins?*, 1538 (P) (Native American)

Wilkinson, Brenda. *Definitely Cool*, 1546 (U) (African American)

   *Not Separate, Not Equal*, 1547 (U) (African American)

Willis, Meredith Sue. *The Secret Super Powers of Marco*, 1560 (M) (Multicultural)

Woodson, Jacqueline. *Last Summer with Maizon*, 1581 (U) (African American)

   *Maizon at Blue Hill*, 1582 (U) (African American)

Wyeth, Sharon Dennis. *The World of Daughter McGuire*, 1588 (U) (Multicultural)

Yashima, Taro. *Crow Boy*, 1595 (P) (Asian—Japan)

## Sea and seashore

Adams, Jeanie. *Going for Oysters*, 22 (P) (Australian—Aborigine)

Albert, Burton. *Where Does the Trail Lead?*, 37 (PS/P) (African American)

Andrews, Jan. *Very Last First Time*, 56 (P/M) (Native American—Inuit)

Bang, Molly. *Yellow Ball*, 88 (PS/P) (African American)

Bowden, Joan Chase. *Why the Tides Ebb and Flow*, 151 (M) (African)

Buffett, Jimmy, and Savannah Jane Buffett. *The Jolly Mon*, 194 (P) (Caribbean)

Bush, Timothy. *Three at Sea*, 208 (P) (Multicultural)

Crespo, George, reteller. *How the Sea Began: A Taino Myth*, 318 (M) (Native American—Taino)

Fox, Paula. *The Slave Dancer: A Novel*, 439 (U) (African American)

George, Jean Craighead. *Shark Beneath the Reef*, 465 (U) (Mexican)

Johnson, Angela. *Joshua by the Sea*, 732 (PS) (African American)

Lee, Huy Voun. *At the Beach*, 856 (P) (Asian—China)

Munsch, Robert, and Michael Kusugak. *A Promise Is a Promise*, 1076 (P) (Native American—Inuit)

Nunes, Susan. *To Find the Way*, 1108 (M) (Tahitian)

O'Dell, Scott. *The Black Pearl*, 1114 (U) (Mexican)

*The Captive*, 1116 (U) (Central American—Mayan)

*Zia*, 1123 (U) (Native American)

Orr, Katherine. *My Grandpa and the Sea*, 1135 (M) (Caribbean)

*Story of a Dolphin*, 1136 (P) (Caribbean)

San Souci, Robert D., reteller. *The Samurai's Daughter: A Japanese Legend*, 1275 (M) (Asian—Japan)

*Song of Sedna*, 1278 (M) (Native American—Inuit)

Sperry, Armstrong. *Call It Courage*, 1362 (U) (Polynesian)

Steiner, Barbara. *Whale Brother*, 1375 (M) (Native American—Eskimo)

Temple, Frances. *Tonight, by Sea*, 1438 (U) (Caribbean—Haiti)

Troughton, Joanna, reteller. *Whale's Canoe: A Folk Tale from Australia*, 1459 (M) (Australian)

Yep, Laurence, reteller. *The Shell Woman & the King: A Chinese Folktale*, 1615 (M) (Asian—China)

## Seasons

Adoff, Arnold. *In for Winter, Out for Spring*, 28 (P/M) (African American)

Anderson, Janet S. *The Key into Winter*, 52 (M) (African American)

Bruchac, Joseph, and Jonathan London. *Thirteen Moons on Turtle's Back: A Native American Year of Moons*, 175 (M) (Native American)

Clifton, Lucille. *Everett Anderson's Year*, 273 (P) (African American)

Demi. *In the Eyes of the Cat: Japanese Poetry for All Seasons*, 354 (M) (Asian—Japan)

Fleming, Denise. *In the Small, Small Pond*, 430 (PS) (Asian heritage)

## Seasons (cont.)

Kroll, Virginia. *The Seasons and Someone*, 829 (M) (Native American—Eskimo)

Larry, Charles, reteller. *Peboan and Seegwun*, 843 (M) (Native American—Ojibway)

Lillie, Patricia. *When This Box Is Full*, 896 (P) (African American)

Lotz, Karen E. *Can't Sit Still*, 917 (P) (African American)

Weiss, Nicki. *On a Hot, Hot Day*, 1535 (P) (Hispanic American)

## Seasons—fall

Bang, Molly. *One Fall Day*, 83 (P) (African American)

Yerxa, Leo. *Last Leaf First Snowflake to Fall*, 1619 (M) (Native American)

## Seasons—spring

Clifton, Lucille. *The Boy Who Didn't Believe in Spring*, 266 (P) (African American)

Lemieux, Margo. *Full Worm Moon*, 864 (M) (Native American—Algonquian)

Wolkstein, Diane. *The Magic Wings: A Tale from China*, 1576 (M) (Asian—China)

## Seasons—summer

Crews, Nina. *One Hot Summer Day*, 321 (PS/P) (African American)

Giovanni, Nikki. *Knoxville, Tennessee*, 479 (P) (African American)

## Seasons—winter

Coutant, Helen. *First Snow*, 314 (P) (Asian American—Vietnam)

Fenner, Carol. *The Skates of Uncle Richard*, 417 (M) (African American)

Keats, Ezra Jack. *The Snowy Day*, 786 (PS/P) (African American)

Shetterly, Susan Hand, reteller. *Muwin and the Magic Hare*, 1318 (M) (Native American—Passamaquoddy)

Spohn, David. *Winter Wood*, 1369 (M) (Multicultural)

Udry, Janice May. *Mary Jo's Grandmother*, 1485 (P) (African American)

Yerxa, Leo. *Last Leaf First Snowflake to Fall*, 1619 (M) (Native American)

## Seeds

Garland, Sherry. *The Lotus Seed*, 458 (P) (Asian American—Vietnam)

## Self-concept

Ada, Alma Flor. *My Name Is María Isabel*, 19 (M) (Hispanic American—Puerto Rico)

Adoff, Arnold. *Hard to Be Six*, 26 (P) (Multicultural)

Altman, Susan, and Susan Lechner. *Followers of the North Star: Rhymes about African American Heroes, Heroines, and Historical Times*, 47 (M/U) (African American)

Ashley, Bernard. *Cleversticks*, 69 (PS/P) (Asian American)

Banks, Jacqueline Turner. *Egg-Drop Blues*, 90 (U) (African American)

Barnes, Joyce Annette. *The Baby Grand, the Moon in July, & Me*, 95 (U) (African American)

Belton, Sandra. *May'naise Sandwiches and Sunshine Tea*, 116 (M) (African American)

Boyd, Candy Dawson. *Fall Secrets*, 155 (U) (African American)

Casler, Leigh. *The Boy Who Dreamed of an Acorn*, 229 (M) (Native American)

Clifton, Lucille. *All Us Come Cross the Water*, 264 (P) (African American)

Cofer, Judith Ortiz. *An Island Like You: Stories of the Barrio*, 286 (U) (Hispanic American—Puerto Rico)

Cumpián, Carlos. *Latino Rainbow: Poems about Latino Americans*, 325 (M/U) (Hispanic American)

Davol, Marguerite W. *Black, White, Just Right!*, 337 (PS/P) (Multicultural)

DeVeaux, Alexis. *An Enchanted Hair Tale*, 366 (M) (African American)

Dobkin, Bonnie. *Everybody Says*, 373 (PS/P) (African American)

Duncan, Alice Faye. *Willie Jerome*, 385 (P) (African American)

Edmiston, Jim. *Little Eagle Lots of Owls*, 391 (M) (Native American)

Feelings, Tom, selector. *Soul Looks Back in Wonder*, 415 (M/U) (African American)

Fenner, Carol. *Yolanda's Genius*, 418 (U) (African American)

Finley, Mary Pierce. *Soaring Eagle*, 422 (U) (Multicultural)

Gilcrist, Jan Spivey. *Indigo and Moonlight Gold*, 474 (P) (African American)

Giovanni, Nikki. *Ego-Tripping: And Other Poems for Young People*, 478 (U) (African American)

Greenfield, Eloise. *Honey, I Love*, 534 (PS/P) (African American)

Hill, Elizabeth Starr. *Evan's Corner*, 646 (P/M) (African American)

*Evan's Corner*, 647 (P/M) (African American)

Hirschfelder, Arlene B., and Beverly R. Singer, selectors. *Rising Voices: Writings of Young Native Americans*, 651 (U) (Native American)

Hoberman, Mary Ann, selector. *My Song Is Beautiful: A Celebration of Multicultural Poems and Pictures*, 654 (P/M) (Multicultural)

Hoffman, Mary. *Amazing Grace*, 658 (P) (African American)

*Boundless Grace*, 659 (P) (African American)

Hudson, Cheryl Willis, and Bernette G. Ford. *Bright Eyes, Brown Skin*, 690 (PS) (African American)

Hudson, Wade. *I'm Gonna Be!*, 692 (P) (African American)

*Pass It On: African-American Poetry for Children*, 694 (P/M) (African American)

Hyppolite, Joanne. *Seth and Samona*, 710 (U) (Caribbean American—Haiti)

Izuki, Steven. *Believers in America: Poems about Americans of Asian and Pacific Islander Descent*, 719 (M/U) (Asian American)

Johnson, Angela. *The Girl Who Wore Snakes*, 731 (P) (African American)

Johnson, Dolores. *The Best Bug to Be*, 743 (P) (African American)

*Papa's Stories*, 745 (P) (African American)

Keats, Ezra Jack. *Peter's Chair*, 785 (PS/P) (African American)

*Whistle for Willie*, 788 (PS/P) (African American)

Kroll, Virginia. *Wood-hoopoe Willie*, 830 (P) (African American)

Lacapa, Kathleen, and Michael Lacapa. *Less Than Half, More Than Whole*, 835 (M) (Multicultural)

Lee, Marie G. *If It Hadn't Been for Yoon Jun*, 861 (U) (Asian American—Korea)

Mandelbaum, Pili. *You Be Me, I'll Be You*, 970 (P) (Multicultural)

## Self-concept (cont.)

Woodson, Jacqueline. *Between Madison and Palmetto*, 1580 (U) (African American)

Wyeth, Sharon Dennis. *The World of Daughter McGuire*, 1588 (U) (Multicultural)

Yarborough, Camille. *Cornrows*, 1591 (M) (African American)
  *The Shimmershine Queens*, 1592 (M/U) (African American)

Yep, Laurence. *The Butterfly Boy*, 1604 (M) (Asian—China)
  *Sea Glass*, 1613 (U) (Asian American—China)

## Senses

McMillan, Bruce. *Sense Suspense: A Guessing Game for the Five Senses*, 960 (P) (Multicultural)

Owen, Roy. *My Night Forest*, 1142 (PS/P) (Hispanic American)

## Senses—seeing

DeArmond, Dale, adapter. *The Seal Oil Lamp: Adapted from an Eskimo Folktale*, 340 (M) (Native American—Eskimo)

Yolen, Jane. *The Seeing Stick*, 1624 (M) (Asian—China)

## Series

### ADVENTURES IN STORYTELLING

Arneach, Lloyd, reteller. *The Animals' Ballgame: A Cherokee Story from the Eastern Band*, 68 (M) (Native American—Cherokee)

*The Baboon's Umbrella: An African Folktale*, 71 (M) (African)

Colman, Warren. *Double Dutch and the Voodoo Shoes: A Modern African-American Urban Tale*, 303 (M) (African American)

The Coyote Rings the Wrong Bell. *The Coyote Rings the Wrong Bell: A Mexican Folktale*, 316 (M) (Mexican)

Garcia, Anamarie, reteller. *The Girl from the Sky: An Inca Folktale from South America*, 456 (M) (South American—Inca)

Hamada, Cheryl, reteller. *The Farmer, the Buffalo, and the Tiger: A Folktale from Vietnam*, 575 (M) (Asian—Vietnam)

*The Fourth Question: A Chinese Folktale*, 576 (M) (Asian—China)

*Kao and the Golden Fish: A Folktale from Thailand*, 577 (M) (Asian—Thailand)

*The White Hare of Inaba: A Japanese Folktale*, 578 (M) (Asian—Japan)

Hilbert, Vi. *Loon and Deer Were Traveling: A Story of the Upper Skagit of Puget Sound*, 645 (M) (Native American—Skagit)

*How Anansi Obtained the Sky God's Stories: An African Folktale from the Ashanti Tribe*, 671 (M) (African—Ashanti)

Mora, Francisco X. *The Tiger and the Rabbit: A Puerto Rican Folktale*, 1054 (M) (Caribbean—Puerto Rico)

Moroney, Lynn, reteller. *The Boy Who Loved Bears: A Pawnee Tale*, 1060 (M) (Native American—Pawnee)

### AFRO-BETS KIDS

Hudson, Wade. *I'm Gonna Be!*, 692 (P) (African American)

## Series (cont.)

AMERICAN GIRLS COLLECTION

Porter, Connie. *Addy Learns a Lesson: A School Story*, 1189 (M) (African American)

*Addy Saves the Day: A Summer Story*, 1190 (M) (African American)

*Addy's Surprise: A Christmas Story*, 1191 (M) (African American)

*Changes for Addy: A Winter Story*, 1192 (M) (African American)

*Happy Birthday, Addy: A Springtime Story*, 1193 (M) (African American)

*Meet Addy: An American Girl*, 1194 (M) (African American)

AUNT MARTHA STORY

Rodriguez, Anita. *Aunt Martha and the Golden Coin*, 1235 (P) (African American)

*Jamal and the Angel*, 1236 (P) (African American)

COUNT YOUR WAY

Haskins, Jim. *Count Your Way Through Africa*, 619 (P) (African)

*Count Your Way Through China*, 620 (P) (Asian—China)

*Count Your Way Through India*, 621 (P) (Asian—India)

*Count Your Way Through Japan*, 622 (P) (Asian—Japan)

*Count Your Way Through Korea*, 623 (P) (Asian—Korea)

*Count Your Way Through Mexico*, 624 (P) (Mexican)

*Count Your Way Through the Arab World*, 625 (P) (Middle Eastern—Arabia)

FESTIVE YEAR

Stock, Catherine. *Halloween Monster*, 1389 (P) (African American)

*Secret Valentine*, 1390 (P) (African American)

FIRST STEPPING STONE

Yarborough, Camille. *Tamika and the Wisdom Rings*, 1593 (M) (African American)

FOLK TALES OF THE WORLD

Loverseed, Amanda, reteller. *Thunder King: A Peruvian Folk Tale*, 920 (M) (South American—Peru)

Makhanlall, David. *Brer Anansi and the Boat Race: A Caribbean Folk Tale*, 969 (M) (Caribbean)

Tate, Carol. *Tale of the Spiteful Spirits: A Kampuchean Folk Tale*, 1411 (M) (Asian—Cambodia)

Troughton, Joanna, reteller. *How Night Came: A Folk Tale from the Amazon*, 1454 (M) (South American—Amazon)

*How Rabbit Stole the Fire: A North American Indian Folk Tale*, 1455 (M) (Native American)

*How the Birds Changed Their Feathers: A South American Indian Folk Tale*, 1456 (M) (South American)

*Make-Believe Tales: A Folk Tale from Burma*, 1457 (M) (Asian—Burma)

*Tortoise's Dream*, 1458 (M) (African)

*Whale's Canoe: A Folk Tale from Australia*, 1459 (M) (Australian)

*What Made Tiddalik Laugh: An Australian Aborigine Folk Tale*, 1460 (M) (Australian—Aborigine)

*Who Will Be the Sun? A North American Indian Folk-tale*, 1461 (M) (Native American—Kutenai)

*The Wizard Punchkin: A Folk Tale from India*, 1462 (M) (Asian—India)

Wade, Gini, reteller. *The Wonderful Bag: An Arabian Tale from The Thousand & One Nights*, 1500 (M) (Middle Eastern—Arabia)

GREENWILLOW READ-ALONE

Bang, Betsy, adapter. *Cucumber Stem: From a Bengali Folktale*, 79 (P) (Asian—India)

*Tuntuni the Tailor Bird: From a Bengali Folktale*, 81 (P) (Asian—India)

Bang, Molly, adapter. *Tye May and the Magic Brush*, 86 (M) (Asian—China)

Hamilton, Virginia. *Jahdu*, 589 (M) (African American)

HELLO READER!

Bolognese, Don. *Little Hawk's New Name*, 147 (P) (Native American)

Cebulash, Mel. *Willie's Wonderful Pet*, 234 (P) (African American)

I CAN READ

Coerr, Eleanor. *Chang's Paper Pony*, 282 (P) (Asian American—China)

Monjo, F. N. *The Drinking Gourd*, 1042 (P/M) (African American)

Pomerantz, Charlotte. *The Outside Dog*, 1186 (P) (Caribbean—Puerto Rico)

I CAN READ HISTORY

Benchley, Nathaniel. *Small Wolf*, 117 (P) (Native American)

Brenner, Barbara. *Wagon Wheels*, 160 (P) (African American)

Lewis, Thomas P. *Hill of Fire*, 891 (P) (Mexican)

JUMP AT THE SUN BOARD

Moore, Dessie. *Getting Dressed*, 1044 (PS) (African American)

*Good Morning*, 1045 (PS) (African American)

*Good Night*, 1046 (PS) (African American)

*Let's Pretend*, 1047 (PS) (African American)

LEGENDS OF THE WORLD

Chang, Cindy, reteller. *The Seventh Sister: A Chinese Legend*, 237 (M) (Asian—China)

Chocolate, Deborah M. Newton, reteller. *Spider and the Sky God: An Akan Legend*, 251 (M) (African—Akan)

*Talk, Talk: An Ashanti Legend*, 252 (M) (African)

Lippert, Margaret H., adapter. *The Sea Serpent's Daughter: A Brazilian Legend*, 899 (M) (South American—Brazil)

Lum, Darrell, reteller. *The Golden Slipper: A Vietnamese Legend*, 923 (M) (Asian—Vietnam)

## Series (cont.)

Mike, Jan M., reteller. *Gift of the Nile: An Ancient Egyptian Legend*, 1015 (M) (African—Egypt)

*Opossum and the Great Firemaker: A Mexican Legend*, 1016 (M) (Mexican)

Palacios, Argentina, adapter. *The Hummingbird King: A Guatemalan Legend*, 1148 (M) (Central American—Guatemala—Mayan)

*The Llama's Secret: A Peruvian Legend*, 1149 (M) (South American—Peru)

Reasoner, Charles, reteller. *The Magic Amber: A Korean Legend*, 1211 (M) (Asian—Korea)

Sakurai, Gail. *Peach Boy: A Japanese Legend*, 1266 (M) (Asian—Japan)

### LET'S READ ALOUD

Greenfield, Eloise. *Honey, I Love*, 534 (PS/P) (African American)

*On My Horse*, 542 (PS/P) (African American)

### MANY VOICES ONE SONG

Altman, Susan, and Susan Lechner. *Followers of the North Star: Rhymes about African American Heroes, Heroines, and Historical Times*, 47 (M/U) (African American)

Cumpián, Carlos. *Latino Rainbow: Poems about Latino Americans*, 325 (M/U) (Hispanic American)

Izuki, Steven. *Believers in America: Poems about Americans of Asian and Pacific Islander Descent*, 719 (M/U) (Asian American)

### NATIVE AMERICAN LEGENDS

Cohlene, Terri, adapter. *Clamshell Boy: A Makah Legend*, 292 (M) (Native American—Makah)

*Dancing Drum: A Cherokee Legend*, 293 (M) (Native American—Cherokee)

*Ka-ha-si and the Loon: An Eskimo Legend*, 294 (M) (Native American—Eskimo)

*Little Firefly: An Algonquian Legend*, 295 (M) (Native American—Algonquian)

*Quillworker: A Cheyenne Legend*, 296 (M) (Native American—Cheyenne)

*Turquoise Boy: A Navajo Legend*, 297 (M) (Native American—Navajo)

### ONCE UPON AMERICA

Goldin, Barbara Diamond. *Red Means Good Fortune: A Story of San Francisco's Chinatown*, 505 (M) (Asian American—China)

Kudlinski, Kathleen V. *Night Bird: A Story of the Seminole Indians*, 832 (M) (Native American—Seminole)

### PUBLISH-A-BOOK CONTEST

Chapman, Christina. *Treasure in the Attic*, 242 (P) (African American)

### READY-TO-READ

Bang, Molly, adapter. *Wiley and the Hairy Man: Adapted from an American Folktale*, 87 (P) (African American)

Hooks, William H. *Peach Boy*, 665 (P) (Asian—Japan)

Mann, Kenny. *"I Am Not Afraid!": Based on a Masai Tale*, 972 (P) (African—Masai)

Schecter, Ellen, reteller. *Sim Chung and the River Dragon: A Folktale from Korea*, 1289 (P) (Asian—Korea)

*The Warrior Maiden: A Hopi Legend*, 1290 (P) (Native American—Hopi)

REDFEATHER

Cohen, Barbara. *213 Valentines*, 288 (M) (African American)

Pfeffer, Susan Beth. *The Riddle Streak*, 1168 (M) (African American)

ROOKIE READER

Boivin, Kelly. *Where Is Mittens?*, 146 (PS/P) (African American)

Dobkin, Bonnie. *Collecting*, 372 (PS/P) (Asian American)

*Everybody Says*, 373 (PS/P) (African American)

*Just a Little Different*, 374 (PS/P) (Multicultural)

Eastman, Patricia. *Sometimes Things Change*, 389 (P) (Multicultural)

Frankel, Julie E. *Oh No, Otis*, 440 (PS/P) (African American)

Greene, Carol. *Hi, Clouds*, 519 (PS/P) (African American)

*Please, Wind*, 520 (PS/P) (African American)

Hamsa, Bobbie. *Polly Wants a Cracker*, 599 (P) (African American)

Javernick, Ellen. *Where's Brooke?*, 726 (PS/P) (Asian American)

Johnson, Mildred D. *Wait, Skates!*, 755 (PS/P) (African American)

Lunn, Carolyn. *Bobby's Zoo*, 924 (PS/P) (African American)

McDonald, Becky Bring. *Katie Couldn't*, 942 (PS/P) (Asian American)

*Larry and the Cookie*, 943 (PS/P) (African American)

McKissack, Patricia, and Fredrick McKissack. *Bugs!*, 953 (P) (African American)

*Constance Stumbles*, 955 (P) (African American)

*Messy Bessey*, 956 (P) (African American)

*Messy Bessey's Closet*, 957 (P) (African American)

*Messy Bessey's Garden*, 958 (P) (African American)

Milios, Rita. *Sneaky Pete*, 1020 (PS/P) (African American)

Moses, Amy. *I Am an Explorer*, 1071 (P) (African American)

Neasi, Barbara J. *Listen to Me*, 1098 (PS/P) (African American)

Petrie, Catherine. *Joshua James Likes Trucks*, 1166 (P) (African American)

Smith, Joanne L. *Show and Tell*, 1341 (P) (African American)

Stevens, Philippa J. *Bonk! Goes the Ball*, 1384 (P) (Asian American)

SPRINGBOARD

Jacobs, Shannon K. *Song of the Giraffe*, 721 (M) (African)

Peters, Julie Anne. *The Stinky Sneakers Contest*, 1164 (M) (African American)

STEP INTO READING

McKissack, Patricia. *Monkey-Monkey's Trick*, 951 (P) (African)

O'Connor, Jane. *Molly the Brave and Me*, 1113 (P) (African American)

Shefelman, Janice. *A Mare for Young Wolf*, 1310 (P) (Native American)

## Series (cont.)

STEPPING STONE

Berends, Polly Berrien. *The Case of the Elevator Duck*, 118 (M) (African American)

Cameron, Ann. *Julian, Dream Doctor*, 215 (M) (African American)
*Julian, Secret Agent*, 216 (M) (African American)
*Julian's Glorious Summer*, 217 (M) (African American)

Chang, Heidi. *Elaine and the Flying Frog*, 238 (M) (Asian American—China)

Fenner, Carol. *The Skates of Uncle Richard*, 417 (M) (African American)

TALES FROM AROUND THE WORLD

Hull, Robert, reteller. *African Stories*, 698 (M) (African)
*Caribbean Stories*, 699 (M) (Caribbean)
*Indian Stories*, 700 (M) (Asian—India)
*Native North American Stories*, 701 (M) (Native American)

TROLL FIRST-START TALL TALE

Jensen, Patsy. *John Henry and His Mighty Hammer*, 729 (P) (African American)

WHAT-A-BABY BOARD

Hudson, Cheryl Willis. *Animal Sounds for Baby*, 686 (PS) (African American)
*Let's Count Baby*, 689 (PS) (African American)

## Shadows

Cendrars, Blaise, and Marcia Brown, translator. *Shadow*, 235 (P) (African)

Hamilton, Virginia. *Jahdu*, 589 (M) (African American)

Keats, Ezra Jack. *Dreams*, 777 (PS/P) (Hispanic American)

## Shells

Howard, Elizabeth Fitzgerald. *Mac & Marie & the Train Toss Surprise*, 674 (P) (African American)

## Shopping

Daly, Niki. *Not So Fast Songololo*, 332 (P) (African—South Africa)

Falwell, Cathryn. *Feast for 10*, 412 (P) (African American)

Heo, Yumi. *One Afternoon*, 639 (P) (Asian American—Korea)

## Short stories

Ada, Alma Flor. *Where the Flame Trees Bloom*, 21 (M) (Caribbean—Cuba)

Anderson, Bernice G., collector. *Trickster Tales from Prairie Lodgefires*, 51 (M) (Native American)

Appiah, Peggy. *Ananse the Spider: Tales from an Ashanti Village*, 60 (M) (African—Ashanti)

Arkhurst, Joyce Cooper, reteller. *The Adventures of Spider: West African Folk Tales*, 62 (M) (African—West Africa)
*More Adventures of Spider: West African Folk Tales*, 63 (M) (African—West Africa)

Baumgartner, Barbara. *Crocodile! Crocodile! Stories Told Around the World*, 99 (M) (Multicultural)

Belting, Natalia. *Moon Was Tired of Walking on Air*, 111 (U) (South American)

Berger, Terry. *Black Fairy Tales*, 119 (M) (African)

Berry, James. *Spiderman Anancy*, 125 (M) (Caribbean)

Bierhorst, John, reteller. *Doctor Coyote: A Native American Aesop's Fables*, 130 (M) (Mexican—Aztec)

   *The Fire Plume: Legends of the American Indians*, 131 (M) (Native American)

   *The Monkey's Haircut: And Other Stories Told by the Maya*, 133 (M/U) (Central American—Mayan)

   *The Naked Bear: Folktales of the Iroquois*, 134 (M/U) (Native American—Iroquois)

   *The Whistling Skeleton: American Indian Tales of the Supernatural*, 136 (M/U) (Native American)

Brenner, Anita. *The Boy Who Could Do Anything: And Other Mexican Folk Tales*, 157 (M/U) (Mexican)

Bruchac, Joseph, reteller. *Flying with the Eagle, Racing the Great Bear: Stories from Native North America*, 170 (U) (Native American)

Bruchac, Joseph, and Michael J. Caduto, retellers. *Native American Stories*, 174 (M/U) (Native American)

Bruchac, Joseph, and Gayle Ross, retellers. *The Girl Who Married the Moon: Tales from Native North America*, 176 (U) (Native American)

Bryan, Ashley. *Beat the Story-Drum, Pum-Pum*, 181 (M) (African)

   *Lion and the Ostrich Chicks: And Other African Folk Tales*, 185 (M) (African)

   *The Ox of the Wonderful Horns and Other African Folktales*, 186 (M) (African)

Cameron, Ann. *More Stories Julian Tells*, 218 (M) (African American)

   *The Stories Julian Tells*, 220 (M) (African American)

Carlson, Lori M., and Cynthia L. Ventura, editors. *Where Angels Glide at Dawn: New Stories from Latin America*, 222 (U) (Latin American)

Climo, Shirley. *Someone Saw a Spider: Spider Facts and Folktales*, 280 (M) (Multicultural)

Cofer, Judith Ortiz. *An Island Like You: Stories of the Barrio*, 286 (U) (Hispanic American—Puerto Rico)

Courlander, Harold, compiler. *The Crest and the Hide: And Other African Stories of Chiefs, Bards, Hunters, Sorcerers, and Common People*, 312 (M/U) (African)

Courlander, Harold, and George Herzog. *The Cow-Tail Switch: And Other West African Stories*, 313 (M/U) (African)

Curry, Jane Louise, reteller. *Back in the Beforetime: Tales of the California Indians*, 326 (M/U) (Native American)

Curtis, Edward S., collector. *The Girl Who Married a Ghost: And Other Tales from "The North American Indian,"* 327 (U) (Native American)

Davison, Katherine. *Moon Magic: Stories from Asia*, 336 (M) (Asian)

DeSpain, Pleasant. *Thirty-Three Multicultural Tales to Tell*, 365 (U) (Multicultural)

deWit, Dorothy, editor. *The Talking Stone: An Anthology of Native American Tales and Legends*, 367 (U) (Native American)

Fairman, Tony, reteller. *Bury My Bones, But Keep My Words: African Tales for Retelling*, 411 (U) (African)

Finger, Charles J. *Tales from Silver Lands*, 421 (U) (South American)

## Short stories (cont.)

Rollins, Charlemae Hill, compiler. *Christmas Gif': An Anthology of Christmas Poems, Songs, and Stories Written by and About Black People*, 1240 (M/U) (African American)

Rosen, Michael, editor. *South and North, East and West: The Oxfam Book of Children's Stories*, 1248 (M) (Multicultural)

Sadler, Catherine Edwards, reteller. *Heaven's Reward: Fairy Tales from China*, 1261 (M) (Asian—China)

   *Treasure Mountain: Folktales from Southern China*, 1262 (M) (Asian—China)

Sanfield, Steve. *The Adventures of High John the Conqueror*, 1269 (M/U) (African American)

San Souci, Robert D. *Larger Than Life: The Adventures of American Legendary Heroes*, 1273 (M) (Multicultural)

   *Short and Shivery: Thirty Chilling Tales*, 1276 (M/U) (Multicultural)

Shannon, George, reteller. *More Stories to Solve: Fifteen Folktales from Around the World*, 1307 (M) (Multicultural)

   *Still More Stories to Solve: Fourteen Folktales from Around the World*, 1308 (M) (Multicultural)

   *Stories to Solve: Folktales from Around the World*, 1309 (M) (Multicultural)

Shepherd, Sandy. *Myths and Legends from Around the World*, 1314 (M) (Multicultural)

Sherlock, Philip, reteller. *Anansi, the Spider Man: Jamaican Folk Tales*, 1315 (M) (Caribbean—Jamaica)

   *West Indian Folk-Tales*, 1316 (M/U) (Caribbean—West Indies)

Soto, Gary. *Baseball in April: And Other Stories*, 1349 (U) (Hispanic American)

   *Local News*, 1354 (U) (Mexican American)

Strickland, Dorothy S., editor. *Listen Children: An Anthology of Black Literature*, 1399 (U) (African American)

Tate, Eleanora E. *Front Porch Stories: At the One-Room School*, 1413 (M) (African American)

Taylor, C. J. *Bones in the Basket: Native Stories of the Origin of People*, 1416 (M) (Native American)

   *How We Saw the World: Nine Native Stories of the Way Things Began*, 1419 (M) (Native American)

Thornhill, Jan. *Crow and Fox: And Other Animal Legends*, 1441 (M) (Multicultural)

Timpanelli, Gioia, reteller. *Tales from the Roof of the World: Folktales of Tibet*, 1443 (M/U) (Asian—Tibet)

Turenne des Prés, François. *Children of Yayoute: Folk Tales of Haiti*, 1466 (U) (Caribbean—Haiti)

Uchida, Yoshiko, reteller. *The Magic Listening Cap: More Folktales from Japan*, 1478 (M/U) (Asian—Japan)

Vuong, Lynette Dyer. *The Brocaded Slipper: And Other Vietnamese Tales*, 1497 (M) (Asian—Vietnam)

   *The Golden Carp: And Other Tales from Vietnam*, 1498 (U) (Asian—Vietnam)

   *Sky Legends of Vietnam*, 1499 (U) (Asian—Vietnam)

Watkins, Yoko Kawashima. *Tales from the Bamboo Grove*, 1528 (M) (Asian—Japan)

Weiss, Jacqueline Shachter, collector and adapter. *Young Brer Rabbit: And Other Trickster Tales from the Americas*, 1534 (M) (Latin American)

Wheeler, M. J. *Fox Tales*, 1540 (M) (Asian—India)

Whitney, Alex. *Stiff Ears: Animal Folktales of the North American Indian*, 1544 (M) (Native American)

Wolkstein, Diane, collector. *The Magic Orange Tree: And Other Haitian Folktales*, 1575 (M/U) (Caribbean—Haiti)

Wood, Marion. *Spirits, Heroes and Hunters from North American Indian Mythology*, 1578 (M/U) (Native American)

Yee, Paul. *Tales from Gold Mountain: Stories of the Chinese in the New World*, 1598 (M) (Asian American—China)

Yellow Robe, Rosebud. *Tonweya and the Eagles: And Other Lakota Tales*, 1600 (U) (Native American—Lakota)

Yeoman, John. *The Singing Tortoise: And Other Animal Folktales*, 1602 (M) (Multicultural)

Yep, Laurence, reteller. *The Rainbow People*, 1612 (M/U) (Asian—China)

*Tongues of Jade*, 1617 (M/U) (Asian American—China)

*Tree of Dreams: Ten Tales from the Garden of Night*, 1618 (U) (Multicultural)

## Sibling rivalry

Adoff, Arnold. *Hard to Be Six*, 26 (P) (Multicultural)

Caines, Jeannette. *Abby*, 210 (PS) (African American)

Climo, Shirley. *The Egyptian Cinderella*, 278 (M) (African—Egypt)

Fitzhugh, Louise. *Nobody's Family Is Going to Change*, 427 (U) (African American)

Greenfield, Eloise. *She Come Bringin Me That Little Baby Girl*, 543 (P) (African American)

Mills, Claudia. *A Visit to Amy-Claire*, 1026 (PS/P) (Asian American)

Pfeffer, Susan Beth. *The Riddle Streak*, 1168 (M) (African American)

Wilson, Johnniece Marshall. *Oh, Brother*, 1564 (M) (African American)

## Sign language

Rankin, Laura. *The Handmade Alphabet*, 1204 (P/M) (Multicultural)

## Singing

Lewis, Richard. *All of You Was Singing*, 888 (M) (Mexican—Aztec)

## Sitting Bull

Bruchac, Joseph. *A Boy Called Slow: The True Story of Sitting Bull*, 168 (M) (Native American—Lakota Sioux)

## Sky

Belting, Natalia. *The Sun Is a Golden Earring*, 113 (M) (Multicultural)

Birdseye, Tom, adapter. *A Song of Stars: An Asian Legend*, 140 (M) (Asian—China)

Chang, Cindy, reteller. *The Seventh Sister: A Chinese Legend*, 237 (M) (Asian—China)

Cummings, Pat. *C.L.O.U.D.S.*, 324 (P) (African American)

Daly, Niki, reteller. *Why the Sun and the Moon Live in the Sky*, 333 (M) (African—Nigeria)

Lyons, Mary E. *Letters from a Slave Girl: The Story of Harriet Jacobs*, 930 (U) (African American)

McKissack, Patricia, and Fredrick McKissack. *Christmas in the Big House, Christmas in the Quarters*, 954 (M) (African American)

Marie, D. *Tears for Ashan*, 974 (M) (African)

Medearis, Angela Shelf. *Dancing with the Indians*, 1001 (P) (Multicultural)

Monjo, F. N. *The Drinking Gourd*, 1042 (P/M) (African American)

O'Dell, Scott. *The Captive*, 1116 (U) (Central American—Mayan)

   *My Name Is Not Angelica*, 1120 (U) (Caribbean)

   *Sing Down the Moon*, 1121 (U) (Native American)

Picó, Fernando. *The Red Comb*, 1171 (M) (Caribbean—Puerto Rico)

Porter, Connie. *Changes for Addy: A Winter Story*, 1192 (M) (African American)

   *Meet Addy: An American Girl*, 1194 (M) (African American)

Price, Leontyne, reteller. *Aida*, 1198 (U) (African)

Ringgold, Faith. *Aunt Harriet's Underground Railroad in the Sky*, 1220 (P/M) (African American)

Robinet, Harriette Gillem. *If You Please, President Lincoln*, 1224 (U) (African American)

Ruby, Lois. *Steal Away Home*, 1254 (U) (African American)

Smucker, Barbara. *Runaway to Freedom: A Story of the Underground Railroad*, 1344 (U) (African American)

Stolz, Mary. *Cezanne Pinto: A Memoir*, 1392 (U) (African American)

Treviño, Elizabeth Borton de. *I, Juan de Pareja*, 1452 (U) (African heritage)

Turner, Ann. *Nettie's Trip South*, 1467 (M) (African American)

Turner, Glennette Tilley. *Running for Our Lives*, 1469 (U) (African American)

Winter, Jeanette. *Follow the Drinking Gourd*, 1567 (M) (African American)

Wright, Courtni C. *Journey to Freedom: A Story of the Underground Railroad*, 1584 (M) (African American)

   *Jumping the Broom*, 1585 (M) (African American)

Yep, Laurence. *Dragon's Gate*, 1606 (U) (Asian American—China)

## Sleep

Bierhorst, John, selector. *On the Road of Stars: Native American Night Poems and Sleep Charms*, 135 (M) (Native American)

Keats, Ezra Jack. *Dreams*, 777 (PS/P) (Hispanic American)

Loh, Morag Jeanette. *Tucking Mommy In*, 909 (P) (Multicultural)

Mwalimu, and Adrienne Kennaway. *Awful Aardvark*, 1078 (M) (African)

Oxenbury, Helen. *Say Goodnight*, 1145 (PS) (Multicultural)

## Songs

Bryan, Ashley. *All Night, All Day: A Child's First Book of African-American Spirituals*, 180 (P/M) (African American)

   *I'm Going to Sing: Black American Spirituals, Vol. 2*, 184 (M) (African American)

   *Walk Together Children: Black American Spirituals*, 191 (M) (African American)

Buffett, Jimmy, and Savannah Jane Buffett. *The Jolly Mon*, 194 (P) (Caribbean)

## Songs (cont.)

Burgie, Irving. *Caribbean Carnival: Songs of the West Indies*, 206 (M) (Caribbean)

Delacre, Lulu, selector. *Arroz Con Leche: Popular Songs and Rhymes from Latin America*, 347 (P/M) (Latin American)

*Las Navidades: Popular Christmas Songs from Latin America*, 348 (P/M) (Latin American)

Fichter, George S. *American Indian Music and Musical Instruments: With Instructions for Making the Instruments*, 419 (M/U) (Native American)

Harris, Joel Chandler. *Jump Again! More Adventures of Brer Rabbit*, 614 (M/U) (African American)

*Jump on Over! The Adventures of Brer Rabbit and His Family*, 615 (M/U) (African American)

Jacobs, Shannon K. *Song of the Giraffe*, 721 (M) (African)

Johnson, James Weldon. *Lift Every Voice and Sing*, 753 (P/M) (African American)

*Lift Ev'ry Voice and Sing*, 754 (M) (African American)

Langstaff, John, editor. *Climbing Jacob's Ladder: Heroes of the Bible in African-American Spirituals*, 839 (P/M) (African American)

*What a Morning! The Christmas Story in Black Spirituals*, 840 (P/M) (African American)

Melmed, Laura Krauss. *The First Song Ever Sung*, 1007 (P) (Asian—Japan)

Orozco, José-Luis, selector, arranger, and translator. *De Colores: And Other Latin-American Folk Songs for Children*, 1134 (M/U) (Latin American)

Politi, Leo. *Juanita*, 1182 (M) (Mexican American)

*Song of the Swallows*, 1183 (M) (Mexican American)

Rollins, Charlemae Hill, compiler. *Christmas Gif': An Anthology of Christmas Poems, Songs, and Stories Written by and About Black People*, 1240 (M/U) (African American)

Seeger, Pete. *Abiyoyo: Based on a South African Lullaby and Folk Song*, 1302 (M) (African—South Africa)

Serwadda, W. Moses. *Songs and Stories from Uganda*, 1304 (M) (African—Uganda)

Weiss, George David, and Bob Thiel. *What a Wonderful World*, 1533 (P) (Multicultural)

Wolkstein, Diane, collector. *The Magic Orange Tree: And Other Haitian Folktales*, 1575 (M/U) (Caribbean—Haiti)

## Spiders

Aardema, Verna, reteller. *The Vingananee and the Tree Toad: A Liberian Tale*, 13 (M) (African—Liberia)

Appiah, Peggy. *Ananse the Spider: Tales from an Ashanti Village*, 60 (M) (African—Ashanti)

Arkhurst, Joyce Cooper, reteller. *The Adventures of Spider: West African Folk Tales*, 62 (M) (African—West Africa)

*More Adventures of Spider: West African Folk Tales*, 63 (M) (African—West Africa)

Berry, James. *Spiderman Anancy*, 125 (M) (Caribbean)

Bryan, Ashley. *The Ox of the Wonderful Horns and Other African Folktales*, 186 (M) (African)

Chocolate, Deborah M. Newton, reteller. *Spider and the Sky God: An Akan Legend*, 251 (M) (African—Akan)

Climo, Shirley. *Someone Saw a Spider: Spider Facts and Folktales*, 280 (M) (Multicultural)

*How Anansi Obtained the Sky God's Stories: An African Folktale from the Ashanti Tribe*, 671 (M) (African—Ashanti)

Kimmel, Eric A., reteller. *Anansi and the Moss-Covered Rock*, 802 (M) (African)

*Anansi and the Talking Melon*, 803 (M) (African)

*Anansi Goes Fishing*, 804 (M) (African)

McDermott, Gerald, adapter. *Anansi the Spider: A Tale from the Ashanti*, 934 (P) (African—Ashanti)

Makhanlall, David. *Brer Anansi and the Boat Race: A Caribbean Folk Tale*, 969 (M) (Caribbean)

Roth, Susan L. *The Story of Light*, 1252 (M) (Native American—Cherokee)

Sherlock, Philip, reteller. *Anansi, the Spider Man: Jamaican Folk Tales*, 1315 (M) (Caribbean—Jamaica)

*West Indian Folk-Tales*, 1316 (M/U) (Caribbean—West Indies)

Temple, Frances, reteller. *Tiger Soup: An Anansi Story from Jamaica*, 1437 (M) (Caribbean—Jamaica)

## Sports

Lankford, Mary D. *Hopscotch Around the World*, 841 (P/M) (Multicultural)

## Sports—baseball

Adoff, Arnold. *OUTside INside Poems*, 32 (M) (African American)

Christopher, Matt. *Shortstop from Tokyo*, 257 (M) (Asian American—Japan)

Cohen, Barbara. *Thank You, Jackie Robinson*, 287 (M) (African American)

Curtis, Gavin. *Grandma's Baseball*, 328 (P) (African American)

Johnson, Dolores. *What Kind of Baby-Sitter Is This?*, 747 (P) (African American)

Lord, Bette Bao. *In the Year of the Boar and Jackie Robinson*, 915 (M) (Asian American—China)

Mochizuki, Ken. *Baseball Saved Us*, 1031 (M) (Asian American—Japan)

Myers, Walter Dean. *Me, Mop, and the Moondance Kid*, 1084 (M/U) (African American)

*Mop, Moondance, and the Nagasaki Knights*, 1085 (M/U) (African American)

Namioka, Lensey. *Yang the Youngest and His Terrible Ear*, 1095 (M) (Asian American—China)

Nelson, Vaunda Micheaux. *Mayfield Crossing*, 1099 (U) (African American)

Slote, Alfred. *Finding Buck McHenry*, 1335 (M) (African American)

Spohn, David. *Home Field*, 1366 (M) (Multicultural)

Stolz, Mary. *Coco Grimes*, 1393 (M) (African American)

*Stealing Home*, 1395 (M/U) (African American)

## Sports—basketball

Brooks, Bruce. *The Moves Make the Man*, 163 (U) (African American)

Soto, Gary. *Taking Sides*, 1359 (U) (Mexican American)

## Sports—bicycling

Bunting, Eve. *Summer Wheels*, 201 (M) (African American)

Cameron, Ann. *Julian's Glorious Summer*, 217 (M) (African American)

McKissack, Patricia, and Fredrick McKissack. *Constance Stumbles*, 955 (P) (African American)

Say, Allen. *The Bicycle Man*, 1282 (M) (Asian—Japan)

Soto, Gary. *Summer on Wheels*, 1358 (U) (Mexican American)

## Sports—figure skating

Fenner, Carol. *The Skates of Uncle Richard*, 417 (M) (African American)

## Sports—fishing

Aardema, Verna, reteller. *Anansi Finds a Fool: An Ashanti Tale*, 1 (M) (African—Ashanti)

Adams, Jeanie. *Going for Oysters*, 22 (P) (Australian—Aborigine)

Cooper, Susan. *Jethro and the Jumbie*, 310 (M) (Caribbean)

Engel, Diana. *Fishing*, 401 (P) (African American)

George, Jean Craighead. *Shark Beneath the Reef*, 465 (U) (Mexican)

Igus, Toyomi. *When I Was Little*, 711 (P) (African American)

Luenn, Nancy. *Nessa's Fish*, 921 (P) (Native American—Inuit)

McKissack, Patricia. *A Million Fish . . . More or Less*, 949 (M) (African American)

Orr, Katherine. *My Grandpa and the Sea*, 1135 (M) (Caribbean)

Say, Allen. *A River Dream*, 1287 (P) (Asian American)

Stock, Catherine. *Armien's Fishing Trip*, 1387 (P) (African—South Africa)

Stolz, Mary. *Go Fish!*, 1394 (M) (African American)

## Sports—football

Mathis, Sharon Bell. *Red Dog, Blue Fly: Football Poems*, 986 (M) (African American)

## Sports—horseback riding

Hewett, Joan. *Laura Loves Horses*, 641 (M) (Hispanic American)

## Sports—hunting

Benchley, Nathaniel. *Small Wolf*, 117 (P) (Native American)

Bernhard, Emery, reteller. *The Girl Who Wanted to Hunt: A Siberian Tale*, 120 (M) (Asian—Siberia)

Davis, Deborah. *The Secret of the Seal*, 334 (M) (Native American—Inuit)

Geraghty, Paul. *The Hunter*, 468 (P) (African)

Hodges, Margaret, reteller. *The Golden Deer*, 655 (M) (Asian—India)

MacDonald, Suse. *Nanta's Lion: A Search-and-Find Adventure*, 945 (P) (African—Masai)

Prusski, Jeffrey. *Bring Back the Deer*, 1200 (P) (Native American)

Rohmer, Harriet, Octavio Chow, and Morris Vidaure. *The Invisible Hunters/Los Cazadores Invisibles: A Legend from the Miskito Indians of Nicaragua/Una Leyenda de los Indios Miskitos de Nicaragua*, 1239 (M) (Central American—Nicaragua)

Roy, Ronald. *A Thousand Pails of Water*, 1253 (P) (Asian)

## Sports—roller skating
Johnson, Mildred D. *Wait, Skates!*, 755 (PS/P) (African American)

## Sports—skateboarding
Richemont, Enid. *The Magic Skateboard*, 1219 (M) (African heritage)

## Sports—sled racing
Gardiner, John Reynolds. *Stone Fox*, 457 (M) (Native American)
O'Dell, Scott. *Black Star, Bright Dawn*, 1115 (U) (Native American—Eskimo)

## Sports—soccer
Stevens, Philippa J. *Bonk! Goes the Ball*, 1384 (P) (Asian American)

## Sports—swimming
Walter, Mildred Pitts. *Mariah Keeps Cool*, 1513 (M) (African American)

## Sports—wrestling
Stamm, Claus. *Three Strong Women: A Tall Tale from Japan*, 1371 (M) (Asian—Japan)

## Stars
Armstrong, Jennifer. *Wan Hu Is in the Stars*, 66 (M) (Asian—China)
Birdseye, Tom, adapter. *A Song of Stars: An Asian Legend*, 140 (M) (Asian—China)
Chang, Cindy, reteller. *The Seventh Sister: A Chinese Legend*, 237 (M) (Asian—China)
Cohlene, Terri, adapter. *Quillworker: A Cheyenne Legend*, 296 (M) (Native American—Cheyenne)
Garcia, Anamarie, reteller. *The Girl from the Sky: An Inca Folktale from South America*, 456 (M) (South American—Inca)
Goble, Paul. *Her Seven Brothers*, 493 (M) (Native American—Cheyenne)
*The Lost Children: The Boys Who Were Neglected*, 499 (M) (Native American—Blackfoot)
*Star Boy*, 501 (M) (Native American—Blackfoot)
Hillman, Elizabeth. *Min-Yo and the Moon Dragon*, 649 (M) (Asian—China)
Hort, Lenny. *How Many Stars in the Sky?*, 667 (P) (African American)
Lee, Jeanne M., reteller. *Legend of the Milky Way*, 858 (M) (Asian—China)
Mayo, Gretchen Will, reteller. *Star Tales: North American Indian Stories about the Stars*, 997 (M/U) (Native American)
Mobley, Jane. *The Star Husband*, 1030 (M) (Native American)
Mollel, Tololwa M. *The Orphan Boy: A Masai Story*, 1038 (M) (African—Masai)
Monjo, F. N. *The Drinking Gourd*, 1042 (P/M) (African American)
Monroe, Jean Guard, and Ray A. Williamson. *They Dance in the Sky: Native American Star Myths*, 1043 (M/U) (Native American)
Oughton, Jerrie. *How the Stars Fell into the Sky: A Navajo Legend*, 1140 (M) (Native American—Navajo)

## Stars (cont.)

Taylor, Harriet Peck, reteller. *Coyote Places the Stars*, 1423 (M) (Native American—Wasco)

Winter, Jeanette. *Follow the Drinking Gourd*, 1567 (M) (African American)

## Stores

Carlstrom, Nancy White. *Baby-O*, 223 (P) (Caribbean)

Chan, Jennifer L. *One Small Girl*, 236 (P) (Asian American—China)

Freeman, Don. *Corduroy*, 445 (PS/P) (African American)

Martel, Cruz. *Yagua Days*, 977 (M) (Hispanic American—Puerto Rico)

Schotter, Roni. *A Fruit and Vegetable Man*, 1293 (P) (Asian American)

Shelby, Anne. *We Keep a Store*, 1312 (P) (African American)

## Storytelling

Arneach, Lloyd, reteller. *The Animals' Ballgame: A Cherokee Story from the Eastern Band*, 68 (M) (Native American—Cherokee)

*The Baboon's Umbrella: An African Folktale*, 71 (M) (African)

Belton, Sandra. *From Miss Ida's Porch*, 115 (M) (African American)

Chocolate, Deborah M. Newton, reteller. *Spider and the Sky God: An Akan Legend*, 251 (M) (African—Akan)

Clifton, Lucille. *The Lucky Stone*, 274 (M) (African American)

Colman, Warren. *Double Dutch and the Voodoo Shoes: A Modern African-American Urban Tale*, 303 (M) (African American)

DeSpain, Pleasant. *Thirty-Three Multicultural Tales to Tell*, 365 (U) (Multicultural)

Dupré, Rick. *The Wishing Chair*, 387 (P) (African American)

Franklin, Kristine L. *The Old, Old Man and the Very Little Boy*, 441 (P) (African)

Garcia, Anamarie, reteller. *The Girl from the Sky: An Inca Folktale from South America*, 456 (M) (South American—Inca)

Grifalconi, Ann. *Osa's Pride*, 557 (P) (African)

Haley, Gail E., reteller. *A Story, a Story*, 574 (M) (African)

Hamada, Cheryl, reteller. *The Farmer, the Buffalo, and the Tiger: A Folktale from Vietnam*, 575 (M) (Asian—Vietnam)

*The Fourth Question: A Chinese Folktale*, 576 (M) (Asian—China)

*Kao and the Golden Fish: A Folktale from Thailand*, 577 (M) (Asian—Thailand)

*The White Hare of Inaba: A Japanese Folktale*, 578 (M) (Asian—Japan)

Hilbert, Vi. *Loon and Deer Were Traveling: A Story of the Upper Skagit of Puget Sound*, 645 (M) (Native American—Skagit)

*How Anansi Obtained the Sky God's Stories: An African Folktale from the Ashanti Tribe*, 671 (M) (African—Ashanti)

Howard, Elizabeth Fitzgerald. *Aunt Flossie's Hats (and Crab Cakes Later)*, 672 (P) (African American)

*Papa Tells Chita a Story*, 675 (P) (African American)

Johnson, Angela. *Tell Me a Story, Mama*, 740 (P) (African American)

Johnson, James Weldon. *The Creation*, 751 (P/M) (African American)

Joseph, Lynn. *The Mermaid's Twin Sister: More Stories from Trinidad*, 773 (M) (Caribbean)

Liddell, Janice. *Imani and the Flying Africans*, 894 (M) (African American)

Luenn, Nancy. *Nessa's Story*, 922 (P) (Native American—Inuit)

McKissack, Patricia. *A Million Fish . . . More or Less*, 949 (M) (African American)

Martin, Bill, Jr., and John Archambault. *Knots on a Counting Rope*, 978 (P/M) (Native American)

Meyer, Carolyn. *Rio Grande Stories*, 1013 (U) (Multicultural)

Milich, Melissa. *Can't Scare Me!*, 1019 (M) (African American)

Miller, Montzalee. *My Grandmother's Cookie Jar*, 1025 (P) (Native American)

Mora, Francisco X. *The Tiger and the Rabbit: A Puerto Rican Folktale*, 1054 (M) (Caribbean—Puerto Rico)

Moroney, Lynn, reteller. *The Boy Who Loved Bears: A Pawnee Tale*, 1060 (M) (Native American—Pawnee)

Pellowski, Anne. *The Family Storytelling Handbook: How to Use Stories, Anecdotes, Rhymes, Handkerchiefs, Paper, and Other Objects to Enrich Your Family Traditions*, 1159 (M/U) (Multicultural)

*Hidden Stories in Plants: Unusual and Easy-to-Tell Stories from Around the World Together with Creative Things to Do While Telling Them*, 1160 (M/U) (Multicultural)

*The Story Vine: A Source Book of Unusual and Easy-to-Tell Stories from Around the World*, 1161 (M/U) (Multicultural)

Robinson, Adjai. *Three African Tales*, 1227 (M) (African)

Rodriguez, Anita. *Aunt Martha and the Golden Coin*, 1235 (P) (African American)

*Jamal and the Angel*, 1236 (P) (African American)

Stolz, Mary. *Go Fish!*, 1394 (M) (African American)

Stroud, Virginia A. *Doesn't Fall Off His Horse*, 1401 (M) (Native American—Kiowa)

Tate, Carol. *Tale of the Spiteful Spirits: A Kampuchean Folk Tale*, 1411 (M) (Asian—Cambodia)

Tate, Eleanora E. *Front Porch Stories: At the One-Room School*, 1413 (M) (African American)

Weisman, Joan. *The Storyteller*, 1532 (P) (Native American—Pueblo)

Welsch, Roger. *Uncle Smoke Stories: Nehawka Tales of Coyote the Trickster*, 1537 (M) (Native American)

## String

Gryski, Camilla. *Cat's Cradle, Owl's Eyes: A Book of String Games*, 564 (M/U) (Multicultural)

*Many Stars & More String Games*, 565 (M) (Multicultural)

*Super String Games*, 566 (M) (Multicultural)

## Summer

Wyeth, Sharon Dennis. *Always My Dad*, 1587 (P) (African American)

## Sun

Baylor, Byrd. *The Way to Start a Day*, 104 (M) (Multicultural)

Belting, Natalia. *The Sun Is a Golden Earring*, 113 (M) (Multicultural)

*The King's Fifth*, 1119 (U) (Mexican)

Paulsen, Gary. *Dogsong*, 1157 (U) (Native American—Inuit)

Robinet, Harriette Gillem. *If You Please, President Lincoln*, 1224 (U) (African American)

Speare, Elizabeth George. *The Sign of the Beaver*, 1361 (M/U) (Native American)

Sperry, Armstrong. *Call It Courage*, 1362 (U) (Polynesian)

Taylor, Theodore. *Timothy of the Cay*, 1434 (U) (Caribbean)

Watkins, Yoko Kawashima. *My Brother, My Sister, and I*, 1526 (U) (Asian—Japan)

   *So Far from the Bamboo Grove*, 1527 (U) (Asian—Korea/Japan)

## Tangrams

Tompert, Ann. *Grandfather Tang's Story*, 1445 (P) (Asian—China)

## Taxis

Best, Cari. *Taxi! Taxi!*, 128 (P) (Hispanic American)

## Television

Wright, Betty Ren. *The Day Our TV Broke Down*, 1583 (P) (African American)

## Theater

Greenfield, Eloise. *Grandpa's Face*, 533 (P) (African American)

## Tides

Bowden, Joan Chase. *Why the Tides Ebb and Flow*, 151 (M) (African)

## Time

Singer, Marilyn. *Nine O'Clock Lullaby*, 1326 (P) (Multicultural)

## Tools

Morris, Ann. *Tools*, 1066 (PS/P) (Multicultural)

## Totems

Hoyt-Goldsmith, Diane. *Totem Pole*, 682 (M) (Native American—Tsimshian)

Siberell, Anne. *Whale in the Sky*, 1324 (M) (Native American—Northwest Coast)

## Toys

Bang, Molly. *One Fall Day*, 83 (P) (African American)

Carlstrom, Nancy White. *Barney Is Best*, 224 (PS/P) (Hispanic American)

Petrie, Catherine. *Joshua James Likes Trucks*, 1166 (P) (African American)

Tagore, Rabindranath. *Paper Boats*, 1406 (P) (Multicultural)

Williams, Karen Lynn. *Galimoto*, 1549 (P/M) (African)

## Toys—balls

Bang, Molly. *Yellow Ball*, 88 (PS/P) (African American)

## Toys—dolls

Greenfield, Eloise. *My Doll, Keshia*, 539 (PS) (African American)

McKissack, Patricia. *Nettie Jo's Friends*, 952 (P) (African American)

Pomerantz, Charlotte. *The Chalk Doll*, 1185 (P) (Caribbean—Jamaica)

Rupert, Rona. *Straw Sense*, 1257 (P) (African)

Tsutsui, Yoriko. *Anna's Special Present*, 1465 (P) (Asian—Japan)

## Toys—teddy bears

Appiah, Sonia. *Amoko and Efua Bear*, 61 (P) (African—Ghana)

Freeman, Don. *Corduroy*, 445 (PS/P) (African American)

  *A Pocket for Corduroy*, 446 (PS/P) (African American)

Smith, Joanne L. *Show and Tell*, 1341 (P) (African American)

Straight, Susan. *Bear E. Bear*, 1398 (P) (Multicultural)

Sun, Chyng Feng. *Mama Bear*, 1403 (P) (Asian American—China)

Young, Ruth. *Golden Bear*, 1635 (PS/P) (African American)

## Trains

Crews, Donald. *Shortcut*, 320 (P) (African American)

Fraser, Mary Ann. *Ten Mile Day: And the Building of the Transcontinental Railroad*, 444 (M) (Asian American—China)

Goble, Paul. *Death of the Iron Horse*, 488 (M) (Native American—Cheyenne)

Howard, Elizabeth Fitzgerald. *Mac & Marie & the Train Toss Surprise*, 674 (P) (African American)

  *The Train to Lulu's*, 676 (P) (African American)

Jensen, Patsy. *John Henry and His Mighty Hammer*, 729 (P) (African American)

Keats, Ezra Jack. *John Henry: An American Legend*, 780 (M) (African American)

Krensky, Stephen. *The Iron Dragon Never Sleeps*, 824 (U) (Asian American—China)

Lester, Julius. *John Henry*, 870 (M) (African American)

Pinkney, Gloria Jean. *The Sunday Outing*, 1176 (P/M) (African American)

Small, Terry. *The Legend of John Henry*, 1336 (M) (African American)

Torres, Leyla. *Subway Sparrow*, 1450 (P) (Multicultural)

Uchida, Yoshiko. *Sumi and the Goat and the Tokyo Express*, 1481 (M) (Asian—Japan)

Yep, Laurence. *Dragon's Gate*, 1606 (U) (Asian American—China)

## Transportation

Baer, Edith. *This Is the Way We Go to School: A Book about Children Around the World*, 73 (P) (Multicultural)

Morris, Ann. *On the Go*, 1065 (PS/P) (Multicultural)

Munsch, Robert. *Where is Gah-Ning?*, 1075 (P) (Asian American—China)

Williams, Karen Lynn. *Tap-Tap*, 1550 (M) (Caribbean—Haiti)

## Treasure

Hamilton, Virginia. *The Mystery of Drear House: The Conclusion of the Dies Drear Chronicle*, 592 (M) (African American)

Myers, Walter Dean. *The Mouse Rap*, 1086 (U) (African American)

*The Righteous Revenge of Artemis Bonner*, 1087 (U) (African American)

## Trees

Adoff, Arnold. *Flamboyán*, 25 (P) (Caribbean—Puerto Rico)

Anderson/Sankofa, David A. *The Rebellion of Humans: An African Spiritual Journey*, 55 (M) (African)

Casler, Leigh. *The Boy Who Dreamed of an Acorn*, 229 (M) (Native American)

Chanin, Michael. *Grandfather Four Winds and the Rising Moon*, 241 (M) (Native American)

Cherry, Lynne. *The Great Kapok Tree: A Tale of the Amazon Rain Forest*, 243 (M) (South American)

Demi. *Under the Shade of the Mulberry Tree*, 359 (M) (Asian—China)

Duarte, Margarida Estrela Bandeira. *The Legend of the Palm Tree*, 382 (M) (South American—Brazil)

Eckewa, T. Obinkaram. *The Ancestor Tree*, 390 (M) (African)

Franklin, Kristine L. *When the Monkeys Came Back*, 443 (P) (Central American—Costa Rica)

Glaser, Linda. *Tanyu's Big Green Dream*, 481 (M) (Multicultural)

Graham, Lorenz. *Song of the Boat*, 513 (M) (African—West Africa)

Hamada, Cheryl, reteller. *Kao and the Golden Fish: A Folktale from Thailand*, 577 (M) (Asian—Thailand)

Howard, Elizabeth Fitzgerald. *Chita's Christmas Tree*, 673 (P) (African American)

Lichtveld, Noni. *I Lost My Arrow in a Kankan Tree*, 893 (M) (South American—Surinam)

Lottridge, Celia Barker, reteller. *The Name of the Tree: A Bantu Folktale*, 916 (M) (African—Bantu)

Lovelace, Maud Hart. *The Trees Kneel at Christmas*, 919 (M) (Middle Eastern American—Lebanon)

McDermott, Gerald, adapter. *The Magic Tree: A Tale from the Congo*, 937 (M) (African—Zaire)

Mattingly, Christobel. *The Miracle Tree*, 989 (M) (Asian—Japan)

Mogensen, Jan. *Kakalambalala*, 1032 (M) (African)

Mora, Pat. *Pablo's Tree*, 1056 (P) (Mexican American)

Rose, Deborah Lee, adapter. *The People Who Hugged the Trees: An Environmental Folktale*, 1242 (M) (Asian—India)

Say, Allen, reteller. *Once Under the Cherry Blossom Tree: An Old Japanese Tale*, 1286 (M) (Asian—Japan)

*Tree of Cranes*, 1288 (P/M) (Asian American—Japan)

Troughton, Joanna, reteller. *Tortoise's Dream*, 1458 (M) (African)

Young, Ed. *Up a Tree*, 1633 (P) (Asian)

## Trucks

Petrie, Catherine. *Joshua James Likes Trucks*, 1166 (P) (African American)

Williams, Karen Lynn. *Tap-Tap*, 1550 (M) (Caribbean—Haiti)

## Twins

Banks, Jacqueline Turner. *Egg-Drop Blues*, 90 (U) (African American)

*The New One*, 91 (U) (African American)

*Project Wheels*, 92 (U) (African American)

Blackman, Malorie. *Girl Wonder and the Terrific Twins*, 142 (M) (African American)

Lattimore, Deborah Nourse. *Punga: The Goddess of Ugly*, 847 (M) (New Zealand—Maori)

## Umbrellas

*The Baboon's Umbrella: An African Folktale*, 71 (M) (African)

Yashima, Taro. *Umbrella*, 1596 (P) (Asian American—Japan)

## Underground Railroad

Armstrong, Jennifer. *Steal Away*, 65 (U) (African American)

Brill, Marlene Targ. *Allen Jay and the Underground Railroad*, 161 (M) (African American)

Hamilton, Virginia. *The House of Dies Drear*, 587 (M) (African American)

*The Mystery of Drear House: The Conclusion of the Dies Drear Chronicle*, 592 (M) (African American)

Hoobler, Dorothy, and Thomas Hoobler. *Next Stop, Freedom: The Story of a Slave Girl*, 662 (M) (African American)

Lawrence, Jacob. *Harriet and the Promised Land*, 853 (M) (African American)

Monjo, F. N. *The Drinking Gourd*, 1042 (P/M) (African American)

Ringgold, Faith. *Aunt Harriet's Underground Railroad in the Sky*, 1220 (P/M) (African American)

Ruby, Lois. *Steal Away Home*, 1254 (U) (African American)

Smucker, Barbara. *Runaway to Freedom: A Story of the Underground Railroad*, 1344 (U) (African American)

Stolz, Mary. *Cezanne Pinto: A Memoir*, 1392 (U) (African American)

Turner, Glennette Tilley. *Running for Our Lives*, 1469 (U) (African American)

Winter, Jeanette. *Follow the Drinking Gourd*, 1567 (M) (African American)

Wright, Courtni C. *Journey to Freedom: A Story of the Underground Railroad*, 1584 (M) (African American)

## U.S. history

Altman, Susan, and Susan Lechner. *Followers of the North Star: Rhymes about African American Heroes, Heroines, and Historical Times*, 47 (M/U) (African American)

Armstrong, Jennifer. *Steal Away*, 65 (U) (African American)

Banks, Sara H. *Remember My Name*, 93 (U) (Native American—Cherokee)

Baylor, Byrd. *Before You Came This Way*, 100 (P/M) (Native American)

Bird, E. J. *The Rainmakers*, 139 (U) (Native American—Anasazi)

Brenner, Barbara. *Wagon Wheels*, 160 (P) (African American)

Brill, Marlene Targ. *Allen Jay and the Underground Railroad*, 161 (M) (African American)

Burchard, Peter. *Bimby*, 202 (M/U) (African American)

## U.S. history (cont.)

*Streams to the River, River to the Sea: A Novel of Sacagawea*, 1122 (U) (Native American)

O'Dell, Scott, and Elizabeth Hall. *Thunder Rolling in the Mountains*, 1124 (U) (Native American—Nez Perce)

Paulsen, Gary. *Canyons*, 1156 (U) (Native American—Apache)

Ringgold, Faith. *Aunt Harriet's Underground Railroad in the Sky*, 1220 (P/M) (African American)

*Dinner at Aunt Connie's House*, 1221 (P/M) (African American)

Robinet, Harriette Gillem. *If You Please, President Lincoln*, 1224 (U) (African American)

*Mississippi Chariot*, 1225 (U) (African American)

Ruby, Lois. *Steal Away Home*, 1254 (U) (African American)

Seattle, Chief. *Brother Eagle, Sister Sky: A Message from Chief Seattle*, 1299 (M) (Native American)

Sewell, Marcia. *People of the Breaking Day*, 1305 (M) (Native American—Wampanoag)

Shor, Pekay, reteller. *When the Corn Is Red*, 1321 (M) (Native American—Tuscaroran)

Stewart, Elisabeth J. *On the Long Trail Home*, 1386 (U) (Native American—Cherokee)

Turner, Ann. *Nettie's Trip South*, 1467 (M) (African American)

Turner, Glennette Tilley. *Running for Our Lives*, 1469 (U) (African American)

Walter, Mildred Pitts. *The Girl on the Outside*, 1509 (U) (African American)

Wheeler, Gloria. *Night of the Full Moon*, 1539 (M) (Native American—Potawatomi)

Winter, Jeanette. *Follow the Drinking Gourd*, 1567 (M) (African American)

Wright, Courtni C. *Journey to Freedom: A Story of the Underground Railroad*, 1584 (M) (African American)

*Wagon Train: A Family Goes West in 1865*, 1586 (M) (African American)

Yep, Laurence. *Dragon's Gate*, 1606 (U) (Asian American—China)

## U.S. history—Civil War

Fleischman, Paul. *Bull Run*, 429 (U) (Multicultural)

Forrester, Sandra. *Sound the Jubilee*, 435 (U) (African American)

Hansen, Joyce. *Which Way Freedom?*, 606 (U) (African American)

Polacco, Patricia. *Pink and Say*, 1181 (M) (African American)

Porter, Connie. *Addy Learns a Lesson: A School Story*, 1189 (M) (African American)

*Addy's Surprise: A Christmas Story*, 1191 (M) (African American)

*Changes for Addy: A Winter Story*, 1192 (M) (African American)

*Happy Birthday, Addy: A Springtime Story*, 1193 (M) (African American)

*Meet Addy: An American Girl*, 1194 (M) (African American)

## U.S. history—Colonial times

Benchley, Nathaniel. *Small Wolf*, 117 (P) (Native American)

Dalgliesh, Alice. *The Courage of Sarah Noble*, 331 (M) (Native American)

Speare, Elizabeth George. *The Sign of the Beaver*, 1361 (M/U) (Native American)

## U.S. history—Depression

Taylor, Mildred D. *The Friendship*, 1424 (M/U) (African American)
  *Let the Circle Be Unbroken*, 1427 (U) (African American)
  *Song of the Trees*, 1431 (M/U) (African American)
  *Mississippi Bridge*, 1428 (M/U) (African American)
  *The Road to Memphis*, 1429 (U) (African American)
  *Roll of Thunder, Hear My Cry*, 1430 (U) (African American)
  *Song of the Trees*, 1431 (M/U) (African American)
Uchida, Yoshiko. *A Jar of Dreams*, 1475 (U) (Asian American—Japan)

## U.S. history—Pilgrims

George, Jean Craighead. *The First Thanksgiving*, 462 (P) (Native American)
Kessel, Joyce K. *Squanto and the First Thanksgiving*, 797 (P) (Native American—Patuxet)

## U.S. history—Revolution

Collier, James Lincoln, and Christopher Collier. *Jump Ship to Freedom*, 300 (U) (African American)
  *War Comes to Willy Freeman*, 301 (U) (African American)
  *Who Is Carrie?*, 302 (U) (African American)

## U.S. history—the 1950s

Taylor, Mildred D. *The Gold Cadillac*, 1426 (M/U) (African American)

## U.S. history—Vietnam War

Boyd, Candy Dawson. *Charlie Pippin*, 153 (U) (African American)
Pettit, Jayne. *My Name Is San Ho*, 1167 (U) (Asian American—Vietnam)

## U.S. history—World War II

Banim, Lisa. *American Dreams*, 89 (M) (Asian American—Japan)
Mochizuki, Ken. *Baseball Saved Us*, 1031 (M) (Asian American—Japan)
Shigekawa, Marlene. *Blue Jay in the Desert*, 1320 (M) (Asian American—Japan)
Uchida, Yoshiko. *The Bracelet*, 1472 (M) (Asian American—Japan)
  *Journey Home*, 1476 (U) (Asian American—Japan)
  *Journey to Topaz: A Story of the Japanese-American Evacuation*, 1477 (U) (Asian American—Japan)
Yep, Laurence. *Hiroshima*, 1609 (U) (Asian—Japan)

## Urban life

Adoff, Arnold, editor. *My Black Me: A Beginning Book of Black Poetry*, 30, 31 (M/U) (African American)
  *Where Wild Willie?*, 33 (P) (African American)

## Urban life (cont.)

Mathis, Sharon Bell. *Sidewalk Story*, 987 (M) (African American)

Mennen, Ingrid, and Niki Daly. *Somewhere in Africa*, 1010 (P) (African)

Miles, Betty. *Sink or Swim*, 1017 (M) (African American)

Mohr, Nicholasa. *Felita*, 1033 (M) (Hispanic American—Puerto Rico)

Moore, Emily. *Whose Side Are You On?*, 1050 (M) (African American)

Myers, Walter Dean. *Fast Sam, Cool Clyde, and Stuff*, 1083 (U) (African American)

   *The Mouse Rap*, 1086 (U) (African American)

   *Scorpions*, 1088 (U) (African American)

   *The Young Landlords*, 1089 (U) (African American)

Patrick, Denise Lewis. *The Car Washing Street*, 1153 (P) (African American)

Quattlebaum, Mary. *Jackson Jones and the Puddle of Thorns*, 1202 (M) (African American)

Ringgold, Faith. *Tar Beach*, 1222 (P/M) (African American)

Rodriguez, Anita. *Aunt Martha and the Golden Coin*, 1235 (P) (African American)

   *Jamal and the Angel*, 1236 (P) (African American)

Smalls-Hector, Irene. *Irene and the Big, Fine Nickel*, 1338 (P/M) (African American)

   *Jonathan and His Mommy*, 1339 (PS/P) (African American)

Sonneborn, Ruth A. *Friday Night Is Papa Night*, 1348 (P) (Caribbean—Puerto Rico)

Spinelli, Eileen. *If You Want to Find Golden*, 1364 (P) (Multicultural)

Wagner, Jane. *J. T.*, 1501 (M) (African American)

Walter, Mildred Pitts. *Lillie of Watts: A Birthday Discovery*, 1512 (M) (Native American)

Weik, Mary Hays. *The Jazz Man*, 1530 (M) (African American)

Weiss, Nicki. *On a Hot, Hot Day*, 1535 (P) (Hispanic American)

Williams, Vera B. *A Chair for My Mother*, 1554 (P) (Hispanic American)

   *Cherries and Cherry Pits*, 1555 (P) (African American)

   *Music, Music for Everyone*, 1557 (P) (Hispanic American)

   *Scooter*, 1558 (M) (Hispanic American)

   *Something Special for Me*, 1559 (P) (Hispanic American)

Willis, Meredith Sue. *The Secret Super Powers of Marco*, 1560 (M) (Multicultural)

Yarborough, Camille. *The Shimmershine Queens*, 1592 (M/U) (African American)

   *Tamika and the Wisdom Rings*, 1593 (M) (African American)

Yashima, Taro. *Umbrella*, 1596 (P) (Asian American—Japan)

## Violence

Davis, Ossie. *Just Like Martin*, 335 (U) (African American)

Maartens, Maretha. *Paper Bird: A Novel of South Africa*, 932 (U) (African—South Africa)

Myers, Walter Dean. *Scorpions*, 1088 (U) (African American)

## Volcanoes

Grifalconi, Ann. *The Village of Round and Square Houses*, 558 (M) (African)

Lewis, Thomas P. *Hill of Fire*, 891 (P) (Mexican)

Czernecki, Stefan, and Timothy Rhodes. *The Hummingbirds' Gift*, 329 (M) (Mexican)

dePaola, Tomie, reteller. *The Legend of the Bluebonnet: An Old Tale of Texas*, 360 (M) (Native American)

Duarte, Margarida Estrela Bandeira. *The Legend of the Palm Tree*, 382 (M) (South American—Brazil)

Guthrie, Donna W. *Nobiuh's Well: A Modern African Folktale*, 569 (M) (African)

Hamilton, Virginia. *Drylongso*, 585 (M) (African American)

Jacobs, Shannon K. *Song of the Giraffe*, 721 (M) (African)

James, Betsy. *The Mud Family*, 724 (M) (Native American— Anasazi)

Lattimore, Deborah Nourse. *The Dragon's Robe*, 845 (M) (Asian—China)

Lawson, Julie, reteller. *The Dragon's Pearl*, 854 (M) (Asian—China)

Lee, Jeanne M., reteller. *Toad Is the Uncle of Heaven: A Vietnamese Folk Tale*, 860 (M) (Asian—Vietnam)

Lottridge, Celia Barker, reteller. *The Name of the Tree: A Bantu Folktale*, 916 (M) (African—Bantu)

Mogensen, Jan. *Kakalambalala*, 1032 (M) (African)

Mollel, Tololwa M. *A Promise to the Sun: An African Story*, 1040 (M) (African)

Oliviero, Jamie. *The Fish Skin*, 1126 (M) (Native American)

Rappaport, Doreen. *The Long-Haired Girl: A Chinese Legend*, 1206 (M) (Asian—China)

Rodanas, Kristina, reteller. *Dragonfly's Tale*, 1232 (M) (Native American—Zuni)

Rosen, Michael, reteller. *How Giraffe Got Such a Long Neck . . . and Why Rhino Is So Grumpy: A Tale from East Africa*, 1246 (M) (African—East Africa)

Yep, Laurence. *The Junior Thunder Lord*, 1610 (M) (Asian—China)

Zubizarreta, Rosalma, Harriet Rohmer, and David Schecter. *The Woman Who Outshone the Sun: The Legend of Lucia Zenteno*, 1637 (M) (Mexican—Zapotec)

## Weather—floods

Alexander, Ellen. *Llama and the Great Flood: A Folktale from Peru*, 39 (M) (South American—Peru)

Bernhard, Emery, reteller. *The Tree That Rains: The Flood Myth of the Huichol Indians of Mexico*, 123 (M) (Native American—Huichol)

Palacios, Argentina, adapter. *The Llama's Secret: A Peruvian Legend*, 1149 (M) (South American—Peru)

Rucki, Ani. *Turkey's Gift to the People*, 1255 (M) (Native American—Navajo)

## Weather—rain

Aardema, Verna, reteller. *Bringing the Rain to Kapiti Plain: A Nandi Tale*, 4 (P/M) (African—Nandi)

Bonnici, Peter. *The First Rains*, 149 (P) (Asian—India)

Browne, Vee, reteller. *Monster Birds: A Navajo Folktale*, 167 (M) (Native American—Navajo)

Crews, Nina. *One Hot Summer Day*, 321 (PS/P) (African American)

Greenfield, Eloise. *Aaron and Gayla's Counting Book*, 524 (PS/P) (African American)

Johnson, Angela. *Rain Feet*, 738 (PS) (African American)

## Weather—rain (cont.)

Lee, Jeanne M., reteller. *Toad Is the Uncle of Heaven: A Vietnamese Folk Tale*, 860 (M) (Asian—Vietnam)

Martel, Cruz. *Yagua Days*, 977 (M) (Hispanic American—Puerto Rico)

Oliviero, Jamie. *The Fish Skin*, 1126 (M) (Native American)

Stanley, Sanna. *The Rains Are Coming*, 1374 (P) (African—Zaire)

Wisniewski, David. *Rain Player*, 1570 (M) (Central American—Mayan)

Yashima, Taro. *Umbrella*, 1596 (P) (Asian American—Japan)

## Weather—rainbows

Yolen, Jane. *Rainbow Rider*, 1623 (M) (Native American)

## Weather—snow

Bushey, Jeanne. *A Sled Dog for Moshi*, 209 (P) (Native American—Inuit)

Conway, Diana Cohen. *Northern Lights: A Hanukkah Story*, 305 (P) (Multicultural)

Keats, Ezra Jack. *The Snowy Day*, 786 (PS/P) (African American)

San Souci, Robert D. *The Snow Wife*, 1277 (M) (Asian—Japan)

Udry, Janice May. *Mary Jo's Grandmother*, 1485 (P) (African American)

## Weather—storms

Hest, Amy. *Ruby's Storm*, 640 (P) (Hispanic American)

Lee, Jeanne M. *Ba-Nam*, 857 (P) (Asian—Vietnam)

Stolz, Mary. *Storm in the Night*, 1396 (P/M) (African American)

## Weather—thunder

Bryan, Ashley. *The Story of Lightning & Thunder*, 189 (M) (African)

Harrell, Beatrice Orcutt. *How Thunder and Lightning Came to Be: A Choctaw Legend*, 608 (M) (Native American—Choctaw)

Loverseed, Amanda, reteller. *Thunder King: A Peruvian Folk Tale*, 920 (M) (South American—Peru)

Yep, Laurence. *The Junior Thunder Lord*, 1610 (M) (Asian—China)

## Weather—tidal waves

Hodges, Margaret. *The Wave*, 657 (M) (Asian—Japan)

## Weather—wind

Ellis, Veronica Freeman. *Land of the Four Winds: Kpa Nieh Kpau*, 397 (M) (African—Liberia)

Ets, Marie Hall. *Gilberto and the Wind*, 407 (P) (Mexican)

Greene, Carol. *Please, Wind*, 520 (PS/P) (African American)

Hamilton, Virginia. *Drylongso*, 585 (M) (African American)

McKissack, Patricia. *Mirandy and Brother Wind*, 950 (P) (African American)

Yolen, Jane. *The Girl Who Loved the Wind*, 1622 (M) (Asian)

## Weddings

Kimmel, Eric A., reteller. *The Greatest of All: A Japanese Folktale*, 805 (M) (Asian—Japan)

Kline, Suzy. *Horrible Harry and the Kickball Wedding*, 812 (M) (Asian American—Korea)

Kwon, Holly H., reteller. *The Moles and the Mireuk: A Korean Folktale*, 834 (M) (Asian—Korea)

Lewin, Hugh. *Jafta and the Wedding*, 880 (P) (African—South Africa)

Rodanas, Kristina, reteller. *The Story of Wali Dâd*, 1233 (M) (Asian—India)

Samuels, Vyanne. *Carry Go Bring Come*, 1268 (P) (Caribbean—Jamaica)

Shepard, Aaron, reteller. *The Gifts of Wali Dad: A Tale of India and Pakistan*, 1313 (M) (Asian—India/Pakistan)

Uchida, Yoshiko. *The Happiest Ending*, 1473 (U) (Asian American—Japan)

Wright, Courtni C. *Jumping the Broom*, 1585 (M) (African American)

## Wishes

Rhee, Nami, reteller. *Magic Spring: A Korean Folktale*, 1216 (M) (Asian—Korea)

## Witchcraft

Konigsburg, E. L. *Jennifer, Hecate, Macbeth, William McKinley, and Me, Elizabeth*, 822 (M) (African American)

## Witches

Kimmel, Eric A., adapter. *The Witch's Face: A Mexican Tale*, 808 (M) (Mexican)

Pitre, Felix, reteller. *Paco and the Witch: A Puerto Rican Folktale*, 1178 (M) (Caribbean—Puerto Rico)

White, Carolyn. *The Tree House Children: An African Tale*, 1542 (M) (African)

## Wizards

Troughton, Joanna, reteller. *The Wizard Punchkin: A Folk Tale from India*, 1462 (M) (Asian—India)

## Women

Riordan, James. *The Woman in the Moon: And Other Tales of Forgotten Heroines*, 1223 (M/U) (Multicultural)

San Souci, Robert D., collector and adapter. *Cut from the Same Cloth: American Women of Myth, Legend, and Tall Tale*, 1271 (U) (Multicultural)

## Wordless books

Alexander, Martha. *Bobo's Dream*, 41 (PS/P) (African American)

Bang, Molly. *The Grey Lady and the Strawberry Snatcher*, 82 (P) (African American)

Young, Ed. *Up a Tree*, 1633 (P) (Asian)

## World

Anno, Mitsumasa, and Raymond Briggs. *All in a Day*, 58 (M) (Multicultural)

## World (cont.)

Gray, Nigel. *A Country Far Away*, 515 (P) (African)

Hamanaka, Sheila. *All the Colors of the Earth*, 579 (PS/P) (Multicultural)

Hoberman, Mary Ann, selector. *My Song Is Beautiful: A Celebration of Multicultural Poems and Pictures*, 654 (P/M) (Multicultural)

Knight, Margy Burns. *Who Belongs Here? An American Story*, 818 (M) (Asian American—Cambodia)

Shepherd, Sandy. *Myths and Legends from Around the World*, 1314 (M) (Multicultural)

Spier, Peter. *People*, 1363 (P/M) (Multicultural)

Weiss, George David, and Bob Thiel. *What a Wonderful World*, 1533 (P) (Multicultural)

## World War II

Chang, Margaret, and Raymond Chang. *In the Eye of War*, 240 (U) (Asian—China)

Choi, Sook Nyul. *Year of Impossible Goodbyes*, 256 (U) (Asian—Korea)

Coerr, Eleanor. *Mieko and the Fifth Treasure*, 283 (M) (Asian—Japan)

Mattingly, Christobel. *The Miracle Tree*, 989 (M) (Asian—Japan)

Taylor, Theodore. *The Cay*, 1433 (U) (Caribbean)

Watkins, Yoko Kawashima. *My Brother, My Sister, and I*, 1526 (U) (Asian—Japan)

*So Far from the Bamboo Grove*, 1527 (U) (Asian—Korea/Japan)

## Zodiac

Van Woerkom, Dorothy, adapter. *The Rat, the Ox, and the Zodiac: A Chinese Legend*, 1491 (M) (Asian—China)

Yen, Clara, reteller. *Why Rat Comes First: A Story of the Chinese Zodiac*, 1601 (M) (Asian—China)

# TITLE INDEX

Note: Numerals refer to entry numbers, not page numbers.

# ILLUSTRATOR INDEX

# CULTURE INDEX

⟩⟩•◦•⟨⟨

*Note:* Numerals refer to entry numbers, not page numbers.

## Native American

# USE LEVEL INDEX

———✦———

*Note:* Numerals refer to entry numbers, not page numbers.

## Middle (M) (cont.)

## Middle/Upper (M/U)